T0076274

Get the eBook FREE!
(PDF, ePub, Kindle, and liveBook all included)

We believe that once you buy a book from us, you should be able to read it in any format we have available. To get electronic versions of this book at no additional cost to you, purchase and then register this book at the Manning website.

Go to https://www.manning.com/freebook and follow the instructions to complete your pBook registration.

That's it!
Thanks from Manning!

Praise for the first edition

"Like all the other great in Action titles from Manning, this book gives you everything you need to become productive quickly."

—Kevin Orr, Sumus Solutions

"Kotlin is fun and easy to learn when you have this book to guide you!"

—Filip Pravica, Info.nl

"Thorough, well written, and easily accessible."

—Jason Lee, NetSuite

"Complete introduction guide on the concepts and the paradigms of the Kotlin programming language."

—Ronald Tischliar, system architect, WWK Insurance

"Kotlin is an exciting yet pragmatic language that every Java programmer should learn, and this is the only book they'll need to learn Kotlin well."

—Tim Lavers, senior software engineer, Pacific Knowledge Systems

"With deep knowledge shown by the authors, it's clear they can convey that material to readers."

—Dylan Scott, software developer, Shred Code

"A perfect and unique book to start learning the Kotlin language, written by two awesome developers from the Kotlin team in JetBrains."

—Paweł Gajda, Android developer, EL Passion

Kotlin in Action

Second Edition

SEBASTIAN AIGNER, ROMAN ELIZAROV,
SVETLANA ISAKOVA, DMITRY JEMEROV

MANNING
SHELTER ISLAND

Manning Publications Co.   Development editor: Marina Michaels
20 Baldwin Road   Technical development editor: Robert Wenner
PO Box 761   Review editors: Aleksandar Dragosavljević and
                                                    Radmila Ercegovac
Shelter Island, NY 11964   Production editor: Keri Hales
                                        Copy editor: Christian Berk
                                        Proofreader: Katie Tennant
                             Technical proofreader: Igor Wojda
                                         Typesetter: Gordan Salinovic
                                     Cover designer: Marija Tudor

ISBN 9781617299605
Printed in the United States of America

brief contents

contents

preface

The idea for Kotlin was conceived at JetBrains in 2010. By that time, JetBrains was an established vendor of development tools for many languages, including Java, C#, JavaScript, Python, Ruby, and PHP. IntelliJ IDEA, the Java IDE that is our flagship product, also included plugins for Groovy and Scala.

The experience of building the tooling for such a diverse set of languages gave us a unique understanding of and perspective on the language design space as a whole. And yet the IntelliJ Platform-based IDEs, including IntelliJ IDEA, were still being developed in Java.

We were somewhat envious of our colleagues on the .NET team who were developing in C#, a modern, powerful, and rapidly evolving language. But we didn't see any language we could use in place of Java. What were our requirements for such a language?

The first and most obvious requirement was static typing. We don't know any other way to develop a multimillion-line codebase over many years without going crazy. Second, we needed full compatibility with the existing Java code. That codebase is a hugely valuable asset for JetBrains, and we couldn't afford to lose it or devalue it through difficulties with interoperability. Third, we didn't want to accept any compromises in terms of tooling quality. Developer productivity is the most important value to JetBrains, and great tooling is essential to achieving that. Finally, we needed a language that was easy to learn and reason about.

When we see an unmet need for our company, we know there are other companies in similar situations, and we expect our solution to find many users outside of JetBrains. With this in mind, we decided to embark on the project of creating a new language: Kotlin.

As it happens, the project took longer than we expected, and Kotlin 1.0 came out more than five years after the first commit to the repository. Since then, the language has found its audience, grown into a wonderful ecosystem of its own, and is here to stay.

Kotlin is named after an island near St. Petersburg, Russia. In using the name of an island, we followed the precedent established by Java and Ceylon. (In English, the name is usually pronounced "cot-lin," not "coat-lin" or "caught-lin.")

As the language was approaching release, we realized it would be valuable to have a book about Kotlin, written by people who were involved in making design decisions for the language and who could confidently explain why things are the way they are in Kotlin. This book is a result of that effort, and we hope it will help you learn and understand the Kotlin language. Good luck, and may you always develop with pleasure!

acknowledgments

First of all, we'd like to thank Sergey Dmitriev and Max Shafirov for believing in the idea of a new language and deciding to invest JetBrains' resources. Without them, neither the language nor this book would exist.

We would especially like to acknowledge Andrey Breslav, who is the main person to blame for designing a language that's a pleasure to write about (and to code in). Andrey, despite having to lead the continuously growing Kotlin team, was able to give us a lot of helpful feedback for the first edition of this book, which we greatly appreciate.

We're grateful to the team at Manning, who guided us through the process of writing this book and helped make the text readable and well structured—particularly our development editors, Dan Maharry and Marina Michaels, who bravely strove to find time to talk despite our busy schedules, as well as Michael Stephens, Helen Stergius, Kevin Sullivan, Tiffany Taylor, Elizabeth Martin, and Marija Tudor. In addition, we thank the rest of the production staff who helped format this book.

The feedback from our technical reviewers, Igor Wojda and Brent Watson, was also invaluable, as were the comments of the reviewers who read the manuscript during the development process: Robert Wenner, Alessandro Campeis, Amit Lamba, Angelo Costa, Boris Vasile, Brendan Grainger, Calvin Fernandes, Christopher Bailey, Christopher Bortz, Conor Redmond, Dylan Scott, Filip Pravica, Jason Lee, Justin Lee, Kevin Orr, Nicolas Frankel, Paweł Gajda, Ronald Tischliar, and Tim Lavers.

Thanks also go to everyone who submitted feedback during the MEAP program and in the book's forum; we've improved the text based on your comments: Alessandro Campeis, Bob Resendes, Didier Garcia, Haim Raman, James Watson, João Miguel

Pires Dias, Jorge Ezequiel Bo, Mark Kotyk, Md Shahriar Anwar, Mikael Dautrey, Nitin Gode, Peter Szabo, Phillip Sorensen, Rani Sharim, Richard Meinsen, Sergio Britos, Simeon Leyzerzon, Steve Prior, Walter Alexander Mata López, and William Morgan.

We're grateful to the entire Kotlin team, who had to listen to frequent reports like, "One more section is finished!" throughout the time we spent writing this book. We want to thank our colleagues who helped us plan the book and gave feedback on its drafts, especially Ilya Ryzhenkov, Michael Glukhikh, Ilya Gorbunov, Vsevolod Tolstopyatov, Dmitry Khalanskiy, and Hadi Hariri. We'd also like to thank our friends who not only were supportive but also had to read the text and provide feedback (sometimes in ski resorts during vacations): Lev Serebryakov, Pavel Nikolaev, Alex Semin, and Alisa Afonina.

Finally, we'd like to thank our families and cats for making this world a better place.

about this book

The second edition of *Kotlin in Action* teaches you the Kotlin programming language and how to use it to build applications running on the Java virtual machine (JVM) and Android. It starts with the basic features of the language and proceeds to cover the more distinctive aspects of Kotlin, such as its support for building high-level abstractions and domain-specific languages. The book also provides the information you need to integrate Kotlin with existing Java projects and helps you introduce Kotlin into your current working environment.

The book covers Kotlin 2.0. For ongoing updates about the new features and changes, please refer to the online documentation at https://kotlinlang.org.

Who should read this book

Kotlin in Action, Second Edition, is primarily focused on developers with some level of Java experience. Kotlin builds on many concepts and techniques from Java, and the book strives to get you up to speed quickly by using your existing knowledge.

If you're experienced with other programming languages such as C# or JavaScript, you may need to refer to other sources of information to understand the more intricate aspects of Kotlin's interaction with the JVM, but you'll still be able to learn Kotlin using this book. We focus on the Kotlin language as a whole and not on a specific problem domain, so the book should be equally useful for server-side developers, Android developers, and everyone else who builds projects targeting the JVM.

How this book is organized: A road map

The book is divided into three parts. Part 1 explains how to get started using Kotlin together with existing libraries and APIs:

- Chapter 1 talks about the key goals, values, and areas of application for Kotlin, and it shows you the different ways to run Kotlin code.
- Chapter 2 explains the essential elements of any Kotlin program, including control structures and variable and function declarations.
- Chapter 3 goes into detail about how functions are declared in Kotlin and introduces the concept of extension functions and properties.
- Chapter 4 is focused on class declarations and introduces the concepts of data classes and companion objects.
- Chapter 5 introduces the use of lambdas in Kotlin and showcases a number of Kotlin standard library functions using lambdas.
- Chapter 6 gives an overview of how you work with collections in Kotlin as well as their lazy counterpart: sequences.
- Chapter 7 familiarizes you with the concept of nullability.
- Chapter 8 describes the Kotlin type system, including an additional focus on collections.

Part 2 teaches you how to build your own APIs and abstractions in Kotlin and covers some of the language's deeper features:

- Chapter 9 talks about the principle of conventions, which assigns special meaning to methods and properties with specific names, and it introduces the concept of delegated properties.
- Chapter 10 shows how to declare higher-order functions—functions that take other functions and parameters or return them. It also introduces the concept of inline functions.
- Chapter 11 is a deep dive into the topic of generics in Kotlin, starting with the basic syntax and going into more advanced areas, such as reified type parameters and variance.
- Chapter 12 covers the use of annotations and reflection and is centered around JKid, a small, real-life JSON serialization library that makes heavy use of those concepts.
- Chapter 13 introduces the concept of domain-specific languages, describes Kotlin's tools for building them, and demonstrates many DSL examples.

Part 3 covers coroutines and flows, the approach to performing concurrent programming in Kotlin:

- Chapter 14 provides an overview of Kotlin's concurrency model, including suspending functions, coroutines, and the basic mechanics of writing concurrent code.

- Chapter 15 talks about the concept of structured concurrency, which helps you manage concurrent tasks and introduces the mechanisms required for cancellation and error handling.
- Chapter 16 introduces flows, the coroutine-based abstraction used for modeling sequential streams of values over time.
- Chapter 17 covers flow operators, which can be used to transform Kotlin flows, in more detail.
- Chapter 18 dives deeper into the subject of error handling and testing your concurrent code.

The book also features three appendixes:

- Appendix A explains how to build Kotlin code with Gradle and Maven.
- Appendix B focuses on writing documentation comments and generating API documentation for Kotlin modules.
- Appendix C is a guide for exploring the Kotlin ecosystem and finding the latest online information.

The book works best when you read it all the way through, but you're also welcome to refer to individual chapters covering specific subjects you're interested in and to follow the cross-references if you run into an unfamiliar concept.

About the code

The following typographical conventions are used throughout this book:

- *Italic font* is used to introduce new terms.
- `Fixed-width font` is used to denote code samples, as well as function names, classes, and other identifiers.

Code annotations accompany many of the code listings and highlight important concepts. Where necessary, the original source code has been reformatted; we've added line breaks and reworked indentation to accommodate the available page space in the book. In rare cases, even this was not enough, and listings include line-continuation markers ( ).

Many source listings in the book show code together with its output. In those cases, we show the output of the code as a line comment following the line that produces the output or below the snippet, like this:

```
fun main() {
    println("Hello World")
    // Hello World
}
```

Some of the examples are intended to be complete runnable programs, whereas others are snippets used to demonstrate certain concepts and may contain omissions (indicated with . . .) or syntax errors (described in the book text or in the examples themselves). The runnable examples can be downloaded as a zip file from the publisher's website at https://www.manning.com/books/kotlin-in-action-second-edition.

liveBook discussion forum

Purchase of *Kotlin in Action, Second Edition*, includes free access to liveBook, Manning's online reading platform. Using liveBook's exclusive discussion features, you can attach comments to the book globally or to specific sections or paragraphs. It's a snap to make notes for yourself, ask and answer technical questions, and receive help from the authors and other users. To access the forum, go to https://livebook.manning.com/book/kotlin-in-action-second-edition/discussion. You can also learn more about Manning's forums and the rules of conduct at https://livebook.manning.com/discussion.

Manning's commitment to our readers is to provide a venue where a meaningful dialogue between individual readers and between readers and authors can take place. It is not a commitment to any specific amount of participation on the part of the authors, whose contribution to the forum remains voluntary (and unpaid). We suggest you try asking them some challenging questions lest their interest stray! The forum and the archives of previous discussions will be accessible from the publisher's website as long as the book is in print.

Other online resources

Kotlin has a lively online community, so if you have questions or want to chat with fellow Kotlin users, you can use the following resources:

- *The Kotlin Slack*—https://slack-chats.kotlinlang.org/
- *The official Kotlin forums*—https://discuss.kotlinlang.org
- *The Kotlin tag on Stack Overflow*—http://stackoverflow.com/questions/tagged/kotlin
- *Kotlin Reddit*—www.reddit.com/r/Kotlin

about the authors

SEBASTIAN AIGNER is a developer advocate at JetBrains. He regularly speaks at conferences and gives workshops on Kotlin-related subjects. Sebastian is a host on the *Talking Kotlin* podcast and creates videos for the official Kotlin YouTube channel. As a member of the Kotlin Foundation, he helps maintain the ecosystem's growth and sustainability.

ROMAN ELIZAROV was the project lead for Kotlin at JetBrains and focused on the design of the Kotlin language in the role of lead language designer for seven years. He previously designed and developed high-performance trading software for leading brokerage firms and market data delivery services that routinely handle millions of events per second. While working on Kotlin at JetBrains, he contributed to the design of Kotlin coroutines and the development of the Kotlin coroutines library.

SVETLANA ISAKOVA began as a member of the Kotlin compiler team and is now a developer advocate for JetBrains. She teaches Kotlin and speaks at conferences worldwide. She is a cocreator of the course Kotlin for Java Developers at Coursera and is a coauthor of the book *Atomic Kotlin* (Mindview LLC, 2021).

DMITRY JEMEROV was one of the initial developers working on Kotlin as the project began. He's deeply familiar with the design of the language and the reasons for the decisions made during its development. During his tenure at JetBrains, Dmitry worked on various Kotlin-related subjects, including the IntelliJ IDEA plug-in for Kotlin and the Kotlin documentation.

about the cover illustration

The figure on the cover of *Kotlin in Action, Second Edition*, "Habit of a Russian Lady at Valday in 1764," is taken from a book by Thomas Jefferys, published between 1757 and 1772.

In those days, it was easy to identify where people lived and what their trade or station in life was just by their dress. Manning celebrates the inventiveness and initiative of the computer business with book covers based on the rich diversity of regional culture centuries ago, brought back to life by pictures from collections such as this one.

Part 1

Introducing Kotlin

The goal of this part of the book is to get you productive writing Kotlin code that uses existing APIs. Chapter 1 will introduce you to the general traits of Kotlin.

In chapters 2–4, you'll learn how basic programming concepts—statements, functions, classes, and types—map to Kotlin code and how Kotlin enriches them to make programming more pleasant. You'll be able to rely on your existing knowledge of other object-oriented languages, like Java, as well as tools, such as IDE coding-assistance features and the Java-to-Kotlin converter, to get up to speed quickly. In chapter 5, you'll find out how lambdas help you avoid repetition and effectively solve common programming tasks. Chapter 6 teaches you how Kotlin allows you to elegantly modify collections using a functional programming approach. In chapter 7, you'll become familiar with one of the key Kotlin specialties: its support for dealing with `null` values. In chapter 8, you'll take a closer look at the basics of Kotlin's type system, from basic numbers to the special `Any` and `Nothing` types. You'll also learn more about collection types, including their read-only and mutable versions, and get introduced to arrays.

Kotlin: What and why

Kotlin is a modern programming language on the Java virtual machine (JVM) and beyond. It's a general-purpose, concise, safe, and pragmatic language. Independent programmers, small software shops, and large enterprises all have embraced Kotlin: millions of developers are now using it to write mobile apps, build server-side applications, and create desktop software, among several other applications.

Kotlin started as a "better Java"—a language with improved developer ergonomics that prevents common categories of errors and embraces modern language design paradigms, all while maintaining the ability to be used everywhere Java was used. Over the last decade, Kotlin has managed to prove itself to be a pragmatic fit for many types of developers, projects, and platforms. Android is now Kotlin first, meaning most of the Android development is done in Kotlin. For server-side development, Kotlin makes a strong alternative to Java, with native and well-documented Kotlin support in prevalent frameworks, like Spring, and pure Kotlin frameworks exploiting the full potential of the language, like Ktor.

Kotlin combines ideas from existing languages that work well but also brings innovative approaches, such as coroutines for asynchronous programming. Despite beginning with a JVM-only focus, Kotlin grew significantly beyond that, providing more "targets" to run on, including technology to create cross-platform solutions. In this chapter, we'll take a detailed look at Kotlin's main traits.

1.1   A taste of Kotlin

Let's start with a small example to demonstrate what Kotlin looks like. Even in this first, short code snippet, you can see a lot of interesting features and concepts in Kotlin—all of which will be discussed in detail throughout the book:

- Defining a `Person` data class with properties without the need to specify a body
- Declaring read-only properties (`name` and `age`) with the `val` keyword
- Providing default values for arguments
- Explicit work with nullable values (`Int?`) in the type system, avoiding the "billion-dollar mistake" of `NullPointerException`s
- Top-level function definitions without nesting them inside classes
- Named arguments when invoking functions and constructors
- Using trailing commas
- Using collection operations with lambda expressions
- Providing fallback values when a variable is `null` via the Elvis operator (`?:`)
- Using string templates as an alternative to manual concatenation
- Using autogenerated functions for data classes, such as `toString`

The code is explained briefly, but don't worry if something isn't clear right away. We will take plenty of time to discuss each and every detail of this code listing throughout the book, so you'll be able to confidently write code just like this yourself.

Listing 1.1   An early taste of Kotlin

```
data class Person(              ◁——— Data class
    val name: String,           ◁——— Read-only property
    val age: Int? = null        ◁———
)                                       Nullable type (Int?)—the default value for the argument

fun main() {                    ◁——— Top-level function
    val persons = listOf(
        Person("Alice", age = 29),      ◁——— Named argument
        Person("Bob"),          ◁———
    )                               Trailing comma
    val oldest = persons.maxBy {        ◁——— Lambda expression
```

```
        it.age ?: 0                  ◁─── Null-coalescing Elvis operator
    }
    println("The oldest is: $oldest")       ◁─── String template
}

// The oldest is: Person(name=Alice, age=29)    ◁─── Autogenerated toString
```

Our first Kotlin code snippet demonstrates how to create a collection in Kotlin, fill it with some `Person` objects, and then find the oldest person in the collection, using default values where no age is specified. When creating the list of people, it omits Bob's age, so `null` is used as a default value. To find the oldest person in the list, the `maxBy` function is used. The lambda expression passed to the function takes one parameter, implicitly named `it` by default (although you can assign other names to the parameter, as well). The *Elvis operator* (`?:`) returns zero if `age` is `null`. Because Bob's age isn't specified, the Elvis operator replaces it with zero, so Alice wins the prize for being the oldest person.

You can also try to run this example on your own. The easiest option to do so is to use the online playground at https://play.kotlinlang.org/. Type in the example and click the Run button, and then the code will be executed.

Do you like what you've seen? Read on to learn more and become a Kotlin expert. We hope that soon you'll see such code in your own projects, not only in this book.

1.2   Kotlin's primary traits

Kotlin is a multiparadigm language. It is statically typed, meaning many errors can be caught at compile time instead of at run time. It combines ideas from object-oriented and functional languages, which helps you write elegant code and make use of additional powerful abstractions. It provides a powerful way to write asynchronous code, which is important in many development areas.

Just based on these short descriptions, you maybe already have an intuitive idea of the type of language Kotlin is. Let's look at these key attributes in greater detail. First, let's see what kinds of applications you can build with Kotlin.

1.2.1   Kotlin use cases: Android, server side, anywhere Java runs, and beyond

Kotlin's target is quite broad. The language doesn't focus on a single problem domain or address a single type of challenge faced by software developers today. Instead, it provides across-the-board productivity improvements for all tasks that come up during the development process and aims for an excellent level of integration with libraries that support specific domains or programming paradigms.

Common Kotlin use cases include the following:

- Building mobile applications that run on Android devices
- Building server-side code (typically, backends of web applications)

The initial goal of Kotlin was to provide a more concise, more productive, safer alternative to Java that's suitable in all contexts Java can be used. That includes a broad variety of environments, from running small edge devices to the largest data centers. In all these use cases Kotlin fits perfectly, and developers can do their job with less code and fewer annoyances along the way.

But Kotlin works in other contexts as well. Using Kotlin Multiplatform, you can create cross-platform applications for desktop, iOS, and Android—and even run Kotlin in the browser. This book is focused mainly on the language itself and intricacies of the JVM target. You can find extensive information about other Kotlin applications on the Kotlin website: https://kotl.in/. Next, let's look at the key qualities of Kotlin as a programming language.

1.2.2   *Static typing makes Kotlin performant, reliable, and maintainable*

Statically typed programming languages come with several advantages, such as performance, reliability, maintainability, and tool support. The key advantage of a statically typed language is that the type of every expression in a program is known at compile time. Kotlin is a statically typed programming language; the Kotlin compiler can validate that the methods and fields you're trying to access on an object actually exist. This helps eliminate an entire class of bugs—rather than crash at run time, if a field is missing or the return type of a function call isn't as expected, you will see these problems at compile time, allowing you to fix them earlier in the development cycle.

The following are some benefits of static typing:

- *Performance*—Calling methods is faster because there's no need to determine which method needs to be called at run time.
- *Reliability*—The compiler uses types to verify the consistency of the program, so there are fewer chances for crashes at run time.
- *Maintainability*—Working with unfamiliar code is easier because you can see what kind of types the code is working with.
- *Tool support*—Static typing enables reliable refactorings, precise code completion, and other IDE features.

This is in contrast to *dynamically typed* programming languages, like Python or JavaScript. Those languages let you define variables and functions that can store or return data of any type and resolve the method and field references at run time. This allows for shorter code and greater flexibility in creating data structures, but the downside is that problems like misspelled names or invalid parameters passed to functions can't be detected during compilation and can lead to run-time errors.

While the type of every expression in your program needs to be *known* at compile time, Kotlin doesn't require you to *specify* the type of every variable explicitly in your source code. In many cases, the type of a variable can automatically be determined from the context, allowing you to omit the type declaration. Here's the simplest possible example of this:

```
val x: Int = 1        ◁——— You can specify the variable type explicitly.
val y = 1      ◁──┐
                  │  But often, you don't have specify it.
```

You're declaring a variable, and because it's initialized with an integer value, Kotlin automatically determines that its type is `Int`. The ability of the compiler to determine types from context is called *type inference*. Type inference in Kotlin means most of the extra verbosity associated with static typing disappears because you don't need to declare types explicitly.

If you look at the specifics of Kotlin's type system, you'll find many concepts familiar from other object-oriented programming languages. Classes and interfaces, for example, work as you may expect. And if you happen to be a Java developer, your knowledge transfers especially easily to Kotlin, including topics like generics.

Something that may stand out to you is Kotlin's support for *nullable types*, which enables you to write more reliable programs by detecting possible `null` pointer exceptions at compile time, rather than experience them in the form of crashes at run time. We'll return to the topic of nullable types in section 1.4.3 and discuss them in detail in chapter 7, where we'll also contrast them with other approaches for `null` values you might be familiar with.

Kotlin's type system also has first-class support for *function types*. To see what this is about, let's look at the main ideas of functional programming to determine how it's supported in Kotlin.

1.2.3 Combining functional and object-oriented programming makes Kotlin safe and flexible

As a multiparadigm programming language, Kotlin combines the *object-oriented* approach with the *functional programming* style. The key concepts of functional programming are as follows:

- *First-class functions*—You work with functions (pieces of behavior) as values. You can store them in variables, pass them as parameters, or return them from other functions.
- *Immutability*—You work with immutable objects, which guarantees their state can't change after their creation.
- *No side effects*—You write *pure functions*, functions that return the same result given the same inputs and don't modify the state of other objects or interact with the outside world.

What benefits can you gain from writing code in the functional style? First, there is the benefit of *conciseness*. Functional code can be more elegant and succinct when compared to its *imperative* counterpart: instead of mutating variables and relying on loops and conditional branching, working with functions as values gives you much more power of abstraction.

Applying a functional programming style also lets you avoid duplication in your code. If you have similar code fragments that implement a similar task but differ in some smaller details, you can easily extract the common part of the logic into a function and pass the differing parts as arguments. Those arguments might themselves be functions. In Kotlin, you can express those using a concise syntax for lambda expressions.

The second benefit of functional code is *safe concurrency*. One of the biggest sources of errors in multithreaded programs is modification of the same data from multiple "actors" (often multiple threads) without proper synchronization. If you use immutable data structures and pure functions, you can be sure that such unsafe modifications won't happen, and you don't need to come up with complicated synchronization schemes.

Finally, functional programming means *easier testing*. Functions without side effects can be tested in isolation without requiring a lot of setup code to construct the entire environment they depend on. When your functions don't interact with the outside world, you'll also have an easier time reasoning about your code and validating its behavior without having to keep a larger, complex system in your head at all times.

Generally, a functional programming style can be used with many programming languages, and many of its parts are advocated as good programming style. But not all languages provide the syntactic and library support required to use it effortlessly. Kotlin has a rich set of features to support functional programming from the get-go. These include the following:

- *Function types*—Allowing functions to receive other functions as arguments or return other functions
- *Lambda expressions*—Letting you pass around blocks of code with minimum boilerplate
- *Member references*—Allowing you to use functions as values and, for instance, pass them as arguments
- *Data classes*—Providing a concise syntax for creating classes that can hold immutable data
- *Standard library APIs*—A rich set in the standard library for working with objects and collections in the functional style

The following snippet demonstrates a chain of actions to be performed with an input sequence. Having a given sequence of messages, the code finds "all unique senders of non-empty unread messages sorted by their names":

```
messages
    .filter { it.body.isNotBlank() && !it.isRead }
    .map(Message::sender)
    .distinct()
    .sortedBy(Sender::name)
```

The Kotlin standard library defines functions like `filter`, `map`, and `sortedBy` for you to use. The Kotlin language supports lambda expressions and member references (like `Message::sender`) so that the arguments passed to these functions are very concise.

When writing code in Kotlin, you can combine both object-oriented and functional approaches and use the tools that are most appropriate for the problem you're solving; you get the full power of functional-style programming in Kotlin, and when you need it, you can work with mutable data and write functions with side effects, all without jumping through extra hoops. And, of course, working with frameworks based on interfaces and class hierarchies is just as easy as you would expect it to be.

1.2.4 Concurrent and asynchronous code becomes natural and structured with coroutines

Whether you're building an application running on a server, a desktop machine, or a mobile phone, *concurrency*—running multiple pieces of your code at the same time—is a topic that's almost unavoidable. User interfaces need to remain responsive while long-running computations are running in the background. When interacting with services on the internet, applications often need to make more than one request at a time. Likewise, server-side applications are expected to keep serving incoming requests, even when a single request is taking much longer than usual. All of these applications need to operate *concurrently*, working on more than one thing at a time.

There have been many approaches to concurrency, including threads, callbacks, futures, promises, reactive extensions, and more. Kotlin approaches the problem of concurrent and asynchronous programming using *suspendable computations* called *coroutines*, where code can suspend its execution and resume its work at a later point.

In this example, you define a function `processUser` making three network calls by calling `authenticate`, `loadUserData`, and `loadImage`:

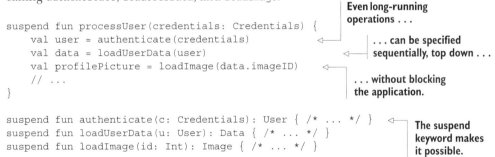

```
suspend fun processUser(credentials: Credentials) {
    val user = authenticate(credentials)
    val data = loadUserData(user)
    val profilePicture = loadImage(data.imageID)
    // ...
}

suspend fun authenticate(c: Credentials): User { /* ... */ }
suspend fun loadUserData(u: User): Data { /* ... */ }
suspend fun loadImage(id: Int): Image { /* ... */ }
```

Even long-running operations . . .

. . . can be specified sequentially, top down . . .

. . . without blocking the application.

The suspend keyword makes it possible.

A network call may take arbitrarily long. When performing each network request, the execution of the `processUser` function is *suspended* while waiting for the result. However, the thread this code is running on (and, by extension, the application itself) isn't *blocked*; while waiting for the result of `processUser`, it can do other tasks in the meantime, such as responding to user inputs. (You'll learn the details of suspending functions in section 14.1.)

You won't be able to write this code sequentially in an imperative fashion, one call after another, without blocking the underlying threads. On the other hand, if you use callbacks or reactive streams, such simple consecutive logic becomes much more complicated.

In the following example, you load two images concurrently using `async` (which you will explore in section 14.6.3) and then wait for the loading to be completed via `await`, returning the combination of the images (e.g., one overlaid on the other) as the result:

```
suspend fun loadAndOverlay(first: String, second: String): Image =
    coroutineScope {
        val firstDeferred = async { loadImage(first) }
        val secondDeferred = async { loadImage(second) }
        combineImages(firstDeferred.await(), secondDeferred.await())
    }
```

Starts loading the first image in a new coroutine

Starts loading the second image in yet another coroutine

When both images are loaded, it overlays them and returns the resulting image.

Structured concurrency, the subject of chapter 15, helps you manage the lifetime of your coroutines. In this example, two loading processes are started in a structured way (from the same *coroutine scope*). This guarantees that if one loading fails, the second one gets automatically canceled.

Coroutines are also a very lightweight abstraction, meaning you can launch millions of concurrent jobs without significant performance penalties. Together with abstractions, like *cold* and *hot flows*, covered in chapter 16, Kotlin coroutines become a powerful tool for building concurrent applications.

The entire third part of this book is dedicated to learning the ins and outs of coroutines, and understanding how you can best apply them for your use cases.

1.2.5   *Kotlin can be used for any purpose: It's free, open source, and open to contributions*

The Kotlin language, including the compiler, libraries, and all related tooling, is entirely open source and free to use for any purpose. It's available under the Apache 2 license; development happens in the open on GitHub (http://github.com/jetbrains/kotlin). There are many ways to contribute to the development of Kotlin and its community:

- The project welcomes code contributions for new features and fixes associated with the Kotlin compiler and its associated tooling.
- By providing bug reports and feedback, you can help improve the experience for everyone when developing with Kotlin.
- Potential new language features are discussed at length in the Kotlin community, and input from Kotlin developers like yourself plays a big role in driving forward and evolving the language.

You also have a choice of multiple open source IDEs for developing your Kotlin applications: IntelliJ IDEA Community Edition and Android Studio are fully supported. (Of course, IntelliJ IDEA Ultimate works as well.) Now that you understand what kind of language Kotlin is, let's see how the benefits of Kotlin work in specific practical applications.

1.3 Areas in which Kotlin is often used

As mentioned earlier, two of the main areas in which Kotlin is often used are server-side and Android development. Let's look at those areas in turn and see why Kotlin is a good fit for them.

1.3.1 Powering backends: Server-side development with Kotlin

Server-side programming is a fairly broad concept. It encompasses all the following types of applications and much more:

- Web applications that return HTML pages to a browser
- Backends for mobile or single-page applications that expose a JSON API over HTTP
- Microservices that communicate with other microservices over an RPC protocol or message bus

Developers have been building these kinds of applications on the JVM for many years and have accumulated a huge stack of frameworks and technologies to help build them. Such applications usually aren't developed in isolation or started from scratch. There's almost always an existing system that is being extended, improved, or replaced, and new code must integrate with existing parts of the system, which may have been written many years ago.

In this environment especially, Kotlin profits from its seamless interoperability with existing Java code. Regardless of whether you're writing a new component or migrating the code of an existing service to Kotlin, Kotlin will fit right in. You won't run into problems when you need to extend Java classes in Kotlin or annotate the methods and fields of a class in a certain way. The benefits are that the code of your system will be more compact, more reliable, and easier to maintain.

Another big advantage of using Kotlin is better reliability for your application. Kotlin's type system, with its precise tracking of `null` values, makes the problem of `null` pointer exceptions much less pressing. Most of the code that would lead to a `Null-PointerException` at run time in Java fails to compile in Kotlin, ensuring that you fix the error before the application gets to the production environment.

Modern frameworks, such as Spring (https://spring.io/), provide first-class support for Kotlin out of the box. Beyond the seamless interoperability, these frameworks include additional extensions and make use of techniques that make it feel as if they were designed for Kotlin in the first place.

In this example, you're defining a simple Spring Boot application, which serves a list of `Greeting` objects, consisting of an ID and some text, as JSON via HTTP, as seen in figure 1.1. Concepts from the Spring framework transfer directly to Kotlin: you use the same annotations (`@SpringBootApplication`, `@RestController`, `@GetMapping`) as you would when using Java, as shown in the following listing.

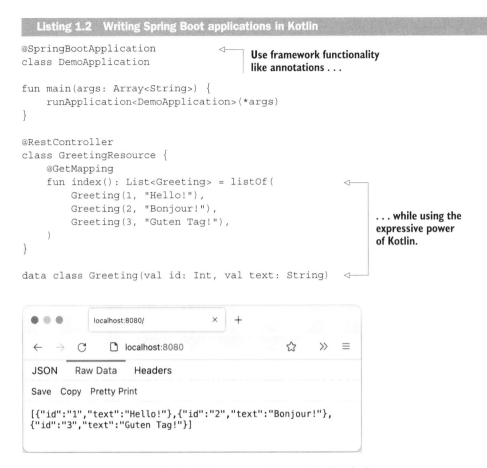

Listing 1.2   Writing Spring Boot applications in Kotlin

```
@SpringBootApplication                  ◁──┐  Use framework functionality
class DemoApplication                       │  like annotations . . .

fun main(args: Array<String>) {
    runApplication<DemoApplication>(*args)
}

@RestController
class GreetingResource {
    @GetMapping
    fun index(): List<Greeting> = listOf(        ◁──┐
        Greeting(1, "Hello!"),                       │
        Greeting(2, "Bonjour!"),                     │  . . . while using the
        Greeting(3, "Guten Tag!"),                   │  expressive power
    )                                                │  of Kotlin.
}                                                    │
                                                     │
data class Greeting(val id: Int, val text: String)  ◁──┘
```

```
● ● ●        localhost:8080/                ×    +

←    →   C        □  localhost:8080            ☆   »   ≡

JSON    Raw Data    Headers

Save   Copy   Pretty Print

[{"id":"1","text":"Hello!"},{"id":"2","text":"Bonjour!"},
{"id":"3","text":"Guten Tag!"}]
```

Figure 1.1   By combining Kotlin with industry-proven frameworks, like Spring, writing an application that serves JSON via HTTP only takes two dozen lines of code.

Check the Kotlin or Spring websites to find more information about using Spring with Kotlin (https://kotlinlang.org/docs/jvm-get-started-spring-boot.html).

Kotlin also enjoys an ever-growing ecosystem of its own libraries, including server-side frameworks. As an example, Ktor (https://ktor.io/) is a connected applications framework for Kotlin, built by JetBrains, which can be used to build server-side applications and make network requests in client and mobile applications. It powers products like JetBrains Space (https://jetbrains.space) and Toolbox (https://jetbrains.com/toolbox) and has been adopted by companies like Adobe.

As a Kotlin framework, Ktor makes full use of the capabilities of the language. For example, it defines a custom *domain-specific language* (DSL) to declare how HTTP requests are routed through the application. Rather than configuring your application using annotations or XML files, you can use a DSL from Ktor to configure the routing of your server-side application, with constructs that look like they are a part of

the Kotlin language but are completely custom for the framework—something you'll
learn how to do yourself in chapter 13.

In the example shown in the following listing, you're defining three routes, `/world`,
`/greet`, and `/greet/{entityId}`, using the `get`, `post`, and `route` DSL constructs from Ktor.

Listing 1.3   A Ktor app uses a DSL to route HTTP requests

```
fun main() {
    embeddedServer(Netty, port = 8000) {         Defines how Ktor handles
        routing {                                incoming HTTP requests . . .
            get ("/world") {
                call.respondText("Hello, world!")    . . . using a DSL that looks like it is
            }                                        built-in Kotlin functionality . . .
            route("/greet") {
                get { /* . . . */ }
                post("/{entityId}") { /* . . . */ }    . . . and that is easily
            }                                          composable
        }
    }.start(wait = true)
}
```

DSLs flexibly combine Kotlin language features and are often used for configuration;
the construction of complex objects; or *object-relational mapping* (ORM) tasks, translating objects into their database representation and vice versa.

Other Kotlin server-side frameworks, like http4k (https://http4k.org/), strongly
embrace the functional nature of Kotlin code and provide simple and uniform abstractions for requests and responses. In short, whether you're looking to use a battle-tested
industry standard framework for your next large project or need a lightweight framework for your next microservice, you can rest assured there's a framework waiting for
you in Kotlin's extensive ecosystem.

1.3.2 Mobile Development: Android is Kotlin first

The most-used mobile operating system in the world, Android, started officially supporting Kotlin as a language for building apps in 2017. Only 2 years later, in 2019,
after a lot of positive feedback from developers, Android became Kotlin first, making
it the default choice for new apps. Since then, Google's development tools, Jetpack
libraries (https://developer.android.com/jetpack), samples, documentation, and
training content all primarily focus on Kotlin.

Kotlin is a good fit for mobile apps: these types of applications usually need to be
delivered quickly while ensuring reliable operation on a large variety of devices.
Kotlin's language features turn Android development into a much more productive
and pleasant experience. Common development tasks can be accomplished with
much less code. The Android KTX library (https://developer.android.com/
kotlin/ktx), built by the Android team, improves your experience even further by
adding Kotlin-friendly adapters around many standard Android APIs.

Google's Jetpack Compose toolkit (https://developer.android.com/jetpack/compose) for building native user interfaces for Android is also designed for Kotlin from the ground up. It embraces Kotlin's language features and gives you the ability to write less, simpler, and easier-to-maintain code when building the UI of your mobile applications.

Here's an example of Jetpack Compose, just to give you a taste of what Android development with Kotlin feels like. The following code shows the message and expands or hides the details on click:

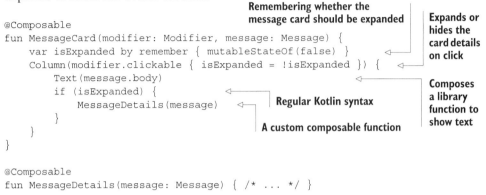

You can write the whole UI in Kotlin and use the regular Kotlin syntax, like `if` expressions or loops. In this example, we show a UI element representing additional details only if the user clicked on the card to get the expanded view. With Kotlin, you can extract custom logic representing different parts of the UI into functions, like `Message-Details`, having more elegant code as a result.

Embracing Kotlin on Android also means more reliable code, fewer `NullPointer-Exceptions`, and fewer messages that read "Unfortunately, process has stopped." As an example, Google managed to reduce the number of `NullPointerException` crashes in their Google Home app by 30% after switching the development of new features to Kotlin.

Using Kotlin doesn't introduce any new compatibility concerns or performance disadvantages to your apps, either. Kotlin is fully compatible with Java 8 and above, and the code generated by the compiler is executed efficiently. The runtime used by Kotlin is fairly small, so you won't experience a large increase in the size of the compiled application package. And when you use lambdas, many of the Kotlin standard library functions will inline them. Inlining lambdas ensures no new objects will be created and the application won't suffer from extra GC pauses. You'll benefit from all the cool new language features of Kotlin, and your users will still be able to run your application on their devices, even if they don't run the latest version of Android.

1.3.3 *Multiplatform: Sharing business logic and minimizing duplicate work on iOS, JVM, JS, and beyond*

Kotlin is also a *multiplatform* language. In addition to the JVM, Kotlin supports the following targets:

- It can be compiled to JavaScript, allowing you to run Kotlin code in the browser and runtimes such as Node.js.
- With Kotlin/Native, you can compile Kotlin code to native binaries, allowing you to target iOS and other platforms with self-contained programs.
- Kotlin/Wasm, a target that is still being developed at the time of writing, will make it possible for you to compile your Kotlin code to the WebAssembly binary instruction format, allowing you to run your code on the WebAssembly virtual machines that ship in modern browsers and other runtimes.

Kotlin also lets you specify which parts of your software should be shared between different targets and which parts have a platform-specific implementation, on a very fine-grained level. Because this control is very fine-grained, you can mix and match the best combination of common and platform-specific code. This mechanism, which Kotlin calls *expect/actual*, allows you to take advantage of platform-specific functionality from your Kotlin code. This effectively mitigates the classic problem of "targeting the lowest common denominator" that cross-platform toolkits usually face, wherein you are limited to a subset of operations available on all platforms you target.

A major use case we have seen for code sharing is mobile applications targeting both Android and iOS. With Kotlin Multiplatform, you only have to write your business logic once, but you can use it in both iOS and Android targets in a completely native fashion and even make use of the respective APIs, toolkits, and capabilities these platforms offer. Similarly, sharing code between a server-side service and a JavaScript application running in the browser helps you reduce duplicate work, keep validation logic in sync, and more.

If you want to learn more about the specifics of these additional platforms, as well as Kotlin's support for sharing code and multiplatform programming, please refer to "Kotlin Multiplatform" on the Kotlin website (https://kotlinlang.org/docs/multiplatform.html). Now that we've looked at a selection of things that make Kotlin great, let's examine Kotlin's philosophy—the main characteristics that distinguish Kotlin from other languages.

1.4 *The philosophy of Kotlin*

When we talk about Kotlin, we like to say that it's a pragmatic, concise, and safe language with a focus on interoperability. What exactly do we mean by each of those words? Let's look at each of them in turn.

1.4.1 Kotlin is a pragmatic language

Being *pragmatic* has a simple meaning to us: Kotlin is a practical language designed to solve real-world problems. Its design is based on many years of industry experience creating large-scale systems, and its features are chosen to address use cases encountered by many software developers. Moreover, developers worldwide have been using Kotlin for roughly a decade now. Their continued feedback has shaped each released version of the language, which makes us confident saying Kotlin helps solve problems in real projects.

Kotlin also is not a research language. It mostly relies on features and solutions that have already appeared in other programming languages and have proven to be successful. This reduces the complexity of the language and makes it easier to learn by letting you rely on familiar concepts. When new features are introduced, they remain in an experimental state for quite a long time. This makes it possible for the language design team to gather feedback and allows the final design of a feature to be tweaked and fine-tuned before it is added as a stable part of the language.

Kotlin doesn't enforce using any particular programming style or paradigm. As you begin to study the language, you can use the style and techniques familiar to you. Later, you'll gradually discover the more powerful features of Kotlin, such as extension functions (section 3.3), its expressive type system (chapters 7 and 8), higher-order functions (chapter 10), and many more. You will learn to apply them in your own code, which will make it concise and idiomatic.

Another aspect of Kotlin's pragmatism is its focus on tooling. A smart development environment is just as essential for a developer's productivity as a good language, and because of that, treating IDE support as an afterthought isn't an option. In the case of Kotlin, the IntelliJ IDEA plug-in is developed in lockstep with the compiler, and language features are always designed with tooling in mind.

The IDE support also plays a major role in helping you discover the features of Kotlin. In many cases, the tools will automatically detect common code patterns that can be replaced by more concise constructs and offer to fix the code for you. By studying the language features used by the automated fixes, you can learn to apply those features in your own code as well.

1.4.2 Kotlin is concise

It's common knowledge that developers spend more time reading existing code than writing new code. Imagine you're a part of a team developing a big project, and you need to add a new feature or fix a bug. What are your first steps? You look for the exact section of code that you need to change, and only then do you implement a fix. You read a lot of code to find out what you have to do. This code might have been written recently by your colleagues or by someone who no longer works on the project—or by you, long ago. Only after understanding the surrounding code can you make the necessary modifications.

The simpler and more concise the code is, the faster you'll understand what's going on. Of course, good design plays a significant role here, and so does the choice of expressive names, ensuring your variables, functions, and classes are accurately described by their names. But the choice of the language and its conciseness are also important. The language is *concise* if its syntax clearly expresses the intent of the code you read and doesn't obscure it with boilerplate required to specify how the intent is accomplished.

Kotlin tries hard to ensure all the code you write carries meaning and isn't just there to satisfy code structure requirements. A lot of the standard boilerplate of object-oriented languages, such as getters, setters, and the logic for assigning constructor parameters to fields, is implicit in Kotlin and doesn't clutter your source code. Semicolons can also be omitted in Kotlin, removing a bit of extra clutter from your code, and its powerful type inference spares you from explicitly specifying types where the compiler can deduce them from the context.

Kotlin has a rich standard library that lets you replace these long, repetitive sections of code with library method calls. Kotlin's support for lambdas and anonymous functions (function literals that are used like expressions) makes it easy to pass small blocks of code to library functions. This lets you encapsulate all the common parts in the library and keep only the unique, task-specific portion in the user code.

At the same time, Kotlin doesn't try to collapse the source code to the smallest number of characters possible. For example, Kotlin supports overloading a fixed set of operators, meaning you can provide custom implementations for +, -, in, or []. However, users can't define their own custom operators. This prevents developers from replacing method names with cryptic punctuation sequences, which would be harder to read and more difficult to find in documentation systems than using expressive names.

More concise code takes less time to write and, more important, less time to read and comprehend. This improves your productivity and empowers you to get things done faster.

1.4.3   Kotlin is safe

In general, when we speak of a programming language as *safe*, we mean its design prevents certain kinds of errors in a program. Of course, this isn't an absolute quality; no language prevents all possible errors. Additionally, preventing errors usually comes at a cost. You need to give the compiler more information about the intended operation of the program, so the compiler can then verify that the information matches what the program does. Because of that, there's always a tradeoff between the level of safety you get and the loss of productivity required to put in more detailed annotations.

Running on the JVM already provides many safety guarantees—for example, memory safety, preventing buffer overflows, and other problems caused by incorrect use of dynamically allocated memory. As a statically typed language on the JVM, Kotlin also ensures the type safety of your applications. And Kotlin goes further: it makes it easy to define read-only variables (via the `val` keyword) and quick to group them in immutable (data) classes, resulting in additional safety for multithreaded applications.

Beyond that, Kotlin aims to prevent errors happening at run time by performing checks during compile time. Most important, Kotlin strives to remove the `NullPointer-Exception` from your program. Kotlin's type system tracks values that can and can't be `null` and forbids operations that can lead to a `NullPointerException` at run time. The additional cost required for this is minimal—marking a type as nullable takes only a single character, a question mark at the end:

```
fun main() {
    var s: String? = null        ⊲────────┐ May be null
    var s2: String = ""          ⊲──── May not be null

    println(s.length)            ⊲──── Won't compile, saving you from a crash
    println(s2.length)           ⊲────┐
}                                     └ Will work as expected
```

To complement this, Kotlin provides many convenient ways to handle nullable data. This helps greatly in eliminating application crashes.

Another type of exception Kotlin helps avoid is the class cast exception, which happens when you cast an object to a type without first checking that it has the right type. Kotlin combines check and cast into a single operation. That means once you've checked the type, you can refer to members of that type without any additional casts, redeclarations, or checks.

In this example, `is` performs a type check on the `value` variable, which may be of `Any` type. The compiler knows that in the `true` branch of the conditional, `value` must be of type `String`, so it can safely permit the usage of methods from that type (a so-called *smart-cast*, which we'll get to know in greater detail in section 2.3.6).

```
fun modify(value: Any) {
    if (value is String) {        ⊲────┐ Checks the type
        println(value.uppercase())  ⊲──┐
    }                                  └ Uses a method callable on
}                                        String without further casts
```

Next, let's talk specifically about Kotlin for JVM targets. Kotlin provides seamless interoperability with Java.

1.4.4   *Kotlin is interoperable*

Regarding interoperability, your first concern probably is, "Can I use my existing libraries?" With Kotlin, the answer is, "Yes, absolutely." Regardless of the kind of APIs the library requires, you can work with them from Kotlin. You can call Java methods, extend Java classes and implement interfaces, apply Java annotations to your Kotlin classes, and so on.

Unlike some other JVM languages, Kotlin goes even further with interoperability, making it effortless to call Kotlin code from Java as well. No tricks are required; Kotlin classes and methods can be called exactly like regular Java classes and methods. This gives you the ultimate flexibility to mix Java and Kotlin code anywhere in your project. When you start adopting Kotlin in your Java project, you can run the Java-to-Kotlin converter on any single class in your codebase, and the rest of the code will continue to compile and work without any modifications. This works regardless of the role of the class you've converted—something we'll take a closer look at in section 1.5.1.

Another area where Kotlin focuses on interoperability is its use of existing Java libraries to the largest degree possible. For example, Kotlin's collections rely almost entirely on Java standard library classes, extending them with additional functions for more convenient use in Kotlin. (We'll look at the mechanism for this in greater detail in section 3.3.) This means you never need to wrap or convert objects when you call Java APIs from Kotlin, or vice versa. All the API richness provided by Kotlin comes at no cost at run time.

The Kotlin tooling also provides full support for cross-language projects. It can compile an arbitrary mix of Java and Kotlin source files, regardless of how they depend on each other. IDE features inside IntelliJ IDEA and Android Studio work across languages as well, allowing you to do the following:

- Navigate freely between Java and Kotlin source files
- Debug mixed-language projects and step between code written in different languages
- Refactor your Java methods and have their use in Kotlin code correctly updated, and vice versa

As an example, figure 1.2 shows how finding usages across a mixed Kotlin and Java codebase works in IntelliJ IDEA.

Hopefully, by now, we've convinced you to give Kotlin a try. But how can you start using it? In the next section, we'll discuss the process of compiling and running Kotlin code, both from the command line and using different tools.

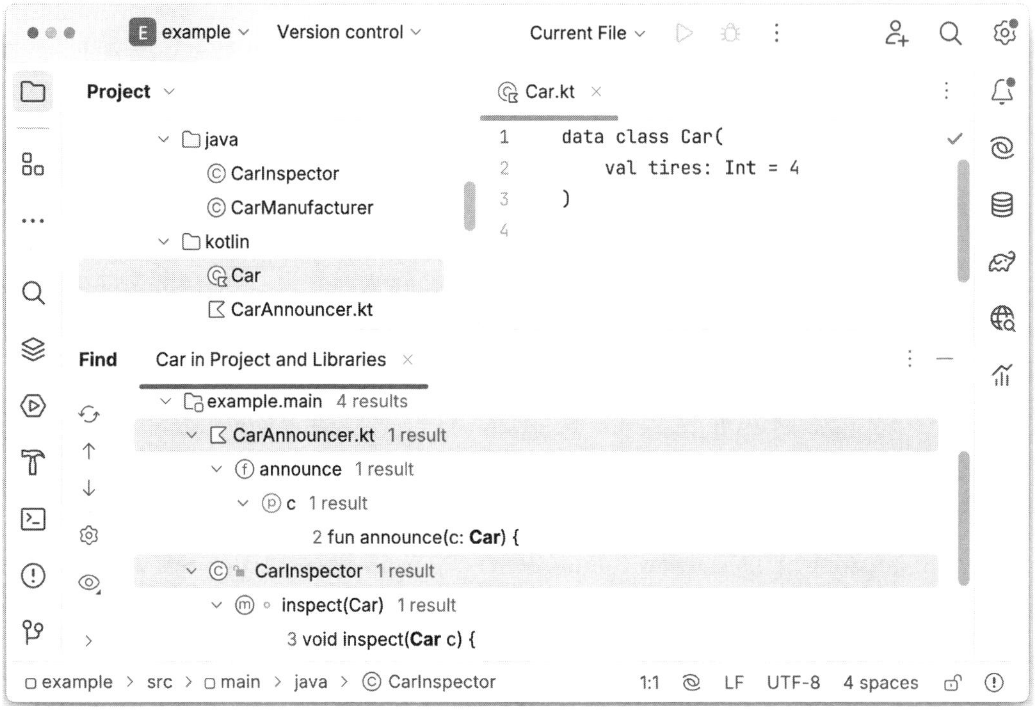

Figure 1.2   When using the Find Usages action in IntelliJ IDEA, it finds results across Kotlin and Java files in the same project. Other IDE features, such as refactorings and navigation, work just as smoothly across both languages.

1.5   Using the Kotlin tools

Let's examine an overview of the Kotlin tools. First, we'll discuss how to set up your environment to run the Kotlin code.

1.5.1   Setting up and running the Kotlin code

You can run small snippets online or install an IDE. You'll get the best experience with IntelliJ IDEA or Android Studio. We provide the basic information here, but the best up-to-date tutorials are available on the Kotlin website. If you need the detailed information about getting your environment set up or information about different compilation targets, please refer to the Getting Started section of the Kotlin website (https://kotlinlang.org/docs/getting-started.html).

TRY KOTLIN WITHOUT INSTALLATION WITH THE KOTLIN ONLINE PLAYGROUND

The easiest way to try Kotlin doesn't require any installation or configuration. At https://play.kotlinlang.org/, you can find an online playground, where you can write, compile, and run small Kotlin programs. The playground has code samples demonstrating the features of Kotlin as well as a series of exercises for learning Kotlin interactively. Alongside it, the Kotlin documentation (https://kotlinlang.org/docs) also has several interactive samples you can run right in the browser.

These are the quickest ways to run short snippets of Kotlin, but they provides less assistance and guidance. It's a very minimal development environment that is missing several convenient features, such as autocomplete or inspections that can tell you how to improve your Kotlin code. The web version also doesn't support user interactions via the standard input stream or working with files and directories; however, these features are all conveniently available inside IntelliJ IDEA and Android Studio.

PLUG-IN FOR INTELLIJ IDEA AND ANDROID STUDIO

The IntelliJ IDEA plug-in for Kotlin has been developed in parallel with the language, and it's a full-featured development environment for Kotlin. It's mature and stable, and it provides a complete set of tools for Kotlin development.

The Kotlin plug-in is included out of the box with IntelliJ IDEA and Android Studio, so no additional setup is necessary. You can use either the free, open source IntelliJ IDEA Community Edition or Android Studio, or the commercial IntelliJ IDEA Ultimate. In IntelliJ IDEA, select Kotlin in the New Project dialog, and you're good to go. In Android Studio, you simply need to create a new project to immediately start writing Kotlin. You can also check the "Get started with Kotlin/JVM" tutorial with detailed instructions and screenshots on how to create a project in IntelliJ IDEA: https://kotlinlang.org/docs/jvm-get-started.html.

THE JAVA-TO-KOTLIN CONVERTER

Getting up to speed with a new language is never effortless. Fortunately, we've built a nice little shortcut that lets you speed up your learning and adoption by relying on your existing knowledge of Java. This tool is the automated Java-to-Kotlin converter.

As you start learning Kotlin, the converter can help you express something when you don't remember the exact syntax. You can write the corresponding snippet in Java and then paste it into a Kotlin file, and the converter will automatically offer to translate the code into Kotlin. The result won't always be the most idiomatic, but it will be working code, and you'll be able to make progress with your task.

The converter is also great for introducing Kotlin into an existing Java project. When you need to write a new class, you can do it in Kotlin right from the beginning. However, if you need to make significant changes to an existing class, you may also want to use Kotlin in the process. That's where the converter comes into play: you convert the class into Kotlin first, and then you add the changes, using all the benefits of a modern language.

Using the converter in IntelliJ IDEA is extremely easy. You can either copy a Java code fragment and paste it into a Kotlin file or invoke the Convert Java File to Kotlin File action if you need to convert an entire file.

1.5.2   Compiling Kotlin code

Kotlin is a compiled language, which means before you can run Kotlin code, you need to compile it. As we discussed in section 1.3.3, the Kotlin code can be compiled to different targets:

- JVM bytecode (stored in .class files) to run on the JVM
- JVM bytecode to be further transformed and run on Android
- Native targets to run natively on different operating systems
- JavaScript (and WebAssembly) to run in a browser

For the Kotlin compiler, it's not important whether the produced JVM bytecode runs on JVM or is further transformed and runs on Android. Android Runtime (ART) transforms the JVM bytecode to Dex bytecode and runs it instead. For more details on how it works on Android, please refer to the documentation: https://source.android .com/devices/tech/dalvik.

Since the main target for this book is Kotlin/JVM, let's discuss how the compilation process works there in greater detail. You can find information about other targets on the Kotlin website.

THE COMPILATION PROCESS FOR KOTLIN/JVM

Kotlin source code is normally stored in files with the extension .kt. When compiling Kotlin code for the JVM target, the compiler analyzes the source code and generates .class files, just like the Java compiler does. The generated .class files are then packaged and executed using the standard procedure for the type of application you're working on.

In the simplest case, you can use the `kotlinc` command to compile your code from the command line and use the `java` command to execute your code:

```
kotlinc <source file or directory> -include-runtime -d <jar name>
java -jar <jar name>
```

A JVM can run .class files compiled from the Kotlin code without knowing whether they were written initially in Java or in Kotlin. Kotlin built-in classes and their APIs, however, differ from those in Java, and to correctly run the compiled code, JVM needs the additional information as a dependency: the *Kotlin runtime library*. When compiling code from the command line, we explicitly invoked `-include-runtime` to include this runtime library into the resulting JAR file.

The Kotlin runtime library, which must be distributed with your application, contains the definitions of Kotlin's basic classes, like `Int` and `String`, and some extensions Kotlin adds to the standard Java APIs. A simplified description of the Kotlin build process is shown in figure 1.3.

In addition, you need the *Kotlin standard library* included as a dependency in your application. In theory, you can write the Kotlin code without it, but in practice, you never need to do so. The standard library contains the definitions of such fundamental classes as `List`, `Map`, and `Sequence` as well as many methods for working with them. We discuss the most important classes and their APIs in detail in this book.

In most real-life cases, you'll be using a build system such as Gradle or Maven to compile your code. Kotlin is compatible with these build systems. All of those build systems also support mixed-language projects that combine Kotlin and Java in the

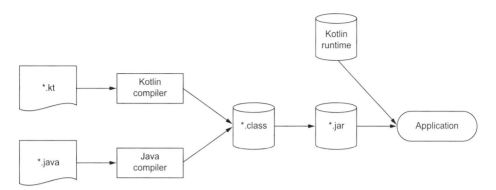

Figure 1.3   Kotlin build process

same codebase. Maven and Gradle take care of including both the Kotlin runtime library and (for the latest versions) Kotlin standard library as dependencies of your application, so you don't need to include them explicitly.

The best and most up-to-date way to check the details of how to set up the project with the build system of your choice is reviewing the following sections of the Kotlin documentation: https://kotlinlang.org/docs/gradle.html and https://kotlinlang.org/docs/maven.html. For a quick start, you don't need to know all the peculiarities; you can simply create a new project, and the correct build file with the necessary dependencies will be generated for you.

Summary

- Kotlin is statically typed and supports type inference, allowing it to maintain correctness and performance while keeping the source code concise.
- Kotlin supports both object-oriented and functional programming styles, enabling higher-level abstractions through first-class functions and simplifying testing and multithreaded development through the support of immutable values.
- Coroutines are a lightweight alternative to threads and help make asynchronous code feel natural by allowing you to write logic that looks similar to sequential code and structure concurrent code in parent–child relationships.
- Kotlin works well for server-side applications, with Kotlin-first frameworks like Ktor and http4k, as well as fully supports all existing Java frameworks, like Spring Boot.
- Android is Kotlin first, with development tools, libraries, samples, and documentation all primarily focused on Kotlin.
- Kotlin Multiplatform brings your Kotlin code to targets beyond the JVM, including iOS and the web.
- Kotlin is free and open source, and it supports multiple build systems and IDEs.
- IntelliJ IDEA and Android Studio allow you to navigate smoothly across code written in both Kotlin and Java.

- The Kotlin playground (https://play.kotlinlang.org) is a fast way to try Kotlin without any setup.
- The automated Java-to-Kotlin converter allows you to bring your existing code and knowledge to Kotlin.
- Kotlin is pragmatic, safe, concise, and interoperable, meaning it focuses on using proven solutions for common tasks, preventing common errors, such as `NullPointerExceptions`; supporting compact and easy-to-read code; and providing unrestricted integration with Java.

Kotlin basics

2

This chapter covers

- Declaring functions, variables, classes, enums, and properties
- Control structures in Kotlin
- Smart casts
- Throwing and handling exceptions

In this chapter, you'll learn the basics of the Kotlin language required to write your first working Kotlin programs. These include basic building blocks that you encounter all throughout Kotlin programs, like variables and functions. You'll also get acquainted with different ways of representing data in Kotlin via enums as well as classes and their properties.

The control structures you'll learn throughout this chapter will give you the tools needed to use conditional logic in your programs as well as iterate using loops. You will also learn what makes these constructs special compared to other languages, like Java.

We'll also introduce the basic mechanics of types in Kotlin, starting with the concept of a *smart cast*, an operation that combines a type check and a cast into one operation. You'll see how this helps you remove redundancy from your code without sacrificing safety. We'll also briefly talk about exception handling and Kotlin's philosophy behind it. By the end of this chapter, you'll already be able to combine these basic bits and pieces of the Kotlin language to write your own working Kotlin code, even if it might not be the most idiomatic.

> **What's idiomatic Kotlin?**
>
> When discussing Kotlin code, a certain phrase often reoccurs: *idiomatic Kotlin*. You'll certainly hear this phrase throughout this book, but you might also hear it when talking to your colleagues, when attending community events, or at conferences. Clearly, it's worth understanding what this means.
>
> Simply put, idiomatic Kotlin is how a "native Kotlin speaker" writes code, using language features and syntactic sugar where appropriate. Such code is made up of *idioms*—recognizable structures that address problems you're trying to solve in "the Kotlin way." Idiomatic code fits in with the programming style generally accepted by the community and follows the recommendations of the language designers.
>
> Like any skill, learning to write idiomatic Kotlin takes time and practice. As you progress through this book, inspect the provided code samples, and write your own code, you will gradually develop an intuition for what idiomatic Kotlin code looks and feels like and will gain the ability to independently apply these learnings in your own code.

2.1   *Basic elements: Functions and variables*

This section introduces you to the basic elements every Kotlin program consists of: functions and variables. You'll write your very first Kotlin program, see how Kotlin lets you omit many type declarations, and learn how it encourages you to avoid using mutable data where possible—and why that's a good thing.

2.1.1   *Writing your first Kotlin program: "Hello, world!"*

Let's start our journey into the world of Kotlin with a classical example: a program that prints "Hello, world!" In Kotlin, it's just one function (figure 2.1).

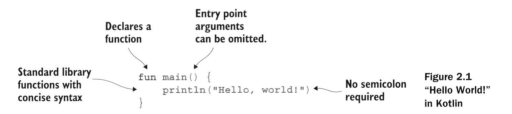

Figure 2.1 "Hello World!" in Kotlin

We can observe several features and elements of the language syntax in this simple code snippet already:

- The `fun` keyword is used to declare a function. Programming in Kotlin is lots of fun, indeed!

- The function can be declared at the top level of any Kotlin file; you don't need to put it in a class.
- You can specify the `main` function as the entry point for your application at the top level and without additional arguments (other languages may require you to always accept an array of command-line parameters, for example).
- Kotlin emphasizes conciseness: you just write `println` to display your text in the console. The Kotlin standard library provides many wrappers around standard Java library functions (e.g., `System.out.println`) with more concise syntax, and `println` is one of them.
- You can (and should) omit the semicolon from the end of a line, just as in many other modern languages.

So far, so good! We'll discuss some of these topics in more detail later. Now, let's explore the function declaration syntax.

2.1.2   *Declaring functions with parameters and return values*

The first function you wrote didn't actually return any meaningful values. However, the purpose of functions is often to compute and subsequently return some kind of result. For example, you may want to write a simple function `max` that takes two integer numbers `a` and `b` and returns the larger of the two. So what would that look like?

The function declaration starts with the `fun` keyword followed by the function name: `max`, in this case. It's followed by the parameter list in parentheses. Here, we declare two parameters, `a` and `b`, both of type `Int`. In Kotlin, you first specify the parameter name, and then you specify the type, separated by a colon. The return type comes after the parameter list, separated from it by a colon:

```
fun max(a: Int, b: Int): Int {
    return if (a > b) a else b
}
```

Figure 2.2 shows you the basic structure of a function. Note that in Kotlin, `if` is an expression with a result value. You can think of `if` as returning a value from either of its branches. This makes it similar to the ternary operator in other languages, like Java, where the same construct might look like `(a > b) ? a : b`.

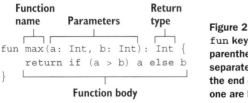

Figure 2.2   A Kotlin function is introduced with the `fun` keyword. Parameters and their types follow in parentheses, each annotated with a name and a type, separated by a colon. Its return type is specified after the end of the parameter list. Functions just like this one are basic building blocks of any Kotlin program.

You can then call your function by using its name, providing the arguments in parentheses. You'll learn about different ways for calling Kotlin functions in section 3.2.1:

```
fun main() {
    println(max(1, 2))
    // 2
}
```

Parameters and return type of the main function

As you already saw in the "Hello, World!" example, the entry point of every Kotlin program is its `main` function. This function can either be declared with no parameters or with an array of strings as its arguments (`args: Array<String>`). In the latter case, each element in the array corresponds to a command-line parameter passed to your application. In any case, the `main` function does not return any value.

The difference between expressions and statements

In Kotlin, `if` is an expression, not a statement. The difference between an expression and a statement is that an expression has a value, which can be used as part of another expression, whereas a statement is always a top-level element in its enclosing block and doesn't have its own value. In Kotlin, most control structures, except the loops (`for`, `while`, and `do/while`), are expressions, which sets it apart from other languages, like Java. Specifically, the ability to combine control structures with other expressions lets you express many common patterns concisely, as you'll see later in the book. As a sneak peek, here are some snippets that are valid in Kotlin:

```
val x = if (myBoolean) 3 else 5
val direction = when (inputString) {
    "u" -> UP
    "d" -> DOWN
    else -> UNKNOWN
}
val number = try {
    inputString.toInt()
} catch (nfe: NumberFormatException) {
    -1
}
```

On the other hand, Kotlin enforces assignments to always be statements—that is, when assigning a value to a variable, this assignment operation doesn't itself return a value.

This helps avoid confusion between comparisons and assignments, which is a common source of mistakes in languages that treat them as expressions, such as Java or C/C++. That means the following isn't valid Kotlin code:

```
val number: Int
val alsoNumber = i = getNumber()
// ERROR: Assignments are not expressions,
// and only expressions are allowed in this context
```

2.1.3 *Making function definitions more concise by using expression bodies*

In fact, you can make your max function even more concise. Since its body consists of a single expression (if (a > b) a else b), you can use that expression as the entire body of the function, removing the curly braces and the return statement. Instead, you can place the single expression right after an equals sign (=):

```
fun max(a: Int, b: Int): Int = if (a > b) a else b
```

If a function is written with its body in curly braces, we say that this function has a *block body*. If it returns an expression directly, it has an *expression body*.

Converting between expression body and block body in IntelliJ IDEA and Android Studio

IntelliJ IDEA and Android Studio provide intention actions to convert between the two styles of functions: Convert to Expression Body and Convert to Block Body. You can find them via the lightbulb icon when your cursor is placed on the function or the Alt-Enter (or Option-Return on macOS) keyboard shortcut.

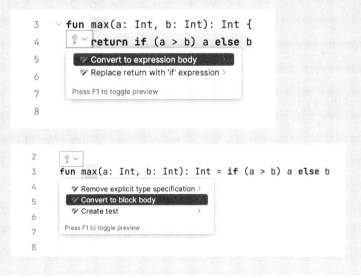

Functions that have an expression body are a frequent occurrence in Kotlin code. You've already seen that they are quite convenient when your function happens to be a trivial one-liner that intends to give a conditional check or an often-used operation a memorable name. But they also find use when functions evaluate a single, more complex expression, such as if, when, or try. You'll see such functions later in this chapter, when we talk about the when construct.

You could simplify your max function even more and omit the return type:

```
fun max(a: Int, b: Int) = if (a > b) a else b
```

At first sight, this might seem puzzling to you. How can there be functions without return-type declarations? You've already learned that Kotlin is a statically typed language—so doesn't it require every expression to have a type at compile time?

Indeed, every variable and every expression has a type, and every function has a return type. But for expression-body functions, the compiler can analyze the expression used as the body of the function and use its type as the function return type, even when it's not specified explicitly. This type of analysis is usually called *type inference*.

Note that omitting the return type is allowed only for functions with an expression body. For functions with a block body that return a value, you must specify the return type and write the `return` statements explicitly. That's a conscious choice. Oftentimes, real-world functions are long and contain several `return` statements; having the return type and the `return` statements written explicitly helps you quickly grasp what can be returned. Let's look at the syntax for variable declarations next.

> **Keep your return types explicit when writing a library**
>
> If you are authoring libraries other developers depend upon, you may want to refrain from using inferred return types for functions that are part of your public API. By explicitly specifying the types of your functions, you can avoid accidental signature changes that could cause errors in the code of your library's consumers. In fact, Kotlin provides tooling in the form of compiler options that can automatically check that you're explicitly specifying return types. You'll learn more about this *explicit API mode* in section 4.1.3.

2.1.4 *Declaring variables to store data*

Another basic building block you'll commonly use in all your Kotlin programs is variables, which allow you to store data. A variable declaration in Kotlin starts with a keyword (`val` or `var`), followed by the name for the variable. While Kotlin lets you omit the type for many variable declarations (thanks to its powerful *type inference*, which you've already seen in section 2.1.3), you can always explicitly put the type after the variable name. For example, if you need to store one of the most famous questions and its respective answer in a Kotlin variable, you could do so by specifying two variables, `question` and `answer`, with their explicit types—`String` for the textual question and `Int` for the integer answer:

```
val question: String =
    "The Ultimate Question of Life, the Universe, and Everything"
val answer: Int = 42
```

You can also omit the type declarations, making the example a bit more concise:

```
val question =
    "The Ultimate Question of Life, the Universe, and Everything"
val answer = 42
```

As with expression-body functions, if you don't specify the type, the compiler analyzes the initializer expression and uses its type as the variable type. In this case, the initializer, `42`, is of type `Int`, so the variable `answer` will have the same type.

If you use a floating-point constant, the variable will have the type `Double`:

```
val yearsToCompute = 7.5e6        ◁——— 7.5 × 10⁶ = 7,500,000.0
```

The number types, along with other basic types, are covered in greater depth in section 8.1.

If you're not initializing your variable immediately, and instead assigning it at a later point, the compiler won't be able to infer the type for the variable. In this case, you need to specify its type explicitly:

```
fun main() {
    val answer: Int
    answer = 42
}
```

2.1.5 Marking a variable as read only or reassignable

To control when a variable can be assigned a new value, Kotlin provides you with two keywords, `val` and `var`, for declaring variables:

- `val` (from *value*) declares a *read-only reference*. A variable declared with `val` can be assigned only once. After it has been initialized, it can't be reassigned a different value. (For comparison, in Java, this would be expressed via the `final` modifier.)
- `var` (from *variable*) declares a *reassignable reference*. You can assign other values to such a variable, even after it has been initialized. (This behavior is analogous to a regular, non-final variable in Java.)

By default, you should strive to declare all variables in Kotlin with the `val` keyword; change it to `var` only if necessary. Using read-only references, immutable objects, and functions without side effects allows you to take advantage of the benefits offered by the *functional programming* style. We briefly touched on its advantages in section 1.2.3, and we'll return to this topic in chapter 5.

A `val` variable must be initialized exactly once during the execution of the block where it's defined. However, you can initialize it with different values depending on some condition, as long as the compiler can ensure only one of the initialization statements will be executed.

You may find yourself in a situation in which you want to assign the contents of a `result` variable that depends on the return value of another function, like `canPerform-Operation`. Because the compiler is smart enough to know that exactly one of the two potential assignments will be executed, you can still specify `result` as a read-only reference using the `val` keyword:

```
fun canPerformOperation(): Boolean {
    return true
}

fun main() {
    val result: String
    if (canPerformOperation()) {
        result = "Success"
    } else {
        result = "Can't perform operation"
    }
}
```

Note that, even though a `val` reference is itself read only and can't be changed once it has been assigned, the object it points to may be mutable. For example, adding an element to a mutable list, which is referenced by a read-only reference, is perfectly okay:

```
fun main() {
    val languages = mutableListOf("Java")      ◁——  Declares a read-only reference
    languages.add("Kotlin")              ◁——  Mutates the object pointed to by the
}                                              reference by adding an element
```

In section 8.2.2, we'll discuss mutable and read-only objects in greater detail.

Even though the `var` keyword allows a variable to change its value, its type is fixed. For example, if you decided midprogram that the `answer` variable should store a string instead of an integer, you would be met with a compile error:

```
fun main() {
    var answer = 42
    answer = "no answer"      ◁——— Error: type mismatch
}
```

There's an error on the string literal because its type (`String`) isn't as expected (`Int`). The compiler infers the variable type only from the initializer and doesn't take subsequent assignments into account when determining the type.

If you need to store a value of a mismatching type in a variable, you must manually convert or coerce the value into the right type. We'll discuss number conversions in section 8.1.4.

Now that you know how to define variables, it's time to see some new tricks for referring to values of those variables. Specifically, you'll see how you can provide some nicer and more structured outputs for your first Kotlin programs.

2.1.6   *Easier string formatting: String templates*

Let's get back to the "Hello World!" example that opened this section and extend it with some extra features that occur commonly in all kinds of Kotlin programs. You'll add a bit of personalization, by having the program greet people by name. If the user specifies a name via the standard input, then your program uses it in the greeting. In case the user doesn't actually provide any input, you'll just have to greet all of Kotlin instead. Such a greeting program could look as follows and showcases a few features you haven't seen before.

Listing 2.1 Using string templates

```
fun main() {
    val input = readln()
    val name = if (input.isNotBlank()) input else "Kotlin"
    println("Hello, $name!")
}
```

◁─── Prints "Hello, Kotlin!" or "Hello, Bob!" if you enter "Bob" via stdin (e.g., your terminal)

This example introduces a feature called *string templates* and also briefly shows an example of how you could read simple user input. In the code, you read `input` from the standard input stream via the `readln()` function (which is available in any Kotlin file, alongside others). You then declare a variable `name` and initialize its value using an `if` expression. If the standard input exists and is not blank, `name` is assigned the value of `input`. Otherwise, it's assigned a default value of `"Kotlin"`. Finally, you use it in the string literal passed to `println`.

Like many scripting languages, Kotlin allows you to refer to local variables in string literals by putting the `$` character in front of the variable name. This is equivalent to Java's string concatenation (`"Hello, " + name + "!"`) but is more compact and just as efficient. And, of course, the expressions are statically checked, and the code won't compile if you try to refer to a variable that doesn't exist.

> **NOTE** For JVM 1.8 targets, the compiled code creates a `StringBuilder` and appends the constant parts and variable values to it. Applications targeting JVM 9 or above compile string concatenations into more efficient dynamic invocations via `invokedynamic`.

If you need to include the `$` character in a string, you escape it with a backslash:

```
fun main() {
    println("\$x")
    // $x
}
```

◁─── Doesn't interpret x as a variable reference

String templates in Kotlin are quite powerful, since they don't limit you to referencing individual variables. If you want your greeting to be a bit more adventurous and greet your user by the length of their name, you can also provide a more complex expression in the string template. All it takes is putting curly braces around the expression:

```
fun main() {
    val name = readln()
    if (name.isNotBlank()) {
        println("Hello, ${name.length}-letter person!")
    }
}
```

Uses the ${} syntax to insert the length property of the name variable to the greeting string ───▷

```
    // Blank input: (no output)
    // "Seb" input: Hello, 3-letter person!
}
```

Now, you can include arbitrary expressions inside string templates, and you already knew that `if` is an expression in Kotlin. Combining the two, you can now rewrite your greeting program to include the conditional directly inside the string template:

```
fun main() {
    val name = readln()
    println("Hello, ${if (name.isBlank()) "someone" else name}!")
    // Blank input: Hello, someone!
    // "Seb" input: Hello, Seb!
}
```

Notice how, within a string template, you can still use an expression that itself contains a double-quoted string! When the expression is evaluated, it returns either the string `someone` or the provided name and inserts it in the surrounding template. In section 3.5, we'll return to strings and talk more about what you can do with them.

Now, you already know a few of the most basic building blocks to write your own Kotlin programs: functions and variables. Let's go one step up in the hierarchy and look at classes and how they help you encapsulate and group related data in an object-oriented fashion. This time, you'll use the Java-to-Kotlin converter to help you get started using the new language features.

2.2   Encapsulating behavior and data: Classes and properties

Just like other object-oriented programming languages, Kotlin provides the abstraction of a *class*. Kotlin's concepts in this area will be familiar to you, but you'll find that many common tasks can be accomplished with much less code than other object-oriented languages. This section will introduce you to the basic syntax for declaring classes. We'll go into more detail in chapter 4.

To begin, let's look at a simple plain old Java object (POJO) `Person` class that so far contains only one property: `name`.

Listing 2.2   Simple Java class `Person`

```
/* Java */
public class Person {
    private final String name;

    public Person(String name) {
        this.name = name;
    }

    public String getName() {
        return name;
    }
}
```

You can see that, in Java, this requires some quite lengthy code. The constructor body is entirely repetitive, as it only assigns the parameters to fields with corresponding names. As per convention, to access the `name` field, the `Person` class should also provide a getter function `getName`, which also just returns the contents of the field. This kind of repetition often happens in Java. In Kotlin, this logic can be expressed without so much boilerplate.

In chapter 1, we introduced the Java-to-Kotlin converter: a tool that automatically replaces Java code with Kotlin code that does the same thing. Let's look at the converter in action and convert the `Person` class to Kotlin.

Listing 2.3 `Person` class converted to Kotlin

```
class Person(val name: String)
```

Looks good, doesn't it? If you've tried another modern object-oriented language, you may have seen something similar. As you can see, Kotlin offers a concise syntax for declaring classes, especially classes that contain only data but no code. We'll discuss their relationship to a very similar concept in Java 14 and above, *records*, in chapter 4.

Note that the modifier `public` disappeared during the conversion from Java to Kotlin. In Kotlin, `public` is the default visibility, so you can omit it.

2.2.1 Associating data with a class and making it accessible: Properties

The idea of a class is to encapsulate data and code that works on that data into a single entity. In Java, the data is stored in fields, which are usually private. If you need to let clients of the class access that data, you provide *accessor methods*: a getter and possibly a setter. You saw an example of this in the `Person` class. The setter can also contain additional logic for validating the passed value, sending notifications about the change and so on.

In Java, the combination of the field and its accessors is often referred to as a *property*, and many frameworks make heavy use of that concept. In Kotlin, properties are a first-class language feature that entirely replaces fields and accessor methods. You declare a property in a class the same way you declare a variable: with the `val` and `var` keywords. A property declared as `val` is read only, whereas a `var` property is mutable and can be changed. For example, you could expand your `Person` class, which already contained a read-only `name` property, with a mutable `isStudent` property.

Listing 2.4 Declaring a mutable property in a class

```
class Person(
    val name: String,          ⟵┐  Read-only property—generates a field and a trivial getter
    var isStudent: Boolean     ⟵── Writable property—a field, getter, and setter
)
```

Basically, when you declare a property, you declare the corresponding accessors (a getter for a read-only property and both a getter and a setter for a writable one). By default, the implementation of these accessors is trivial; a field is created to store the value, the getter returns the value of this field, and the setter updates its value. But if you want, you may declare a custom accessor that uses different logic to compute or update the property value.

The concise declaration of the Person class in listing 2.4 hides the same underlying implementation as the original Java code: it's a class with private fields that is initialized in the constructor and can be accessed through the corresponding getter. That means you can use this class from Java and from Kotlin the same way, independent of where it was declared. The use looks identical. Here's how you can use the Kotlin class Person from Java code, creating a new Person object with the name Bob who is a student—until he graduates.

Listing 2.5 Using the Person class from Java

```java
public class Demo {
    public static void main(String[] args) {
        Person person = new Person("Bob", true);
        System.out.println(person.getName());
        // Bob
        System.out.println(person.isStudent());
        // true
        person.setStudent(false); // Graduation!
        System.out.println(person.isStudent());
        // false
    }
}
```

Note that this looks the same when Person is defined in Java and Kotlin. Kotlin's name property is exposed to Java as a getter method called getName. The getter and setter naming rule has an exception: if the property name starts with is, no additional prefix for the getter is added and, in the setter name, is is replaced with set. Thus, from Java, you can call isStudent() and setStudent() to access the isStudent property .

If you convert listing 2.5 to Kotlin, you get the following result.

Listing 2.6 Using the Person class from Kotlin

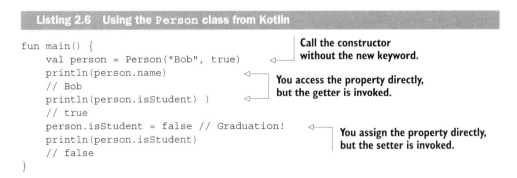

```kotlin
fun main() {
    val person = Person("Bob", true)        ◁── Call the constructor
    println(person.name)                          without the new keyword.
    // Bob                                   ◁── You access the property directly,
    println(person.isStudent) )                   but the getter is invoked.
    // true
    person.isStudent = false // Graduation!  ◁── You assign the property directly,
    println(person.isStudent)                     but the setter is invoked.
    // false
}
```

Now, instead of invoking the getter explicitly, you reference the property directly. The logic stays the same, but the code is more concise. Setters of mutable properties work the same way. While, in Java, you use `person.setStudent(false)` to symbolize a graduation, in Kotlin, you use the property syntax directly and write `person.isStudent = false`.

> **TIP** You can also use the Kotlin property syntax for classes defined in Java. Getters in a Java class can be accessed as `val` properties from Kotlin, and getter–setter pairs can be accessed as `var` properties. For example, if a Java class defines methods called `getName` and `setName`, you can access it as a property called `name`. If it defines `isStudent` and `setStudent` methods, the name of the corresponding Kotlin property will be `isStudent`.

In most cases, the property has a corresponding backing field that simply stores the property value (you'll learn more about backing fields in Kotlin in section 4.2.4.) But if the value can be computed on the fly (e.g., by deriving it from other properties) you can express that using a custom getter.

2.2.2 *Computing properties instead of storing their values: Custom accessors*

Let's see how you could provide a custom implementation of a property accessor. One common case for this is when a property is a direct result of some other properties in the object. If you have a `Rectangle` class that stores `width` and `height`, you can provide a property `isSquare` that is `true` when `width` and `height` are equal. Because this is a property, you can check "on the go," computing it on access; you don't need to store that information as a separate field. Instead, you can provide a custom getter, whose implementation computes the "squareness" of the `Rectangle` every time the property is accessed:

```
class Rectangle(val height: Int, val width: Int) {
    val isSquare: Boolean
        get() {                          ⟵——— Property getter declaration
            return height == width
        }
}
```

Note that you don't have to use the full syntax with curly braces. Just like any other function, you can define the getter using expression-body syntax you learned about in section 2.1.3 and write `val isSquare get() = height == width`, as well. As you can see, the expression-body syntax also allows you to omit explicitly specifying the property type, having the compiler infer the type for you instead.

Regardless of the syntax you choose, the invocation of a property like `isSquare` stays the same:

```
fun main() {
    val rectangle = Rectangle(41, 43)
    println(rectangle.isSquare)
    // false
}
```

If you need to access this property from Java, you call the `isSquare` method as before.

You might ask whether it's better to declare a property with a custom getter or define a function inside the class (referred to as a *member function* or *method* in Kotlin). Both options are similar: there is no difference in implementation or performance; they only differ in readability. Generally, if you describe the characteristic (the property) of a class, you should declare it as a property. If you are describing the behavior of a class, choose a member function instead.

In chapter 4, you'll take a look at more examples that use classes, properties, and member functions as well as look at the syntax to explicitly declare constructors. If you're impatient and happen to know the equivalents of these topics in Java, you can always use the Java-to-Kotlin converter in the meantime to peek ahead. Before we move on to other language features, let's briefly examine how code in Kotlin projects is generally structured.

2.2.3   *Kotlin source code layout: Directories and packages*

As your programs grow in complexity, consisting of more and more functions, classes, and other language constructs, you'll inevitably need to start thinking about how to organize your source code in order for your project to stay maintainable and navigable. Let's examine how Kotlin projects are typically structured.

Kotlin uses the concept of *packages* to organize classes (similar to what you may be familiar with from Java). Every Kotlin file can have a `package` statement at the beginning, and all declarations (classes, functions, and properties) defined in the file will be placed in that package.

The following listing shows an example of a source file showing the syntax for the package declaration statement.

> **Listing 2.7 Putting a class and a function declaration in a package**

```
package geometry.shapes          ⬍——— Package declaration

class Rectangle(val height: Int, val width: Int) {
    val isSquare: Boolean
        get() = height == width
}

fun createUnitSquare(): Rectangle {
    return Rectangle(1, 1)
}
```

Declarations defined in other files can be used directly if they're in the same package; they need to be *imported* if they're in a different package. This happens using the `import` keyword at the beginning of the file, placed directly below the `package` directive.

Kotlin doesn't make a distinction between importing classes or functions, and it allows you to import any kind of declaration using the `import` keyword. If you are writing a demo project in the `geometry.example` package, then you can use the class

`Rectangle` and the function `createUnitSquare` from the `geometry.shapes` package simply by importing them by name.

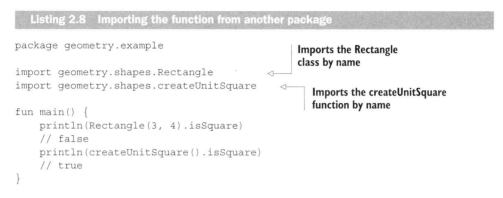

Listing 2.8   Importing the function from another package

```
package geometry.example

import geometry.shapes.Rectangle                    ◁──  Imports the Rectangle
import geometry.shapes.createUnitSquare                   class by name

fun main() {                                        ◁──  Imports the createUnitSquare
    println(Rectangle(3, 4).isSquare)                     function by name
    // false
    println(createUnitSquare().isSquare)
    // true
}
```

You can also import all declarations defined in a particular package by writing .* after the package name. Note that this *star import* (also called *wildcard import*) makes everything defined in the package visible—not only classes but also top-level functions and properties. In listing 2.8, writing `import geometry.shapes.*` instead of the explicit import makes the code compile correctly as well.

In Java, you put your classes into a structure of files and directories that matches the package structure. For example, if you have a package named shapes with several classes, you need to put every class into a separate file with a matching name and store those files in a directory also called shapes. The following listing shows how the geometry package and its subpackages could be organized in Java. Assume the `createUnitSquare` function is located in a separate file, called RectangleUtil (see figure 2.3).

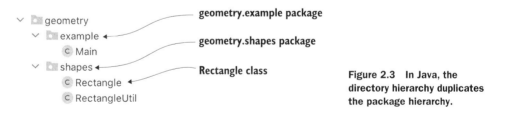

Figure 2.3   In Java, the directory hierarchy duplicates the package hierarchy.

In Kotlin, you can put multiple classes in the same file and choose any name for that file. Kotlin also doesn't impose any restrictions on the layout of source files on disk; you can use any directory structure to organize your files. For instance, you can define all the content of the package `geometry.shapes` in the file shapes.kt and place this file in the geometry folder without creating a separate shapes folder (see figure 2.4).

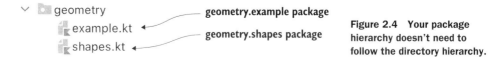

Figure 2.4   Your package hierarchy doesn't need to follow the directory hierarchy.

In most cases, however, it's still a good practice to organize source files into directories according to the package structure, following Java's directory layout. Sticking to that structure is especially important in projects where Kotlin is mixed with Java because doing so allows you to migrate the code gradually without introducing any surprises. But you shouldn't hesitate to pull multiple classes into the same file, especially if the classes are small (and, in Kotlin, they often are).

Now, you know how programs are structured. Let's return to our journey through the basic concepts of Kotlin and have a look at how to handle different choices in Kotlin beyond the `if` expression.

2.3   *Representing and handling choices: Enums and when*

In this section, we'll look at an example of declaring enums in Kotlin and talk about the `when` construct. The latter can be thought of as a more powerful and often-used replacement for the `switch` construct in Java. We will also discuss the concept of *smart casts*, which combine type checks and casts.

2.3.1   *Declaring enum classes and enum constants*

It's time we add a splash of color to this book! Given manufacturing constraints, you'll have to rely on your imagination to visualize them in all their glory—here, you'll have to realize them as Kotlin code—specifically, an enum of color constants.

Listing 2.9   Declaring a simple enum class

```
package ch02.colors

enum class Color {
    RED, ORANGE, YELLOW, GREEN, BLUE, INDIGO, VIOLET
}
```

This is a rare case in which a Kotlin declaration uses more keywords than the corresponding Java one: `enum class` versus just `enum` in Java.

> **enum is a soft keyword**
>
> In Kotlin, `enum` is a so-called *soft keyword*: it has a special meaning when it comes before `class`, but you can use it as a regular name (e.g., for a function, variable name, or parameter) in other places. On the other hand, `class` is a *hard keyword*, meaning you can't use it as an identifier: you have to use an alternate spelling or phrasing, like `clazz` or `aClass`.

Having colors stored in an enum is useful, but we can do better. Color values are often represented using their red, green, and blue components. Enum constants use the same constructor and property declaration syntax, as you saw earlier for regular classes. You can use this to expand your `Color` enum: you can associate each enum constant with its r, g, and b values. You can also declare properties, like rgb, which creates a combined numerical color value from the components, and methods, like printColor, using familiar syntax.

Listing 2.10 Declaring an enum class with properties

```
package ch02.colors

enum class Color(
    val r: Int,                     Declares properties
    val g: Int,                     of enum constants
    val b: Int
) {
    RED(255, 0, 0),                 Specifies property values when
    ORANGE(255, 165, 0),            each constant is created
    YELLOW(255, 255, 0),
    GREEN(0, 255, 0),
    BLUE(0, 0, 255),
    INDIGO(75, 0, 130),             The semicolon here is required.
    VIOLET(238, 130, 238);
    val rgb = (r * 256 + g) * 256 + b    Defines a property on the enum class
    fun printColor() = println("$this is $rgb")
}                                        Defines a method
                                         on the enum class
fun main() {
    println(Color.BLUE.rgb)
    // 255
    Color.GREEN.printColor()
    // GREEN is 65280
}
```

Note that this example shows the only place in the Kotlin syntax where you're required to use semicolons: if you define any methods in the enum class, the semicolon separates the enum constant list from the method definitions. Now that we have a fully fledged Colors enum, let's see how Kotlin lets you easily work with these constants.

2.3.2 Using the when expression to deal with enum classes

Do you remember any of the mnemonic phrases children use to memorize the colors of the rainbow? Here's one: *Richard Of York Gave Battle In Vain!* Imagine you need a function that gives you a mnemonic for each color (and you don't want to store this information in the enum itself). In Java, you could use a switch statement or, since Java 13, a switch expression for this. The corresponding Kotlin construct is when.

Like if, when is an expression that returns a value, so you can write a function with an expression body, returning the when expression directly. When we talked about functions at the beginning of the chapter, we promised an example of a multiline function with an expression body. The following listing shows such an example.

Listing 2.11 Using when for choosing the right enum value

```
fun getMnemonic(color: Color) =          ◁──── Returns a when expression directly
    when (color) {                       ◁┐
        Color.RED -> "Richard"            │  Returns the corresponding string if
        Color.ORANGE -> "Of"              │  the color equals the enum constant
        Color.YELLOW -> "York"
        Color.GREEN -> "Gave"
        Color.BLUE -> "Battle"
        Color.INDIGO -> "In"
        Color.VIOLET -> "Vain"
    }

fun main() {
    println(getMnemonic(Color.BLUE))
    // Battle
}
```

The code finds the branch corresponding to the passed `color` value; note that you don't need to write `break` statements for each branch. (In Java, a missing `break` in a `switch` statement is often a cause for bugs.) If a match is successful, only the corresponding branch is executed. You can also combine multiple values in the same branch if you separate them with commas. So to use different branches based on the "warmth" of the color, you could group your enum constants accordingly in your `when` expression.

Listing 2.12 Combining options in one when branch

```
fun measureColor() = Color.ORANGE
// as a stand-in for more complex measurement logic

fun getWarmthFromSensor(): String {
    val color = measureColor()
    return when(color) {
        Color.RED, Color.ORANGE, Color.YELLOW -> "warm (red = ${color.r})"
        Color.GREEN -> "neutral (green = ${color.g})"
        Color.BLUE, Color.INDIGO, Color.VIOLET -> "cold (blue = ${color.b})"
    }
}

fun main() {
    println(getWarmthFromSensor())
    // warm (red = 255)
}
```

These examples use enum constants by their full name, specifying the `Color` enum class name every time one of the enum's constants is referenced. By importing the constant values, you can simplify this code and save yourself some repetition, as shown in the following listing.

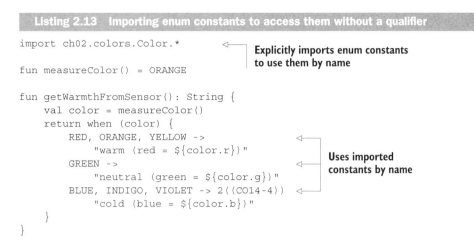

Listing 2.13   Importing enum constants to access them without a qualifier

```
import ch02.colors.Color.*         ◁─┐   Explicitly imports enum constants
                                     │   to use them by name
fun measureColor() = ORANGE

fun getWarmthFromSensor(): String {
    val color = measureColor()
    return when (color) {
        RED, ORANGE, YELLOW ->               ◁─┐
            "warm (red = ${color.r})"          │
        GREEN ->                             ◁─┤  Uses imported
            "neutral (green = ${color.g})"      │  constants by name
        BLUE, INDIGO, VIOLET -> 2((CO14-4))  ◁─┘
            "cold (blue = ${color.b})"
    }
}
```

2.3.3   Capturing the subject of a when expression in a variable

In the previous examples, the subject of the when expression was the color variable, which you obtained by invoking the measureColor() function. To avoid cluttering the surrounding code with extraneous variables, like color in this case, the when expression can also capture its subject in a variable. In this case, the captured variable's scope is restricted to the body of the when expression, while still providing access to its properties inside the branches of the when expression.

Listing 2.14   Assigning the subject of a when to a variable

```
import ch02.colors.Color.*      ◁──── Imports the constants (RED, ORANGE, etc.)

fun measureColor() = ORANGE                     Captures the subject of the when
                                                expression in a variable called
fun getWarmthFromSensor() =                     color, whose scope is restricted
    when (val color = measureColor()) {    ◁─   to the when body
        RED, ORANGE, YELLOW -> "warm (red = ${color.r})"  ◁─┐
        GREEN -> "neutral (green = ${color.g})"             │ We can access the
        BLUE, INDIGO, VIOLET -> "cold (blue = ${color.b}"   │ properties of the
    }                                                       │ captured variable.
```

In future examples, we'll use the short enum names but omit the explicit imports for simplicity. Note that anytime when is used as an expression (meaning its result is used in an assignment or as a return value), the compiler enforces the construct to be *exhaustive*. This means *all possible paths* must return a value.

In the previous example, we cover all enum constants, making the when construct exhaustive. Instead, we could also provide a default case using the else keyword. In cases where the compiler can't deduce whether all possible paths are covered, it forces us to provide a default case. We'll look at such an example in the next section.

2.3.4   *Using the when expression with arbitrary objects*

The `when` construct in Kotlin is actually more flexible than you might be used to from other languages—you can use any kind of object as a branch condition. Let's write a function that mixes two colors if they can be mixed in this small palette. You don't have many options, and you can easily enumerate them all.

Listing 2.15   Using different objects in `when` branches

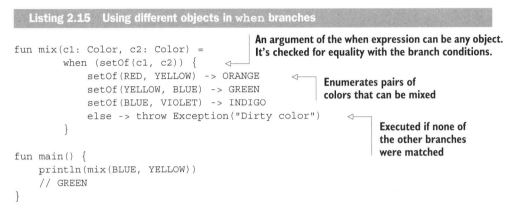

```
fun mix(c1: Color, c2: Color) =                    An argument of the when expression can be any object.
        when (setOf(c1, c2)) {         ◁           It's checked for equality with the branch conditions.
            setOf(RED, YELLOW) -> ORANGE    ◁
            setOf(YELLOW, BLUE) -> GREEN           Enumerates pairs of
            setOf(BLUE, VIOLET) -> INDIGO          colors that can be mixed
            else -> throw Exception("Dirty color")    ◁
        }                                                   Executed if none of
                                                            the other branches
fun main() {                                                were matched
    println(mix(BLUE, YELLOW))
    // GREEN
}
```

If colors `c1` and `c2` are `RED` and `YELLOW` (or vice versa), the result of mixing them is `ORANGE`, and so on. To implement this, you use *set comparison*. The Kotlin standard library contains a function `setOf`, which creates a `Set` containing the objects specified as its arguments. A *set* is a collection for which the order of items doesn't matter; two sets are equal if they contain the same items. Thus, if the sets `setOf(c1, c2)` and `setOf(RED, YELLOW)` are equal, either `c1` is `RED` and `c2` is `YELLOW`, or vice versa. This is exactly what you want to check.

The `when` expression matches its argument against all branches in order until some branch condition is satisfied. Thus, `setOf(c1, c2)` is checked for equality, first with `setOf(RED, YELLOW)` and then with other sets of colors, one after another. If none of the other branch conditions are satisfied, the `else` branch is evaluated. Since the Kotlin compiler can't deduce that we have covered all possible combinations of color sets, and the result of the `when` expression is used as the return value for the `mix` function, we're forced to provide a default case to guarantee that the `when` expression is, indeed, exhaustive.

Being able to use any expression as a `when` branch condition lets you write concise and beautiful code, in many cases. In this example, the condition is an equality check; next, you'll see how the condition may be any Boolean expression.

2.3.5   *Using the when expression without an argument*

You may have noticed that listing 2.15 is somewhat inefficient. Every time you call this function, it creates several `Set` instances that are used only to check whether two given colors match the other two colors. Normally, this isn't an issue, but if the function is called often, it's worth rewriting the code in a different way to avoid creating many short-lived objects, which need to be cleaned up by the garbage collector. You can do this by using the when expression without an argument, as shown in the following listing. The code is less readable, but that's the price you often have to pay to achieve better performance.

Listing 2.16   Using when without an argument

```
fun mixOptimized(c1: Color, c2: Color) =
    when {
        (c1 == RED && c2 == YELLOW) ||        <──── No argument for when
        (c1 == YELLOW && c2 == RED) ->
            ORANGE

        (c1 == YELLOW && c2 == BLUE) ||
        (c1 == BLUE && c2 == YELLOW) ->
            GREEN

        (c1 == BLUE && c2 == VIOLET) ||
        (c1 == VIOLET && c2 == BLUE) ->
            INDIGO
                                                        Used as an expression, the
                                                        when statement needs to
        else -> throw Exception("Dirty color")  <──┘   be exhaustive.
    }

fun main() {
    println(mixOptimized(BLUE, YELLOW))
    // GREEN
}
```

If no argument is supplied for the when expression, the branch condition is any Boolean expression. The mixOptimized function does the same thing mix did earlier. Its advantage is that it doesn't create any extra objects, but the cost is that it's harder to read. Let's move on and look at examples of the when construct in which *smart casts* come into play.

2.3.6   Smart casts: Combining type checks and casts

Now that you've successfully mixed a few colors with Kotlin, let's move on to a bit more complex example. You'll write a function that evaluates simple arithmetic expressions, like (1 + 2) + 4. The expressions will contain only one type of operation: the sum of two numbers. Other arithmetic operations (e.g., subtraction, multiplication, and division) can be implemented in a similar way, and you can do that as an exercise. In the process, you'll learn about how *smart casts* make it much easier to work with Kotlin objects of different types.

First, how do you encode the expressions? Traditionally, you store them in a tree-like structure, where each node is either a sum (Sum) or a number (Num). Num is always a leaf node, whereas a Sum node has two children: the arguments of the sum operation. Listing 2.17 shows a simple structure of classes used to encode the expressions: an interface, called `Expr`, and two classes, `Num` and `Sum`, that implement it (figure 2.5). Note that the `Expr` interface doesn't declare any methods; it's used as a *marker interface* to provide a common type for different kinds of expressions. To mark that a class implements an interface, you use a colon (`:`) followed by the interface name, as shown in the following listing (you'll take a closer look at interfaces in section 4.1.1).

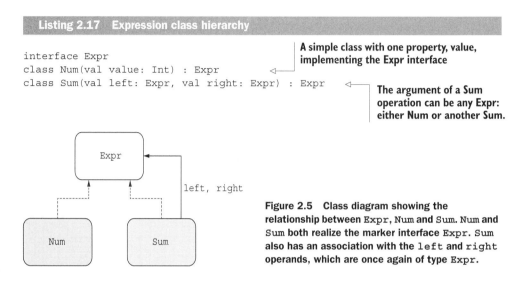

Listing 2.17 Expression class hierarchy

```
interface Expr
class Num(val value: Int) : Expr
class Sum(val left: Expr, val right: Expr) : Expr
```

A simple class with one property, value, implementing the Expr interface

The argument of a Sum operation can be any Expr: either Num or another Sum.

Figure 2.5 Class diagram showing the relationship between `Expr`, `Num` and `Sum`. `Num` and `Sum` both realize the marker interface `Expr`. `Sum` also has an association with the `left` and `right` operands, which are once again of type `Expr`.

`Sum` stores references to the `left` and `right` arguments of type `Expr`. In your example, that means they can be either `Num` or `Sum`. To store the expression `(1 + 2) + 4` mentioned earlier, you create a structure of `Expr` objects, specifically `Sum(Sum(Num(1), Num(2)), Num(4))`. Figure 2.6 shows its tree representation.

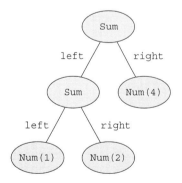

Figure 2.6 A representation of the expression `Sum(Sum(Num(1), Num(2)), Num(4))` describing the mathematical expression `(1 + 2) + 4`. We use this representation as the input for our evaluation function.

Your goal is to evaluate this kind of expression, consisting of `Sum` and `Num` objects, computing the resulting value. Let's take a look at that next.

The `Expr` interface has two implementations, so you have to try two options to evaluate a result value for an expression:

1   If an expression is a number, you return the corresponding value.

2   If it's a sum, you must evaluate the left and right expressions recursively and return their sum.

First, we'll look at an implementation of this function written in a style similar to what you might see in Java code. Then, we'll refactor it to reflect idiomatic Kotlin.

Initially, you might write a function reminiscent of the style you may see in other languages, using a sequence of `if` expressions to check the different subtypes of `Expr`. In Kotlin, you check whether a variable is of a certain type by using an `is` check, so an implementation might look like this.

Listing 2.18   Evaluating expressions with an `if` cascade

```
fun eval(e: Expr): Int {
    if (e is Num) {
        val n = e as Num          ⟵——  This explicit cast to
        return n.value                   Num is redundant.
    }
    if (e is Sum) {
        return eval(e.right) + eval(e.left)      ⟵——  The variable e is smart cast.
    }
    throw IllegalArgumentException("Unknown expression")
}

fun main() {
    println(eval(Sum(Sum(Num(1), Num(2)), Num(4))))
    // 7
}
```

The `is` syntax might be familiar to you if you've programmed in C#, and Java developers might recognize it as the equivalent of `instanceof`.

Kotlin's `is` check provides some additional convenience: if you check the variable for a certain type, you don't need to cast it afterward; you can use it as having the type you checked for. In effect, the compiler performs the cast for you, something we call a *smart cast*.

In the `eval` function, after you check whether the variable `e` has the `Num` type, the compiler smartly interprets it as a variable of type `Num`. You can then access the `value` property of `Num` without having to do an explicit cast: `e.value`. The same goes for the `right` and `left` properties of `Sum`: you write only `e.right` and `e.left` in the corresponding context. In IntelliJ IDEA and Android Studio, these smart-cast values are emphasized with a background color, so it's easy to grasp that this value was checked beforehand (see figure 2.7).

```
if (e is Sum) {
    return eval(e.right) + eval(e.left)
}
```

Figure 2.7   The IDE highlights smart casts with a background color, visible in the e-book version.

The smart cast works only if a variable couldn't have changed after the `is` check. When you're using a smart cast with a property of a class, as in this example, the property has to be a `val` and it can't have a custom accessor. Otherwise, it would not be possible to verify that every access to the property would return the same value. As you'll see later, smart casts also work together with other Kotlin language features, such as nullability, which we'll discuss in greater detail in chapter 7, and Kotlin's final-by-default classes, which you will explore in section 4.1.2.

An explicit cast to the specific type is expressed via the `as` keyword:

```
val n = e as Num
```

But as you may have guessed, this implementation isn't yet considered idiomatic Kotlin. Let's look at how to refactor the `eval` function.

2.3.7   *Refactoring: Replacing an if with a when expression*

In section 2.1.2, you have already seen that `if` is an *expression* in Kotlin. This is also why there is no ternary operator in Kotlin—the `if` expression can already return a value. That means you can rewrite the `eval` function to use the expression-body syntax, removing the `return` statement and the curly braces and using the `if` expression as the function body instead.

Listing 2.19   Using `if` expressions that return values

```
fun eval(e: Expr): Int =
    if (e is Num) {
        e.value
    } else if (e is Sum) {
        eval(e.right) + eval(e.left)
    } else {
        throw IllegalArgumentException("Unknown expression")
    }

fun main() {
    println(eval(Sum(Num(1), Num(2))))
    // 3
}
```

And you can make this code even more concise: the curly braces are optional if there's only one expression in an `if` branch—for an `if` branch with a block, the last expression is returned as a result. A shortened version of the `eval` expression using cascading `if` expressions could look like this:

```
fun eval(e: Expr): Int =
    if (e is Num) e.value
    else if (e is Sum) eval(e.right) + eval(e.left)
    else throw IllegalArgumentException("Unknown expression")
```

But you've already gotten to know an even better language construct for expressing multiple choices in section 2.3.2—let's polish this code even more and rewrite it using when.

The when expression isn't restricted to checking values for equality, which is what you saw earlier. Here, you use a different form of when branches, allowing you to check the type of the when argument value. Just as in the if example in listing 2.19, the type check applies a smart cast, so you can access members of Num and Sum without extra casts.

Listing 2.20   Using a when instead of an if cascade

```
fun eval(e: Expr): Int =                              when branches that
    when (e) {                                        check and smart cast
        is Num -> e.value                             the argument type
        is Sum -> eval(e.right) + eval(e.left)
        else -> throw IllegalArgumentException("Unknown expr")
    }
```

Compare the last two Kotlin versions of the eval function, and think about how you can apply when as a replacement for sequences of if expressions in your own code as well. For branch logic containing multiple operations, you can use a block expression as a branch body. Let's see how this works.

2.3.8   Blocks as branches of if and when

Both if and when can have blocks as branches. In this case, the last expression in the block is the result. Let's say you want to gain a deeper understanding of how your eval function computes the result. One way to do so is to add println statements that log what the function is currently calculating. You can add them in the block for each branch in your when expression. The last expression in the block is what will be returned.

Listing 2.21   Using when with compound actions in branches

```
fun evalWithLogging(e: Expr): Int =
    when (e) {
        is Num -> {
            println("num: ${e.value}")        This is the last expression in
            e.value                            the block and is returned if e
        }                                      is of type Num.
        is Sum -> {
            val left = evalWithLogging(e.left)
            val right = evalWithLogging(e.right)
            println("sum: $left + $right")
            left + right                       This expression is returned if e is of type Sum.
        }
        else -> throw IllegalArgumentException("Unknown expression")
    }
```

Now, you can look at the logs printed by the `evalWithLogging` function and follow the order of computation:

```
fun main() {
    println(evalWithLogging(Sum(Sum(Num(1), Num(2)), Num(4))))
    // num: 1
    // num: 2
    // sum: 1 + 2
    // num: 4
    // sum: 3 + 4
    // 7
}
```

The rule that *the last expression in a block is the result* holds in all cases in which a block can be used and a result is expected. As you'll see in section 2.5.2, the same rule works for the `try` body and `catch` clauses, and in section 5.1.3 we'll discuss the application of this rule to lambda expressions. But as we mentioned in section 2.1.3, this rule doesn't hold for regular functions. A function can have either an expression body that can't be a block or a block body with explicit `return` statements inside. By now, you've seen multiple ways of choosing the right things among many in your Kotlin code, so it seems now would be a good time to see how you can iterate over things.

2.4   *Iterating over things: while and for loops*

Iteration in Kotlin is very similar to what you are probably used to from Java, C#, or other languages. The `while` loop takes the same traditional form it does in other languages, so you'll only take a brief look at it. You'll also find the `for` loop, which is written `for (<item> in <elements>)`, reminiscent of Java's `for-each` loop, for example. Let's explore what kind of looping scenarios you can cover with these two forms of loops.

2.4.1   *Repeating code while a condition is true: The while loop*

Kotlin has `while` and `do-while` loops, and their syntax is probably familiar to you from other programming languages. Let's briefly review it:

```
while (condition) {           ◁──── The body is executed while the condition is true.
    /*...*/
    if (shouldExit) break     ◁──── break terminates the enclosing loop.
}

do {
    if (shouldSkip) continue      ◁──── continue proceeds to the next loop step.
    /*...*/
} while (condition)        ◁──┐ The body is executed for the first time unconditionally.
                              │ After that, it's executed while the condition is true.
```

For nested loops, Kotlin allows you to specify a *label*, which you can then reference when using `break` or `continue`. A label is an identifier followed by the at sign (`@`):

```
outer@ while (outerCondition) {        ◄─── Marks the loop with the label outer
    while (innerCondition) {
        if (shouldExitInner) break         break and continue without labels always
        if (shouldSkipInner) continue      operate on the closest enclosing loop.
        if (shouldExit) break@outer
        if (shouldSkip) continue@outer      break and continue with labels
        // ...                              break out of the specified loop.
    }
    // ...
}
```

Let's move on to discuss the various uses of the `for` loop and see how it covers not just the iteration over collection items but over *ranges* as well.

2.4.2 Iterating over numbers: Ranges and progressions

As we just mentioned, in Kotlin, there's no C-style `for` loop, where you initialize a variable, update its value on every step through the loop, and exit the loop when the value reaches a certain bound (the classical `int i = 0; i < 10; i++`). To replace the most common use cases of such loops, Kotlin uses the concepts of *ranges*.

A range is essentially just an interval between two values, usually numbers: a start and an end. You write it using the `..` operator:

```
val oneToTen = 1..10
```

Note that in Kotlin, these ranges are *closed* or *inclusive*, meaning the second value is always a part of the range.

The most basic thing you can do with integer ranges is loop over all the values. If you can iterate over all the values in a range, such a range is called a *progression*.

Let's use integer ranges to play the *Fizz-Buzz game*. It's a nice way to survive a long trip in a car and remember your forgotten division skills. Implementing this game is also a popular task for programming interviews!

To play Fizz-Buzz, players take turns counting incrementally, replacing any number divisible by 3 with the word *fizz* and any number divisible by 5 with the word *buzz*. If a number is a multiple of both 3 and 5, you say, "Fizz-Buzz."

The code in the following listing prints the right answers for the numbers from 1 to 100. Note how you check the possible conditions with a `when` expression without an argument.

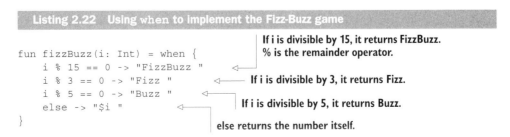

Listing 2.22   Using when to implement the Fizz-Buzz game

```
                                            If i is divisible by 15, it returns FizzBuzz.
                                            % is the remainder operator.
fun fizzBuzz(i: Int) = when {
    i % 15 == 0 -> "FizzBuzz "    ◄
    i % 3 == 0 -> "Fizz "         ◄─── If i is divisible by 3, it returns Fizz.
    i % 5 == 0 -> "Buzz "         ◄
    else -> "$i "                 ◄        If i is divisible by 5, it returns Buzz.
}
                                       else returns the number itself.
```

```
fun main() {
    for (i in 1..100) {          ◁——— Iterates over the integer range 1..100
        print(fizzBuzz(i))
    }
    // 1 2 Fizz 4 Buzz Fizz 7 ...
}
```

Suppose you get tired of these rules after an hour of driving and want to complicate things a bit. Let's start counting backward from 100 and include only even numbers.

Listing 2.23 Iterating over a range with a step

```
fun main() {
    for (i in 100 downTo 1 step 2) {
        print(fizzBuzz(i))
    }
    // Buzz 98 Fizz 94 92 FizzBuzz 88 ...
}
```

Now, you're iterating over a progression that has a *step*, which allows it to skip some numbers. The step can also be negative, in which case the progression goes backward rather than forward. In this example, 100 downTo 1 is a progression that goes backward (with step –1). Then, step changes the absolute value of the step to 2 while keeping the direction (in effect, setting the step to –2).

As we mentioned earlier, the .. syntax always creates a range that includes the end point (the value to the right of ..). In many cases, it's more convenient to iterate over half-closed ranges, which don't include the specified end point. To create such a range, use ..<. For example, the loop for (x in 0..<size) is equivalent to for (x in 0..size-1), but it expresses the idea somewhat more clearly. In section 3.4.3, you'll learn more about the syntax used by downTo and step in these examples.

You can see how working with ranges and progressions helped you cope with the advanced rules for the Fizz-Buzz game. But the for loop in Kotlin can do more than that. Let's look at some other examples.

2.4.3 *Iterating over maps*

We've mentioned that the most common scenario of using a for (x in y) loop is iterating over a collection. You are most likely already familiar with its behavior—the loop is executed for each element in the input collection. In this case, you simply print each element from the collection of colors. Inside the loop, the individual colors can be addressed with color, as shown in the following listing, since that is the name used in the for loop.

Listing 2.24 Iterating over a map with a `for` loop

```
fun main() {
    val collection = listOf("red", "green", "blue")
```

```
        for (color in collection) {
            print("$color ")
        }
        // red green blue
}
```

Instead of spending more time on this, let's see something more interesting instead: how to iterate over a map. As an example, we'll look at a small program that prints binary representations for characters—providing you with a simple lookup table that will help you decipher binary-encoded text, like `1000100  1000101  1000011  1000001 1000110`, by hand! You'll store these binary representations in a map (just for illustrative purposes).

The following code creates a map, fills it with binary representations of some letters, and then prints the map's contents. As you can see, the `..` syntax to create a range works not only for numbers but also for characters. Here, you use it to iterate over all characters from `A` up to and including `F`.

Listing 2.25   Initializing and iterating over a map

```
fun main() {
    val binaryReps = mutableMapOf<Char, String>()      ⟵  Mutable maps preserve element
                                                           iteration order in Kotlin.
    for (char in 'A'..'F') {                           ⟵  Iterates over the characters
                                                           from A to F, using a range
                                                           of characters
        val binary = char.code.toString(radix = 2)     ⟵  Converts ASCII code to binary
        binaryReps[char] = binary                      ⟵  Stores the value in a map by the c key
    }

    for ((letter, binary) in binaryReps) {             ⟵  Iterates over a map, assigning the
        println("$letter = $binary")                       map key to letter and the associated
    }                                                      value to binary
    // A = 1000001    D = 1000100
    // B = 1000010    E = 1000101
    // C = 1000011    F = 1000110
    // (output split into columns for conciseness)
}
```

Listing 2. 25 shows that the `for` loop allows you to unpack an element of a collection you're iterating over (in this case, a collection of key–value pairs in the map). You store the result of the unpacking in two separate variables: `letter` receives the key, and `binary` receives the value. In section 9.4, you'll learn more about this destructuring syntax.

Another nice trick used in listing 2.25 is the shorthand syntax for getting and updating the values of a map by key. Instead of having to call functions like `get` and `put`, you can use `map[key]` to read values and `map[key] = value` to set them. That means instead of having to use the Java-style version of `binaryReps.put(char, binary)`, you can use the equivalent, but more elegant, `binaryReps[char] = binary`.

You can use the same unpacking syntax to iterate over a collection while keeping track of the index of the current item. This allows you to avoid creating a separate variable to store the index and incrementing it by hand. In this case, you're printing the elements of a collection with their respective indices using the `withIndex` function:

```
fun main() {
    val list = listOf("10", "11", "1001")        Iterates over a
    for ((index, element) in list.withIndex()) {  ◁── collection with an index
        println("$index: $element")
    }
    // 0: 10
    // 1: 11
    // 2: 1001
}
```

We'll dig into the whereabouts of `withIndex` in section 3.3.

You've seen how you can use the `in` keyword to iterate over a range or a collection. Beyond that, you can also use `in` to check whether a value belongs to a range or collection. Let's take a closer look.

2.4.4   *Using in to check collection and range membership*

You use the `in` operator to check whether a value is in a range or its opposite, `!in`, to check whether a value isn't in a range. For example, when validating the input of a user, you often have to check whether an input character is, indeed, a letter or excludes digits. Here's how you could use `in` to write some small helper functions, `isLetter` and `isNotDigit`, that check whether a character belongs to a range of characters.

Listing 2.26   Checking range membership using `in`

```
fun isLetter(c: Char) = c in 'a'..'z' || c in 'A'..'Z'
fun isNotDigit(c: Char) = c !in '0'..'9'

fun main() {
    println(isLetter('q'))
    // true
    println(isNotDigit('x'))
    // true
}
```

This technique for checking whether a character is a letter looks simple. Under the hood, nothing tricky happens: you still check that the character's code is somewhere between the code of the first letter and the code of the last one. But this logic is concisely hidden in the implementation of the range classes in the standard library:

```
c in 'a'..'z'        ◁──── Transforms to 'a' <= c && c <= 'z'
```

The `in` and `!in` operators also work in `when` expressions, which becomes even more convenient when you have a number of different ranges that you want to check.

Listing 2.27 Using in checks as when branches

```
fun recognize(c: Char) = when (c) {
    in '0'..'9' -> "It's a digit!"
    in 'a'..'z', in 'A'..'Z' -> "It's a letter!"
    else -> "I don't know..."
}

fun main() {
    println(recognize('8'))
    // It's a digit!
}
```

> **Checks whether the value is in the range from 0 to 9**

> **You can combine multiple ranges.**

Ranges aren't restricted to characters, either. If you have any class that supports comparing instances (by implementing the `kotlin.Comparable` interface you'll learn more about in section 9.2.2), you can create ranges of objects of that type. If you have such a range, you can't enumerate all objects in the range. Think about it: can you, for example, enumerate all strings that are alphabetically between *Java* and *Kotlin*? No, you can't. But you can still check whether another object belongs to the range, using the `in` operator:

```
fun main() {
    println("Kotlin" in "Java".."Scala")
    // true
}
```

> **The same as "Java" <= "Kotlin" && "Kotlin" <= "Scala"**

Note that the strings are compared alphabetically here because that's how the `String` class implements the `Comparable` interface. In alphabetical sorting, `"Java"` comes before `"Kotlin"` and `"Kotlin"` comes before `"Scala"`, so `"Kotlin"` is in the range between the two strings.

The same `in` check works with collections as well:

```
fun main() {
    println("Kotlin" in setOf("Java", "Scala"))
    // false
}
```

> **This set doesn't contain the string "Kotlin".**

In section 9.3.2, you'll see how to use ranges and progressions with your own data types and what objects in general you can use `in` checks with. To round out our overview of basic building blocks of Kotlin programs, there's one more topic we want to look at in this chapter: dealing with exceptions.

2.5   *Throwing and catching exceptions in Kotlin*

Exception handling in Kotlin is similar to the way it's done in Java and many other languages. A function can complete in a normal way or throw an exception if an error occurs. The function caller can catch this exception and process it; if it doesn't, the exception is rethrown further up the stack.

You throw an exception using the `throw` keyword—in this case, to indicate that the calling function has provided an invalid percentage value:

```
if (percentage !in 0..100) {
    throw IllegalArgumentException(
        "A percentage value must be between 0 and 100: $percentage"
    )
}
```

This is a good time to remind yourself that Kotlin doesn't have a `new` keyword. Creating an exception instance is no different.

In Kotlin, the `throw` construct is an *expression* and can be used as a part of other expressions:

```
val percentage =
    if (number in 0..100)
        number
    else                                                   throw is an expression.
        throw IllegalArgumentException(        ◁
            "A percentage value must be between 0 and 100: $number"
        )
```

In this example, if the condition is satisfied, the program behaves correctly, and the `percentage` variable is initialized with `number`. Otherwise, an exception is thrown, and the variable isn't initialized. We'll discuss the technical details of `throw` as a part of other expressions in section 8.1.7, where we'll also discover more about its return type, among other things.

2.5.1   *Handling exceptions and recovering from errors: try, catch, and finally*

If you're on the other side—trying to recover from errors, rather than throw them— you use the `try` construct with `catch` and `finally` clauses to handle exceptions. You can see it in the following listing, which reads a line of text from a `BufferedReader`, tries to parse it as a number, and returns either the number or `null`, if the line isn't a valid number.

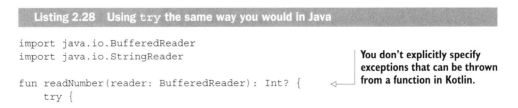

Listing 2.28   Using `try` the same way you would in Java

```
import java.io.BufferedReader
import java.io.StringReader                            You don't explicitly specify
                                                       exceptions that can be thrown
fun readNumber(reader: BufferedReader): Int? {    ◁   from a function in Kotlin.
    try {
```

```
        val line = reader.readLine()
        return Integer.parseInt(line)
    } catch (e: NumberFormatException) {      ◁——— The exception type is on the right.
        return null
    } finally {                    ◁——— finally works just as it does in Java.
        reader.close()
    }
}

fun main() {
    val reader = BufferedReader(StringReader("239"))
    println(readNumber(reader))
    // 239
}
```

An important difference from Java is Kotlin doesn't have a `throws` clause. If you wrote this function in Java, you'd explicitly write `throws` `IOException` after the function declaration.

Listing 2.29 In Java, checked exceptions are part of the method signature

```
Integer readNumber(BufferedReader reader) throws IOException
```

You'd need to do this because Java's `readLine` and `close` may throw an `IOException`, which is a *checked exception*. In the Java world, this describes a type of exception that needs to be handled explicitly. You must declare all checked exceptions your function can throw, and if you call another function, you need to handle its checked exceptions or declare that your function can throw them, too.

Just like many other modern JVM languages, Kotlin doesn't differentiate between checked and unchecked exceptions. You don't specify the exceptions thrown by a function, and you may or may not handle any exceptions. This design decision is based on the practice of using checked exceptions in Java. Experience has shown that the Java rules often require a lot of meaningless code to rethrow or ignore exceptions, and the rules don't consistently protect you from the errors that can happen.

For example, in listing 2.28, `NumberFormatException` isn't a checked exception. Therefore, the Java compiler doesn't force you to catch it, and you can easily see the exception happen at run time. This is unfortunate because invalid input data is a common situation and should be handled gracefully. At the same time, the `BufferedReader.close` method can throw an `IOException`, which is a checked exception and needs to be handled. Most programs can't take any meaningful action if closing a stream fails, so the code required to catch the exception from the `close` method is boilerplate.

As a result of this design decision, you get to decide yourself which exceptions you do and don't want to handle. If you wanted to, you could implement the `readNumber` function without any `try-catch` constructs at all, as shown in the following listing.

```
fun readNumber(reader: BufferedReader): Int {
    val line = reader.readLine()
    reader.close()
    return Integer.parseInt(line)
}
```

What about Java's `try-with-resources`? Kotlin doesn't have any special syntax for this; it's implemented as a library function. In chapter 10, you'll see how this is possible.

2.5.2   *Using try as an expression*

So far, you've only seen the `try` construct used as a statement. But since `try` is an *expression* (just like `if` and `when`), you can modify your example a little to take advantage of that and assign the value of your `try` expression to a variable. For brevity, let's remove the `finally` section (only because you've already seen how this works—don't use it as an excuse to not close your streams!) and add some code to print the number you read from the file.

Listing 2.31   Using `try` as an expression

```
fun readNumber(reader: BufferedReader) {
    val number = try {
        Integer.parseInt(reader.readLine())    ◁────   Becomes the value of
    } catch (e: NumberFormatException) {                the try expression
        return
    }

    println(number)
}

fun main() {
    val reader = BufferedReader(StringReader("not a number"))
    readNumber(reader)          ◁────   Nothing is printed.
}
```

It's worth pointing out that, unlike with `if`, you always need to enclose the statement body in curly braces. Just as in other statements, if the body contains multiple expressions, the value of the `try` expression as a whole is the value of the last expression.

   This example puts a `return` statement in the `catch` block, so the execution of the function doesn't continue after the `catch` block. If you want to continue execution, the `catch` clause also needs to have a value, which will be the value of the last expression in it. Here's how this works.

Listing 2.32   Returning a value in `catch`

```
fun readNumber(reader: BufferedReader) {
    val number = try {
        Integer.parseInt(reader.readLine())    ◁────   This value is used when
                                                        no exception happens.
```

```
    } catch (e: NumberFormatException) {
        null                              ⟵——  The null value is used in
    }                                           case of an exception.

    println(number)
}

fun main() {
    val reader = BufferedReader(StringReader("not a number"))
    readNumber(reader)
    // null                          ⟵——  An exception is thrown, so
}                                          the function prints null.
```

If the execution of a `try` code block behaves normally, the last expression in the block is the result. If an exception is caught, the last expression in a corresponding `catch` block is the result. In listing 2.32, the result value is `null` if a `NumberFormatException` is caught.

Using `try` as an expression can help you make your code a bit more concise by avoiding the introduction of additional intermediate variables, and it allows you to easily assign fallback values or return from the enclosing function outright. At this point, if you're impatient, you can start writing programs in Kotlin by combining the basic building blocks you've seen so far. As you read this book, you'll continue to learn how to change your habitual ways of thinking and use the full power of Kotlin!

Summary

- The `fun` keyword is used to declare a function. The `val` and `var` keywords declare read-only and mutable variables, respectively.
- While a `val` reference is read only, the object that it points to may still be mutable.
- String templates help you avoid noisy string concatenation. Add the prefix `$` to a variable name or surround an expression with `${}` to have its value injected into the string.
- Classes can be expressed in a concise way in Kotlin.
- The familiar `if` is now an expression with a return value.
- The `when` expression is analogous to `switch` in Java but is more powerful.
- You don't have to cast a variable explicitly after checking it has a certain type: the compiler casts it for you automatically using a smart cast.
- The `for`, `while`, and `do-while` loops are similar to their counterparts in Java, but the `for` loop is now more convenient, especially when you need to iterate over a map or a collection with an index.
- The concise syntax `1..5` (and `1..<5`) creates a range. Ranges and progressions allow Kotlin to use a uniform syntax and set of abstractions in `for` loops and also work with the `in` and `!in` operators, which check whether a value belongs to a range.
- Exception handling in Kotlin is very similar to Java, except Kotlin doesn't require you to declare the exceptions that can be thrown by a function.

Defining and calling functions

3

This chapter covers

- Functions for working with collections, strings, and regular expressions
- Using named arguments, default parameter values, and the infix call syntax
- Adapting Java libraries to Kotlin through extension functions and properties
- Structuring code with top-level and local functions and properties

By now, you should be fairly comfortable with using Kotlin on a basic level, the same way you might have used other object-oriented languages, like Java, before. You've seen how the concepts familiar to you from Java translate to Kotlin and how Kotlin often makes them more concise and readable.

In this chapter, you'll see how Kotlin improves on one of the key elements of every program: declaring and calling functions. We'll also look into the possibilities for adapting Java libraries to the Kotlin style through the use of extension functions, allowing you to gain the full benefits of Kotlin in mixed-language projects.

To make our discussion more useful and less abstract, we'll focus on Kotlin collections, strings, and regular expressions as our problem domain. As an introduction, let's look at how to create collections in Kotlin.

3.1 Creating collections in Kotlin

Before you can use collections in interesting ways, you'll need to learn how to create them. In chapter 2, you bumped into the way to create a new set (a collection for which the order of items doesn't matter—two sets are equal if they contain the same items): the `setOf` function. You created a set of colors then, but for now, let's keep it simple and work with numbers:

```
val set = setOf(1, 7, 53)
```

You create a list or a map in a similar way:

```
val list = listOf(1, 7, 53)
val map = mapOf(1 to "one", 7 to "seven", 53 to "fifty-three")
```

Note that `to` isn't a special construct but a normal function. We'll return to it later in the chapter, in section 3.4.3.

Can you guess the classes of objects that are created here? Run the following example to see this for yourself:

```
fun main() {
    val set = setOf(1, 7, 53)
    val list = listOf(1, 7, 53)
    val map = mapOf(1 to "one", 7 to "seven", 53 to "fifty-three")

    println(set.javaClass)                    ◁─┐  javaClass is Kotlin's equivalent
    // class java.util.LinkedHashSet             └  of Java's getClass().

    println(list.javaClass)
    // class java.util.Arrays$ArrayList

    println(map.javaClass)
    // class java.util.LinkedHashMap
}
```

As you can see, Kotlin uses the standard Java collection classes. This is good news for Java developers: Kotlin doesn't reimplement collection classes. All of your existing knowledge about Java collections still applies here. It is worth noting, however, that unlike in Java, Kotlin's collection interfaces are read only by default. We will explore further details on this topic as well as the mutable counterparts for these interfaces in chapter 8.

Using the standard Java collections makes it much easier to interact with Java code. You don't need to convert collections one way or the other when you call Java functions from Kotlin or vice versa.

Even though Kotlin's basic collections are exactly the same classes as Java collections, you can do much more with them in Kotlin. For example, you can get the last element from a list, get a shuffled version of a list, or sum up a collection (given it's a collection of numbers):

```
fun main() {
    val strings = listOf("first", "second", "fourteenth")

    strings.last()
    // fourteenth

    println(strings.shuffled())
    // [fourteenth, second, first]

    val numbers = setOf(1, 14, 2)
    println(numbers.sum())
    // 17
}
```

In this chapter, we'll explore in detail how this works and where all the new methods on the Java classes come from. In future chapters, when we start talking about lambdas, you'll see much more that you can do with collections, but we'll continue using the same standard Java collection classes. And in chapter 8, you'll learn how the Java collection classes are represented in the Kotlin type system. Before discussing how the functions `last` and `sum` can work directly on Java collections, let's learn some new concepts for declaring a function.

3.2   *Making functions easier to call*

Now that you know how to create a collection of elements, let's do something straightforward: print its contents. Don't worry if this seems overly simple; along the way, you'll meet a bunch of important concepts.

Java collections have a default `toString` implementation, but the formatting of the output is fixed and not always what you need:

```
fun main() {
    val list = listOf(1, 2, 3)
    println(list)              ◁─── Invokes toString()
    // [1, 2, 3]
}
```

Imagine you need the elements to be separated by semicolons and surrounded by parentheses, instead of the brackets used by the default implementation: `(1; 2; 3)`. To solve this, Java projects use third-party libraries, such as Guava and Apache Commons, or reimplement the logic inside the project. In Kotlin, a function to handle this is part of the standard library.

In this section, you'll implement this function yourself. You'll begin with a straight-forward implementation that doesn't use Kotlin's facilities for simplifying function declarations, and then you'll rewrite it in a more idiomatic style.

The `joinToString` function shown next appends the elements of the collection to a `StringBuilder` (a mutable sequence of characters) with a separator between them, a prefix at the beginning, and a postfix at the end. The function is generic; it works on collections that contain elements of any type. The syntax for generics is similar to Java. (A more detailed discussion of generics will be the subject of chapter 11.)

Listing 3.1   Initial implementation of `joinToString()`

```
fun <T> joinToString(
        collection: Collection<T>,
        separator: String,
        prefix: String,
        postfix: String
): String {

    val result = StringBuilder(prefix)

    for ((index, element) in collection.withIndex()) {      Don't append a separator
        if (index > 0) result.append(separator)         ◁    before the first element.
        result.append(element)
    }

    result.append(postfix)
    return result.toString()
}
```

Let's verify the function works as intended:

```
fun main() {
    val list = listOf(1, 2, 3)
    println(joinToString(list, "; ", "(", ")"))
    // (1; 2; 3)
}
```

The implementation is fine, and you'll mostly leave it as is. Instead, we'll focus on the declaration—how can you change it to make calls of this function less verbose? Maybe you could avoid having to pass four arguments every time you call the function. Let's see what you can do.

3.2.1   Named arguments

The first problem we'll address concerns the readability of function calls. For example, look at the following call of `joinToString`:

```
joinToString(collection, " ", " ", ".")
```

Can you tell what parameters all these `Strings` correspond to? Are the elements separated by the whitespace or the dot? These questions are hard to answer without looking at the signature of the function. Maybe you remember it or maybe your IDE can help you, but it's not obvious from the calling code.

This problem is especially common with Boolean flags. To solve it, some Java coding styles recommend creating enum types instead of using Booleans. Others even require you to specify the parameter names explicitly in a comment, as in the following example:

```
/* Java */
joinToString(collection, /* separator */ " ",  /* prefix */ " ",
    /* postfix */ ".");
```

With Kotlin, you can do better:

```
joinToString(collection, separator = " ", prefix = " ", postfix = ".")
```

When calling a function written in Kotlin, you can specify the names of some (or all) of the arguments you're passing to the function. If you specify the names of all arguments passed to the function, you can even change their order:

```
joinToString(
    postfix = ".",
    separator = " ",
    collection = collection,
    prefix = " "
)
```

Named arguments work especially well with default parameter values, which we'll look at next.

> **TIP** IntelliJ IDEA and Android Studio can keep explicitly written argument names up to date if you rename the parameter of the function being called; instead of editing the parameter names by hand, use the Rename or Change Signature action. Both actions can be found by right-clicking on the function name and choosing the Refactor option.

3.2.2   *Default parameter values*

Another common Java problem is the overabundance of overloaded methods in some classes. Just look at `java.lang.Thread` (http://mng.bz/4KZC) and its eight constructors! The overloads can be provided for the sake of backward compatibility, the convenience of API users, or other reasons, but the end result is the same: duplication. The parameter names and types are repeated over and over, and if you want to be thorough, you also have to repeat most of the documentation in every overload. At the same time, if you call an overload that omits some parameters, it's not always clear which values are used for them.

In Kotlin, you can often avoid creating overloads because you can specify default values for parameters in a function declaration. Let's use that to improve the `joinTo-String` function. For most cases, the strings can be separated by commas without any prefix or postfix. So let's make these values the defaults.

Listing 3.2   Declaring `joinToString()` with default parameter values

```
fun <T> joinToString(
        collection: Collection<T>,
        separator: String = ", ",        Parameters with
        prefix: String = "",             default values
        postfix: String = ""
): String { /* ... */ }
```

Now, you can either invoke the function with all the arguments or omit some of them:

```
fun main() {
    joinToString(list, ", ", "", "")
    // 1, 2, 3
    joinToString(list)
    // 1, 2, 3
    joinToString(list, "; ")
    // 1; 2; 3
}
```

When using the regular call syntax, you have to specify the arguments in the same order as in the function declaration, and you can omit only trailing arguments. If you use named arguments, you can omit some arguments from the middle of the parameter list and specify only the ones you need, in any order you want:

```
fun main() {
    joinToString(list, postfix = ";", prefix = "# ")
    // # 1, 2, 3;
}
```

Note that the default values of the parameters are encoded in the function being called, not at the call site. If you change the default value and recompile the class containing the function, the callers that haven't specified a value for the parameter will start using the new default value.

Default values and Java

Given that Java doesn't have the concept of default parameter values, you have to specify all the parameter values explicitly when you call a Kotlin function with default parameter values from Java. If you frequently need to call a function from Java and want to make it easier to use for Java callers, you can annotate it with `@JvmOverloads`. This instructs the compiler to generate Java overloaded methods, omitting each of the parameters one by one, starting from the last one. For example, you may annotate your `joinToString` function with `@JvmOverloads`, as shown in the following listing.

(continued)

Listing 3.3　Declaring `joinToString()` with default parameter values

```
@JvmOverloads
fun <T> joinToString(
        collection: Collection<T>,
        separator: String = ", ",
        prefix: String = "",
        postfix: String = ""
): String { /* ... */ }
```

This means the following overloads are generated:

```
/* Java */
String joinToString(Collection<T> collection, String separator,
    String prefix, String postfix);

String joinToString(Collection<T> collection, String separator,
    String prefix);

String joinToString(Collection<T> collection, String separator);

String joinToString(Collection<T> collection);
```

Each overload uses the default values for the parameters that have been omitted from the signature.

So far, you've been working on your utility function without paying much attention to the surrounding context. Surely, it must have been a method of some class that wasn't shown in the example listings, right? In fact, Kotlin makes this unnecessary.

3.2.3　*Getting rid of static utility classes: Top-level functions and properties*

We all know that Java, as an object-oriented language, requires all code to be written as methods of classes. Usually, this works out nicely, but in reality, almost every large project ends up with a lot of code that doesn't clearly belong to any single class. Sometimes, an operation works with objects of two different classes that play an equally important role for it. Other times, there is one primary object, but you don't want to bloat its API by adding the operation as an instance method.

As a result, you end up with classes that don't contain any state or instance methods. Such classes only act as containers for several static methods. A perfect example is the `Collections` class in the JDK. To find other examples in your own code, look for classes that have `Util` as part of the name.

In Kotlin, you don't need to create all those meaningless classes. Instead, you can place functions directly at the top level of a source file, outside of any class. Such functions are still members of the package declared at the top of the file, and you still need to import them if you want to call them from other packages, but the unnecessary extra level of nesting no longer exists.

Let's put the `joinToString` function into the `strings` package directly. Create a file called join.kt with the following contents (this choice is arbitrary; any other filename would work just as well).

Listing 3.4 Declaring `joinToString()` as a top-level function

```
package strings

fun joinToString( /* ... */ ): String { /* ... */ }
```

How does this run? When you compile the file, some classes will be produced because the JVM can only execute code in classes. When you work only with Kotlin, that's all you need to know. But if you need to call such a function from Java, you have to understand how it will be compiled. To make this clear, let's look at the Java code that would compile to the same class:

```
/* Java */
package strings;                        ┐  Corresponds to join.kt,
                                        │  the filename of listing 3.4
public class JoinKt {            ◁──────┘
    public static String joinToString(/* ... */) { /* ... */ }
}
```

You can see that the name of the class generated by the Kotlin compiler corresponds to the name of the file containing the function—capitalized to match Java's naming scheme and suffixed with `Kt`. All top-level functions in the file are compiled to static methods of that class. Therefore, calling this function from Java is as easy as calling any other static method:

```
/* Java */
import strings.JoinKt;

/* ... */

JoinKt.joinToString(list, ", ", "", "");
```

Changing the file class name

By default, the class name generated by the compiler corresponds to the filename, together with a `Kt` suffix. To change the name of the generated class that contains Kotlin top-level functions, add a file-wide annotation: `@file:JvmName("...")`. Place it at the beginning of the file, before the package name:.

```
@file:JvmName("StringFunctions")      ◁────── Annotation to specify the class name

package strings                 ◁────── The package statement follows the file annotations.

fun joinToString(/* ... */): String { /* ... */ }
```

> **(continued)**
> Now, the function can be called as follows:
>
> ```
> /* Java */
> import strings.StringFunctions;
> StringFunctions.joinToString(list, ", ", "", "");
> ```
>
> A detailed discussion of the annotation syntax comes later, in chapter 12.

TOP-LEVEL PROPERTIES

Just like functions, properties can be placed at the top level of a file. Storing individual pieces of data outside of a class isn't needed as often but is still useful. For example, you can use a `var` property to count the number of times some operation has been performed:

```
var opCount = 0          ◁──── Declares a top-level property

fun performOperation() {
    opCount++            ◁──── Changes the value of the property
    // ...
}

fun reportOperationCount() {                              Reads the value
    println("Operation performed $opCount times")   ◁──┘ of the property
}
```

The value of such a property will be stored in a static field.

Top-level properties also allow you to define constants in your code:

```
val UNIX_LINE_SEPARATOR = "\n"
```

By default, top-level properties, just like any other properties, are exposed to Java code as accessor methods (a getter for a `val` property and a getter–setter pair for a `var` property). If you want to expose a constant to Java code as a `public static final` field, to make its use more natural, you can mark it with the `const` modifier (this is allowed for properties of primitive types as well as `String`):

```
const val UNIX_LINE_SEPARATOR = "\n"
```

This gets you the equivalent of the following Java code:

```
/* Java */
public static final String UNIX_LINE_SEPARATOR = "\n";
```

You've improved the initial `joinToString` utility function quite a lot. Now, let's look at how to make it even handier.

NOTE   The Kotlin standard library also contains several useful top-level functions and properties. An example of this is the `kotlin.math` package. It provides useful functions for typical mathematical and trigonometric operations,
such as the `max` function to compute the maximum of two numbers. It also
comes with a number of mathematical constants, like Euler's number or pi:

```
fun main() {
    println(max(PI, E))
    // 3.141592653589793
}
```

3.3   Adding methods to other people's classes: Extension functions and properties

One of the main themes of Kotlin is smooth integration with existing code. Even pure
Kotlin projects are built on top of Java libraries, such as the JDK, the Android framework, and other third-party frameworks. And when you integrate Kotlin into a Java
project, you're also dealing with the existing code that hasn't been or won't be converted to Kotlin. Wouldn't it be nice to be able to use all the niceties of Kotlin when
working with those APIs, without having to rewrite them? That's what extension functions allow you to do.

   Conceptually, an *extension function* is a simple thing: a function that can be called as
a member of a class but is defined outside of it. To demonstrate one, let's add a
method for computing the last character of a string (ignoring the edge case of working with empty strings for now):

```
package strings

fun String.lastChar(): Char = this.get(this.length - 1)
```

All you need to do is put the name of the class or interface you're extending before
the name of the function you're adding. This class name is called the *receiver type*; the
value on which you're calling the extension function is called the *receiver object*. This is
illustrated in figure 3.1.

Figure 3.1   In an extension function declaration, the *receiver type* is the type on which the extension
is defined. You use it to specify the type your function extends. The *receiver object* is the instance of
that type. You use it to access properties and methods of the type you're extending.

You can call the function using the same syntax you use for ordinary class members:

```
fun main() {
    println("Kotlin".lastChar())
    // n
}
```

In this example, `String` is the receiver type and `"Kotlin"` is the receiver object.

In a sense, you've added your own method to the `String` class. Even though `String` isn't part of your code, and you may not even have the source code to that class, you can still extend it with the methods you need in your project. It doesn't even matter whether `String` is written in Java, Kotlin, or some other JVM language, such as Groovy, or even whether it is marked as `final`, preventing subclassing. As long as it's compiled to a Java class, you can add your own extensions to that class.

In the body of an extension function, you use `this` the same way you would use it in a method. And as in a regular method, you can omit it:

```
package strings

fun String.lastChar(): Char = get(length - 1)
```
Receiver object members can be accessed without this.

In the extension function, you can directly access the methods and properties of the class you're extending, as in methods defined in the class itself. Note that extension functions don't allow you to break encapsulation. Unlike methods defined in the class, extension functions don't have access to private or protected members of the class.

Later, we'll use the term *method* for both members of the class and extension functions. For instance, we can say that in the body of the extension function, you can call any method on the receiver, meaning you can call both members and extension functions. On the call site, extension functions are indistinguishable from members, and often, it doesn't matter whether the particular method is a member or an extension.

3.3.1 *Imports and extension functions*

When you define an extension function, it doesn't automatically become available across your entire project. Instead, it needs to be imported, just like any other class or function. This helps avoid accidental name conflicts. Kotlin allows you to import individual functions using the same syntax you use for classes:

```
import strings.lastChar

val c = "Kotlin".lastChar()
```

Of course, `*` imports work as well:

```
import strings.*

val c = "Kotlin".lastChar()
```

You can change the name of the class or function you're importing using the `as` keyword:

```
import strings.lastChar as last

val c = "Kotlin".last()
```

Changing a name on import is useful when you have several functions with the same name in different packages and you want to use them in the same file. For regular classes or functions, you have another choice in this situation: you can use a fully qualified name to refer to the class or function (and whether you can import a class or function at all also depends on its visibility modifier, as you'll see in section 4.1.3). For extension functions, the syntax requires you to use the short name, so the `as` keyword in an import statement is the only way to resolve the conflict.

3.3.2 Calling extension functions from Java

Under the hood, an extension function is a static method that accepts the receiver object as its first argument. Calling it doesn't involve creating adapter objects or any other run-time overhead.

That makes using extension functions from Java pretty easy: you call the static method and pass the receiver object instance. Just as with other top-level functions, the name of the Java class containing the method is determined from the name of the file where the function is declared. Let's say it was declared in a StringUtil.kt file:

```
/* Java */
char c = StringUtilKt.lastChar("Java");
```

This extension function is declared as a top-level function, so it's compiled to a static method. You can import the `lastChar` method statically from Java, simplifying the use to just `lastChar("Java")`. This code is somewhat less readable than the Kotlin version, but it's idiomatic, from the Java point of view.

3.3.3 Utility functions as extensions

Now, you can write the final version of the `joinToString` function. This is almost exactly what you'll find in the Kotlin standard library.

Listing 3.5 Declaring `joinToString()` as an extension

```
fun <T> Collection<T>.joinToString(          ⟵  Declares an extension function on Collection<T>
        separator: String = ", ",
        prefix: String = "",                     Assigns default values
        postfix: String = ""                     for parameters
): String {
    val result = StringBuilder(prefix)

    for ((index, element) in this.withIndex()) {   ⟵  The keyword this refers
        if (index > 0) result.append(separator)        to the receiver object:
        result.append(element)                          a collection of T.
    }

    result.append(postfix)
    return result.toString()
}
```

```
fun main() {
    val list = listOf(1, 2, 3)
    println(
        list.joinToString(
            separator = "; ",
            prefix = "(",
            postfix = ")"
        )
    )
    // (1; 2; 3)
}
```

You make it an extension to a collection of elements (meaning it works on lists, sets, and the like), and you provide default values for all the arguments. Now, you can invoke joinToString like a member of a class:

```
fun main() {
    val list = listOf(1, 2, 3)
    println(list.joinToString(" "))
    // 1 2 3
}
```

Because extension functions are effectively syntactic sugar over static method calls, you can use a more specific type as a receiver type, not only a class. Let's say you want to have a join function that can be invoked only on collections of strings:

```
fun Collection<String>.join(
        separator: String = ", ",
        prefix: String = "",
        postfix: String = ""
) = joinToString(separator, prefix, postfix)

fun main() {
    println(listOf("one", "two", "eight").join(" "))
    // one two eight
}
```

Calling this function with a list of objects of another type won't work:

```
fun main() {
    listOf(1, 2, 8).join()
    // Error: None of the following candidates is applicable because of
    // receiver type mismatch:
    // public fun Collection<String>.join(...): String
    // defined in root package
}
```

The static nature of extensions also means extension functions can't be overridden in subclasses. Let's look at an example.

3.3.4 No overriding for extension functions

Method overriding in Kotlin works as usual for member functions, but you can't override an extension function. Let's say you have two classes, `View` and `Button`. `Button` is a subclass of `View` and overrides the `click` function from the superclass. To implement this, you mark `View` and `click` with the `open` modifier to allow overriding and use the `override` modifier to provide an an implementation in the subclass (we'll take a closer look at this syntax in section 4.1.1 and learn more about the syntax for instantiating subclasses in section 4.2.1).

Listing 3.6 Overriding a member function

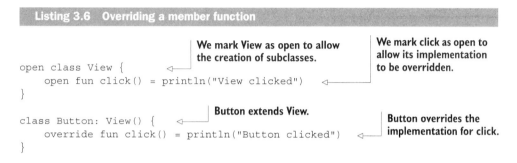

We mark View as open to allow the creation of subclasses.

We mark click as open to allow its implementation to be overridden.

```
open class View {
    open fun click() = println("View clicked")
}

class Button: View() {
    override fun click() = println("Button clicked")
}
```

Button extends View.

Button overrides the implementation for click.

If you declare a variable of type `View`, you can store a value of type `Button` in that variable because `Button` is a subtype of `View`. If you call a regular method, such as `click`, on this variable and that method is overridden in the `Button` class, the overridden implementation from the `Button` class will be used:

```
fun main() {
    val view: View = Button()
    view.click()
    // Button clicked
}
```

Determines the method to call based on the actual value of view

But it doesn't work that way for extensions. Extension functions aren't a part of the class; they're declared externally to it, as shown in figure 3.2.

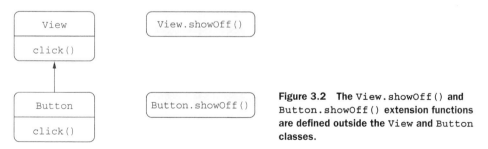

Figure 3.2 The `View.showOff()` and `Button.showOff()` extension functions are defined outside the `View` and `Button` classes.

Even though you can define extension functions with the same name and parameter types for a base class and its subclass, the function that's called depends on the declared static type of the variable, determined at compile time, not the run-time type of the value stored in that variable.

The following example shows two `showOff` extension functions declared on the `View` and `Button` classes. When you call `showOff` on a variable of type `View`, the corresponding extension is called, even though the actual type of the value is `Button`.

Listing 3.7 No overriding for extension functions

```
fun View.showOff() = println("I'm a view!")
fun Button.showOff() = println("I'm a button!")

fun main() {
    val view: View = Button()
    view.showOff()              <────── The extension function is resolved statically.
    // I'm a view!
}
```

It might help to recall that an extension function is compiled to a static function in Java with the receiver as the first argument. Java would choose the function the same way:

```
/* Java */
class Demo {
    public static void main(String[] args) {
        View view = new Button();
        ExtensionsKt.showOff(view);       showOff functions are declared
        // I'm a view!                    in the extensions.kt file.
    }
}
```

As you can see, overriding doesn't apply to extension functions; Kotlin resolves them statically.

> **NOTE** If the class has a member function with the same signature as an extension function, the member function always takes precedence. You should keep this in mind when extending the API of classes: if you add a member function with the same signature as an extension function a client of your class has defined and they then recompile their code, it will change its meaning and start referring to the new member function. Your IDE will also warn you that the extension function is shadowed by a member function.

We've discussed how to provide additional methods for external classes. Now, let's see how to do the same with properties.

3.3.5 *Extension properties*

You've already gotten to know the syntax for declaring Kotlin properties in section 2.2.1, and just like extension functions, you can also specify *extension properties*. These allow you to extend classes with APIs that can be accessed using the property syntax, rather than the function syntax. Even though they're called *properties*, they can't have any state because there's no proper place to store it—it's not possible to add extra fields to existing instances of Java objects. As a result, extension properties always have to define custom accessors, like the ones you learned about in section 2.2.2. Still, they provide a shorter, more concise calling convention, which can still come in handy sometimes.

In the previous section, you defined a function `lastChar()`. Now, let's convert it into a property, allowing you to call `"myText".lastChar` instead of `"myText".lastChar()`.

Listing 3.8 Declaring an extension property

```
val String.lastChar: Char
    get() = this.get(length - 1)
```

You can see that, just as with functions, an extension property looks like a regular property with a receiver type added. The getter must always be defined because there's no backing field and, therefore, no default getter implementation. Initializers aren't allowed for the same reason: there's nowhere to store the value specified as the initializer.

If you define the same property on a `StringBuilder`, you can make it a `var` because the contents of a `StringBuilder` can be modified.

Listing 3.9 Declaring a mutable extension property

```
var StringBuilder.lastChar: Char
    get() = this.get(length - 1)          ← Property getter
    set(value) {                          ← Property setter
        this.setCharAt(length - 1, value)
    }
```

You access extension properties exactly like member properties:

```
fun main() {
    val sb = StringBuilder("Kotlin?")
    println(sb.lastChar)
    // ?
    sb.lastChar = '!'
    println(sb)
    // Kotlin!
}
```

Note that when you need to access an extension property from Java, you have to invoke its getter and setter explicitly: `StringUtilKt.getLastChar("Java")` and `StringUtilKt.setLastChar(sb, '!')`.

Now that we've discussed the concept of extensions in general, let's return to the topic of collections. In the following subsection, we'll look at a few more library functions that help you handle them as well as language features that come up in those functions.

3.4   *Working with collections: varargs, infix calls, and library support*

This section shows some of the functions from the Kotlin standard library for working with collections. Along the way, it describes a few related language features:

- The `vararg` keyword, which allows you to declare a function taking an arbitrary number of arguments
- An *infix* notation that lets you call some one-argument functions without ceremony
- *Destructuring declarations* that allow you to unpack a single composite value into multiple variables

3.4.1   *Extending the Java collections API*

We started this chapter with the idea that collections in Kotlin are the same classes as in Java but with an extended API. Among others, you saw examples of getting the last element in a list and computing the sum of a collection of numbers:

```
fun main() {
    val strings: List<String> = listOf("first", "second", "fourteenth")
    strings.last()
    // fourteenth

    val numbers: Collection<Int> = setOf(1, 14, 2)
    numbers.sum()
    // 17
}
```

We were interested in how it works—why it's possible to do so many things with collections in Kotlin out of the box, even though they're instances of the Java library classes. Now, the answer should be clear: the `last` and `sum` functions are declared as extension functions and are always imported by default in your Kotlin files!

The `last` function is no more complex than `lastChar` for `String`, discussed in the previous section; it's an extension on the `List` class. For `sum`, we show a simplified declaration (the real library function works not only for `Int` numbers but for any number types):

```
fun <T> List<T>.last(): T { /* returns the last element */ }
fun Collection<Int>.sum(): Int { /* sum up all elements */ }
```

Many extension functions are declared in the Kotlin standard library, and we won't list all of them here. You may wonder what the best way to learn everything in the Kotlin standard library is. You don't have to—anytime you need to do something with a collection or any other object, the code completion in the IDE will show you all the possible functions available for that type of object. The list includes both regular methods and extension functions; you can choose the function you need. In addition to that, the standard library reference (https://kotlinlang.org/api/latest/jvm/stdlib/) lists all the methods available for each library class—members as well as extensions.

At the beginning of the chapter, you also saw functions for creating collections. A common trait of those functions is that they can be called with an arbitrary number of arguments. In the following section, you'll see the syntax for declaring such functions.

3.4.2 *Varargs: Functions that accept an arbitrary number of arguments*

When you call a function to create a list, you can pass any number of arguments to it:

```
val list = listOf(2, 3, 5, 7, 11)
```

If you look up how this function is declared in the standard library, you'll find the following signature:

```
fun listOf<T>(vararg values: T): List<T> { /* implementation */ }
```

This method makes use of a language feature that allows you to pass an arbitrary number of values to a method by packing them in an array: varargs. Kotlin's varargs are similar to those in Java, but the syntax is slightly different: instead of three dots after the type, Kotlin uses the `vararg` modifier on the parameter.

Another difference between Kotlin and Java is the syntax of calling the function when the arguments you need to pass are already packed in an array. In Java, you pass the array as is, whereas Kotlin requires you to explicitly unpack the array so that every array element becomes a separate argument to the function being called. This feature is called a *spread operator*, and using it is as simple as putting the `*` character before the corresponding argument. In this snippet, you're "spreading" the `args` array, which contains the command-line arguments passed to your `main` function, to use it as the variable arguments for the `listOf` function:

```
fun main(args: Array<String>) {
    val list = listOf("args: ", *args)        ◁─── The spread operator unpacks
    println(list)                                   the array contents.
}
```

This example shows that the spread operator lets you combine the values from an array and some fixed values in a single call. This isn't supported in Java.

Now, let's move on to maps. We'll briefly discuss another way to improve the readability of Kotlin function invocations: the *infix call*.

3.4.3 *Working with pairs: Infix calls and destructuring declarations*

To create maps, you use the `mapOf` function:

```
val map = mapOf(1 to "one", 7 to "seven", 53 to "fifty-three")
```

This is a good time to provide another explanation we promised you at the beginning of the chapter. The word `to` in this line of code isn't a built-in construct but, rather, a method invocation of a special kind, an *infix call*.

In an infix call, the method name is placed immediately between the target object name and the parameter, with no extra separators. The following two calls are equivalent:

```
1.to("one")        ◁───┐  Calls the to function the regular way
1 to "one"         ◁────  Calls the to function using an infix notation
```

Infix calls can be used with regular methods and extension functions that have exactly one required parameter. To allow a function to be called using the infix notation, you need to mark it with the `infix` modifier. Here's a simplified version of the declaration of the `to` function:

```
infix fun Any.to(other: Any) = Pair(this, other)
```

The `to` function returns an instance of `Pair`, which is a Kotlin standard library class that, unsurprisingly, represents a pair of elements. The actual declarations of `Pair` and `to` use generics, but we're omitting them here to keep things simple.

Note that you can initialize two variables with the contents of a `Pair` directly:

```
val (number, name) = 1 to "one"
```

This feature is called a *destructuring declaration*. Figure 3.3 illustrates how it works with pairs.

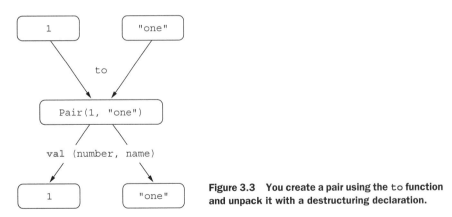

Figure 3.3 You create a pair using the `to` function and unpack it with a destructuring declaration.

The destructuring-declaration feature isn't limited to pairs. For example, you can also initialize two variables, `key` and `value`, with the contents of a map entry (something you've already seen very briefly in chapter 2).

This also works with loops, as you've seen in the implementation of `joinToString`, which uses the `withIndex` function:

```
for ((index, element) in collection.withIndex()) {
    println("$index: $element")
}
```

Chapter 9 will describe the general rules for destructuring an expression and using it to initialize several variables.

The `to` function is an extension function. You can create a pair of any elements, which means it's an extension to a generic receiver: you can write `1 to "one"`, `"one" to 1`, `list to list.size()`, and so on. Let's look at the signature of the `mapOf` function:

```
fun <K, V> mapOf(vararg values: Pair<K, V>): Map<K, V>
```

Like `listOf`, `mapOf` accepts a variable number of arguments, but this time, they should be pairs of keys and values. Even though the creation of a new map may look like a special construct in Kotlin, it's a regular function with a concise syntax. Next, let's discuss how extensions simplify dealing with strings and regular expressions.

3.5 *Working with strings and regular expressions*

Kotlin strings are exactly the same as Java strings. You can pass a string created in Kotlin code to any Java method, and you can use any Kotlin standard library methods on strings you receive from Java code. No conversion is involved, and no additional wrapper objects are created.

Kotlin makes working with standard Java strings more enjoyable by providing several useful extension functions. Also, it hides some confusing methods, adding extensions that are clearer. As our first example of the API differences, let's look at how Kotlin handles splitting strings.

3.5.1 *Splitting strings*

You're probably familiar with the `split` method on `String`. Everyone uses it, but sometimes, people complain about it on Stack Overflow (http://stackoverflow.com): "The `split` method in Java doesn't work with a dot." It's a common trap to write `"12.345-6 .A".split(".")` and expect an array `[12, 345-6, A]` as a result. But Java's `split` method returns an empty array! That happens because it takes a regular expression as a parameter and splits a string into several strings according to the expression. Here, the dot (`.`) is a regular expression that denotes any character.

Kotlin hides the confusing method and provides as replacements several overloaded extensions named `split` that have different arguments. The one that takes a regular expression requires a value of type `Regex` or `Pattern`, not `String`. This ensures it's always clear whether a string passed to a method is interpreted as plain text or a regular expression.

Here's how you'd split the string with either a dot or dash:

```
fun main() {
    println("12.345-6.A".split("\\.|-".toRegex()))
    // [12, 345, 6, A]
}
```
⊲─┐ **Creates a regular**
   expression explicitly

Kotlin uses exactly the same regular expression syntax as Java. The pattern here matches a dot (we escaped it to indicate that we mean a literal character, not a wildcard) or dash. The APIs for working with regular expressions are also similar to the standard Java library APIs, but they're more idiomatic. For instance, in Kotlin, you use an extension function `toRegex` to convert a string into a regular expression.

But for such a simple case, you don't need to use regular expressions. The other overload of the `split` extension function in Kotlin takes an arbitrary number of delimiters as plain-text strings:

```
fun main() {
    println("12.345-6.A".split(".", "-"))
    // [12, 345, 6, A]
}
```
⊲─── **Specifies several delimiters**

Note that you can specify character arguments instead and write `"12.345-6.A"` `.split('.', '-')`, which will lead to the same result. This method replaces the similar Java method, which can take only one character as a delimiter.

3.5.2   Regular expressions and triple-quoted strings

Let's look at another example with two different implementations: the first one will use extensions on `String`, and the second will work with regular expressions. Your task will be to parse a file's full path name into its components: a directory, a filename, and an extension. The Kotlin standard library contains functions to get the substring before (or after) the first (or last) occurrence of the given delimiter. Listing 3.10 shows how you can use them to solve this task (also see figure 3.4).

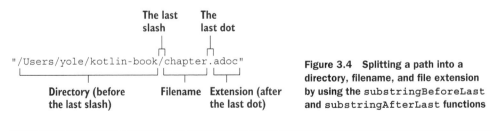

Figure 3.4   Splitting a path into a directory, filename, and file extension by using the `substringBeforeLast` and `substringAfterLast` functions

Listing 3.10   Using `String` extensions for parsing paths

```
fun parsePath(path: String) {
    val directory = path.substringBeforeLast("/")
    val fullName = path.substringAfterLast("/")
```

```
    val fileName = fullName.substringBeforeLast(".")
    val extension = fullName.substringAfterLast(".")

    println("Dir: $directory, name: $fileName, ext: $extension")
}

fun main() {
    parsePath("/Users/yole/kotlin-book/chapter.adoc")
    // Dir: /Users/yole/kotlin-book, name: chapter, ext: adoc
}
```

The substring before the last slash symbol of the file `path` is the path to an enclosing directory, the substring after the last dot is a file extension, and the filename goes between them.

Kotlin makes it easier to work with strings without resorting to regular expressions, which are powerful but also sometimes hard to understand after they've been written. If you want to use regular expressions, the Kotlin standard library can help. The following listing shows how the same task can be done using regular expressions.

Listing 3.11   Using regular expressions for parsing paths

```
fun parsePathRegex(path: String) {
    val regex = """(.+)/(.+)\.(.+)""".toRegex()
    val matchResult = regex.matchEntire(path)
    if (matchResult != null) {
        val (directory, filename, extension) = matchResult.destructured
        println("Dir: $directory, name: $filename, ext: $extension")
    }
}

fun main() {
    parsePathRegex("/Users/yole/kotlin-book/chapter.adoc")
    // Dir: /Users/yole/kotlin-book, name: chapter, ext: adoc
}
```

In this example, the regular expression is written in a *triple-quoted string*. In such a string, you don't need to escape any characters, including the backslash, so you can encode a regular expression matching a literal dot with \., rather than \\., as you'd write in an ordinary string literal (see figure 3.5).

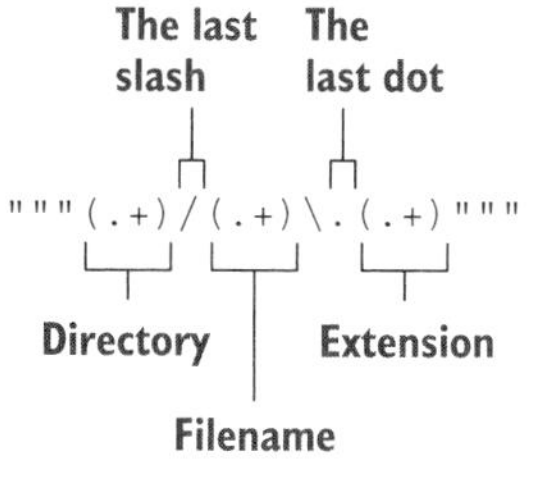

Figure 3.5   The regular expression for splitting a path into a directory, a filename, and a file extension

This regular expression divides a path into three groups separated by a slash and a dot. The pattern . matches any character from the beginning, so the first group (.+) contains the substring before the last slash. This substring includes all the previous slashes because they match the "any character" pattern. Similarly, the second group contains the substring before the last dot (and after the last slash), and the third group contains the remaining part.

Now, let's discuss the implementation of the `parsePathRegex` function from the previous example. You create a regular expression and match it against an input path. If the match is successful (the result isn't `null`), you assign the value of its `destructured` property to the corresponding variables. This is the same syntax used when you initialized two variables with a `Pair`; section 9.4 will cover the details.

3.5.3   *Multiline triple-quoted strings*

The purpose of triple-quoted strings is not only to avoid escaping characters. Such a string literal can contain any characters, including line breaks. That gives you an easy way to embed in your programs text containing line breaks. As an example, let's draw some ASCII art:

```
val kotlinLogo =
    """
    | //
    |//
    |/ \
    """.trimIndent()

fun main() {
    println(kotlinLogo)
    // | //
    // |//
    // |/ \
}
```

The multiline string contains all the characters between the triple quotes. That includes the line breaks and indents used to format the code. In cases like this, you are most likely only interested in the actual content of your string. By calling `trimIndent`, you can remove that common minimal indent of all the lines of your string and remove the first and last lines of the string, given they are blank.

> **NOTE** Different operating systems use different characters to mark the end of a line in a file: Windows uses CRLF (Carriage Return Line Feed), Linux and macOS uses LF (Line Feed). Regardless of the used operating system, Kotlin interprets CRLF, LF, and CR as line breaks.

As you saw in the previous example, a triple-quoted string can contain line breaks; however, you can't use special characters, like \n. On the other hand, you don't have to escape \, so the Windows-style path `"C:\\Users\\yole\\kotlin-book"` can be written as `"""C:\Users\yole\kotlin-book"""`.

You can also use string templates in multiline strings. Because multiline strings don't support escape sequences, you have to use an embedded expression if you need to use a literal dollar sign or an escaped Unicode symbol in the contents of your string. So rather than write `val think = """Hmm \uD83E\uDD14"""`, you'll have to write the following to properly interpret the escaped symbol encoded in this string: `val think = """Hmm ${"\uD83E\uDD14"}"""`.

One of the areas multiline strings can be useful in your programs (besides games that use ASCII art) is tests. In tests, it's fairly common to execute an operation that produces multiline text (e.g., a web page fragment or other structured text) and compare the result with the expected output. Multiline strings give you a perfect solution for including the expected output as part of your tests. There is no need for clumsy escaping or loading the text from external files—just put in some quotation marks and place the expected HTML, XML, JSON, or other output between them. And for better formatting, use the aforementioned `trimIndent` function, which is another example of an extension function:

```
val expectedPage = """
    <html lang="en">
        <head>
        <title>A page</title>
        </head>
    <body>
        <p>Hello, Kotlin!</p>
    </body>
    </html>
""".trimIndent()

val expectedObject = """
    {
        "name": "Sebastian",
        "age": 27,
        "homeTown": "Munich"
    }
""".trimIndent()
```

Syntax highlighting inside triple-quoted strings in IntelliJ IDEA and Android Studio

Using triple-quoted strings for formatted text, like HTML or JSON, provides an additional benefit: IntelliJ IDEA and Android Studio can provide you with syntax highlighting inside those string literals. To enable highlighting, place your cursor inside the string and press Alt-Enter (or Option-Return on macOS) or click the floating yellow lightbulb icon and select Inject Language or Reference. Next, select the type of language you're using in the string (e.g., JSON). Your multiline string then becomes properly syntax-highlighted JSON. If your text snippet happens to be malformed JSON, you'll even get warnings and descriptive error messages, all within your Kotlin string. By default, this highlighting is temporary. To instruct your IDE to always inject a string literal with a given language, you can use the `@Language("JSON")` annotation.

(continued)

```
13 ∨  val expectedObject : String   = """
14 ∨      {
15            "name": "Sebastian",
16            "age": 27,
17            "homeTown": "Munich"
18        }
19    """.trimIndent()
20
```

- ✓ Do not show property type hints   >
- ✓ Convert property initializer to getter >
- ✓ Convert to lazy property   >
- ✓ **Inject language or reference**

🔍 JSON   ✕

JSON (JSON)
{} JSON Lines (JSON lines)
{} JSON5 (JSON5)
{} JSONPath (JSONPath)
{} MongoDB-JSON-Query (MongoDB JSON Query)

```
13    val expectedObject : String   = """
14        {
15            "name": "Sebastian",
16            "age": 27,
17            "homeTown": "Munich"
18        }
19    """.trimIndent()
```

```
14    @Language("JSON")
15    val expectedObject : String   = """
16        {
17            "name": "Sebastian",
18            "age": 27,
19            "homeTown": "Munich"
20        }
21    """.trimIndent()
```

For more information on language injections in IntelliJ IDEA and Android Studio, take a look at https://www.jetbrains.com/help/idea/using-language-injections.html.

You can now see that extension functions are a powerful way to extend the APIs of existing libraries and adapt them to the idioms of the Kotlin language. And indeed, a large portion of the Kotlin standard library is made up of extension functions for standard Java classes. You can also find many community-developed libraries that provide Kotlin-friendly extensions for third-party libraries.

Now that you can see how Kotlin gives you better APIs for the libraries you use, let's turn our attention back to your code. You'll see some new uses for extension functions, and we'll also discuss a new concept: *local functions.*

3.6 *Making your code tidy: Local functions and extensions*

Many developers believe one of the most important qualities of good code is a lack of duplication. There's even a special name for this principle: don't repeat yourself (DRY). But when you write in Java, following this principle isn't always trivial. In many cases, it's possible to use the Extract Method refactoring feature of your IDE to break longer methods into smaller chunks and then reuse those chunks. But this can make code more difficult to understand because you end up with a class with many small methods and no clear relationship between them. You can go even further and group the extracted methods into an inner class, which lets you maintain the structure, but this approach requires a significant amount of boilerplate.

Kotlin gives you a cleaner solution: you can nest the functions you've extracted in the containing function. This way, you have the structure you need without any extra syntactic overhead.

Let's see how to use local functions to fix a fairly common case of code duplication. In the next listing, a function saves a user to a database, and you need to make sure the user object contains valid data.

Listing 3.12 A function with repetitive code

```kotlin
class User(val id: Int, val name: String, val address: String)

fun saveUser(user: User) {
    if (user.name.isEmpty()) {
        throw IllegalArgumentException(                    ◁──┐
            "Can't save user ${user.id}: empty Name")         │  Field validation
    }                                                         │  is duplicated.
                                                              │
    if (user.address.isEmpty()) {                      ◁──────┘
        throw IllegalArgumentException(
            "Can't save user ${user.id}: empty Address")
    }

    // Save user to the database
}

fun main() {
    saveUser(User(1, "", ""))
    // java.lang.IllegalArgumentException: Can't save user 1: empty Name
}
```

The amount of duplicated code here is fairly small, and you probably won't want to have a full-blown method in your class that handles one special case of validating a user. But if you put the validation code into a local function, you can get rid of the duplication and still maintain a clear code structure. Here's how it works.

Listing 3.13   Extracting a local function to avoid repetition

```
class User(val id: Int, val name: String, val address: String)

fun saveUser(user: User) {

    fun validate(user: User,                        ◁─── Declares a local function
                 value: String,                          to validate any field
                 fieldName: String) {
        if (value.isEmpty()) {
            throw IllegalArgumentException(
                "Can't save user ${user.id}: empty $fieldName")
        }
    }
    validate(user, user.name, "Name")               ◁─── Calls the local function to
    validate(user, user.address, "Address")              validate the specific fields

    // Save user to the database
}
```

This looks better; the validation logic isn't duplicated, but it's still confined to the scope of the `validate` function. As the project evolves, you can easily add more validations if you need to add other fields to `User`. However, passing the `User` object to the validation function is somewhat ugly. The good news is that it's entirely unnecessary because local functions have access to all parameters and variables of the enclosing function. Let's take advantage of that and get rid of the extra `User` parameter.

Listing 3.14   Accessing outer function parameters in a local function

```
class User(val id: Int, val name: String, val address: String)

fun saveUser(user: User) {                           Now, you don't duplicate
    fun validate(value: String, fieldName: String) {  ◁── the user parameter of the
        if (value.isEmpty()) {                             saveUser function.
            throw IllegalArgumentException(
                "Can't save user ${user.id}: " +      ◁── You can access parameters of
                    "empty $fieldName")                   the outer function directly.
        }
    }

    validate(user.name, "Name")
    validate(user.address, "Address")

    // Save user to the database
}
```

To further improve this example, you can move the validation logic into an extension function of the `User` class.

Listing 3.15 Extracting the logic into an extension function

```
class User(val id: Int, val name: String, val address: String)

fun User.validateBeforeSave() {
    fun validate(value: String, fieldName: String) {
        if (value.isEmpty()) {
            throw IllegalArgumentException(
                "Can't save user $id: empty $fieldName")          You can access
        }                                                         properties of
    }                                                             User directly.

    validate(name, "Name")
    validate(address, "Address")
}

fun saveUser(user: User) {
    user.validateBeforeSave()          Calls the extension function

    // Save user to the database
}
```

Extracting a piece of code into an extension function turns out to be surprisingly useful. Even though `User` is a part of your codebase and not a library class, you don't want to put this logic into a method of `User` because it's not relevant to any other places `User` is used. If you follow this approach, the API of the class contains only the essential methods used everywhere, so the class remains small and easy to wrap your head around. On the other hand, functions that primarily deal with a single object and don't need access to its private data can access its members without extra qualification, as in listing 3.15.

Extension functions can also be declared as local functions, so you could go even further and include `User.validateBeforeSave` as a local function in `saveUser`. But deeply nested local functions are usually fairly hard to read, so as a general rule, we don't recommend using more than one level of nesting. Having looked at all the cool things you can do with functions, in the next chapter, we'll examine what you can do with classes.

Summary

- Kotlin enhances the Java collection classes with a richer API.
- Defining default values for function parameters greatly reduces the need to define overloaded functions, and the named-argument syntax makes calls to functions with many parameters much more readable.
- Functions and properties can be declared directly in a file, not just as members of a class, allowing for a more flexible code structure.

- Extension functions and properties allow you to extend the API of any class, including classes defined in external libraries, without modifying its source code and with no run-time overhead.

- Infix calls provide a clean syntax for calling operator-like methods with a single argument.

- Kotlin provides a large number of convenient string-handling functions for both regular expressions and plain strings.

- Triple-quoted strings provide a clean way to write expressions that would require a lot of noisy escaping and string concatenation in Java.

- Local functions help you structure your code more cleanly and eliminate duplication.

Classes, objects, and interfaces

In this chapter, you'll gain a deeper understanding of working with classes and interfaces in Kotlin. You already saw the basic syntax for declaring a class in section 2.2, and you know how to declare methods and properties, use simple primary constructors (aren't they nice?), and work with enums. But there's a lot more to see and learn on the topic! Kotlin's classes and interfaces differ a bit from what you might be used to from Java: for example, interfaces can contain property declarations. Kotlin's declarations are `final` and `public`, by default. In addition, nested classes aren't inner by default; they don't contain an implicit reference to their outer class.

For constructors, the short primary constructor syntax works great for the majority of cases, but Kotlin also comes with full syntax that lets you declare constructors with nontrivial initialization logic. The same works for properties: the concise syntax is nice, but you can easily define your own implementations of accessors.

The Kotlin compiler can generate useful methods to avoid verbosity. Declaring a class as a `data` class instructs the compiler to generate several standard methods for this class. You can also avoid writing delegating methods by hand, since the delegation pattern is supported natively in Kotlin.

You'll also get to see Kotlin's `object` keyword, which declares a class and also creates an instance of the class. The keyword is used to express singleton objects, companion objects, and object expressions (analogous to Java anonymous classes). Let's start by talking about classes and interfaces and the details of defining class hierarchies in Kotlin.

4.1   Defining class hierarchies

In this section, you'll take a look at how class hierarchies are defined in Kotlin. You'll look at Kotlin's visibility and access modifiers as well as which defaults Kotlin chooses for them. You'll also learn about the `sealed` modifier, which restricts the possible subclasses of a class or implementations of an interface.

4.1.1   Interfaces in Kotlin

We'll begin with a look at defining and implementing interfaces. Kotlin interfaces can contain definitions of abstract methods as well as implementations of non-abstract methods; however, they can't contain any state.

To declare an interface in Kotlin, use the `interface` keyword instead of `class`. An interface that indicates that an element is clickable—like a button or hyperlink—could look like the code in the following listing.

Listing 4.1   Declaring a simple interface

```
interface Clickable {
    fun click()
}
```

This declares an interface with a single abstract method named `click`, which doesn't return any value. All non-abstract classes implementing the interface need to provide an implementation of this method.

> **NOTE**   Technically, it does return a value: `Unit`, the Kotlin equivalent of Java's `void`. You'll take a detailed look at this in section 8.1.6.

To mark a button as `Clickable`, you put the interface name behind a colon after the class name and provide an implementation for the `click` function.

```
class Button : Clickable {
    override fun click() = println("I was clicked")
}

fun main() {
    Button().click()
    // I was clicked
}
```

Kotlin uses the colon after the class name for both *composition* (that is, implementing interfaces) and *inheritance* (that is, subclassing, as you'll see in section 4.1.2). A class can implement as many interfaces as it wants, but it can extend only one class.

The `override` modifier is used to mark methods and properties that override those from the superclass or interface. Unlike Java, which uses the optional `@Override` annotation, using the `override` modifier is *mandatory* in Kotlin. This saves you from accidentally overriding a method if it's added after you wrote your implementation; your code won't compile unless you explicitly mark the method as `override` or rename it.

An interface method can have a default implementation. To do so, you just provide a method body. In this case, you could add a function `showOff` with a default implementation to the `Clickable` interface that simply prints some text.

```
interface Clickable {          Regular method declaration
    fun click()          <────┘
    fun showOff() = println("I'm clickable!")   <───┐ Method with a default
}                                                    implementation
```

If you implement this interface, you are forced to provide an implementation for `click`. You can redefine the behavior of the `showOff` method, or you can omit it if you're fine with the default behavior.

Now, let's suppose another interface also defines a `showOff` method and has the following implementation for it.

```
interface Focusable {
    fun setFocus(b: Boolean) =
        println("I ${if (b) "got" else "lost"} focus.")

    fun showOff() = println("I'm focusable!")
}
```

What happens if you need to implement both interfaces in your class? Each of them contains a `showOff` method with a default implementation, so which implementation wins? Neither wins. Instead, you get the following compiler error if you don't implement `showOff` explicitly:

```
The class 'Button' must override public open fun showOff()
because it inherits many implementations of it.
```

The Kotlin compiler forces you to provide your own implementation.

Listing 4.5   Invoking an inherited interface method implementation

```
class Button : Clickable, Focusable {
    override fun click() = println("I was clicked")

    override fun showOff() {
        super<Clickable>.showOff()
        super<Focusable>.showOff()
    }
}
```

> **You must provide an explicit implementation if more than one implementation for the same member is inherited.**

> **Here, super being qualified by the supertype name in angle brackets specifies the parent whose method you want to call.**

The `Button` class now implements two interfaces. You implement `showOff()` by calling both implementations you inherited from supertypes. To invoke an inherited implementation, you use the `super` keyword together with the base type name in angle brackets: `super<Clickable>.showOff()` (a different syntax from Java's `Clickable.super`
`.showOff()`).

If you only need to invoke one inherited implementation, you can use the expression body syntax and write this:

```
override fun showOff() = super<Clickable>.showOff()
```

To verify that everything you've read so far is actually true, you can create an instance of your `Button` class and invoke all the inherited methods—the overridden `showOff` and `click` functions, as well as the `setFocus` function from the `Focusable` interface, which provided a default implementation.

Listing 4.6   Calling inherited and overridden methods

```
fun main() {
    val button = Button()
    button.showOff()
    // I'm clickable!
    // I'm focusable!
    button.setFocus(true)
    // I got focus.
    button.click()
    // I was clicked.
}
```

Implementing interfaces with method bodies in Java

Kotlin compiles each interface with default methods to a combination of a regular interface and a class containing the method bodies as static methods. The interface contains only declarations, and the class contains all the implementations as static methods. Therefore, if you need to implement such an interface in a Java class, you must define your own implementations of all methods, including those that have method bodies in Kotlin. For example, a `JavaButton` that implements `Clickable` needs to provide implementations for both `click` and `showOff`, even though Kotlin provides a default implementation for the latter, as shown in listing 4.7.

Listing 4.7   Calling inherited and overridden methods

```
class JavaButton implements Clickable {
    @Override
    public void click() {
        System.out.println("I was clicked");
    }

    @Override
    public void showOff() {                          Java code can't use Kotlin's
        System.out.println("I'm showing off");   ◁── default implementations.
    }
}
```

Now that you've seen how Kotlin allows you to implement methods defined in interfaces, let's look at the second half of that story: overriding members defined in base classes.

4.1.2   Open, final, and abstract modifiers: Final by default

By default, you can't create a subclass for a Kotlin class or override any methods from a base class—all classes and methods are *final*, by default.

This sets it apart from Java, where you are allowed to create subclasses of any class and can override any method, unless it has been explicitly marked with the `final` keyword. But why didn't Kotlin follow this approach? Because while this is often convenient, it can also be problematic.

The so-called *fragile base class* problem occurs when modifications of a base class can cause incorrect behavior of subclasses because the changed code of the base class no longer matches the assumptions in its subclasses. If the class doesn't provide exact rules for how it should be subclassed (which methods should be overridden and how), the clients are at risk of overriding the methods in a way the author of the base class didn't expect. Because it's impossible to analyze all the subclasses, the base class is "fragile," in the sense that any change in it may lead to unexpected changes of behavior in subclasses.

To protect against this problem, *Effective Java* by Joshua Bloch (Addison-Wesley, 2008), one of the best-known books on good Java programming style, recommends that you "design and document for inheritance or else prohibit it." This means all classes and methods that aren't specifically intended to be overridden in subclasses must be explicitly marked as `final`. Kotlin follows this philosophy, making its classes, methods, and properties `final` by default.

If you want to allow the creation of subclasses of a class, you need to mark the class with the `open` modifier. In addition, you need to add the `open` modifier to every property or method that can be overridden.

Let's say you want to spice up your user interface beyond a simple button and create a clickable `RichButton`. Subclasses of this class should be able to provide their own animations but shouldn't be able to break basic behavior, such as disabling the button. You could declare the class as follows.

Listing 4.8   Declaring an open class with an open method

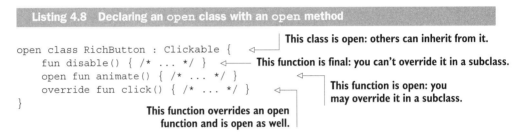

This means a subclass of `RichButton` could, in turn, look like the following.

Listing 4.9   Declaring a subclass of an open class that overrides open methods

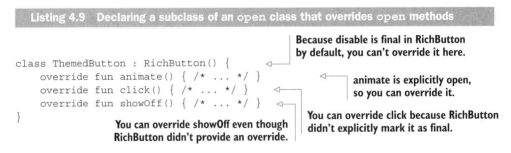

Note that if you override a member of a base class or interface, the overriding member will also be `open` by default. If you want to change this and forbid the subclasses of your class from overriding your implementation, you can explicitly mark the overriding member as `final`.

Listing 4.10   Forbidding an override

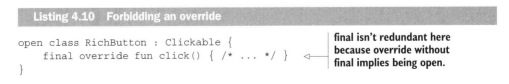

Open classes and smart casts

One significant benefit of classes that are `final` by default is that they enable smart casts in a larger variety of scenarios. As we mentioned in section 2.3.6, the compiler can only perform a smart cast (an automatic cast that allows you to access members without further manual casting) for variables that couldn't have changed after the type check.

For a class, this means smart casts can only be used with a class property that is a `val` and doesn't have a custom accessor. This requirement means the property must be `final`, because otherwise, a subclass could override the property and define a custom accessor, breaking the key requirement of smart casts.

Because properties are `final` by default, you can use smart casts with most properties without thinking about it explicitly, which improves the expressiveness of your code.

You can also declare a class as `abstract`, making it so the class can't be instantiated. An abstract class usually contains abstract members that don't have implementations and must be overridden in subclasses. Abstract members are always open, so you don't need to use an explicit `open` modifier (just like you don't need an explicit `open` modifier in an `interface`).

An example of an abstract class is a class that defines the properties of an animation, like the animation speed and number of frames, as well as behavior for running the animation. Since these properties and methods only make sense when implemented by another object, `Animated` is marked as `abstract`.

Listing 4.11 Declaring an abstract class

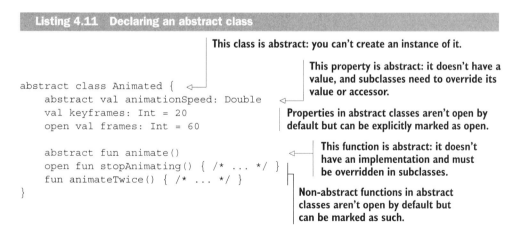

This class is abstract: you can't create an instance of it.

This property is abstract: it doesn't have a value, and subclasses need to override its value or accessor.

```
abstract class Animated {
    abstract val animationSpeed: Double
    val keyframes: Int = 20
    open val frames: Int = 60

    abstract fun animate()
    open fun stopAnimating() { /* ... */ }
    fun animateTwice() { /* ... */ }
}
```

Properties in abstract classes aren't open by default but can be explicitly marked as open.

This function is abstract: it doesn't have an implementation and must be overridden in subclasses.

Non-abstract functions in abstract classes aren't open by default but can be marked as such.

Table 4.1 lists the access modifiers in Kotlin. The comments in the table are applicable to modifiers in classes; in interfaces, you don't use `final`, `open`, or `abstract`. A member in an interface is always `open` ; you can't declare it as `final`. It's `abstract` if it has no body but the keyword isn't required.

Table 4.1 The meaning of access modifiers in a class

Modifier	Corresponding member	Comments
`final`	Can't be overridden	Used by default for class members
`open`	Can be overridden	Should be specified explicitly
`abstract`	Must be overridden	Can be used only in abstract classes; abstract members can't have an implementation
`override`	Overrides a member in a superclass or interface	Overridden member is open by default, if not marked `final`

Now that we've discussed the modifiers that control inheritance, let's take a look at the role visibility modifiers play in Kotlin.

4.1.3 *Visibility modifiers: Public by default*

Visibility modifiers help to control access to declarations in your code base. By restricting the visibility of a class's implementation details, you ensure that you can change them without the risk of breaking code that depends on the class.

Kotlin provides `public`, `protected`, and `private` modifiers, which are analogous to their Java counterparts: `public` declarations are visible everywhere; `protected` declarations are visible in subclasses; and `private` declarations are visible inside a class or, in the case of top-level declarations, visible inside a file. In Kotlin, not specifying a modifier means the declaration is `public`.

> **NOTE** Public by default differs from what you might know from Java, but it is a convenient convention for application developers. Library authors, on the other hand, usually want to make sure that no parts of their API are accidentally exposed. Hiding a previously public API after the fact would be a breaking change, after all. For this case, Kotlin provides an *explicit API mode*. In explicit mode, you need to specify the visibility for declarations that would be exposed as a public API and explicitly specify the type for properties and functions that are part of the public API, as well. Explicit API mode can be enabled using the `-Xexplicit-api={strict|warning}` compiler option or via your build system.

For restricting visibility inside a module, Kotlin provides the visibility modifier `internal`. A *module* is a set of Kotlin files compiled together. This could be a Gradle source set, a Maven project, or an IntelliJ IDEA module.

> **NOTE** When using Gradle, the `test` source set can access declarations marked as `internal` from your `main` source set.

No package private in Kotlin

Kotlin doesn't have the concept of package-private visibility, which is the default visibility in Java. Kotlin uses packages only as a way of organizing code in namespaces; it doesn't use them for visibility control.

The advantage of `internal` visibility is that it provides real encapsulation for the implementation details of your module. In Java, the encapsulation can be easily broken because external code can define classes in the same packages used by your code and, thus, gain access to your package-private declarations.

Kotlin also allows you to use `private` visibility for top-level declarations, including classes, functions, and properties. Such declarations are visible only in the file where they are declared. This is another useful way to hide the implementation details of a subsystem. Table 4.2 summarizes all the visibility modifiers.

Table 4.2   Kotlin visibility modifiers

Modifier	Class member	Top-level declaration
`public` (default)	Visible everywhere	Visible everywhere
`internal`	Visible in a module	Visible in a module
`protected`	Visible in subclasses	—
`private`	Visible in a class	Visible in a file

Let's look at an example. Every line in the `giveSpeech` function tries to violate the visibility rules. It compiles with an error.

Listing 4.12   Using different visibility modifiers

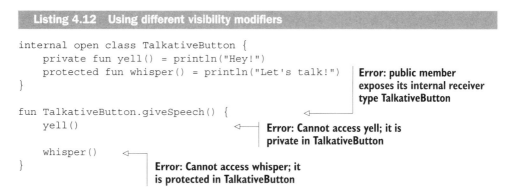

```
internal open class TalkativeButton {
    private fun yell() = println("Hey!")
    protected fun whisper() = println("Let's talk!")   Error: public member
}                                                        exposes its internal receiver
                                                         type TalkativeButton
fun TalkativeButton.giveSpeech() {
    yell()                              Error: Cannot access yell; it is
                                        private in TalkativeButton
    whisper()
}                  Error: Cannot access whisper; it
                   is protected in TalkativeButton
```

Kotlin forbids you to reference the less-visible type `TalkativeButton` (`internal`, in this case) from the `public` function `giveSpeech`. This is a case of a more general rule: all types used in the list of base types and type parameters of a class or the signature of a method must be as visible as the class or method itself. This rule means that you always have access to all types you might need to invoke the function or extend a class. To solve the problem, you can either make the `giveSpeech` extension function `internal` or make the `TalkativeButton` class `public`.

Note the difference in behavior for the `protected` modifier in Java and in Kotlin. In Java, you can access a `protected` member from the same package, but Kotlin doesn't allow that.

In Kotlin, visibility rules are simple, and a `protected` member is *only* visible in the class and its subclasses. Also note that extension functions of a class don't get access to its `private` or `protected` members. This is also why you can't call the `protected` `whisper` function from the extension function `giveSpeech`.

Kotlin's visibility modifiers and Java

In Kotlin, `public`, `protected`, and `private` modifiers are preserved when compiling to Java bytecode. You use such Kotlin declarations from Java code as if they were declared with the same visibility in Java. The only exception is a `private` class: it's compiled to a package-private declaration under the hood (you can't make a class `private` in Java).

But you may ask, what happens with the `internal` modifier? There's no direct analogue in Java. Package-private visibility is a totally different thing: a module usually consists of several packages, and different modules may contain declarations from the same package. Thus, an `internal` modifier becomes `public` in the bytecode.

This correspondence between Kotlin declarations and their Java analogues (or their bytecode representation) explains why sometimes you can access something from Java code that you can't access from Kotlin. For instance, you can access an `internal` class or a top-level declaration from Java code in another module or a `protected` member from Java code in the same package.

But note that the names of `internal` members of a class are mangled. Technically, `internal` members can be used from Java, but they look ugly in the Java code. That helps avoid unexpected clashes in overrides when you extend a class from another module, and it prevents you from accidentally using `internal` classes.

Another difference in visibility rules between Kotlin and Java is that an outer class doesn't see `private` members of its inner (or nested) classes in Kotlin. Let's discuss inner and nested classes in Kotlin next and look at an example.

4.1.4   *Inner and nested classes: Nested by default*

If you want to encapsulate a helper class or keep code close to where it is used, you can declare a class inside another class. However, unlike in Java, nested classes in Kotlin don't have access to the outer class instance, unless you specifically request that. Let's look at an example showing why this is important.

Imagine you want to define a `View` element, the state of which can be serialized. It may not be easy to serialize a view, but you can copy all the necessary data to another helper class. You declare the `State` interface that implements `Serializable`. The `View` interface declares `getCurrentState` and `restoreState` methods that can be used to save the state of a view.

Listing 4.13   Declaring a view with serializable state

```
interface State : Serializable

interface View {
    fun getCurrentState(): State
    fun restoreState(state: State) { /* ... */ }
}
```

It's handy to define a class that saves a button state in the `Button` class. Let's see how it can be done in Java (the similar Kotlin code will be shown in a moment).

Listing 4.14   Implementing `View` in Java with an inner class

```
/* Java */
public class Button implements View {
    @Override
    public State getCurrentState() {
        return new ButtonState();
    }

    @Override
    public void restoreState(State state) { /*...*/ }

    public class ButtonState implements State { /*...*/ }
}
```

You define the `ButtonState` class that implements the `State` interface and holds specific information for `Button`. In the `getCurrentState` method, you create a new instance of this class. In a real case, you'd initialize `ButtonState` with all necessary data.

What's wrong with this code? Why do you get a `java.io.NotSerializableException:` `Button` exception if you try to serialize the state of the declared button? This may look strange at first: the variable you serialize is `state` of the `ButtonState` type, not the `Button` type.

Everything becomes clear when you recall that in Java, when you declare a class in another class, it becomes an inner class by default. The `ButtonState` class in the example implicitly stores a reference to its outer `Button` class. That explains why `ButtonState` can't be serialized: `Button` isn't serializable, and the reference to it breaks the serialization of `ButtonState`.

To fix this problem, you need to declare the `ButtonState` class as `static`. Declaring a nested class as `static` removes the implicit reference from that class to its enclosing class.

In Kotlin, the default behavior of inner classes is the opposite of what we've just described, as shown next.

Listing 4.15   Implementing `View` **in Kotlin with a nested class**

```
class Button : View {
    override fun getCurrentState(): State = ButtonState()

    override fun restoreState(state: State) { /*...*/ }

    class ButtonState : State { /*...*/ }
}
```

> This class is an analogue of a static nested class in Java.

A nested class in Kotlin with no explicit modifiers is the same as a `static` nested class in Java. To turn it into an inner class so that it contains a reference to an outer class, you use the `inner` modifier. Table 4.3 describes the differences in this behavior between Java and Kotlin, and the difference between nested and inner classes is illustrated in figure 4.1.

Table 4.3   Correspondence between nested and inner classes in Java and Kotlin

Class A declared within another class B	In Java	In Kotlin
Nested class (doesn't store a reference to an outer class)	static class A	class A
Inner class (stores a reference to an outer class)	class A	inner class A

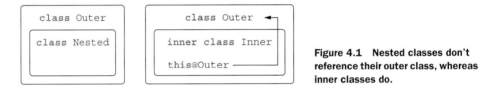

Figure 4.1   Nested classes don't reference their outer class, whereas inner classes do.

The syntax to reference an instance of an outer class in Kotlin also differs from Java. You write `this@Outer` to access the `Outer` class from the `Inner` class:

```
class Outer {
    inner class Inner {
        fun getOuterReference(): Outer = this@Outer
    }
}
```

Now, you've learned the difference between inner and nested classes in Java and in Kotlin. Next, let's discuss how to create a hierarchy containing a limited number of classes.

4.1.5   Sealed classes: Defining restricted class hierarchies

Before this chapter, you had already made your first acquaintance with class hierarchies in Kotlin. Recall the expression hierarchy example from section 2.3.6, which you used to encode expressions like `(1 + 2) + 4`. The interface `Expr` is implemented by `Num`, which represents a number; and `Sum`, which represents a sum of two expressions.

It's convenient to handle all the possible cases in a `when` expression. But you must provide the `else` branch to specify what should happen if none of the other branches match.

Listing 4.16 Expressions as interface implementations

```
interface Expr
class Num(val value: Int) : Expr
class Sum(val left: Expr, val right: Expr) : Expr

fun eval(e: Expr): Int =
    when (e) {
        is Num -> e.value                              You have to check
        is Sum -> eval(e.right) + eval(e.left)         the else branch.
        else ->
            throw IllegalArgumentException("Unknown expression")
    }
```

Because you're using the `when` construct as an expression (that is, using its return value), it needs to be exhaustive: the Kotlin compiler forces you to check for the default option. In this example, you can't return something meaningful, so you throw an exception.

Always having to add a default branch isn't convenient. This can also become a problem, since if you (or a colleague or the author of a dependency you use) add a new subclass, the compiler won't alert you that you're missing a case. If you forget to add a branch to handle that new subclass, it will simply choose the default branch, which can lead to subtle bugs.

Kotlin comes with a solution to this problem: `sealed` classes. You mark a superclass with the `sealed` modifier, which restricts the possibility of creating subclasses. All *direct* subclasses of a sealed class must be known at compile time and declared in the same package as the sealed class itself, and *all* subclasses need to be located within the same module.

Instead of using an interface, you could make `Expr` a `sealed class` and have `Num` and `Sum` subclass it.

Listing 4.17 Expressions as sealed classes

```
sealed class Expr                              Mark a base class as sealed ...
class Num(val value: Int) : Expr()
class Sum(val left: Expr, val right: Expr) : Expr()      ... and list all the
                                                         possible subclasses.
fun eval(e: Expr): Int =
    when (e) {                        The when expression covers all possible
        is Num -> e.value             cases, so no else branch is needed.
        is Sum -> eval(e.right) + eval(e.left)
    }
```

If you handle all subclasses of a `sealed` class in a `when` expression, you don't need to provide the default branch—the compiler can ensure you've covered all possible branches. Note that the `sealed` modifier implies that the class is abstract; you don't need an explicit `abstract` modifier and can declare abstract members. The behavior of sealed classes is illustrated in figure 4.2.

Figure 4.2   All direct subclasses of a sealed class must be known at compile time.

When you use `when` with `sealed` classes and add a new subclass, the `when` expression returning a value fails to compile, which points you to the code that must be changed—for example, when you define a multiplication operator `Mul` but don't handle it in the `eval` function.

Listing 4.18   Adding a new class to a sealed hierarchy

```
sealed class Expr
class Num(val value: Int) : Expr()
class Sum(val left: Expr, val right: Expr) : Expr()
class Mul(val left: Expr, val right: Expr): Expr()

fun eval(e: Expr): Int =
    when (e) {
        is Num -> e.value
        is Sum -> eval(e.right) + eval(e.left)
        // ERROR: 'when' expression must be exhaustive,
        // add necessary 'is Mul' branch or 'else' branch instead
    }
```

Besides classes, you can also use the `sealed` modifier to define a `sealed interface`. Sealed interfaces follow the same rules: once the module that contains the sealed interface is compiled, no new implementations for it can be provided:

```
sealed interface Toggleable {
    fun toggle()
}
```
As usual, sealed interfaces define functions and properties...

```
class LightSwitch: Toggleable {
    override fun toggle() = println("Lights!")
}
```
...and classes implement them.

```
class Camera: Toggleable {
    override fun toggle() = println("Camera!")
}
```

Handling all implementations of a `sealed interface` in a `when` statement also means you do not have to specify an `else` branch.

As you'll recall, in Kotlin, you use a colon both to extend a class and to implement an interface:

```
class Num(val value: Int) : Expr()      ◁──┐  Num is a subclass.
class LightSwitch: Toggleable      ◁────── LightSwitch implements an interface.
```

What we have yet to discuss is the meaning of the parentheses after the class name in `Expr()`. We'll talk about it in the next section, which covers initializing classes in Kotlin.

4.2 Declaring a class with nontrivial constructors or properties

In object-oriented languages, classes can typically have one or more constructors. Kotlin is the same, but it makes an important, explicit distinction: it differentiates between a *primary* constructor (which is usually the main, concise way to initialize a class and is declared outside of the class body) and a *secondary* constructor (which is declared in the class body). It also allows you to put additional initialization logic in *initializer blocks*. First, we'll look at the syntax of declaring the primary constructor and initializer blocks, and then we'll explain how to declare several constructors. After that, we'll talk more about properties.

4.2.1 Initializing classes: Primary constructor and initializer blocks

In section 2.2, you saw how to declare a simple class:

```
class User(val nickname: String)
```

Typically, all declarations in a class go inside curly braces, so you may wonder why this class is different. It has no curly braces, and instead, it has only a declaration in parentheses. This block of code surrounded by parentheses is called a *primary constructor*. It serves two purposes: specifying constructor parameters and defining properties that are initialized by those parameters. Let's unpack what happens here and look at the most explicit code you can write that does the same thing:

```
class User constructor(_nickname: String) {      ◁──┐  Primary constructor
    val nickname: String                                 with one parameter

    init {                          ◁────── Initializer block
        nickname = _nickname
    }
}
```

In this example, you see two new Kotlin keywords: `constructor` and `init`. The `constructor` keyword begins the declaration of a primary or secondary constructor, and the `init` keyword introduces an *initializer block*. Such blocks contain initialization code that's executed when the class is created and are intended to be used together with primary constructors. Because the primary constructor has a constrained syntax, it can't contain the initialization code; that's why you have initializer blocks. If you want, you can declare several initializer blocks in one class.

The underscore in the constructor parameter `_nickname` serves to distinguish the name of the property from the name of the constructor parameter. An alternative possibility is to use the same name and write `this` to remove the ambiguity: `this.nickname = nickname`.

In this example, you don't need to place the initialization code in the initializer block, because it can be combined with the declaration of the `nickname` property. You can also omit the `constructor` keyword if there are no annotations or visibility modifiers on the primary constructor. If you apply those changes, you get the following:

```
class User(_nickname: String) {        ◁——— Primary constructor with one parameter
    val nickname = _nickname           ◁
}                                         The property is initialized with the parameter.
```

This is another way to declare the same class. Note how you can refer to primary constructor parameters in property initializers and initializer blocks.

The two previous examples declared the property by using the `val` keyword in the body of the class. If the property is initialized with the corresponding constructor parameter, the code can be simplified by adding the `val` keyword before the parameter. This replaces the property definition in the class body:

```
class User(val nickname: String)    ◁——— val means the corresponding property is
                                          generated for the constructor parameter.
```

All these declarations of the `User` class achieve the same thing, but the last one uses the most concise syntax.

You can declare default values for constructor parameters just as you can for function parameters:

```
class User(
    val nickname: String,                      Provides a default value for
    val isSubscribed: Boolean = true    ◁——— the constructor parameter
)
```

To create an instance of a class, you call the constructor directly, without any extra keywords, like `new`. Let's demonstrate how our potential users Alice got subscribed to the mailing list by default, Bob and Carol read the terms and conditions carefully and deselected the default option, and Dave is explicitly interested in what our marketing department has to share:

```
fun main() {                               Uses the default value true for
    val alice = User("Alice")    ◁——— the isSubscribed parameter
    println(alice.isSubscribed)
    // true                                You can specify all parameters
    val bob = User("Bob", false)    ◁——— according to declaration order.
```

```
    println(bob.isSubscribed)
    // false                                                You can explicitly specify names
    val carol = User("Carol", isSubscribed = false)  ◁─┘   for some constructor arguments.
    println(carol.isSubscribed)
    // false                                                You can specify names
    val dave = User(nickname = "Dave", isSubscribed = true)  ◁─  for all constructor
    println(dave.isSubscribed)                                  arguments.
    // true
}
```

> **NOTE** If all the constructor parameters have default values, the compiler generates an additional constructor without parameters that uses all the default values. That makes it easier to use Kotlin with libraries that instantiate classes via parameterless constructors. If you have Java code that needs to call a Kotlin constructor with some default parameters, you can specify the constructor as `@JvmOverloads constructor`. This instructs the compiler to generate the appropriate overloads for use from Java, as discussed in section 3.2.2.

If the constructor of a superclass takes arguments, then the primary constructor of your class also needs to initialize them. You can do so by providing the superclass constructor parameters after the superclass reference in the base class list:

```
open class User(val nickname: String) { /* ... */ }

class SocialUser(nickname: String) : User(nickname) { /* ... */ }
```

If you don't declare any constructors for a class, a default constructor without parameters that does nothing will be generated for you:

```
open class Button      ◁──── A default constructor without arguments is generated.
```

If you inherit from the `Button` class and don't provide any constructors, you have to explicitly invoke the constructor of the superclass even if it doesn't have any parameters. That's why you need empty parentheses after the name of the superclass:

```
class RadioButton: Button()
```

Note the difference with interfaces: interfaces don't have constructors, so if you implement an interface, you never put parentheses after its name in the supertype list.

If you want to ensure that your class can't be instantiated by code outside the class itself, you have to make the constructor `private`. Here's how you make the primary constructor `private`:

```
                                                          This class has a
                                                          private constructor.
class Secret private constructor(private val agentName: String) {}   ◁──┘
```

Because the `Secret` class has only a `private` constructor, code outside the class can't instantiate it. Later, in section 4.4.2, we'll talk about companion objects, which may be a good place to call such constructors.

> ### Alternatives to private constructors
> In Java, you can use a `private` constructor that prohibits class instantiation to express a more general idea: the class is a container of static utility members or is a singleton. Kotlin has built-in language features for these purposes. You use top-level functions (which you saw in section 3.2.3) as static utilities. To express singletons, you use object declarations, as you'll see in section 4.4.1.

In most real use cases, the constructor of a class is straightforward: it contains no parameters or assigns the parameters to the corresponding properties. That's why Kotlin has concise syntax for primary constructors: it works great in the majority of cases. But life isn't always that easy, so Kotlin allows you to define as many constructors as your class needs. Let's see how this works.

4.2.2   *Secondary constructors: Initializing the superclass in different ways*

Generally speaking, classes with multiple constructors are much less common in Kotlin code than in Java. Most situations where you'd need overloaded constructors are covered by Kotlin's support for default parameter values and named argument syntax.

> **TIP**   Don't declare multiple secondary constructors to overload and provide default values for arguments. Instead, specify default values directly.

But there are still situations when multiple constructors are required. The most common one comes up when you need to extend a framework class that provides multiple constructors that initialize the class in different ways. Take, for example, a `Downloader` class that's declared in Java and has two constructors—one taking a `String` and the other a `URI` as its parameter:

```
import java.net.URI;

public class Downloader {
    public Downloader(String url) {
        // some code
    }

    public Downloader(URI uri) {
        // some code
    }
}
```

In Kotlin, the same declaration would look as follows:

```
open class Downloader {
    constructor(url: String?) {          ⟵———— Secondary constructors
        // some code
    }

    constructor(uri: URI?) {
        // some code
    }
}
```

This class doesn't declare a primary constructor (as you can tell by the lack of paren-theses after the class name in the class header), but it declares two secondary con-structors. A secondary constructor is introduced using the `constructor` keyword. You can declare as many secondary constructors as you need.

If you want to extend this class, you can declare the same constructors:

```
class MyDownloader : Downloader {
    constructor(url: String?) : super(url) {     ⟵⎤
        // ...                                        ⎮ Calling superclass
    }                                                 ⎮ constructors
    constructor(uri: URI?) : super(uri) {        ⟵⎦
        // ...
    }
}
```

Here, you define two constructors, each calling the corresponding constructor of the superclass using the `super()` keyword. This is illustrated in figure 4.3; an arrow shows which constructor is delegated to.

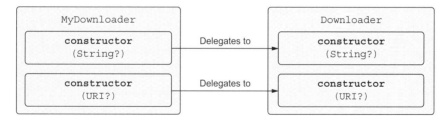

Figure 4.3   Using different superclass constructors

Just as in Java, you also have an option to call another constructor of your own class from a constructor, using the `this()` keyword. Here's how this works:

```
class MyDownloader : Downloader {
    constructor(url: String?) : this(URI(url))     ⟵⎤ Delegates to another
    constructor(uri: URI?) : super(uri)                ⎦ constructor of the class
}
```

You change the MyDownloader class so that one of the constructors delegates to the other constructor of the same class (using this), creating a URI object from the url string, as shown in figure 4.4. The second constructor continues to call super().

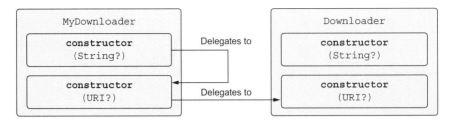

Figure 4.4 Delegating to a constructor of the same class

If the class has no primary constructor, then each secondary constructor must initialize the base class or delegate to another constructor that does so. Thinking in terms of the previous figures, each secondary constructor must have an outgoing arrow starting a path that ends at any constructor of the base class.

The main use case for when you need to use secondary constructors is Java interoperability. But there's another possible case: when you have multiple ways to create instances of your class with different parameter lists. We'll discuss an example in section 4.4.2.

We've discussed how to define nontrivial constructors. Now, let's turn our attention to nontrivial properties.

4.2.3   *Implementing properties declared in interfaces*

In Kotlin, an interface can contain abstract property declarations. Here's an example of an interface definition with such a declaration:

```
interface User {
    val nickname: String
}
```

This means classes implementing the User interface need to provide a way to obtain the value of nickname. The interface doesn't specify whether the value should be stored in a backing field or obtained through a getter. Therefore, the interface itself doesn't contain any state. Classes implementing the interface may store the value if they need to or simply compute it when accessed, as you have seen in section 2.2.2.

Let's look at a few possible implementations for the interface: PrivateUser, who fills in only their nickname; SubscribingUser, who apparently was forced to provide an email address to register; and SocialUser, who rashly shared their account ID from a social network. All of these classes implement the abstract property in the interface in different ways.

Listing 4.19   Implementing an interface property

```
class PrivateUser(override val nickname: String) : User
                                                              Primary constructor
class SubscribingUser(val email: String) : User {             property
    override val nickname: String
        get() = email.substringBefore('@')         ⊲──── Custom getter
}

class SocialUser(val accountId: Int) : User {
    override val nickname = getNameFromSocialNetwork(accountId)   ⊲──
}                                                                        Property
                                                                         initializer
fun getNameFromSocialNetwork(accountId: Int) =
    "kodee$accountId"

fun main() {
    println(PrivateUser("kodee").nickname)
    // kodee
    println(SubscribingUser("test@kotlinlang.org").nickname)
    // test
    println(SocialUser(123).nickname)
    // kodee123
}
```

For `PrivateUser`, you use the concise syntax to declare a property directly in the primary constructor. This property implements the abstract property from `User`, so you mark it as `override`.

For `SubscribingUser`, the `nickname` property is implemented through a custom getter. This property doesn't have a backing field to store its value; it only has a getter that calculates a nickname from the email on every invocation.

For `SocialUser`, you assign the value to the `nickname` property in its initializer. You use a `getNameFromSocialNetwork` function that's supposed to return the name of a social user, given their account ID. In real life, this function would be costly: it needs to establish a connection with the social network provider to get the desired data. That's why you decide to invoke it once during the initialization phase.

Pay attention to the different implementations of `nickname` in `SubscribingUser` and `SocialUser`. Although they look similar, the property of `SubscribingUser` has a custom getter that calculates `substringBefore` on every access, whereas the property in `Social-User` has a backing field that stores the data computed during the class initialization.

In addition to abstract property declarations, an interface can contain properties with getters and setters, as long as they don't reference a backing field. (A backing field would require storing state in an interface, which isn't allowed.) Let's look at an example:

```
interface EmailUser {
    val email: String
    val nickname: String                             The property doesn't have a
        get() = email.substringBefore('@')   ⊲──     backing field: the result value
}                                                    is computed on each access.
```

This interface contains the abstract property `email` as well as the `nickname` property with a custom getter. The first property must be overridden in subclasses, whereas the second one can be inherited (or overridden, as needed).

> **When to prefer properties to functions**
>
> In section 2.2.2, we briefly touched upon when to declare a function without parameters or a read-only property with a custom getter. We established that *characteristics* of a class should generally be declared as properties and *behavior* should be declared as methods. There are a few additional stylistic conventions in Kotlin for using read-only properties instead of functions. If the code in question has any of the following qualities, prefer a property over a function:
>
> - Doesn't throw exceptions
> - Is cheap to calculate (or cached on the first run)
> - Returns the same result across multiple invocations if the object state hasn't changed
>
> Otherwise, consider using a function instead.

Unlike properties implemented in interfaces, properties implemented in classes have full access to backing fields. Let's see how you can refer to them from accessors.

4.2.4 *Accessing a backing field from a getter or setter*

You've seen a few examples of two kinds of properties: properties that store values and properties with custom accessors that calculate values on every access. Now, let's see how you can combine the two and implement a property that stores a value and provides additional logic that's executed when the value is accessed or modified. To support that, you need to be able to access the property's backing field from its accessors.

Let's say you're building a contact management system that keeps track of `User` objects, their `name`, as well as their `address`. Then, you want to log any change of data stored in a property, like `address`. To do so, you declare a mutable property and execute the additional code on each setter access.

Listing 4.20 Accessing the backing field in a setter

```
class User(val name: String) {
    var address: String = "unspecified"
        set(value: String) {
            println(
                """
                Address was changed for $name:
                "$field" -> "$value".            ⟵——— Reads the backing field value
                """.trimIndent()
            )
            field = value      ⟵——┐  Updates the backing field value
        }                          │  with the provided string
}
```

```
fun main() {
    val user = User("Alice")
    user.address = "Christoph-Rapparini-Bogen 23"
    // Address was changed for Alice:
    // "unspecified" -> "Christoph-Rapparini-Bogen 23".
}
```

You change a property value as usual by saying `user.address = "new value"`, which invokes its setter under the hood. In this example, the setter is redefined, so the additional logging code is executed (for simplicity, in this case you print it out).

In the body of the setter, you use the special identifier `field` to access the value of the backing field. In a getter, you can only read the value, and in a setter, you can both read and modify it.

Note that if your getter or setter for a mutable property is trivial, you can choose to define only the accessor where you need custom behavior without redefining the other one. For example, the getter in listing 4.20 is trivial and only returns the field value, so you don't need to redefine it.

You may wonder what the difference is between making a property that has a backing field and one that doesn't. The way you access the property doesn't depend on whether it has a backing field; the compiler will generate the backing field for the property if you either reference it explicitly or use the default accessor implementation. If you provide custom accessor implementations that don't use `field` (for the getter if the property is a `val` and for both accessors if it's a mutable property), the compiler understands that the property doesn't need to store any information itself, so no backing field will be generated. The following listing illustrates this with a property, `ageIn2050`, that is purely defined in terms of the `birthYear` of a `Person`.

> **Listing 4.21 A property that doesn't store information itself**

```
class Person(var birthYear: Int) {
    var ageIn2050
        get() = 2050 - birthYear        ◁——— No field reference in getter …
        set(value) {
            birthYear = 2050 - value     ◁——┐  … or setter means no
        }                                     │  backing field is generated.
}
```

Sometimes, you don't need to change the default implementation of an accessor, but you still need to change its visibility. Let's see how you can do this.

4.2.5 Changing accessor visibility

By default, the accessor's visibility is the same as the property's. However, you can change this if you need to, by putting a visibility modifier before the `get` or `set` keyword. To see how you can use it, let's look at an example—a small class called `Length-Counter` that keeps track of the total length of words added to it.

Listing 4.22   Declaring a property with a private setter

```
class LengthCounter {
    var counter: Int = 0
        private set                          You can't change this
                                             property outside of the class.
    fun addWord(word: String) {
        counter += word.length
    }
}
```

The `counter` property, which holds the total length, is `public` because it's part of the API the class provides to its clients. But you need to make sure it's only modified in the class, because otherwise external code could change it and store an incorrect value. Therefore, you let the compiler generate a getter with the default visibility and change the visibility of the setter to `private`.

Here's how you can use this class:

```
fun main() {
    val lengthCounter = LengthCounter()
    lengthCounter.addWord("Hi!")
    println(lengthCounter.counter)
    // 3
}
```

You create an instance of `LengthCounter`, and then you add a word `"Hi!"` of length `3`. Now, the `counter` property stores `3`. As anticipated, attempting to write to the property from outside the class results in a compile-time error:

```
fun main() {
    // ...
    lengthCounter.counter = 0
    // Error: Cannot assign to 'counter': the setter is private in
    ⇒ 'LengthCounter'
}
```

More about properties

Later in the book, we'll continue our discussion of properties. Here are some references:

- The `lateinit` modifier on a non-null property specifies that this property is initialized later, after the constructor is called, which is a common case in some frameworks. This feature will be covered in section 7.9.
- Lazy initialized properties, as part of the more general *delegated properties* feature, will be covered in section 9.5.
- For compatibility with Java frameworks, you can use annotations that emulate Java features in Kotlin. For instance, the `@JvmField` annotation on a property exposes a `public` field without accessors. You'll learn more about annotations in chapter 12.
- The `const` modifier makes working with annotations more convenient and lets you use a property of a primitive type or `String` as an annotation argument. Section 12.1.1 provides details.

That concludes our discussion of writing nontrivial constructors and properties in Kotlin. Next, you'll see how to make classes whose main purpose is to make holding multiple pieces of information even friendlier: using `data` classes.

4.3 Compiler-generated methods: Data classes and class delegation

The Java platform defines several methods that need to be present in many classes and are usually implemented in a mechanical way, such as `equals` (indicating whether two objects are equal to each other), `hashCode` (providing a hash code for the object, as required by data structures like hash maps), and `toString` (returning a textual representation of the object).

Fortunately, IDEs can automate the generation of these methods, so you usually don't need to write them by hand. But in this case, your codebase still contains boilerplate code you have to maintain. The Kotlin compiler takes things a step further: it can perform the mechanical code generation behind the scenes, without cluttering your source code files with the results.

You already saw how this works for trivial class constructor and property accessors. Let's look at more examples of cases where the Kotlin compiler generates typical methods useful for simple data classes and greatly simplifies the class-delegation pattern.

4.3.1 Universal object methods

All Kotlin classes have several methods you may want to override, just like in Java: `toString`, `equals`, and `hashCode`. Let's look at what these methods are and how Kotlin can help you generate their implementations automatically. As a starting point, you'll use a simple `Customer` class that stores a customer's name and postal code.

Listing 4.23 Initial declaration of the `Customer` class

```
class Customer(val name: String, val postalCode: Int)
```

Let's see how class instances are represented as strings.

STRING REPRESENTATION: TOSTRING()

All classes in Kotlin, just as in Java, provide a way to get a string representation of the class's objects. This is primarily used for debugging and logging, although you can use this functionality in other contexts as well. By default, the string representation of an object looks like `Customer@5e9f23b4` (the class name and the memory address at which the object is stored), which, in practice, isn't very useful. To change this, you need to override the `toString` method.

Listing 4.24 Implementing `toString()` for `Customer`

```
class Customer(val name: String, val postalCode: Int) {
    override fun toString() = "Customer(name=$name, postalCode=$postalCode)"
}
```

Now, the representation of a customer looks like this:

```
fun main() {
    val customer1 = Customer("Alice", 342562)
    println(customer1)
    // Customer(name=Alice, postalCode=342562)
}
```

That's much more informative, isn't it?

OBJECT EQUALITY: EQUALS()

All computations with the `Customer` class take place outside of it. This class just stores the data; it's meant to be plain and transparent. Nevertheless, you may have some requirements for the behavior of such a class. For example, suppose you want the objects to be considered equal if they contain the same data:

```
fun main() {
    val customer1 = Customer("Alice", 342562)
    val customer2 = Customer("Alice", 342562)
    println(customer1 == customer2)
    // false
}
```

> In Kotlin, == checks whether the objects are equal, not the references. It is compiled to a call of equals.

You see that the objects aren't equal. To address this, you must override `equals` for the `Customer` class.

== for equality

In Java, you can use the `==` operator to compare primitive and reference types. If applied to primitive types, Java's `==` compares values, whereas `==` on reference types compares references. Thus, in Java, there's the well-known practice of always calling `equals`, and there's the well-known problem of forgetting to do so.

In Kotlin, the `==` operator is the default way to compare two objects: it compares their values by calling equals under the hood. Thus, if `equals` is overridden in your class, you can safely compare its instances using `==`. For reference comparison, you can use the `===` operator, which works exactly the same as `==` in Java by comparing the object references. In other words, `===` checks whether two references point to the same object in memory. The negated analogues of `==` and `===`, `!=` and `!==`, behave accordingly.

Let's look at the changed `Customer` class. In Kotlin, the `equals` function takes the nullable parameter `other` of type `Any`—the superclass of all classes in Kotlin, which you'll get to know more intimately in section 8.1.5.

Listing 4.25   Implementing `equals()` for `Customer`

```
class Customer(val name: String, val postalCode: Int) {
    override fun equals(other: Any?): Boolean {
```

> Any is the analogue of java.lang .Object: a superclass of all classes in Kotlin. The nullable type Any? means other can be null.

```
        if (other == null || other !is Customer)       ⊲─── Checks whether
            return false                                     other is a Customer
        return name == other.name &&          ⊲───
            postalCode == other.postalCode         Checks whether the corresponding
    }                                              properties are equal
    override fun toString() = "Customer(name=$name, postalCode=$postalCode)"
}
```

Just to remind you, the `is` operator checks whether a value has the specified type and smart casts `other` to the `Customer` type (it is the analogue of `instanceof` in Java). Like the `!in` operator, which is a negation for the `in` check (we discussed both in section 2.4.4), the `!is` operator denotes the negation of the `is` check. Such operators make your code easier to read. In chapter 7, we'll discuss nullable types in detail and why the condition `other == null || other !is Customer` can be simplified to `other !is Customer`.

Because in Kotlin the `override` modifier is mandatory, you're protected from accidentally writing `fun equals(other: Customer)`, which would add a new method instead of overriding `equals`. After you override `equals`, you may expect that customers with the same property values are equal. Indeed, the equality check `customer1 == customer2` in the previous example returns `true` now. But if you want to do more complicated things with customers, it doesn't work. The usual interview question is, "What's broken, and what's the problem?" You may say that the problem is that `hashCode` is missing. That is, in fact, the case, and we'll now discuss why this is important.

HASH CONTAINERS: HASHCODE()

The `hashCode` method should be always overridden together with `equals`. This section explains why.

Create a set with one element: a customer named Alice. Then, create a new `Customer` instance containing the same data, and check whether it's contained in the set. You'd expect the check to return `true` because the two instances are equal, but in fact, it returns `false`:

```
fun main() {
    val processed = hashSetOf(Customer("Alice", 342562))
    println(processed.contains(Customer("Alice", 342562)))
    // false
}
```

This is because the `Customer` class is missing the `hashCode` method. Therefore, it violates the general `hashCode` contract: if two objects are equal, they must have the same hash code. The `processed` set is a `HashSet`. Values in a `HashSet` are compared in an optimized way: at first, their hash codes are compared, and then, only if their hash codes are equal, the actual values are compared. The hash codes are different for two different instances of the `Customer` class in the previous example, so the set decides it doesn't contain the second object, even though `equals` would return `true`. Therefore, if the rule isn't followed, data structures like `HashSet` can't work correctly with such objects. To fix this, you must provide an appropriate implementation of `hashCode` to the class.

Listing 4.26 Implementing `hashCode()` for `Customer`

```
class Customer(val name: String, val postalCode: Int) {
    /* ... */
    override fun hashCode(): Int = name.hashCode() * 31 + postalCode
}
```

Now, you have a class that works as expected in all scenarios—but notice how much code you've had to write. Fortunately, the Kotlin compiler can help you by generating all of those methods automatically. Let's see how you can ask it to do that.

4.3.2 *Data classes: Autogenerated implementations of universal methods*

If you want your class to be a convenient holder for your data, you need to override these methods: `toString`, `equals`, and `hashCode`. Usually, the implementations of those methods are straightforward, and IDEs like IntelliJ IDEA can help you generate them automatically as well as verify that they're implemented correctly and consistently.

The good news is you don't have to generate all of these methods in Kotlin. If you add the modifier `data` to your class, as shown in the following listing, the necessary methods are automatically generated for you.

Listing 4.27 `Customer` as a data class

```
data class Customer(val name: String, val postalCode: Int)
```

Easy, right? Now, you have a class that overrides all the standard methods you usually need:

- `equals` for comparing instances
- `hashCode` for using instances as keys in hash-based containers, such as `HashMap`
- `toString` for generating string representations showing all the fields in declaration order

The `equals` and `hashCode` methods take into account all the properties declared in the primary constructor. The generated `equals` method checks that the values of all the properties are equal. The `hashCode` method returns a value that depends on the hash codes of all the properties. Note that properties that aren't declared in the primary constructor don't take part in the equality checks and hash code calculation. The following listing shows an example to help you believe this "magic."

Listing 4.28 The `Customer` data class has implementations for all standard methods

```
fun main() {
    val c1 = Customer("Sam", 11521)
```

```
    val c2 = Customer("Mart", 15500)
    val c3 = Customer("Sam", 11521)
    println(c1)
    // Customer(name=Sam, postalCode=11521)
    println(c1 == c2)
    // false
    println(c1 == c3)
    // true
    println(c1.hashCode())
    // 2580770
    println(c3.hashCode())
    // 2580770
}
```

This isn't a complete list of useful methods generated for `data` classes. The next section reveals one more, and section 9.4 fills in the rest.

DATA CLASSES AND IMMUTABILITY: THE COPY METHOD

Note that even though the properties of a data class aren't required to be `val`—you can use `var` as well—it's strongly recommended to only use read-only properties, making the instances of the data class *immutable*. This is required if you want to use such instances as keys in a `HashMap` or a similar container because, otherwise, the container could get into an invalid state if the object used as a key was modified after being added to the container. Immutable objects are also much easier to reason about, especially in multithreaded code: once an object has been created, it remains in its original state, and you don't need to worry about other threads modifying the object while your code is working with it.

To make it even easier to use data classes as immutable objects, the Kotlin compiler generates one more method for them: a method that allows you to *copy* the instances of your classes, changing the values of some properties. Creating a copy is usually a preferable alternative to modifying the instance in place: the copy has a separate life cycle and can't affect the places in the code that refer to the original instance. Here's what the `copy` method would look like if you implemented it manually:

```
class Customer(val name: String, val postalCode: Int) {
    /* ... */
    fun copy(name: String = this.name,
            postalCode: Int = this.postalCode) =
        Customer(name, postalCode)
}
```

And here's how the `copy` method can be used:

```
fun main() {
    val bob = Customer("Bob", 973293)
    println(bob.copy(postalCode = 382555))
    // Customer(name=Bob, postalCode=382555)
}
```

Kotlin data classes and Java records

Records were first introduced in Java 14. Conceptually, they are very similar to Kotlin's data classes, in that they hold immutable groups of values. Records also autogenerate some methods based on their values, such as `toString`, `hashCode` and `equals`. Other convenience functions, like the `copy` method, are absent in records.

Compared to Kotlin data classes, Java records also impose more structural restrictions:

- All properties are required to be `private` and `final`.
- A record can't extend a superclass.
- You can't specify additional properties in the class body.

For interoperability purposes, you can declare record classes in Kotlin by annotating a `data class` with the `@JvmRecord` annotation. In this case, the data class needs to adhere to the same structural restrictions that apply to records.

You've seen how the `data` modifier makes value-object classes more convenient to use. Now, let's talk about the other Kotlin feature that lets you avoid IDE-generated boilerplate code: class delegation.

4.3.3 *Class delegation: Using the by keyword*

A common problem in the design of large object-oriented systems is fragility caused by implementation inheritance. When you extend a class and override some of its methods, your code becomes dependent on the implementation details of the class you're extending. When the system evolves and the implementation of the base class changes or new methods are added to it, the assumptions about its behavior you've made in your class can become invalid, so your code may end up not behaving correctly.

The design of Kotlin recognizes this problem and treats classes as `final` by default, as you have seen in section 4.1.2. This ensures that only those classes designed for extensibility can be inherited from. When working on such a class, you see that it's open, and you can keep in mind that modifications need to be compatible with derived classes.

But often, you need to add behavior to another class, even if it wasn't designed to be extended. A common way to implement this is known as the *decorator* design pattern. The essence of the pattern is that a new class is created, implementing the same interface as the original class and storing the instance of the original class as a field. Methods in which the behavior of the original class doesn't need to be modified are forwarded to the original class instance.

One downside of this approach is that it requires a fairly large amount of boilerplate code (so much that several IDEs, like IntelliJ IDEA, have dedicated features to generate that code for you). For example, this is how much code you need for a decorator that implements an interface as simple as `Collection`, even when you don't modify any behavior:

```
class DelegatingCollection<T> : Collection<T> {
    private val innerList = arrayListOf<T>()

    override val size: Int get() = innerList.size
    override fun isEmpty(): Boolean = innerList.isEmpty()
    override fun contains(element: T): Boolean = innerList.contains(element)
    override fun iterator(): Iterator<T> = innerList.iterator()
    override fun containsAll(elements: Collection<T>): Boolean =
            innerList.containsAll(elements)
}
```

The good news is that Kotlin includes first-class support for delegation as a language feature. Whenever you're implementing an interface, you can say that you're *delegating* the implementation of the interface to another object, using the `by` keyword. Here's how you can use this approach to rewrite the previous example:

```
class DelegatingCollection<T>(
    innerList: Collection<T> = mutableListOf<T>()
) : Collection<T> by innerList
```

All the method implementations in the class are gone. The compiler will generate them, and the implementation is similar to that in the `DelegatingCollection` example. Because there's little interesting content in the code, there's no point in writing it manually when the compiler can do the same job for you automatically.

Now, when you need to change the behavior of some methods, you can override them, and your code will be called instead of the generated methods. You can leave out methods for which you're satisfied with the default implementation of delegating to the underlying instance.

Let's see how you can use this technique to implement a collection that counts the number of attempts to add an element to it. For example, if you're performing some kind of deduplication, you can use such a collection to measure how efficient the process is by comparing the number of attempts to add an element with the resulting size of the collection.

Listing 4.29   Using class delegation

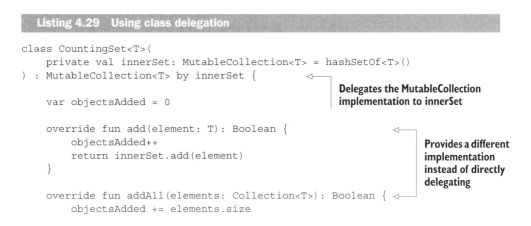

```
class CountingSet<T>(
    private val innerSet: MutableCollection<T> = hashSetOf<T>()
) : MutableCollection<T> by innerSet {          ◁─── Delegates the MutableCollection
                                                     implementation to innerSet
    var objectsAdded = 0

    override fun add(element: T): Boolean {      ◁───
        objectsAdded++                                Provides a different
        return innerSet.add(element)                  implementation
    }                                                 instead of directly
                                                      delegating
    override fun addAll(elements: Collection<T>): Boolean {  ◁──┘
        objectsAdded += elements.size
```

```
            return innerSet.addAll(elements)
    }
}

fun main() {
    val cset = CountingSet<Int>()
    cset.addAll(listOf(1, 1, 2))
    println("Added ${cset.objectsAdded} objects, ${cset.size} uniques.")
    // Added 3 objects, 2 uniques.
}
```

As you see, you override the `add` and `addAll` methods to increment the count, and you delegate the rest of the implementation of the `MutableCollection` interface to the container you're wrapping.

The important part is that you aren't introducing any dependency on how the underlying collection is implemented. For example, you don't care whether that collection implements `addAll` by calling `add` in a loop or it uses a different implementation optimized for a particular case. You have full control over what happens when the client code calls your class, and you rely only on the documented API of the underlying collection to implement your operations, so you can rely on it continuing to work.

You've now seen how the Kotlin compiler can generate useful methods for classes. Let's proceed to the final big part of Kotlin's class story: the `object` keyword and the different situations in which it comes into play.

4.4 *The object keyword: Declaring a class and creating an instance, combined*

The `object` keyword comes up in Kotlin in a number of cases, but they all share the same core idea: the keyword defines a class and creates an instance (in other words, an object) of that class at the same time. Let's look at the different situations when it's used:

- *Object declaration*—A way to define a singleton.
- *Companion objects*—Can contain factory methods and other methods related to this class but which don't require a class instance to be called. Their members can be accessed via class name.
- *Object expressions*—Used instead of Java's anonymous inner class.

It's time to discuss these Kotlin features in detail.

4.4.1 *Object declarations: Singletons made easy*

A fairly common occurrence in the design of object-oriented systems is a class for which you need only one instance. This is usually implemented using the *singleton* pattern in languages like Java: you define a class with a `private` constructor and a static field holding the only existing instance of the class.

Kotlin provides first-class language support for this using the *object declaration* feature. The object declaration combines a *class declaration* and a declaration of a *single instance* of that class.

For example, you can use an object declaration to represent the payroll of an organization. You probably don't have multiple payrolls, so—depending on the overall complexity of your application—using an object for this could be reasonable:

```
object Payroll {
    val allEmployees = mutableListOf<Person>()

    fun calculateSalary() {
        for (person in allEmployees) {
            /* ... */
        }
    }
}
```

Object declarations are introduced with the `object` keyword. An object declaration effectively defines a class and a variable of that class with the same name in a single statement.

Just like a class, an object declaration can contain declarations of properties, methods, initializer blocks, and so on. The only things that aren't allowed are constructors (either primary or secondary). Unlike instances of regular classes, object declarations are created immediately at the point of definition, not through constructor calls from other places in the code. Therefore, defining a constructor for an object declaration doesn't make sense. Likewise, any initial state you want to give to your object declaration needs to be provided as a part of that object's body.

And just like a variable, an object declaration lets you call methods and access properties, using the object name to the left of the . character:

```
Payroll.allEmployees.add(Person(/* ... */))
```

```
Payroll.calculateSalary()
```

Object declarations can also inherit from classes and interfaces. This is often useful when the framework you're using requires you to implement an interface, but your implementation doesn't contain any state. For example, let's take the `Comparator` interface. A `Comparator` implementation receives two objects and returns an integer indicating which of the objects is greater. Comparators almost never store any data, so you usually need just a single `Comparator` instance for a particular way of comparing objects. That's a perfect use case for an object declaration.

As an example, let's implement a comparator that compares file paths case insensitively.

Listing 4.30   Implementing `Comparator` with an object

```
object CaseInsensitiveFileComparator : Comparator<File> {
    override fun compare(file1: File, file2: File): Int {
        return file1.path.compareTo(file2.path,
                ignoreCase = true)
```

```
        }
    }

fun main() {
    println(
        CaseInsensitiveFileComparator.compare(
            File("/User"), File("/user")
        )
    )
    // 0
}
```

You use singleton objects in any context where an ordinary object (an instance of a class) can be used. For example, you can pass this object as an argument to a function that takes a Comparator:

```
fun main() {
    val files = listOf(File("/Z"), File("/a"))
    println(files.sortedWith(CaseInsensitiveFileComparator))
    // [/a, /Z]
}
```

Here, you're using the sortedWith function, which returns a list sorted according to the specified Comparator.

Singletons and dependency injection

Just like the singleton pattern, object declarations aren't always ideal for use in large software systems. They're great for small pieces of code that have few or no dependencies but not for large components that interact with many other parts of the system. The main reason is that you don't have any control over the instantiation of objects and can't specify parameters for the constructors.

This means you can't replace the implementations of the object itself, or other classes the object depends on, in unit tests or different configurations of the software system. If you need to do that, you should use regular Kotlin classes and dependency injection.

You can also declare objects in a class. Such objects also have only a single instance; they don't have a separate instance for each instance of the containing class. For example, it's logical to place a comparator comparing objects of a particular class inside that class.

Listing 4.31 Implementing Comparator with a nested object

```
data class Person(val name: String) {
    object NameComparator : Comparator<Person> {
        override fun compare(p1: Person, p2: Person): Int =
            p1.name.compareTo(p2.name)
    }
}
```

```
fun main() {
    val persons = listOf(Person("Bob"), Person("Alice"))
    println(persons.sortedWith(Person.NameComparator))
    // [Person(name=Alice), Person(name=Bob)]
}
```

Using Kotlin objects from Java

An object declaration in Kotlin is compiled as a class with a static field holding its single instance, which is always named INSTANCE. If you implemented the singleton pattern in Java, you'd probably do the same thing by hand. Thus, to use a Kotlin object from the Java code, you access the static INSTANCE field:

```
/* Java */
CaseInsensitiveFileComparator.INSTANCE.compare(file1, file2);
Person.NameComparator.INSTANCE.compare(person1,  person2)
```

In this example, the INSTANCE fields have type CaseInsensitiveFileComparator and NameComparator, respectively.

Now, let's look at a special case of objects nested inside a class: *companion objects*.

4.4.2 *Companion objects: A place for factory methods and static members*

Classes in Kotlin can't have static members. In fact, Kotlin doesn't have a static keyword, like Java does. Instead, Kotlin relies on package-level functions (which can replace static methods in many situations) and object declarations (which serve to replace static methods as well as static fields in other cases). In most cases, it's recommended to use top-level functions. But top-level functions can't access private members of a class, as illustrated in figure 4.5. An example of such a function that needs access to private members is a *factory method*. Factory methods are responsible for the creation of an object, and as such, they often need access to its private members.

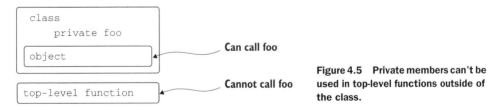

Figure 4.5 Private members can't be used in top-level functions outside of the class.

To write a function that can be called without having a class instance but which has access to the internals of a class, you can write it as a member of an object declaration inside that class. Exactly one of the object declarations defined in a class can be marked with a special keyword: companion. If you do that, you gain the ability to access the methods and properties of that object directly through the name of the containing class, without specifying the name of the object explicitly. The resulting syntax looks exactly like static method invocation in Java. Here's a basic example showing the syntax:

```
class MyClass {
    companion object {
        fun callMe() {
            println("Companion object called")
        }
    }
}

fun main() {
    MyClass.callMe()
    // Companion object called
}
```

It's important to keep in mind that a companion object belongs to its respective class. You can't access the companion object's members on an instance of the class. This also sets them apart from static members in Java:

```
fun main() {
    val myObject = MyClass()
    myObject.callMe()
    // Error: Unresolved reference: callMe
}
```

Remember when we promised you a good place to call a `private` constructor in section 4.2.1? That's the companion object. The companion object has access to all `private` members of the class, including the `private` constructor. That makes it an ideal candidate to implement the factory pattern.

Let's look at an example of declaring two constructors and then change it to use factory methods declared in the companion object. We'll build on listing 4.19 with `SocialUser` and `SubscribingUser`. Previously, these entities were different classes implementing the common interface `User`. Now, you decide to manage with only one class but to provide different means of creating it.

> **Listing 4.32   Defining a class with multiple secondary constructors**

```
class User {
    val nickname: String

    constructor(email: String) {            ◁─┐
        nickname = email.substringBefore('@')  │
    }                                          │  Secondary constructors
                                               │
    constructor(socialAccountId: Int) {     ◁─┘
        nickname = getSocialNetworkName(socialAccountId)
    }
}
```

An alternative approach to express the same logic, which can be beneficial for many reasons, is to use factory methods to create instances of the class. The `User` instance is created through factory methods, not multiple constructors.

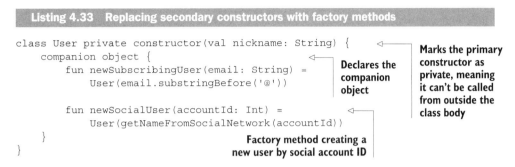

Listing 4.33 Replacing secondary constructors with factory methods

```
class User private constructor(val nickname: String) {
    companion object {
        fun newSubscribingUser(email: String) =
            User(email.substringBefore('@'))

        fun newSocialUser(accountId: Int) =
            User(getNameFromSocialNetwork(accountId))
    }
}
```

Marks the primary constructor as private, meaning it can't be called from outside the class body

Declares the companion object

Factory method creating a new user by social account ID

You can invoke the methods of `companion object` via the class name:

```
fun main() {
    val subscribingUser = User.newSubscribingUser("bob@gmail.com")
    val socialUser = User.newSocialUser(4)
    println(subscribingUser.nickname)
    // bob
}
```

Factory methods are very useful. They can be named according to their purpose, as shown in the example. In addition, a factory method can return subclasses of the class where the method is declared, as in the example in which `SubscribingUser` and `SocialUser` are classes. You can also avoid creating new objects when it's not necessary. For example, you can ensure every email corresponds to a unique `User` instance and returns an existing instance instead of a new one when the factory method is called with an email that's already in the cache. But if you need to extend such classes, using several constructors may be a better solution because companion object members can't be overridden in subclasses.

4.4.3 Companion objects as regular objects

A *companion object* is a regular object declared in a class. Just like other object declarations, it can be named, implement an interface, or have extension functions or properties. In this section, we'll look at an example.

Suppose you're working on a web service for a company's payroll, and you need to serialize and deserialize objects as JSON. You can place the serialization logic in a companion object.

Listing 4.34 Declaring a named companion object

```
class Person(val name: String) {
    companion object Loader {
```

Declares a companion object named Loader

```
        fun fromJSON(jsonText: String): Person = /* ... */
    }
}
```
**You can use both ways
to call fromJSON.**
```
fun main() {
    val person = Person.Loader.fromJSON("""{"name": "Dmitry"}""")    ◁
    println(person.name)
    // Dmitry
    val person2 = Person.fromJSON("""{"name": "Brent"}""")           ◁
    println(person2.name)
    // Brent
}
```

In most cases, you refer to the companion object via the name of its containing class, so you don't need to worry about its name. But you can specify a name for it if needed, as in listing 4.34: companion object Loader.

Your class can only have one companion object, and regardless of whether you give it a name, you'll always be able to access its members via the class name. If you omit the name of the companion object, the default name assigned to it is Companion. You'll see some examples using this name later in the section titled "Companion-object extensions."

You can find a number of such singleton companion objects in the Kotlin standard library as well. For example, the companion object Default for Kotlin's Random class provides access to the default random number generator:

**Both invocations use
Kotlin's default random
number generator.**

```
val chance = Random.nextInt(from = 0, until = 100)
val coin = Random.Default.nextBoolean()
```

IMPLEMENTING INTERFACES IN COMPANION OBJECTS

Just like any other object declaration, a companion object can implement interfaces. As you'll see in a moment, you can use the name of the containing class directly as an instance of an object implementing the interface.

Suppose you have many kinds of objects in your system, including Person. You want to provide a common way to create objects of all types. Let's say you have an interface JSONFactory for objects that can be deserialized from JSON, and all objects in your system should be created through this factory. You can provide an implementation of that interface for your Person class via the companion object. (The following example uses generics you'll get to know in chapter 11, but hopefully, it is still clear.)

Listing 4.35 Implementing an interface in a companion object

```
interface JSONFactory<T> {
    fun fromJSON(jsonText: String): T
}

class Person(val name: String) {
```

```
    companion object : JSONFactory<Person> {
        override fun fromJSON(jsonText: String): Person = /* ... */
    }                                                                    ◁─┐
}                                      Companion object implementing an interface │
```

Then, if you have a function that uses an abstract factory to load entities, you can pass the `Person` object to it:

```
fun <T> loadFromJSON(factory: JSONFactory<T>): T {
    /* ... */
}
loadFromJSON(Person)      ◁─┘ instance to the function
```
Passes the companion-object instance to the function

Note that the name of the `Person` class is used as an instance of `JSONFactory`.

> ## Kotlin companion objects and static members
>
> The companion object for a class is compiled similarly to a regular object: a static field in a class refers to its instance. If the companion object isn't named, it can be accessed through the `Companion` reference from the Java code:
>
> ```
> /* Java */
> Person.Companion.fromJSON("...");
> ```
>
> If a companion object has a name, you use this name instead of `Companion`.
>
> But you may need to work with Java code that requires a member of your class to be static. You can achieve this with the `@JvmStatic` annotation on the corresponding member. If you want to declare a `static` field, use the `@JvmField` annotation on a top-level property or a property declared in an `object`. These features exist specifically for interoperability purposes and are not, strictly speaking, part of the core language. We'll cover annotations in detail in chapter 12. Note that Kotlin can access static methods and fields declared in Java classes, using the same syntax as Java.

COMPANION-OBJECT EXTENSIONS

As you saw in section 3.3, extension functions allow you to define methods that can be called on *instances of a class* defined elsewhere in the codebase. But what if you need to define functions that can be called on *the class itself*, using the same syntax as companion-object methods? If the class has a companion object, you can do so by defining extension functions on it. More specifically, if class `C` has a companion object and you define an extension function `func` on `C.Companion`, you can call it as `C.func()`.

For example, imagine you want to have a cleaner separation of concerns for your `Person` class. The class itself will be part of the core business logic module, but you don't want to couple that module to any specific data format. Because of that, the deserialization function needs to be defined in the module responsible for client–server communication. To keep the same nice syntax for invoking the deserialization function, you can use an extension function on the companion object, as shown in the following listing. Note how you use the default name (`Companion`) to refer to the companion object that was declared without an explicit name.

> **Listing 4.36   Defining an extension function for a companion object**

```
// business logic module
class Person(val firstName: String, val lastName: String) {
    companion object {                    ◁───┐
    }                                          │ Declares an empty companion object
}

// client/server communication module                Declares an
fun Person.Companion.fromJSON(json: String): Person {  ◁──┘ extension function
    /* ... */
}

val p = Person.fromJSON(json)
```

You call `fromJSON` as if it was defined as a method of the companion object, but it's actually defined outside of it as an extension function. As always, this extension function looks like a member, but it's not (and just like other extension functions, extending a companion object does not give you access to its private members). But note that you must declare a companion object in your class, even an empty one, to be able to define extensions to it.

You've seen how useful companion objects can be. Now, let's move to the next feature in Kotlin that's expressed with the same `object` keyword: object expressions.

4.4.4   *Object expressions: Anonymous inner classes rephrased*

The `object` keyword can be used not only for declaring named singleton-like objects but also for declaring *anonymous objects*. Anonymous objects replace Java's use of anonymous inner classes.

For example, let's see how you could provide a typical *event listener* in Kotlin. Let's say you are working with a `Button` class that takes an instance of the `MouseListener` interface to specify the behavior when the user interacts with the button:

```
interface MouseListener {
    fun onEnter()
    fun onClick()
}

class Button(private val listener: MouseListener) { /* ... */ }
```

You can use an object expression to create an ad hoc implementation of the `Mouse-Listener` interface and then pass it to the `Button` constructor.

Listing 4.37 Implementing an event listener with an anonymous object

```
fun main() {
    Button(object : MouseListener {
        override fun onEnter() { /* ... */ }
        override fun onClick() { /* ... */ }
    })
}
```

Declares an anonymous object
implementing MouseListener

Overrides MouseListener
methods

The syntax is the same as with object declarations, except that you omit the name of the object. However, unlike object declarations, anonymous objects aren't singletons. Every time an object expression is executed, a new instance of the object is created.

The object expression declares a class and creates an instance of that class, but it doesn't assign a name to the class or the instance. Typically, neither is necessary because you'll use the object as a parameter in a function call. If you do need to assign a name to the object, you can store it in a variable:

```
val listener = object : MouseListener {
    override fun onEnter() { /* ... */ }
    override fun onClick() { /* ... */ }
}
```

Anonymous objects in Kotlin are quite flexible: they can implement one interface, multiple interfaces, or no interfaces at all.

Code in an object expression can access the variables in the function where it was created—just like in Java's anonymous classes. But unlike in Java, this isn't restricted to `final` variables. In Kotlin, you can also modify the values of variables from within an object expression. For example, let's see how you can use the listener to count the number of clicks in a window.

Listing 4.38 Accessing local variables from an anonymous object

```
fun main() {
    var clickCount = 0
    Button(object : MouseListener {
        override fun onEnter() { /* ... */ }
        override fun onClick() {
            clickCount++
        }
    })
}
```

Declares a local variable

Updates the value of the variable

NOTE   Object expressions are mostly useful when you need to override multiple methods in your anonymous object. If you only need to implement a single-method interface (such as `Runnable`), you can rely on Kotlin's support for SAM conversion (converting a function literal to an implementation of an interface with a single abstract method) and write your implementation as a function literal (lambda). We'll discuss lambdas and SAM conversion in much greater detail in section 5.2.

4.5 *Extra type safety without overhead: Inline classes*

With data classes, you've already seen how code generated by the compiler can help you keep your code readable and clutter free. Let's look at another example that shows off the power of the Kotlin compiler: *inline classes.*

Assume, for a moment, you're building a simple system to keep track of your expenses:

```
fun addExpense(expense: Int) {
    // save the expense as USD cent
}
```

During your next trip to Japan, you want to add the invoice for a tasty Nikuman (a steamed bun), which costs you ¥200:

```
addExpense(200) // Japanese Yen
```

The problem becomes apparent quite quickly: because the signature of your function accepts a plain `Int`, there is nothing preventing callers of the function from passing values that actually have different semantics. In this case, there is nothing preventing the caller from interpreting the parameter as "yen," even though the actual implementation requires the value passed to mean "USD cent."

The classical approach to preventing this is to use a class instead of a plain `Int`:

```
class UsdCent(val amount: Int)

fun addExpense(expense: UsdCent) {
    // save the expense as USD cent
}

fun main() {
    addExpense(UsdCent(147))
}
```

While this approach makes it far less likely to accidentally pass a value with the wrong semantics to the function, it comes with a few performance considerations: a new `UsdCent` object needs to be created for each `addExpense` function call, which is then unwrapped inside the function body and discarded. If this function is called a lot, a large number of short-lived objects need to be allocated and subsequently garbage collected.

This is where *inline classes* come into play. They allow you to introduce a layer of type safety without compromising performance.

To turn the `UsdCent` class into an inline class, mark it with the `value` keyword, and then annotate it with `@JvmInline`:

```
@JvmInline
value class UsdCent(val amount: Int)
```

This small change avoids the needless instantiation of objects without giving up on the type safety provided by your `UsdCent` wrapper type. At run time, instances of `UsdCent` will be represented as the wrapped property. This is also where inline classes get their name from: the data of the class is *inlined* at the usage sites.

> **NOTE**   To be entirely accurate, the Kotlin compiler represents the inline class as its underlying type *wherever possible*. There are cases in which it is necessary to keep the wrapper type—most notably, when the inline class is used as a type parameter. You can find a discussion of these special cases in the Kotlin documentation (https://kotlinlang.org/docs/inline-classes.html). We'll take a closer look at the idea of wrapping and unwrapping for types in chapter 7.

To qualify as "inline," your class must have exactly one property, which needs to be initialized in the primary constructor. Inline classes also don't participate in class hierarchies: they don't extend other classes and can't be extended themselves. However, they can still implement interfaces, define methods, or provide computed properties (which you learned about in section 2.2.2):

```
interface PrettyPrintable {
    fun prettyPrint()
}

@JvmInline
value class UsdCent(val amount: Int): PrettyPrintable {
    val salesTax get() = amount * 0.06
    override fun prettyPrint() = println("${amount}¢")
}

fun main() {
    val expense = UsdCent(1_99)
    println(expense.salesTax)
    // 11.94
    expense.prettyPrint()
    // 199¢
}
```

You'll mostly find yourself reaching for inline classes to make the semantics of basic values explicit, such as indicating units of measurement used for plain number types or differentiating the meaning of different strings. They prevent function callers from accidentally passing compatible values with differing semantics. We'll see another prime example of inline classes in section 8.1.2.

   We've finished our discussion of classes, interfaces, and objects. In the next chapter, we'll move on to one of the most interesting areas of Kotlin: lambdas and functional programming.

Inline classes and Project Valhalla

Currently, inline classes are a feature of the Kotlin compiler. It knows how to emit code that doesn't incur the performance penalty of allocating objects in most cases. But that won't have to be the case forever. Project Valhalla (https://openjdk.org/projects/valhalla/) is a set of JDK enhancement proposals (JEPs) that aim to bring support for inline classes (now referred to as *primitive classes* and previously known as *value classes*) into the JVM itself. This means the runtime environment would natively understand the concept of inline classes.

Thus, Valhalla is also the reason inline classes in Kotlin are currently annotated with `@JvmInline`: this makes it explicit that inline classes currently get special treatment from the Kotlin compiler. When a Valhalla-based implementation is available in the future, you'll be able to declare your inline classes in Kotlin without the annotation and make use of the built-in JVM support by default.

Summary

- Interfaces in Kotlin are similar to Java's but can contain default implementations and properties.
- All declarations are `final` and `public`, by default.
- To make a declaration non-`final`, mark it as `open`.
- `internal` declarations are visible in the same module.
- Nested classes aren't inner by default. Use the keyword `inner` to store a reference to the outer class.
- All direct subclasses of `sealed` classes and all implementations of `sealed` interfaces need to be known at compile time.
- Initializer blocks and secondary constructors provide flexibility for initializing class instances.
- You use the `field` identifier to reference a property backing field from the accessor body.
- Data classes provide compiler-generated `equals`, `hashCode`, `toString`, `copy`, and other methods.
- Class delegation helps avoid many similar delegating methods in your code.
- Object declaration is Kotlin's way to define a singleton class.
- Companion objects (along with package-level functions and properties) replace Java's static method and field definitions.
- Companion objects, like other objects, can implement interfaces as well as have extension functions and properties.
- Object expressions are Kotlin's replacement for Java's anonymous inner classes, with added power, such as the ability to implement multiple interfaces and modify the variables defined in the scope where the object is created.
- Inline classes allow you to introduce a layer of type safety to your program while avoiding potential performance hits caused by allocating many short-lived objects.

Programming
with lambdas

Lambda expressions, or simply *lambdas*, are essentially small chunks of code that can be passed to other functions. With lambdas, you can easily extract common code structures into library functions, allowing you to reuse more code and be more expressive while you're at it. The Kotlin standard library makes heavy use of them. In this chapter, you'll learn what a lambda is, see examples of some typical use cases for lambda functions, see what they look like in Kotlin, and learn their relationship to *member references.*

You'll also see how lambdas are fully interoperable with Java APIs and libraries—even those that weren't originally designed with lambdas in mind—and how you can use functional interfaces in Kotlin to make code dealing with function types even more expressive. Finally, we'll look at *lambdas with receivers*—a special kind of lambdas where the body is executed in a different context than the surrounding code.

5.1 Lambda expressions and member references

The introduction of lambdas to Java 8 was one of the longest-awaited changes in the evolution of the language. Why was it such a big deal? In this section, you'll find out why lambdas are so useful and what their syntax looks like in Kotlin.

5.1.1 Introduction to lambdas: Blocks of code as values

Passing and storing pieces of behavior in your code is a frequent task. For example, you often need to express ideas like, "When an event happens, run this handler" or "Apply this operation to all elements in a data structure." In older versions of Java, you could accomplish this through anonymous inner classes. While anonymous inner classes get the job done, they require verbose syntax.

There is another approach to solve this problem: the ability to *treat functions as values.* Instead of declaring a class and passing an instance of that class to a function, you can pass a function directly. With lambda expressions, the code is even more concise. You don't need to declare a function; instead, you can, effectively, pass a block of code directly as a function parameter. This approach of treating functions as values and combining functions to express behavior is also one of the main pillars of *functional programming.*

A quick refresher on functional programming

In section 1.2.3, we briefly covered Kotlin's nature as a multiparadigm language and the benefits that functional programming can bring to your projects: succinctness, a focus on immutability, and an even stronger power of abstraction. To refresh your memory, here are some of the hallmarks of functional programming again:

- *First-class functions*—Functions (pieces of behavior) are treated as values. You can store them in variables, pass them as parameters, or return them from other functions. Lambdas, as you will explore in this chapter, are one of Kotlin's language features that enables comfortably treating functions as first-class citizens.
- *Immutability*—You design your objects in a way that guarantees their internal state can't change after their creation: they cannot mutate.
- *No side effects*—You structure your functions to return the same result given the same inputs without modifying the state of other objects or the outside world. Such functions are called *pure.*

Let's look at an example to illustrate where the approach of using lambda expressions really shines. Imagine you need to define the behavior for clicking a button. To do so, a `Button` object may require you to pass an instance of the corresponding `OnClick-Listener` interface for handling the click. This interface specifies one method, onClick. In Kotlin, you could implement it by using an `object` declaration, as introduced in section 4.4.1.

Listing 5.1   Implementing a listener with an `object` declaration

```
button.setOnClickListener(object: OnClickListener {
    override fun onClick(v: View) {
        println("I was clicked!")
    }
})
```

The verbosity required to declare an object like this becomes irritating when repeated many times. A notation to express just the *behavior*—what should be done on clicking—helps you eliminate redundant code: you can rewrite the preceding snippet using a lambda.

Listing 5.2   Implementing a listener with a lambda

```
button.setOnClickListener {
    println("I was clicked!")
}
```

This Kotlin code does the same thing as using an anonymous object, but it is more concise and readable. We'll discuss the details of this example (and why it can be used to implement an interface like `OnClickListener`) later in this section.

You saw how a lambda can be used as an alternative to an anonymous object with only one method. Let's now continue and briefly explore another classical use of lambda expressions: working with collections.

5.1.2   *Lambdas and collections*

One of the main tenets of good programming style is to avoid duplication in your code. Most of the tasks we perform with collections follow a few common patterns. Lambdas enable Kotlin to provide a good, convenient standard library that provides powerful functionality to work with collections.

Let's look at an example. You'll use the `Person` class, which contains information about a person's name and age:

```
data class Person(val name: String, val age: Int)
```

Suppose you have a list of people, and you need to find the oldest of them. If you had no experience with lambdas, you might rush to implement the search manually. You'd introduce two intermediate variables—one to hold the maximum age and another to store the first found person of this age—and then iterate over the list, updating these variables.

Listing 5.3   Searching through a collection manually via a `for` loop

```
fun findTheOldest(people: List<Person>) {
    var maxAge = 0                              ⟵——— Stores the maximum age
    var theOldest: Person? = null      ⟵
    for (person in people) {                      Stores a person of the maximum age
        if (person.age > maxAge) {     ⟵
            maxAge = person.age            If the next person is older than the current
            theOldest = person             oldest person, changes the maximum
        }
    }
    println(theOldest)
}

fun main() {
    val people = listOf(Person("Alice", 29), Person("Bob", 31))
    findTheOldest(people)
    // Person(name=Bob, age=31)
}
```

With enough experience, you can bang out such loops pretty quickly. But there's quite a lot of code here, and it's easy to make mistakes. For example, you might get the comparison wrong and find the minimum element instead of the maximum.

In Kotlin, there's a better way. You can use a function from the standard library, as shown next.

Listing 5.4   Searching through a collection by using the `maxByOrNull` function

```
fun main() {
    val people = listOf(Person("Alice", 29), Person("Bob", 31))
    println(people.maxByOrNull { it.age })      ⟵
    // Person(name=Bob, age=31)                     Finds the maximum by
}                                                    comparing the ages
```

The `maxByOrNull` function can be called on any collection and takes one argument: the function that specifies which values should be compared to find the maximum element. The code in curly braces { `it.age` } is a lambda implementing this *selector logic*; it receives a collection element as an argument and returns a value to compare. Because the lambda only takes one argument (the collection item) and we don't specify an explicit name for it, we refer to it using the implicit name `it`. In this example, the collection element is a `Person` object, and the value to compare is its age, stored in the `age` property.

If a lambda just delegates to a function or property, it can be replaced by a member reference.

Listing 5.5   Searching using a member reference

```
people.maxByOrNull(Person::age)
```

This code means the same thing as listing 5.4. The details of this will be covered in section 5.1.5.

Most of the what we typically do with collections can be concisely expressed with library functions taking lambdas or member references. The resulting code is much shorter and easier to understand, and it often communicates your intent (that is, what your code is trying to achieve) more clearly than its loop-based counterpart. To help you start getting used to it, let's look at the syntax for lambda expressions. Later, in chapter 6, we will take a more detailed look at what functionality is available to you for manipulating collections using lambdas.

5.1.3   Syntax for lambda expressions

As we've mentioned, a lambda encodes a small piece of behavior that you can pass around as a value. It can be declared independently and stored in a variable. But more frequently, it's declared directly when passed to a function. Figure 5.1 shows the syntax for declaring lambda expressions.

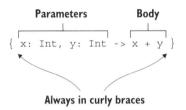

Figure 5.1   Lambda expression syntax—a lambda is always surrounded by curly braces, specifies a number of parameters, and provides a body of the lambda which contains the actual logic.

A lambda expression in Kotlin is always surrounded by curly braces. Note that there are no parentheses around the arguments. The arrow separates the argument list from the body of the lambda.

You can store a lambda expression in a variable and then treat this variable like a normal function (call it with the corresponding arguments):

```
fun main() {
    val sum = { x: Int, y: Int -> x + y }
    println(sum(1, 2))                        <----- Calls the lambda stored in a variable
    // 3
}
```

If you want, you can also call a lambda expression directly:

```
fun main() {
    { println(42) }()
    // 42
}
```

But such syntax isn't readable and doesn't make much sense (it's equivalent to executing the lambda body directly). If you need to enclose a piece of code in a block, you can use the library function `run` that executes the lambda passed to it:

```
fun main() {
    run { println(42) }          ◁────── Runs the code in the lambda
    // 42
}
```

The `run` function becomes especially useful when you need to execute a block of several statements in a place where an expression is expected. Consider a declaration of a top-level variable that performs some setup or does some additional work:

```
val myFavoriteNumber = run {
    println("I'm thinking!")
    println("I'm doing some more work...")
    42
}
```

In section 10.2, you'll learn why such invocations—unlike the creation of a lambda expression and calling it directly via {…}()—have no runtime overhead and are as efficient as built-in language constructs. Let's return to listing 5.4, which finds the oldest person in a list:

```
fun main() {
    val people = listOf(Person("Alice", 29), Person("Bob", 31))
    println(people.maxByOrNull { it.age })
    // Person(name=Bob, age=31)
}
```

If you rewrite this example without using any syntax shortcuts, you get the following:

```
people.maxByOrNull({ p: Person -> p.age })
```

It should be clear what happens here: the piece of code in curly braces is a lambda expression, and you pass it as an argument to the function. The lambda expression takes one argument of type `Person` and returns its age.

But this code is verbose. First, there's too much punctuation, which hurts readability. Second, the type can be inferred from the context and, therefore, omitted. Finally, you don't need to assign a name to the lambda argument in this case.

Let's make these improvements, starting with the braces. In Kotlin, a syntactic convention lets you move a lambda expression out of parentheses if it's the last argument in a function call. In this example, the lambda is the only argument, so it can be placed after the parentheses:

```
people.maxByOrNull() { p: Person -> p.age }
```

When the lambda is the only argument to a function, you can also remove the empty parentheses from the call:

```
people.maxByOrNull { p: Person -> p.age }
```

All three syntactic forms mean the same thing, but the last one is the easiest to read. If a lambda is the only argument, you'll definitely want to write it without the parentheses. If a function takes several arguments and only the last argument is a lambda, it's also considered good style in Kotlin to keep the lambda outside the parentheses. If you want to pass two or more lambdas, you can't move more than one out, so it's usually better to keep all of them inside the parentheses.

To see what these options look like with a more complex call, let's return to the joinToString function you used extensively in chapter 3. It's also defined in the Kotlin standard library, with the difference being the standard library version takes a function as an additional parameter. This function can be used to convert an element to a string differently than its toString function. Here's how you can use it to print only names.

Listing 5.6 Passing a lambda as a named argument

```
fun main() {
    val people = listOf(Person("Alice", 29), Person("Bob", 31))
    val names = people.joinToString(
        separator = " ",
        transform = { p: Person -> p.name }
    )
    println(names)
    // Alice Bob
}
```

And here's how you can rewrite that call with the lambda outside the parentheses.

Listing 5.7 Passing a lambda outside of parentheses

```
people.joinToString(" ") { p: Person -> p.name }
```

Listing 5.6 uses a named argument to pass the lambda, making it clear what the lambda is used for. Listing 5.7 is more concise, but it doesn't express explicitly what the lambda is used for, so it may be harder to understand for people not familiar with the function being called.

> **TIP** IntelliJ IDEA and Android Studio allow you to automatically convert between the two syntactic forms of where to place a last-argument lambda. To convert one form to the other, place your cursor on the lambda (see figure 5.2). Press Alt-Enter (or Option-Return on macOS) or click the floating yellow lightbulb icon, and then select Move Lambda Argument Out of Parentheses and Move Lambda Argument Into Parentheses.

Let's move on to simplifying the syntax and removing the parameter type.

```
10 ▶  fun main() {
11  ⁝    people.maxByOrNull({ it.age })
12    }
```

● Move lambda argument out of parentheses

- ⟿ Introduce local variable   ›
- ⟿ Convert lambda to reference   ›
- ⟿ Convert to multi-line lambda   ›
- ⟿ Convert to run   ›
- ⟿ Convert to with   ›
- ⟿ Use destructuring declaration   ›
- ⟿ Convert to anonymous function   ›
- ⟿ Disable a trailing comma by default in the formatter   ›
- ⟿ Specify explicit lambda signature   ›

Press F1 to toggle preview

```
10 ▶  fun main() {
11  ⁝    people.maxByOrNull { it.age }
12    }
```

Figure 5.2 The "Move lambda …" action allows you to move a lambda argument out of the surrounding parentheses.

Listing 5.8 Omitting the lambda parameter type

```
people.maxByOrNull { p: Person -> p.age }        ⟵──── Parameter type explicitly written
people.maxByOrNull { p -> p.age }                ⟵──┐
                                                    └─ Parameter type inferred
```

As with local variables, if the type of a lambda parameter can be inferred, you don't need to specify it explicitly. With the maxByOrNull function, the parameter type is always the same as the collection element type. The compiler knows you're calling maxByOrNull on a collection of Person objects, so it can understand that the lambda parameter will also be of type Person.

There are cases when the compiler can't infer the lambda parameter type, but we won't discuss them here. The simple rule you can follow is to always start without the types; if the compiler complains, specify them.

You can specify some of the argument types while leaving others with just names. Doing so may be convenient if the compiler can't infer one of the types or an explicit type improves readability.

The last simplification you can make in this example is to replace a parameter with the default parameter name: it. This name is generated if the context expects a lambda with only one argument and its type can be inferred. You can see all the simplification steps in figure 5.3.

Listing 5.9 Using the default parameter name it

```
people.maxByOrNull { it.age }     ⟵──── it is an autogenerated parameter name.
```

This default name is generated only if you don't specify the argument name explicitly.

> **NOTE** The `it` convention is great for shortening your code, but you shouldn't abuse it. In particular, in the case of nested lambdas, it's better to declare the parameter of each lambda explicitly; otherwise, it's difficult to understand which value the `it` refers to (and you will get a warning along the lines of "Implicit parameter `it` of enclosing lambda is shadowed"). It's also useful to declare parameters explicitly if the meaning or type of the parameter isn't clear from the context.

1 `people.maxByOrNull({ p: Person -> p.age })`

2 `people.maxByOrNull() { p: Person -> p.age }`

3 `people.maxByOrNull { p: Person -> p.age }`

4 `people.maxByOrNull { p -> p.age }`

5 `people.maxByOrNull { it.age }`

6 `people.maxByOrNull(Person::age)`

Figure 5.3 You simplified your `maxByOrNull` call to get the oldest person from the `people` collection in six steps. You (1) moved the lambda out of the parentheses, (2) removed the now empty pair of parentheses, (3) instead of specifying the parameter type for `p` explicitly, (4) you used the Kotlin compiler's type inference, and (5) used the implicit name for the only lambda parameter `it`. You also (6) learned an additional shorthand in the form of member references.

If you store a lambda in a variable, there's no context from which to infer the parameter types, so you must specify them explicitly:

```
val getAge = { p: Person -> p.age }
people.maxByOrNull(getAge)
```

So far, you've only seen examples with lambdas that consist of one expression or statement. But lambdas aren't constrained to such a small size and can contain multiple statements. In this case, the last expression is the result—no explicit `return` statement needed:

```
fun main() {
    val sum = { x: Int, y: Int ->
       println("Computing the sum of $x and $y...")
       x + y
    }
    println(sum(1, 2))
    // Computing the sum of 1 and 2...
    // 3
}
```

Next, let's talk about a concept that often goes hand in hand with lambda expressions: capturing variables from the context.

5.1.4   *Accessing variables in scope*

You know that when you declare an anonymous inner class in a function, you can refer to parameters and local variables of that function from inside the class. With lambdas, you can do exactly the same thing. If you use a lambda in a function, you can access the parameters of that function as well as the local variables declared before the lambda (see figure 5.4).

To demonstrate, let's use the `forEach` standard library function. It's one of the most basic collection-manipulation functions; all it does is call the given lambda on every element in the collection. The `forEach` function is somewhat more concise than a regular `for` loop, but it doesn't have many other advantages, so you don't need to rush to convert all your loops to lambdas. The following listing takes a list of messages and prints each with the same prefix.

Listing 5.10   Using function parameters in a lambda

```
fun printMessagesWithPrefix(messages: Collection<String>, prefix: String) {
    messages.forEach {
        println("$prefix $it")
    }
}
```

→ Accesses the prefix parameter in the lambda

→ Takes as an argument a lambda specifying what to do with each element

```
fun main() {
    val errors = listOf("403 Forbidden", "404 Not Found")
    printMessagesWithPrefix(errors, "Error:")
    // Error: 403 Forbidden
    // Error: 404 Not Found
}
```

Figure 5.4   The `forEach` lambda can access the `prefix` variable defined in the surrounding scope and any other variables defined in surrounding scopes—all the way up to the surrounding class and file scopes.

One important difference in using lambdas between Kotlin and Java is that, in Kotlin, you aren't restricted to accessing final variables: you can also modify variables from within a lambda. In the next listing, you're counting the number of client and server errors in a given collection of response status codes. You do so by incrementing the `clientErrors` and `serverErrors` variables defined in the `printProblemCounts` functions from within the `forEach` lambda.

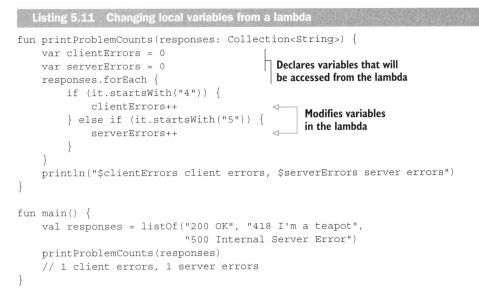

```
fun printProblemCounts(responses: Collection<String>) {
    var clientErrors = 0
    var serverErrors = 0                    Declares variables that will
    responses.forEach {                     be accessed from the lambda
        if (it.startsWith("4")) {
            clientErrors++                   Modifies variables
        } else if (it.startsWith("5")) {     in the lambda
            serverErrors++
        }
    }
    println("$clientErrors client errors, $serverErrors server errors")
}

fun main() {
    val responses = listOf("200 OK", "418 I'm a teapot",
                           "500 Internal Server Error")
    printProblemCounts(responses)
    // 1 client errors, 1 server errors
}
```

As you can see, Kotlin allows you to access (and modify) nonfinal variables in a lambda. External variables accessed from a lambda, such as `prefix`, `clientErrors`, and `serverErrors`, in these examples, are said to be *captured* by the lambda.

Note that, by default, the lifetime of a local variable is constrained by the function in which the variable is declared. But if it's captured by the lambda, the code that uses this variable can be stored and executed later. You may ask how this works. When you capture a final variable, its value is stored together with the lambda code that uses it. For nonfinal variables, the value is enclosed in a special wrapper that lets you change it, and the reference to the wrapper is stored together with the lambda.

Capturing a mutable variable: Implementation details

Java allows you to capture only final variables. When you want to capture a mutable variable, you can use one of the following tricks: either declare an array of one element in which to store the mutable value or create an instance of a wrapper class that stores the reference that can be changed. If you used this technique explicitly in Kotlin, the code would be as follows:

```
class Ref<T>(var value: T)     Class used to simulate capturing a mutable variable

fun main() {
    val counter = Ref(0)                    Formally, an immutable variable
    val inc = { counter.value++ }           is captured, but the actual value is
}                                           stored in a field and can be changed.
```

(continued)

In real code, you don't need to create such wrappers. Instead, you can mutate the variable directly:

```
fun main() {
    var counter = 0
    val inc = { counter++ }
}
```

How does it work? The first example shows how the second example works under the hood. Any time you capture a final variable (`val`), its value is copied, as in Java. When you capture a mutable variable (`var`), its value is stored as an instance of a `Ref` class. The `Ref` variable is final and can be easily captured, whereas the actual value is stored in a field and can be changed from the lambda.

An important caveat is that if a lambda is used as an event handler or is otherwise executed asynchronously, the modifications to local variables will occur only when the lambda is executed. For example, the following code isn't a correct way to count button clicks:

```
fun tryToCountButtonClicks(button: Button): Int {
    var clicks = 0
    button.onClick { clicks++ }
    return clicks
}
```

This function will always return 0. Even though the `onClick` handler will modify the value of `clicks`, you won't be able to observe the modification because the `onClick` handler will be called after the function returns. A correct implementation of the function would need to store the click count not in a local variable but in a location that remains accessible outside the function—for example, in a property of a class.

We've discussed the syntax for declaring lambdas and how variables are captured in lambdas. Now, let's talk about member references, a feature that lets you easily pass references to existing functions.

5.1.5   *Member references*

You've seen how lambdas allow you to pass a block of code as a parameter to a function, but what if the code you need to pass as a parameter is already defined as a function? Of course, you can pass a lambda that calls that function, but doing so is somewhat redundant. Can you pass the function directly?

In Kotlin, just like in Java 8, you can do so if you convert the function to a value. You use the `::` operator for that:

```
val getAge = Person::age
```

This expression is called *member reference*, and it provides a short syntax for creating a function value that calls exactly one method or accesses a property. A double colon separates the name of a class from the name of the member you need to reference (a method or property), as shown in figure 5.5.

Class   Member

Person::age

Separated by a double colon

Figure 5.5   Member reference syntax

This is a more concise expression of a lambda that does the same thing:

```
val getAge = { person: Person -> person.age }
```

Note that, regardless of whether you're referencing a function or a property, you shouldn't put parentheses after its name in a member reference. After all, you're not invoking it but working with a reference to it.

A member reference has the same type as a lambda that calls that function or property, so you can use the two interchangeably:

```
people.maxByOrNull(Person::age)
people.maxByOrNull { person: Person -> person.age }
```
These calls are equivalent.

You can have a reference to a function that's declared at the top level (and isn't a member of a class), as well:

```
fun salute() = println("Salute!")

fun main() {
    run(::salute)      ⟵——— Reference to the top-level function
    // Salute!
}
```

In this case, you omit the class name and start with `::`. The member reference `::salute` is passed as an argument to the library function `run`, which calls the corresponding function.

When a lambda delegates to a function that takes several parameters, it's especially convenient to provide a member reference—it lets you avoid repeating the parameter names and their types:

```
val action = { person: Person, message: String ->
    sendEmail(person, message)
}
val nextAction = ::sendEmail
```
This lambda delegates to a sendEmail function.
You can use a member reference instead.

You can store or postpone the action of creating an instance of a class using a *constructor reference*. The constructor reference is formed by specifying the class name after the double colons:

```
data class Person(val name: String, val age: Int)

fun main() {
    val createPerson = ::Person
```
An action of creating an instance of Person is saved as a value.

```
    val p = createPerson("Alice", 29)
    println(p)
    // Person(name=Alice, age=29)
}
```

Note that you can also reference extension functions in the same way:

```
fun Person.isAdult() = age >= 21
val predicate = Person::isAdult
```

Although `isAdult` isn't a member of the `Person` class, you can access it via reference, just as you can access it as a member on an instance: `person.isAdult()`.

5.1.6 *Bound callable references*

So far, our member references have always pointed to a member of a class. Using bound callable references, we can use the same member reference syntax to capture a reference to a method on a specific object instance. In this example, the variable `personsAgeFunction` is a regular member reference: given an object of type `Person` as a parameter, invoking it returns the age of that person. `sebsAgeFunction`, on the other hand, returns the age of a specific person when invoked (and as such also takes no arguments):

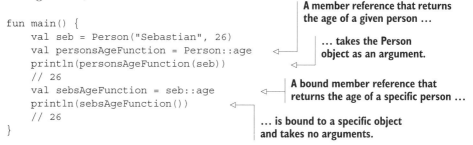

```
fun main() {
    val seb = Person("Sebastian", 26)
    val personsAgeFunction = Person::age
    println(personsAgeFunction(seb))
    // 26
    val sebsAgeFunction = seb::age
    println(sebsAgeFunction())
    // 26
}
```

A member reference that returns the age of a given person …

… takes the Person object as an argument.

A bound member reference that returns the age of a specific person …

… is bound to a specific object and takes no arguments.

As you can see, the way we defined `sebsAgeFunction` in this example—`seb::age`—is equivalent to writing the lambda `{ seb.age }` explicitly, but it's more concise (figure 5.6).

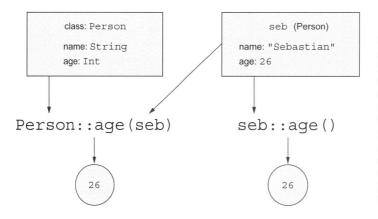

Figure 5.6 A regular member reference, like `Person::age`, takes an instance of an object as a parameter and returns the value of the member. A bound member reference like `seb::age` takes no arguments and returns the value of the member belonging to the object it is bound to.

In the following section, we'll look at many library functions that work great with lambda expressions as well as member references.

We've thoroughly discussed a frequently used application of lambda expressions: using them to simplify manipulating collections. Now, let's continue with another important topic: using lambdas with an existing Java API.

5.2   *Using Java functional interfaces: Single abstract methods*

There are already a lot of libraries in the JVM ecosystem written in Kotlin, and those libraries can directly make use of Kotlin's lambdas. However, there is a good chance you may want to use a library written in Java in your Kotlin project. The good news is that Kotlin lambdas are fully interoperable with Java APIs. In this section, you'll see exactly how this works.

At the beginning of the chapter, you saw an example of passing a lambda to a Java method:

```
button.setOnClickListener {          ◁──── Passes the lambda as an argument
    println("I was clicked!")
}
```

The `Button` class sets a new listener to a button via a `setOnClickListener` method that takes an argument of type `OnClickListener`:

```
/* Java */
public class Button {
    public void setOnClickListener(OnClickListener l) { ... }
}
```

The `OnClickListener` interface declares one method, `onClick`:

```
/* Java */
public interface OnClickListener {
    void onClick(View v);
}
```

Depending on the Java version, implementing the `OnClickListener` interface can be quite involved. Prior to Java 8, you had to create a new instance of an anonymous class to pass it as an argument to the `setOnClickListener` method:

```
/* Before Java 8 */
button.setOnClickListener(new OnClickListener() {
    @Override
    public void onClick(View v) {
        /* ... */
    }
}

/* Only since Java 8 */
button.setOnClickListener(view -> { /* ... */ });
```

In Kotlin, you simply pass a lambda:

```
button.setOnClickListener { view -> /* ... */ }
```

The lambda used to implement `OnClickListener` has one parameter of type `View`, as in the `onClick` method. The mapping is illustrated in figure 5.7.

```
public interface OnClickListener {
    void onClick(View v);                    { view -> ... }
}
```

Figure 5.7　Parameters of the lambda correspond to method parameters in the interface with a single abstract method.

This works because the `OnClickListener` interface has only one abstract method. Such interfaces are called *functional interfaces,* or *single abstract method (SAM) interfaces.* The Java API is full of functional interfaces, like `Runnable` and `Callable`, as well as methods working with them. Kotlin allows you to use lambdas when calling Java methods that take functional interfaces as parameters, ensuring your Kotlin code remains clean and idiomatic. Let's look in detail at what happens when you pass a lambda to a method that expects an argument of a functional interface type.

5.2.1　*Passing a lambda as a parameter to a Java method*

You can pass a lambda to any Java method that expects a functional interface. For example, consider this method, which has a parameter of type `Runnable`:

```
/* Java */
void postponeComputation(int delay, Runnable computation);
```

In Kotlin, you can invoke it and pass a lambda as an argument. The compiler will automatically convert it into an instance of `Runnable`:

```
postponeComputation(1000) { println(42) }
```

Note that when we say "an instance of `Runnable`," we mean "an instance of an anonymous class implementing `Runnable`." The compiler will create that for you and will use the lambda as the body of the single abstract method—the `run` method, in this case.

You can achieve the same effect by creating an anonymous object that implements `Runnable` explicitly:

```
postponeComputation(1000, object : Runnable {        Passes an object expression
    override fun run() {                             as an implementation of a
        println(42)                                  functional interface
    }
})
```

But there's a difference. When you explicitly declare an object, a new instance is created on each invocation. With a lambda, the situation is different: if the lambda doesn't access any variables from the function where it's defined, the corresponding anonymous class instance is reused between calls:

```
postponeComputation(1000) { println(42) }
```

One instance of Runnable is created for the entire program.

If the lambda captures variables from the surrounding scope, it's no longer possible to reuse the same instance for every invocation. In that case, the compiler creates a new object for every call and stores the values of the captured variables in that object. For example, in the following function, every invocation uses a new `Runnable` instance, storing the `id` value as a field:

```
fun handleComputation(id: String) {
    postponeComputation(1000) {
        println(id)
    }
}
```

Creates a new instance of Runnable on each handleComputation call

Captures the variable id in a lambda

Note that the discussion of creating an anonymous class and an instance of this class for a lambda is valid for Java methods expecting functional interfaces but does not apply to working with collections using Kotlin extension methods. If you pass a lambda to a Kotlin function that's marked `inline`, no anonymous classes are created. And most of the library functions are marked `inline`. Details of how this works are discussed in section 10.2.

As you've seen, in most cases, the conversion of a lambda to an instance of a functional interface happens automatically, without any effort on your part. But there are cases when you need to perform the conversion explicitly. Let's see how to do that.

5.2.2   SAM constructors: Explicit conversion of lambdas to functional interfaces

A *SAM constructor* is a compiler-generated function that lets you perform an explicit conversion of a lambda into an instance of an interface with a single abstract method. You can use it in contexts when the compiler doesn't apply the conversion automatically. For instance, if you have a method that returns an instance of a functional interface, you can't return a lambda directly; you need to wrap it into a SAM constructor. Here's a simple example.

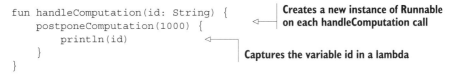
Listing 5.12   Using a SAM constructor to return a value

```
fun createAllDoneRunnable(): Runnable {
    return Runnable { println("All done!") }
}

fun main() {
    createAllDoneRunnable().run()
    // All done!
}
```

The name of the SAM constructor is the same as the name of the underlying functional interface. The SAM constructor takes a single argument—a lambda that will be used as the body of the single abstract method in the functional interface—and returns an instance of the class implementing the interface.

In addition to returning values, SAM constructors are used when you need to store a functional interface instance generated from a lambda in a variable. Suppose you want to reuse one listener for several buttons, as in the following listing (in an Android application, this code can be a part of the `Activity.onCreate` method).

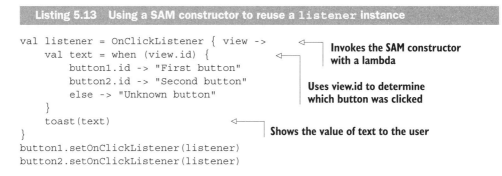

Listing 5.13 Using a SAM constructor to reuse a `listener` instance

```
val listener = OnClickListener { view ->          ◁——  Invokes the SAM constructor
    val text = when (view.id) {          ◁——         with a lambda
        button1.id -> "First button"
        button2.id -> "Second button"                Uses view.id to determine
        else -> "Unknown button"                     which button was clicked
    }
    toast(text)                  ◁——
}                                           Shows the value of text to the user
button1.setOnClickListener(listener)
button2.setOnClickListener(listener)
```

`listener` checks which button was the source of the click and behaves accordingly. You could define a listener by using an object declaration that implements `OnClick-Listener`, but SAM constructors give you a more concise option.

> **Lambdas and adding or removing listeners**
>
> Note that there's no `this` in a lambda, as there is in an anonymous object; there's no way to refer to the anonymous class instance into which the lambda is converted. From the compiler's point of view, the lambda is a block of code, not an object, and you can't refer to it as an object. The `this` reference in a lambda refers to a surrounding class.
>
> If your event listener needs to unsubscribe itself while handling an event, you can't use a lambda for that. Use an anonymous object to implement a listener, instead. In an anonymous object, the `this` keyword refers to the instance of that object, and you can pass it to the API that removes the listener.

Also, even though SAM conversion in method calls typically happens automatically, there are cases when the compiler can't choose the right overload when you pass a lambda as an argument to an overloaded method. In those cases, applying an explicit SAM constructor is a good way to resolve the compilation error.

5.3 *Defining SAM interfaces in Kotlin: fun interfaces*

In Kotlin, you can often use function types to express behavior where you would otherwise have to use a functional interface. In section 11.3.7, we'll see a way to give more expressive names to function types in Kotlin through type aliases.

However, there may be a few cases where you want to be more explicit in your code. By declaring a `fun interface` in Kotlin, you can define your own functional interfaces.

Functional interfaces in Kotlin contain exactly one abstract method but can also contain several additional non-abstract methods. This can help you express more complex constructs you couldn't fit into a function type's signature.

In the following example, you define a functional interface called `IntCondition` with an abstract method `check`. You define an additional, non-abstract method called `checkString`, which invokes check after converting its parameter to an integer. As with Java SAMs, you use the SAM constructor to instantiate the interface with a lambda that specifies the implementation of `check`.

Listing 5.14 A functional interface in Kotlin contains exactly one abstract method

```
fun interface IntCondition {                          Exactly one abstract method ...
    fun check(i: Int): Boolean        ◄─┘
    fun checkString(s: String) = check(s.toInt())       ... and additional
    fun checkChar(c: Char) = check(c.digitToInt())      non-abstract methods
}

fun main() {
    val isOdd = IntCondition { it % 2 != 0 }
    println(isOdd.check(1))
    // true
    println(isOdd.checkString("2"))
    // false
    println(isOdd.checkChar('3'))
    // true
}
```

When a function accepts a parameter whose type is defined as a `fun interface`, you may once again also just provide a lambda implementation directly or pass a reference to a lambda, both of which dynamically instantiate the interface implementation.

In the following example, you're defining a `checkCondition` function that takes an `IntCondition` as we previously defined it. You then have multiple options of calling that function—for example, by passing a lambda directly or passing a reference to a function that has the correct type (`(Int) -> Boolean`—you'll learn more about this syntax, and lambdas in general, in section 10.1).

Listing 5.15 The functional interface is dynamically instantiated

```
fun checkCondition(i: Int, condition: IntCondition): Boolean {
    return condition.check(i)
}

fun main() {
    checkCondition(1) { it % 2 != 0 }          ◄─── Either pass a lambda directly ...
    // true
    val isOdd: (Int) -> Boolean = { it % 2 != 0 }
    checkCondition(1, isOdd)   ◄─┐
    // true                       └─ ... or reference a lambda with a matching signature.
}
```

Cleaner Java call sites with functional interfaces

If you're writing code that you expect to be used from both Java and Kotlin code, using a `fun interface` can also improve the cleanliness of the Java call sites. Kotlin function types are translated as objects whose generic types are the parameters and return types. For functions that don't return anything, Kotlin uses `Unit` as its analog to Java's `void` (we will talk about the necessity and usefulness of the `Unit` type in greater depth in section 8.1.6).

That also means that when such a Kotlin function type is invoked from Java, the caller needs to explicitly return `Unit.INSTANCE`. Using a `fun interface` removes that requirement, making the call site more concise. In this example, the functions `consumeHello` and `consumeHelloFunctional` do the same thing but are defined once using a functional interface and once using Kotlin functional types:

```
fun interface StringConsumer {
    fun consume(s: String)
}

fun consumeHello(t: StringConsumer) {
    t.consume("Hello")
}

fun consumeHelloFunctional(t: (String) -> Unit) {
    t("Hello")
}
```

When used from Java, the variant of the function using a `fun interface` can be called with a simple lambda, whereas the variant using Kotlin functional types requires the lambda to explicitly return Kotlin's `Unit.INSTANCE`:

```
import kotlin.Unit;

public class MyApp {
    public static void main(String[] args) {
        /* Java */
        MainKt.consumeHello(s -> System.out.println(s.toUpperCase()));
        MainKt.consumeHelloFunctional(s -> {
            System.out.println(s.toUpperCase());      ⎫ Using Kotlin function types
            return Unit.INSTANCE;                 ◁───┤ from Java may require you to
        });                                           ⎭ explicitly return Unit.INSTANCE.
    }
}
```

As a general rule, simple functional types work well if your API can accept any function that takes a specific set of parameters and returns a specific type. When you need to express more complex contracts or operations you can't express in a functional type signature, a functional interface is a good choice.

We'll further discuss the use of function types in function declarations in section 10.1 and take a closer look at type aliases in Kotlin in section 11.3.7.

To finish our discussion of lambda syntax and usage, let's look at lambdas with receivers and how they're used to define convenient library functions that look like built-in constructs.

5.4   Lambdas with receivers: with, apply, and also

This section demonstrates the `with`, `apply`, and `also` functions from the Kotlin standard library. These functions are convenient, and you'll find many uses for them, even without understanding how they're declared. In section 13.2.1, you'll see how you can declare similar functions for your own needs. The explanations in this section, however, help you become familiar with a unique feature of Kotlin's lambdas that isn't available with Java: the ability to call methods of a different object in the body of a lambda without any additional qualifiers. Such lambdas are called *lambdas with receivers*. Let's begin by looking at the `with` function, which uses a lambda with a receiver.

5.4.1   Performing multiple operations on the same object: with

Many languages have special statements you can use to perform multiple operations on the same object without repeating its name. Kotlin also has this facility, but it's provided as a library function called `with`, not as a special language construct. To see how it can be useful, consider the following example, which you'll then refactor using `with`.

Listing 5.16   Building the alphabet

```
fun alphabet(): String {
    val result = StringBuilder()
    for (letter in 'A'..'Z') {
        result.append(letter)
    }
    result.append("\nNow I know the alphabet!")
    return result.toString()
}

fun main() {
    println(alphabet())
    // ABCDEFGHIJKLMNOPQRSTUVWXYZ
    // Now I know the alphabet!
}
```

In this example, you call several different methods on the `result` instance and repeat the `result` name in each call. This isn't too bad, but what if the expression you were using was longer or repeated more often? Here's how you can rewrite the code using `with`.

Listing 5.17   Using `with` to build the alphabet

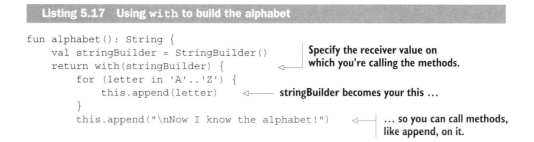

```
fun alphabet(): String {
    val stringBuilder = StringBuilder()          Specify the receiver value on
    return with(stringBuilder) {                 which you're calling the methods.
        for (letter in 'A'..'Z') {
            this.append(letter)            stringBuilder becomes your this ...
        }
        this.append("\nNow I know the alphabet!")    ... so you can call methods,
                                                      like append, on it.
```

```
        this.toString()
    }
}
```
Return a value from with.

The with structure looks like a special construct, but it's a function that takes two arguments: stringBuilder, in this case, and a lambda. The convention of putting the lambda outside of the parentheses works here, and the entire invocation looks like a built-in feature of the language. Alternatively, you could write this as with(string-Builder, { … }), but it's less readable.

The with function converts its first argument into a *receiver* of the lambda that's passed as a second argument. You can access this receiver via an explicit this reference. Alternatively, as usual for a this reference, you can omit it and access methods or properties of this value without any additional qualifiers (figure 5.8).

```
val stringBuilder = StringBuilder()
with(stringBuilder) { this: StringBuilder

    // . . .

}
```

Figure 5.8   Inside the lambda of the with function, the first argument is available as the receiver type this. IDEs, like IntelliJ IDEA and Android Studio, have the option to visualize this receiver type via an inlay hint after the opening parenthesis.

In listing 5.17, this refers to stringBuilder, which is passed to with as the first argument. You can access methods on stringBuilder via explicit this references, as in this.append (letter), or directly, making your code even more concise.

Listing 5.18   You don't need to specify this explicitly inside the with lambda

```
fun alphabet(): String {
    val stringBuilder = StringBuilder()
    return with(stringBuilder) {
        for (letter in 'A'..'Z') {
            append(letter)
        }
        append("\nNow I know the alphabet!")
        toString()
    }
}
```
You can omit the explicit this inside the lambda.

Lambdas with receiver and extension functions

You may recall that you saw a similar concept, with this referring to the function receiver. In the body of an extension function, this refers to the instance of the type the function is extending, and it can be omitted to give you direct access to the receiver's members.

Note that an extension function is, in a sense, a function with a receiver. The following analogy can be applied:

| Regular function | Regular lambda |
| Extension function | Lambda with a receiver |

A lambda is a way to define behavior similar to a regular function. A lambda with a receiver is a way to define behavior similar to an extension function.

Let's refactor the initial `alphabet` function even further and get rid of the extra `stringBuilder` variable.

Listing 5.19   Using `with` and an expression body to build the alphabet

```
fun alphabet() = with(StringBuilder()) {
    for (letter in 'A'..'Z') {
        append(letter)
    }
    append("\nNow I know the alphabet!")
    toString()
}
```

This function now only returns an expression, so it's rewritten using the expression-body syntax. You create a new instance of `StringBuilder` and pass it directly as an argument, and then you reference it without the explicit `this` in the lambda.

> **Method–name conflicts**
>
> What happens if the object you pass as a parameter to `with` has a method with the same name as the class in which you're using `with`? In this case, you can add an explicit label to the `this` reference to specify which method you need to call.
>
> Imagine the `alphabet` function is a method of the class `OuterClass`. If you need to refer to the `toString` method defined in the outer class instead of the one in `StringBuilder`, you can do so using the following syntax:
>
> ```
> this@OuterClass.toString()
> ```

The value `with` returns is the result of executing the lambda code. The result is the last expression in the lambda. But sometimes, you want the call to return the receiver object, not the result of executing the lambda. That's where the `apply` library function can be of use.

5.4.2   *Initializing and configuring objects: The apply function*

The `apply` function works almost exactly the same as `with` ; the main difference is that `apply` always returns the object passed to it as an argument (in other words, the receiver object). Let's refactor the `alphabet` function again, this time using `apply`.

Listing 5.20   Using `apply` to build the alphabet

```
fun alphabet() = StringBuilder().apply {
    for (letter in 'A'..'Z') {
        append(letter)
    }
    append("\nNow I know the alphabet!")
}.toString()
```

You can call the `apply` function as an extension function on any type—in this case, you're calling it on your newly created `StringBuilder` instance. The object you're calling `apply` on becomes the receiver of the lambda passed as an argument (see figure 5.9). The result of executing `apply` is `StringBuilder`, so you call `toString` to convert it to `String` afterward.

val result : StringBuilder = **StringBuilder().*apply* {** this: StringBuilder

   // . . .

}

Figure 5.9   Like the `with` function, `apply` makes the object it was called on the receiver type inside the lambda. `apply` also returns the object it was called on. Inlay hints in IntelliJ IDEA and Android Studio help visualize this.

One of many cases in which this is useful is when you're creating an instance of an object and need to initialize some properties right away. In Java, this is usually accomplished through a separate `Builder` object, and in Kotlin, you can use `apply` on any object without any special support from the library where the object is defined.

To see how `apply` is used for such cases, let's look at an example that creates an Android `TextView` component with some custom attributes.

Listing 5.21   Using `apply` to initialize a `TextView`

```
fun createViewWithCustomAttributes(context: Context) =
    TextView(context).apply {
        text = "Sample Text"
        textSize = 20.0
        setPadding(10, 0, 0, 0)
    }
```

The `apply` function allows you to use the compact expression body style for the function. You create a new `TextView` instance and immediately pass it to `apply`. In the lambda passed to `apply`, the `TextView` instance becomes the receiver, so you can call methods and set properties on it. After the lambda is executed, `apply` returns that instance, which is already initialized; it becomes the result of the `createViewWith-CustomAttributes` function.

The `with` and `apply` functions are basic generic examples of using lambdas with receivers. More specific functions can also use the same pattern. For example, you can simplify the `alphabet` function even further by using the `buildString` standard library function, which will take care of creating a `StringBuilder` and calling `toString`. The argument of `buildString` is a lambda with a receiver, and the receiver is always a `StringBuilder`.

Listing 5.22 Using `buildString` to build the alphabet

```
fun alphabet() = buildString {
    for (letter in 'A'..'Z') {
        append(letter)
    }
    append("\nNow I know the alphabet!")
}
```

The `buildString` function is an elegant solution for the task of creating a `String` with the help of `StringBuilder`. The Kotlin standard library also comes with collection builder functions, which help you create a read-only , `List`, `Set`, or `Map`, while allowing you to treat the collection as mutable during the construction phase.

Listing 5.23 Using `buildList`, `buildSet`, and `buildMap` to create collections

```
val fibonacci = buildList {
    addAll(listOf(1, 1, 2))
    add(3)
    add(index = 0, element = 3)
}

val shouldAdd = true

val fruits = buildSet {
    add("Apple")
    if (shouldAdd) {
        addAll(listOf("Apple", "Banana", "Cherry"))
    }
}

val medals = buildMap<String, Int> {
    put("Gold", 1)
    putAll(listOf("Silver" to 2, "Bronze" to 3))
}
```

5.4.3 Performing additional actions with an object: also

Just like `apply`, you can use the `also` function to take a receiver object, perform an action on it, and then return the receiver object (see figure 5.10). The main difference is that within the lambda of `also`, you access the receiver object as an argument—either by giving it a name, or using the default name `it`. This makes `also` a good fit for running actions that take the original receiver object as an argument (as opposed to operations that work on the object's properties and functions). When you see `also` in the code, you can interpret it as executing additional effects: "… and also do the following with the object."

```
val x : List<Int> = listOf(1, 2, 3).also { it: List<Int>
    // . . .
}
```

Figure 5.10   When using `also`, the object doesn't become the receiver type inside the lambda but makes the object available as an argument, named `it` by default. The `also` function returns the object it was called on, as you can see in these inlay hints.

In the following example, you're mapping a collection of fruits to their uppercased names and *also* adding the result of that mapping to an additional collection. You then filter for those fruits from the collection whose name is longer than five characters and *also* print that result, before finally reversing the list.

Listing 5.24   Using `also` to perform additional effects

```
fun main() {
    val fruits = listOf("Apple", "Banana", "Cherry")
    val uppercaseFruits = mutableListOf<String>()
    val reversedLongFruits = fruits
        .map { it.uppercase() }
        .also { uppercaseFruits.addAll(it) }
        .filter { it.length > 5 }
        .also { println(it) }
        .reversed()
    // [BANANA, CHERRY]
    println(uppercaseFruits)
    // [APPLE, BANANA, CHERRY]
    println(reversedLongFruits)
    // [CHERRY, BANANA]
}
```

You'll see more interesting examples for lambdas with receivers in section 13.2, when we begin discussing domain-specific languages (DSLs). Lambdas with receivers are great tools for building DSLs; we'll show you how to use them for that purpose and how to define your own functions that call lambdas with receivers.

Summary

- Lambdas allow you to pass chunks of code as arguments to functions, so you can easily extract common code structures.
- Kotlin lets you pass lambdas to functions outside of parentheses to make your code clean and concise.
- If a lambda only takes a single parameter, you can refer to it with its implicit name `it`. This saves you the effort of explicitly naming the only lambda parameter in short and simple lambdas.

- Lambdas can *capture* external variables. That means you can, for example, use your lambdas to access and modify variables in the function containing the call to the lambda.

- You can create references to methods, constructors, and properties by prefixing the name of the function with ::. You can pass such references to functions instead of lambdas as a shorthand.

- To implement interfaces with a single abstract method (aka SAM interfaces), you can simply pass lambdas instead of creating an object implementing the interface explicitly.

- *Lambdas with receivers* are lambdas that allow you to directly call methods on a special receiver object. Because the body of these lambdas is executed in a different context than the surrounding code, they can help with structuring your code.

- The `with` standard library function allows you to call multiple methods on the same object without repeating the reference to the object. `apply` lets you construct and initialize any object, using a builder-style API. `also` lets you perform additional actions with an object.

Working with
collections and sequences

This chapter covers

- Working with collections in a functional style
- Sequences: performing collection operations lazily

In chapter 5, you learned about lambdas as a way of passing small blocks of code to other functions. One of the most common uses for lambdas is *working with collections*. In this chapter, you will see how replacing common collection access patterns with a combination of standard library functions and your own lambdas can make your code more expressive, elegant, and concise—whether you are filtering your data based on predicates, need to group data, or want to transform collection items from one form to another.

You will also explore *sequences* as an alternative way to apply multiple collection operations efficiently and without creating much overhead. You will learn the difference between *eager* and *lazy* execution of collection operations in Kotlin and how to use either one in your programs.

160

6.1   *Functional APIs for collections*

A functional programming style provides many benefits when it comes to manipulating collections. For most tasks, you can use functions provided by the standard library and customize their behavior by passing lambdas as arguments to these functions. Compared to navigating through collections and aggregating data manually, this allows you to express common operations consistently, using a vocabulary of functions you share with other Kotlin developers.

In this section, we'll explore some of the functions in the Kotlin standard library you might find yourself reaching for when working with collections. We'll start with staple functions like `filter` and `map` that help you transform collections as well as the concepts behind these functions. We'll also cover other useful functions and provide tips on how to avoid overusing them as well as how to write clear and comprehensible code.

Note that these functions weren't invented by the designers of Kotlin. These and similar functions are available for all languages that support lambdas, including C#, Groovy, and Scala. If you're already familiar with these concepts, you can quickly look through the following examples and skip the explanations.

6.1.1   *Removing and transforming elements: filter and map*

The `filter` and `map` functions form the basis for manipulating collections. Many collection operations can be expressed with their help. Whenever you're faced with the task of filtering a collection based on a specific predicate, or you need to transform each element of a collection into a different form, these functions should come to mind.

For each function, we'll provide one example with numbers and one using the familiar `Person` class:

```
data class Person(val name: String, val age: Int)
```

The `filter` function goes through a collection and selects the elements for which the given lambda returns `true`. For example, given a list of some numbers, `filter` can help you extract only the even numbers (where the remainder of a division by 2 is 0):

```
fun main() {
    val list = listOf(1, 2, 3, 4)
    println(list.filter { it % 2 == 0 })        ◁——— Only even numbers remain.
    // [2, 4]
}
```

The result is a new collection that contains only the elements from the input collection that satisfy the predicate, as illustrated in figure 6.1.

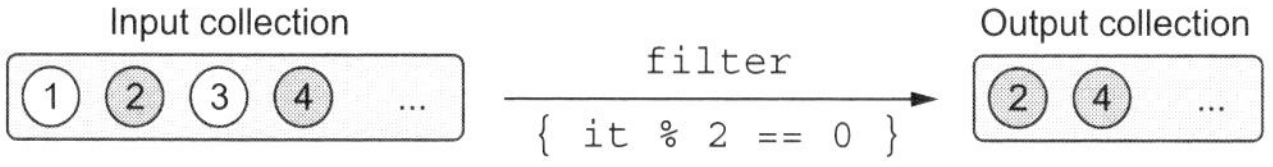

Figure 6.1   The `filter` function selects elements matching a given predicate.

If you want a collection of only people older than 30, you can use `filter` again:

```
fun main() {
    val people = listOf(Person("Alice", 29), Person("Bob", 31))
    println(people.filter { it.age > 30 })
    // [Person(name=Bob, age=31)]
}
```

The `filter` function can create a new collection of elements that match a given predicate but do not *transform* the elements in the process—your output is still a collection of `Person` objects. You can think of it as "extracting" entries from your collection, without changing their type.

Compare this to the `map` function, which allows you to transform the elements of your input collection. It applies the given function to each element in the collection and collects the return values into a new collection. You could use it to transform a list of numbers into a list of their squares, as in the following example:

```
fun main() {
    val list = listOf(1, 2, 3, 4)
    println(list.map { it * it })
    // [1, 4, 9, 16]
}
```

The result is a new collection that contains the same number of elements, but each element has been transformed according to the given predicate function (see figure 6.2).

Figure 6.2 The `map` function applies a lambda to all elements in a collection.

If you want to print just a list of names, not a list of people, you can transform the list using `map`. This turns the list of `Person` objects into a list of `String` objects representing their names, which you can easily print:

```
fun main() {
    val people = listOf(Person("Alice", 29), Person("Bob", 31))
    println(people.map { it.name })
    // [Alice, Bob]
}
```

Note that this example can be nicely rewritten using member references:

```
people.map(Person::name)
```

You can easily chain several calls like that. For example, let's find the names of people older than 30:

```
println(people.filter { it.age > 30 }.map(Person::name))
// [Bob]
```

Now, let's say you need to find the oldest people in the group. You can find the maximum age of the people in the group and return everyone who is that age (or `null` if no such person exists—more on nullability in chapter 7). It's easy to write such code using lambdas:

```
people.filter {
    val oldestPerson = people.maxByOrNull(Person::age)
    it.age == oldestPerson?.age
}
```

But note that this code repeats the process of finding the maximum age for every person, so if there are 100 people in the collection, the search for the maximum age will be performed 100 times!

The following solution improves on that and calculates the maximum age just once:

```
val maxAge = people.maxByOrNull(Person::age)?.age
people.filter { it.age == maxAge }
```

Don't repeat a calculation if you don't need to! Simple-looking code using lambda expressions can sometimes obscure the complexity of the underlying operations. Always keep in mind what is happening in the code you write.

If your filtering and transformation operations depend on the index of the elements in addition to their actual values, you can use the sibling functions `filterIndexed` and `mapIndexed`, which provide your lambda with the (zero-based) index of an element as well as the element itself. In this example, you're filtering a list of numbers to only contain those values at an even index and greater than 3. You are also mapping a second list to sum the index number and the numerical value of each element:

```
fun main() {
    val numbers = listOf(1, 2, 3, 4, 5, 6, 7)
    val filtered = numbers.filterIndexed { index, element ->
        index % 2 == 0 && element > 3
    }
    println(filtered)
    // [5, 7]

    val mapped = numbers.mapIndexed { index, element ->
        index + element
    }
    println(mapped)
    // [1, 3, 5, 7, 9, 11, 13]
}
```

Filter and transformation functions can also be applied to maps:

```
fun main() {
    val numbers = mapOf(0 to "zero", 1 to "one")
    println(numbers.mapValues { it.value.uppercase() })
    // {0=ZERO, 1=ONE}
}
```

There are separate functions to handle keys and values. `filterKeys` and `mapKeys` filter and transform the keys of a map, respectively, whereas `filterValues` and `mapValues` filter and transform the corresponding values.

6.1.2   *Accumulating values for collections: reduce and fold*

In addition to the `filter` and `map` functions, `reduce` and `fold` are two more essential building blocks when working with collections in a functional style. These functions are used to *aggregate* information from a collection: given a collection of items, they return a single value. This value is gradually built up in an "accumulator." Your lambda is invoked for each element and needs to return a new accumulator value.

When using `reduce`, you start with the first element of your collection in the accumulator (so don't call it on an empty collection!). Your lambda is then called with the accumulator and the second element. In this example, you use `reduce` to sum and multiply the values of the input collection, respectively (the same behavior is illustrated in figure 6.3):

```
fun main() {
    val list = listOf(1, 2, 3, 4)
    val summed = list.reduce { acc, element ->
        acc + element
    }
    println(summed)
    // 10
    val multiplied = list.reduce { acc, element ->
        acc * element
    }
    println(multiplied)
    // 24
}
```

The `fold` function is conceptually very similar to `reduce`, but instead of putting the first element of your collection into the accumulator at the beginning, you can choose an arbitrary start value. In this example, you're concatenating the `name` property of two `Person` objects using `fold` (a job usually tailored for the `joinToString` function we explored earlier, but an illustrative example, nonetheless). You initialize the accumulator with an empty string and then gradually build up the final text in your lambda (you can see this behavior illustrated in figure 6.4):

```
fun main() {
    val people = listOf(
        Person("Alex", 29),
        Person("Natalia", 28)
    )
    val folded = people.fold("") { acc, person ->
        acc + person.name
    }
    println(folded)
}
// AlexNatalia
```

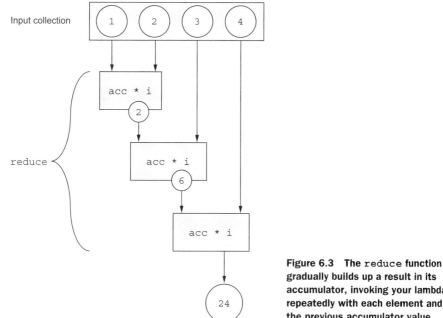

Figure 6.3   **The** `reduce` **function gradually builds up a result in its accumulator, invoking your lambda repeatedly with each element and the previous accumulator value.**

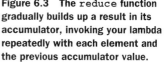

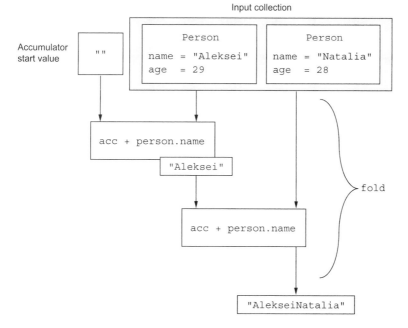

Figure 6.4   **The** `fold` **function allows you to specify the initial value and type of the accumulator. The result is gradually built up in the accumulator, applying your lambda repeatedly on each accumulator–element pair.**

There are many algorithms you can express concisely using a `fold` or `reduce` operation. In cases where you want to retrieve all intermittent values of the `reduce` or `fold` operations, the `runningReduce` and `runningFold` functions come to the rescue. Their only difference compared to the previously discussed `reduce` and `fold` functions is that these functions return a *list*. It contains all intermittent accumulator values alongside the final result. In this example, you're using the `running` counterpart of the snippets discussed in the previous paragraphs:

```
fun main() {
    val list = listOf(1, 2, 3, 4)
    val summed = list.runningReduce { acc, element ->
        acc + element
    }
    println(summed)
    // [1, 3, 6, 10]
    val multiplied = list.runningReduce { acc, element ->
        acc * element
    }
    println(multiplied)
    // [1, 2, 6, 24]
    val people = listOf(
        Person("Alex", 29),
        Person("Natalia", 28)
    )
    println(people.runningFold("") { acc, person ->
        acc + person.name
    })
    // [, Alex, AlexNatalia]
}
```

While the final result is the same, the running functions return all intermediate values as well.

6.1.3 Applying a predicate to a collection: all, any, none, count, and find

Another common task is checking whether all, some, or no elements in a collection match a certain condition. In Kotlin, this is expressed using the `all`, `any`, and `none` functions. The `count` function checks how many elements satisfy the predicate, and the `find` function returns the first matching element.

To demonstrate those functions, let's define the predicate `canBeInClub27` to check whether a person is 27 or younger:

```
val canBeInClub27 = { p: Person -> p.age <= 27 }
```

If you're interested in whether all the elements satisfy this predicate, you use the `all` function:

```
fun main() {
    val people = listOf(Person("Alice", 27), Person("Bob", 31))
    println(people.all(canBeInClub27))
    // false
}
```

If you need to check whether there's at least one matching element, use `any`:

```
fun main() {
    println(people.any(canBeInClub27))
    // true
}
```

Note that `!all` ("not all") with a condition can be replaced with `any` with a negation of that condition, and vice versa. To make your code easier to understand, you should choose a function that doesn't require you to put a negation sign before it:

```
fun main() {
    val list = listOf(1, 2, 3)
    println(!list.all { it == 3 })
    // true
    println(list.any { it != 3 })
    // true
}
```

The negation `!` isn't noticeable, so it's better to use any in this case.

The condition in the argument has changed to its opposite.

The first check ensures that not all elements are equal to 3. That's the same as having at least one non-3, which is what you check using `any` on the second line.

Likewise, you can replace `!any` with `none`:

```
fun main() {
    val list = listOf(1, 2, 3)
    println(!list.any { it == 4 })
    // true
    println(list.none { it == 4 })
    // true
}
```

Rather than using a call to any and negating its result …

… we can use none with the same condition.

The first invocation checks whether any elements in the collection are equal to 4 and negates that result. A more natural way of expressing this, both in code and words, is to check whether none of the elements are equal to 4.

Predicates and empty collections

While reading the description of the different types of predicates—`any`, `none`, and `all`—you may have started to wonder what these functions return when called on empty collections. Let's address this mystery.

In the case of `any`, the collection contains no elements that can satisfy the provided predicate. That means it returns `false`:

```
fun main() {
    println(emptyList<Int>().any { it > 42 })
    // false
}
```

(continued)
Note also that this snippet shows off a more expressive way of creating empty lists in Kotlin: via the `emptyList` function.

As you've seen, the `none` function is the inverse of the `any` function. That's also reflected in the case of an empty collection: there is no element that can violate the predicate, so the function returns `true`:

```
fun main() {
    println(emptyList<Int>().none { it > 42 })
    // true
}
```

The function with perhaps the largest mind-bending potential is `all`. Regardless of the predicate, it returns `true` when called on an empty collection:

```
fun main() {
    println(emptyList<Int>().all { it > 42 })
    // true
}
```

This might surprise you at first, but upon further investigation, you'll find that this is a very reasonable return value. You can't name an element that violates the predicate, so the predicate clearly has to be true for *all* elements in the collection—even if there are none! This concept is known as the *vacuous truth* and, in most cases, actually ends up a good fit for conditionals that should also work with empty collections.

If you want to know how many elements satisfy a predicate, use `count`:

```
fun main() {
    val people = listOf(Person("Alice", 27), Person("Bob", 31))
    println(people.count(canBeInClub27))
    // 1
}
```

Using the right function for the job: count vs. size
It's easy to forget about `count` and implement it by filtering the collection and getting its size:

```
println(people.filter(canBeInClub27).size)
// 1
```

But in this case, an intermediate collection is created to store all the elements that satisfy the predicate. On the other hand, the `count` method tracks only the number of matching elements, not the elements themselves, and is, therefore, more efficient. As a general rule, try to find the most appropriate operation that suits your needs.

To find an element that satisfies the predicate, use the `find` function:

```
fun main() {
    val people = listOf(Person("Alice", 27), Person("Bob", 31))
    println(people.find(canBeInClub27))
    // Person(name=Alice, age=27)
}
```

This returns the first matching element if there are many or `null` if nothing satisfies the predicate. A synonym of `find` is `firstOrNull`, which you can use if it expresses the idea more clearly for you.

6.1.4 Splitting a list into a pair of lists: partition

In some situations, you need to divide a collection into two groups based on a given predicate: elements that fulfill a Boolean predicate and those that don't. If you need both groups, you could use the functions `filter` and its sibling `filterNot` (which inverts the predicate) to create these two lists. In this example, you're finding out who is allowed in the club—and who isn't:

```
fun main() {
    val people = listOf(
        Person("Alice", 26),
        Person("Bob", 29),
        Person("Carol", 31)
    )
    val comeIn = people.filter(canBeInClub27)
    val stayOut = people.filterNot(canBeInClub27)
    println(comeIn)
    // [Person(name=Alice, age=26)]
    println(stayOut)
    // [Person(name=Bob, age=29), Person(name=Carol, age=31)]
}
```

But there is also a more concise way to do this: using the `partition` function. It returns this pair of lists, without having to repeat the predicate and without having to iterate the input collection twice. This means you can express the same logic from the previous code snippet as follows (illustrated in figure 6.5):

```
val (comeIn, stayOut) = people.partition(canBeInClub27)
println(comeIn)
// [Person(name=Alice, age=26)]
println(stayOut)
// [Person(name=Bob, age=29), Person(name=Carol, age=31)]
```

The destructuring declaration takes care of splitting the returned pair of lists into two variables based on a Boolean predicate.

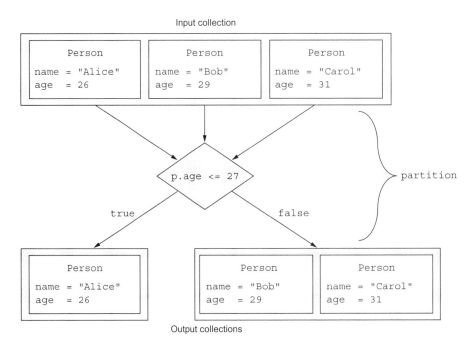

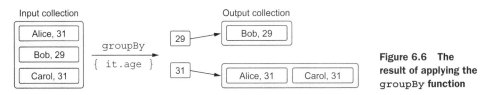

Figure 6.5 The `partition` function returns a pair consisting of two lists: those that satisfy the given Boolean predicate and those that don't.

6.1.5 *Converting a list to a map of groups: groupBy*

Often enough, the elements in a collection can't be clustered into just the "true" and "false" groups that `partition` returns. Instead, you may want to divide all elements into different groups according to some *quality*. For example, you want to group people of the same age. It's convenient to pass this quality directly as a parameter. The `groupBy` function can do this for you:

```
fun main() {
    val people = listOf(
        Person("Alice", 31),
        Person("Bob", 29),
        Person("Carol", 31)
    )
    println(people.groupBy { it.age })
}
```

The result of this operation is a map from the key by which the elements are grouped (age, in this case) to the groups of elements (persons); see figure 6.6.

Figure 6.6 The result of applying the `groupBy` function

For this example, the output is as follows:

```
{31=[Person(s=Alice, age=31), Person(s=Carol, age=31)],
29=[Person(s=Bob, age=29)]}
```

Each group is stored in a list, so the result type is `Map<Int, List<Person>>`. You can make further modifications with this map, using functions such as `mapKeys` and `mapValues`.

As another example, let's see how to group strings by their first character using member references:

```
fun main() {
    val list = listOf("apple", "apricot", "banana", "cantaloupe")
    println(list.groupBy(String::first))
    // {a=[apple, apricot], b=[banana], c=[cantaloupe]}
}
```

Note that `first` here isn't a member of the `String` class—it's an extension. Nevertheless, you can access it as a member reference.

6.1.6 Transforming collections into maps: associate, associateWith, and associateBy

With `groupBy`, you now already know a way of creating an associative data structure from a list—by grouping elements based on a common property. If you want to create a map from the elements of a collection *without* grouping elements, the `associate` function comes into play. You provide it with a lambda that expresses a transformation from an item in your input collection to a key–value pair that will be put into a map. In this example, you use the `associate` function to turn a list of `Person` objects into a map of names to ages and query an example value, like you would with any other `Map<String, Int>`. You use the infix function `to`, which we introduced in section 3.4.3 to specify the individual key–value pairs (illustrated in figure 6.7):

```
fun main() {
    val people = listOf(Person("Joe", 22), Person("Mary", 31))
    val nameToAge = people.associate { it.name to it.age }    ◁─┐  The infix function
    println(nameToAge)                                           │  to creates a Pair
    // {Joe=22, Mary=31}                                         │  of its left and
    println(nameToAge["Joe"])                                    │  right operand.
    // 22
}
```

Instead of creating pairs of custom keys *and* custom values, you may want to create an association between the elements of your collection with another certain value. You can do this with the `associateWith` and `associateBy` functions.

`associateWith` uses the original elements of your collection as keys. The lambda you provide generates the corresponding value for each key. On the other hand, `associateBy` uses the original elements of your collection as values and uses your lambda to generate the keys of the map.

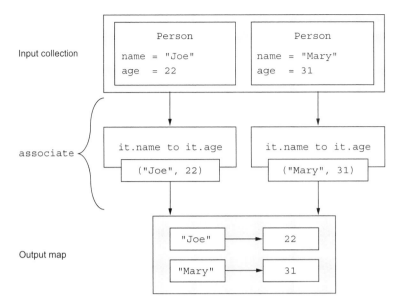

Figure 6.7   The `associate` function turns a list into a map based on the pairs of keys and values returned by your lambda.

In this example, you're first creating a map of people to their ages by using the `associateWith` function. You create the inverse map, from ages to people, using the `associateBy` function:

```
fun main() {
    val people = listOf(
        Person("Joe", 22),
        Person("Mary", 31),
        Person("Jamie", 22)
    )
    val personToAge = people.associateWith { it.age }
    println(personToAge)
    // {Person(name=Joe, age=22)=22, Person(name=Mary, age=31)=31,
    //   Person(name=Jamie, age=22)=22}
    val ageToPerson = people.associateBy { it.age }
    println(ageToPerson)
    // {22=Person(name=Jamie, age=22), 31=Person(name=Mary, age=31)}
}
```

> Joe and Jamie have the same age ...
>
> ... which is being used as a key ...
>
> ... so only the latter shows up in the map.

Keep in mind that keys for maps have to be unique, and the ones generated by `associate`, `associateBy`, and `associateWith` are no exception. If your transformation function would result in the same key being added multiple times, the last result overwrites any previous assignments.

6.1.7   Replacing elements in mutable collections: replaceAll and fill

Generally, a functional programming style encourages you to work with immutable collections, but there may still be some situations in which it is more ergonomic to work with mutable collections. For those situations, the Kotlin standard library comes with a few convenience functions to help you change the contents of your collections.

When applied to a `MutableList`, the `replaceAll` function replaces each element in the list with a result from the lambda you specify. For the special case of replacing all elements in the mutable list with the same value, you can use the `fill` function as a shorthand. In this example, you first replace all elements in your input collection with their uppercase variant and then replace all names with placeholder text:

```
fun main() {
    val names = mutableListOf("Martin", "Samuel")
    println(names)
    // [Martin, Samuel]
    names.replaceAll { it.uppercase() }
    println(names)
    // [MARTIN, SAMUEL]
    names.fill("(redacted)")
    println(names)
    // [(redacted), (redacted)]
}
```

6.1.8   *Handling special cases for collections: ifEmpty*

Often, it only makes sense for a program to proceed if an input collection is not empty—so that there are some actual elements to process. With the `ifEmpty` function, you can provide a lambda that generates a default value in case your collection does not contain any elements:

```
fun main() {
    val empty = emptyList<String>()
    val full = listOf("apple", "orange", "banana")
    println(empty.ifEmpty { listOf("no", "values", "here") })
    // [no, values, here]
    println(full.ifEmpty { listOf("no", "values", "here") })
    // [apple, orange, banana]
}
```

> **ifBlank: ifEmpty's sibling function for strings**
>
> When working with text (which we often also simply treat as a collection of characters), we sometimes relax the requirement of "empty" to "blank": strings containing only whitespace characters are seldom more expressive than pure empty strings. To generate a default value for them, we can use the `ifBlank` function:
>
> ```
> fun main() {
>     val blankName = " "
>     val name = "J. Doe"
>     println(blankName.ifEmpty { "(unnamed)" })
>     //
>     println(blankName.ifBlank { "(unnamed)" })
>     // (unnamed)
>     println(name.ifBlank { "(unnamed)" })
>     // J. Doe
> }
> ```

6.1.9   *Splitting collections: chunked and windowed*

When the data in your collection represents a series of information, you may want to work with multiple consecutive values at a time. Consider, for example, a list of daily measurements of a temperature sensor:

```
val temperatures = listOf(27.7, 29.8, 22.0, 35.5, 19.1)
```

To get a three-day average for each set of days in this list of values, you would use a *sliding window* of size 3; you would first average the first three values: 27.7, 29.8, and 22.0. Then, you would "slide" the window over by one index, averaging 29.8, 22.0, and 35.5. You would keep sliding until you reach the final three values—22.0, 35.5, and 19.1.

To generate these kinds of sliding windows, you can use the `windowed` function. `windowed` optionally lets you pass a lambda that transforms the output. In the case of temperature measurements, that could be calculating the average of each window (illustrated in figure 6.8):

```
fun main() {
    println(temperatures.windowed(3))
    // [[27.7, 29.8, 22.0], [29.8, 22.0, 35.5], [22.0, 35.5, 19.1]]
    println(temperatures.windowed(3) { it.sum() / it.size })
    // [26.5, 29.099999999999998, 25.53333333333333]
}
```

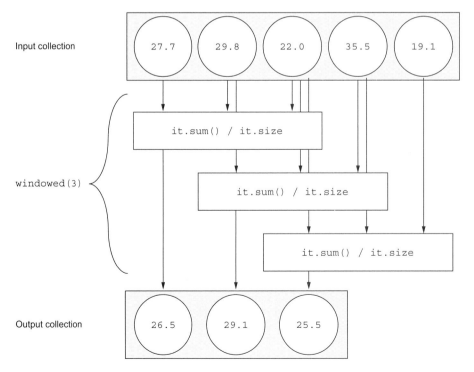

Figure 6.8   The `windowed` function processes your input collection using a sliding window.

Instead of running a sliding window over your input collection, you may want to break the collection into distinct parts of a given size. The `chunked` function helps you achieve this. Once again, you can also pass a lambda, which transforms the output (illustrated in figure 6.9):

```
fun main() {
    println(temperatures.chunked(2))
    // [[27.7, 29.8], [22.0, 35.5], [19.1]]
    println(temperatures.chunked(2) { it.sum() })
    // [57.5, 57.5, 19.1]
}
```

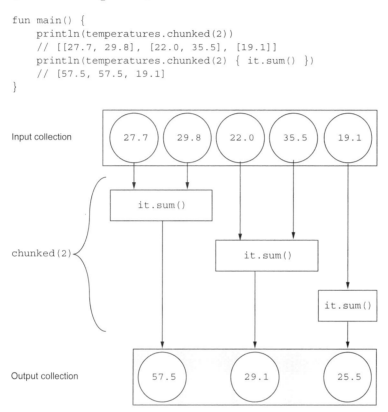

Figure 6.9 **The `chunked` function processes your input collection in nonoverlapping segments of the specified size.**

Note that in the preceding example, even though you specify a chunk size of 2, the last generated chunk may have a smaller size: since the input collection has an odd number of items, the `chunked` function creates two chunks of size 2 and puts the remaining item in a third chunk.

6.1.10 Merging collections: zip

Sometimes, you may have to work with separate lists that contain related data, and aggregate this information. For example, instead of a list of `Person` objects, you have two lists, for people's names and ages, respectively:

```
val names = listOf("Joe", "Mary", "Jamie")
val ages = listOf(22, 31, 31, 44, 0)
```

If you know that the values in each list correspond to their index (that is, the name at index 0, Joe, corresponds to the age at index 0, 22), you can use the zip function to create a list of pairs from values at the same index from two collections. Passing a lambda to the function also allows you to specify how the output should be transformed. In this example, you create a list of Person objects from each pair of name and age (illustrated in figure 6.10):

```
fun main() {
    val names = listOf("Joe", "Mary", "Jamie")
    val ages = listOf(22, 31, 31, 44, 0)
    println(names.zip(ages))
    // [(Joe, 22), (Mary, 31), (Jamie, 31)]
    println(names.zip(ages) { name, age -> Person(name, age) })
    // [Person(name=Joe, age=22), Person(name=Mary, age=31),
    // Person(name=Jamie, age=31)]
}
```

Values that don't have a counterpart in the other collection are ignored by zip.

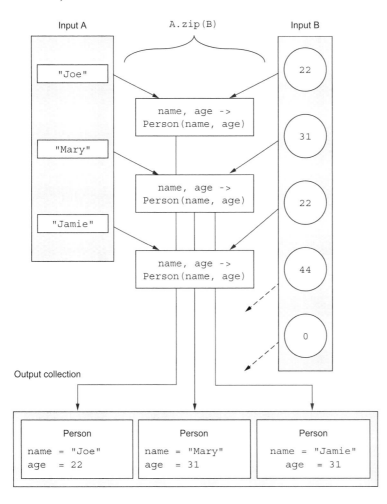

Figure 6.10   The zip function correlates each element of its two inputs at the same index using the lambda you pass to it; otherwise, it creates pairs of the elements . Elements that don't have a counter-part in the other collection are ignored.

Note that the size of the resulting collection is the same as the shorter of the two lists: zip only processes items at those indexes that exist in both input collections.

Like the to function to create Pair objects, the zip function can also be called as an *infix* function (as introduced in section 3.4.3)—though you won't be able to pass a transforming lambda in this case:

```
println(names zip ages)
// [(Joe, 22), (Mary, 31), (Jamie, 31)]
```

Like any other function, you can chain multiple zip calls to combine more than two lists, even when using the infix syntax. Since zip always operates on two lists, though, you'll need to be aware that your resulting structure will consist of nested pairs, rather than simply a list of lists:

```
val countries = listOf("DE", "NL", "US")
println(names zip ages zip countries)
// [((Joe, 22), DE), ((Mary, 31), NL), ((Jamie, 31), US)]
```

> **Combining multiple calls to zip results in a list of nested pairs. Note the extra parentheses around the names and ages.**

6.1.11 *Processing elements in nested collections: flatMap and flatten*

Let's put aside our discussion of people and switch to books. Suppose you have a collection of books, represented by the Book class:

```
class Book(val title: String, val authors: List<String>)
```

Each book was written by one or more authors, and you have a number of books in your library:

```
val library = listOf(
 Book("Kotlin in Action", listOf("Isakova", "Elizarov", "Aigner", "Jemerov")),
 Book("Atomic Kotlin", listOf("Eckel", "Isakova")),
 Book("The Three-Body Problem", listOf("Liu"))
)
```

If you want to compute all authors in your library, you might start by using the map function you got to know in section 6.1.1:

```
fun main() {
    val authors = library.map { it.authors }
    println(authors)
    // [[Isakova, Elizarov, Aigner, Jemerov], [Eckel, Isakova], [Liu]]
}
```

Likely, this isn't the result you had in mind, though. Because authors is a List<String> in itself, your resulting collection is a List<List<String>>—a nested collection.

With the flatMap function, you can compute the set of all the authors in your library, without any extra nesting. It does two things: at first it transforms (or *maps*) each element to a collection, according to the function given as an argument (just like you saw with the map function), and then it combines (or *flattens*) these lists into one.

```
fun main() {
    val authors = library.flatMap { it.authors }          List of all authors
    println(authors)                                       in your library
    // [Isakova, Elizarov, Aigner, Jemerov, Eckel, Isakova, Liu]
    println(authors.toSet())
    // [Isakova, Elizarov, Aigner, Jemerov, Eckel, Liu]   Set of all authors in your
}                                                          library, without duplicates
```

Each book can be written by multiple authors, and the `book.authors` property stores a list of authors. In listing 6.1, you use the `flatMap` function to combine the authors of all the books in a single, flat list. The `toSet` call removes duplicates from the resulting collection—so in this example, Svetlana `Isakova` is listed only once in the output.

You may think of `flatMap` when you're stuck with a collection of collections of elements (e.g., `List<List<Int>>`) that have to be combined into one (i.e., `List<Int>`). Note that if you don't need to transform anything and just need to flatten such a collection of collections, you can use the `flatten` function: `listOfLists.flatten()`.

We've highlighted a few of the collection operation functions in the Kotlin standard library, but there are many more. We won't cover them all, for reasons of space as well as because showing a long list of functions is boring. Our general advice when you write code that works with collections is to think of how the operation could be expressed as a general transformation and to look for a standard library function that performs such a transformation—either by looking through your IDE's autocomplete suggestions or by consulting the Kotlin standard library reference (https://kotlinlang.org/api/latest/jvm/stdlib/). It's likely you'll be able to find one and use it to solve your problem more quickly than with a manual implementation.

Now, let's take a closer look at the performance of code that chains collection operations. In the next section, you'll see the different ways such operations can be executed.

6.2   *Lazy collection operations: Sequences*

In the previous section, you saw several examples of chained collection functions, such as `map` and `filter`. These functions create intermediate collections *eagerly*, meaning the intermediate result of each step is stored in a temporary list. *Sequences* give you an alternative way to perform such computations that avoids the creation of intermediate temporary objects, similar to how Java 8's streams do. Here's an example:

```
people.map(Person::name).filter { it.startsWith("A") }
```

The Kotlin standard library reference says that both `map` and `filter` return a list. That means this chain of calls will create two lists: one to hold the results of the `map` function and another for the results of `filter`. This isn't a problem when the source list contains two elements, but it becomes much less efficient if you have a million.

To make this more efficient, you can convert the operation so that it uses sequences instead of collections directly:

```
people
    .asSequence()                    Converts the initial collection to Sequence
    .map(Person::name)
    .filter { it.startsWith("A") }   Sequences support the same API as collections.
    .toList()
                                     Converts the resulting Sequence back into a list
```

The result of applying this operation is the same as in the previous example: a list of people's names that start with the letter *A*. But in the second example, no intermediate collections to store the elements are created, so performance for a large number of elements will be noticeably better.

The entry point for lazy collection operations in Kotlin is the `Sequence` interface. The interface represents just that: a sequence of elements that can be enumerated one by one. `Sequence` provides only one method, `iterator`, that you can use to obtain the values from the sequence.

The strength of the `Sequence` interface is in the way operations on it are implemented. The elements in a sequence are evaluated *lazily*. Therefore, you can use sequences to efficiently perform chains of operations on elements of a collection without creating collections to hold intermediate results of the processing. You'll also notice that we can use functions we already know from regular list processing, such as `map` and `filter`, with sequences as well.

Any collection can be converted to a sequence by calling the extension function `asSequence`. To do the opposite conversion, from a sequence to a plain list, you call `toList`.

Why do you need to convert the sequence back to a collection? Wouldn't it be more convenient to use sequences instead of collections if they're so much better? The answer is sometimes. If you only need to iterate over the elements in a sequence, you can use the sequence directly. If you need to use other API methods, such as accessing the elements by index, then you need to convert the sequence to a list.

> **NOTE** As a rule, use a sequence whenever you have a chain of operations on a *large* collection. In section 10.2, we'll discuss why eager operations on regular collections are efficient in Kotlin, in spite of creating intermediate collections. But if the collection contains a large number of elements, the intermediate rearranging of elements costs a lot, so lazy evaluation is preferable.

Because operations on a sequence are lazy, to perform them, you need to iterate over the sequence's elements directly or by converting it to a collection. The next section explains this process.

6.2.1 *Executing sequence operations: Intermediate and terminal operations*

Operations on a sequence are divided into two categories: intermediate and terminal. An *intermediate operation* returns another sequence, which knows how to transform the elements of the original sequence. A *terminal operation* returns a result, which may be a collection, an element, a number, or any other object that's somehow obtained by the sequence of transformations of the initial collection (see figure 6.11).

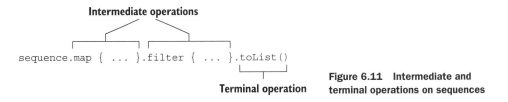

Figure 6.11   Intermediate and terminal operations on sequences

Intermediate operations are always lazy. Look at this example, where the terminal operation is missing:

```
fun main() {
    println(
        listOf(1, 2, 3, 4)
            .asSequence()
            .map {
                print("map($it) ")
                it * it
            }.filter {
                print("filter($it) ")
                it % 2 == 0
            }
    )
    // kotlin.sequences.FilteringSequence@506e1b77
}
```

Executing this code snippet doesn't print the expected result to the console—rather than seeing the result of these operations, you only see the Sequence object itself. The execution of the map and filter transformations are postponed and will be applied only when the result is obtained (that is, when a terminal operation is called):

```
fun main() {
    listOf(1, 2, 3, 4)
        .asSequence()
        .map {
            print("map($it) ")
            it * it
        }.filter {
            print("filter($it) ")
            it % 2 == 0
        }.toList()
}
```

The terminal operation (toList) causes all the postponed computations to be performed.

One more important thing to notice in this example is the order in which the computations are performed. The naive approach would be to call the map function on each element first and then call the filter function on each element of the resulting sequence. That's how map and filter work on collections but not on sequences. For sequences, all operations are applied to each element sequentially: the first element is processed (mapped, then filtered), and then the second element is processed, and so on.

This approach means some elements aren't transformed at all if the result is obtained before they are reached. Let's look at an example with map and find operations. First, you map a number to its square, and then you find the first item that's greater than 3:

```
fun main() {
    println(
        listOf(1, 2, 3, 4)
            .asSequence()
            .map { it * it }
            .find { it > 3 }
    )
    // 4
}
```

If the same operations are applied to a collection instead of a sequence, then the result of map is evaluated first, transforming all elements in the initial collection. In the second step, an element satisfying the predicate is found in the intermediate collection. With sequences, the lazy approach means you can skip processing some of the elements. Figure 6.12 illustrates the difference between evaluating this code in an eager (using collections) versus lazy (using sequences) manner.

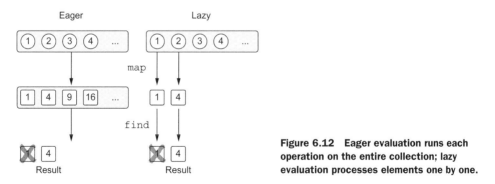

Figure 6.12   Eager evaluation runs each operation on the entire collection; lazy evaluation processes elements one by one.

In the first case, when you work with collections, the list is transformed into another list, so the map transformation is applied to each element, including 3 and 4. Afterward, the first element satisfying the predicate is found: the square of 2.

In the second case, the find call begins processing the elements one by one. You take a number from the original sequence, transform it with map, and then check whether it matches the predicate passed to find. When you reach 2, you see that its square is greater than 3 and return it as the result of the `find` operation. You don't need to look at 3 and 4 because the result was found before you reached them.

The order of the operations you perform on a collection can affect performance as well. Imagine you have a collection of people, and you want to print their names if they're shorter than a certain limit. You need to do two things: map each person to their name, and then filter out those names that are too long. You can apply `map` and `filter` operations in any order in this case. Both approaches give the same result, but they differ in the total number of transformations that should be performed (see figure 6.13):

```kotlin
fun main() {
    val people = listOf(
        Person("Alice", 29),
        Person("Bob", 31),
        Person("Charles", 31),
        Person("Dan", 21)
    )
    println(
        people
            .asSequence()
            .map(Person::name)        ⟵——— map goes first, and then filter.
            .filter { it.length < 4 }
            .toList()
    )
    // [Bob, Dan]
    println(
        people
            .asSequence()
            .filter { it.name.length < 4 }
            .map(Person::name)
            .toList()                 ⟵——— map goes after filter.
    )
    // [Bob, Dan]
}
```

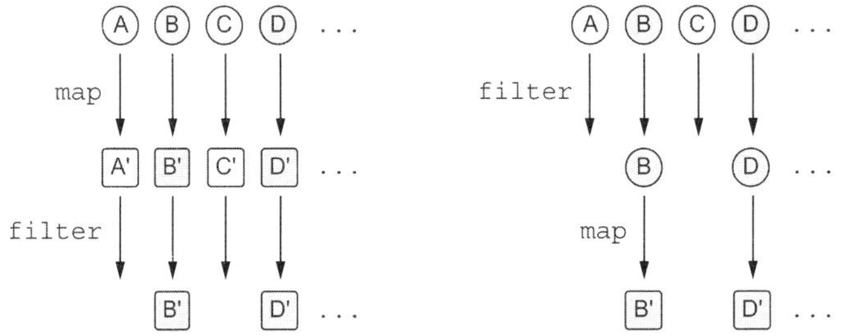

Figure 6.13 Applying `filter` first helps to reduce the total number of transformations.

If `map` goes first, each element is transformed, even if it is discarded in the next step and never used again. If you apply `filter` first, inappropriate elements are filtered out as soon as possible and aren't transformed. As a rule of thumb, the earlier you can remove elements from your chain of operations (without compromising the logic of your code, of course), the more performant your code will be.

6.2.2   Creating sequences

The previous examples used the same method to create a sequence: you called asSequence() on a collection. Another possibility is to use the generateSequence function. This function calculates the next element in a sequence, given the previous one. For example, here's how you can use generateSequence to calculate the sum of all natural numbers up to 100. First, you generate a sequence of all natural numbers. Then, you use the takeWhile function to take elements from that sequence if they're less than or equal to 100. Finally, you use sum to calculate the sum of these numbers.

Listing 6.2   Generating and using a sequence of natural numbers

```
fun main() {
    val naturalNumbers = generateSequence(0) { it + 1 }
    val numbersTo100 = naturalNumbers.takeWhile { it <= 100 }
    println(numbersTo100.sum())
    // 5050
}
```
All the delayed operations are performed when the result sum is obtained.

Note that naturalNumbers (an infinite sequence) and numbersTo100 (a finite sequence) in this example are both sequences with postponed computation. The actual numbers in those sequences won't be evaluated until you call the terminal operation (sum, in this case).

Another common use case is a sequence of parents. If an element has parents of its own type, you may be interested in qualities of the sequence of all of its ancestors. Typical examples for this might be the lineage for a human being or the parent folder structure for a given file (on the JVM, both files and folders are typically represented by the same type: File). In the following example, you inquire whether the file is located in a hidden directory by generating a sequence of its parent directories and checking this attribute on each of the directories.

Listing 6.3   Generating and using a sequence of parent directories

```
import java.io.File

fun File.isInsideHiddenDirectory() =
        generateSequence(this) { it.parentFile }.any { it.isHidden }

fun main() {
    val file = File("/Users/svtk/.HiddenDir/a.txt")
    println(file.isInsideHiddenDirectory())
    // true
}
```

Once again, you generate a sequence by providing the first element and a way to get each subsequent element. By replacing any with find, you'll get the actual directory that is hidden, instead of just a Boolean value indicating there is a hidden file somewhere in the path. Note that using sequences allows you to stop traversing the parents as soon as you find the required directory.

Summary

- Instead of manually iterating over elements in a collection, most common operations can be performed by combining existing functions from the standard library with your own lambdas. Kotlin comes with a wide variety of such functions.
- The `filter` and `map` functions form the basis for manipulating collections and make it easy to extract elements that match a certain predicate or transform elements into a new form.
- The `reduce` and `fold` operations *aggregate* information from a collection, helping you compute a single value given a collection of items.
- Functions from the `associate` and `groupBy` families help you turn flat lists into maps, so you can structure your data by your own criteria.
- For data in collections that is related by its indices, the `chunked`, `windowed`, and `zip` functions make it possible to create subgroups of collection elements or merge together multiple collections.
- Using *predicates*, lambda functions that return `Boolean`, the `all`, `any`, `none`, and other sibling functions allow you to check whether certain invariants apply to your collections.
- To deal with nested collections, the `flatten` function can help you extract the nested items, while the `flatMap` function even makes it possible to perform a transformation in the same step.
- Sequences allow you to combine multiple operations on a collection *lazily* and without creating collections to hold intermediate results, making your code more efficient. You can use the same functions you use for collections to manipulate sequences.

Working with
nullable values

7

This chapter covers

- Nullable types
- Syntax for dealing with values that are potentially null
- Converting between nullable and non-nullable types
- Interoperability between Kotlin's concept of nullability and Java code

By now, you've seen a large part of Kotlin's syntax in action. You've moved beyond creating basic code in Kotlin and are ready to enjoy some of Kotlin's productivity features that can make your code more compact and readable. One of the essential features in Kotlin that helps improve the reliability of your code is its support for *nullable types*. Let's look at the details.

185

7.1   *Avoiding NullPointerExceptions and handling the absence of values: Nullability*

Nullability is a feature of the Kotlin type system that helps you avoid `NullPointerException` (NPE) errors. As a user of a program, you've probably seen an error message similar to "An error has occurred: `java.lang.NullPointerException`," with no additional details. On Android, you may have seen another version of this message, along the lines of "Unfortunately, application X has stopped," which often also conceals a `NullPointerException` as a cause. Such errors occurring at run time are troublesome for both users and developers.

The approach of modern languages, including Kotlin, is to convert these problems from run-time errors into compile-time errors. By supporting nullability as part of the type system, the compiler can detect many possible errors during compilation and reduce the possibility of having exceptions thrown at run time.

In this section, we'll discuss nullable types in Kotlin: how Kotlin marks values that are allowed to be `null` and the tools Kotlin provides to deal with such values. Moving beyond that, we'll cover the details of mixing Kotlin and Java code with respect to nullable types.

7.2   *Making possibly null variables explicit with nullable types*

The first and probably most important difference between Kotlin's and Java's type systems is Kotlin's explicit support for *nullable types*. What does this mean? It's a way to indicate which variables or properties in your program are allowed to be `null`. If a variable can be `null`, calling a method on it isn't safe because it can cause a `NullPointerException`. Kotlin disallows such calls and thereby prevents many possible exceptions. To see how this works in practice, let's look at the following Java function, which accepts a `String` and calls the `length` function on it:

```
/* Java */
int strLen(String s) {
    return s.length();
}
```

Is this function safe? Well, a seasoned developer would probably quickly spot that if the function is called with a `null` argument, it will throw a `NullPointerException`. Do you need to add a check for `null` to the function? It depends on the function's intended use.

Let's rewrite this function in Kotlin. This is the first question you must answer: do you expect the function to be called with a `null` argument? We mean not only the `null` literal directly, as in `strLen(null)`, but also any variable or other expression that may have the value `null` at run time.

If you don't expect it to happen, you declare this function in Kotlin as follows:

```
fun strLen(s: String) = s.length
```

Calling `strLen` with an argument that may be `null` isn't allowed and will be flagged as an error at compile time:

```
fun main() {
    strLen(null)
    // ERROR: Null can not be a value of a non-null type String
}
```

The parameter is declared as type `String`, and in Kotlin, this means it must always contain a `String` instance. The compiler enforces that, so you can't pass an argument containing `null`. This gives you the guarantee that the `strLen` function will never throw a `NullPointerException` at run time.

If you want to allow the use of this function with all arguments, including those that can be `null`, you need to mark this explicitly by putting a question mark after the type name:

```
fun strLenSafe(s: String?) = ...
```

You can put a question mark after any type, to indicate that the variables of this type can store `null` references: `String?`, `Int?`, `MyCustomType?`, and so on (see figure 7.1).

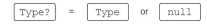

Figure 7.1 The question mark after a type name indicates it is nullable. A variable of nullable type can store a `null` reference.

To reiterate, a type without a question mark denotes that variables of this type can't store `null` references. This means all regular types are non-nullable by default, unless explicitly marked as nullable.

Once you have a value of nullable type, the set of operations you can perform on it is restricted. For example, you can no longer call methods on it. The compiler will now complain about the call to `length` in the function body:

```
fun strLenSafe(s: String?) = s.length()
// ERROR: only safe (?.) or non-null asserted (!!.) calls are allowed
// on a nullable receiver of type kotlin.String?
```

You also can't assign a value of nullable type to a variable of a non-nullable type:

```
fun main() {
    val x: String? = null
    var y: String = x
    // ERROR: Type mismatch:
    // inferred type is String? but String was expected
}
```

You can't pass a value of nullable type as an argument to a function having a non-nullable parameter:

```
fun main() {
    val x: String? = null
    strLen(x)
    // ERROR: Type mismatch:
    // inferred type is String? but String was expected
}
```

So what can you do with a value of nullable type? The most important thing is to compare it with `null`. And once you perform the comparison, the compiler remembers that and treats the value as non-nullable in the scope where the check has been performed. For example, the following code is perfectly valid.

Listing 7.1   Handling `null` values using `if` checks

```
fun strLenSafe(s: String?): Int =
    if (s != null) s.length else 0          ◁———    By adding the check for null,
                                                     the code now compiles.
fun main() {
    val x: String? = null
    println(strLenSafe(x))
    // 0
    println(strLenSafe("abc"))
    // 3
}
```

If using `if` checks was the only tool for tackling nullability, your code would become verbose fairly quickly. Fortunately, Kotlin provides a number of other tools to help deal with nullable values in a more concise manner. But before we look at those tools, let's spend some time discussing the meaning of *nullability* and what variable types are.

7.3   *Taking a closer look at the meaning of types*

Let's think about the most general questions: what are types, and why do variables have them? In 1976, David Parnas had already defined types as a set of possible values and a set of operations that can be performed on these values ("Abstract types defined as classes of variables," https://dl.acm.org/doi/10.1145/800237.807133).

Let's try to apply this definition to some of the Java types, starting with the `double` type. As you know, a `double` is a 64-bit floating-point number. You can perform standard mathematical operations on these values. All of those functions are equally applicable to all values of type `double`. Therefore, if you have a variable of type `double`, you can be certain that any operation on its value that's allowed by the compiler will execute successfully.

Now, let's contrast this with a variable of type `String`. In Java, such a variable can hold one of two kinds of values: an instance of the class `String` or `null`. Those kinds of values are completely unlike each other: even Java's own `instanceof` operator will tell you that `null` isn't a `String`. The operations that can be done on the value of the variable are also completely different: an actual `String` instance allows you to call any methods on the string, whereas a `null` value allows only a limited set of operations.

This means Java's type system isn't doing a good job in this case. Even though the variable has a declared type—`String`—you don't know what you can do with values of this variable unless you perform additional checks. Often, you skip those checks because you know from the general flow of data in your program that a value can't be `null` at a certain point. Sometimes you're wrong, and your program then crashes with a `NullPointerException`.

Other ways to cope with NullPointerException errors

Java has some tools to help solve the problem of `NullPointerException`. For example, some people use annotations (e.g., `@Nullable` and `@NotNull`) to express the nullability of values. There are tools (e.g., IntelliJ IDEA's built-in code inspections) that can use these annotations to detect places where a `NullPointerException` can be thrown. But such tools aren't part of the standard Java compilation process, so it's hard to ensure they're applied consistently. It's also difficult to annotate the entire codebase, including the libraries used by the project, so that all possible error locations can be detected. Our own experience at JetBrains shows that even widespread use of nullability annotations in Java doesn't completely solve the problem of NPEs.

Another path to solving this problem is to never use `null` values in code and to use a special wrapper type, such as the `Optional` type introduced in Java 8, to represent values that may or may not be defined. This approach has several downsides: the code gets more verbose, the extra wrapper instances affect performance at run time, and it's not used consistently across the entire ecosystem. Even if you do use `Optional` everywhere in your own code, you'll still need to deal with `null` values returned from methods of the JDK, the Android framework, and other third-party libraries.

Nullable types in Kotlin provide a comprehensive solution to this problem. Distinguishing nullable and non-nullable types provides a clear understanding of what operations are allowed on the value and what operations can lead to exceptions at run time and are therefore forbidden.

> **NOTE** Objects of nullable or non-nullable types at run time are the same; a nullable type isn't a wrapper for a non-null type. Besides some automatically generated intrinsic checks (https://kotlinlang.org/docs/java-to-kotlin-nullability-guide.html#support-for-nullable-types), which have very little performance impact, working with nullable types in Kotlin has essentially no run-time overhead.

Now, let's see how to work with nullable types in Kotlin and why dealing with them is by no means annoying. We'll start with the special operator for safely accessing a nullable value.

7.4 Combining null checks and method calls with the safe call operator: ?.

One of the most useful tools in Kotlin's arsenal is the *safe-call* operator: `?.`. This operator allows you to combine a `null` check and a method call into a single operation. For example, the expression str?.uppercase() is equivalent to the following, more cumbersome one: if (str != null) str.uppercase() else null.

In other words, if the value on which you're trying to call the method isn't null, the method call is executed normally. If it's null, the call is skipped, and null is used as the value instead. Figure 7.2 illustrates this.

Figure 7.2   The safe-call operator calls methods only on non-null values. If the value happens to be null, no call is made, and null is returned directly. This allows you to safely call methods without having to write a null check by hand.

Note that the result type of such an invocation is nullable. Although String.uppercase returns a value of type String, the result type of an expression s?.uppercase() when s is nullable will be String?:

```
fun printAllCaps(str: String?) {
    val allCaps: String? = str?.uppercase()      ⊲———— allCaps may be null.
    println(allCaps)
}

fun main() {
    printAllCaps("abc")
    // ABC
    printAllCaps(null)
    // null
}
```

As shown in the following listing, safe calls can be used for accessing properties as well, not just for method calls. The following example shows a simple Kotlin class, Employee, with a nullable property, manager, and demonstrates the use of a safe-call operator for accessing that property in the managerName function.

Listing 7.2   Using safe calls to deal with nullable properties

```
class Employee(val name: String, val manager: Employee?)

fun managerName(employee: Employee): String? = employee.manager?.name

fun main() {
    val ceo = Employee("Da Boss", null)
    val developer = Employee("Bob Smith", ceo)
    println(managerName(developer))
    // Da Boss
```

```
    println(managerName(ceo))
    // null
}
```

If you have an object graph in which multiple properties have nullable types, it's often convenient to use multiple safe calls in the same expression. Say you store information about a person, their company, and the address of the company using different classes. Both the company and its address may be omitted. With the `?.` operator, you can access the `country` property for a `Person` in one line, without any additional checks.

Listing 7.3   Chaining multiple safe-call operators

```
class Address(val streetAddress: String, val zipCode: Int,
              val city: String, val country: String)

class Company(val name: String, val address: Address?)

class Person(val name: String, val company: Company?)

fun Person.countryName(): String {                          ◁── Several safe-call
    val country = this.company?.address?.country                 operators can
    return if (country != null) country else "Unknown"           be in a chain.
}

fun main() {
    val person = Person("Dmitry", null)
    println(person.countryName())
    // Unknown
}
```

Sequences of calls with `null` checks are a common sight in Java code, and you've now seen how Kotlin makes them more concise. But listing 7.3 contains unnecessary repetition: you're comparing a value to `null` and returning either that value or something else if it's `null`. Let's see how Kotlin can help eliminate that repetition.

7.5   Providing default values in null cases with the Elvis operator: ?:

Kotlin has a handy operator to provide default values instead of `null`; it's called the *Elvis operator* (or the *null-coalescing operator*, if you prefer more serious-sounding names). It looks like this: `?:` (you can visualize it being Elvis if you turn your head sideways). Here's how it's used:

```
fun greet(name: String?) {                          If name is null, recipient will
    val recipient: String = name ?: "unnamed"   ◁── be set to unnamed instead.
    println("Hello, $recipient!")
}
```

The operator takes two values, and its result is the first value if it isn't `null` or the second value if the first one is `null`. Figure 7.3 shows how it works.

Figure 7.3   The Elvis operator substitutes a specified value for `null`. This allows you to provide a default value, should the left-hand expression happen to be `null`.

The Elvis operator is often used together with the safe-call operator to substitute a value other than `null` when the object on which the method is called is `null`. Here's how you can use this pattern to simplify listing 7.1.

Listing 7.4   Using the Elvis operator to deal with `null` values

```
fun strLenSafe(s: String?): Int = s?.length ?: 0

fun main() {
    println(strLenSafe("abc"))
    // 3
    println(strLenSafe(null))
    // 0
}
```

The implementation of the `countryName` function from listing 7.3 now also fits in a single, elegant expression:

```
fun Person.countryName() = company?.address?.country ?: "Unknown"
```

What makes the Elvis operator particularly handy in Kotlin is that operations such as `return` and `throw` work as expressions and, therefore, can be used on the operator's right side. In that case, if the value on the left side is `null`, the function will immediately return a value or throw the exception you specified. This is helpful for checking preconditions in a function.

Let's see how you can use this operator to implement a function to print a shipping label with the person's company address. The next listing repeats the declarations of all the classes—in Kotlin, they're so concise that it's not a problem.

Listing 7.5   Using `throw` together with the Elvis operator

```
class Address(val streetAddress: String, val zipCode: Int,
              val city: String, val country: String)

class Company(val name: String, val address: Address?)

class Person(val name: String, val company: Company?)
```

```
fun printShippingLabel(person: Person) {
    val address = person.company?.address
        ?: throw IllegalArgumentException("No address")    ⟵——┐ Throws an exception if
    with (address) {                              ⟵————————————┐ the address is absent
        println(streetAddress)       address is non-null.
        println("$zipCode $city, $country")
    }
}

fun main() {
    val address = Address("Elsestr. 47", 80687, "Munich", "Germany")
    val jetbrains = Company("JetBrains", address)
    val person = Person("Dmitry", jetbrains)
    printShippingLabel(person)
    // Elsestr. 47
    // 80687 Munich, Germany
    printShippingLabel(Person("Alexey", null))
    // java.lang.IllegalArgumentException: No address
}
```

The function `printShippingLabel` prints a label if everything is correct. If there's no address, it doesn't just throw a `NullPointerException` with a line number but instead reports a meaningful error. If an address is present, the label consists of the street address, zip code, city, and country. Note how the `with` function, which you saw in section 5.4.1, is used to avoid repeating `address` four times in a row.

Now, you know the Kotlin way to perform "if not `null`" checks. Next, let's talk about the Kotlin-safe version of `instanceof` checks: the *safe-cast operator*, which often appears together with safe calls and Elvis operators.

7.6 *Safely casting values without throwing exceptions: as?*

In chapter 2, you saw the regular Kotlin operator for type casts: the `as` operator. Just like a regular Java type cast, `as` throws a `ClassCastException` if the value doesn't have the type you're trying to cast it to. Of course, you can combine it with an `is` check to ensure it does have the proper type. But as a safe and concise language, doesn't Kotlin provide a better solution? Indeed it does.

The `as?` operator tries to cast a value to the specified type and returns `null` if the value doesn't have the proper type. Figure 7.4 illustrates this.

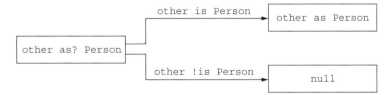

Figure 7.4   The safe-cast operator `as?` gives you the tools to safely work with the possibility that a cast may not succeed. It tries to cast a value to the given type and returns `null` if the type differs.

One common pattern of using a safe cast, shown in the following listing, is combining it with the Elvis operator. For example, this comes in handy for implementing the `equals` method.

Listing 7.6   Using a safe cast to implement `equals`

```
class Person(val firstName: String, val lastName: String) {
    override fun equals(other: Any?): Boolean {
        val otherPerson = other as? Person ?: return false

        return otherPerson.firstName == firstName &&
                otherPerson.lastName == lastName
    }

    override fun hashCode(): Int =
        firstName.hashCode() * 37 + lastName.hashCode()
}

fun main() {
    val p1 = Person("Dmitry", "Jemerov")
    val p2 = Person("Dmitry", "Jemerov")
    println(p1 == null)
    // false
    println(p1 == p2)
    // true
    println(p1.equals(42))
    // false
}
```

Checks the type and returns false if there is no match

After the safe cast, the variable otherPerson is smart cast to the Person type.

The == operator calls the equals method.

With this pattern, you can easily check whether the parameter has a proper type, cast it, and return `false` if the type isn't right—all in the same expression. Of course, smart casts also apply in this context: after you've checked the type and rejected `null` values, the compiler knows that the type of the `otherPerson` variable's value is `Person` and lets you use it accordingly.

The safe-call, safe-cast, and Elvis operators are useful and appear often in Kotlin code. But sometimes, you don't need Kotlin's support in handling `null` values; you just need to tell the compiler that the value is, in fact, not `null`. Let's see how you can achieve that.

7.7   *Making promises to the compiler with the non-null assertion operator: !!*

The *non-null assertion* is the simplest and bluntest tool Kotlin gives you for dealing with a value of nullable type. It's represented by a double exclamation mark and converts any value to a non-nullable type. For `null` values, an exception is thrown. The logic is illustrated in figure 7.5.

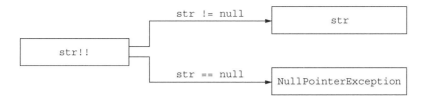

Figure 7.5   By using a non-null assertion, you don't have to explicitly handle your value being `null`. Instead, it throws an exception when encountering a `null` value.

Here's a trivial example of a function that uses the assertion to convert a nullable argument to a non-null one.

Listing 7.7   Using a non-null assertion

```
fun ignoreNulls(str: String?) {
    val strNotNull: String = str!!      ⊲─── The exception points to this line.
    println(strNotNull.length)
}

fun main() {
    ignoreNulls(null)
    // Exception in thread "main" java.lang.NullPointerException
    //   at <...>.ignoreNulls(07_NotnullAssertions.kt:2)
}
```

What happens if `str` is `null` in this function? Kotlin doesn't have much choice: it will throw an exception at run time. But note that the place where the exception is thrown is the assertion itself, not a subsequent line where you're trying to use the value. Essentially, you're telling the compiler, "I know the value isn't `null`, and I'm ready for an exception if it turns out I'm wrong."

> **NOTE** You may notice that the double exclamation mark looks a bit rude: it's almost like you're yelling at the compiler. This is intentional. The designers of Kotlin are trying to nudge you toward a better solution that doesn't involve making assertions that can't be verified by the compiler.

But there are situations where non-null assertions are the appropriate solution for a problem. When you check for `null` in one function and use the value in another function, the compiler can't recognize that the use is safe. If you're certain the check is always performed in another function, you may not want to duplicate it before using the value; then, you can use a non-null assertion instead.

This happens in practice with action classes, which you might encounter in UI frameworks. In an action class, there are separate methods for updating the state of an action (to enable or disable it) and for executing it. The checks performed in the `update` method ensure the `execute` method won't be called if the conditions aren't met, but there's no way for the compiler to recognize that.

Let's look at a hypothetical example of an action class that uses a non-null assertion in this situation. The `CopyRowAction` action, which operates on a `SelectableText-List`, is supposed to copy the value of the selected row in a list to the clipboard. We've omitted all the unnecessary details, keeping only the code responsible for checking whether any row was selected (meaning, therefore, the action can be performed) and obtaining the value for the selected row. We imply here that that `executeCopyRow` is called only when `isActionEnabled` is true. That also means that `list.selectedIndex` will never be `null` when `executeCopyRow` is invoked (even though the compiler doesn't know this).

Listing 7.8   Using a non-null assertion in an action class

```
class SelectableTextList(
    val contents: List<String>,
    var selectedIndex: Int? = null,
)

class CopyRowAction(val list: SelectableTextList) {
    fun isActionEnabled(): Boolean =
        list.selectedIndex != null
                                                    executeCopyRow is called only if
    fun executeCopyRow() {              ◁────────   isActionEnabled returns true.
        val index = list.selectedIndex!!
        val value = list.contents[index]
        // copy value to clipboard
    }
}
```

Note that if you don't want to use `!!` in this case, you can write `val index = list.selectedIndex ?: return` to obtain the index as a non-nullable type. If you use that pattern, a nullable value of `list.selectedIndex` will cause an early return from the function, so `value` will always be non-null. Although the non-null check using the Elvis operator is redundant here, it may be a good protection against `isActionEnabled` becoming more complicated later.

There's one more caveat to keep in mind: when you use `!!` and it results in an exception, the stack trace identifies the line number in which the exception was thrown but not a specific expression. To make it clear exactly which value was `null`, it's best to avoid using multiple `!!` assertions on the same line:

```
person.company!!.address!!.country        ◁────── Don't write code like this!
```

If you get an exception in this line, you won't be able to tell whether it was `company` or `address` that held a `null` value.

So far, we've discussed mostly how to *access* the values of nullable types. But what should you do if you need to pass a nullable value as an argument to a function that expects a non-nullable value? The compiler doesn't allow you to do that without a check because doing so is unsafe. The Kotlin language doesn't have any special support for this case, but there's a standard library function that can help you: `let`.

7.8   *Dealing with nullable expressions: The let function*

The `let` function makes it easier to deal with nullable expressions. Together with the safe-call operator, it allows you to evaluate an expression, check the result for `null`, and store the result in a variable, all in a single, concise expression.

One of its most common uses is handling a nullable argument that should be passed to a function that expects a non-nullable parameter. Let's say the function `sendEmailTo` takes one parameter of type `String` and sends an email to that address. This function is written in Kotlin and requires a non-nullable parameter:

```
fun sendEmailTo(email: String) { /*...*/ }
```

You can't pass a value of nullable type to this function:

```
fun main() {
    val email: String? = "foo@bar.com"
    sendEmailTo(email)
    //ERROR: Type mismatch: inferred type is String? but String was expected
}
```

You have to check explicitly whether this value isn't `null`:

```
if (email != null) sendEmailTo(email)
```

But you can go another way: use the `let` function, and call it via a safe call. All the `let` function does is turn the object on which it's called into a parameter of the lambda. In that way, it is similar to some of the other scope functions you got to know in section 5.4. However, if you combine it with the safe-call syntax, it effectively converts an object of nullable type on which you call `let` into one of non-nullable type (see figure 7.6).

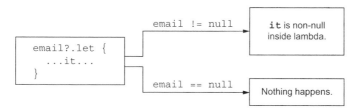

Figure 7.6   Together with the safe-call operator, `let` allows you to specify a lambda that is executed only if your expression isn't `null`. This is particularly useful when you are working with the result of a chain of expressions that happens to be nullable.

The `let` function will be called only if the email value is non-null, so you use the email as a non-nullable argument of the lambda:

```
email?.let { email -> sendEmailTo(email) }
```

Switching to the short syntax using the autogenerated name `it`, the result is much more concise: `email?.let { sendEmailTo(it) }`. Here's a more complete example that shows this pattern.

Listing 7.9   Using `let` to call a function with a non-nullable parameter

```
fun sendEmailTo(email: String) {
    println("Sending email to $email")
}

fun main() {
    var email: String? = "yole@example.com"
    email?.let { sendEmailTo(it) }
    // Sending email to yole@example.com
    email = null
    email?.let { sendEmailTo(it) }
}
```

Note that the `let` notation is especially convenient when you have to use the value of a longer expression if it's not `null`. You don't have to create a separate variable in this case. Compare this explicit `if` check

```
val person: Person? = getTheBestPersonInTheWorld()
if (person != null) sendEmailTo(person.email)
```

to the same code without an extra variable:

```
getTheBestPersonInTheWorld()?.let { sendEmailTo(it.email) }
```

This function returns `null`, so the code in the lambda will never be executed:

```
fun getTheBestPersonInTheWorld(): Person? = null
```

When you need to check multiple values for `null`, you can use nested `let` calls to handle them. But in most cases, such code ends up fairly verbose and hard to follow. It's generally easier to use a regular `if` expression to check all the values together.

> **Comparing Kotlin's scope functions: When to use with, apply, let, run, and also**
>
> Over the last few chapters, you've taken a detailed look at multiple functions with very similar signatures: `with`, `apply`, `let`, `run`, and `also`.
>
> All of these *scope functions* execute a block of code in the context of an object. They differ in how you refer to the object in question from inside the lambda as well as their return value:

Function	Access to x via	Return value
x.let { … }	it	Result of lambda
x.also { … }	it	x
x.apply { … }	this	x
x.run { … }	this	Result of lambda
with(x) { … }	this	Result of lambda

Their differences are quite subtle. Thus, it's worth once again pointing out the tasks each of them is particularly suited for, so you can compare them side by side:

- Use let together with the safe call operator ?. to execute a block of code only when the object you are working with is not null. Use a standalone let to turn an expression into a variable, limited to the scope of its lambda.
- Use apply to configure properties of your object using a builder-style API (e.g., when creating an instance).
- Use also to execute additional actions that use your object, while passing the original object to further chained operations.
- Use with to group function calls on the same object, without having to repeat its name.
- Use run to configure an object *and* compute a custom result.

The usage of the different scope functions differs mainly in the details, so you might find yourself in a situation where more than one scope function seems like a good fit. For those cases, it makes sense to agree on conventions used in your team or for your project.

One other common situation is properties that are effectively non-nullable but can't be initialized with a non-null value in the constructor. Let's see how Kotlin allows you to deal with that situation.

7.9   Non-null types without immediate initialization: Late-initialized properties

Many frameworks initialize objects in dedicated methods called after the object instance has been created. For example, in Android, the activity initialization happens in the onCreate method. In JUnit, it is customary to put initialization logic in methods annotated with @BeforeAll or @BeforeEach.

But you can't leave a non-nullable property without an initializer in the constructor and only initialize it in a special method. Kotlin normally requires you to initialize all properties in the constructor, and if a property has a non-nullable type, you have to provide a non-null initializer value. If you can't provide that value, you have to use a nullable type instead. If you do that, every access to the property requires either a null check or the !! operator.

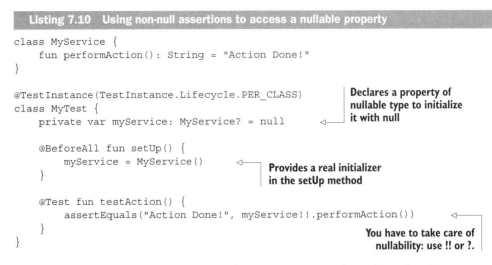

```
class MyService {
    fun performAction(): String = "Action Done!"
}

@TestInstance(TestInstance.Lifecycle.PER_CLASS)
class MyTest {
    private var myService: MyService? = null

    @BeforeAll fun setUp() {
        myService = MyService()
    }

    @Test fun testAction() {
        assertEquals("Action Done!", myService!!.performAction())
    }
}
```

Declares a property of
nullable type to initialize
it with null

Provides a real initializer
in the setUp method

You have to take care of
nullability: use !! or ?.

This looks ugly, especially if you access the property many times. To solve this, you can declare the `myService` property as *late initialized*. This is done by applying the `lateinit` modifier.

Listing 7.11   Using a late-initialized property

```
class MyService {
    fun performAction(): String = "Action Done!"
}

@TestInstance(TestInstance.Lifecycle.PER_CLASS)
class MyTest {
    private lateinit var myService: MyService

    @BeforeAll fun setUp() {
        myService = MyService()
    }

    @Test fun testAction() {
        assertEquals("Action Done!", myService.performAction())
    }
}
```

Declares a property of a
non-null type without an
initializer

Initializes the property in the
setUp method as before

Accesses the property
without extra null checks

Note that a late-initialized property is always a `var` because you need to be able to change its value outside of the constructor, and `val` properties are compiled into final fields that must be initialized in the constructor. But you no longer need to initialize it in a constructor, even though the property has a non-nullable type. If you access the property before it's been initialized, you get the following:

```
kotlin.UninitializedPropertyAccessException:
    lateinit property myService has not been initialized
```

It clearly identifies what has happened and is much easier to understand than a generic `NullPointerException` (figure 7.7).

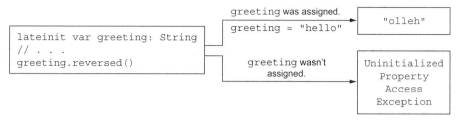

Figure 7.7 A `lateinit` property is has a non-nullable type but doesn't need to be assigned a value right away. It is your responsibility not to access the variable before it was assigned a value.

`lateinit` properties are commonly used in conjunction with Java dependency injection frameworks, like Google Guice. In that scenario, the values of `lateinit` properties are set externally by the framework. To ensure compatibility with a broad range of Java frameworks, Kotlin generates a field with the same visibility as the `lateinit` property. If the property is declared as `public`, the field will be `public` as well.

> **NOTE** The `lateinit` modifier isn't restricted to properties of classes. You can also specify local variables inside a function body or lambda, as well as top-level properties, to be late initialized.

Now, let's look at how you can extend Kotlin's set of tools for dealing with `null` values. You'll learn to do this by defining extension functions for nullable types.

7.10 *Extending types without the safe-call operator: Extensions for nullable types*

Defining extension functions for nullable types is one more powerful way to deal with `null` values. Rather than ensuring a variable can't be `null` before a method call, you can allow the calls with `null` as a receiver and deal with `null` in the function. This is only possible for extension functions; regular member calls are dispatched through the object instance and, therefore, can never be performed when the instance is `null`.

As an example, consider the functions `isEmpty` and `isBlank`, defined as extensions of `String` in the Kotlin standard library. The first one checks whether the string is an empty string `""`, and the second one checks whether it's empty or if it consists solely of whitespace characters. You'll generally use these functions to check that the string is nontrivial to do something meaningful with it. You may think it would be useful to handle `null` in the same way as trivial empty or blank strings. And indeed, you can do so: the functions `isNullOrEmpty` and `isNullOrBlank` can be called with a receiver of type `String?`.

Listing 7.12 Calling an extension function with a nullable receiver

```
fun verifyUserInput(input: String?) {
    if (input.isNullOrBlank()) {        ⟵── No safe call is needed.
```

```
        println("Please fill in the required fields")
    }
}

fun main() {
    verifyUserInput(" ")
    // Please fill in the required fields
    verifyUserInput(null)
    // Please fill in the required fields
}
```

> No exception happens when you call isNullOrBlank with null as a receiver.

You can call an extension function that was declared for a nullable receiver without safe access (see figure 7.8). The function handles possible `null` values.

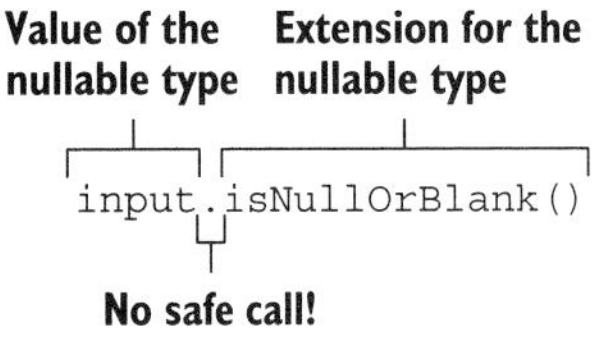

Value of the   **Extension for the**
nullable type   **nullable type**

```
input.isNullOrBlank()
```

No safe call!

Figure 7.8 **Extensions for nullable types know how to handle the `null` case for their receiver themselves. Therefore, they can be accessed without a safe call.**

The function `isNullOrBlank` checks explicitly for `null`, returning `true` in this case, and then calls `isBlank`, which can be called on a non-nullable `String` only:

```
fun String?.isNullOrBlank(): Boolean =        ◁── Extension for a nullable String
        this == null || this.isBlank()    ◁─
```
                                           │ A smart cast is applied to the second this.

When you declare an extension function for a nullable type (ending with `?`), you can call this function on nullable values; `this` in a function body can be `null`, so you have to check for that explicitly. In Java, `this` is always non-null because it references the instance of a class you're in. In Kotlin, that's no longer the case: in an extension function for a nullable type, `this` can be `null`.

Note that the `let` function we discussed earlier can be called on a nullable receiver as well, but it doesn't check whether the value is `null`. If you invoke it on a nullable type without using the safe-call operator, the lambda argument will also be nullable. This also means the passed block of code will always be executed, whether the value turns out to be `null` or not:

```
fun sendEmailTo(email: String) {
    println("Sending email to $email")
}

fun main() {
    val recipient: String? = null
    recipient.let { sendEmailTo(it) }    ◁─ No safe call, so it
    // ERROR: Type mismatch:                  has a nullable type
    // inferred type is String? but String was expected
}
```

Therefore, if you want to check the arguments for being non-null with `let`, you have to use the safe-call operator `?.`, as you saw earlier: `recipient?.let { sendEmailTo(it) }`.

> **NOTE**   When you define your own extension function, you need to consider whether you should define it as an extension for a nullable type. By default, define it as an extension for a non-nullable type. You can safely change it later (no code will be broken) if it turns out it's used mostly on nullable values, and the `null` value can be reasonably handled.

This section showed you something unexpected. If you dereference a variable without an extra check, as in `s.isNullOrBlank()`, it doesn't immediately mean the variable is non-null—the function can be an extension for a nullable type. Next, let's discuss another case that may surprise you: a type parameter can be nullable even without a question mark at the end.

7.11   *Nullability of type parameters*

By default, all generic type parameters of functions and classes in Kotlin are nullable. Any type, including a nullable type, can be substituted for a type parameter; in this case, declarations using the type parameter as a type are allowed to be `null`, even though the type parameter `T` doesn't end with a question mark. Consider the following example.

Listing 7.13   Dealing with a nullable type parameter

```
fun <T> printHashCode(t: T) {
    println(t?.hashCode())           ◁──┐  You have to use a safe call
}                                        │  because t might be null.

fun main() {
    printHashCode(null)       ◁─────  T is inferred as Any?.
    // null
}
```

In the `printHashCode` call, the inferred type for the type parameter `T` is a nullable type, `Any?`. Therefore, the parameter `t` is allowed to hold `null`, even without a question mark after `T`.

To make the type parameter non-nullable, you need to specify a non-nullable upper bound for it. That will reject a nullable value as an argument.

Listing 7.14   Declaring a non-nullable upper bound for a type parameter

```
fun <T: Any> printHashCode(t: T) {      ◁───  Now, T can't be nullable.
    println(t.hashCode())
}

fun main() {                            ┌  This code doesn't compile: you can't pass
    printHashCode(null)       ◁────┘  null because a non-null value is expected.
}
```

```
        // Error: Type parameter bound for `T` is not satisfied
        printHashCode(42)
        // 42
}
```

Section 11.1.4 covers generics in Kotlin in greater detail. Note that type parameters are the only exception to the rule that a question mark at the end is required to mark a type as nullable, and types without a question mark are non-nullable. The next section shows another special case of nullability: types that come from the Java code.

7.12   *Nullability and Java*

The previous discussion covered the tools for working with `null` values in the Kotlin world. But Kotlin prides itself on its Java interoperability, and you know that Java doesn't support nullability in its type system. So what happens when you combine Kotlin and Java? Do you lose all safety, or do you have to check every value for `null`? Or is there a better solution? Let's find out.

First, as we mentioned, sometimes, Java code contains information about nullability, expressed using annotations. When this information is present in the code, Kotlin uses it. Thus `@Nullable String` in Java is seen as `String?` by Kotlin, and `@NotNull String` is just `String` (see figure 7.9).

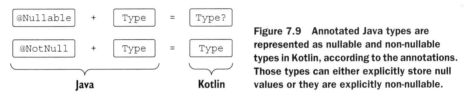

Figure 7.9   **Annotated Java types are represented as nullable and non-nullable types in Kotlin, according to the annotations. Those types can either explicitly store null values or they are explicitly non-nullable.**

Kotlin recognizes many different flavors of nullability annotations, including those from the JSR-305 standard (in the `javax.annotation` package), the Android ones (`android.support.annotation`), and those supported by JetBrains tools (`org.jetbrains.annotations`). The interesting question is what happens when the annotations aren't present. In that case, the Java type becomes a *platform type* in Kotlin.

7.12.1   *Platform types*

A *platform type* is essentially a type for which Kotlin doesn't have nullability information; you can work with it as either a nullable or non-nullable type (see figure 7.10). This means, just as in Java, you have full responsibility for the operations you perform with that type. The compiler will allow all operations. It also won't highlight any `null`-safe operations on such values as redundant, which it normally does when you perform a `null`-safe operation on a value of a non-nullable type. If you know the value can be `null`, you can

Figure 7.10   **Java types without special annotations are represented in Kotlin as platform types. You can choose to use them either as nullable or non-nullable types.**

compare it with `null` before use. If you know it's not `null`, you can use it directly. Just as in Java, you'll get a `NullPointerException` at the usage site if you get this wrong.

Let's say the `Person` class is declared in Java.

Listing 7.15 A Java class without nullability annotations

```
/* Java */
public class Person {
    private final String name;

    public Person(String name) {
        this.name = name;
    }

    public String getName() {
        return name;
    }
}
```

Can `getName` return `null` or not? The Kotlin compiler knows nothing about nullability of the `String` type in this case, so you have to deal with it yourself. If you're sure the name isn't `null`, you can dereference it in a usual way, as in Java, without additional checks. But be ready to get an exception in this case.

Listing 7.16 Accessing a Java class without `null` checks

```
fun yellAt(person: Person) {
    println(person.name.uppercase() + "!!!")      ◁──┐  The receiver person.name of
}                                                     │  the uppercase() call is null,
                                                      │  so an exception is thrown.
fun main() {
    yellAt(Person(null))
    // java.lang.NullPointerException: person.name must not be null
}
```

Your other option is to interpret the return type of `getName()` as nullable and access it safely.

Listing 7.17 Accessing a Java class with `null` checks

```
fun yellAtSafe(person: Person) {
    println((person.name ?: "Anyone").uppercase() + "!!!")
}

fun main() {
    yellAtSafe(Person(null))
    // ANYONE!!!
}
```

In this example, `null` values are handled properly, and no run-time exception is thrown.

Be careful while working with Java APIs. Most of the libraries aren't annotated, so you may interpret all the types as non-nullable, but that can lead to errors. To avoid errors, you should check the documentation (and, if needed, the implementation) of the Java methods you're using to find out when they can return `null` and add checks for those methods.

Why platform types?

Wouldn't it be safer for Kotlin to treat all values coming from Java as nullable? Such a design would be possible, but it would require a large number of redundant `null` checks for values that can never be `null` because the Kotlin compiler wouldn't be able to see that information.

The situation would be especially bad with generics—for example, every `Array-List<String>` coming from Java would be an `ArrayList<String?>?` in Kotlin, and you'd need to check values for `null` on every access or use a cast, which would defeat the safety benefits. Writing such checks is extremely annoying, so the designers of Kotlin went with the pragmatic option and allowed the developers to take responsibility for correctly handling values coming from Java.

You can't declare a variable of a platform type in Kotlin; these types can only come from Java code. But you may see them in error messages and in the IDE:

```
val i: Int = person.name
// ERROR: Type mismatch: inferred type is String! but Int was expected
```

The `String!` notation is how the Kotlin compiler and Kotlin IDEs, like IntelliJ IDEA and Android Studio, denote platform types coming from Java code (figure 7.11). You can't use this syntax in your own code, and usually, this exclamation mark isn't connected with the source of a problem, so you can usually ignore it. It just emphasizes that the nullability of the type is unknown.

```
fun main() {
    val s : String!  = p.name
}
```

Figure 7.11 When using type inference for a Java property, IntelliJ IDEA and Android Studio indicate that you are working with a platform type if inlay hints for Kotlin Types are enabled. The exclamation point allows you to spot these platform types at a glance.

As we said already, you may interpret platform types any way you like—as nullable or non-nullable—so both of the following declarations are valid:

```
val s: String? = person.name          ⟵——— Java's property can be seen as nullable ...
val s1: String = person.name          ⟵———
                                           └── ... or non-null.
```

In this case, just as with the method calls, you need to make sure you get the nullability right. If you try to assign a `null` value coming from Java to a non-nullable Kotlin variable, you'll get an exception at the point of assignment.

We've discussed how Java types are seen from Kotlin. Let's now talk about some pitfalls of creating mixed Kotlin and Java hierarchies.

7.12.2 Inheritance

When overriding a Java method in Kotlin, you have a choice of whether to declare the parameters and the return type as nullable or non-nullable. For example, let's look at a `StringProcessor` interface in Java.

Listing 7.18   A Java interface with a `String` parameter

```
/* Java */
interface StringProcessor {
    void process(String value);
}
```

In Kotlin, both of the following implementations will be accepted by the compiler.

Listing 7.19   Implementing the Java interface with different parameter nullability

```
class StringPrinter : StringProcessor {
    override fun process(value: String) {
        println(value)
    }
}

class NullableStringPrinter : StringProcessor {
    override fun process(value: String?) {
        if (value != null) {
            println(value)
        }
    }
}
```

Note that it's important to get nullability right when implementing methods from Java classes or interfaces. Because the implementation methods can be called from non-Kotlin code, the Kotlin compiler will generate non-null assertions for every parameter you declare with a non-nullable type. If the Java code does pass a `null` value to the method, the assertion will trigger, and you'll get an exception, even if you never access the parameter value in your implementation.

Let's summarize our discussion of nullability. We've discussed nullable and non-nullable types and the means of working with them: operators for safe operations (safe call `?.`, the Elvis operator `?:`, and safe cast `as?`) as well as the operator for unsafe dereference (the non-null assertion `!!`). You've seen how the library function `let` can help you accomplish concise non-null checks and how extensions for nullable types can help move a non-null check into a function. We've also discussed platform types that represent Java types in Kotlin.

Summary

- Kotlin's support of nullable types detects possible `NullPointerException` errors at compile time.
- Regular types are non-nullable by default unless they are explicitly marked as nullable. A question mark after a type name indicates it is nullable.
- Kotlin provides a variety of tools for dealing with nullable types concisely.
- Safe calls (`?.`) allow you to call methods and access properties on nullable objects.
- The Elvis operator (`?:`) makes it possible to provide a default value for an expression that may be `null`, return from execution, or throw an exception.
- You can use non-null assertions (`!!`) to promise the compiler that a given value is not `null` (but you will have to expect an exception if you break that promise).
- The `let` scope function turns the object on which it is called into the parameter for a lambda. Together with the safe-call operator, it effectively converts an object of nullable type into one of non-nullable type.
- The `as?` operator provides an easy way to cast a value to a type and handle the case in which it has a different type.

Basic types, collections, and arrays

This chapter covers

- Primitive and other basic types and their correspondence to the Java types
- Kotlin collections, arrays, and their nullability and interoperability stories

Beyond its support for nullability, Kotlin's type system has several essential features to improve the reliability of your code and implements many lessons learned from other type systems, including Java's. These decisions shape the way you work with everything in Kotlin code, from primitive values and basic types to the hierarchy of collections found in the Kotlin standard library. Kotlin introduces features such as *read-only collections* and refines or doesn't expose parts of the type system that have turned out to be problematic or unnecessary, such as first-class support for arrays. Let's take a closer look, starting with the basic building blocks.

8.1   *Primitive and other basic types*

This section describes the basic types used in programs, such as Int, Boolean, and Any. Unlike Java, Kotlin doesn't differentiate primitive types and wrappers. You'll shortly learn why and how it works under the hood. You'll see the correspondence between Kotlin types and such Java types as Object and Void, as well.

8.1.1   *Representing integers, floating-point numbers, characters, and Booleans with primitive types*

As you may know, Java makes a distinction between primitive types and reference types. A variable of a *primitive type* (such as int) holds its value directly. A variable of a *reference type* (such as String) holds a reference to the memory location containing the object.

Values of primitive types can be stored and passed around more efficiently, but you can't call methods on such values or store them in collections. Java provides special wrapper types (such as java.lang.Integer) that encapsulate primitive types in situations when an object is needed. Thus, to define a collection of integers, you can't write Collection<int>; you have to use Collection<Integer> instead.

Kotlin doesn't distinguish between primitive types and wrapper types. You always use the same type (e.g., Int):

```
val i: Int = 1
val list: List<Int> = listOf(1, 2, 3)
```

That's convenient. What's more, you can call methods on values of a number type. For example, consider this snippet, which uses the coerceIn standard library function to restrict the value to the specified range:

```
fun showProgress(progress: Int) {
    val percent = progress.coerceIn(0, 100)
    println("We're $percent % done!")
}

fun main() {
    showProgress(146)
    // We're 100 % done!
}
```

If primitive and reference types are the same, does that mean Kotlin represents all numbers as objects? Wouldn't that be terribly inefficient? Indeed it would, so Kotlin doesn't do that.

At run time, the number types are represented in the most efficient way possible. In most cases—for variables, properties, parameters, and return types—Kotlin's Int type is compiled to the Java primitive type int. The only case in which this isn't possible is generic classes, such as collections. A primitive type used as a type argument of a generic class is compiled to the corresponding Java wrapper type. For example, if the

`Int` type is used as a type argument of the collection, then the collection will store instances of `java.lang.Integer`, the corresponding wrapper type.

The full list of types that correspond to Java primitive types is as follows:

- *Integer types*—`Byte`, `Short`, `Int`, and `Long`
- *Floating-point number types*—`Float` and `Double`
- *Character type*—`Char`
- *Boolean type*—`Boolean`

8.1.2   *Using the full bit range to represent positive numbers: Unsigned number types*

There are situations when you need to utilize the full bit range of an integer number representing positive values—for example, when you're working on the bit-and-byte level, manipulating the pixels in a bitmap, the bytes in a file, or other binary data. In situations like these, Kotlin extends the regular primitive types on the Java virtual machine (JVM) with types for unsigned integer numbers. Specifically, there are four unsigned number types, shown in table 8.1.

Table 8.1   Unsigned number types in Kotlin

Type	Size	Value range
`UByte`	8 bit	`0 - 255`
`UShort`	16 bit	`0 - 65535`
`UInt`	32 bit	`0 - 2^32 - 1`
`ULong`	64 bit	`0- 2^64 - 1`

Unsigned number types "shift" the value range compared to their signed counterparts, allowing you to store larger non-negative numbers in the same amount of memory. A regular `Int`, for example, allows you to store numbers from roughly negative 2 billion to positive 2 billion. A `UInt`, on the other hand, can represent numbers between 0 and roughly 4 billion (you can see this in figure 8.1).

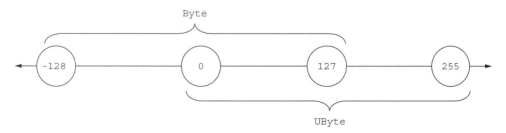

Figure 8.1   Unsigned number types shift the value range, allowing you to store larger non-negative numbers in the same amount of memory. Where a regular, signed `Byte` can store values between `-128` and `127`, a `UByte` can store values between `0` and `255`.

Like other primitive types, unsigned numbers in Kotlin are only wrapped when required. Otherwise, they have the performance characteristics of primitive types.

> **NOTE** It may be tempting to use unsigned integers in situations where you want to express that non-negative integers are required. However, that's not the goal of Kotlin's unsigned number types. In cases where you don't explicitly need the full bit range, you are generally better served with regular integers and checking that a non-negative value was passed to your function.

Unsigned number types: Implementation details

If you take a look at the JVM specification (http://mng.bz/nJa4), you'll notice that the JVM itself does not specify or provide primitives for unsigned numbers. Kotlin can't change that, so it provides its own abstractions on top of the existing signed primitives.

It does so using a concept you learned about in section 4.5: inline classes. Each class representing an unsigned number is actually an inline class, which uses its signed counterpart as storage. That's right: under the hood, your `UInt` is just a regular `Int`. Because the Kotlin compiler takes care of replacing inline classes by the underlying property they wrap wherever possible, you can expect unsigned number types to perform equally to signed number types.

The Kotlin compiler can easily convert a type like `Int` to the corresponding primitive type on the JVM because both types are capable of representing the same set of values (and neither can store a `null` reference). Likewise, when you use a Java declaration from Kotlin, Java primitive types become non-nullable types (not platform types) because they can't hold `null` values. Now, let's discuss the nullable versions of the same types.

8.1.3   *Nullable primitive types: Int?, Boolean?, and more*

Nullable types in Kotlin can't be represented by Java primitive types because `null` can only be stored in a variable of a Java reference type. That means whenever you use a nullable version of a primitive type in Kotlin, it's compiled to the corresponding wrapper type.

To see the nullable types in use, let's go back to the opening example of the book and recall the `Person` class declared there. The class represents a person whose name is always known and whose age can be either known or unspecified. Let's add a function that checks whether one person is older than another.

Listing 8.1   Using nullable primitive types

```
data class Person(val name: String,
                  val age: Int? = null) {

    fun isOlderThan(other: Person): Boolean? {
        if (age == null || other.age == null)
            return null
        return age > other.age
```

```
    }
}
fun main() {
    println(Person("Sam", 35).isOlderThan(Person("Amy", 42)))
    // false
    println(Person("Sam", 35).isOlderThan(Person("Jane")))
    // null
}
```

Note how the regular nullability rules apply here. You can't just compare two values of type `Int?` because one of them may be `null`. Instead, you have to check that both values aren't `null`. After that, the compiler allows you to work with them normally.

The value of the `age` property declared in the class `Person` is stored as a `java.lang.Integer`. But this detail only matters if you're working with the class from Java. To choose the right type in Kotlin, you only need to consider whether `null` is a possible value for the variable or property.

As mentioned earlier, generic classes are another case when wrapper types come into play. If you use a primitive type as a type argument of a class, Kotlin uses the boxed representation of the type. For example, this creates a list of boxed `Integer` values, even though you've never specified a nullable type or used a `null` value:

```
val listOfInts = listOf(1, 2, 3)
```

This happens because of the way generics are implemented on the JVM. The JVM currently doesn't support using a primitive type as a type argument, so a generic class (both in Java and in Kotlin) must always use a boxed representation of the type. As a consequence, if you need to efficiently store large collections of primitive types, you must either use a third-party library that provides support for such collections, like Eclipse Collections (https://github.com/eclipse/eclipse-collections), or store them in arrays. We'll discuss arrays in detail at the end of this chapter. Now, let's look at how you can convert values between different primitive types.

8.1.4   *Kotlin makes number conversions explicit*

One important difference between Kotlin and Java is the way they handle numeric conversions. Kotlin doesn't automatically convert numbers from one type to another, even when the type you're assigning your value to is larger and could comfortably hold the value you're trying to assign. For example, the following code won't compile in Kotlin:

```
val i = 1
val l: Long = i          ⟵——— Error: type mismatch
```

Instead, you need to apply the conversion explicitly:

```
val i = 1
val l: Long = i.toLong()
```

Conversion functions are defined for every primitive type (except `Boolean`): `toByte()`, `toShort()`, `toChar()`, and so on. The functions support converting in both directions: extending a smaller type to a larger one, like `Int.toLong()`, and truncating a larger type to a smaller one, like `Long.toInt()`.

Kotlin makes the conversion explicit to avoid surprises, especially when comparing boxed values. The `equals` method for two boxed values checks the box type, not just the value stored in it. Thus, in Java, `Integer.valueOf(42).equals(Long.valueOf(42))` returns `false`. If Kotlin supported implicit conversions, you could write something like this:

```
val x = 1                              ◁──────┐ Int variable
val list = listOf(1L, 2L, 3L)          ◁────── List of Long values
x in list                              ◁──────┐
                                              │ False if Kotlin supported implicit conversions
```

This would evaluate to `false`, contrary to expectations. Thus, the line `x in list` from this example doesn't compile. Kotlin requires you to convert the types explicitly so that only values of the same type are compared:

```
fun main() {
    val x = 1
    println(x.toLong() in listOf(1L, 2L, 3L))
    // true
}
```

If you use different number types in your code at the same time, you must convert variables explicitly to avoid unexpected behavior.

Primitive type literals

Kotlin supports the following ways to write number literals in source code, in addition to simple decimal numbers:

- Literals of type `Long` use the `L` suffix: `123L`.
- Literals of type `Double` use the standard representation of floating-point numbers: `0.12`, `2.0`, `1.2e10`, and `1.2e-10`.
- Literals of type `Float` use the `f` or `F` suffix: `123.4f`, `.456F`, and `1e3f`.
- Hexadecimal literals use the `0x` or `0X` prefix (e.g., `0xCAFEBABE` or `0xbcdL`).
- Binary literals use the `0b` or `0B` prefix (e.g., `0b000000101`).
- Unsigned number literals use the `U` suffix: `123U`, `123UL`, and `0x10cU`.

For character literals, you use mostly the same syntax as in Java. You write the character in single quotes, and you can also use escape sequences if you need to. The following are examples of valid Kotlin character literals: `'1'`, `'\t'` (the tab character), and `'\u0009'` (the tab character represented using a Unicode escape sequence).

Note that when you're writing a number literal, you usually don't need to use conversion functions. One possibility is to use the special syntax to mark the type of the constant explicitly, such as `42L` or `42.0f`. And even if you don't use it, the necessary conversion is applied automatically if you use a number literal to initialize a variable of a known type or pass it as an argument to a function. In addition, arithmetic operators are overloaded to accept all appropriate numeric types. For example, the following code works correctly without any explicit conversions:

```
fun printALong(l: Long) = println(l)

fun main() {
    val b: Byte = 1           ◁─── Constant value gets the correct type.
    val l = b + 1L            ◁──── + works with Byte and Long arguments.
    printALong(42)     ◁──
    // 42                       The compiler interprets 42 as a Long value.
}
```

Note that the behavior of Kotlin arithmetic operators with regard to number-range overflow and underflow is exactly the same in Java; Kotlin doesn't introduce any extra overflow checks:

```
fun main() {
    println(Int.MAX_VALUE + 1)       An overflow causes the value to
    -2147483648                  ◁─  wrap around to the minimum ...
    println(Int.MIN_VALUE - 1)
    2147483647                  ◁──── ... and an underflow to the maximum.
}
```

Conversion from String

The Kotlin standard library provides a set of extension functions to convert a string into a primitive type: `toInt`, `toByte`, `toBoolean`, and so on. Each of these functions tries to parse the contents of the string as the corresponding type and throws a `NumberFormatException` if the parsing fails:

```
fun main() {
    println("42".toInt())
    // 42
}
```

However, if you're expecting the conversion from string to primitive type to fail often, it can be cumbersome to always handle the `NumberFormatException` explicitly. For this case, each of these extension functions also comes with a counterpart that returns `null` if the conversion fails: `toIntOrNull`, `toByteOrNull`, and so on:

```
fun main() {
    println("seven".toIntOrNull())
    // null
}
```

A special case is the conversion of strings to Boolean values. These conversion functions are defined on a nullable receiver, as introduced in chapter 7.

(continued)

The `toBoolean` function returns `true` if the string it is called on is not `null`, and its content is equal to the word *true* (ignoring capitalization). Otherwise, it returns `false`:

```
fun main() {
    println("trUE".toBoolean())
    // true
    println("7".toBoolean())
    // false
    println(null.toBoolean())
    // false
}
```

For exact matches on the strings `"true"` and `"false"` during conversion, use the `toBooleanStrict` function, which only accepts these two values and throws an exception otherwise.

Before we move on to other types, there are three more special types we need to mention: `Any`, `Unit`, and `Nothing`.

8.1.5   *Any and Any?: The root of the Kotlin type hierarchy*

Similar to how `Object` is the root of the class hierarchy in Java, the `Any` type is the supertype of all non-nullable types in Kotlin. But in Java, `Object` is a supertype of all reference types only, and primitive types aren't part of the hierarchy. That means you have to use wrapper types such as `java.lang.Integer` to represent a primitive type value when `Object` is required. In Kotlin, `Any` is a supertype of all types, including the primitive types, such as `Int`.

Just as in Java, assigning a value of a primitive type to a variable of type `Any` performs automatic boxing:

```
val answer: Any = 42        ⟵——— The value 42 is boxed because Any is a reference type.
```

Note that `Any` is a non-nullable type, so a variable of the type `Any` can't hold the value `null`. If you need a variable that can hold any possible value in Kotlin, including `null`, you must use the `Any?` type.

Under the hood, the `Any` type corresponds to `java.lang.Object`. The `Object` type used in parameters and return types of Java methods is seen as `Any` in Kotlin. (More specifically, it's viewed as a platform type because its nullability is unknown.) When a Kotlin function uses `Any`, it's compiled to `Object` in the Java bytecode.

As you saw in chapter 4, all Kotlin classes have the following three methods: `toString`, `equals`, and `hashCode`. These methods are inherited from `Any`. Other methods defined on `java.lang.Object` (e.g., `wait` and `notify`) aren't available on `Any`, but you can call them if you manually cast the value to `java.lang.Object`.

8.1.6   *The Unit type: Kotlin's void*

The Unit type in Kotlin fulfills the same function as void in Java. It can be used as a return type of a function that has nothing interesting to return:

```
fun f(): Unit { /* ... */ }
```

Syntactically, it's the same as writing a function with a block body without a type declaration:

```
fun f() { /* ... */ }        ◁——— Explicit Unit declaration is omitted.
```

In most cases, you won't notice the difference between void and Unit. If your Kotlin function has the Unit return type and doesn't override a generic function, it's compiled to a good-old void function under the hood. If you override it from Java, the Java function just needs to return void.

What distinguishes Kotlin's Unit from Java's void, then? Unit is a full-fledged type, and unlike void, it can be used as a type argument. Only one value of this type exists; it's also called Unit and is returned *implicitly*. This is useful when you override a function that returns a generic parameter and make it return a value of the Unit type:

```
interface Processor<T> {
    fun process(): T
}

class NoResultProcessor : Processor<Unit> {        │ Returns Unit, but you omit
    override fun process() {                      ◁─┘ the type specification
        // do stuff
    }                         ◁——— You don't need an explicit return here.
}
```

The signature of the interface requires the process function to return a value, and because the Unit type does have a value, it's no problem to return it from the method. But you don't need to write an explicit return statement in NoResultProcessor.process because return Unit is added implicitly by the compiler.

Contrast this with Java, where neither of the possibilities for solving the problem of using "no value" as a type argument are as nice as the Kotlin solution. One option is to use separate interfaces (e.g., Callable and Runnable) to represent interfaces that don't and do return a value. The other is to use the special java.lang.Void type as the type parameter. If you use the second option, you still need to put in an explicit return null; to return the only possible value matching that type because if the return type isn't void, you must always have an explicit return statement.

You may wonder why we chose a different name for Unit and didn't call it Void. The name Unit is used traditionally in functional languages to mean "only one instance," and that's exactly what distinguishes Kotlin's Unit from Java's void. We could have used the customary Void name, but Kotlin has a type called Nothing that performs an entirely different function. Having two types called `Void` and `Nothing` would be confusing because their meanings are so close. So what's this `Nothing` type about? Let's find out.

8.1.7 *The Nothing type: "This function never returns"*

For some functions in Kotlin, the concept of a "return value" doesn't make sense because they never complete successfully. For example, many testing libraries have a function called `fail` that fails the current test by throwing an exception with a specified message. A function that has an infinite loop in it will also never complete successfully.

When analyzing code that calls such a function, it's useful to know that the function will never terminate normally. To express that, Kotlin uses a special return type called `Nothing`:

```
fun fail(message: String): Nothing {
    throw IllegalStateException(message)
}

fun main() {
    fail("Error occurred")
    // java.lang.IllegalStateException: Error occurred
}
```

The `Nothing` type doesn't have any values, so it only makes sense to use it as a function return type or as a type argument for a type parameter that's used as a generic function return type. In all other cases, declaring a variable where you can't store any value doesn't make sense.

Note that functions returning `Nothing` can be used on the right side of the Elvis operator to perform precondition checking:

```
val address = company.address ?: fail("No address")
println(address.city)
```

This example shows why having `Nothing` in the type system is extremely useful. The compiler knows that a function with this return type never terminates normally and uses that information when analyzing the code calling the function. In the previous example, the compiler infers that the type of `address` is non-null because the branch handling the case when it's `null` always throws an exception and won't continue the execution of the code that follows. The Kotlin standard library also has such a function built in: the `error` function throws an `IllegalStateException`, and it's return type is `Nothing`.

We've finished our discussion of the basic types in Kotlin: primitive types, `Any`, `Unit`, and `Nothing`. Now, let's look at the collection types and how they differ from their Java counterparts.

8.2   Collections and arrays

You've already seen many examples of code that uses various collection APIs, and as discussed in section 3.1, Kotlin builds on the Java collections library and augments it with features added through extension functions. There's more to the story of the collection support in Kotlin and the correspondence between Java and Kotlin collections, and now is a good time to look at the details.

8.2.1   Collections of nullable values and nullable collections

In chapter 7, we discussed the concept of nullable types, but we only briefly touched on nullability of type arguments. But this is essential for a consistent type system: it's no less important to know whether a collection can hold `null` values than to know whether the value of a variable can be `null`. The good news is that Kotlin fully supports nullability for type arguments. Just as the type of a variable can have a ? character appended to indicate that the variable can hold `null`, a type used as a type argument can be marked in the same way. To see how this works, let's look at an example of a function that takes an input text and tries to parse each line in the input string as a number.

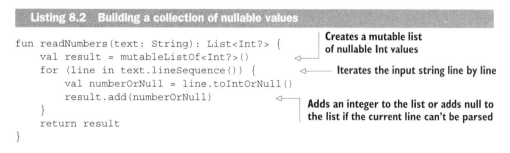

Listing 8.2   Building a collection of nullable values

```
fun readNumbers(text: String): List<Int?> {
    val result = mutableListOf<Int?>()          ← Creates a mutable list of nullable Int values
    for (line in text.lineSequence()) {         ← Iterates the input string line by line
        val numberOrNull = line.toIntOrNull()
        result.add(numberOrNull)                 ← Adds an integer to the list or adds null to the list if the current line can't be parsed
    }
    return result
}
```

`List<Int?>` is a list that can hold values of type `Int?`—in other words, `Int` or `null`. You add an integer to the `result` list if the line can be parsed or `null` otherwise.

Note how the nullability of the type of the variable itself is distinct from the nullability of the type used as a type argument. The difference between a list of nullable `Int`s and a nullable list of `Int`s is illustrated in figure 8.2.

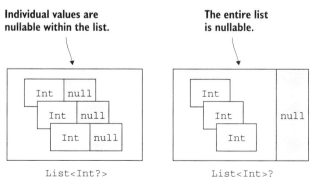

Individual values are nullable within the list.

The entire list is nullable.

List<Int?>   List<Int>?

Figure 8.2   Carefully consider how you intend to use your collection when thinking about nullability. Should the whole collection itself be nullable, or should individual elements inside the collection be nullable?

In the first case, the list itself is always non-null, but each value in the list can be `null`. A variable of the second type may contain a `null` reference instead of a list instance, but the elements in the list are guaranteed to be non-null.

By the way, given our knowledge of functional programming and lambdas, we can actually shrink this example by using the `map` function, which we first saw in chapter 6. It applies a given function—in this case, `toIntOrNull`—to each element in the input sequence, which we can then collect in a result list.

Listing 8.3   Shortening the `readNumbers` method with `map`

```
fun readNumbers2(text: String): List<Int?> =
    text.lineSequence().map { it.toIntOrNull() }.toList()
```

You may also find yourself in a situation where you would like to declare a variable that holds a nullable list of nullable numbers. This allows you to express that individual elements in the list can be absent but also that the list as a whole may be absent. The Kotlin way to write this is `List<Int?>?`, with two question marks (illustrated in figure 8.3). The inner question mark specifies that the *elements* of the list are nullable. The outer question mark specifies that the *list itself* is nullable. You need to apply `null` checks both when using the value of the variable as well as when using the value of every element in the list.

To see how you can work with a list of nullable values, let's write a function to add all the valid numbers together and count the invalid numbers separately.

The entire list and its individual values are nullable.

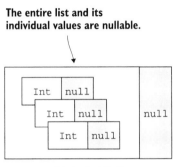

List<Int?>?

Figure 8.3   A nullable collection of nullable integers can be `null` itself or store elements that are potentially `null`.

Listing 8.4   Working with a collection of nullable values

```
fun addValidNumbers(numbers: List<Int?>) {
    var sumOfValidNumbers = 0
    var invalidNumbers = 0
    for (number in numbers) {                    Reads a nullable value from the list
        if (number != null) {                    Checks the value for null
            sumOfValidNumbers += number
        } else {
            invalidNumbers++
        }
    }
    println("Sum of valid numbers: $sumOfValidNumbers")
    println("Invalid numbers: $invalidNumbers")
}

fun main() {
    val input = """
```

```
        1
        abc
        42
    """.trimIndent()                    ◁─── Defines a multiline input string
    val numbers = readNumbers(input)
    addValidNumbers(numbers)
    // Sum of valid numbers: 43
    // Invalid numbers: 1
}
```

There isn't much special going on here. When you access an element of the list, you get back a value of type Int?, and you need to check it for null before you can use it in arithmetic operations.

Taking a collection of nullable values and filtering out null is such a common operation that Kotlin provides a standard library function filterNotNull to perform it. Here's how you can use it to greatly simplify the previous example.

Listing 8.5 Using `filterNotNull` with a collection of nullable values

```
fun addValidNumbers(numbers: List<Int?>) {
    val validNumbers = numbers.filterNotNull()
    println("Sum of valid numbers: ${validNumbers.sum()}")
    println("Invalid numbers: ${numbers.size - validNumbers.size}")
}
```

Of course, the filtering also affects the type of the collection. The type of validNumbers is List<Int> because the filtering ensures the collection doesn't contain any null elements (you can see this in figure 8.4).

Figure 8.4 The `filterNotNull` function returns a new collection with all the `null` elements from the input collection removed. This new collection is also of non-nullable type, meaning you won't have to do any further `null` handling down the line.

Now you understand how Kotlin distinguishes between collections that hold nullable and non-null elements. In the next section, let's look at another major distinction introduced by Kotlin: read-only versus mutable collections.

8.2.2 *Read-only and mutable collections*

An important trait that sets apart Kotlin's collection design from Java's is that it separates the interfaces for accessing the data in a collection and for modifying the data. This distinction exists, starting with the most basic interface for working with collections: kotlin.collections.Collection. Using this interface, you can iterate over the elements in a collection, obtain its size, check whether it contains a certain element, and perform other operations that read data from the collection. But this interface doesn't have any methods for adding or removing elements.

To modify the data in the collection, use the `kotlin.collections.MutableCollection` interface. It extends the regular `kotlin.collections.Collection` and provides methods for adding and removing the elements, clearing the collection, and so on. Figure 8.5 shows the key methods defined in the two interfaces.

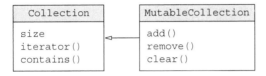

Figure 8.5   The `Collections` interface is read-only. `MutableCollection` extends it and adds methods to modify a collection's contents.

As a general rule, you should use read-only interfaces everywhere in your code. Use the mutable variants only if the code will modify the collection.

Just like the separation between `val` and `var`, the separation between read-only and mutable interfaces for collections makes it much easier to understand what's happening with data in your program. If a function takes a parameter that is a `Collection` but not a `MutableCollection`, you know it's not going to modify the collection but only read data from it. And if a function requires you to pass a `MutableCollection`, you can assume it will modify the data. If you have a collection that's part of the internal state of your component, you may need to make a copy of that collection before passing it to such a function. (This pattern is usually called a *defensive copy*.) For example, you can clearly see that the following `copyElements` function will modify the target collection but not the source collection.

Listing 8.6   Using read-only and mutable collection interfaces

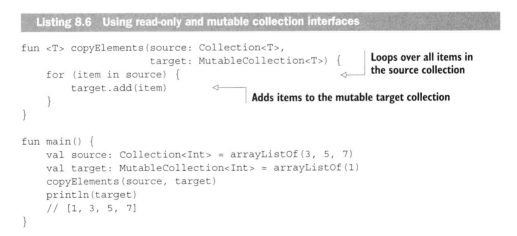

```kotlin
fun <T> copyElements(source: Collection<T>,
                     target: MutableCollection<T>) {        Loops over all items in
    for (item in source) {                                  the source collection
        target.add(item)
    }                              Adds items to the mutable target collection
}

fun main() {
    val source: Collection<Int> = arrayListOf(3, 5, 7)
    val target: MutableCollection<Int> = arrayListOf(1)
    copyElements(source, target)
    println(target)
    // [1, 3, 5, 7]
}
```

You can't pass a variable of a read-only collection type as the `target` argument, even if its value is a mutable collection:

```
fun main() {
    val source: Collection<Int> = arrayListOf(3, 5, 7)
    val target: Collection<Int> = arrayListOf(1)
    copyElements(source, target)          ◁—————  Error on the target argument
    // Error: Type mismatch: inferred type is Collection<Int>
    // but MutableCollection<Int> was expected
}
```

A key idea to keep in mind when working with collection interfaces is that *read-only collections aren't necessarily immutable*. If you're working with a variable that has a read-only interface type, this can be just one of the many references to the same collection. Other references can have a mutable interface type, as illustrated in figure 8.6.

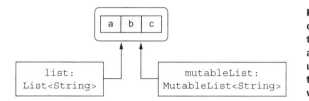

Figure 8.6   Two different references, one read only and one mutable, pointing to the same collection object. Code accessing `list` can't change the underlying collection but may still have to deal with changes done by code working with the `mutableList`.

If one part of your code holds a reference to the collection that is mutable, then another part of your code holding a read-only "view" on that same collection can't rely on the assumption that the collection isn't modified by the first part simultaneously. When the collection is modified while your code is working on it, it may lead to ConcurrentModificationException errors and other problems.

Therefore, it's essential to understand that *read-only collections aren't always thread safe*: what your function may receive as a "view" on a collection may actually be a mutable collection under the hood. So if you're working with data in a multithreaded environment, you need to ensure that your code properly synchronizes access to the data or uses data structures that support concurrent access.

> **NOTE** While immutable collections aren't available in the standard library, the kotlinx.collections.immutable library (https://github.com/Kotlin/kotlinx.collections.immutable) provides immutable collection interfaces and implementation prototypes for Kotlin.

How does the separation between read-only and mutable collections work? Didn't we say earlier that Kotlin collections are the same as Java collections? Isn't there a contradiction? Let's see what really happens here.

8.2.3   Kotlin collections and Java collections are deeply related

It's true that every Kotlin collection is an instance of the corresponding Java collection interface. No conversion is involved when moving between Kotlin and Java; there's no need for wrappers or copying data. But every Java collection interface has two *representations* in Kotlin: a read-only one and a mutable one, as you can see in figure 8.7.

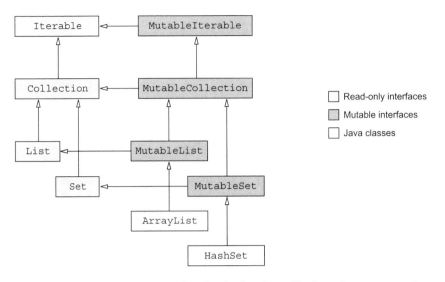

Figure 8.7   The hierarchy of the Kotlin collection interfaces. The Java classes `ArrayList` and `HashSet`, among others, extend Kotlin mutable interfaces.

All collection interfaces shown in figure 8.7 are declared in Kotlin. The basic structure of the Kotlin read-only and mutable interfaces is parallel to the structure of the Java collection interfaces in the `java.util` package. In addition, each mutable interface extends the corresponding read-only interface. Mutable interfaces correspond directly to the interfaces in the `java.util` package, whereas the read-only versions lack all the mutating methods.

Figure 8.7 also contains the Java classes `java.util.ArrayList` and `java.util.HashSet` to show how Java standard classes are treated in Kotlin. Kotlin sees them as if they inherited from the Kotlin's `MutableList` and `MutableSet` interfaces, respectively. Other implementations from the Java collection library (`LinkedList`, `SortedSet`, and so on) aren't presented here, but from the Kotlin perspective, they have similar supertypes. This way, you get both compatibility and clear separation of mutable and read-only interfaces.

In addition to the collections, the `Map` class (which doesn't extend `Collection` or `Iterable`) is also represented in Kotlin as two distinct versions: `Map` and `MutableMap`. Table 8.2 shows the functions you can use to create collections of different types.

Table 8.2   Collection-creation functions

Collection type	Read-only	Mutable
List	listOf, List	mutableListOf, MutableList, arrayListOf, buildList
Set	setOf	mutableSetOf, hashSetOf, linkedSetOf, sortedSetOf, buildSet
Map	mapOf	mutableMapOf, hashMapOf, linkedMapOf, sortedMapOf, buildMap

Note that `setOf()` and `mapOf()` return instances of the `Set` and `Map` read-only interfaces but that are mutable *under the hood*. (On the JVM, collections can be wrapped in a call to `Collections.unmodifiable` to make changes impossible. However, since this introduces indirection overhead, Kotlin doesn't do this for your collections automatically.) But you shouldn't rely on that: it's possible that a future version of Kotlin will use truly immutable implementation classes as return values of `setOf` and `mapOf`.

When you need to call a Java method and pass a collection as an argument, you can do so directly without any extra steps. For example, if you have a Java method that takes a `java.util.Collection` as a parameter, you can pass any `Collection` or `Mutable-Collection` value as an argument to that parameter.

This has important consequences with regard to mutability of collections. Because Java doesn't distinguish between read-only and mutable collections, Java code *can modify the collection*, even if it's declared as a read-only `Collection` on the Kotlin side. The Kotlin compiler can't fully analyze what's being done to the collection in the Java code, and therefore, there's no way for Kotlin to reject a call passing a read-only `Collection` to Java code that modifies it. For example, the following two snippets of code form a compilable cross-language Kotlin–Java program:

```java
/* Java */
// CollectionUtils.java
public class CollectionUtils {
    public static List<String> uppercaseAll(List<String> items) {
        for (int i = 0; i < items.size(); i++) {
            items.set(i, items.get(i).toUpperCase());
        }
        return items;
    }
}
```

```kotlin
// Kotlin
// collections.kt
fun printInUppercase(list: List<String>) {          ← Declares a read-only parameter
    println(CollectionUtils.uppercaseAll(list))      ← Calls a Java function that
    println(list.first())                            ← modifies the collection
}                                                      Shows that the collection has been modified

fun main() {
    val list = listOf("a", "b", "c")
    printInUppercase(list)
    // [A, B, C]
    // A
}
```

Therefore, if you're writing a Kotlin function that takes a collection and passes it to Java, *it's your responsibility to use the correct type for the parameter*, depending on whether the Java code you're calling will modify the collection.

Note that this caveat also applies to collections with non-null element types. If you pass such a collection to a Java method, the method can put a `null` value into it; there's no way for Kotlin to forbid that or even to detect that it has happened without compromising performance. Because of that, you need to take special precautions when you pass collections to Java code that can modify them, to make sure the Kotlin types correctly reflect all the possible modifications to the collection. Now, let's take a closer look at how Kotlin deals with collections declared in Java code.

8.2.4 *Collections declared in Java are seen as platform types in Kotlin*

If you recall the discussion of nullability earlier in this chapter, you'll remember that types defined in Java code are seen as *platform types* in Kotlin. For platform types, Kotlin doesn't have the nullability information, so the compiler allows Kotlin code to treat them as either nullable or non-null. In the same way, variables of collection types declared in Java are also seen as platform types. A collection with a platform type is essentially a collection of unknown mutability—the Kotlin code can treat it as either read only or mutable. Usually, this doesn't matter, because in effect, all the operations you may want to perform just work.

The difference becomes important when you're overriding or implementing a Java method that has a collection type in its signature. Here, as with platform types for nullability, you need to decide which Kotlin type you're going to use to represent a Java type coming from the method you're overriding or implementing.

You need to make multiple choices in this situation, all of which will be reflected in the resulting parameter type in Kotlin:

- Is the collection nullable?
- Are the elements in the collection nullable?
- Will your method modify the collection?

To see the difference, consider the following cases. In the first example, a Java interface represents an object that processes text in a file.

> **Listing 8.7   A Java interface with a collection parameter**

```
/* Java */
interface FileContentProcessor {
    void processContents(
        File path,
        byte[] binaryContents,
        List<String> textContents
    );
}
```

A Kotlin implementation of this interface needs to make the following choices:

- The list will be nullable because some files are binary and their contents can't be represented as text.
- The elements in the list will be non-nullable because lines in a file are never `null`.
- The list will be read only because it represents the contents of a file, and those contents aren't going to be modified.

Here's how this implementation looks.

Listing 8.8 Kotlin implementation of `FileContentProcessor`

```
class FileIndexer : FileContentProcessor {
    override fun processContents(
        path: File,
        binaryContents: ByteArray?,
        textContents: List<String>?
    ) {
        // ...
    }
}
```

Contrast this with another interface. Here, the implementations of the interface parse some data from a text form into a list of objects, append those objects to the output list, and report errors detected when parsing by adding the messages to a separate list.

Listing 8.9 Another Java interface with a collection parameter

```
/* Java */
interface DataParser<T> {
    void parseData(
        String input,
        List<T> output,
        List<String> errors
    );
}
```

The choices in this case are different:

- `List<String>` will be non-null because the callers always need to receive error messages.
- The elements in the list will be nullable because not every item in the output list will have an associated error message.
- `List<String>` will be mutable because the implementing code needs to add elements to it.

Here's how you can implement that interface in Kotlin.

Listing 8.10 Kotlin implementation of `DataParser`

```
class PersonParser : DataParser<Person> {
    override fun parseData(
        input: String,
        output: MutableList<Person>,
        errors: MutableList<String?>
    ) {
        // ...
    }
}
```

Note how the same Java type—`List<String>`—is represented by two different Kotlin types: a `List<String>?` (nullable list of strings) in one case and a `MutableList<String?>` (mutable list of nullable strings) in the other. To make these choices correctly, you must know the exact contract the Java interface or class needs to follow. This is usually easy to understand based on what your implementation needs to do.

Now that we've discussed collections, it's time to look at arrays. As we've mentioned before, you should prefer using collections to arrays by default. But because many Java APIs still use arrays, we'll cover how to work with them in Kotlin.

8.2.5   *Creating arrays of objects and primitive types for interoperability and performance reasons*

You have already encountered arrays quite early in your Kotlin journey because an array can be part of the signature of the Kotlin `main` function. Here's a reminder of how it looks.

Listing 8.11   Using arrays

```
fun main(args: Array<String>) {
    for (i in args.indices) {          ← Uses the array.indices extension property
        println("Argument $i is: ${args[i]}")     to iterate over the range of indices
    }                                  ← Accesses elements by
}                                        index with array[index]
```

An array in Kotlin is a class with a type parameter, and the element type is specified as the corresponding type argument.

To create an array in Kotlin, you have the following possibilities:

- The `arrayOf` function creates an array containing the elements specified as arguments to this function.
- The `arrayOfNulls` function creates an array of a given size containing `null` elements. Of course, it can only be used to create arrays where the element type is nullable.
- The `Array` constructor takes the size of the array and a lambda and initializes each array element by calling the lambda. This is how you can initialize an array with a non-null element type without passing each element explicitly.

As a simple example, here's how you can use the `Array` function to create an array of strings from `"a"` to `"z"`.

Listing 8.12   Creating an array of characters

```
fun main() {
    val letters = Array<String>(26) { i -> ('a' + i).toString() }
    println(letters.joinToString(""))
    // abcdefghijklmnopqrstuvwxyz
}
```

The lambda takes the index of the array element and returns the value to be placed in the array at that index. Here, you calculate the value by adding the index to the `'a'` character and converting the result to a string. The array element type is shown for clarity; you can omit it in real code because the compiler can infer it:

```
fun main() {
    val letters = Array(26) { i -> ('a' + i).toString() }
    println(letters.joinToString())
    // a, b, c, d, e, f, g, h, i, j
}
```

> **NOTE** This type of construction isn't actually exclusive to arrays. Kotlin also provides `List` and `MutableList` functions that instantiate their elements based on a size parameter and an initialization lambda.

Having said that, one of the most common cases for creating an array in Kotlin code is when you need to call a Java method that takes an array or a Kotlin function with a `vararg` parameter, as shown in the following listing. In those situations, you often have the data already stored in a collection, and you just need to convert it into an array. You can do this using the `toTypedArray` method.

Listing 8.13 Passing a collection to a `vararg` method

```
fun main() {
    val strings = listOf("a", "b", "c")
    println("%s/%s/%s".format(*strings.toTypedArray()))
    // a/b/c
}
```
The spread operator (*) is used to pass an array when vararg parameters are expected.

As with other types, type arguments of array types always become object types. Therefore, if you declare something like an `Array<Int>`, it will become an array of boxed integers (its Java type will be `java.lang.Integer[]`). If you need to create an array of values of a primitive type without boxing, you must use one of the specialized classes for arrays of primitive types.

To represent arrays of primitive types, Kotlin provides a number of separate classes—one for each primitive type. For example, an array of values of type `Int` is called `IntArray`. For other types, Kotlin provides `ByteArray`, `CharArray`, `BooleanArray`, and so on. All of these types are compiled to regular Java primitive type arrays, such as `int[]`, `byte[]`, `char[]`, and so on. Therefore, values in such an array are stored without boxing, in the most efficient manner possible.

> **NOTE** Just like other number type arrays that prevent boxing, Kotlin also allows you to create arrays of unsigned types, such as `UByteArray`, `UShortArray`, `UIntArray`, and `ULongArray`. At the time of writing, unsigned arrays and operations on them are not yet stable.

To create an array of a primitive type, you have the following options:

- The constructor of the type takes a `size` parameter and returns an array initialized with default values for the corresponding primitive type (usually zeros).
- The factory function (`intArrayOf` for `IntArray` and so on for other array types) takes a variable number of values as arguments and creates an array holding those values.
- Another constructor takes a size and a lambda used to initialize each element.

Here's how the first two options work for creating an integer array holding five zeros:

```
val fiveZeros = IntArray(5)
val fiveZerosToo = intArrayOf(0, 0, 0, 0, 0)
```

Here's how you can use the constructor accepting a lambda:

```
fun main() {
    val squares = IntArray(5) { i -> (i+1) * (i+1) }
    println(squares.joinToString())
    // 1, 4, 9, 16, 25
}
```

Alternatively, if you have an array or a collection holding boxed values of a primitive type, you can convert them to an array of that primitive type using the corresponding conversion function, such as `toIntArray`.

Next, let's look at some of the things you can do with arrays. In addition to the basic operations (getting the array's length and getting and setting elements), the Kotlin standard library supports the same set of extension functions for arrays as for collections. All the functions you saw in chapter 6 (`filter`, `map`, and so on) work for arrays as well, including the arrays of primitive types. (Note that the return values of these functions are lists, not arrays.)

Let's see how to rewrite listing 8.11 using the `forEachIndexed` function and a lambda. The lambda passed to that function is called for each element of the array and receives two arguments: the index of the element and the element itself.

Listing 8.14   Using `forEachIndexed` with an array

```
fun main(args: Array<String>) {
    args.forEachIndexed { index, element ->
        println("Argument $index is: $element")
    }
}
```

Now, you know how to use arrays in your code. Working with them is as simple as working with collections in Kotlin.

Summary

- Types representing basic numbers (e.g., `Int`) look and function like regular classes but are usually compiled to Java primitive types. Kotlin's unsigned number classes, which don't have an exact equivalent on the JVM, are transformed via inline classes to behave and perform like primitive types.

- Nullable primitive types (e.g., `Int?`) correspond to boxed primitive types in Java (e.g., `java.lang.Integer`).

- The `Any` type is a supertype of all other types and is analogous to Java's `Object`. `Unit` is an analogue of `void`.

- The `Nothing` type is used as a return type of functions that don't terminate normally.

- Types coming from Java are interpreted as platform types in Kotlin, allowing the developer to treat them as either nullable or non-null.

- Kotlin uses the standard Java classes for collections and enhances them with a distinction between read-only and mutable collections.

- You must carefully consider nullability and mutability of parameters when you extend Java classes or implement Java interfaces in Kotlin.

- You can use arrays in Kotlin, but it's generally recommended to prefer collections by default.

- Kotlin's `Array` class looks like a regular generic class but is compiled to a Java array.

- Arrays of primitive types are represented by special classes, such as `IntArray`.

Part 2

Embracing Kotlin

By now, you should be very familiar with using Kotlin to access existing APIs. In this part of the book, you'll learn how to build your own APIs in Kotlin. It's important to remember that building APIs isn't restricted to library authors: every time you have two interacting classes in your program, one of them provides an API to the other.

In chapter 9, you'll learn about the principle of *conventions*, which are used in Kotlin to implement operator overloading and other abstraction techniques such as delegated properties. Chapter 10 takes a closer look at lambdas, and you'll see how you can declare your own functions that take lambdas as parameters. You'll become familiar with Kotlin's take on some more advanced concepts, such as generics (chapter 11) and annotations and reflection (chapter 12). Also in chapter 12, you'll study a fairly large real-world Kotlin project: JKid, a JSON serialization and deserialization library. And finally, in chapter 13, you'll reach one of Kotlin's crown jewels: its support for building domain-specific languages.

Operator overloading and other conventions

9

This chapter covers

- Operator overloading
- Conventions: special named functions supporting various operations
- Delegated properties

Kotlin has a number of features where specific language constructs are implemented by calling functions that you define in your own code. You already may be familiar with these types of constructs from Java, where objects that implement the `java.lang.Iterable` interface can be used in `for` loops and objects that implement the `java.lang.AutoCloseable` interface can be used in try-with-resources statements.

In Kotlin, such features are tied to functions with specific names (and not bound to some special interfaces in the standard library, like they are in Java). For example, if your class defines a special method named `plus`, then by convention, you can use the + operator on instances of this class. Because of that, in Kotlin, we refer to this technique as *conventions*. In this chapter, we'll look at different conventions supported by Kotlin and how they can be used.

235

Kotlin uses the principle of conventions, instead of relying on types as Java does, because this allows developers to adapt existing Java classes to the requirements of Kotlin language features. Kotlin code can't modify third-party classes so that they would implement additional interfaces. On the other hand, defining new methods for a class is possible through the mechanism of extension functions. You can define any convention methods as extensions and thereby adapt any existing Java class without modifying its code.

As a running example in this chapter, we'll use a simple `Point` class, representing a point on a screen. Such classes are available in most UI frameworks, and you can easily adapt the definitions shown here to your environment:

```
data class Point(val x: Int, val y: Int)
```

Let's begin by defining some arithmetic operators on the `Point` class.

9.1   Overloading arithmetic operators makes operations for arbitrary classes more convenient

The most straightforward example of the use of conventions in Kotlin is arithmetic operators. In Java, the full set of arithmetic operations can be used only with primitive types, and additionally, the `+` operator can be used with `String` values. But these operations could be convenient in other cases as well. For example, if you're working with numbers through the `BigInteger` class, it would be more elegant to sum them using `+` than to call the `add` method explicitly. To add an element to a collection, you may want to use the `+=` operator. Kotlin allows you to do that, and in this section, we'll show you how it works.

9.1.1   Plus, times, divide, and more: Overloading binary arithmetic operations

The first operation you'll support is adding two points together. This operation sums up the points' x- and y-coordinates. Here's how you can implement it.

Listing 9.1   Defining the `plus` operator

```kotlin
data class Point(val x: Int, val y: Int) {
    operator fun plus(other: Point): Point {       ◁──  Defines an operator
        return Point(x + other.x, y + other.y)           function named plus
    }                                              ◁──
}                                                        Adds the coordinates
                                                         and returns a new point

fun main() {
    val p1 = Point(10, 20)
    val p2 = Point(30, 40)
    println(p1 + p2)        ◁──── Calls the plus function using the + sign
    // Point(x=40, y=60)
}
```

Note how you use the `operator` keyword to declare the `plus` function. All functions used to overload operators need to be marked with that keyword. This makes it explicit that you intend to use the function as an implementation of the corresponding convention and that you didn't define a function that accidentally had a matching name.

After you declare the `plus` function with the `operator` modifier, you can sum up your objects using just the + sign. Under the hood, the `plus` function is referred to, as shown in figure 9.1.

Figure 9.1 The + operator is transformed into a `plus` function call.

As an alternative to declaring the operator as a member, you can define the operator as an extension function.

Listing 9.2 Defining an operator as an extension function

```kotlin
operator fun Point.plus(other: Point): Point {
    return Point(x + other.x, y + other.y)
}
```

The implementation is exactly the same. Future examples will use the extension function syntax because it's a common pattern to define convention extension functions for external library classes, and the same syntax will work nicely for your own classes as well.

Compared to some other languages, defining and using overloaded operators in Kotlin is simpler because you can't define your own operators. For cases in which you want to be able to use a function between two operands (i.e., `a myOp b`), Kotlin offers *infix functions*, which were covered in section 3.4 and you will revisit again in section 13.4.1. These allow you to use the main syntax benefit of custom operators—having operands on each side of the function call—without introducing arbitrary symbol combinations whose meaning you will have to painstakingly remember.

Kotlin has a limited set of operators you can overload, and each one corresponds to the name of the function you need to define in your class. Table 9.1 lists all the binary operators you can define and the corresponding function names.

Table 9.1 Overloadable binary arithmetic operators

Expression	Function name
a * b	times
a / b	div
a % b	mod
a + b	plus
a - b	minus

Operators for your own types always use the same precedence as the standard numeric types. For example, if you write `a + b * c`, the multiplication will always be executed before the addition, even if you've defined those operators yourself. The operators *, /, and % have the same precedence, which is higher than the precedence of the + and - operators.

Operator functions and Java

Kotlin operators are easy to call from Java: because every overloaded operator is defined as a Kotlin function (with the `operator` modifier), you call them as regular functions using the full name. When you call Java from Kotlin, you can use the operator syntax for any methods with names matching the Kotlin conventions. Because Java doesn't define any syntax for marking operator functions, the requirement to use the `operator` modifier doesn't apply, and the matching name and number of parameters are the only constraints. If a Java class defines a method with the behavior you need but gives it a different name, you can define an extension function with the correct name that would delegate to the existing Java method.

When you define an operator, you don't need to use the same types for the two operands. For example, let's define an operator that will allow you to scale a point by a certain number. You can use it to translate points between different coordinate systems.

Listing 9.3   Defining an operator with different operand types

```
operator fun Point.times(scale: Double): Point {
    return Point((x * scale).toInt(), (y * scale).toInt())
}

fun main() {
    val p = Point(10, 20)
    println(p * 1.5)
    // Point(x=15, y=30)
}
```

Note that Kotlin operators don't automatically support *commutativity* (the ability to swap the left and right sides of an operator). If you want users to be able to write `1.5 * p` in addition to `p * 1.5`, you need to define a separate operator for that: `operator fun Double.times(p: Point): Point`.

The return type of an operator function can also be different from either of the operand types. For example, you can define an operator to create a string by repeating a character a number of times.

Listing 9.4   Defining an operator with a different return type

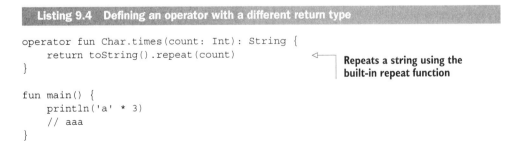

```
operator fun Char.times(count: Int): String {
    return toString().repeat(count)
}

fun main() {
    println('a' * 3)
    // aaa
}
```

Repeats a string using the built-in repeat function

This operator takes a `Char` as the left operand and an `Int` as the right operand and has `String` as the result type. Such combinations of operand and result types are perfectly acceptable.

Note that you can overload `operator` functions like regular functions: you can define multiple methods with different parameter types for the same method name.

No special operators for bitwise operations

Kotlin doesn't define any bitwise operators for standard number types (both signed and unsigned, as you have gotten to know in section 8.1); consequently, it doesn't allow you to define them for your own types. Instead, it uses regular functions supporting the infix call syntax, which you saw in section 3.4. You can define similar functions that work with your own types.

Here's the full list of functions provided by Kotlin for performing bitwise operations:

- `shl`—Signed shift left
- `shr`—Signed shift right
- `ushr`—Unsigned shift right
- `and`—Bitwise and
- `or`—Bitwise or
- `xor`—Bitwise xor
- `inv`—Bitwise inversion

The following example demonstrates the use of some of these functions:

```
fun main() {
    println(0x0F and 0xF0)
    // 0
    println(0x0F or 0xF0)
    // 255
    println(0x1 shl 4)
    // 16
}
```

Now, let's discuss the operators like `+=` that merge two actions: assignment and the corresponding arithmetic operator.

9.1.2 *Applying an operation and immediately assigning its value: Overloading compound assignment operators*

Normally, when you define an operator such as `plus`, as you've done in section 9.1.1, Kotlin supports not only the + operation but += as well. Operators such as +=, -=, and so on are called *compound assignment operators.* Here's an example:

```
fun main() {
    var point = Point(1, 2)
    point += Point(3, 4)
    println(point)
    // Point(x=4, y=6)
}
```

This is the same as writing `point = point + Point(3, 4)`. Of course, that works only if the `point` variable is mutable.

In some cases, it makes sense to define the `+=` operation that would modify an object referenced by the variable on which it's used, but not reassign the reference. One such case is adding an element to a mutable collection:

```
fun main() {
    val numbers = mutableListOf<Int>()
    numbers += 42
    println(numbers[0])
    // 42
}
```

If you define a function named `plusAssign` with the `Unit` return type and mark it with the `operator` keyword, Kotlin will call it when the `+=` operator is used. Other binary arithmetic operators have similarly named counterparts: `minusAssign`, `timesAssign`, and so on.

The Kotlin standard library defines a function `plusAssign` on a mutable collection, and the previous example uses it (`+=`):

```
operator fun <T> MutableCollection<T>.plusAssign(element: T) {
    this.add(element)
}
```

When you write `+=` in your code, theoretically, both `plus` and `plusAssign` functions can be called (see figure 9.2). If this is the case and both functions are defined and applicable, the compiler reports an error. One possibility to resolve it is replacing your use of the operator with a regular function call. Another is to replace a `var` with a `val`, so that the `plusAssign` operation becomes inapplicable. But in general, it's best to design new classes consistently: try not to add both `plus` and `plusAssign` operations at the same time. If your class is immutable, like `Point` in one of the earlier examples, you should provide only operations that return a new value (such as `plus`). If you design a mutable class, like a builder, provide only `plusAssign` and similar operations.

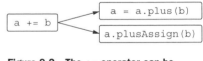
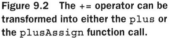

Figure 9.2   The `+=` operator can be transformed into either the `plus` or the `plusAssign` function call.

The Kotlin standard library supports both approaches for collections. The `+` and `-` operators always return a new collection. The `+=` and `-=` operators work on mutable collections by modifying them in place, and on read-only collections by returning a modified copy. (This means `+=` and `-=` can only be used with a read-only collection if the variable referencing it is declared as a `var`.) As operands of those operators, you can use either individual elements or other collections with a matching element type:

```
fun main() {
    val list = mutableListOf(1, 2)
    list += 3                          ⟵——— += changes list.
```

```
    val newList = list + listOf(4, 5)
    println(list)
    // [1, 2, 3]
    println(newList)
    // [1, 2, 3, 4, 5]
}
```

⟵┐ **+ returns a new list containing
   all the elements.**

So far, we've discussed overloading of *binary* operators—operators that are applied to two values, such as `a + b`. In addition, Kotlin allows you to overload *unary* operators, which are applied to a single value, as in `-a`.

9.1.3   *Operators with only one operand: Overloading unary operators*

The procedure for overloading a unary operator is the same as you saw previously: declare a function (member or extension) with a predefined name, and then mark it with the modifier `operator`. Let's look at an example.

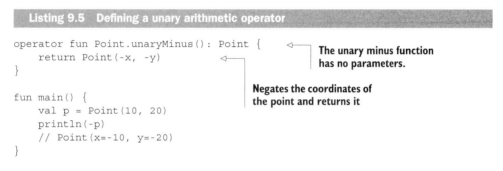

Listing 9.5   Defining a unary arithmetic operator

```
operator fun Point.unaryMinus(): Point {
    return Point(-x, -y)
}

fun main() {
    val p = Point(10, 20)
    println(-p)
    // Point(x=-10, y=-20)
}
```

⟵ **The unary minus function
   has no parameters.**

**Negates the coordinates of
the point and returns it**

Functions used to overload unary operators don't take any arguments. As shown in figure 9.3, the unary plus operator works the same way. Table 9.2 lists all the unary operators you can overload.

**Figure 9.3   The unary + operator
is transformed into a `unaryPlus`
function call.**

Table 9.2   Overloadable unary arithmetic operators

Expression	Function name
+a	unaryPlus
-a	unaryMinus
!a	not
++a, a++	inc
--a, a--	dec

When you define the `inc` and `dec` functions to overload increment and decrement operators, the compiler automatically supports the same semantics for pre- and post-increment operators as for the regular number types. Consider the following example, which overloads the ++ operator for the BigDecimal class from the Java standard library.

Listing 9.6   Defining an increment operator

```
import java.math.BigDecimal

operator fun BigDecimal.inc() = this + BigDecimal.ONE

fun main() {
    var bd = BigDecimal.ZERO          Increments after the first
    println(bd++)          ◁——┘       println statement executes
    // 0
    println(bd)
    // 1                     Increments before the second
    println(++bd)    ◁——┘    println statement executes
    // 2
}
```

The postfix operation ++ first returns the current value of the bd variable and after that increases it, whereas the prefix operation works the other way round. The printed values are the same as you'd see if you used a variable of type Int, and you didn't need to do anything special to support this.

9.2   *Overloading comparison operators makes it easy to check relationships between objects*

Just as with arithmetic operators, Kotlin lets you use comparison operators (==, !=, >, <, and so on) with any object, not just with primitive types. Instead of calling equals or compareTo, as in Java, you can use comparison operators directly, which is intuitive and concise. In this section, we'll look at the conventions used to support these operators.

9.2.1   *Equality operators: equals (==)*

We touched on the topic of equality in chapter 4. You saw that using the == operator in Kotlin is translated into a call of the equals method. This is just one more application of the principle of conventions we've been discussing.

Using the != operator is also translated into a call of equals, with the obvious difference that the result is inverted. Note that unlike all other operators, == and != can be used with nullable operands because those operators check equality to null under the hood. The comparison a == b checks whether a isn't null, and if it's not, calls a.equals(b) (see figure 9.4). Otherwise, the result is true only if both arguments are null references.

```
a == b  ——▶  a?.equals(b) ?: (b == null)
```

Figure 9.4   An equality check == is transformed into an equals call and a null check.

For the `Point` class, the implementation of `equals` is automatically generated by the compiler because you've marked it as a `data` class (section 4.3.2 explained the details). But if you did implement it manually, here's what the code could look like (note that a full implementation should also provide a `hashCode` implementation; we've omitted it here for brevity).

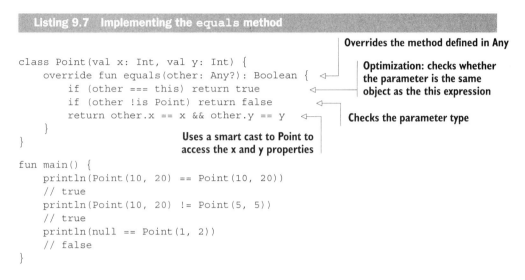

Listing 9.7   Implementing the `equals` method

```kotlin
class Point(val x: Int, val y: Int) {
    override fun equals(other: Any?): Boolean {
        if (other === this) return true
        if (other !is Point) return false
        return other.x == x && other.y == y
    }
}
fun main() {
    println(Point(10, 20) == Point(10, 20))
    // true
    println(Point(10, 20) != Point(5, 5))
    // true
    println(null == Point(1, 2))
    // false
}
```

Overrides the method defined in Any

Optimization: checks whether the parameter is the same object as the this expression

Checks the parameter type

Uses a smart cast to Point to access the x and y properties

You use the *identity equals* operator (`===`) to check whether the parameter to `equals` is the same object as the one on which `equals` is called. The identity equals operator does exactly the same thing as the `==` operator in Java: it checks that both of its arguments reference the same object (or have the same value if they have a primitive type). Using this operator is a common optimization when implementing `equals`. Note that the `===` operator can't be overloaded.

The `equals` function is marked as `override` because, unlike other conventions, the method implementing it is defined in the `Any` class (equality comparison is supported for all objects in Kotlin). That also explains why you don't need to mark it as `operator`: the base method in `Any` is marked as such, and the `operator` modifier on a method applies also to all methods that implement or override it. Also note that `equals` can't be implemented as an extension because the implementation inherited from the `Any` class would always take precedence over the extension.

Listing 9.7 also shows that using the `!=` operator is also translated into a call of the `equals` method. The compiler automatically negates the return value, so you don't need to do anything for this to work correctly.

What about other comparison operators?

9.2.2 *Ordering operators: compareTo (<, >, ?, and >=)*

In Java, classes can implement the `Comparable` interface in order to be used in algorithms that compare values, such as finding a maximum or sorting. The `compareTo` method defined in that interface is used to determine whether one object is larger than another. But in Java, there's no shorthand syntax for calling this method. Only values of primitive types can be compared using `<` and `>`; all other types require you to write `element1.compareTo(element2)` explicitly.

Kotlin supports the same `Comparable` interface. But the `compareTo` method defined in that interface can be called by convention and uses of comparison operators (`<`, `>`, `?`, and `>=`) are translated into calls of `compareTo`, as shown in figure 9.5. The return type of `compareTo` has to be `Int`. The expression `p1 < p2` is equivalent to `p1.compareTo(p2) < 0`. Other comparison operators work exactly the same way.

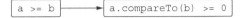

Figure 9.5   A comparison of two objects is transformed into a comparison of the result of the `compareTo` call with zero.

Because there's no obviously right way to compare two-dimensional points with one another, let's use the good-old `Person` class to show how the method can be implemented. The implementation will use address book ordering (compare by last name, and then, if the last name is the same, compare by first name).

Listing 9.8   Implementing the `compareTo` method

```kotlin
class Person(
        val firstName: String, val lastName: String
) : Comparable<Person> {

    override fun compareTo(other: Person): Int {
        return compareValuesBy(this, other,
            Person::lastName, Person::firstName)
    }
}

fun main() {
    val p1 = Person("Alice", "Smith")
    val p2 = Person("Bob", "Johnson")
    println(p1 < p2)
    // false
}
```

Evaluates the given function or property references in order and compares values

In this case, you implement the `Comparable` interface so that the `Person` objects can be compared not only by Kotlin code but also by Java functions, such as the functions used to sort collections. Just as with `equals`, the `operator` modifier is applied to the function in the base interface, so you don't need to repeat the keyword when you override the function.

Note that you can use the `compareValuesBy` function from the Kotlin standard library to implement the `compareTo` method easily and concisely. This function receives a list of selector functions that calculate values to be compared. The function calls each selector in order for both objects and compares the return values. If the values are different, it returns the result of the comparison. If they're the same, it proceeds to the next selector function, or returns 0 if there are no more functions to call. These selectors can be passed as lambdas or, as you do here, as property references.

Note, however, that a direct implementation comparing fields by hand would be faster, although it would contain more code. As always, you should prefer the concise version and worry about performance only if you know the implementation will be called frequently.

All classes that implement the `Comparable` interface can be compared in Kotlin using the concise operator syntax. That also includes `String`, for example:

```
fun main() {
    println("abc" < "bac")
    // true
}
```

You don't need to add any extensions to make that work.

9.3   *Conventions used for collections and ranges*

Some of the most common operations for working with collections are getting and setting elements by index as well as checking whether an element belongs to a collection. All of these operations are supported via operator syntax: to get or set an element by index, you use the syntax `a[b]` (called the *indexed access operator*). The `in` operator can be used to check whether an element is in a collection or range and also to iterate over a collection. You can add those operations for your own classes that act as collections. Let's now look at the conventions used to support those operations.

9.3.1   *Accessing elements by index: The get and set conventions*

You already know that in Kotlin, you can access the elements in a map similarly to how you access arrays in Java—via square brackets:

```
val value = map[key]
```

You can use the same operator to change the value for a key in a mutable map:

```
mutableMap[key] = newValue
```

Now, it's time to see how this works. In Kotlin, the indexed access operator is one more convention. Reading an element using the indexed access operator is translated into a call of the `get` operator method, and writing an element becomes a call to `set`. The methods are already defined for the `Map` and `MutableMap` interfaces. Let's see how to add similar methods to your own class.

You'll allow the use of square brackets to reference the coordinates of the point: `p[0]` to access the x coordinate and `p[1]` to access the y coordinate. Here's how to implement and use them.

Listing 9.9   Implementing the `get` convention

```
operator fun Point.get(index: Int): Int {      ⟵── Defines an operator function named get
    return when(index) {
        0 -> x                 ⟵┐  Gets the coordinate corresponding
        1 -> y                   │  to the given index
        else ->
            throw IndexOutOfBoundsException("Invalid coordinate $index")
    }
}

fun main() {
    val p = Point(10, 20)
    println(p[1])
    // 20
}
```

All you need to do is define a function named `get` and mark it as `operator`. Once you do that, expressions like `p[1]`, where `p` has type `Point`, will be translated into calls to the `get` method.

Note that the parameter of `get` can be any type, not just `Int`. For example, when you use the indexing operator on a map, the parameter type is the key type of the map, which can be an arbitrary type. You can also define a `get` method with multiple parameters. For example, if you're implementing a class to represent a two-dimensional array or matrix, you can define a method, such as `operator fun get(rowIndex: Int, colIndex: Int)`, and call it as `matrix[row, col]`, as shown in figure 9.6. You can define multiple overloaded `get` methods with different parameter types if your collection can be accessed with different key types.

```
x[a, b] ──────▶ x.get(a, b)
```

Figure 9.6   Access via square brackets is transformed into a `get` function call.

In a similar way, you can define a function that lets you change the value at a given index using the bracket syntax. The `Point` class is immutable, so it doesn't make sense to define such a method for `Point`. Let's define another class to represent a mutable point and use that as an example.

Listing 9.10   Implementing the `set` convention

```
data class MutablePoint(var x: Int, var y: Int)
                                                              ⟵┐ Defines an operator
operator fun MutablePoint.set(index: Int, value: Int) {   ⟵──┘ function named set
    when(index) {
        0 -> x = value         ⟵┐  Changes the coordinate corresponding
        1 -> y = value           │  to the specified index
        else ->
            throw IndexOutOfBoundsException("Invalid coordinate $index")
    }
}

fun main() {
```

```
        val p = MutablePoint(10, 20)
        p[1] = 42
        println(p)
        // MutablePoint(x=10, y=42)
}
```

This example is also simple: to allow the use of the indexed access operator in assignments, you just need to define a function named `set`. The last parameter to `set` receives the value used on the right side of the assignment, and the other arguments (in the case of `Point`, only the `index`) are taken from the indices used inside the brackets. The general form of this is visualized in figure 9.7.

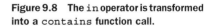

Figure 9.7   Assignment through square brackets is transformed into a `set` function call.

9.3.2   Checking whether an object belongs to a collection: The `in` convention

One other operator supported by collections is the `in` operator, which is used to check whether an object belongs to a collection. The corresponding function is called `contains`. Let's implement it so that you can use the `in` operator to check whether a point belongs to a rectangle.

Listing 9.11   Implementing the `in` convention

```
data class Rectangle(val upperLeft: Point, val lowerRight: Point)

operator fun Rectangle.contains(p: Point): Boolean {
    return p.x in upperLeft.x..<lowerRight.x &&
           p.y in upperLeft.y..<lowerRight.y
}

fun main() {
    val rect = Rectangle(Point(10, 20), Point(50, 50))
    println(Point(20, 30) in rect)
    // true
    println(Point(5, 5) in rect)
    // false
}
```

Builds a range and checks that coordinate x belongs to this range

Uses the < operator to build an open range

The object on the right side of `in` becomes the object on which the `contains` method is called, and the object on the left side becomes the argument passed to the method (see figure 9.8).

In the implementation of `Rectangle.contains`, you use the `..<` operator to build an *open range* and then you use the `in` operator on a range to check that a point belongs to it.

Figure 9.8   The `in` operator is transformed into a `contains` function call.

An *open range* is a range that doesn't include its ending point. For example, if you build a regular (closed) range using `10..20`, this range includes all numbers from 10 to 20, including 20. An open range `10..<20` includes numbers from 10 to 19 but doesn't include 20. A rectangle class is often defined in such a way that its bottom and right coordinates aren't part of the rectangle, so the use of open ranges is appropriate here.

9.3.3   *Creating ranges from objects: The rangeTo and rangeUntil conventions*

To create a range, you use the `..` syntax: for instance, `1..10` represents the numbers from 1 to 10. You met ranges in chapter 2, but now, let's discuss the convention that helps create one. The `..` operator is a concise way to call the `rangeTo` function (see figure 9.9).

The `rangeTo` function returns a range. You can define this operator for your own class. But if your class implements the `Comparable` interface, you

Figure 9.9   The `..` operator is transformed into a rangeTo function call.

don't need that: you can create a range of any comparable elements by means of the Kotlin standard library. The library defines the `rangeTo` function that can be called on any comparable element:

```
operator fun <T: Comparable<T>> T.rangeTo(that: T): ClosedRange<T>
```

This function returns a range that allows you to check whether different elements belong to it.

As an example, let's build a range of dates using the `LocalDate` class (defined in the Java 8 standard library).

Listing 9.12   Working with a range of dates

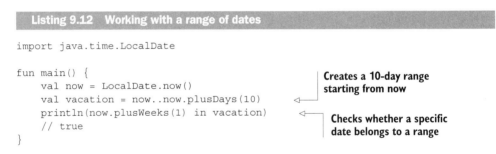

```
import java.time.LocalDate

fun main() {
    val now = LocalDate.now()
    val vacation = now..now.plusDays(10)          Creates a 10-day range
    println(now.plusWeeks(1) in vacation)          starting from now
    // true
}                                                  Checks whether a specific
                                                   date belongs to a range
```

The expression `now..now.plusDays(10)` is transformed into `now.rangeTo(now.plusDays(10))` by the compiler. The `rangeTo` function isn't a member of `LocalDate` but rather is an extension function on `Comparable`, as shown earlier.

The `rangeTo` operator has lower priority than arithmetic operators. But it's better to use parentheses for its arguments to avoid confusion:

```
fun main() {
    val n = 9                        You can write 0..n + 1, but
    println(0..(n + 1))              parentheses make it clearer.
    // 0..10
}
```

Also note that the expression `0..n.forEach {}` won't compile because you must surround a range expression with parentheses to call a method on it:

```
fun main() {
    val n = 9
    (0..n).forEach { print(it) }         ◁─┐ Put a range in parentheses
    // 0123456789                            to call a method on it.
}
```

Analogue to the `rangeTo` operator, the `rangeUntil` operator (`..<`) returns an open-end range, which doesn't include the specified upper bound:

```
fun main() {
    (0..<9).forEach { print(it) }
    // 012345678
}
```

Now, let's discuss how conventions allow you to iterate over a collection or a range.

9.3.4 *Making it possible to loop over your types: The iterator convention*

As we discussed in section 2.4, `for` loops in Kotlin use the same `in` operator as range checks. But its meaning is different in this context: it's used to perform iteration. This means a statement such as `for (x in list) { … }` will be translated into a call of `list.iterator()`, on which the `hasNext` and `next` methods are then repeatedly called, just like in Java.

Note that in Kotlin, it's also a convention, which means the `iterator` method can be defined as an extension. That explains why it's possible to iterate over a regular string: the Kotlin standard library defines an extension function `iterator` on `Char-Sequence`, a superclass of `String`:

```
operator fun CharSequence.iterator(): CharIterator      ◁─┐ This library function
                                                            makes it possible to
fun main() {                                                iterate over a string.
    for (c in "abc") { }
}
```

You can define the `iterator` function as a method in your own classes, or as an extension function for third-party classes that you are using. As in the following example, you could define an extension function that makes it possible to iterate over `LocalDate` objects. Because the `iterator` function should return an object implementing the `Iterator<LocalDate>` interface, you use an object declaration (as you got to know in section 4.4.1) to specify implementations for the `hasNext` and `next` functions expected by the interface.

Listing 9.13   Implementing a date range iterator

```
import java.time.LocalDate

operator fun ClosedRange<LocalDate>.iterator(): Iterator<LocalDate> =
    object : Iterator<LocalDate> {                    ◁──── This object implements an Iterator
        var current = start                                  over LocalDate elements.

        override fun hasNext() =
            current <= endInclusive        ◁────── Note the compareTo
                                                   convention used for dates.
        override fun next(): LocalDate {
            val thisDate = current
            current = current.plusDays(1)     ◁────── Increments the current
            return thisDate        ◁──────                date by one day
        }                  Returns the pre-
    }                      incremented date

fun main() {
    val newYear = LocalDate.ofYearDay(2042, 1)
    val daysOff = newYear.minusDays(1)..newYear       ┌─ Iterates over daysOff when
    for (dayOff in daysOff) { println(dayOff) }   ◁───┤  the corresponding iterator
    // 2041-12-31                                     └─ function is available
    // 2042-01-01
}
```

Note how you define the `iterator` method on a custom range type: you use `LocalDate`
as a type argument. The `rangeTo` library function, shown in the previous section,
returns an instance of `ClosedRange`, and the `iterator` extension on `ClosedRange<Local-
Date>` allows you to use an instance of the range in a `for` loop.

9.4 Making destructuring declarations possible with component functions

When we discussed data classes in chapter 4, we mentioned that some of their features
would be revealed later. Now that you're familiar with the principle of conventions, we
can look at the final feature: *destructuring declarations*. This feature allows you to
unpack a single composite value and use it to initialize several separate local variables.

Here's how it works:

```
fun main() {
    val p = Point(10, 20)           Declares variables x and y,
    val (x, y) = p          ◁──────  initialized with components of p
    println(x)
    // 10
    println(y)
    // 20
}
```

A destructuring declaration looks like a regular variable declaration, but it has multiple variables grouped in parentheses.

Under the hood, the destructuring declaration once again uses the principle of conventions. To initialize each variable in a destructuring declaration, a function named componentN is called, where N is the position of the variable in the declaration. In other words, the previous example would be transformed, as shown in figure 9.10.

Figure 9.10 Destructuring declarations are transformed into componentN function calls.

For a data class, the compiler generates a componentN function for every property declared in the primary constructor. The following example shows how you can declare these functions manually for a non-data class:

```
class Point(val x: Int, val y: Int) {
    operator fun component1() = x
    operator fun component2() = y
}
```

One of the main use cases where destructuring declarations are helpful is returning multiple values from a function. If you need to do that, you can define a data class to hold the values you need to return and use it as the return type of the function. The destructuring declaration syntax makes it easy to unpack and use the values after you call the function. To demonstrate, let's write a simple function to split a filename into a name and an extension.

Listing 9.14 Using a destructuring declaration to return multiple values

```
data class NameComponents(val name: String,         ◁—— Declares a data class
                          val extension: String)        to hold the values

fun splitFilename(fullName: String): NameComponents {
    val result = fullName.split('.', limit = 2)
    return NameComponents(result[0], result[1])     ◁—— Returns an instance of the
}                                                        data class from the function

fun main() {
    val (name, ext) = splitFilename("example.kt")   ◁—— Uses the destructuring
    println(name)                                        declaration syntax to
    // example                                           unpack the class
    println(ext)
    // kt
}
```

You can improve this example even further if you note that componentN functions are also defined on arrays and collections. This is useful when you're dealing with collections of a known size—and this is such a case, with split returning a list of two elements.

```
data class NameComponents(
        val name: String,
        val extension: String)

fun splitFilename(fullName: String): NameComponents {
    val (name, extension) = fullName.split('.', limit = 2)
    return NameComponents(name, extension)
}
```

Of course, it's not possible to define an infinite number of such `componentN` functions so the syntax would work with an arbitrary number of items, but that wouldn't be useful, either. The standard library allows you to use this syntax to access the first five elements of a container.

A simpler way to return multiple values from a function is to use the `Pair` and `Triple` classes from the standard library. While this may require less code than defining your own class, you're also giving up valuable expressiveness in your code because `Pair` and `Triple` don't make it clear what is contained in the returned object.

9.4.1   *Destructuring declarations and loops*

Destructuring declarations work not only as top-level statements in functions but also in other places where you can declare variables—for example, in loops. One good use for that is enumerating entries in a map. Here's a small example using this syntax to print all entries in a given map.

```
fun printEntries(map: Map<String, String>) {
    for ((key, value) in map) {          ◁──┐ Destructuring
        println("$key -> $value")             │ declaration in a loop
    }
}

fun main() {
    val map = mapOf("Oracle" to "Java", "JetBrains" to "Kotlin")
    printEntries(map)
    // Oracle -> Java
    // JetBrains -> Kotlin
}
```

This simple example uses two Kotlin conventions: one to iterate over an object and another to destructure declarations. The Kotlin standard library contains an extension function `iterator` on `Map` that returns an iterator over map entries. Thus, unlike Java, you can iterate over a map directly. It also contains extensions functions `component1` and `component2` on `Map.Entry`, returning its key and value, respectively. In effect, the previous loop is translated to the equivalent of the following code:

```
for (entry in map.entries) {
    val key = entry.component1()
    val value = entry.component2()
    // ...
}
```

You can also use destructuring declarations when a lambda receives a composite value like a `data class` or a map. In this example, you are yet again printing all entries in a given map, but this time you use the `.forEach` function, which you got to know in chapter 5:

```
map.forEach { (key, value) ->
    println("$key -> $value")
}
```

These examples again illustrate the importance of extension functions to support Kotlin's conventions.

9.4.2 *Ignoring destructured values using the _ character*

When you're destructuring an object with many components, there's a chance you might not actually need all of them. In this example, you're destructuring a `Person` class, but really only use the `firstName` and `age` fields.

Listing 9.17 Destructuring a `Person` object

```
data class Person(
    val firstName: String,
    val lastName: String,
    val age: Int,
    val city: String,
)

fun introducePerson(p: Person) {
    val (firstName, lastName, age, city) = p
    println("This is $firstName, aged $age.")
}
```

In this case, declaring a local `lastName` and `city` variable doesn't provide any value for our code. Rather, it clutters the body of the function with unused variables—something that is generally best avoided.

Since we're not forced to destructure the whole object, we can leave trailing destructuring declarations (in this case, `city`) out of the destructuring declaration. Instead, you only destructure the first three elements:

```
val (firstName, lastName, age) = p
```

To get rid of the `lastName` declaration, you have to take a slightly different route. Were we to just remove it (leaving us with `(firstName, age)`), we would falsely assign the contents of `Person.lastName` to the `age` variable (remember that under the hood, this destructuring declaration only calls the `component1` and `component2` functions, regardless of the name you give them). To deal with this case, Kotlin allows you to assign unused declarations during destructuring by assigning them to the reserved _ character.

Equipped with this knowledge, you can make the implementation for `introduce-Person` more concise—renaming `lastName` to `_`, and removing `city` during the destructuring entirely:

```
fun introducePerson(p: Person) {
    val (firstName, _, age) = p          ◁—— To ignore a component during
    println("This is $firstName, aged $age.")     destructuring, assign it to _.
}
```

Limitations and drawbacks of destructuring in Kotlin

Kotlin's implementation of destructuring declarations is *positional*, meaning the result of a destructuring operation depends entirely on the positions of the arguments. For the `Person` data class from listing 9.17, this means variables during destructuring will always be assigned the values in the same order as they appear in the constructor:

```
val (firstName, lastName, age, city) = p
```

The names of the variables to which the result of the destructuring is assigned do not matter—because destructuring declarations iterates through the `component`N functions one after the other, this code works just as well:

```
val (f, l, a, c) = p
```

This can lead to subtle problems when, during refactoring, you change the order of properties in a data class:

```
data class Person(
    val lastName: String,        firstName and lastName
    val firstName: String,       have traded places.
    val age: Int,
    val city: String,
)
```

Now, the previous code snippet still works, but it falsely assigns the value of `lastName` to `firstName`, and vice versa:

```
val (firstName, lastName, age, city) = p
```

This behavior means destructuring declarations are best only used for small container classes (such as key–value pairs or index–value pairs) or classes that are very unlikely to change in the future. They should be avoided for more complex entities.

A potential solution to this problem is the introduction of *name-based destructuring*, a topic that at the time of writing is being considered for Kotlin's value classes (http://mng.bz/v17r); multi-filed value classes are planned to be added in a future version of Kotlin.

9.5   *Reusing property accessor logic: Delegated properties*

To conclude this chapter, let's look at one more feature that relies on conventions and is one of the most unique and powerful in Kotlin: *delegated properties*. This feature lets you easily implement properties that work in a more complex way than storing values in backing fields, without duplicating the logic in each accessor. For example, properties can store their values in database tables, in a browser session, in a map, and so on.

The foundation for this feature is *delegation*: a design pattern where an object, instead of performing a task, delegates that task to another helper object. The helper object is called a *delegate*. You saw this pattern earlier, in section 4.3.3, when we were discussing class delegation. Here this pattern is applied to a property, which can also delegate the logic of its accessors to a helper object. You could implement that by hand—or use a better solution: take advantage of Kotlin's language support. You'll see examples for both in a moment, but first, let's have a look at a general explanation.

9.5.1   *Basic syntax and inner workings of delegated properties*

The general syntax of a delegated property is as follows:

```
var p: Type by Delegate()
```

The property p delegates the logic of its accessors to another object: in this case, a new instance of the Delegate class. The object is obtained by evaluating the expression following the by keyword, which can be anything that satisfies the rules of the convention for property delegates.

Let's take a look at what happens under the hood for a class that defines a delegated property, such as this:

```
class Foo {
    var p: Type by Delegate()
}
```

The compiler creates a hidden helper property, initialized with the instance of the delegate object, to which the initial property p delegates. For simplicity, let's call it delegate:

```
class Foo {
    private val delegate = Delegate()   ◁——   This helper property is generated by the compiler.

    var p: Type   ◁——
        set(value: Type) = delegate.setValue(/* ... */, value)
        get() = delegate.getValue(/* ... */)
}
```

Generated accessors of the p property call the getValue and setValue methods on delegate.

By convention, the Delegate class must have getValue and setValue operator functions, although the latter is required only for mutable properties (i.e., when defining var delegate = …). Additionally, they can (but don't have to) also provide an implementation for the `provideDelegate` function, in which you can perform validation logic or change the way the delegate is instantiated when it is first created. As usual, they can be implemented as members or extensions. To simplify the explanation, we omit their parameters; the exact signatures will be covered later in this chapter. In a simple form, the `Delegate` class might look like the following:

```
                                  The getValue method contains the
                                   logic for implementing a getter.        The setValue method
class Delegate {                                                           contains the logic for
    operator fun getValue(/* ... */) { /* ... */ }    ◁─┘                  implementing a setter.

    operator fun setValue(/* ... */, value: Type) { /* ... */ }    ◁──────┘

    operator fun provideDelegate(/* ... */): Delegate { /* ... */ }    ◁──┐
}                                                                          │
                                  The provideDelegate method contains the logic
                                   for providing or constructing a delegate.

class Foo {
    var p: Type by Delegate()    ◁──┤  The by keyword associates a property with a delegate
}                                       object (here, a new instance of the Delegate class).

fun main() {                      Creating a type with a delegated property
    val foo = Foo()    ◁──────┤   calls delegate.provideDelegate(), if present.
    val oldValue = foo.p    ◁──────┐
    foo.p = newValue ◁───────┐         Accessing a property foo.p calls
}                              │         delegate.getValue(...) under the hood.
                               │
                   Changing a property value calls delegate.setValue(..., newValue).
```

You use `foo.p` as a regular property, but under the hood the methods on the helper property of the `Delegate` type are called. To investigate how this mechanism is used in practice, we'll begin by looking at one example of the power of delegated properties: library support for lazy initialization. Afterward, we'll explore how you can define your own delegated properties and when this is useful.

9.5.2 *Using delegated properties: Lazy initialization and by lazy()*

Lazy initialization is a common pattern that entails creating part of an object on demand when it's accessed for the first time. This is helpful when the initialization process consumes significant resources, and the data isn't always required when the object is used.

For example, consider a `Person` class that lets you access a list of the emails written by a person. The emails are stored in a database and take a long time to access. You want to load the emails on first access to the property and do so only once. Let's say you have the following function `loadEmails`, which retrieves the emails from the database:

```
class Email { /*...*/ }
fun loadEmails(person: Person): List<Email> {
    println("Load emails for ${person.name}")
    return listOf(/*...*/)
}
```

Here's how you can implement lazy loading using an additional `_emails` property that stores `null` before anything is loaded and the list of emails afterward. The `emails` property itself uses a custom accessor as you got to know them in section 2.2.2.

Listing 9.18 Implementing lazy initialization using a backing property

```
class Person(val name: String) {
    private var _emails: List<Email>? = null
```
> The _emails property, which stores the data and to which emails delegates

```
    val emails: List<Email>
        get() {
            if (_emails == null) {
                _emails = loadEmails(this)
```
> Loads the data on access

```
            }
            return _emails!!
```
> If the data was loaded before, it returns it

```
        }
}

fun main() {
    val p = Person("Alice")
    p.emails
```
> Emails are loaded on first access.

```
    // Load emails for Alice
    p.emails
}
```

Here you use the so-called *backing property* technique. You have one property, `_emails`, which stores the value, and another, `emails`, which provides read access to it. You need to use two properties because the properties have different types: `_emails` is nullable, whereas `emails` is non-null. Their naming follows a simple convention: when your class has two properties representing the same concept, the private property is prefixed with an underscore (`_emails`), while the public property has no prefix (`emails`).

This technique can be used fairly often, so it's worth getting familiar with it. But the code is somewhat cumbersome: imagine how much longer it would become if you had several lazy properties. What's more, it doesn't always work correctly: the implementation isn't thread safe. If two threads both access the `emails` property, there's no mechanism in place to prevent the expensive `loadEmails` function from being called twice. At best, this only wastes some resources, but at worst, you end up with an inconsistent state in your application. Surely Kotlin provides a better solution.

The code becomes much simpler with the use of a delegated property, which can encapsulate both the backing property used to store the value and the logic ensuring that the value is initialized only once. The delegate you can use here is returned by the `lazy` standard library function.

Listing 9.19 Implementing lazy initialization using a delegated property

```
class Person(val name: String) {
    val emails by lazy { loadEmails(this) }
}
```

The `lazy` function returns an object that has a method called `getValue` with the proper signature, so you can use it together with the `by` keyword to create a delegated property. The argument of `lazy` is a lambda that it calls to initialize the value. The `lazy` function is thread safe by default; and if you need to, you can specify additional options to tell it which lock to use or to bypass the synchronization entirely if the class is never used in a multithreaded environment.

In the next section, we'll dive into details of how the mechanism of delegated properties works and discuss the conventions in play here.

9.5.3 *Implementing your own delegated properties*

To see how delegated properties are implemented, let's take another example: the task of notifying listeners when a property of an object changes. This is useful in many different cases—for example, when objects are presented in a UI and you want to automatically update the UI when the objects change.

This is typically called an *observable*. Let's see how we could implement it in Kotlin. First, let's look at a variant that doesn't use delegated properties. Then, let's refactor the code to use delegated properties.

The `Observable` class manages a list of `Observers`. When `notifyObservers` is called, it calls the `onChange` function for each registered `Observer` with the old and new property values. An `Observer` only needs to provide an implementation for this `onChange` method, so it would be suitable to use a functional interface as you've seen them in chapter 5:

```
fun interface Observer {
    fun onChange(name: String, oldValue: Any?, newValue: Any?)
}

open class Observable {
    val observers = mutableListOf<Observer>()
    fun notifyObservers(propName: String, oldValue: Any?, newValue: Any?) {
        for (obs in observers) {
            obs.onChange(propName, oldValue, newValue)
        }
    }
}
```

Now, let's write a `Person` class. You'll define a read-only property (the person's name, which typically doesn't change) and two writable properties: the age and the salary. The class will notify its observers when either the age or the salary of the person is changed.

Listing 9.20   Implementing observer notifications for changed properties manually

```
class Person(val name: String, age: Int, salary: Int): Observable() {
    var age: Int = age
        set(newValue) {
```

```
                val oldValue = field
                field = newValue
                notifyObservers(
                    "age", oldValue, newValue
                )
            }

    var salary: Int = salary
        set(newValue) {
            val oldValue = field
            field = newValue
            notifyObservers(
                "salary", oldValue, newValue
            )
        }
}

fun main() {
    val p = Person("Seb", 28, 1000)
    p.observers += Observer { propName, oldValue, newValue ->
        println(
            """
            Property $propName changed from $oldValue to $newValue!
            """.trimIndent()
        )
    }
    p.age = 29
    // Property age changed from 28 to 29!
    p.salary = 1500
    // Property salary changed from 1000 to 1500!
}
```

- The field identifier lets you access the property backing field.
- Notifies observers about the property change
- Creates an observer using the shorthand available for fun interfaces and attaches it, awaiting property changes

Note how this code uses the `field` identifier to access the backing field of the `age` and `salary` properties, as we discussed in chapter 4.

There's quite a bit of repeated code in the setters. Let's try to extract a class that will store the value of the property and fire the necessary notification.

Listing 9.21 Using observer notifications for changed properties with a helper class

```
class ObservableProperty(
    val propName: String,
    var propValue:
    Int,
    val observable: Observable
) {
    fun getValue(): Int = propValue
    fun setValue(newValue: Int) {
        val oldValue = propValue
        propValue = newValue
        observable.notifyObservers(propName, oldValue, newValue)
    }
}
```

```
class Person(val name: String, age: Int, salary: Int): Observable() {
    val _age = ObservableProperty("age", age, this)
    var age: Int
        get() = _age.getValue()
        set(newValue) {
            _age.setValue(newValue)
        }

    val _salary = ObservableProperty("salary", salary, this)
    var salary: Int
        get() = _salary.getValue()
        set(newValue) {
            _salary.setValue(newValue)
        }
}
```

Now, you're close to understanding how delegated properties work in Kotlin. You created a class that stores the value of the property and automatically notifies observers when it's modified. You removed the duplication in the logic, but instead quite a bit of boilerplate is required to create the `ObservableProperty` instance for each property and to delegate the getter and setter to it. Kotlin's delegated property feature lets you get rid of that boilerplate. But before you can do that, you need to change the signatures of the `ObservableProperty` methods to match those required by Kotlin conventions.

Listing 9.22 `ObservableProperty` as a property delegate

```
import kotlin.reflect.KProperty

class ObservableProperty(var propValue: Int, val observable: Observable) {
    operator fun getValue(thisRef: Any?, prop: KProperty<*>): Int = propValue

    operator fun setValue(thisRef: Any?, prop: KProperty<*>, newValue: Int) {
        val oldValue = propValue
        propValue = newValue
        observable.notifyObservers(prop.name, oldValue, newValue)
    }
}
```

Compared to the previous version, this code has the following changes:

- The `getValue` and `setValue` functions are now marked as `operator`, as required for all functions used through conventions.
- You add two parameters to those functions: one to receive the instance for which the property is get or set (`thisRef`), and the second to represent the property itself (`prop`). The property is represented as an object of type `KProperty`. We'll look at it in greater detail in chapter 12; for now, all you need to know is that you can access the name of the property as `KProperty.name`.
- You remove the `name` property from the primary constructor because you can now access the property name through `KProperty`.

You can finally use the magic of Kotlin's delegated properties. See how much shorter the code becomes?

Listing 9.23 Using delegated properties to make properties observable

```
class Person(val name: String, age: Int, salary: Int) : Observable() {
    var age by ObservableProperty(age, this)
    var salary by ObservableProperty(salary, this)
}
```

With the `by` keyword, the Kotlin compiler does automatically what you did manually in the previous version of the code. Compare this code to the previous version of the `Person` class: the generated code when you use delegated properties is very similar. The object to the right of `by` is called the *delegate*. Kotlin automatically stores the delegate in a hidden property and calls `getValue` and `setValue` on the delegate when you access or modify the main property.

Instead of implementing the observable property logic by hand, you can use the Kotlin standard library. It turns out the standard library already contains its own `ObservableProperty` class. However, the standard library class doesn't know anything about the `Observable` interface that you defined earlier, so you need to pass it a lambda that tells it how to report the changes in the property value. The following listing shows how you can do that.

Listing 9.24 Using `Delegates.observable` for property change notifications

```
import kotlin.properties.Delegates

class Person(val name: String, age: Int, salary: Int) : Observable() {
    private val onChange = { property: KProperty<*>, oldValue: Any?,
        newValue: Any? ->
        notifyObservers(property.name, oldValue, newValue)
    }

    var age by Delegates.observable(age, onChange)
    var salary by Delegates.observable(salary, onChange)
}
```

The expression to the right of `by` doesn't have to be a new instance creation. It can also be a function call, another property, or any other expression, as long as the value of this expression is an object on which the compiler can call `getValue` and `setValue` with the correct parameter types. As with other conventions, `getValue` and `setValue` can be either methods declared on the object itself or extension functions.

Note that to keep the examples simple, we've only shown you how to work with delegated properties of type `Int`. The delegated properties mechanism is fully generic and works with any other type, too.

9.5.4 *Delegated properties are translated to hidden properties with custom accessors*

Let's summarize the rules for how delegated properties work. Suppose you have a class with a delegated property:

```
class C {
    var prop: Type by MyDelegate()
}

val c = C()
```

The instance of `MyDelegate` will be stored in a hidden property, which we'll refer to as `<delegate>`. The compiler will also use an object of type `KProperty` to represent the property. We'll refer to this object as `<property>`.

The compiler generates the following code:

```
class C {
    private val <delegate> = MyDelegate()

    var prop: Type
        get() = <delegate>.getValue(this, <property>)
        set(value: Type) = <delegate>.setValue(this, <property>, value)
}
```

Thus, inside every property accessor, the compiler generates calls to the corresponding `getValue` and `setValue` methods, as shown in figure 9.11.

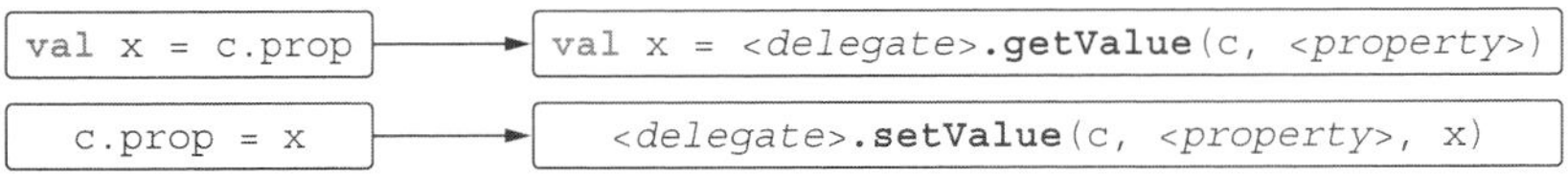

```
val x = c.prop  ──────▶  val x = <delegate>.getValue(c, <property>)

c.prop = x      ──────▶  <delegate>.setValue(c, <property>, x)
```

Figure 9.11 When you access a property, the `getValue` **and** `setValue` **functions on** `<delegate>` **are called.**

The mechanism is fairly simple, yet it enables many interesting scenarios. You can customize where the value of the property is stored (in a map, a database table, or the cookies of a user session) and also what happens when the property is accessed (to add validation, change notifications, and so on). All of this can be accomplished with compact code. Let's look at one more use for delegated properties in the standard library and then see how you can use them in your own frameworks.

9.5.5 *Accessing dynamic attributes by delegating to maps*

Another common pattern where delegated properties come into play is objects that have a dynamically defined set of attributes associated with them. (Other languages, such as C#, call such objects *expando objects*.) For example, consider a contact-management system that allows you to store arbitrary information about your contacts.

Each person in the system has a few required properties (such as a name) that are handled in a special way. Each person also has any number of additional attributes that can be different for each of them (e.g., their youngest child's birthday).

One way to implement such a system is to store all the attributes of a person in a map and provide properties for accessing the information that requires special handling. Here's an example.

Listing 9.25 Defining a property that stores its value in a map

```
class Person {
    private val _attributes = mutableMapOf<String, String>()

    fun setAttribute(attrName: String, value: String) {
        _attributes[attrName] = value
    }

    var name: String
        get() = _attributes["name"]!!          ◁─┐ Retrieves the attribute
        set(value) {                               from the map
            _attributes["name"] = value   ◁─┐
        }                                     Stores the attribute
}                                             in the map

fun main() {
    val p = Person()
    val data = mapOf("name" to "Seb", "company" to "JetBrains")
    for ((attrName, value) in data)
        p.setAttribute(attrName, value)
    println(p.name)
    // Seb
    p.name = "Sebastian"
    println(p.name)
    // Sebastian
}
```

Here, you use a generic API to load the data into the object (in a real project, this could be JSON deserialization or something similar) and then a specific API to access the value of one property. Changing this to use a delegated property is trivial; you can put the map directly after the `by` keyword.

Listing 9.26 Using a delegated property that stores its value in a map

```
class Person {
    private val _attributes = mutableMapOf<String, String>()

    fun setAttribute(attrName: String, value: String) {
        _attributes[attrName] = value
    }

    var name: String by _attributes        ◁─── Uses the map as a delegated property
}
```

This works because the standard library defines `getValue` and `setValue` extension functions on the standard `Map` and `MutableMap` interfaces. The name of the property is automatically used as the key to store the value in the map. As in listing 9.25, `p.name` hides the call of `_attributes.getValue(p, prop)`, which, in turn, is implemented as `_attributes[prop.name]`.

9.5.6   *How a real-life framework might use delegated properties*

Changing the way the properties of an object are stored and modified is extremely useful for framework developers. This section shows an example case of how delegated properties improve framework development and usage and dives into the details of how they work.

Let's say your database contains the table `Users` with two columns: the `name` of type string and the `age` of the type integer. You can define the classes `Users` and `User` in Kotlin. Then, all the user entities stored in the database can be loaded and changed in Kotlin code via instances of the `User` class.

Listing 9.27   Accessing database columns using delegated properties

```
object Users : IdTable() {          ◁───┤ The object corresponds to a table in the database.
    val name = varchar("name", length = 50).index()   ◁───┐
    val age = integer("age")                                │  Properties correspond to
}                                                           │  columns in this table.

class User(id: EntityID) : Entity(id) {   ◁───┤ Each instance of User corresponds
    var name: String by Users.name   ◁───┐        to a specific entity in the table.
    var age: Int by Users.age             │
}                                  The value of name is the value stored
                                   in the database for that user.
```

The `Users` object describes a database table; it's declared as an object because it describes the table as a whole, so you only need one instance of it. Properties of the object represent columns of the table.

The `Entity` class, the superclass of `User`, contains a mapping of database columns to their values for the entity. The properties for the specific `User` have the values `name` and `age` specified in the database for this user.

Using the framework is especially convenient because accessing the property automatically retrieves the corresponding value from the mapping in the `Entity` class, and modifying it marks the object as dirty so that it can be saved to the database when needed. You can write `user.age += 1` in your Kotlin code, and the corresponding entity in the database will be automatically updated.

Now, you know enough to understand how a framework with such an API can be implemented. Each of the entity attributes (`name`, `age`) is implemented as a delegated property, using the column object (`Users.name`, `Users.age`) as the delegate:

```
class User(id: EntityID) : Entity(id) {
    var name: String by Users.name
    var age: Int by Users.age
}
```

> Users.name is a delegate
> for the name property.

Let's look at the explicitly specified types of columns:

```
object Users : IdTable() {
    val name: Column<String> = varchar("name", 50).index()
    val age: Column<Int> = integer("age")
}
```

For the `Column` class, the framework defines the `getValue` and `setValue` methods, satisfying the Kotlin convention for delegates:

```
operator fun <T> Column<T>.getValue(o: Entity, desc: KProperty<*>): T
{
    // retrieve the value from the database
}
operator fun <T> Column<T>.setValue(o: Entity, desc: KProperty<*>, value: T)
{
    // update the value in the database
}
```

You can use the `Column` property (`Users.name`) as a delegate for a delegated property (`name`). When you write `user.age += 1` in your code, the code will perform something similar to `user.ageDelegate.setValue(user.ageDelegate.getValue() + 1)` (omitting the parameters for the property and object instances). The `getValue` and `setValue` methods take care of retrieving and updating the information in the database.

The full implementation of the classes in this example can be found in the source code for the Exposed framework (https://github.com/JetBrains/Exposed). We'll return to this framework in chapter 13, to explore the DSL design techniques used there.

Summary

- Kotlin allows you to overload some of the standard mathematical operations by defining functions with the corresponding names. You can't define your own operators, but you can use infix functions as a more expressive alternative.
- You can use comparison operators (`==`, `!=`, `>`, `<`, and so on) with any object. They are mapped to calls of the `equals` and `compareTo` methods.
- By defining functions named `get`, `set`, and `contains`, you can support the `[]` and `in` operators to make your class similar to Kotlin collections.
- Creating ranges and iterating over collections and arrays also work through conventions.

- Destructuring declarations allow you to initialize multiple variables by unpacking a single object, which is handy for returning multiple values from a function. They work with data classes automatically, and you can support them for your own classes by defining functions named `componentN`.
- Delegated properties allow you to reuse logic controlling how property values are stored, initialized, accessed, and modified, which is a powerful tool for building frameworks.
- The `lazy` standard library function provides an easy way to implement lazily initialized properties.
- The `Delegates.observable` function allows you to add an observer of property changes.
- Delegated properties can use any map as a property delegate, providing a flexible way to work with objects that have variable sets of attributes.

10
Higher-order functions:
Lambdas as parameters
and return values

This chapter covers

- Function types
- Higher-order functions and their use for structuring code
- Inline functions
- Non-local returns and labels
- Anonymous functions

You were introduced to lambdas in chapter 5, where you explored the general concept, and dove deeper into the standard library functions that use lambdas in chapter 6. Lambdas are a great tool for building abstractions, and, of course, their power isn't restricted to collections and other classes in the standard library. In this chapter, you'll learn how to create *higher-order functions*—your own functions that take lambdas as arguments or return them. You'll see how higher-order functions can help simplify your code, remove code duplication, and build nice abstractions. You'll also become acquainted with *inline functions*—a powerful Kotlin feature that removes the performance overhead associated with using lambdas and enables more flexible control flow within lambdas.

10.1 Declaring functions that return or receive other functions: Higher-order functions

The key new idea of this chapter is the concept of *higher-order functions*. By definition, a higher-order function is a function that takes another function as an argument or returns one. In Kotlin, functions can be represented as values either by using lambdas or via function references. Therefore, a higher-order function is any function to which you can pass a lambda or a function reference as an argument, or a function that returns one, or both. For example, the `filter` standard library function takes a predicate function as an argument and is, therefore, a higher-order function:

```
list.filter { x > 0 }
```

In chapter 6, you saw many other higher-order functions declared in the Kotlin standard library: `map`, `with`, and so on. Now you'll learn how you can declare such functions in your own code. To do this, you must first be introduced to *function types*.

10.1.1 Function types specify the parameter types and return values of a lambda

In order to declare a function that takes a lambda as an argument, you need to know how to declare the type of the corresponding parameter. Before we get to this, let's look at a simpler case and store a lambda in a local variable. You already saw how you can do this without declaring the type, relying on Kotlin's type inference:

```
val sum = { x: Int, y: Int -> x + y }
val action = { println(42) }
```

In this case, the compiler infers that both the `sum` and `action` variables have function types (your IDE can help you visualize this, see figure 10.1).

```
val sum : (Int, Int) -> Int = { x: Int, y: Int -> x + y }
val action : () -> Unit = { println(42) }
```

Figure 10.1   Optional inlay hints in IntelliJ IDEA and Android Studio help visualize the inferred function types of lambdas like `sum` and `action`.

Now let's see what an explicit type declaration for these variables looks like:

```
val sum: (Int, Int) -> Int = { x, y -> x + y }    ← Function that takes two Int
                                                    parameters and returns an Int value
val action: () -> Unit = { println(42) }    ← Function that takes no arguments
                                               and doesn't return a value
```

To declare a function type, you put the function parameter types in parentheses, followed by an arrow and the return type of the function (see figure 10.2).

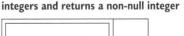

Parameter types   Return type

```
(Int, String) -> Unit
```

Figure 10.2   Function type syntax in Kotlin

As you'll remember from chapter 8, the Unit type is used to specify that a function returns no meaningful value. The Unit return type can be omitted when you declare a regular function, but a function type declaration always requires an explicit return type, so you can't omit Unit in this context.

Note how you can omit the types of the parameters x, y in the lambda expression { x, y -> x + y }. Because they're specified in the function type as part of the variable declaration, you don't need to repeat them in the lambda itself.

As with any other function, the return type of a function type can be marked as nullable:

```
var canReturnNull: (Int, Int) -> Int? = { x, y -> null }
```

You can also define a nullable variable of a function type. To specify that the variable itself, rather than the return type of the function, is nullable, you need to enclose the entire function type definition in parentheses and put the question mark after the closing parenthesis:

```
var funOrNull: ((Int, Int) -> Int)? = null
```

Note the subtle difference between this example and the previous one. If you omit the parentheses, you'll declare a function type with a nullable return type, and not a nullable variable of a function type. Figure 10.3 illustrates this.

A function that takes two integers and returns a nullable integer

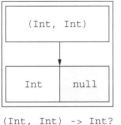

A nullable function that takes two integers and returns a non-null integer

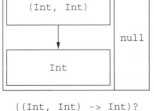

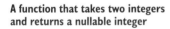

Figure 10.3   The parentheses decide whether a function type has a nullable return type or is nullable itself.

10.1.2 Calling functions passed as arguments

Now that you know how to specify a functional type in Kotlin in a local variable, let's discuss how to implement a higher-order function. The first example is as simple as possible and uses the same type declaration as the sum lambda you saw earlier. The function performs an arbitrary operation on two numbers, 2 and 3, and prints the result.

Listing 10.1   Defining a simple higher-order function

```
fun twoAndThree(operation: (Int, Int) -> Int) {            Declares a parameter
    val result = operation(2, 3)                           of a function type
    println("The result is $result")
}
                                                           Calls the parameter
fun main() {                                               of a function type
    twoAndThree { a, b -> a + b }
    // The result is 5
    twoAndThree { a, b -> a * b }
    // The result is 6
}
```

The syntax for calling the function passed as an argument is the same as calling a regular function: you put the parentheses after the function name and the parameters inside the parentheses.

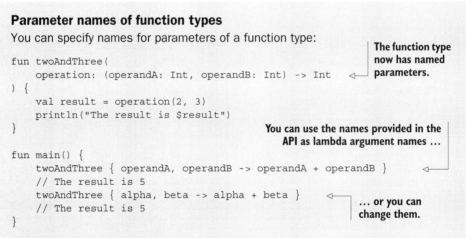

Parameter names of function types

You can specify names for parameters of a function type:

```
fun twoAndThree(
    operation: (operandA: Int, operandB: Int) -> Int
) {
    val result = operation(2, 3)
    println("The result is $result")
}

fun main() {
    twoAndThree { operandA, operandB -> operandA + operandB }
    // The result is 5
    twoAndThree { alpha, beta -> alpha + beta }
    // The result is 5
}
```

The function type now has named parameters.

You can use the names provided in the API as lambda argument names …

… or you can change them.

Parameter names don't affect type matching. When you declare a lambda, you don't have to use the same parameter names as the ones used in the function type declaration. However, the names improve the readability of the code and can be used in the IDE for code completion.

As a more interesting example, let's reimplement one of the most commonly used standard library functions: the filter function. You've used filter earlier, in chapter 6, but now, it's time to engage with its inner workings. To keep things simple, you'll implement the `filter` function on `String`, but the generic version that works on a collection of any elements is similar. The declaration of the `filter` function is shown in figure 10.4.

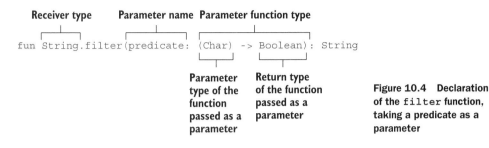

Figure 10.4   Declaration of the `filter` function, taking a predicate as a parameter

The `filter` function takes a predicate as a parameter. The type of `predicate` is a function that takes a character parameter and returns a Boolean result. When `predicate` returns `true` for a given character, it needs to be present in the resulting string. If it returns `false`, it should not be included. Here's how the function can be implemented.

The `filter` function implementation is straightforward. It checks whether each character satisfies the predicate. For those characters that do, it uses the `append` function of the `StringBuilder` provided by `buildString` (as you have gotten to know it in chapter 5), gradually building up the result, and then returning it. This is particularly simple because of the iterator convention that you've seen previously in chapter 9, allowing you to iterate over the `String` just like any other Kotlin collection.

Because both the extension function and the `buildString` function define a receiver, you use a labeled `this` expression to access the outer receiver of the `filter` function (the input string) rather than the receiver of the `buildString` lambda (a `StringBuilder` instance). You'll take a closer look at the labeled `this` expression in figure 10.6.

Listing 10.2   Implementing a simple version of the `filter` function

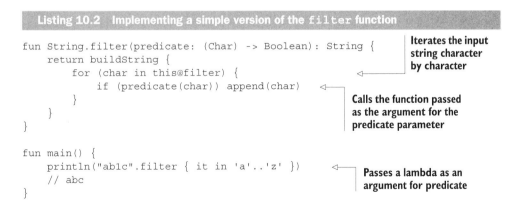

```
fun String.filter(predicate: (Char) -> Boolean): String {
    return buildString {
        for (char in this@filter) {
            if (predicate(char)) append(char)
        }
    }
}

fun main() {
    println("ab1c".filter { it in 'a'..'z' })
    // abc
}
```

Iterates the input string character by character

Calls the function passed as the argument for the predicate parameter

Passes a lambda as an argument for predicate

INTELLIJ IDEA TIP   IntelliJ IDEA supports smart stepping into lambda code in the debugger. If you step through the previous example, you'll see how execution moves between the body of the `filter` function and the lambda you pass through it, as the function processes each element in the input list.

10.1.3   *Java lambdas are automatically converted to Kotlin function types*

As you already discovered in chapter 5, you can pass a Kotlin lambda to any Java method that expects a functional interface through automatic SAM (single abstract method) conversion. This means that your Kotlin code can rely on Java libraries and call higher-order functions defined in Java without problems. Likewise, Kotlin functions that use function types can be called easily from Java. Java lambdas are automatically converted to values of function types, as shown in the following listing.

Listing 10.3   ProcessTheAnswer.kt

```
/* Kotlin declaration */
fun processTheAnswer(f: (Int) -> Int) {
    println(f(42))
}


/* Java call */
processTheAnswer(number -> number + 1);
// 43
```

In Java, you can easily use extension functions from the Kotlin standard library that expect lambdas as arguments. Note, however, that they don't look as nice as in Kotlin—you have to pass a receiver object as a first argument explicitly:

```
/* Java */
import kotlin.collections.CollectionsKt;

// ...
public static void main(String[] args) {
    List<String> strings = new ArrayList();          You can use a function from
    strings.add("42");                               the Kotlin standard library
    CollectionsKt.forEach(strings, s -> {            in Java code.
        System.out.println(s);
        return Unit.INSTANCE;                         You have to return a value
    });                                               of Unit type explicitly.
}
```

In Java, your function or lambda can return `Unit`. But because the `Unit` type has a value in Kotlin, you need to return it explicitly. You can't pass a lambda returning `void` as an argument of a function type that returns `Unit`, like `(String) -> Unit` in the previous example.

Function types: Implementation details

Under the hood, Kotlin function types are regular interfaces: a variable of a function type is an implementation of a `FunctionN` interface. The interfaces you can use are enumerated by their number of function arguments: `Function0<R>` (this function takes no arguments, and only specifies its return type), `Function1<P1, R>` (this function takes one argument), and so on. Each interface defines a single `invoke` method, and calling it will execute the function. (We'll discuss the `invoke` operator in more detail in chapter 13.) In short, `FunctionN` interfaces look like this:

```
interface Function1<P1, out R> {
    operator fun invoke(p1: P1): R
}
```

A variable of a function type is an instance of a class implementing the corresponding `FunctionN` interface, with the `invoke` method containing the body of the lambda. Under the hood, that means listing 10.3 looks approximately like this:

```
fun processTheAnswer(f: Function1<Int, Int>) {
    println(f.invoke(42))
}
```

Because these functional types are really just Kotlin interfaces, they can be used wherever you can use an interface. For example, a class could inherit from a `FunctionN` interface or its equivalent functional type (although this is rarely used in practice):

```
class Adder : (Int, Int) -> Int {          ◁───┐  Equivalent to
    override operator fun invoke(                 Function2<Int, Int, Int>
        p1: Int,
        p2: Int
    ): Int {
        return p1 + p2
    }
}
```

The `FunctionN` interfaces are *synthetic compiler-generated types*, meaning you won't find their declarations in the Kotlin standard library. Instead, the compiler generates them for you when necessary, meaning you can use an interface for a function with any number of parameters without artificial restrictions on the possible number of function type parameters.

10.1.4 Parameters with function types can provide defaults or be nullable

When you declare a parameter of a function type, you can also specify its default value. To see where this can be useful, let's go back to the `joinToString` function that we discussed in chapter 3. Here's the implementation we ended up with.

Listing 10.4 `joinToString` with hardcoded `toString` conversion

```
fun <T> Collection<T>.joinToString(
        separator: String = ", ",
        prefix: String = "",
        postfix: String = ""
```

```
): String {
    val result = StringBuilder(prefix)

    for ((index, element) in this.withIndex()) {
        if (index > 0) result.append(separator)
        result.append(element)                        ◁—  Converts the object to a
    }                                                      string, using the default
                                                           toString method
    result.append(postfix)
    return result.toString()
}
```

This implementation is flexible, but it doesn't let you control one key aspect of the conversion: how individual values in the collection are converted to strings. The code uses `StringBuilder.append(o: Any?)`, which always converts the object to a string using the `toString` method. This works well in many cases but not always. You now know that you can pass a lambda to specify how values are converted into strings. But requiring all callers to pass that lambda would be cumbersome because most of them are okay with the default behavior. To solve this, you can define a parameter of a function type and specify a default value for it as a lambda.

Listing 10.5   Specifying a default value for a parameter of a function type

```
fun <T> Collection<T>.joinToString(
        separator: String = ", ",                              Declares a parameter
        prefix: String = "",                                   of a function type
        postfix: String = "",                                  with a lambda as
        transform: (T) -> String = { it.toString() }   ◁—      a default value
): String {
    val result = StringBuilder(prefix)

    for ((index, element) in this.withIndex()) {        Calls the function passed
        if (index > 0) result.append(separator)         as an argument for the
        result.append(transform(element))         ◁—    transform parameter
    }

    result.append(postfix)
    return result.toString()
}

fun main() {                                          Uses the default
    val letters = listOf("Alpha", "Beta")             conversion function
    println(letters.joinToString())          ◁—
    // Alpha, Beta
    println(letters.joinToString { it.lowercase() })   ◁—   Passes a lambda
    // alpha, beta                                           as an argument
    println(letters.joinToString(separator = "! ", postfix = "! ",
            transform = { it.uppercase() }))   ◁—
    // ALPHA! BETA!                              Uses the named argument syntax for
}                                               passing several arguments, including
                                                a lambda
```

Note that this function is generic: it has a type parameter T, denoting the type of the element in a collection. The transform lambda will receive an argument of that type.

Declaring a default value of a function type requires no special syntax—you just put the value as a lambda after the = sign. Listing 10.5 shows different ways of calling the function: omitting the lambda entirely (so that the default toString() conversion is used), passing it outside of the parentheses (because it is the last argument of the joinToString function), and passing it as a named argument.

An alternative approach is to declare a parameter of a nullable function type. Note that you can't call the function passed in such a parameter directly: Kotlin will refuse to compile such code because it detects the possibility of null pointer exceptions in this case. One option is to check for null explicitly:

```
fun foo(callback: (() -> Unit)?) {
    // ...
    if (callback != null) {
        callback()
    }
}
```

A shorter version makes use of the fact that a function type is an implementation of an interface with an invoke method. As a regular method, invoke can be called through the safe-call syntax: callback?.invoke(). The following listing shows how you can use this technique to rewrite the joinToString function.

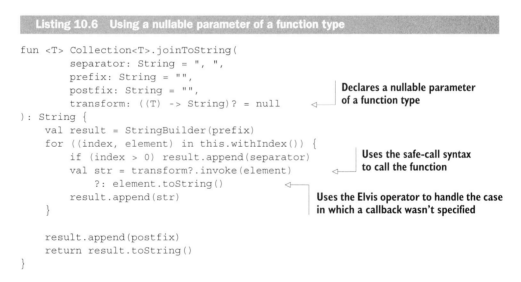

Listing 10.6 Using a nullable parameter of a function type

```
fun <T> Collection<T>.joinToString(
        separator: String = ", ",
        prefix: String = "",
        postfix: String = "",
        transform: ((T) -> String)? = null          ◁──┐ Declares a nullable parameter
): String {                                                of a function type
    val result = StringBuilder(prefix)
    for ((index, element) in this.withIndex()) {
        if (index > 0) result.append(separator)
        val str = transform?.invoke(element)         ◁──┐ Uses the safe-call syntax
            ?: element.toString()          ◁──┐            to call the function
        result.append(str)
    }                                       Uses the Elvis operator to handle the case
                                            in which a callback wasn't specified

    result.append(postfix)
    return result.toString()
}
```

This example is also a good chance to remind yourself once more of the function type syntax discussed in figure 10.2: transform is a parameter of a nullable function type but has a non-nullable return type. If transform is not null, it is guaranteed to return a non-null value of type String.

Now you know how to write functions that take functions as arguments. Let's look next at the other kind of higher-order functions: functions that return other functions.

10.1.5 Returning functions from functions

The requirement to return a function from another function doesn't come up as often as passing functions to other functions, but it's still useful. For instance, imagine a piece of logic in a program that can vary, depending on the state of the program or other conditions—for example, calculating the cost of shipping, depending on the selected shipping method. You can define a function that chooses the appropriate logic variant and returns it as another function. The following listing shows how this looks as code.

Listing 10.7   Defining a function that returns another function

```
enum class Delivery { STANDARD, EXPEDITED }

class Order(val itemCount: Int)                          Declares a function that
                                                         returns a function
fun getShippingCostCalculator(delivery: Delivery): (Order) -> Double {    ◁──┘
    if (delivery == Delivery.EXPEDITED) {
        return { order -> 6 + 2.1 * order.itemCount }    ◁──┐
    }                                                        Returns lambdas
                                                             from the function
    return { order -> 1.2 * order.itemCount }            ◁──┘
}
                                            Stores the returned function in a variable
fun main() {
    val calculator = getShippingCostCalculator(Delivery.EXPEDITED)    ◁──┘
    println("Shipping costs ${calculator(Order(3))}")    ◁──┐
    // Shipping costs 12.3                                    Invokes the
}                                                             returned function
```

To declare a function that returns another function, you specify a function type as its return type. In listing 10.7, `getShippingCostCalculator` returns a function that takes an `Order` and returns a `Double`. To return a function, you write a `return` expression followed by a lambda; a member reference; or another expression of a function type, such as a local variable.

Let's see another example where returning functions from functions is useful. Suppose you're working on a GUI contact-management application, and you need to determine which contacts should be displayed, based on the state of the UI. Let's say the UI allows you to type a string and then shows only contacts with names starting with that string; it also lets you hide contacts that don't have a phone number specified. You'll use the `ContactListFilters` class to store the state of the options:

```
class ContactListFilters {
    var prefix: String = ""
    var onlyWithPhoneNumber: Boolean = false
}
```

When a user types D to see the contacts whose first or last name starts with D, the prefix value is updated. We've omitted the code that makes the necessary changes. (A full UI application would be too much code for the book, so we provide a simplified example here.)

To decouple the contact list display logic from the filtering UI, you can define a function that creates a predicate used to filter the contact list, as shown in the following listing. This predicate checks the prefix and also checks that the phone number is present, if required.

Listing 10.8   Using functions that return functions in UI code

```
data class Person(
        val firstName: String,
        val lastName: String,
        val phoneNumber: String?
)

class ContactListFilters {
    var prefix: String = ""
    var onlyWithPhoneNumber: Boolean = false

    fun getPredicate(): (Person) -> Boolean {          // Declares a function that returns a function
        val startsWithPrefix = { p: Person ->
            p.firstName.startsWith(prefix) || p.lastName.startsWith(prefix)
        }
        if (!onlyWithPhoneNumber) {
            return startsWithPrefix                    // Returns a variable of a function type
        }
        return { startsWithPrefix(it)
                && it.phoneNumber != null }            // Returns a lambda from this function
    }
}

fun main() {
    val contacts = listOf(
        Person("Dmitry", "Jemerov", "123-4567"),
        Person("Svetlana", "Isakova", null)
    )
    val contactListFilters = ContactListFilters()
    with (contactListFilters) {
        prefix = "Dm"
        onlyWithPhoneNumber = true
    }
    println(
        contacts.filter(contactListFilters.getPredicate())   // Passes the function returned by getPredicate as an argument to filter
    )
    // [Person(firstName=Dmitry, lastName=Jemerov, phoneNumber=123-4567)]
}
```

The getPredicate method returns a function value that you pass to the filter function as an argument. Kotlin function types allow you to do this just as easily as for values of other types, such as strings.

Higher-order functions are an extremely powerful tool for improving the structure of your code and removing duplication. Next, let's see how lambdas can help extract repeated logic from your code.

10.1.6 *Making code more reusable by reducing duplication with lambdas*

Together, function types and lambda expressions constitute a great tool to create reusable code. Many kinds of code duplication that previously could be avoided only through cumbersome constructions can now be eliminated by using succinct lambda expressions.

Let's look at an example that analyzes visits to a website. The class `SiteVisit` stores the path of each visit, its duration, and the user's OS. Various OSs are represented with an enum.

Listing 10.9   Defining the site visit data

```
data class SiteVisit(
    val path: String,
    val duration: Double,
    val os: OS
)

enum class OS { WINDOWS, LINUX, MAC, IOS, ANDROID }

val log = listOf(
    SiteVisit("/", 34.0, OS.WINDOWS),
    SiteVisit("/", 22.0, OS.MAC),
    SiteVisit("/login", 12.0, OS.WINDOWS),
    SiteVisit("/signup", 8.0, OS.IOS),
    SiteVisit("/", 16.3, OS.ANDROID)
)
```

Imagine you need to display the average duration of visits from Windows machines. You can perform the task using the `average` function.

Listing 10.10   Analyzing site visit data with hardcoded filters

```
val averageWindowsDuration = log
    .filter { it.os == OS.WINDOWS }
    .map(SiteVisit::duration)
    .average()

fun main() {
    println(averageWindowsDuration)
    // 23.0
}
```

Now, suppose you need to calculate the same statistics for Mac users. To avoid duplication, you can extract the platform as a parameter.

Listing 10.11 Removing duplication with a regular function

```
fun List<SiteVisit>.averageDurationFor(os: OS) =
        filter { it.os == os }.map(SiteVisit::duration).average()    ◄────── Duplicated
                                                                             code
fun main() {                                                                 extracted
    println(log.averageDurationFor(OS.WINDOWS))                              into the
    // 23.0                                                                  function
    println(log.averageDurationFor(OS.MAC))
    // 22.0
}
```

Note how making this function an extension improves readability. You can even declare this function as a local extension function if it makes sense only in the local context.

But it's not powerful enough. Imagine you're interested in the average duration of visits from the mobile platforms (currently you recognize two of them: iOS and Android).

Listing 10.12 Analyzing site visit data with a complex hardcoded filter

```
fun main() {
    val averageMobileDuration = log
        .filter { it.os in setOf(OS.IOS, OS.ANDROID) }
        .map(SiteVisit::duration)
        .average()
    println(averageMobileDuration)
    // 12.15
}
```

Now, a simple parameter representing the platform doesn't do the job. It's also likely that you'll want to query the log with more complex conditions, such as, "What's the average duration of visits to the signup page from iOS?" Lambdas can help. You can use function types to extract the required condition into a parameter.

Listing 10.13 Removing duplication with a higher-order function

```
fun List<SiteVisit>.averageDurationFor(predicate: (SiteVisit) -> Boolean) =
        filter(predicate).map(SiteVisit::duration).average()

fun main() {
    println(
        log.averageDurationFor {
            it.os in setOf(OS.ANDROID, OS.IOS)
        }
    )
    // 12.15
    println(
        log.averageDurationFor {
            it.os == OS.IOS && it.path == "/signup"
```

```
        }
     )
    // 8.0
}
```

Function types can help eliminate code duplication. If you're tempted to copy and paste a piece of the code, it's likely that the duplication can be avoided. With lambdas, you can extract not only the data that's repeated, but the behavior as well.

> **NOTE**   Some well-known design patterns can be simplified using function types and lambda expressions. Let's consider the strategy pattern, for example. Without lambda expressions, it requires you to declare an interface with several implementations for each possible strategy. With function types in your language, you can use a general function type to describe the strategy and pass different lambda expressions as different strategies.

We've discussed how to create higher-order functions. Next, let's look at their performance. Won't your code be slower if you begin using higher-order functions for everything, instead of writing good-old loops and conditions? The next section discusses why this isn't always the case and how the `inline` keyword can help.

10.2   *Removing the overhead of lambdas with inline functions*

You've probably noticed that the shorthand syntax for passing a lambda as an argument to a function in Kotlin looks similar to the syntax of regular statements, such as `if` and `for`. You saw this during our discussion of the `with` and `apply` functions in chapter 5. But what about performance? Aren't we creating unpleasant surprises by defining functions that look exactly like Java statements but run much more slowly?

In chapter 5, we explained that lambdas are normally compiled to anonymous classes. But that means every time you use a lambda expression, an extra class is created, and if the lambda captures some variables, then a new object is created on every invocation. This introduces runtime overhead, causing an implementation that uses a lambda to be less efficient than a function that executes the same code directly.

Could it be possible to tell the compiler to generate code that's as efficient as directly executing the code, but still let you extract the repeated logic into a library function? Indeed, the Kotlin compiler allows you to do that. If you mark a function with the `inline` modifier, the compiler won't generate a function call when this function is used and, instead, will replace every call to the function with the actual code implementing the function. Let's explore how that works in detail and review some examples.

10.2.1   *Inlining means substituting a function body to each call site*

When you declare a function as `inline`, its body is inlined—in other words, it's substituted directly into places where the function is called instead of being invoked normally. Let's look at an example to understand the resulting code.

The function in listing 10.14 can be used to ensure that a shared resource isn't accessed concurrently by multiple threads. The function locks a `Lock` object, executes the given block of code, and then releases the lock.

Listing 10.14 Defining an inline function

```
import java.util.concurrent.locks.Lock
import java.util.concurrent.locks.ReentrantLock

inline fun <T> synchronized(lock: Lock, action: () -> T): T {
    lock.lock()
    try {
        return action()
    }
    finally {
        lock.unlock()
    }
}

fun main() {
    val l = ReentrantLock()
    synchronized(l) {
        // ...
    }
}
```

The body of a function marked as inline is substituted into places where the function is called.

The syntax for calling this function looks exactly like using the `synchronized` statement in Java. The difference is that the Java `synchronized` statement can be used with any object, whereas this function requires you to pass a `Lock` instance. The definition shown here is just an example; the Kotlin standard library also defines an implementation of `synchronized`: one that accepts any object as an argument.

But using explicit locks for synchronization provides for more reliable and maintainable code. In section 10.2.5, we'll introduce the `withLock` function from the Kotlin standard library, which you should prefer for executing the given action under a lock.

Because you've declared the `synchronized` function as `inline`, the code generated for every call to it is the same as for a `synchronized` statement in Java. Consider this example of using `synchronized()`:

```
fun foo(l: Lock) {
    println("Before sync")
    synchronized(l) {
        println("Action")
    }
    println("After sync")
}
```

Figure 10.5 shows the equivalent code, which will be compiled to the same bytecode.

Note that the inlining is applied to the lambda expression as well as the implementation of the `synchronized` function. The bytecode generated from the lambda

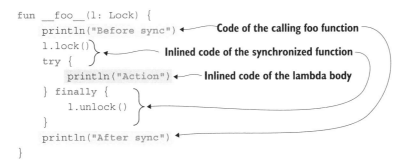

Figure 10.5   The compiled version of the `foo` function

becomes part of the definition of the calling function and isn't wrapped in an anonymous class implementing a function interface.

It's also possible to call an inline function and pass the parameter of a function type from a variable:

```
class LockOwner(val lock: Lock) {
    fun runUnderLock(body: () -> Unit) {
        synchronized(lock, body)
    }
}
```

A variable of a function type is passed as an argument, not a lambda.

In this case, the lambda's code isn't available at the site where the inline function is called; therefore, it isn't inlined. Only the body of the `synchronized` function is inlined—the lambda is called as usual. The `runUnderLock` function will be compiled to bytecode similar to the following function:

This function is similar to the bytecode the real **runUnderLock** is compiled to.

```
class LockOwner(val lock: Lock) {
    fun __runUnderLock__(body: () -> Unit) {
        lock.lock()
        try {
            body()
        }
        finally {
            lock.unlock()
        }
    }
}
```

The body isn't inlined because there's no lambda at the invocation.

If you have two uses of an inline function in different locations with different lambdas, then every call site will be inlined independently. The code of the inline function will be copied to both locations where you use it, with different lambdas substituted into it.

In addition to functions, you can also mark your property accessors (`get`, `set`) as `inline`. This becomes useful when making use of Kotlin's *reified generics*. We'll discuss examples and their details in chapter 11.

10.2.2 *Restrictions on inline functions*

Due to the way inlining is performed, not every function that uses lambdas can be inlined. When the function is inlined, the body of the lambda expression that's passed as an argument is substituted directly into the resulting code. This restricts the possible uses of the corresponding parameter in the function body. If the lambda parameter is invoked, such code can be easily inlined. But if the parameter is stored somewhere for further use, the code of the lambda expression can't be inlined because there must be an object that contains this code:

```
class FunctionStorage {
    var myStoredFunction: ((Int) -> Unit)? = null
    inline fun storeFunction(f: (Int) -> Unit) {
        myStoredFunction = f
    }
}
```

Stores the passed parameter, meaning the compiler can't substitute the code at every call site, and reports an illegal use of the inline parameter f

Generally, the parameter can be inlined if it's called directly or passed as an argument to another `inline` function. Otherwise, the compiler will prohibit the inlining of the parameter with the following error message: "Illegal usage of inline-parameter."

For example, various functions that work on sequences return instances of classes that represent the corresponding sequence operation and receive the lambda as a constructor parameter. Here's how the `Sequence.map` function is defined:

```
fun <T, R> Sequence<T>.map(transform: (T) -> R): Sequence<R> {
    return TransformingSequence(this, transform)
}
```

The `map` function doesn't call the function passed as the `transform` parameter directly. Instead, it passes this function to the constructor of a class that stores it in a property. To support that, the lambda passed as the `transform` argument needs to be compiled into the standard non-inline representation, as an anonymous class implementing a function interface.

If you have a function that expects two or more lambdas as arguments, you may choose to inline only some of them. This makes sense when one of the lambdas is expected to contain a lot of code or is used in a way that doesn't allow inlining. You can mark the parameters that accept such non-inlineable lambdas with the `noinline` modifier:

```
inline fun foo(inlined: () -> Unit, noinline notInlined: () -> Unit) {
  // ...
}
```

Note that the compiler fully supports inlining functions across modules or those defined in third-party libraries. You can also call most inline functions from Java; such calls will not be inlined but will be compiled as regular function calls. In chapter 11, you'll see another case where it makes sense to use `noinline` (with some constraints on Java interoperability, however).

10.2.3 Inlining collection operations

Let's consider the performance of Kotlin standard library functions that work on collections. Most of the collection functions in the standard library take lambda expressions as arguments. Would it be more efficient to implement these operations directly, instead of using the standard library functions? For example, let's compare the ways you can filter a list of people, as shown in the next two listings.

Listing 10.15   Filtering a collection using a lambda

```
data class Person(val name: String, val age: Int)

val people = listOf(Person("Alice", 29), Person("Bob", 31))

fun main() {
    println(people.filter { it.age < 30 })
    // [Person(name=Alice, age=29)]
}
```

The previous code can be rewritten without lambda expressions.

Listing 10.16   Filtering a collection manually

```
fun main() {
    val result = mutableListOf<Person>()
    for (person in people) {
        if (person.age < 30) result.add(person)
    }
    println(result)
    // [Person(name=Alice, age=29)]
}
```

In Kotlin, the `filter` function is declared as inline. It means the bytecode of the `filter` function, together with the bytecode of the lambda passed to it, will be inlined where `filter` is called. As a result, the bytecode generated for the first version that uses `filter` is roughly the same as the bytecode generated for the second version. You can safely use idiomatic operations on collections, and Kotlin's support for inline functions ensures that you don't need to worry about performance.

Imagine now that you apply two operations, `filter` and `map`, in a chain:

```
fun main() {
    println(
        people.filter { it.age > 30 }
            .map(Person::name)
    )
    // [Bob]
}
```

This example uses a lambda expression and a member reference. Once again, both `filter` and `map` are declared as `inline`, so their bodies are inlined, and no extra classes or objects are created. However, the code creates an intermediate collection to store the result of filtering the list. The code generated from the `filter` function adds elements to that collection, and the code generated from `map` reads from it.

If the number of elements to process is large and the overhead of an intermediate collection becomes a concern, you can use a sequence instead, by adding an `asSequence` call to the chain. We discussed sequences in chapter 6, but as you saw in section 10.2.2, lambdas used to process a sequence aren't inlined. Each intermediate sequence is represented as an object storing a lambda in its field, and the terminal operation causes a chain of calls through each intermediate sequence to be performed. Therefore, even though operations on sequences are lazy, you shouldn't strive to insert an `asSequence` call into every chain of collection operations in your code. This helps only for large collections; smaller ones can be processed nicely with regular collection operations.

10.2.4 Deciding when to declare functions as inline

Now that you've learned about the benefits of the `inline` keyword, you might consider using `inline` throughout your codebase, in an attempt to make it run faster. As it turns out, this isn't a good idea. Using the `inline` keyword is likely to improve performance only with functions that take lambdas as arguments; all other cases require additional investigation, measuring, and profiling of your application.

For regular function calls, the JVM already provides powerful inlining support. It analyzes the execution of your code and inlines calls whenever doing so provides the most benefit. This happens automatically while translating bytecode to machine code. In bytecode, the implementation of each function is repeated only once and doesn't need to be copied to every place where the function is called, as with Kotlin's `inline` functions. What's more, the stacktrace is clearer if the function is called directly.

On the other hand, inlining functions with lambda arguments is beneficial. First, the overhead you avoid through inlining is more significant. You save not only on the call, but also on the creation of the extra class for each lambda and an object for the lambda instance. Second, the JVM currently isn't smart enough to always perform inlining through the call and the lambda. Finally, inlining lets you use features that are impossible to make work with regular lambdas, such as non-local returns, which we'll discuss later in this chapter.

You should still pay attention to the code size when deciding whether to use the `inline` modifier. If the function you want to inline is large, copying its bytecode into every call site could be expensive in terms of bytecode size. In that case, you should try to extract the code not related to the lambda arguments into a separate non-inline function. You can verify for yourself that the `inline` functions in the Kotlin standard library are always small. Next, let's see how higher-order functions can help you improve your code.

10.2.5 *Using inlined lambdas for resource management with withLock, use, and useLines*

One common pattern where lambdas can remove duplicate code is resource management: acquiring a resource before an operation and releasing it afterward. *Resource* here can mean many different things: a file, a lock, a database transaction, and so on. The standard way to implement such a pattern is to use a `try/finally` statement in which the resource is acquired before the `try` block and released in the `finally` block, or to use specialized language constructs like Java's try-with-resources.

In section 10.2.1, you saw an example of how you can encapsulate the logic of the `try/finally` statement in a function and pass the code using the resource as a lambda to that function. The example showed the `synchronized` function, which has the same syntax as the `synchronized` statement in Java: it takes the lock object as an argument. The Kotlin standard library defines another function called `withLock`, which has a more idiomatic API for the same task: it's an extension function on the `Lock` interface. Here's how it can be used:

```
val l: Lock = ReentrantLock()            Executes the given
l.withLock {                      ◁───┐  action under the lock
    // access the resource protected by this lock
}
```

The `withLock` function is defined as follows in the Kotlin library:

```
inline fun <T> Lock.withLock(action: () -> T): T {    ◁──┐  The idiom of
    lock()                                                  working with locks
    try {                                                   is extracted into a
        return action()                                     separate function.
    } finally {
        unlock()
    }
}
```

In section 14.7.4, while diving deeper into Kotlin coroutines and concurrent programming, you'll encounter `Mutex`, which also provides a `withLock` function that acts as an analog to the `Lock` variant you've just explored.

Files are another common type of resource where this pattern is used. Listing 10.17 shows a Kotlin function that reads the first line from a file. To do so, it uses the `use` function from the Kotlin standard library. The `use` function is an extension function called on a closable resource (an object implementing the `Closable` interface); it receives a lambda as an argument. The function calls the lambda and ensures the resource is closed, regardless of whether the lambda completes normally or throws an exception. In this example, it ensures the `BufferedReader` and `FileReader`, both of which implement `Closeable`, are properly closed down after use.

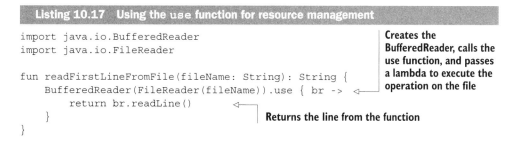

Listing 10.17 Using the `use` function for resource management

```
import java.io.BufferedReader
import java.io.FileReader

fun readFirstLineFromFile(fileName: String): String {
    BufferedReader(FileReader(fileName)).use { br ->
        return br.readLine()
    }
}
```

Creates the
BufferedReader, calls the
use function, and passes
a lambda to execute the
operation on the file

Returns the line from the function

Of course, the `use` function is inlined, so its use doesn't incur any performance overhead.

As in many other cases, the Kotlin standard library also comes with more specialized extension functions. While `use` is designed to work with any type of `Closeable`, the `useLines` function is defined for `File` and `Path` objects and gives the lambda access to a sequence of strings (as you've gotten to know them in chapter 6). This allows you to make the code more concise and idiomatic.

Listing 10.18 The specialized `useLines` extension function

```
import kotlin.io.path.Path
import kotlin.io.path.useLines

fun readFirstLineFromFile(fileName: String): String {
    Path(fileName).useLines {
        return it.first()
    }
}
```

The it is a sequence of strings containing
the lines of text in the input file.

No try-with-resources in Kotlin

Java has a special syntax for working with closable resources such as files: the try-with-resources statement. The equivalent Java code to listing 10.17 to read the first line from a file would look like this:

```
/* Java */
static String readFirstLineFromFile(String fileName) throws IOException {
    try (BufferedReader br =
                    new BufferedReader(new FileReader(fileName))) {
        return br.readLine();
    }
}
```

Kotlin doesn't have an equivalent special syntax because the same task can be accomplished just as seamlessly via `use`. This once again illustrates nicely how versatile higher-order functions (functions expecting lambdas as arguments) can be.

Note that in the body of the lambdas (in both listings 10.17 and 10.18), you use a non-local `return` to return a value from the `readFirstLineFromFile` function—you return from `readFirstLineFromFile`, whose body contains the invocation of lambda, not just from the lambda itself. Let's discuss the use of `return` expressions in lambdas in detail.

10.3 Returning from lambdas: Control flow in higher-order functions

When you start using lambdas to replace imperative code constructs such as loops, you quickly run into the problem of `return` expressions. Putting a `return` statement in the middle of a loop is a no-brainer. But what if you convert the loop into the use of a function such as `filter`? How does `return` work in that case? Let's look at some examples.

10.3.1 Return statements in lambdas: returning from an enclosing function

We'll compare two different ways of iterating over a collection. In the following listing, it's clear that if the person's name is Alice, you return from the function `lookForAlice`.

Listing 10.19   Using `return` in a regular loop

```
data class Person(val name: String, val age: Int)

val people = listOf(Person("Alice", 29), Person("Bob", 31))

fun lookForAlice(people: List<Person>) {
    for (person in people) {
        if (person.name == "Alice") {
            println("Found!")
            return
        }
    }
    println("Alice is not found")        ⟵──┐  This line is printed if there's
}                                            └─ no Alice among people.

fun main() {
    lookForAlice(people)
    // Found!
}
```

Is it safe to rewrite this code using `forEach` iteration? Will the `return` statement mean the same thing? Yes, it's safe to use the `forEach` function instead, as shown next.

Listing 10.20   Using `return` in a lambda passed to `forEach`

```
fun lookForAlice(people: List<Person>) {
    people.forEach {
        if (it.name == "Alice") {
            println("Found!")
            return          ⟵──  Returns from a function, as in listing 10.19
        }
    }
    println("Alice is not found")
}
```

If you use the `return` keyword in a lambda, it *returns from the function in which you called the lambda*, not just from the lambda itself. Such a `return` statement is called a *non-local return* because it returns from a larger block than the block containing the `return` statement.

To understand the logic behind the rule, think about using a `return` keyword in a `for` loop or a `synchronized` block in a Java method. It's obvious that it returns from the function and not from the loop or block. Kotlin allows you to preserve the same behavior when you switch from language features to functions that take lambdas as arguments.

Note that the return from the outer function is possible *only if the function that takes the lambda as an argument is inlined*. In listing 10.20, the body of the `forEach` function is inlined together with the body of the lambda, so it's easy to compile the `return` expression so that it returns from the enclosing function. Using the `return` expression in lambdas passed to non-inline functions isn't allowed, since a non-inline function could store the lambda passed to it in a variable. That means it may execute the lambda later, when the function has already returned, so it's too late for the lambda to affect when the surrounding function returns.

10.3.2 Returning from lambdas: Return with a label

You can write a *local* return from a lambda expression as well. A local return stops the execution of the lambda and continues execution of the code from which the lambda was invoked. To distinguish a local return from a non-local one, you use *labels*, which you've briefly seen in chapter 2. You can label a lambda expression from which you want to return, and then refer to this label after the `return` keyword. In this example, you use `forEach` to iterate all elements in the input collection `people`, and use a labeled `return` to skip over elements where the `name` property is not `"Alice"`.

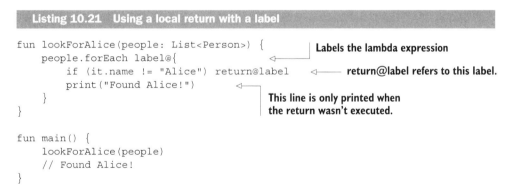

Listing 10.21 Using a local return with a label

```
fun lookForAlice(people: List<Person>) {
    people.forEach label@{                              ◁────  Labels the lambda expression
        if (it.name != "Alice") return@label           ◁────  return@label refers to this label.
        print("Found Alice!")      ◁─┐
    }                                 │ This line is only printed when
}                                     │ the return wasn't executed.

fun main() {
    lookForAlice(people)
    // Found Alice!
}
```

To label a lambda expression, put the label name (which can be any identifier) followed by the `@` character before the opening curly brace of the lambda. To return from a lambda, put the `@` character followed by the label name after the `return` keyword. This is illustrated in figure 10.6.

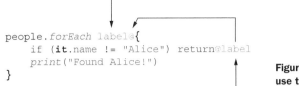

```
people.forEach label@{
    if (it.name != "Alice") return@label
    print("Found Alice!")
}
```

Figure 10.6   Returns from a lambda use the @ character to mark a label.

Alternatively, the name of the function that takes this lambda as an argument can be used as a label.

Listing 10.22   Using the function name as a `return` label

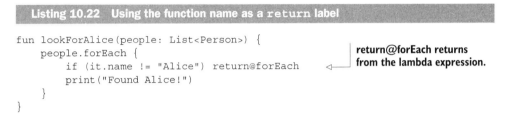

```
fun lookForAlice(people: List<Person>) {
    people.forEach {
        if (it.name != "Alice") return@forEach
        print("Found Alice!")
    }
}
```

return@forEach returns from the lambda expression.

Note that if you specify the label of the lambda expression explicitly, labeling using the function name doesn't work. A lambda expression can't have more than one label.

Labeled this expressions

The same rules apply to the labels of `this` expressions. In chapter 5, we discussed lambdas with receivers—lambdas that contain an implicit receiver object that can be accessed via a `this` reference in a lambda. (Chapter 13 will explain how to write your own functions that expect lambdas with receivers as arguments.) If you specify the label of a lambda with a receiver, you can access its implicit receiver using the corresponding labeled `this` expression:

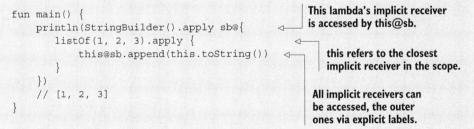

```
fun main() {
    println(StringBuilder().apply sb@{
        listOf(1, 2, 3).apply {
            this@sb.append(this.toString())
        }
    })
    // [1, 2, 3]
}
```

This lambda's implicit receiver is accessed by this@sb.

this refers to the closest implicit receiver in the scope.

All implicit receivers can be accessed, the outer ones via explicit labels.

As with labels for `return` expressions, you can specify the label of the lambda expression explicitly or use the function name instead.

The non-local return syntax is fairly verbose and becomes cumbersome if a lambda contains multiple return expressions. As a solution, you can use an alternate syntax to pass around blocks of code: *anonymous functions.*

10.3.3 *Anonymous functions: Local returns by default*

An anonymous function is another syntactic form of writing a lambda expression. As such, using anonymous functions is another way to write blocks of code that can be passed to other functions. However, they differ in the way you can use `return` expressions. Let's take a closer look, and start with an example.

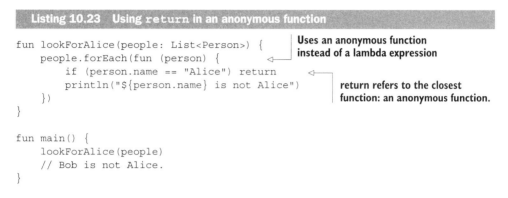

Listing 10.23   Using `return` in an anonymous function

```
fun lookForAlice(people: List<Person>) {
    people.forEach(fun (person) {
        if (person.name == "Alice") return
        println("${person.name} is not Alice")
    })
}

fun main() {
    lookForAlice(people)
    // Bob is not Alice.
}
```

Uses an anonymous function instead of a lambda expression

return refers to the closest function: an anonymous function.

You can see that an anonymous function looks similar to a regular function, except that its name is omitted, and parameter types can be inferred. Here's another example.

Listing 10.24   Using an anonymous function with `filter`

```
people.filter(fun (person): Boolean {
    return person.age < 30
})
```

Anonymous functions follow the same rules as regular functions for specifying the return type. Anonymous functions with a block body, such as the one in listing 10.24, require the return type to be specified explicitly. If you use an expression body, you can omit the return type.

Listing 10.25   Using an anonymous function with an expression body

```
people.filter(fun (person) = person.age < 30)
```

Inside an anonymous function, a `return` expression without a label returns from the anonymous function, not the enclosing one. The rule is simple: `return` *returns from the closest function declared using the* `fun` *keyword*. Lambda expressions don't use the `fun` keyword, so a `return` in a lambda returns from the outer function. Anonymous functions do use `fun`; therefore, in the previous example, the anonymous function is the closest matching function. Consequently, the `return` expression returns from the anonymous function, not from the enclosing one. The difference is illustrated in figure 10.7.

```
fun lookForAlice(people: List<Person>) {
    people.forEach(fun(person) {
        if (person.name == "Alice") return
    })
}
fun lookForAlice(people: List<Person>) {
    people.forEach {
        if (it.name == "Alice") return
    }
}
```

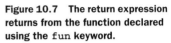

Figure 10.7   The return expression returns from the function declared using the `fun` **keyword.**

Note that despite the fact that an anonymous function looks similar to a regular function declaration, it's another syntactic form of a lambda expression. Generally, you will use the lambda syntax you have seen so far throughout the book. Anonymous functions mainly help shorten code that has a lot of early `return` statements, which would need to be labeled when using the lambda syntax.

The discussion of how lambda expressions are implemented and how they're inlined for inline functions applies to anonymous functions as well.

Summary

- Function types allow you to declare a variable, parameter, or function return value that holds a reference to a function.
- Higher-order functions take other functions as arguments or return them. You can create such functions by using a function type as the type of a function parameter or return value.
- When an inline function is compiled, its bytecode, along with the bytecode of a lambda passed to it, is inserted directly into the code of the calling function. This ensures the call happens with no overhead compared to similar code written directly.
- Higher-order functions facilitate code reuse within the parts of a single component and enable you to build powerful generic and general-purpose libraries.
- Inline functions allow you to use *non-local returns*—return expressions placed in a lambda that return from the enclosing function.
- Anonymous functions provide an alternative syntax to lambda expressions with different rules for resolving the `return` expressions. You can use them if you need to write a block of code with multiple exit points.

Generics

You've already seen a few code examples that use generics in this book. The basic concepts of declaring and using generic classes and functions in Kotlin are similar to Java, so the earlier examples should have been clear without a detailed explanation. In this chapter, we'll return to some of the examples and look at them in more detail.

We'll then go deeper into the topic of generics and explore new concepts introduced in Kotlin, such as reified type parameters and declaration-site variance. These concepts may be novel to you, but don't worry; the chapter covers them thoroughly.

Reified type parameters allow you to refer at run time to the specific types used as type arguments in an inline function call. (For normal classes or functions, this isn't possible because type arguments are erased at run time.)

Declaration-site variance lets you specify whether a generic type with a type argument is a subtype or a supertype of another generic type with the same base type and a different type argument. For example, it regulates whether it's possible to pass arguments of type List<Int> to functions expecting List<Any>.

Use-site variance achieves the same goal for a specific use of a generic type and, therefore, accomplishes the same task as Java's wildcards.

Let's discuss these topics in details, starting with generic type parameters in general.

11.1   *Creating types with type arguments: Generic type parameters*

Generics allow you to define types that have *type parameters*. When an instance of such a type is created, type parameters are substituted with specific types called *type arguments*. For example, if you have a variable of type List, it's useful to know what kind of things are stored in that list. The type parameter lets you specify exactly that—instead of "This variable holds a list," you can say something like "This variable holds a list of strings." Kotlin's syntax for saying "a list of strings" looks the same as in Java: List<String>. You can also declare multiple type parameters for a class. For example, the Map class has type parameters for the key type and the value type: class Map<K, V>. We can instantiate it with specific arguments: Map<String, Person>. So far, everything looks exactly as it does in Java.

Just as with types in general, type arguments can often be inferred by the Kotlin compiler:

```
val authors = listOf("Sveta", "Seb", "Dima", "Roman")
```

Because all values passed to the listOf function are strings, the compiler infers that you're creating a List<String> (your IDE can help you visualize this; see figure 11.1).

```
val authors : List<String>  = listOf("Sveta", "Seb", "Dima", "Roman")
```

Figure 11.1   Optional inlay hints in IntelliJ IDEA and Android Studio help visualize inferred generic types.

On the other hand, if you need to create an empty list, there's nothing from which to infer the type argument, so you need to specify it explicitly. In the case of creating a list, you have a choice between specifying the type as part of the variable declaration and specifying a type argument for the function that creates a list. The following example shows how this is done:

```
val readers: MutableList<String> = mutableListOf()

val readers = mutableListOf<String>()
```

These declarations are equivalent. Note that collection-creation functions are covered in section 8.2.

> ### There are no raw types in Kotlin
>
> Unlike Java, Kotlin always requires type arguments to be either specified explicitly or inferred by the compiler. Because generics were only added to Java in version 1.5, it had to maintain compatibility with code written for older versions, so it allows you to use a generic type without type arguments—a so-called *raw type*. For example, in Java, you can declare a variable of type ArrayList without specifying what kind of things it contains:

```
List aList = new ArrayList();
```

Because Kotlin has had generics from the beginning, it doesn't support raw types, and the type arguments must always be defined. If your program receives a variable with a raw type from Java code, it's treated as having a generic parameter of type `Any!`—a platform type, as you've gotten to know them in section 7.12.

11.1.1   Functions and properties that work with generic types

If you're going to write a function that works with a list and you want it to work with any list (a generic one), not a list of elements of a specific type, you need to write a *generic function*. A generic function has type parameters of its own. These type parameters must be replaced with the specific type arguments on each function invocation.

Most of the library functions working with collections are generic. For example, let's look at the `slice` function declaration, shown in figure 11.2. This function returns a list containing only elements at indices in the specified range.

Type parameter declaration

```
fun <T> List<T>.slice(indices: IntRange): List<T>
```

The type parameter is used in receiver and return types.

Figure 11.2   The generic function `slice` has the type parameter T, allowing it to work with lists of arbitrary elements. This type parameter is used both in the receiver type of the extension function, and the return type of the function.

The function's type parameter `T` is used in the receiver type and the return type; both of them are `List<T>`. When you call such a function on a specific list, you can specify the type argument explicitly. But in almost all cases you don't need to because the compiler infers it, as shown next.

Listing 11.1   Calling a generic function

```
fun main() {
    val letters = ('a'..'z').toList()
    println(letters.slice<Char>(0..2))        ◁─── Specifies the type argument explicitly
    // [a, b, c]
    println(letters.slice(10..13))            ◁─── The compiler infers that T is Char here.
    // [k, l, m, n]
}
```

The result type of both of these calls is `List<Char>`. The compiler substitutes the inferred type `Char` for `T` in the function return type `List<T>`.

In section 10.1.1, you saw the declaration of the `filter` function, which takes a parameter of the function type `(T) -> Boolean`. It had the following signature:

```
fun <T> List<T>.filter(predicate: (T) -> Boolean): List<T>
```

Let's see how you can apply it to the `readers` and `authors` variables from the previous examples.

Listing 11.2   Calling a generic higher-order function

```
fun main() {
    val authors = listOf("Sveta", "Seb", "Roman", "Dima")
    val readers = mutableListOf<String>("Seb", "Hadi")
    println(readers.filter { it !in authors })
    // [Hadi]
}
```

The type of the autogenerated lambda parameter `it` is `String` in this case. The compiler has to (and can) infer that: after all, in the declaration of the function, the lambda parameter has a generic type `T` (it's the type of the function parameter in `(T) ->` `Boolean`). The compiler understands `T` is `String` because it knows the function should be called on `List<T>`, and the actual type of its receiver, `readers`, is `List<String>`.

You can declare type parameters on methods of classes or interfaces, top-level functions, and extension functions. In the last case, the type parameter can be used in the types of the receiver and the parameters, as in listings 11.1 and 11.2: the type parameter `T` is part of the receiver type `List<T>`, and it's used in the parameter function type `(T) -> Boolean` as well.

You can also declare generic extension properties using the same syntax. For example, here's an extension property that returns the penultimate element in a list—that is, the element before the last one:

```
val <T> List<T>.penultimate: T          ← This generic extension property
    get() = this[size - 2]                can be called on a list of any kind.

fun main() {                            ← The type parameter T is inferred
    println(listOf(1, 2, 3, 4).penultimate)   to be Int in this invocation.
    // 3
}
```

> ### You can't declare a generic non-extension property
>
> Regular (non-extension) properties can't have type parameters. It's not possible to store multiple values of different types in a property of a class; therefore, declaring a generic non-extension property doesn't make sense. If you try to do that, the compiler reports an error:
>
> ```
> val <T> x: T = TODO()
> // Error: type parameter of a property must be used in its receiver type
> ```

Now, let's recap how you can declare generic classes.

11.1.2 Generic classes are declared with the angle bracket syntax

Just as in Java, you declare a Kotlin generic class or interface by putting angle brackets after the class name and the type parameters inside the angle brackets. Once you do that, you can use the type parameters in the body of the class, just like any other types. Let's look at how a basic interface like `List`, as you know it from the standard library, could be declared in Kotlin. To simplify it, we've omitted the majority of the methods:

```
interface List<T> {                              The List interface defines a type parameter T.
    operator fun get(index: Int): T              T can be used as a regular type
    // ...                                        in an interface or a class.
}
```

Later, in section 11.3, when we get to the topic of variance, you'll improve on this example and see how `List` is declared in the Kotlin standard library.

If your class extends a generic class (or implements a generic interface), you must provide a type argument for the generic parameter of the base type. It can be either a specific type or another type parameter:

```
class StringList: List<String> {                 This class implements List, providing
    override fun get(index: Int): String = TODO()   a specific type argument: String.
    // . . .                                      Note how String is
}                                                 used instead of T.

class ArrayList<T> : List<T> {                    Now, the generic type parameter T of
    override fun get(index: Int): T = TODO()      ArrayList is a type argument for List.
    // ...
}
```

The `StringList` class is declared to contain only `String` elements, so it uses `String` as the type argument of the base type. Any function from the subclass substitutes this proper type instead of `T`. That means, instead of `fun get(Int): T`, you have a signature `fun get(Int): String`.

The `ArrayList` class defines its own type parameter `T` and specifies that as a type argument of the superclass. Note that `T` in `ArrayList<T>` *is not the same* as in `List<T>`—it's a new type parameter, and it doesn't need to have the same name.

A class can even refer to itself as a type argument. Classes implementing the `Comparable` interface are the classic example of this pattern. Any comparable element must define how to compare it with objects of the same type:

```
interface Comparable<T> {
    fun compareTo(other: T): Int
}

class String : Comparable<String> {
    override fun compareTo(other: String): Int = TODO()
}
```

The `String` class implements the generic `Comparable` interface, providing the type `String` for the type parameter `T`.

So far, generics look similar to those in Java. We'll talk about the differences later in the chapter, in sections 11.2 and 11.3. Now, let's discuss another concept that works similar to Java: the one that allows you to write useful functions for working with comparable items.

11.1.3 Restricting the type a generic class or function can use: Type parameter constraints

Type parameter constraints let you restrict the types that can be used as type arguments for a class or function. For example, consider a function that calculates the sum of elements in a list. It can be used on a `List<Int>` or a `List<Double>`, but not, for example, a `List<String>`. To express this, you can define a type parameter constraint that specifies that the type parameter of `sum` must be a number.

When you specify a type as an *upper bound* constraint for a type parameter of a generic type, the corresponding type arguments in specific instantiations of the generic type must be either the specified type or its subtypes. (For now, you can think of *subtype* as a synonym for *subclass*. Section 11.3.2 will highlight the difference.)

To specify a constraint, you put a colon after the type parameter name, followed by the type that's the upper bound for the type parameter (see figure 11.3). In Java, you use the keyword `extends` to express the same concept: `<T extends Number> T sum(List<T> list)`.

Type parameter

```
fun <T : Number> List<T>.sum(): T
```

Upper bound

Figure 11.3   Constraints are defined by specifying an upper bound after a type parameter. In this case, the `sum` function is constrained to lists of a type whose upper bound is `Number`.

This function invocation is allowed because the actual type argument (`Int` in the following example) extends the abstract class `Number`, a superclass of all classes representing numeric values, from the Kotlin standard library:

```
fun main() {
    println(listOf(1, 2, 3).sum())
    // 6
}
```

Once you've specified a bound for a type parameter `T`, you can use values of type `T` as values of its upper bound. For example, you can invoke methods defined in the class used as the bound:

Specifies Number as the type parameter upper bound

```
fun <T : Number> oneHalf(value: T): Double {
    return value.toDouble() / 2.0
}
```

Invokes a method defined in the Number class

```
fun main() {
    println(oneHalf(3))
    // 1.5
}
```

Now, let's write a generic function that finds the maximum of two items. Because it's only possible to find a maximum of items that can be compared to each other, you need to specify that in the signature of the function. Here's how you do that. You constrain the max function to accept parameters `first` and `second` of type `T`, and constrain `T` to implement `Comparable<T>`, which ensures that only objects that can be compared to `T` can be used.

Listing 11.3   Declaring a function with a type parameter constraint

```
fun <T: Comparable<T>> max(first: T, second: T): T {      ◁——  The arguments of
    return if (first > second) first else second                this function must
}                                                               be comparable
                                                                elements.
fun main() {
    println(max("kotlin", "java"))
    // kotlin
}
```

When you try to call `max` on incomparable items, the code won't compile:

```
println(max("kotlin", 42))
ERROR: Type parameter bound for T is not satisfied:
 inferred type Any is not a subtype of Comparable<Any>
```

The upper bound for `T` is a generic type `Comparable<T>`. As you saw earlier, the `String` class extends `Comparable<String>`, which makes `String` a valid type argument for the `max` function.

Remember, the short form `first > second` is compiled to `first.compareTo(second) > 0`, according to the Kotlin operator conventions as you have seen them in section 9.2.2. This comparison is possible because the type of `first`, which is `T`, extends from `Comparable<T>`, and thus you can compare `first` to another element of type `T`.

In the rare case when you need to specify multiple constraints on a type parameter, you use a slightly different syntax. For example, the following listing is a generic way to ensure that the given `CharSequence` has a period at the end. In this case, you specify that the type used as a type argument must implement both the `CharSequence` and `Appendable` interfaces. This means both the operation accessing the data (`endsWith`) as well as the operation modifying it (`append`) can be used with values of that type. One class that implements both `CharSequence` and `Appendable` is the `StringBuilder` class, which represents a mutable sequence of characters (you briefly encountered `StringBuilder` in section 3.2).

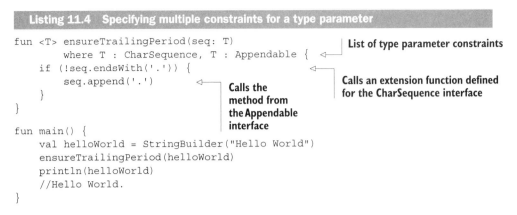

Listing 11.4   Specifying multiple constraints for a type parameter

```
fun <T> ensureTrailingPeriod(seq: T)                              List of type parameter constraints
        where T : CharSequence, T : Appendable {
    if (!seq.endsWith('.')) {
        seq.append('.')                                           Calls an extension function defined
    }                                        Calls the            for the CharSequence interface
}                                            method from
                                             the Appendable
fun main() {                                 interface
    val helloWorld = StringBuilder("Hello World")
    ensureTrailingPeriod(helloWorld)
    println(helloWorld)
    //Hello World.
}
```

Next, we'll discuss another case when type parameter constraints are common: when you want to declare a non-null type parameter.

11.1.4   *Excluding nullable type arguments by explicitly marking type parameters as non-null*

If you declare a generic class or function, any type arguments, including nullable ones, can be substituted for its type parameters. In effect, a type parameter with no upper bound specified will have the upper bound of Any?. Consider the following example:

```
class Processor<T> {
    fun process(value: T) {               value is nullable, so you
        value?.hashCode()                 have to use a safe call.
    }
}
```

In the process function, the parameter value is nullable, even though T isn't marked with a question mark. This is the case because specific instantiations of the Processor class can use a nullable type for T—there are no constraints to forbid the type T to be nullable (e.g., String?):

String?, which is a nullable
type, is substituted for T.

```
val nullableStringProcessor = Processor<String?>()
nullableStringProcessor.process(null)
```

This code compiles fine, having
null as the value argument.

If you want to guarantee that a non-null type will always be substituted for a type parameter, you can achieve this by specifying a constraint. If you don't have any restrictions other than nullability, you can use Any as the upper bound, replacing the default Any?:

```
class Processor<T : Any> {              Specifying a non-null upper bound
    fun process(value: T) {
        value.hashCode()                The value of type T is now non-null.
    }
}
```

The `<T : Any>` constraint ensures that the `T` type will always be a non-nullable type. The code `Processor<String?>` won't be accepted by the compiler because the type argument `String?` isn't a subtype of `Any` (it's a subtype of `Any?`, which is a less specific type):

```
val nullableStringProcessor = Processor<String?>()
// Error: Type argument is not within its bounds: should be subtype of 'Any'
```

Note that you can make a type parameter non-null by specifying any non-null type as an upper bound, not only the type `Any`.

Marking generic types as "definitely non-nullable" when interoperating with Java

A special case worth pointing out is when implementing generic interfaces from Java that are annotated with nullability annotations as you've gotten to know them in section 7.12. For example, this generic `JBox` interface restricts the `put` method to only be called with a non-null parameter of type `T`. Note that the interface itself doesn't make such constraints on the type `T` in general, allowing other methods like `putIfNotNull` to accept nullable values:

```
import org.jetbrains.annotations.NotNull;

public interface JBox<T> {
    /**
     * Puts a non-null value into the box.
     */
    void put(@NotNull T t);

    /**
     * Puts a value into the box if it is not null,
     * doesn't do anything for null values.
     */
    void putIfNotNull(T t);
}
```

With the syntax you have seen so far, you couldn't directly convert this constraint to Kotlin code. If a Kotlin implementation specifies the non-null constraint for the generic type via `T : Any`, nullable values can't be used with the implementation at all anymore—which would differ from the constraint given by the Java interface:

```
class KBox<T : Any>: JBox<T> {          ⟵  Because the generic type T was already
    override fun put(t: T) { /* ... */ }        constrained to be non-nullable here ...
    override fun putIfNotNull(t: T) { /* Problem! */ }      ⟵
}
                              ... you can no longer relax this constraint for a
                              function that expects a nullable parameter.
```

Now, `T` is non-nullable everywhere in the `KBox` implementation—not only in the `put` method.

> **(continued)**
>
> To address this, Kotlin provides a way of marking a type as *definitely non-nullable* at its use site (rather than at the place where the generic parameter is first defined). Syntactically, it is expressed as `T & Any` (a form you may recognize from the notation of intersection types in other languages):
>
> ```
> class KBox<T>: JBox<T> {
>     override fun put(t: T & Any) { /* ... */ }
>     override fun putIfNotNull(t: T) { /* ... */ }
> }
> ```
>
> Using definitely non-nullable types, you can now express the same nullability constraints defined in the Java code in Kotlin.

So far, we've covered the basics of generics—the topics that are most similar to Java. Now, let's discuss another concept that may be somewhat familiar if you're a Java developer: how generics behave at run time.

11.2 Generics at run time: Erased and reified type parameters

From an implementation perspective, generics on the Java virtual machine (JVM) are normally implemented through *type erasure*. This means the type arguments of an instance of a generic class aren't preserved at run time. In this section, we'll discuss the practical implications of type erasure for Kotlin, and how you can get around its limitations by declaring a function as `inline`. You can declare an `inline` function so that its type arguments aren't erased (or, in Kotlin terms, are reified). We'll discuss reified type parameters in detail and look at examples when they're useful.

11.2.1 Limitations to finding type information of a generic class at run time: Type checks and casts

Kotlin's generics are *erased* at run time. This means an instance of a generic class doesn't carry information about the type arguments used to create that instance. For example, if you create a `List<String>` and put a bunch of strings into it, at run time, you'll only be able to see that it's a `List` (an effect that you can also see in Java). It's not possible to identify which type of elements the list was intended to contain. (Of course, you can get an element and check its type, but that won't give you any guarantees because other elements may have different types.)

Consider what happens with these two lists when you run the code (shown in figure 11.4):

```
val list1: List<String> = listOf("a", "b")
val list2: List<Int> = listOf(1, 2, 3)
```

Even though the compiler sees two distinct types for the lists, at execution time, they look exactly the same (see figure 11.4). Despite that, you can normally be sure a `List<String>` contains only strings and a `List<Int>` contains only integers because the compiler knows the type arguments and ensures only elements of the correct type are stored in each list. (You can deceive the compiler through type casts or by using Java raw types to access the list, but you need to make a special effort to do that.)

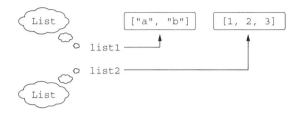

Figure 11.4   At run time, you don't know whether `list1` and `list2` were declared as lists of strings or integers. Each of them is just `List`. This introduces additional constraints to working with type arguments.

Let's talk next about the constraints that go with erasing the type information. Because type arguments aren't stored, you can't check them—for example, you can't check whether a list is a list of strings rather than other objects. As a general rule, it's not possible to use types with type arguments in `is` checks. This can prove to be a hurdle when you want to create a function that should exhibit different behavior based on the type argument of its parameter.

For example, you might have a function `readNumbersOrWords`, which, depending on the user input, either returns a `List<String>` or `List<Int>`. Trying to discern between the list of numbers and words via `is` checks inside the `printList` function doesn't compile:

```
fun readNumbersOrWords(): List<Any> {
    val input = readln()
    val words: List<String> = input.split(",")
    val numbers: List<Int> = words.mapNotNull { it.toIntOrNull() }
    return numbers.ifEmpty { words }
}

fun printList(l: List<Any>) {
    when(l) {
        is List<String> -> println("Strings: $l")      Error: Cannot check for an
        is List<Int> -> println("Integers: $l")         instance of erased type
    }
}

fun main() {
    val list = readNumbersOrWords()
    printList(list)
}
```

Even though it's perfectly possible to find out at run time that value is a `List`, you can't tell whether it's a list of strings, persons, or something else: that information has been erased. Note that erasing generic type information has its benefits: the overall amount of memory used by your application is smaller because less type information needs to be saved in memory.

As we stated earlier, Kotlin doesn't let you use a generic type without specifying type arguments. Thus, you may wonder how to check that the value is a list, rather than a set or another object. You can do that by using the special *star-projection* syntax:

```
if (value is List<*>) { /* ... */ }
```

Effectively, you need to include a `*` for every type parameter the type has. We'll discuss the star projection in detail (including why it's called a *projection*) in section 11.3.6; for now, you can think of it as a type with unknown arguments (or an analog of Java's `List<?>`). In the previous example, you check whether a `value` is a `List`, and you don't get any information about its element type.

Note that you can still use normal generic types in `as` and `as?` casts. But the cast won't fail if the class has the correct base type and an incorrect type argument because the type argument isn't known at run time when the cast is performed. Because of that, the compiler will emit an "unchecked cast" warning on such a cast. It's only a warning, so you can later use the value as having the necessary type, as shown next.

Listing 11.5   Using a type cast with a generic type

```
fun printSum(c: Collection<*>) {                          Warning here: Unchecked
    val intList = c as? List<Int>          ◄──────        cast: List<*> to List<Int>
        ?: throw IllegalArgumentException("List is expected")
    println(intList.sum())
}
```

Everything compiles fine: the compiler only issues a warning, which means this code is legitimate. If you call the `printSum` function on a list or a set of integers, it works as expected—it prints a sum in the first case and throws an `IllegalArgumentException` in the second case:

```
fun main() {                        With lists, everything works as expected.
    printSum(listOf(1, 2, 3))   ◄──┘
    // 6                                         The set isn't a list, so an
    printSum(setOf(1, 2, 3))   ◄────────         exception is thrown.
    // IllegalArgumentException: List is expected
}
```

But if you pass in a value of a wrong type, you'll get a `ClassCastException` at run time:

```
                                    The cast succeeds, but since strings cannot be
fun main() {                        summed, another exception is thrown later.
    printSum(listOf("a", "b", "c"))   ◄────┘
    // ClassCastException: String cannot be cast to Number
}
```

Let's discuss the exception that's thrown if you call the `printSum` function on a list of strings. You don't get an `IllegalArgumentException` because you can't check whether the argument is a `List<Int>`. Therefore, the cast succeeds, and the function `sum` is called on such a list anyway. During its execution, an exception is thrown. This happens because the function tries to get Number values from the list and add them together. An attempt to use a String as a Number results in a ClassCastException at run time.

Note that the Kotlin compiler is smart enough to allow is checks when the corresponding type information is already known at compile time.

Listing 11.6 Using a type check with a known type argument

```
fun printSum(c: Collection<Int>) {                          ⟵──┐ Because the element type Int
    when (c) {                                                  │ is known at compile time ...
        is List<Int> -> println("List sum: ${c.sum()}")      ┐
        is Set<Int> -> println("Set sum: ${c.sum()}")        │ ... these checks
    }                                                        ┘ are legitimate.
}

fun main() {
    printSum(listOf(1,2,3))
    // List sum: 6
    printSum(setOf(3,4,5))
    // Set sum: 12
}
```

In listing 11.6, the check whether c has type List<Int> is possible because you know at compile time that this collection (no matter whether it's a list or another kind of collection) contains integer numbers—unlike the example you saw in listing 11.5, where no information about the type was available.

Generally, the Kotlin compiler takes care of letting you know which checks are dangerous (forbidding is checks and emitting warnings for as casts) and which are possible. You just have to know the meaning of those warnings and understand which operations are safe.

As we already mentioned, Kotlin does have a special construct that allows you to use specific type arguments in the body of a function, but that's only possible for inline functions. Let's look at this feature.

11.2.2 Functions with reified type parameters can refer to actual type arguments at run time

As we discussed earlier, Kotlin generics are erased at run time, which means if you have an instance of a generic class, you can't find out the type arguments used when the instance was created. The same holds for type arguments of a function. When you call a generic function, in its body, you can't determine the type arguments it was invoked with the following:

```
fun <T> isA(value: Any) = value is T
// Error: Cannot check for instance of erased type: T
```

This is true in general, but there's one case where this limitation can be avoided: inline functions. Type parameters of inline functions can be *reified*, which means you can refer to actual type arguments at run time.

We discussed `inline` functions in detail in section 10.2. As a reminder, if you mark a function with the `inline` keyword, the compiler will replace every call to the function with the actual code implementing the function. Making the function `inline` may improve performance if this function uses lambdas as arguments: the lambda code can be inlined as well, so no anonymous class will be created. This section shows another case when `inline` functions are helpful: their type arguments can be reified.

If you declare the previous `isA` function as `inline` and mark the type parameter as `reified`, you can check `value` to see whether it's an instance of `T`.

Listing 11.7 Declaring a function with a reified type parameter

```
inline fun <reified T> isA(value: Any) = value is T      ⏎ Now, this code compiles.

fun main() {
    println(isA<String>("abc"))
    // true
    println(isA<String>(123))
    // false
}
```

Let's look at some less trivial examples of the use of reified type parameters. One of the simplest examples where reified type parameters come into play is the `filterIs-Instance` standard library function. The function takes a collection, selects instances of the specified class, and returns only those instances. Here's how it can be used.

Listing 11.8 Using the `filterIsInstance` standard library function

```
fun main() {
    val items = listOf("one", 2, "three")
    println(items.filterIsInstance<String>())
    // [one, three]
}
```

You say that you're interested in strings only by specifying `<String>` as a type argument for the function. The return type of the function will, therefore, be `List<String>`. In this case, *the type argument is known at run time*, and `filterIsInstance` uses it to check which values in the list are instances of the class specified as the type argument.

Here's a simplified version of the declaration of `filterIsInstance` from the Kotlin standard library.

Listing 11.9 A simplified implementation of `filterIsInstance`

```
inline fun <reified T>                               ⏎  reified declares that this type
        Iterable<*>.filterIsInstance(): List<T> {       parameter will not be erased
    val destination = mutableListOf<T>()                at run time.
    for (element in this) {
        if (element is T) {                          ⏎  You can check whether the element is an instance
            destination.add(element)                    of the class specified as a type argument.
```

```
        }
    }
    return destination
}
```

Why reification works for inline functions only

How does this work? Why are you allowed to write `element is T` in an `inline` function, but not in a regular class or function?

As we discussed in section 10.2, the compiler inserts the bytecode implementing the inline function into every place where it's called. Every time you call the function with a reified type parameter, the compiler knows the exact type used as the type argument in that particular call. Therefore, the compiler can generate the bytecode that references the specific class used as a type argument. In effect, for the `filterIsInstance<String>` call shown in listing 11.8, the generated code will be equivalent to the following:

```
for (element in this) {
    if (element is String)  ⟵── References a specific class
        destination.add(element)
    }
}
```

Because the generated bytecode references a specific class, not a type parameter, it isn't affected by the type argument erasure that happens at run time.

Note that `inline` function with `reified` type parameters can't be called from Java code. Normal inline functions are accessible to Java as regular functions—they can be called but aren't inlined. Functions with reified type parameters require additional processing to substitute the type argument values into the bytecode; therefore, they must always be inlined. This makes it impossible to call them in a regular way, as the Java code does.

An inline function can have multiple reified type parameters, and it can have non-reified type parameters in addition to the reified ones. Note that the `filterIsInstance` function is marked as `inline` even though it doesn't expect any lambdas as arguments. In section 10.2.4, we discussed that marking a function as inline only has performance benefits when the function has function type parameters and the corresponding arguments—lambdas—are inlined together with the function. But in this case, you aren't marking the function as `inline` for performance reasons; instead, you're doing it to enable the use of reified type parameters.

To ensure good performance, you still need to keep track of the size of the function marked as `inline`. If the function becomes large, it's better to extract the code that doesn't depend on the reified type parameters into separate non-inline functions.

11.2.3 Avoiding java.lang.Class parameters by replacing class references with reified type parameters

One common use case for reified type parameters is building adapters for APIs that take parameters of type `java.lang.Class`. An example of such an API is `ServiceLoader` from the JDK. It takes a `java.lang.Class` representing an interface or an abstract class and returns an instance of a service class implementing that interface based on a previously provided configuration. Let's look at how you can use reified type parameters to make those APIs simpler to call.

To load a service using the standard Java API of `ServiceLoader`, you use the following call:

```
val serviceImpl = ServiceLoader.load(Service::class.java)
```

The `::class.java` syntax shows how you can get a `java.lang.Class` corresponding to a Kotlin class. This is an exact equivalent of `Service.class` in Java. We'll cover this in much more detail in section 12.2, in our discussion of reflection.

Now, let's rewrite this example using a function with a reified type parameter, specifying the class of the service to load as a type argument of the `loadService` function:

```
val serviceImpl = loadService<Service>()
```

Much shorter, isn't it? Specifying a class as a type argument is easier to read because it's shorter than the `::class.java` syntax you need to use otherwise.

Next, let's see how this `loadService` function can be defined:

```
inline fun <reified T> loadService() {        ◁──  The type parameter is marked as reified.
    return ServiceLoader.load(T::class.java)   ◁──┐ Accesses the class of the
}                                                  │ type parameter as T::class
```

You can use the same `::class.java` syntax on reified type parameters that you can use on regular classes. Using this syntax gives you the `java.lang.Class` corresponding to the class specified as the type parameter, which you can then use normally.

Simplifying the startActivity function on Android

If you're an Android developer, you may find another example to be more familiar: showing activities. Instead of passing the class of the activity as a `java.lang.Class`, you can also use a reified type parameter:

```
inline fun <reified T : Activity>
        Context.startActivity() {        ◁──  The type parameter is marked as reified.
    val intent = Intent(this, T::class.java)  ◁──┐ Accesses the class of the
    startActivity(intent)                        │ type parameter as T::class
}

startActivity<DetailActivity>()   ◁───  Invokes the method to show an activity
```

11.2.4 Declaring accessors with reified type parameters

Functions are not the only constructs in Kotlin that can be inlined and use reified type parameters. You already saw in section 2.2.2 that property accessors can provide custom implementations for getters and setters. If a property accessor is defined on a generic type, marking the property as `inline` and the type parameter as `reified` allows you to reference the specific class used as the type argument.

In this example, you're providing an extension property `canonical`, which returns the canonical name of a generic class. Just like in section 11.2.3, this provides a more convenient way of accessing the `canonicalName` property, wrapping the call to `T::class.java`:

```
inline val <reified T> T.canonical: String
    get() = T::class.java.canonicalName

fun main() {
    println(listOf(1, 2, 3).canonical)
    // java.util.List
    println(1.canonical)
    // java.lang.Integer
}
```

11.2.5 Reified type parameters come with restrictions

Even though reified type parameters are a handy tool, they have certain restrictions. Some are inherent to the concept, and others are determined by the current implementation and may be relaxed in future versions of Kotlin.

More specifically, here's how you can use a reified type parameter:

- In type checks and casts (`is`, `!is`, `as`, `as?`)
- To use the Kotlin reflection APIs, as we'll discuss in chapter 12 (`::class`)
- To get the corresponding `java.lang.Class` (`::class.java`)
- As a type argument to call other functions

You *can't* do the following:

- Create new instances of the class specified as a type parameter
- Call methods on the companion object of the type parameter class
- Use a non-reified type parameter as a type argument when calling a function with a reified type parameter
- Mark type parameters of classes or non-inline functions as `reified`

The last constraint leads to an interesting consequence: because reified type parameters can only be used in inline functions, using a reified type parameter means the function along with all the lambdas passed to it are inlined. If the lambdas can't be inlined because of the way the inline function uses them or if you don't want them to be inlined for performance reasons, you can use the `noinline` modifier introduced in section 10.2.2 to mark them as non-inlineable.

Now, that we've discussed how generics work as a language feature, let's explore the concepts of subtyping and variance. We'll do so by taking a more detailed look at the most common generic types that come up in every Kotlin program: collections and their subclasses.

11.3   Variance describes the subtyping relationship between generic arguments

The concept of *variance* describes how types with the same base type and different type arguments relate to each other: for example, `List<String>` and `List<Any>`. First, we'll discuss why this relation is important in general, and then we'll look at how it's expressed in Kotlin. Understanding variance is essential when you write your own generic classes or functions: it helps you create APIs that don't restrict users in inconvenient ways and don't break their type-safety expectations.

11.3.1   Variance determines whether it is safe to pass an argument to a function

Imagine that you have a function that takes a `List<Any>` as an argument. Is it safe to pass a variable of type `List<String>` to this function? It's definitely safe to pass a string to a function expecting `Any` because the `String` class extends `Any`. But when `Any` and `String` become type arguments of the `List` interface, it's not so clear anymore.

For example, let's consider a function that prints the contents of the list:

```
fun printContents(list: List<Any>) {
    println(list.joinToString())
}

fun main() {
    printContents(listOf("abc", "bac"))
    // abc, bac
}
```

It looks like a list of strings works fine here. The function treats each element as `Any`, and because every string is `Any`, it's totally safe.

Now, let's look at another function, which modifies the list (and, therefore, takes `MutableList` as a parameter):

```
fun addAnswer(list: MutableList<Any>) {
    list.add(42)
}
```

Can anything bad happen if you pass a list of strings to this function?

```
fun main() {
    val strings = mutableListOf("abc", "bac")       If this line would compile ...
    addAnswer(strings)
    println(strings.maxBy { it.length })
    // ClassCastException: Integer cannot be cast to String     ... you'd get an
}                                                                exception at run time.
```

You declare a variable `strings` of type `MutableList<String>`. Then you try to pass it to the function. If the compiler accepted it (which it doesn't), you'd be able to add an integer to a list of strings, which would then lead to a run-time exception when you tried to access the contents of the list as strings. For that reason, this call doesn't compile. This example shows that it's not safe to pass a `MutableList<String>` as an argument when a `MutableList<Any>` is expected; the Kotlin compiler correctly forbids that.

Now, you can answer the question of whether it's safe to pass a list of strings to a function that expects a list of `Any` objects. It's not safe if the function adds or replaces elements in the list because this creates the possibility of type inconsistencies. It's safe otherwise (we'll discuss why in more detail later in this section). In Kotlin, this can be easily controlled by choosing the right interface, depending on whether the list is mutable. If a function accepts a read-only list, you can pass a `List` with a more specific element type. If the list is mutable, you can't do that.

Later in this section, we'll generalize the same question for any generic class, not only `List`. You'll also see why the two interfaces `List` and `MutableList` are different with regard to their type argument. But before that, we need to discuss the concepts of *type* and *subtype*.

11.3.2 Understanding the differences between classes, types, and subtypes

As we discussed in section 7.3, the type of a variable specifies the possible values for this variable. We've sometimes used the terms *type* and *class* interchangeably, but they aren't—and now is the time to look at the difference.

In the simplest case, with a nongeneric class, the name of the class can be used directly as a type. For example, if you write `var x: String`, you declare a variable that can hold instances of the `String` class. But note that the same class name can also be used to declare a nullable type: `var x: String?`. This means each Kotlin class can be used to construct at least two types.

The story becomes even more complicated with generic classes. To get a valid type, you have to substitute a specific type as a type argument for the class's type parameter. `List` isn't a type (it's a class), but all of the following substitutions are valid types: `List<Int>`, `List<String?>`, `List<List<String>>`, and so on. Each generic class produces a potentially infinite number of types.

In order for us to discuss the relation between types, you need to be familiar with the term *subtype*. A type `B` is a subtype of a type `A` if you can use the value of the type `B` whenever a value of the type `A` is required. For instance, `Int` is a subtype of `Number`, but `Int` isn't a subtype of `String`. This definition also indicates that a type is considered a subtype of itself. Figure 11.5 illustrates this.

The term *supertype* is the opposite of *subtype*. If `A` is a subtype of `B`, then `B` is a supertype of `A`.

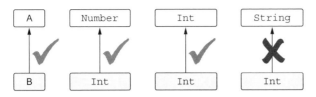

Figure 11.5 `B` is a subtype of `A` if you can use it when `A` is expected. Since you can use an `Int` where a `Number` is expected, it is a subtype. Likewise, you can use an `Int` where an `Int` is expected; it is also a subtype of itself. Because you can't use an `Int` where a `String` is expected, it can't be considered a subtype.

Why is it important whether one type is a subtype of another? The compiler performs this check every time when you assign a value to a variable or pass an argument to a function. Consider the following example.

Listing 11.10   Checking whether a type is a subtype of another

```
fun test(i: Int) {
    val n: Number = i       ◁—— Compiles because Int is a subtype of Number

    fun f(s: String) { /*...*/ }
    f(i)                    ◁—— Doesn't compile because Int isn't a subtype of String
}
```

Storing a value in a variable is allowed only when the value type is a subtype of the variable type; for instance, the type `Int` of the variable initializer `i` is a subtype of the variable type `Number`, so the declaration of `n` is valid. Passing an expression to a function is allowed only when the type of the expression is a subtype of the function parameter type. In the example, the type `Int` of the argument `i` isn't a subtype of the function parameter `String`, so the invocation of the `f` function doesn't compile.

In simple cases, *subtype* means essentially the same thing as *subclass*. For example, the `Int` class is a subclass of `Number`; therefore, the `Int` type is a subtype of the `Number` type. If a class implements an interface, its type is a subtype of the interface type: `String` is a subtype of `CharSequence`.

Nullable types provide an example of when *subtype* isn't the same as *subclass* (see figure 11.6).

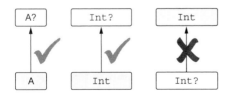

Figure 11.6 A non-null type `A` is a subtype of nullable `A?`, but not vice versa: you can use an `Int` where an `Int?` is expected, but you can't use an `Int?` where an `Int` is expected.

A non-null type is a subtype of its nullable version, but they both correspond to one class. You can always store the value of a non-nullable type in a variable of a nullable type, but not vice versa (`null` isn't an acceptable value for a variable of a non-nullable type). That makes the non-nullable type a subtype of the nullable type:

```
val s: String  = "abc"
val t: String? = s
```
This assignment is legal because String is a subtype of String?.

The difference between subclasses and subtypes becomes especially important when we start talking about generic types. The question from the previous section of whether it's safe to pass a variable of type `List<String>` to a function expecting `List<Any>` now can be reformulated in terms of subtyping: is `List<String>` a subtype of `List<Any>`? You've seen why it's not safe to treat `MutableList<String>` as a subtype of `MutableList<Any>`. Clearly, the reverse isn't true either: `MutableList<Any>` isn't a subtype of `MutableList<String>`.

A generic class—for instance, `MutableList`—is called *invariant* on the type parameter if, for any two different types A and B, `MutableList<A>` isn't a subtype or a supertype of `MutableList<B>`. In Java, all classes are invariant (even though specific uses of those classes can be marked as non-invariant, as you'll see soon).

In the previous section, you saw a class for which the subtyping rules are different: `List`. The `List` interface in Kotlin represents a read-only collection. If A is a subtype of B, then `List<A>` is a subtype of `List<B>`. Such classes or interfaces are called *covariant*. The next section discusses the concept of covariance in detail and explains when it's possible to declare a class or interface as covariant.

11.3.3 *Covariance preserves the subtyping relation*

A *covariant class* is a generic class (we'll use `Producer<T>` as an example) for which the following holds: `Producer<A>` is a subtype of `Producer<B>` if A is a subtype of B. We say that *the subtyping is preserved*. For example, `Producer<Cat>` is a subtype of `Producer<Animal>` because `Cat` is a subtype of `Animal`.

In Kotlin, to declare the class to be covariant on a certain type parameter, you put the `out` keyword before the name of the type parameter:

```
interface Producer<out T> {        ⟵──── This class is declared as a covariant on T.
    fun produce(): T
}
```

Marking a type parameter of a class as covariant makes it possible to pass values of that class as function arguments and return values when the type arguments don't *exactly match* the ones in the function definition. For example, imagine a function that takes care of feeding a group of animals, represented by the `Herd` class. The type parameter of the `Herd` class identifies the type of animal in the herd.

> **Listing 11.11   Defining an invariant collection-like class**

```
open class Animal {
    fun feed() { /* ... */ }
```

```
}
class Herd<T : Animal> {                    ◁──┐  The type parameter isn't
    val size: Int get() = /* ... */              declared as covariant.
    operator fun get(i: Int): T { /* ... */ }
}

fun feedAll(animals: Herd<Animal>) {
    for (i in 0..<animals.size) {
        animals[i].feed()
    }
}
```

Suppose a user of your code has a herd of cats and needs to take care of them.

Listing 11.12 Using an invariant collection-like class

```
class Cat : Animal() {          ◁──── A Cat is an Animal.
    fun cleanLitter() { /* ... */ }
}

fun takeCareOfCats(cats: Herd<Cat>) {
    for (i in 0..<cats.size) {
        cats[i].cleanLitter()
    }                           ┌── Error: inferred type is Herd<Cat>,
    // feedAll(cats)       ◁────┘   but Herd<Animal> was expected.
}
```

Unfortunately, the cats will remain hungry; if you tried to pass the herd to the feedAll function, you'd get a type-mismatch error during compilation. Because you don't use any variance modifier on the T type parameter in the Herd class, making it invariant, the herd of cats isn't a subclass of the herd of animals. You could use an explicit cast to work around the problem, but that approach is verbose, error prone, and almost never a correct way to deal with a type-mismatch problem.

Because the Herd class has an API similar to List and doesn't allow its clients to add or change the animals in the herd, you can make it covariant and change the calling code accordingly.

Listing 11.13 Using a covariant collection-like class

```
class Herd<out T : Animal> {          ◁──── The T parameter is now covariant.
    /* ... */
}

fun takeCareOfCats(cats: Herd<Cat>) {
    for (i in 0..<cats.size) {
        cats[i].cleanLitter()
    }
    feedAll(cats)               ◁──── You don't need a cast.
}
```

You can't make any class covariant, as that would be unsafe. Making the class covariant on a certain type parameter constrains the possible uses of this type parameter in the class. To guarantee type safety, it can be used only in so-called *out* positions, meaning the class can produce values of type T but not consume them.

Uses of a type parameter in declarations of class members can be divided into `in` and `out` positions. Let's consider a class that declares a type parameter T and contains a function that uses T. We say that if T is used as the return type of a function, it's in the `out` position. In this case, the function *produces* values of type T. If T is used as the type of a function parameter, it's in the `in` position. Such a function *consumes* values of type T. Figure 11.7 illustrates this.

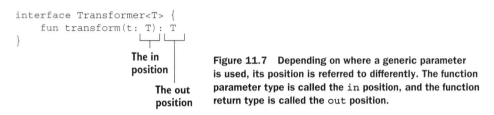

```
interface Transformer<T> {
    fun transform(t: T): T
}
```

The in position

The out position

Figure 11.7 Depending on where a generic parameter is used, its position is referred to differently. The function parameter type is called the `in` position, and the function return type is called the `out` position.

The `out` keyword on a type parameter of the class requires that all methods using T have T only in `out` positions and not in `in` positions. This keyword constrains possible use of T, which guarantees safety of the corresponding subtype relation.

As an example, consider the `Herd` class. It uses the type parameter T in only one place: in the return value of the `get` method.

```
class Herd<out T : Animal> {
    val size: Int get() = /* ... */
    operator fun get(i: Int): T { /* ... */ }        ⟵——— Uses T as the return type
}
```

This is an `out` position, which makes it safe to declare the class as covariant. Any code calling `get` on a `Herd<Animal>` will work perfectly if the method returns a `Cat` because `Cat` is a subtype of `Animal`.

To reiterate, the `out` keyword on the type parameter T means two things:

- The subtyping is preserved (`Producer<Cat>` is a subtype of `Producer<Animal>`).
- T can be used only in `out` positions.

Now, let's look at the `List<T>` interface. `List` is read-only in Kotlin, so it has a method `get` that returns an element of type T but doesn't define any methods that store a value of type T in the list. Therefore, it's also covariant.

```
interface List<out T> : Collection<T> {
    operator fun get(index: Int): T       ⟵——┐  Read-only interface that defines
    // ...                                     only methods that return T (so T
}                                              is in the out position)
```

Note that a type parameter can be used not only as a parameter type or return type directly, but also as a type argument of another type. For example, the `List` interface contains a method `subList` that returns `List<T>`.

```
interface List<out T> : Collection<T> {
    fun subList(fromIndex: Int, toIndex: Int): List<T>     ◁─── Here, T is in the out
    // ...                                                       position as well.
}
```

In this case, `T` in the function `subList` is used in the `out` position. We won't go deep into detail here; if you're interested in the exact algorithm that determines which position is `out` and which is `in`, you can find this information in the Kotlin language documentation.

Note that you can't declare `MutableList<T>` as covariant on its type parameter because it contains methods that take values of type `T` as parameters and return such values (therefore, `T` appears in both `in` and `out` positions). The compiler enforces this restriction. The following code, which attempts to declare the interface as covariant via the `out` keyword, reports an error, `Type parameter T is declared as 'out' but occurs in the 'in' position`:

```
                                      MutableList can't be declared as
                                      covariant (via the out keyword) on T ...
interface MutableList<out T>     ◁──┘
       : List<T>, MutableCollection<T> {
    override fun add(element: T): Boolean     ◁───┐
}                                                  ... because T is used in the in position (T is
                                                   used as the type of a function parameter).
```

Note that constructor parameters are in neither the `in` nor the `out` position. Even if a type parameter is declared as `out`, you can still use it in a constructor parameter declaration:

```
class Herd<out T: Animal>(vararg animals: T) { /* ... */ }
```

The variance protects the class instance from misuse if you're working with it as an instance of a more generic type: you just can't call the potentially dangerous methods. The constructor isn't a method that can be called later (after an instance creation); therefore, it can't be potentially dangerous.

If you use the `val` or `var` keyword with a constructor parameter, however, you also declare a getter and a setter (if the property is mutable). Therefore, the type parameter is used in the `out` position for a read-only property and in both `out` and `in` positions for a mutable property:

```
class Herd<T: Animal>(var leadAnimal: T, vararg animals: T) { /* ... */ }
```

In this case, `T` can't be marked as `out` because the class contains a setter for the `leadAnimal` property that uses `T` in the `in` position.

Also note that the position rules cover only the externally visible (`public`, `protected`, and `internal`) API of a class. Parameters of private methods are in neither the `in` nor the out position. The variance rules protect a class from misuse by external clients and don't come into play in the implementation of the class itself:

```
class Herd<out T: Animal>(private var leadAnimal: T,
    vararg animals: T) { /* ... */ }
```

Now, it's safe to make `Herd` covariant on `T` because the `leadAnimal` property has been made private.

You may ask what happens with classes or interfaces where the type parameter is used only in an `in` position. In that case, the reverse relation holds. The next section presents the details.

11.3.4   *Contravariance reverses the subtyping relation*

The concept of *contravariance* can be thought of as a mirror to covariance: for a contravariant class, the subtyping relation is the opposite of the subtyping relations of classes used as its type arguments. Let's start with an example: the `Comparator` interface. This interface defines one method, `compare`, which compares two given objects:

```
interface Comparator<in T>  {
    fun compare(e1: T, e2: T): Int { /* ... */ }      ⟵——— Uses T in in positions
}
```

You can see that the method of this interface only consumes values of type `T`. That means `T` is used only in `in` positions; therefore, its declaration can be preceded by the `in` keyword.

A comparator defined for values of a certain type can, of course, compare the values of any subtype of that type. For example, you might have a simple hierarchy of fruits—apples and oranges—that both share a common property, `weight`:

```
sealed class Fruit {
    abstract val weight: Int
}

data class Apple(
    override val weight: Int,
    val color: String,
): Fruit()

data class Orange(
    override val weight: Int,
    val juicy: Boolean,
): Fruit()
```

If you now create a `Comparator<Fruit>`, you can use it to compare values of any specific type:

```
fun main() {
    val weightComparator = Comparator<Fruit> { a, b ->
        a.weight - b.weight
```

```
}
val fruits: List<Fruit> = listOf(
    Orange(180, true),
    Apple(100, "green")
)
val apples: List<Apple> = listOf(
    Apple(50, "red"),
    Apple(120, "green"),
    Apple(155, "yellow")
)
println(fruits.sortedWith(weightComparator))   ◁
// [Apple(weight=100, color=green), Orange(weight=180, juicy=true)]
println(apples.sortedWith(weightComparator))
// [Apple(weight=50, color=red), Apple(weight=120, color=green),
    Apple(weight=155, color=yellow)]
}
```

> **You can use the weight comparator for any collection of objects that are a subtype of Fruit, such as apples and oranges.**

The `sortedWith` function expects a `Comparator<String>` (a comparator that can compare strings), and it's safe to pass one that can compare more general types. If you need to perform comparisons on objects of a certain type, you can use a comparator that handles either that type or any of its supertypes. This means `Comparator<Any>` is a *subtype* of `Comparator<String>`, where `Any` is a *supertype* of `String`. The subtyping relation between comparators for two different types goes in the opposite direction of the subtyping relation between those types.

Now, you're ready for the full definition of contravariance. A class that is *contravariant* on the type parameter is a generic class (let's consider `Consumer<T>` as an example) for which the following holds: `Consumer<A>` is a subtype of `Consumer<B>` if B is a subtype of A. The type arguments A and B changed places, so we say the subtyping is reversed. For example, `Consumer<Animal>` is a subtype of `Consumer<Cat>`.

Figure 11.8 shows the difference between the subtyping relation for classes that are covariant and contravariant on a type parameter. You can see that for the `Producer` class, the subtyping relation replicates the subtyping relation for its type arguments, whereas for the `Consumer` class, the relation is reversed.

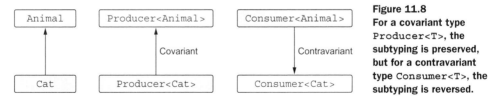

Figure 11.8
For a covariant type `Producer<T>`, **the subtyping is preserved, but for a contravariant type** `Consumer<T>`, **the subtyping is reversed.**

The `in` keyword means values of the corresponding type are *passed in* to methods of this class and consumed by those methods. Similar to the covariant case, constraining use of the type parameter leads to the specific subtyping relation. The `in` keyword on the type parameter T means the subtyping is reversed and T can be used only in `in` positions. Table 11.1 summarizes the differences between the possible variance choices.

Table 11.1   Covariant, contravariant, and invariant classes

Covariant	Contravariant	Invariant
Producer<out T>	Consumer<in T>	MutableList<T>
Subtyping for the class is preserved: Producer<Cat> is a subtype of Producer<Animal>.	Subtyping is reversed: Consumer<Animal> is a subtype of Consumer<Cat>.	No subtyping.
T only in out positions	T only in in positions	T in any position

A class or interface can be covariant on one type parameter and contravariant on another. The classic example is the Function interface. The following declaration shows a one-parameter Function:

```
interface Function1<in P, out R> {
    operator fun invoke(p: P): R
}
```

The Kotlin notation (P) -> R is another, more readable form to express Function1 <P, R>. You can see that P (the parameter type) is used only in the in position and is marked with the in keyword, whereas R (the return type) is used only in the out position and is marked with the out keyword. That means the subtyping for the function type is reversed for its first type argument and preserved for the second. For example, if you have a higher-order function that tries to enumerate your cats, you can pass a lambda accepting any animals:

```
fun enumerateCats(f: (Cat) -> Number) { /* ... */ }
fun Animal.getIndex(): Int = /* ... */

fun main() {
    enumerateCats(Animal::getIndex)
}
```

This code is legal in Kotlin. Animal is a supertype of Cat, and Int is a subtype of Number.

Figure 11.9 illustrates the subtyping relationships in the previous example.

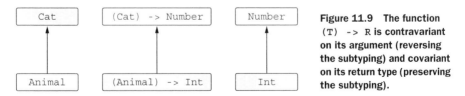

Figure 11.9   The function (T) -> R is contravariant on its argument (reversing the subtyping) and covariant on its return type (preserving the subtyping).

Note that in all the examples so far, the variance of a class is specified directly in its declaration and applies to all places where the class is used. Java doesn't support that and instead uses wildcards to specify the variance for specific uses of a class. Let's look at the difference between the two approaches and see how you can use the second approach in Kotlin.

11.3.5 *Specifying variance for type occurrences via use-site variance*

The ability to specify variance modifiers on class declarations is convenient because the modifiers apply to all places where the class is used. This is called *declaration-site variance*. If you're familiar with Java's wildcard types (`?` `extends` and `?` `super`), you'll realize that Java handles variance differently. In Java, every time you use a type with a type parameter, you can also specify whether this type parameter can be replaced with its subtypes or supertypes. This is called *use-site variance*.

> ### Declaration-site variance in Kotlin vs. Java wildcards
>
> Declaration-site variance allows for more concise code because you specify the variance modifiers once, and clients of your class don't have to think about them. In Java, to create APIs that behave according to users' expectations, the library writer must use wildcards all the time: `Function<? super T, ? extends R>`. If you examine the source code of the Java 8 standard library, you'll find wildcards on every use of the `Function` interface. For example, here's how the `Stream.map` method is declared:
>
> ```
> /* Java */
> public interface Stream<T> {
>     <R> Stream<R> map(Function<? super T, ? extends R> mapper);
> }
> ```
>
> Specifying the variance once on the declaration makes the code much more concise and elegant.

Kotlin supports use-site variance too, allowing you to specify the variance for a specific occurrence of a type parameter even when it can't be declared as covariant or contravariant in the class declaration. Let's see how that works.

You've seen that many interfaces, like `MutableList`, aren't covariant or contravariant in a general case because they can both produce and consume values of types specified by their type parameters. But it's common for a variable of that type in a particular function to be used in only one of those roles: a producer or consumer. For example, consider this simple function.

Listing 11.14 A data copy function with invariant parameter types

```
fun <T> copyData(source: MutableList<T>,
                 destination: MutableList<T>) {
    for (item in source) {
        destination.add(item)
    }
}
```

This function copies elements from one collection to another. Even though both collections have an invariant type, the source collection is only used for reading, and the destination collection is only used for writing. In this situation, elements of a specific type can be copied into a collection that stores a supertype of these elements. For example, it's perfectly valid to copy a collection of strings into a collection with the generic type `Any`.

To make this function work with lists of different types, you can introduce the second generic parameter.

Listing 11.15   A data copy function with two type parameters

```
fun <T: R, R> copyData(source: MutableList<T>,                    ◁─── The source's
                       destination: MutableList<R>) {                  element type
    for (item in source) {                                             should be a
        destination.add(item)                                          subtype of the
    }                                                                   destination's
}                                                                      element type.
fun main() {
    val ints = mutableListOf(1, 2, 3)
    val anyItems = mutableListOf<Any>()
    copyData(ints, anyItems)           ◁─── You can call this function
    println(anyItems)                       because Int is a subtype of Any.
    // [1, 2, 3]
}
```

You declare two generic parameters representing the element types in the source and destination lists. To be able to copy elements from one list to the other, the source element type should be a subtype of elements in the `destination` list, like `Int` is a subtype of `Any` in listing 11.16.

But Kotlin provides a more elegant way to express this. When the implementation of a function only calls methods that have the type parameter in the `out` (or only in the `in`) position, you can take advantage of it and add variance modifiers to the particular usages of the type parameter in the function definition.

Listing 11.16   A data copy function with an out-projected type parameter

```
fun <T> copyData(source: MutableList<out T>,          ◁─── You can add the out keyword
                 destination: MutableList<T>) {             to the type usage: no methods
    for (item in source) {                                  with T in the in position are
        destination.add(item)                               used.
    }
}
```

You can specify a variance modifier on any usage of a type parameter in a type declaration, for a parameter type (as in listing 11.16), local variable type, function return type, and so on. What happens here is called *type projection*: we say that `source` isn't a regular `MutableList` but a *projected* (restricted) one. You can only call methods that return the generic type parameter or, strictly speaking, use it in the `out` position only. The compiler prohibits calling methods where this type parameter is used as an argument (in the `in` position):

```
fun main() {
    val list: MutableList<out Number> = mutableListOf()
    list.add(42)
    // Error: Out-projected type 'MutableList<out Number>' prohibits
    // the use of 'fun add(element: E): Boolean'
}
```

Don't be surprised that you can't call some of the methods if you're using a projected type. If you need to call them, you must use a regular type instead of a projection. This may require you to declare a second type parameter that depends on the one that was originally a projection, as in listing 11.15.

Of course, the right way to implement the function `copyData` would be to use `List<T>` as a type of the `source` argument because we're only using the methods declared in `List`, not in `MutableList`, and the variance of the `List` type parameter is specified in its declaration. But this example is still important for illustrating the concept, especially keeping in mind that most classes don't have a separate covariant read interface and an invariant read–write interface, such as `List` and `MutableList`.

There is no sense in having an `out` projection of a type parameter that already has `out` variance, such as `List<out T>`. That would mean the same as `List<T>` because `List` is declared as `class List<out T>`. The Kotlin compiler will warn that such a projection is redundant.

In a similar way, you can use the `in` modifier on a type parameter to indicate that, in this location, the corresponding value acts as a consumer and the type parameter can be substituted with any of its supertypes. Here's how you can rewrite listing 11.16 using an `in` projection.

> **Listing 11.17   A data copy function with an `in`-projected type parameter**

```
fun <T> copyData(source: MutableList<T>,
                 destination: MutableList<in T>) {       ◁—  Allows the destination
    for (item in source) {                                   element type to be a
        destination.add(item)                                supertype of the source
    }                                                        element type
}
```

NOTE   Use-site variance declarations in Kotlin correspond directly to Java bounded wildcards. `MutableList<out T>` in Kotlin means the same as `Mutable-List<? extends T>` in Java. The `in`-projected `MutableList<in T>` corresponds to Java's `MutableList<? super T>`.

Use-site projections can help to widen the range of acceptable types. Now, let's discuss the extreme case: when types with all possible type arguments become acceptable.

11.3.6   Star projection: Using the * character to indicate a lack of information about a generic argument

While talking about type checks and casts earlier in this chapter, we mentioned the special *star-projection* syntax you can use to indicate that you have no information about a generic argument. For example, a list of elements of an unknown type is expressed using that syntax as `List<*>`. Let's explore the semantics of star projections in detail.

First, note that `MutableList<*>` isn't the same as `MutableList<Any?>` (it's important here that `MutableList<T>` is invariant on `T`). A `MutableList<Any?>` is a list that you know can contain elements of any type. On the other hand, a `MutableList<*>` is a list that contains elements of a specific type you don't know. The list was created as a list of elements of a specific type, such as `String` (you can't create a new `ArrayList<*>`), and the code that created it expects it will only contain elements of that type. Because you don't know what the type is, you can't put anything into the list because any value you put there might violate the expectations of the calling code. But it's possible to get the elements from the list because you know for certain that all values stored there will match the type `Any?`, which is the supertype of all Kotlin types:

```
import kotlin.random.Random
```

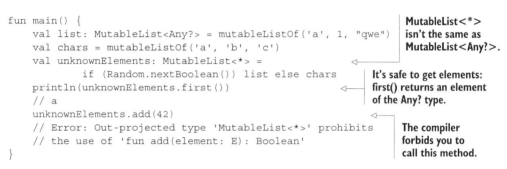

```
fun main() {
    val list: MutableList<Any?> = mutableListOf('a', 1, "qwe")
    val chars = mutableListOf('a', 'b', 'c')
    val unknownElements: MutableList<*> =
            if (Random.nextBoolean()) list else chars
    println(unknownElements.first())
    // a
    unknownElements.add(42)
    // Error: Out-projected type 'MutableList<*>' prohibits
    // the use of 'fun add(element: E): Boolean'
}
```

`MutableList<*>` isn't the same as `MutableList<Any?>`.

It's safe to get elements: first() returns an element of the Any? type.

The compiler forbids you to call this method.

Why does the compiler refer to `MutableList<*>` as an `out`-projected type? In this context, `MutableList<*>` is projected to (acts as) `MutableList<out Any?>`: when you know nothing about the type of the element, it's safe to get elements of `Any?` type, but it's not safe to put elements into the list. Regarding Java wildcards, Kotlin's `MyType<*>` corresponds to Java's `MyType<?>`.

> **NOTE** For contravariant type parameters such as `Consumer<in T>`, a star projection is equivalent to `<in Nothing>`. In effect, you can't call any methods that have `T` in the signature on such a star projection. If the type parameter is contravariant, it acts only as a consumer, and as we discussed earlier, you don't know exactly what it can consume. Therefore, you can't give it anything to consume. If you're interested in more details, see the Kotlin online documentation (http://mng.bz/3Ed7).

You can use the star-projection syntax when the information about type arguments isn't important: you don't use any methods that refer to the type parameter in the signature, or you only read the data and you don't care about its specific type. For instance, you can implement the `printFirst` function taking `List<*>` as a parameter:

```
fun printFirst(list: List<*>) {          ◁─── Every list is a possible argument.
    if (list.isNotEmpty()) {        ◁─┐
        println(list.first())     ◁─┐ │   isNotEmpty() doesn't use
    }                                │ │   the generic type parameter.
}                                    │
                                     │   first() now returns Any?, but
fun main() {                         │   in this case, that's enough.
    printFirst(listOf("Sveta", "Seb", "Dima", "Roman"))
    // Sveta
}
```

As in the case with use-site variance, you have an alternative—to introduce a generic type parameter:

```
fun <T> printFirst(list: List<T>) {       ◁─── Again, every list is a possible argument.
    if (list.isNotEmpty()) {
        println(list.first())          ◁─── first() now returns a value of T.
    }
}
```

The syntax with star projection is more concise, but it works only if you aren't interested in the exact value of the generic type parameter: you use only methods that produce values, and you don't care about the types of those values.

Now, let's look at another example of using a type with a star projection and common traps you may fall into while using that approach. Let's say you need to validate user input, and you declare an interface `FieldValidator`. It contains its type parameter in the `in` position only, so it can be declared as contravariant. And indeed, it's correct to use the validator that can validate any elements when a validator of strings is expected (that's what declaring it as contravariant lets you do). You also declare two validators that handle `String` and `Int` inputs.

Listing 11.18 Interfaces for input validation

```
interface FieldValidator<in T> {          ◁─── Interface declared as contravariant on T
    fun validate(input: T): Boolean    ◁─┐
}                                         │   T is used only in the in position (this
                                          │   method consumes a value of T).
object DefaultStringValidator : FieldValidator<String> {
    override fun validate(input: String) = input.isNotEmpty()
}

object DefaultIntValidator : FieldValidator<Int> {
    override fun validate(input: Int) = input >= 0
}
```

Now, imagine that you want to store all validators in the same container and get the right validator according to the type of input. Your first attempt might use a map to store them. You need to store validators for any types, so you declare a map from

KClass (which represents a Kotlin class—chapter 12 will cover KClass in detail) to
FieldValidator<*> (which may refer to a validator of any type):

```
import kotlin.reflect.KClass

fun main() {
    val validators = mutableMapOf<KClass<*>, FieldValidator<*>>()
    validators[String::class] = DefaultStringValidator
    validators[Int::class] = DefaultIntValidator
}
```

Once you do that, you may have difficulties when trying to use the validators. You
can't validate a string with a validator of the type FieldValidator<*>. It's unsafe
because the compiler doesn't know what kind of validator it is:

```
validators[String::class]!!.validate("")          ◁──  The value stored in
// Error: Out-projected type 'FieldValidator<*>' prohibits   the map has the type
// the use of 'fun validate(input: T): Boolean'              FieldValidator<*>.
```

You saw this error earlier when you tried to put an element into MutableList<*>. In this
case, this error means it's unsafe to give a value of a specific type to a validator for an
unknown type. One of the ways to fix that is to cast a validator explicitly to the type
you need. It's not safe and isn't recommended, but we show it here as a fast trick to
make your code compile so that you can refactor it afterward.

Listing 11.19 Retrieving a validator using an explicit cast

```
val stringValidator = validators[String::class] as FieldValidator<String>   ◁─┐
println(stringValidator.validate(""))
// false                                            Warning: "unchecked cast"
```

The compiler emits a warning about the unchecked cast. Note, however, that this code
will fail on validation only, not when you make the cast because, at run time, all the
generic type information is erased.

Listing 11.20 Incorrectly retrieving a validator

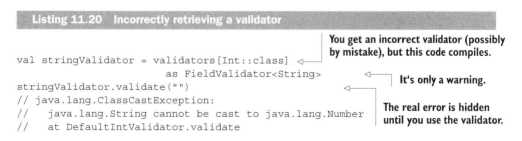

```
                                          You get an incorrect validator (possibly
                                          by mistake), but this code compiles.
val stringValidator = validators[Int::class]   ◁──
                  as FieldValidator<String>            ◁──┐  It's only a warning.
stringValidator.validate("")                       ◁──
// java.lang.ClassCastException:                        The real error is hidden
//   java.lang.String cannot be cast to java.lang.Number   until you use the validator.
//   at DefaultIntValidator.validate
```

This incorrect code and listing 11.19 are similar, in the sense that in both cases, only a
warning is emitted. It becomes your responsibility to cast only values of the correct
type.

This solution isn't type safe and is error prone. So, let's investigate what other options you have if you want to store validators for different types in one place.

The solution in listing 11.21 uses the same `validators` map but encapsulates all the access to it into two generic methods responsible for having only correct validators registered and returned. This code also emits a warning about the unchecked cast (the same one), but here, the object `Validators` controls all access to the map, which guarantees no one will change the map incorrectly.

Listing 11.21 Encapsulating access to the validator collection

```
object Validators {                                        Uses the same map as before, but
    private val validators =                               now, you can't access it outside
            mutableMapOf<KClass<*>, FieldValidator<*>>()
                                                                            Puts only the
    fun <T: Any> registerValidator(                                         correct key–
            kClass: KClass<T>, fieldValidator: FieldValidator<T>) {         value pairs into
        validators[kClass] = fieldValidator                                 the map, when
    }                                                                       a validator
                                                                            corresponds
    @Suppress("UNCHECKED_CAST")                                             to a class
    operator fun <T: Any> get(kClass: KClass<T>): FieldValidator<T> =
        validators[kClass] as? FieldValidator<T>
            ?: throw IllegalArgumentException(              Suppresses the
            "No validator for ${kClass.simpleName}")        warning about the
}                                                           unchecked cast to
                                                            FieldValidator<T>
fun main() {
    Validators.registerValidator(String::class, DefaultStringValidator)
    Validators.registerValidator(Int::class, DefaultIntValidator)

    println(Validators[String::class].validate("Kotlin"))
    // true
    println(Validators[Int::class].validate(42))
    // true
}
```

Now, you have a type-safe API. All the unsafe logic is hidden in the body of the class, and by localizing it, you guarantee it can't be used incorrectly. The compiler forbids you to use an incorrect validator because the `Validators` object always gives you the correct validator implementation:

Now, the get method returns an instance of FieldValidator<String>.

```
println(Validators[String::class].validate(42))
// Error: The integer literal does not conform to the expected type String
```

This pattern can be easily extended to the storage of any custom generic classes. Localizing unsafe code in a separate place prevents misuse and makes use of a container safe. Note that the pattern described here isn't specific to Kotlin; you can use the same approach in Java as well.

Java generics and variance are generally considered the trickiest part of the language. In Kotlin, we've tried hard to come up with a design that is easier to understand and easier to work with, while remaining interoperable with Java.

11.3.7 *Type aliases*

When you're working with types that combine multiple generics, it can sometimes be cumbersome to keep track of the meaning behind a type signature. It may not immediately be obvious what the purpose of a collection with the type `List<(String, Int) -> String>` is, and you may want to avoid repeating the same complex combination of generic and functional types whenever you want to refer to it.

For cases like this, Kotlin allows you to define *type aliases*: alternative names for existing types. You introduce a type alias using the `typealias` keyword, followed by the alias. Then, after an `=` sign, specify the original, underlying type.

You may find type aliases specifically useful when looking to shorten long generic types. In this example, you declare a function to combine the names of the four authors of this book, `combineAuthors`. The behavior of *how* the authors are combined can be passed in using a parameter of a functional type that takes four strings and returns a new, combined string. This is often convenient, since its type signature, `(String, String, String, String) -> String`, may be somewhat cumbersome to repeat for every use. Using a type alias, you can give this functional type a new name, `Name-Combiner`. This alias can then be used wherever you would've previously used the underlying type:

> **A type alias is defined using the typealias keyword, the alias, and the underlying type.**

```
typealias NameCombiner = (String, String, String, String) -> String

val authorsCombiner: NameCombiner = { a, b, c, d -> "$a et al." }
val bandCombiner: NameCombiner = { a, b, c, d -> "$a, $b & The Gang" }

fun combineAuthors(combiner: NameCombiner) {
    println(combiner("Sveta", "Seb", "Dima", "Roman"))
}

fun main() {
    combineAuthors(bandCombiner)
    // Sveta, Seb & The Gang
    combineAuthors(authorsCombiner)
    // Sveta et al.
    combineAuthors { a, b, c, d -> "$d, $c & Co."}
    // Roman, Dima & Co.
}
```

> **Type aliases can be used wherever you would've used the underlying type, like variable declarations …**
>
> **… or function parameter declarations.**
>
> **The type alias resolves to the underlying type. So it's perfectly fine to pass a NameCombiner …**
>
> **… or a lambda taking four strings and returning a single string.**

By introducing a type alias, you managed to imbue the functional type with additional context that may aid in reading the code. However, it's also worth keeping in mind that developers not familiar with your codebase might have to spend additional time mentally resolving the `NameCombiner` alias back to its underlying type when reading code or making changes. Determining when to introduce type aliases in your code base is ultimately a tradeoff you will have to decide for yourself.

It's also worth noting that from the perspective of the compiler, type aliases don't introduce any new constraints or changes—during compilation, aliases are expanded entirely to their underlying type. So, while they provide a useful shorthand, type aliases do not provide any additional type safety.

Inline classes and type aliases: When to use each

Type aliases provide a useful shorthand, but they do not provide any additional type safety. That means they can't be used for introducing additional safeguards that prevent accidentally using two types in each other's stead; the following example illustrates this. Introducing a typealias `ValidatedInput` for `String` helps make the signature of the `save` function clearer by signaling a validated input is expected; however, the compiler will accept any `String` without complaint:

```
typealias ValidatedInput = String

fun save(v: ValidatedInput): Unit = TODO()

fun main() {
    val rawInput = "needs validating!"
    save(rawInput)
}
```

Type aliases introduce no extra compile-time guarantees.

If added type safety with minimized run-time overhead is your goal, make sure you use inline classes (as discussed in section 4.5). Since the types of inline classes are checked just like any other type, the preceding example would not compile because of a type mismatch between `ValidatedInput` and `String`, forcing the user of the `save` function to make the conversion from `String` to `ValidatedInput` explicit, thus catching potential bugs early:

```
@JvmInline
value class ValidatedInput(val s: String)

fun save(v: ValidatedInput): Unit = TODO()

fun main() {
    val rawInput = "needs validating!"
    save(rawInput)
}
```

Won't compile because of the type mismatch between ValidatedInput and String

Summary

- Kotlin's generics are fairly similar to those in Java: you declare a generic function or class in the same way.
- As in Java, type arguments for generic types only exist at compile time.
- You can't use types with type arguments together with the `is` operator because type arguments are erased at run time.

- Type parameters of inline functions can be marked as reified, which allows you to use them at run time to perform `is` checks and obtain `java.lang.Class` instances.

- Variance is a way to specify whether one of two generic types with the same base class and different type arguments is a subtype or a supertype of the other one when one of the type arguments is the subtype of the other one.

- You can declare a class as covariant on a type parameter if the parameter is used only in `out` positions.

- The opposite is true for contravariant cases: you can declare a class as contravariant on a type parameter if it's used only in `in` positions.

- The read-only interface `List` in Kotlin is declared as covariant, which means `List<String>` is a subtype of `List<Any>`.

- The function interface is declared as contravariant on its first type parameter and covariant on its second, which makes `(Animal) -> Int` a subtype of `(Cat) -> Number`.

- Kotlin allows you to specify variance both for a generic class as a whole (*declaration-site variance*) and for a specific use of a generic type (*use-site variance*).

- The star-projection syntax can be used when the exact type arguments are unknown or unimportant.

- Type aliases allow you to provide alternative or shortened names for types. They are expanded to their underlying type at compile time.

Annotations and reflection

This chapter covers
- Applying and defining annotations
- Using reflection to introspect classes at run time
- A real example of a Kotlin project

Up to this point, you've seen many features for working with classes and functions, but they all require you to specify the exact names of classes and functions you're using as part of the program source code. To call a function, you need to know the class in which it was defined as well as its name and parameter types. *Annotations* and *reflection* give you the power to go beyond that and to write code that deals with arbitrary classes that aren't known in advance. You can use annotations to add additional metadata and semantics to declarations. For example, you could use them to indicate whether a declaration is deprecated (as you'll see in section 12.1.1), you could use them for integrations with the compiler, your IDE, and external tools (as you'll see in section 12.1.2), or you could use them to construct library-specific and custom semantics. Reflection allows you to analyze your declarations at run time.

Applying annotations is straightforward, but writing your own annotations, and especially writing the code that handles them, is less trivial. The syntax for using annotations is exactly the same as in Java, whereas the syntax for declaring your own annotation classes is a bit different. The general structure of the reflection APIs is also similar to Java, but the details differ.

As a demonstration of the use of annotations and reflection, we'll walk you through an implementation of a real-life project: a JSON serialization and deserialization library called JKid. The library uses reflection to access properties of arbitrary Kotlin objects at run time as well as to create objects based on data provided in JSON files. Annotations allow you to customize how specific classes and properties are serialized and deserialized by the library.

12.1   Declaring and applying annotations

Annotations allow you to associate additional *metadata* with a declaration. The metadata can then be accessed by tools that work with source code, with compiled class files, or at run time, depending on how the annotation is configured.

12.1.1   Applying annotations to mark declarations

In Kotlin, to apply an annotation, you put its name, prefixed with the @ character, at the beginning of the declaration you're annotating. You can annotate different declarations in your code, such as functions and classes.

For instance, if you're using the `kotlin.test` library together with the JUnit framework (https://junit.org/junit5/), you can mark a test method with the `@Test` annotation:

```
import kotlin.test.*
class MyTest {
    @Test                           The @Test annotation
    fun testTrue() {                instructs the framework to
        assertTrue(1 + 1 == 2)      invoke this method as a test.
    }
}
```

As a more interesting example, let's look at the `@Deprecated` annotation. It marks a declaration as deprecated, indicating it should no longer be used in code—usually because it has been replaced by a different declaration or the functionality it provides is no longer supported.

The `@Deprecated` annotation takes up to three parameters. First, a `message` explains the reason for the deprecation. An optional `replaceWith` parameter allows you to provide a replacement pattern to support a smooth transition to a new version of the API. You can also provide a `level` that helps with gradual deprecation—whereas `WARNING` serves as a mere notification to users of a declaration, `ERROR` and `HIDDEN` prevent new Kotlin code from being compiled against these APIs, with the latter only keeping binary compatibility for previously compiled code.

The following example shows how you can provide arguments for the annotation (specifically, a deprecation message and a replacement pattern). The arguments are passed in parentheses, just as in a regular function call. Here, the `remove` function is annotated to indicate that `removeAt(index)` is the preferred replacement:

```
@Deprecated("Use removeAt(index) instead.", ReplaceWith("removeAt(index)"))
fun remove(index: Int) { /* ... */ }
```

With this declaration, if someone uses the `remove` function, IntelliJ IDEA will not only show what function should be used instead (`removeAt`, in this case) but also offer a quick fix to replace it automatically (see figure 12.1).

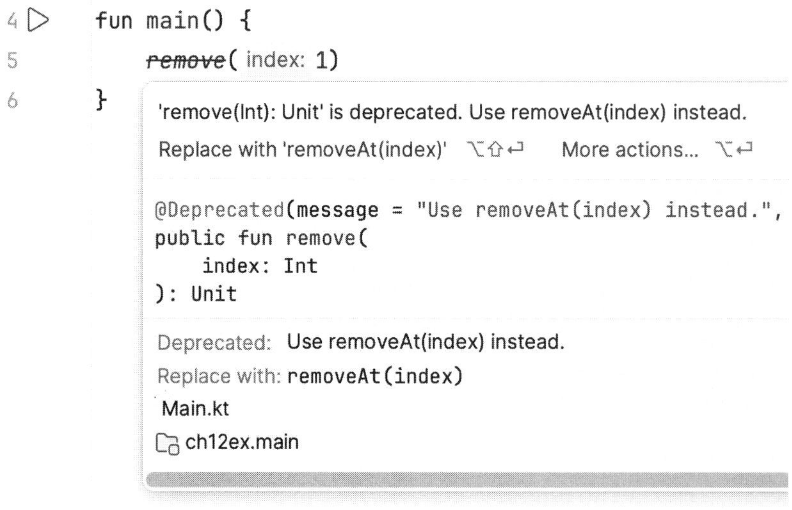

```
4 ▷   fun main() {
5         remove( index: 1)
6     }
```

'remove(Int): Unit' is deprecated. Use removeAt(index) instead.

Replace with 'removeAt(index)' ⌥⇧↵   More actions... ⌥↵

```
@Deprecated(message = "Use removeAt(index) instead.",
public fun remove(
    index: Int
): Unit
```

Deprecated: Use removeAt(index) instead.

Replace with: `removeAt(index)`

Main.kt

ch12ex.main

Figure 12.1   IntelliJ IDEA offers a quick fix to replace calls to functions that are annotated with `@Deprecated`.

Annotations can only have parameters of primitive types, strings, enums, class references, other annotation classes, and arrays thereof. The syntax for specifying annotation arguments looks as follows:

- *Specifying a class as an annotation argument*—Put `::class` after the class name: `@MyAnnotation(MyClass::class)`. For instance, a serialization library (as we will discuss later in this chapter) may provide an annotation that expects a class as an argument to establish the mapping between interfaces and the implementation used during the deserialization process: `@DeserializeInterface(CompanyImpl::class)`.
- *Specifying another annotation as an argument*—Don't put the `@` character before the annotation name. For instance, `ReplaceWith` in the previous example is an annotation, but you don't use `@` when you specify it as an argument of the `Deprecated` annotation.
- *Specifying an array as an argument*—You can use brackets: `@RequestMapping(path = ["/foo", "/bar"])`. Alternatively, you can also use the `arrayOf` function to specify the array. (If you are using an annotation class declared in Java, the `value` parameter is automatically converted to a `vararg` parameter if necessary.)

Annotation arguments need to be known at compile time, so you can't refer to arbitrary properties as arguments. To use a property as an annotation argument, you need to mark it with a `const` modifier, which tells the compiler that the property is a *compile-time constant.* Here's an example of JUnit's `@Timeout` annotation that specifies the timeout for the test in seconds:

```
const val TEST_TIMEOUT = 10L          ◁———— Omitting the const modifier …

class MyTest {
    @Test
    @Timeout(TEST_TIMEOUT)            ◁——┐  … results in the following compile-time
    fun testMethod() {                   │  error: "Only const val can be used in
        // ...                           │  constant expressions."
    }
}
```

As discussed in section 3.2.3, properties annotated with `const` need to be declared at the top level of a file or in an `object` and must be initialized with values of primitive types or `String`. If you try to use a regular property as an annotation argument, you'll get the following error: "Only `const val` can be used in constant expressions."

12.1.2 Specifying the exact declaration an annotation refers to: Annotation targets

In many cases, a single declaration in the Kotlin source code produces multiple Java declarations, and each of them can carry annotations. For example, a Kotlin property corresponds to a Java field, a getter, and possibly a setter and its parameter. A property declared in the primary constructor has one more corresponding element: the constructor parameter. Therefore, it may be necessary to specify which of these elements needs to be annotated.

You specify the element to be annotated with a *use-site target* declaration. The use-site target is placed between the `@` sign and the annotation name and is separated from the name with a colon. The word `get` in figure 12.2 causes the annotation `@JvmName` to be applied to the property getter.

Use-site target
```
    ┌─┴─┐
    @get:JvmName("obtainCertificate")
         └──┬──┘
      Annotation name
```

Figure 12.2   The use-site target (like `get` or `set`) is placed between the `@` sign and the annotation name, and is separated from the name with a colon.

If you want to change the way a function or property is accessed from Java, you can use the `@JvmName` annotation, which you briefly saw in section 3.2.3. Here, you use it to make the `calculate` function callable from Java code via `performCalculation()`:

```
@JvmName("performCalculation")
fun calculate(): Int {
    return (2 + 2) - 1
}
```

You can do the same with properties in Kotlin too; as you may remember from section 2.2.1, Kotlin properties automatically define a getter and setter. To explicitly apply the `@JvmName` annotation to the getter or setter of a property, use `@get:JvmName()` and `@set:JvmName()`, respectively:

```
                                           ┌──┤ Sets the JVM name for the getter
class CertificateManager {                 │
    @get:JvmName("obtainCertificate")  ◄───┘┌─┤ Sets the JVM name for the setter
    @set:JvmName("putCertificate")      ◄────┘
    var certificate: String = "-----BEGIN PRIVATE KEY-----"
}
```

With these annotations in place, Java code can now access the `certificate` property using the renamed `obtainCertificate` and `putCertificate` functions:

```
class Foo {
    public static void main(String[] args) {
        var certManager = new CertificateManager();
        var cert = certManager.obtainCertificate();
        certManager.putCertificate("-----BEGIN CERTIFICATE-----");
    }
}
```

If the annotation you are using happens to be declared in Java, then it is applied to the corresponding field in Kotlin by default. For annotations defined in Kotlin, you can also declare them so that they can be directly applied to properties.

The full list of supported use-site targets is as follows:

- `property`—Property (Java annotations can't be applied with this use-site target)
- `field`—Field generated for the property
- `get`—Property getter
- `set`—Property setter
- `receiver`—Receiver parameter of an extension function or property
- `param`—Constructor parameter
- `setparam`—Property setter parameter
- `delegate`—Field storing the delegate instance for a delegated property
- `file`—Class containing top-level functions and properties declared in the file

Any annotation with the `file` target needs to be placed at the top level of the file, before the `package` directive. One of the annotations commonly applied to files is `@JvmName`, which changes the name of the corresponding class. Section 3.2.3 included an example: `@file:JvmName("StringFunctions")`.

Kotlin allows you to apply annotations to arbitrary expressions, not only to class and function declarations or types. The most common example is the `@Suppress` annotation, which you can use to suppress a specific compiler warning in the context of the annotated expression. Here's an example that annotates a local variable declaration to suppress an unchecked cast warning:

```
fun test(list: List<*>) {
    @Suppress("UNCHECKED_CAST")
    val strings = list as List<String>
    // ...
}
```

TIP Note that IntelliJ IDEA and Android studio offer "Suppress" as a quick fix when you press Alt-Enter on a compiler warning. Selecting this intention will insert the `@Suppress` annotation for you.

Controlling the Java API with annotations

Kotlin provides a variety of annotations to control how declarations written in Kotlin are compiled to Java bytecode and exposed to Java callers. Some of those annotations replace the corresponding keywords of the Java language (e.g., the `@Volatile` annotation serves as a direct replacement for Java's `volatile` keyword). Others are used to change how Kotlin's declarations are visible to Java callers:

- `@JvmName` changes the name of a Java method or field generated from a Kotlin declaration.
- `@JvmStatic` can be applied to methods of an object declaration or a companion object to expose them as static Java methods.
- `@JvmOverloads`, mentioned in section 3.2.2, instructs the Kotlin compiler to generate overloads for a function or constructor that has default parameter values.
- `@JvmField` can be applied to a property to expose that property as a public Java field with no getters or setters.
- `@JvmRecord` can be applied to a `data class` to declare a Java record class, as introduced in section 4.3.2.

You can find more details on the use of those annotations in their documentation comments and in the Java interop section of the online documentation.

12.1.3 *Using annotations to customize JSON serialization*

One of the classic use cases for annotations is customizing object serialization. *Serialization* is the process of converting an object to a binary or text representation that can then be stored or sent over the network. The reverse process, *deserialization*, converts such a representation back to an object. One of the most common formats used for serialization is JSON. There are several widely used Kotlin libraries for serializing Kotlin objects to JSON, including kotlinx.serialization (https://github.com/Kotlin/kotlinx.serialization), which is developed by the Kotlin team at JetBrains. Additionally, libraries like Jackson (https://github.com/FasterXML/jackson) and Gson (https://github.com/google/gson) that are designed to turn Java objects into JSON are also fully compatible with Kotlin.

Over the course of this chapter, we'll discuss the implementation of a pure Kotlin serialization library for this purpose, called JKid. It's small enough for you to read all of its source code easily, and we encourage you to do that while reading this chapter.

The JKid library source code and exercises

The full implementation is available as part of the book's source code as well as online at https://github.com/Kotlin/kotlin-in-action-2e-jkid. To study the library implementation and examples, open the repository as a Gradle project in your IDE. The examples can be found in the project under `src/test/kotlin/examples`. The library isn't as full-featured or flexible as kotlinx.serialization or other libraries, but provides a solid case study for how to perform annotation processing and reflection in Kotlin.

Because we will examine the most significant parts of a whole library, you may find it useful to keep the project open on your computer as you read this chapter. This gives you the opportunity to explore the structure and see how the individually discussed aspects of JKid fit together.

The JKid project features a series of exercises you can work through after you finish reading the chapter to ensure that you understand the concepts. You can find a description of the exercises in the project's `README.md` file or read it at the project page on GitHub.

Let's start with the simplest example to test the library: serializing and deserializing an instance of a class representing a `Person`. You pass the instance to the `serialize` function, and it returns a string containing its JSON representation:

```
data class Person(val name: String, val age: Int)

fun main() {
    val person = Person("Alice", 29)
    println(serialize(person))
    // {"age": 29, "name": "Alice"}
}
```

The JSON representation of an object consists of key–value pairs: pairs of property names and their values for the specific instance, such as `"age": 29`.

To get a Kotlin object back from the JSON representation, you call the `deserialize` function. When you create an instance from JSON data, you must specify the class explicitly as a type argument because JSON doesn't store object types. In this case, you pass the `Person` class:

```
fun main() {
    val json = """{"name": "Alice", "age": 29}"""
    println(deserialize<Person>(json))
    // Person(name=Alice, age=29)
}
```

Figure 12.3 illustrates the equivalence between an object and its JSON representation. Note that the serialized class can contain not only values of primitive types or strings, as shown in the figure, but also collections and instances of other value object classes.

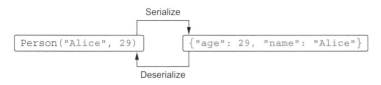

Figure 12.3 Serialization and deserialization of the `Person` instance. Kotlin objects are converted into their textual JSON representation and back.

You can use annotations to customize the way objects are serialized and deserialized. When serializing an object to JSON, by default, the library tries to serialize all the properties and uses the property names as keys. The annotations allow you to change the defaults. In this section, we'll discuss two annotations, `@JsonExclude` and `@JsonName`, and you'll see their implementation later in the chapter:

- The `@JsonExclude` annotation is used to mark a property that should be excluded from serialization and deserialization.
- The `@JsonName` annotation allows you to specify that the key in the key–value pair representing the property should be the given string, not the name of the property.

Consider this example, in which you annotate the property `firstName` to change the key used to represent it in JSON. You also annotate the property `age` to exclude it from serialization and deserialization:

```
data class Person(
    @JsonName("alias") val firstName: String,
    @JsonExclude val age: Int? = null
)
```

Note that you must specify the default value of the property `age`. Otherwise, you wouldn't be able to create a new instance of `Person` during deserialization. Figure 12.4 shows how the representation of an instance of the `Person` class changes.

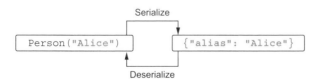

Figure 12.4 Serialization and deserialization of the `Person` instance with annotations applied. The annotation changes the `firstName` field to be serialized to (and deserialized from) a field named `alias`, instead.

With that, you've seen most of the features available in JKid: `serialize()`, `deserialize()`, `@JsonName`, and `@JsonExclude`. Now, let's begin our investigation of its implementation, starting with the annotation declarations.

12.1.4 *Creating your own annotation declarations*

In this section, you'll learn how to declare annotations, using the annotations from JKid as an example. The `@JsonExclude` annotation has the simplest form because it doesn't have any parameters. The syntax looks like a regular class declaration, with the added `annotation` modifier before the `class` keyword:

```
annotation class JsonExclude
```

Because annotation classes are only used to define the structure of metadata associated with declarations and expressions, they can't contain any code. Therefore, the compiler prohibits specifying a body for an annotation class.

For annotations that have parameters, the parameters are declared in the primary constructor of the class. You use the regular primary constructor declaration syntax, and mark all parameters as `val` (this is mandatory for parameters of an annotation class):

```
annotation class JsonName(val name: String)
```

> **Comparison with Java annotations**
>
> For comparison, here's how you would have declared the same annotation in Java:
>
> ```
> /* Java */
> public @interface JsonName {
>     String value();
> }
> ```
>
> Note how the Java annotation has a method called `value`, whereas the Kotlin annotation has a `name` property. In Java, the `value` method is special: when you apply an annotation, you need to provide explicit names for all attributes you're specifying except `value`.
>
> In Kotlin, on the other hand, applying an annotation is a regular constructor call. You can use the named-argument syntax to make the argument names explicit; you only specify the names for some arguments or omit the argument names entirely. In the case of the `JsonName` annotation, `@JsonName(name = "first_name")` is the same as `@JsonName("first_name")` in practice because `name` is the first parameter of the `Json-Name` constructor. If you need to apply an annotation declared in Java to a Kotlin element, however, you're required to use the named-argument syntax for all arguments except `value`, which Kotlin also recognizes as special.

Next, let's discuss how to control annotation usage and how you can apply annotations to other annotations.

12.1.5 *Meta-annotations: Controlling how an annotation is processed*

A Kotlin annotation class itself can be annotated. The annotations that can be applied to annotation classes are called *meta-annotations*. The standard library defines several of them, and they control how the compiler processes annotations. Other frameworks use meta-annotations as well—for example, many dependency-injection libraries use meta-annotations to mark annotations used to identify different injectable objects of the same type.

Of the meta-annotations defined in the standard library, the most common is `@Target`. The declarations of `JsonExclude` and `JsonName` in JKid use it to specify the valid targets for those annotations. Here's how it's applied:

```
@Target(AnnotationTarget.PROPERTY)
annotation class JsonExclude
```

The `@Target` meta-annotation specifies the types of elements to which the annotation can be applied. If you don't use it, the annotation will be applicable to all declarations. That wouldn't make sense for JKid because the library processes only property annotations.

The list of values of the `AnnotationTarget` enum gives the full range of possible targets for an annotation. It includes classes, files, functions, properties, property accessors, types, all expressions, and so on. You can declare multiple targets if you need to: `@Target(AnnotationTarget.CLASS, AnnotationTarget.METHOD)`.

To declare your own meta-annotation, use `ANNOTATION_CLASS` as its target:

```
@Target(AnnotationTarget.ANNOTATION_CLASS)
annotation class BindingAnnotation

@BindingAnnotation
annotation class MyBinding
```

Note that you can't use annotations with a `property` target from Java code. To make such an annotation usable from Java, you can add the second target `AnnotationTarget.FIELD`. In this case, the annotation will be applied to properties in Kotlin and fields in Java.

The @Retention annotation

In Java, you may have seen another important meta-annotation: `@Retention`. You can use it to specify whether the annotation you declare will be stored in the .class file and whether it will be accessible at run time through reflection. Java by default retains annotations in .class files but doesn't make them accessible at run time. That means, by default, Java's annotations are only visible at compile time and for programs working directly on the .class files, such as bytecode analysis tools. Usually, most annotations do need to be present at run time, so in Kotlin, the default is different: annotations have `RUNTIME` retention. That means even though the JKid annotations don't have an explicitly specified retention, you'll be able to access them for reflection, as you'll see in section 12.2.3.

12.1.6 *Passing classes as annotation parameters to further control behavior*

You've seen how to define an annotation that holds static data as its arguments, but sometimes, you need something different: the ability to refer to a *class* as declaration metadata. You can do so by declaring an annotation class that has a class reference as a parameter. In the JKid library, this comes up in the @DeserializeInterface annotation, which allows you to control the deserialization of properties that have an interface type. You can't create an instance of an interface directly, so you need to specify which class is used as the implementation created during deserialization.

Here's a simple example showing how the @DeserializeInterface annotation could be used to specify which class should be used to implement the interface:

```
interface Company {
    val name: String
}

data class CompanyImpl(override val name: String) : Company

data class Person(
    val name: String,
    @DeserializeInterface(CompanyImpl::class) val company: Company
)
```

Upon deserialization, whenever JKid reads a nested company object for a Person instance, it creates and deserializes an instance of CompanyImpl and stores it in the company property. To specify this, you use CompanyImpl::class as an argument of the @DeserializeInterface annotation. In general, to refer to a class, you use its name followed by the ::class keyword.

Now, let's see how the annotation itself is declared. Its single argument is a class reference, as in @DeserializeInterface(CompanyImpl::class):

```
annotation class DeserializeInterface(val targetClass: KClass<out Any>)
```

The KClass type is used to hold references to Kotlin classes; you'll see what it lets you do with those classes in section 12.2.

The type parameter of KClass specifies which Kotlin classes can be referred to by this reference. For instance, CompanyImpl::class has a type KClass<CompanyImpl>, which is a subtype of the annotation parameter type (see figure 12.5).

If you wrote KClass<Any> without the out modifier, you wouldn't be able to pass CompanyImpl::class as an argument; the only allowed argument would be Any::class. The out keyword specifies that you're allowed to refer to classes that extend Any, not

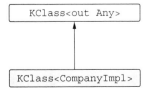

Figure 12.5 The type of the annotation argument
CompanyImpl::class (KClass<CompanyImpl>) **is a**
subtype of the annotation parameter type (KClass<out Any>).

just to `Any` itself. The next section shows one more annotation that takes a reference to generic class as a parameter.

12.1.7 Generic classes as annotation parameters

By default, JKid serializes properties of nonprimitive types as nested objects. But you can change this behavior and provide your own serialization logic for some values.

The `@CustomSerializer` annotation takes a reference to a custom serializer class as an argument. The serializer class should implement the `ValueSerializer` interface, providing a conversion from a Kotlin object to its JSON representation, and likewise, from a JSON value back to a Kotlin object:

```
interface ValueSerializer<T> {
    fun toJsonValue(value: T): Any?
    fun fromJsonValue(jsonValue: Any?): T
}
```

Suppose you need to support serialization of dates, and you've created your own `DateSerializer` class for that, implementing the `ValueSerializer<Date>` interface. This class is provided as an example in the JKid source code (http://mng.bz/e1vQ). Here's how you apply it to the `Person` class:

```
data class Person(
    val name: String,
    @CustomSerializer(DateSerializer::class) val birthDate: Date
)
```

Now, let's see how the `@CustomSerializer` annotation is declared. The `ValueSerializer` class is generic and defines a type parameter, so you need to provide a type argument value whenever you refer to the type. Because you know nothing about the types of properties with which this annotation will be used, you can use a star projection (discussed in section 11.3.6) as the argument:

```
annotation class CustomSerializer(
    val serializerClass: KClass<out ValueSerializer<*>>
)
```

Figure 12.6 examines the type of the `serializerClass` parameter and explains its different parts. You need to ensure the annotation can only refer to classes that implement the `ValueSerializer` interface. For instance, writing `@CustomSerializer(Date::class)` should be prohibited because `Date` doesn't implement the `ValueSerializer` interface.

While this may seem tricky, the good news is that you can apply the same pattern every time you need to use a class as an annotation argument. You can write `KClass<out YourClassName>`, and if `YourClassName` has its own type arguments, replace them with `*`.

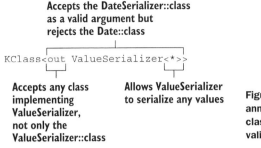

Accepts the DateSerializer::class
as a valid argument but
rejects the Date::class

```
KClass<out ValueSerializer<*>>
```

Accepts any class
implementing
ValueSerializer,
not only the
ValueSerializer::class

Allows ValueSerializer
to serialize any values

Figure 12.6   The type of the `serializerClass` annotation parameter. Only class references to classes that extend `ValueSerializer` will be valid annotation arguments.

You've now seen all the important aspects of declaring and applying annotations in Kotlin. The next step is to find out how to access the data stored in the annotations. For this, you need to use *reflection*.

12.2   *Reflection: Introspecting Kotlin objects at run time*

Reflection is, simply put, a way to access properties and methods of objects *dynamically* at run time, without knowing in advance what those properties are. Normally, when you access a method or a property of an object, the source code of your program references a specific declaration, and the compiler *statically* resolves the reference and ensures the declaration exists. But sometimes, you need to write code that can work with objects of any type or where the names of methods and properties to be accessed are only known at run time. A serialization library is a great example of such code; it needs to be able to serialize any object to JSON, so it can't reference specific classes and properties. This is where reflection comes into play.

When working with reflection in Kotlin, you usually deal with the Kotlin reflection API. It's defined in the `kotlin.reflect` and `kotlin.reflect.full` packages. It gives you access to all Kotlin concepts, such as data classes, properties, and nullable types. An important note is that the Kotlin reflection API isn't restricted to Kotlin classes; you can use the same API to access classes written in any JVM language.

As a fallback, you can also use standard Java reflection, as defined in the `java.lang.reflect` package. Because Kotlin classes are compiled to regular Java byte-code, the Java reflection API supports them perfectly well. In particular, this means Java libraries that use the reflection API are fully compatible with Kotlin code.

> **NOTE**   To reduce the runtime library size on platforms where it matters, such as Android, the Kotlin reflection API is packaged into a separate JAR file, kotlin-reflect.jar, which isn't added to the dependencies of new projects by default. If you're using the Kotlin reflection API, you need to make sure the library is added as a dependency. The Maven group/artifact ID for the library is `org.jetbrains.kotlin:kotlin-reflect`.

In this section, you'll see how JKid uses the reflection API. We'll walk you through the serialization part first because it's more straightforward and easier for us to explain and then proceed to JSON parsing and deserialization. But first, let's take a close look at the contents of the reflection API.

12.2.1   The Kotlin reflection API: KClass, KCallable, KFunction, and KProperty

The main entry point of the Kotlin reflection API is `KClass`, which represents a class. You can use it to enumerate and access all the declarations contained in the class, its superclasses, and so on. You get an instance of `KClass` by writing `MyClass::class`. Likewise, to get the class of an object `myObject` at run time, you write `myObject::class`:

```
import kotlin.reflect.full.*

class Person(val name: String, val age: Int)

fun main() {
    val person = Person("Alice", 29)
    val kClass = person::class                    ◁────── Returns an instance of KClass<out Person>
    println(kClass.simpleName)
    // Person
    kClass.memberProperties.forEach { println(it.name) }
    // age
    // name
}
```

This simple example prints the name of the class and the names of its properties and uses `.memberProperties` to collect all nonextension properties defined in the class as well as in all of its superclasses.

   If you browse the declaration of `KClass`, you'll see that it contains a bunch of useful methods for accessing the contents of the class:

```
interface KClass<T : Any> {
    val simpleName: String?
    val qualifiedName: String?
    val members: Collection<KCallable<*>>
    val constructors: Collection<KFunction<T>>
    val nestedClasses: Collection<KClass<*>>
    // ...
}
```

Many other useful features of `KClass`, including `memberProperties` used in the previous example, are declared as extensions. You can see the full list of methods on `KClass` (including extensions) in the standard library reference (http://mng.bz/em4i).

> **NOTE**   You might expect the `simpleName` and `qualifiedName` properties to be non-nullable. However, recall that section 4.4.4 showed you how to use `object` expressions to create anonymous objects. While these objects are still an instance of a class, that class is anonymous. As such, it has neither a `simpleName` nor a `qualifiedName`. Accessing those fields from a `KClass` instance will return `null`.

You may have noticed that `members`, the list of all members for a class, is a collection of `KCallable` instances. `KCallable` is a superinterface for functions and properties. It declares the `call` method, which allows you to call the corresponding function or the getter of the property:

```
interface KCallable<out R> {
    fun call(vararg args: Any?): R
    // ...
}
```

You provide the function arguments in a `vararg` list. The following code demonstrates how you can use `call` to call a function through reflection:

```
fun foo(x: Int) = println(x)

fun main() {
    val kFunction = ::foo          ◁──┐   Obtains a reference of type
    kFunction.call(42)             ◁──    KFunction1<Int, Unit> to foo
    // 42                              ┌─ Calls the function with
}                                         the argument 42
```

You saw the `::foo` syntax in section 5.1.5, and now you can see that the value of this expression is an instance of the `KFunction` class from the reflection API. To call the referenced function, you use the `KCallable.call` method. In this case, you need to provide a single argument: `42`. If you try to call the function with an incorrect number of arguments, such as `kFunction.call()`, it will throw a run-time exception: "IllegalArgument-Exception: Callable expects 1 argument, but 0 were provided."

In this case, however, you can use a more specific method to call the function. The type of the `::foo` expression is `KFunction1<Int, Unit>`, which contains information about parameter and return types. `KFunction1` denotes that this function takes one parameter. To call the function through this interface, you use the `invoke` method. It accepts a fixed number of arguments (one, in this case), and their types correspond to the type parameters of the `KFunction1` interface. The parameter is of type `Int`, and the return type of the function is of type `Unit`. You can also call `kFunction` directly (section 13.3 will explain the details of why it's possible to call `kFunction` without an explicit `invoke`):

```
import kotlin.reflect.KFunction2

fun sum(x: Int, y: Int) = x + y

fun main() {
    val kFunction: KFunction2<Int, Int, Int> = ::sum
    println(kFunction.invoke(1, 2) + kFunction(3, 4))
    // 10
    kFunction(1)
    // ERROR: No value passed for parameter p2
}
```

Using `invoke`, rather than `call`, on kFunction prevents you from accidentally passing an incorrect number of arguments to the function—the code won't compile. Therefore, if you have a KFunction of a specific type with known parameters and return type, it's preferable to use its `invoke` method. The `call` method is a generic approach that works for all types of functions but doesn't provide type safety.

How and where are KFunctionN interfaces defined?

Types such as `KFunction1` represent functions with different numbers of parameters. Each type extends `KFunction` and adds one additional member `invoke` with the appropriate number of parameters. For example, `KFunction2` declares `operator fun invoke(p1: P1, p2: P2): R`, where `P1` and `P2` represent the function parameter types and `R` represents the return type.

These function types are *synthetic compiler-generated types*, and you won't find their declarations in the `kotlin.reflect` package. That means you can use an interface for a function with any number of parameters, without artificial restrictions on the possible number of function type parameters.

You can invoke the `call` method on a KProperty instance as well, and it will call the getter of the property. But the property interface provides you with a better way to obtain the property value: the `get` method.

To access the `get` method, you need to use the correct interface for the property, depending on how it's declared. Top-level read-only and mutable properties are represented by instances of the KProperty0 and KMutableProperty0 interfaces, respectively—both of which have a no-argument `get` method:

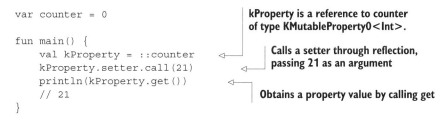

```
var counter = 0                          kProperty is a reference to counter
                                         of type KMutableProperty0<Int>.
fun main() {
    val kProperty = ::counter            Calls a setter through reflection,
    kProperty.setter.call(21)            passing 21 as an argument
    println(kProperty.get())
    // 21                                Obtains a property value by calling get
}
```

A *member property* is represented by an instance of KProperty1 or KMutableProperty1, which both provide a one-argument `get` method. To access its value, you must provide the object instance for which you want to retrieve the value. The following example stores a reference to the property in a `memberProperty` variable; then, you call `memberProperty.get(person)` to obtain the value of this property for the specific `person` instance. So if a `memberProperty` refers to the `age` property of the `Person` class, `memberProperty.get(person)` is a way to dynamically get the value of `person.age`. You previously encountered this concept in section 5.1.6:

```
class Person(val name: String, val age: Int)

fun main() {
    val person = Person("Alice", 29)
    val memberProperty = Person::age
    println(memberProperty.get(person))
    // 29
}
```

Note that `KProperty1` is a generic class. The `memberProperty` variable has the type `KProperty1<Person, Int>`, where the first type parameter denotes the type of the receiver and the second type parameter stands for the property type. Thus, you can call its `get` method only with a receiver of the right type; the call `memberProperty.get("Alice")` won't compile.

Also note that you can only use reflection to access properties defined at the top level or in a class but not local variables of a function. If you define a local variable `x` and try to get a reference to it using `::x`, you'll get a compilation error saying, "References to variables aren't supported yet."

Figure 12.7 shows a hierarchy of interfaces that you can use to access source code elements at run time. Because all declarations can be annotated, the interfaces that represent declaration at run time, such as `KClass`, `KFunction`, and `KParameter`, all extend `KAnnotatedElement`. `KClass` is used to represent both classes and objects. `KProperty` can represent any property, whereas its subclass, `KMutableProperty`, represents a mutable property, which you declare with `var`. You can use the special interfaces `Getter` and `Setter` declared in `Property` and `KMutableProperty` to work with property accessors as functions (e.g., if you need to retrieve their annotations). Both interfaces for accessors extend `KFunction`. For simplicity, we've omitted the specific interfaces for properties like `KProperty0` in the figure.

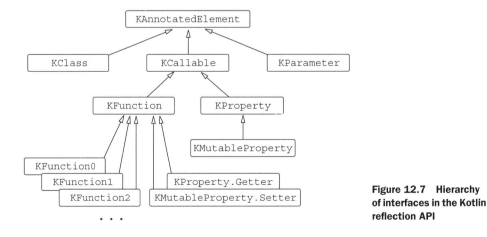

Figure 12.7 Hierarchy of interfaces in the Kotlin reflection API

Now that you're acquainted with the basics of the Kotlin reflection API, let's investigate how the JKid library is implemented.

12.2.2   Implementing object serialization using reflection

First, let's recall the declaration of the serialization function in JKid:

```
fun serialize(obj: Any): String
```

This function takes an object and returns its JSON representation as a string. It'll build up the resulting JSON in a `StringBuilder` instance. As it serializes object properties and their values, it'll append them to this `StringBuilder` object. To make the `append` calls more concise, let's put the implementation in an extension function to `StringBuilder`. That way, you can conveniently call the `append` method without a qualifier:

```
private fun StringBuilder.serializeObject(x: Any) {
    append(/*...*/)
}
```

Converting a function parameter into an extension function receiver is a common pattern in Kotlin code, and we'll discuss it in detail in section 13.2.1. Note that `serializeObject` doesn't extend the `StringBuilder` API; it performs operations that make no sense outside of this context, so it's marked `private` to ensure it can't be used elsewhere. It's declared as an extension to emphasize a particular object as primary for this code block and to make it easier to work with that object.

Consequently, the `serialize` function delegates all the work to `serializeObject`:

```
fun serialize(obj: Any): String = buildString { serializeObject(obj) }
```

As you saw in section 5.4.1, `buildString` creates a `StringBuilder` and allows you to fill it with content in a lambda. In this case, the content is provided by the call to `serialize-Object(obj)`.

Now, let's discuss the behavior of the serialization function. By default, it will serialize all properties of the object. Primitive types and strings will be serialized as JSON numbers, Booleans, and string values, as appropriate. Collections will be serialized as JSON arrays. Properties of other types will be serialized as nested objects. As we discussed in the previous section, this behavior can be customized through annotations.

Let's look at the implementation of `serializeObject`, where you can observe the reflection API in a real scenario.

> **NOTE**   In the repository, this function is called `serializeObjectWithoutAnnotation`—we'll rework this function, as you'll see later.

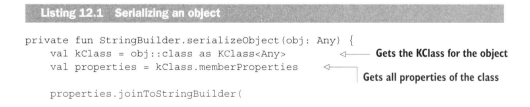

Listing 12.1   Serializing an object

```
private fun StringBuilder.serializeObject(obj: Any) {
    val kClass = obj::class as KClass<Any>         ⟵── Gets the KClass for the object
    val properties = kClass.memberProperties   ⟵─┐
                                                  └ Gets all properties of the class
    properties.joinToStringBuilder(
```

```
        this, prefix = "{", postfix = "}") { prop ->
        serializeString(prop.name)              ◁——— Gets the property name
        append(": ")
        serializePropertyValue(prop.get(obj))   ◁——— Gets the property value
    }
}
```

The implementation of this function should be clear: you serialize each property of the class, one after another. The resulting JSON will look like this: { "prop1": value1, "prop2": value2 }. The joinToStringBuilder function ensures that properties are separated with commas; the serializeString function escapes special characters, as required by the JSON format; and the serializePropertyValue function checks whether a value is a primitive value, string, collection, or nested object, serializing its content accordingly.

In the previous section, we discussed a way to obtain the value of the KProperty instance: the get method. In that case, you worked with the member reference Person::age of the type KProperty1<Person, Int>, which lets the compiler know the exact types of the receiver and the property value. In this example, however, the exact types are unknown because you enumerate all the properties of an object's class. Therefore, the prop variable has the type KProperty1<Any, *>, and prop.get(obj) returns a value of Any? type. You don't get any compile-time checks for the receiver type, but because you're passing the same object from which you obtained the list of properties, the receiver type will be correct. Next, let's see how the annotations used to customize serialization are implemented.

12.2.3 *Customizing serialization with annotations*

Earlier in this chapter, you saw the definitions of annotations that let you customize the process of JSON serialization. In particular, we discussed the @JsonExclude, @JsonName, and @CustomSerializer annotations. Now, it's time to see how these annotations can be handled by the serializeObject function.

We'll start with @JsonExclude. This annotation allows you to exclude some properties from serialization. Let's investigate how the implementation of the serializeObject function needs to change to support that.

Recall that to get all member properties of the class, you use the extension property memberProperties on the KClass instance. But now, the task gets more complicated: properties annotated with @JsonExclude need to be filtered out. Let's see how this is done.

The KAnnotatedElement interface defines the property annotations, a collection of all annotation instances (with run-time retention) that are applied to the element in the source code. Because KProperty extends KAnnotatedElement, you can access all annotations for a property via property.annotations.

But the code responsible for excluding properties actually needs to find a specific annotation. For this case, you can use the findAnnotation function, which can be called on a KAnnotatedElement. This function returns an annotation of a type specified as an argument if such an annotation is present.

Combining findAnnotation with the filter standard library function, you can filter out the properties annotated with @JsonExclude:

```
val properties = kClass.memberProperties
        .filter { it.findAnnotation<JsonExclude>() == null }
```

The next annotation is @JsonName. As a reminder, we'll repeat its declaration and an example of its usage:

```
annotation class JsonName(val name: String)

data class Person(
    @JsonName("alias") val firstName: String,
    val age: Int
)
```

In this case, you're interested not only in its presence but also in its argument: the name that should be used for the annotated property in JSON. Once again, the find-Annotation function helps here:

Gets an instance of the @JsonName annotation if it exists

```
val jsonNameAnn = prop.findAnnotation<JsonName>()
val propName = jsonNameAnn?.name ?: prop.name
```

Gets its name argument or uses prop.name as a fallback

If a property isn't annotated with @JsonName, then jsonNameAnn is null and you still use prop.name as the name for the property in JSON. If the property is annotated, you use the specified name instead.

Let's look at the serialization of an instance of the Person class declared earlier. During the serialization of the firstName property, jsonNameAnn contains the corresponding instance of the annotation class JsonName. Thus, jsonNameAnn?.name returns the non-null value "alias", which is used as a key in JSON. When the age property is serialized, the annotation isn't found, so the property name age is used as a key. As such, the serialized JSON output for a Person("Alice", 35) object is { "alias": "Alice", "age": 35 }

Let's combine the changes discussed so far and look at the resulting implementation of the serialization logic in the following listing.

Listing 12.2 Serializing an object with property filtering

```
private fun StringBuilder.serializeObject(obj: Any) {
    (obj::class as KClass<Any>)
        .memberProperties
        .filter { it.findAnnotation<JsonExclude>() == null }
        .joinToStringBuilder(this, prefix = "{", postfix = "}") {
```

```
            serializeProperty(it, obj)
        }
    }
}
```

Now, the properties annotated with `@JsonExclude` are filtered out. We've also extracted the logic responsible for property serialization into a separate `serializeProperty` function, as shown in the following listing.

```
private fun StringBuilder.serializeProperty(
        prop: KProperty1<Any, *>, obj: Any
) {
    val jsonNameAnn = prop.findAnnotation<JsonName>()
    val propName = jsonNameAnn?.name ?: prop.name
    serializeString(propName)
    append(": ")

    serializePropertyValue(prop.get(obj))
}
```

The property name is processed according to the `@JsonName` annotation discussed earlier.

Next, let's implement the remaining annotation, `@CustomSerializer`. The implementation is based on the function `getSerializer`, which returns the `ValueSerializer` instance registered via the `@CustomSerializer` annotation. For example, if you declare the `Person` class, as shown next, and call `getSerializer()` when serializing the `birth-Date` property, it will return an instance of `DateSerializer`:

```
import java.util.Date

data class Person(
    val name: String,
    @CustomSerializer(DateSerializer::class) val birthDate: Date
)
```

Here's a reminder of how the `@CustomSerializer` annotation is declared to help you better understand the implementation of `getSerializer`:

```
annotation class CustomSerializer(
    val serializerClass: KClass<out ValueSerializer<*>>
)
```

Here's how the `getSerializer` function is implemented.

```
fun KProperty<*>.getSerializer(): ValueSerializer<Any?>? {
    val customSerializerAnn = findAnnotation<CustomSerializer>()
```

```
        ?: return null
    val serializerClass = customSerializerAnn.serializerClass

    val valueSerializer = serializerClass.objectInstance
        ?: serializerClass.createInstance()
    @Suppress("UNCHECKED_CAST")
    return valueSerializer as ValueSerializer<Any?>
}
```

getSerializer is an extension function to KProperty because the function operates on the property. It calls the findAnnotation function to get an instance of the @Custom-Serializer annotation if it exists. Its argument, serializerClass, specifies the class for which you need to obtain an instance.

The most interesting part here is the way you handle both classes and objects (Kotlin's singletons) as values of the @CustomSerializer annotation. They're both represented by the KClass class. The difference is that objects have a non-null value of the objectInstance property, which can be used to access the singleton instance created for the object. For example, DateSerializer is declared as an object, so its object-Instance property stores the singleton DateSerializer instance. You'll use that instance to serialize all objects, and createInstance won't be called. If the KClass represents a regular class, you create a new instance by calling createInstance().

Finally, you can use getSerializer in the implementation of serializeProperty. The following listing shows the final version of the function.

Listing 12.5 Serializing a property with custom serializer support

```
private fun StringBuilder.serializeProperty(
    prop: KProperty1<Any, *>, obj: Any
) {
    val jsonNameAnn = prop.findAnnotation<JsonName>()
    val propName = jsonNameAnn?.name ?: prop.name
    serializeString(propName)
    append(": ")

    val value = prop.get(obj)
    val jsonValue = prop.getSerializer()?.toJsonValue(value)          ← Uses a custom serializer
        ?: value                                                          for the property if it exists
    serializePropertyValue(jsonValue)      ←  Otherwise, uses the
}                                             property value, as before
```

serializeProperty uses the serializer to convert the property value to a JSON-compatible format by calling toJsonValue. If the property doesn't have a custom serializer, it uses the property value.

Now that you've seen an overview of the implementation of the JSON serialization part of the library, we'll move to parsing and deserialization. The deserialization part requires quite a bit more code, so we won't examine all of it, but we'll look at the structure of the implementation and explain how reflection is used to deserialize objects.

12.2.4 *JSON parsing and object deserialization*

Let's start with the second part of the story: implementing the deserialization logic. First, recall that the API, like the one used for serialization, consists of a single function. The function needs access to its type parameter at run time so that it is able to construct the correct resulting object during deserialization. As we previously discussed in section 11.2, this means its type parameter needs to be marked as `reified`, which also forces the function to be marked as `inline`:

```
inline fun <reified T: Any> deserialize(json: String): T
```

Here's an example of its use:

```
data class Author(val name: String)
data class Book(val title: String, val author: Author)

fun main() {
    val json = """{"title": "Catch-22", "author": {"name": "J. Heller"}}"""
    val book = deserialize<Book>(json)
    println(book)
    // Book(title=Catch-22, author=Author(name=J. Heller))
}
```

You pass the type of object to be deserialized as a reified type parameter to the `deserialize` function and get back a new object instance.

Deserializing JSON is a more difficult task than serializing because it involves parsing the JSON string input in addition to using reflection to access object internals. The JSON deserializer in JKid is implemented in a fairly conventional way and consists of three main stages: a lexical analyzer, usually referred to as a *lexer*; a syntax analyzer, or *parser*; and the deserialization component itself.

The lexical analysis splits an input string consisting of characters into a list of tokens. There are two kinds of tokens: *character tokens*, which represent characters with special meanings in the JSON syntax (comma, colon, braces, and brackets), and *value tokens*, which correspond to string, number, Boolean, and `null` constants. A left brace ({), a string value (`"Catch-22"`), and an integer value (42) are examples of different tokens.

The parser is generally responsible for converting a plain list of tokens into a structured representation. Its task in JKid is to understand the higher-level structure of JSON and to convert individual tokens into semantic elements supported in JSON: key–value pairs, objects, and arrays.

The `JsonObject` interface keeps track of the object or array currently being deserialized. The parser calls the corresponding methods when it discovers new properties of the current object (simple values, composite properties, or arrays).

> **Listing 12.6 JSON parser callback interface**

```
interface JsonObject {
    fun setSimpleProperty(propertyName: String, value: Any?)
```

```
    fun createObject(propertyName: String): JsonObject

    fun createArray(propertyName: String): JsonObject
}
```

The `propertyName` parameter in these methods receives the JSON key. Thus, when the parser encounters an `author` property with an object as its value, the `create-Object("author")` method is called. Simple value properties call `setSimpleProperty`, with the actual token value passed as the `value` argument. The `JsonObject` implementations are responsible for creating new objects for properties and storing references to them in the outer object.

Figure 12.8 shows the input and output of each stage for lexical and syntactic analyses when deserializing a sample string. Once again, the lexical analysis divides an input string into a list of tokens; then, the syntactic analysis (the parser) processes this list of tokens and invokes an appropriate method of `JSONObject` on each new meaningful element.

Figure 12.8   **The process of parsing JSON: first, the lexer takes the input text and divides it into tokens. Then, the parser processes the different semantic elements. Finally, the deserializer turns them into the final Kotlin objects.**

The deserializer then provides an implementation for `JsonObject` that gradually builds a new instance of the corresponding type. It needs to find the correspondence between class properties and JSON keys (`title`, `author`, and `name` in figure 12.8) and build nested object values (an instance of `Author`); only after that can it create a new instance of the required class (`Book`).

The JKid library is intended to be used with data classes, and, as such, it passes all the name–value pairs loaded from the JSON file as parameters to the constructor of the class being deserialized. It doesn't support setting properties on object instances after they've been created. This means it needs to store the data somewhere while reading it from JSON, before the construction of the actual object begins.

The requirement to save the components before creating the object looks similar to the traditional *builder* pattern, with the difference that builders are generally tailored to create a specific kind of object. In the case of deserialization, the solution needs to be completely generic. To avoid being boring, we use the term *seed* for the implementation. In JSON, you need to build different types of composite structures: objects, collections, and maps. The classes ObjectSeed, ObjectListSeed, and ValueList-Seed are responsible for building objects and lists of composite objects or simple values appropriately. The construction of maps is left as an exercise for you.

The basic Seed interface extends JsonObject and provides an additional spawn method to get the resulting instance after the building process is finished. It also declares the createCompositeProperty method used to create both nested objects and nested lists (they use the same underlying logic to create instances through seeds).

Listing 12.7   Interface for creating objects from JSON data

```
interface Seed : JsonObject {
    fun spawn(): Any?

    fun createCompositeProperty(
        propertyName: String,
        isList: Boolean
    ): JsonObject

    override fun createObject(propertyName: String) =
        createCompositeProperty(propertyName, false)

    override fun createArray(propertyName: String) =
        createCompositeProperty(propertyName, true)

    // ...
}
```

You may think of spawn as an analogue of build—a method that returns the result value. It returns the constructed object for ObjectSeed and the resulting list for Object-ListSeed or ValueListSeed. We won't discuss in detail how lists are deserialized. Instead, we'll focus our attention on creating objects, which is more complicated and serves to demonstrate the general idea.

But before that, let's study the main deserialize function, shown in the following listing, which does all the work of deserializing a value.

Listing 12.8   The top-level deserialization function

```
fun <T: Any> deserialize(json: Reader, targetClass: KClass<T>): T {
    val seed = ObjectSeed(targetClass, ClassInfoCache())
```

```
        Parser(json, seed).parse()
        return seed.spawn()
}
```

To start the parsing, you create an `ObjectSeed` to store the properties of the object being deserialized, and then you invoke the parser and pass the input stream reader `json` to it. Once you reach the end of the input data, you call the `spawn` function to build the resulting object.

Now, let's focus on the implementation of `ObjectSeed`, which stores the state of an object being constructed. `ObjectSeed` takes a reference to the resulting class and a `classInfoCache` object containing cached information about the properties of the class. This cached information will be used later to create instances of that class. `ClassInfo-Cache` and `ClassInfo` are helper classes, which we'll discuss in the next section.

Listing 12.9 Deserializing an object

```
class ObjectSeed<out T: Any>(
        targetClass: KClass<T>,
        override val classInfoCache: ClassInfoCache
) : Seed {
    private val classInfo: ClassInfo<T> =          ◁── Caches the information needed to
        classInfoCache[targetClass]                    create an instance of targetClass

    private val valueArguments = mutableMapOf<KParameter, Any?>()    Builds a map
    private val seedArguments = mutableMapOf<KParameter, Seed>()     from constructor
                                                                     parameters to
    private val arguments: Map<KParameter, Any?>    ◁──             their values
        get() = valueArguments +
                seedArguments.mapValues { it.value.spawn() }

    override fun setSimpleProperty(propertyName: String, value: Any?) {
        val param = classInfo.getConstructorParameter(propertyName)
        valueArguments[param] =                                             ◁──
            classInfo.deserializeConstructorArgument(param, value)
    }
            Records a value for the constructor parameter if it's a simple value

    override fun createCompositeProperty(
        propertyName: String, isList: Boolean    Loads the value of the DeserializeInterface
    ): Seed {                                       annotation for the property, if any
        val param = classInfo.getConstructorParameter(propertyName)
        val deserializeAs =
            classInfo.getDeserializeClass(propertyName)?.starProjectedType    ◁──
        val seed = createSeedForType(                   ◁──
            deserializeAs ?: param.type, isList               Creates an
        )                                                     ObjectSeed or
        return seed.apply { seedArguments[param] = this }  ◁──  CollectionSeed
    }                                                         according to the
            ... and records it in the seedArguments map       parameter type ...

    override fun spawn(): T =                       ◁──
        classInfo.createInstance(arguments)             Creates the resulting instance of
}                                                       targetClass, passing an arguments map
```

`ObjectSeed` builds a map from constructor parameters to their values. Two mutable maps are used for that: `valueArguments` for simple value properties and `seedArguments` for composite properties. While the result is being built, new arguments are added to the `valueArguments` map by calling `setSimpleProperty` as well as to the `seedArguments` map by calling `createCompositeProperty`. New composite seeds are added in an empty state and are then filled with data coming from the input stream. Finally, the `spawn` method builds all nested seeds recursively by calling `spawn` on each.

Note how calling `arguments` in the body of the `spawn` method launches the recursive building of composite (seed) arguments: the custom getter of `arguments` calls the `spawn` methods on each of the `seedArguments`. The `createSeedForType` function analyzes the type of the parameter and creates either `ObjectSeed`, `ObjectListSeed`, or `ValueList-Seed`, depending on whether the parameter is some kind of collection. We'll leave the investigation into how it's implemented to you. Next, let's see how the `ClassInfo`
`.createInstance` function creates an instance of `targetClass`.

12.2.5   *The final step of deserialization: callBy() and creating objects using reflection*

The last part you need to understand is the `ClassInfo` class, which builds the resulting instance and caches information about constructor parameters. It is used in `Object-Seed`. But before we dive into the implementation details, let's look at the APIs that you use to create objects through reflection.

You've already seen the `KCallable.call` method, which calls a function or a constructor by taking a list of arguments. This method works great in many cases, but it has a restriction: it doesn't support default parameter values. In this case, if a user is trying to deserialize an object with a constructor that has default parameter values, you definitely don't want to require those arguments to be specified in the JSON. Therefore, you need to use another method that does support default parameter values: `KCallable.callBy`:

```
interface KCallable<out R> {
    fun callBy(args: Map<KParameter, Any?>): R
    // ...
}
```

The method takes a map of parameters to their corresponding values that will be passed as arguments. If a parameter is missing from the map, its default value will be used if possible. This also provides the extra convenience that you don't have to put the parameters in the correct order; you can read the name–value pairs from JSON, find the parameter corresponding to each argument name, and put its value in the map.

However, you do need to take care of getting the types right. The type of the value in the `args` map needs to match the constructor parameter type; otherwise, you'll get an `IllegalArgumentException` at run time. This is particularly important for numeric types; you need to know whether the parameter takes an `Int`, a `Long`, a `Double`, or another primitive type, and you need to convert the numeric value coming from JSON to the correct type. To do that, you use the `KParameter.type` property.

The type conversion works via the same `ValueSerializer` interface used for custom serialization. If a property doesn't have an `@CustomSerializer` annotation, you retrieve a standard implementation based on its type.

To do so, you can provide a small function `serializerForType` that provides the mapping between a `KType` and the corresponding built-in `ValueSerializer` objects. To obtain a run-time representation of the types JKid knows about—`Byte`, `Int`, `Boolean`, and so on—you can use the `typeOf<>()` function to return their respective `KType` instances.

Listing 12.10 Getting a serializer based on the type of the value

```
fun serializerForType(type: KType): ValueSerializer<out Any?>? =
        when (type) {
            typeOf<Byte>() -> ByteSerializer
            typeOf<Int>() -> IntSerializer
            typeOf<Boolean>() -> BooleanSerializer
            // ...
            else -> null
        }
```

The corresponding `ValueSerializer` implementations then perform the necessary type checking or conversion. As shown in the following example, the serializer for `Boolean` values checks that `jsonValue` is indeed a `Boolean` upon deserialization.

Listing 12.11 Serializer for `Boolean` values

```
object BooleanSerializer : ValueSerializer<Boolean> {
    override fun fromJsonValue(jsonValue: Any?): Boolean {
        if (jsonValue !is Boolean) throw JKidException("Boolean expected")
        return jsonValue
    }

    override fun toJsonValue(value: Boolean) = value
}
```

The `callBy` method gives you a way to invoke the primary constructor of an object, passing a map of parameters and corresponding values. The `ValueSerializer` mechanism ensures the values in the map have the right types. Now, let's see how you invoke this API.

The `ClassInfoCache` class is intended to reduce the overhead of reflection operations. Recall that the annotations used to control the serialization and deserialization process (`@JsonName` and `@CustomSerializer`) are applied to properties, rather than parameters. When you're deserializing an object, you're dealing with constructor parameters, not properties. To retrieve the annotations, you need to find the corresponding property. Performing this search when reading every key–value pair would be exceedingly slow, so you do this once per class and cache the information. The following listing shows the entire implementation of `ClassInfoCache`.

Listing 12.12   Storage of cached reflection data

```
class ClassInfoCache {
    private val cacheData = mutableMapOf<KClass<*>, ClassInfo<*>>()

    @Suppress("UNCHECKED_CAST")
    operator fun <T : Any> get(cls: KClass<T>): ClassInfo<T> =
            cacheData.getOrPut(cls) { ClassInfo(cls) } as ClassInfo<T>
}
```

You use the same pattern we discussed in section 11.3.6: you remove the type information when you store the values in the map, but the implementation of the `get` method guarantees the returned `ClassInfo<T>` has the right type argument. Note the use of `getOrPut`: if the `cacheData` map already contains an entry for `cls`, this call simply returns that entry. Otherwise, you call the passed lambda, which calculates the value for the key, stores the value in the map, and returns it.

The `ClassInfo` class is responsible for creating a new instance of the target class and caching the necessary information. To simplify the code, we've omitted some functions and trivial initializers. Also, you may notice that instead of `!!`, the actual JKid code in the repository throws an exception with an informative message (which is a good pattern for your own code, as well). Here, it is simply omitted for brevity.

Listing 12.13   Cache of constructor parameter and annotation data

```
class ClassInfo<T : Any>(cls: KClass<T>) {
    private val constructor = cls.primaryConstructor!!

    private val jsonNameToParamMap = hashMapOf<String, KParameter>()
    private val paramToSerializerMap =
        hashMapOf<KParameter, ValueSerializer<out Any?>>()
    private val jsonNameToDeserializeClassMap =
        hashMapOf<String, KClass<out Any>?>()

    init {
        constructor.parameters.forEach { cacheDataForParameter(cls, it) }
    }

    fun getConstructorParameter(propertyName: String): KParameter =
            jsonNameToParam[propertyName]!!

    fun deserializeConstructorArgument(
            param: KParameter, value: Any?): Any? {
        val serializer = paramToSerializer[param]
        if (serializer != null) return serializer.fromJsonValue(value)

        validateArgumentType(param, value)
        return value
```

```
    }

    fun createInstance(arguments: Map<KParameter, Any?>): T {
        ensureAllParametersPresent(arguments)
        return constructor.callBy(arguments)
    }

    // ...
}
```

On initialization, this code locates the property corresponding to each constructor parameter and retrieves its annotations. It stores the data in three maps: jsonNameToParam specifies the parameter corresponding to each key in the JSON file, paramToSerializer stores the serializer for each parameter, and jsonNameToDeserializeClass stores the class specified as the @DeserializeInterface argument, if any. ClassInfo can then provide a constructor parameter by the property name, and the calling code uses the parameter as a key for the parameter-to-argument map.

The cacheDataForParameter, validateArgumentType, and ensureAllParametersPresent functions are private functions in this class. The following listing shows the implementation of ensureAllParametersPresent; you can browse the code of the others yourself.

Listing 12.14   Validating that required parameters are provided

```
private fun ensureAllParametersPresent(arguments: Map<KParameter, Any?>) {
    for (param in constructor.parameters) {
        if (arguments[param] == null &&
                !param.isOptional && !param.type.isMarkedNullable) {
            throw JKidException("Missing value for parameter ${param.name}")
        }
    }
}
```

This function checks that you provide all required values for parameters. Note how the reflection API helps you here. If a parameter has a default value, then param.isOptional is true and you can omit an argument for it; the default one will be used instead. If the parameter type is nullable (type.isMarkedNullable tells you that), null will be used as the default parameter value. For all other parameters, you must provide the corresponding arguments; otherwise, an exception will be thrown. The reflection cache ensures the search for annotations that customize the deserialization process is performed only once, rather than for every property you see in the JSON data.

This completes our discussion of the JKid library implementation. Over the course of this chapter, we've explored the implementation of a JSON serialization and deserialization library, implemented on top of the reflection APIs, and used annotations to customize its behavior. Of course, all the techniques and approaches demonstrated in this chapter can be used for your own frameworks as well.

Summary

- Annotations in Kotlin are applied using the `@MyAnnotation(params)` syntax.
- Kotlin lets you apply annotations to a broad range of targets, including files and expressions.
- An annotation argument can be a primitive value, a string, an enum, a class reference, an instance of another annotation class, or an array thereof.
- Specifying the use-site target for an annotation, as in `@get:JvmName`, allows you to choose how the annotation is applied if a single Kotlin declaration produces multiple bytecode elements.
- You declare an `annotation class` as a class with a primary constructor, where all parameters are marked as `val` properties and without a body.
- Meta-annotations can be used to specify the target, retention mode, and other attributes of annotations.
- The reflection API allows you to enumerate and access the methods and properties of an object dynamically at run time. It has interfaces representing different kinds of declarations, such as classes (`KClass`), functions (`KFunction`), and so on.
- To obtain a `KClass` instance, you can use `ClassName::class` for classes or `objName::class` for object instances.
- The `KFunction` and `KProperty` interfaces both extend `KCallable`, which provides the generic `call` method.
- The `KCallable.callBy` method can be used to invoke methods with default parameter values.
- `KFunction0`, `KFunction1`, and so on are functions with different numbers of parameters that can be called using the `invoke` method.
- `KProperty0` and `KProperty1` are properties with different numbers of receivers that support the `get` method for retrieving the value. `KMutableProperty0` and `KMutableProperty1` extend those interfaces to support changing property values via the `set` method.
- To obtain a run-time representation for a `KType`, you can use the `typeOf<T>()` function.

DSL construction

This chapter covers

- Building domain-specific languages
- Using lambdas with receivers
- Applying the `invoke` convention
- Examples of existing Kotlin DSLs

In this chapter, we'll discuss how you can design expressive and idiomatic APIs for your Kotlin classes through the use of *domain-specific languages* (DSLs). We'll explore the differences between traditional and DSL-style APIs, and you'll see how DSL-style APIs can be applied to a wide variety of practical problems in areas as diverse as database access, HTML generation, testing, writing build scripts, and many others.

Kotlin DSL design relies on many language features, two of which we haven't yet fully explored. One of them you saw briefly in chapter 5: lambdas with receivers. They allow you to create a DSL structure by defining code-block-specific functions, properties, and behavior. The other is new: the `invoke` convention, which enables more flexibility in combining lambdas and property assignments in DSL code. We'll study those features in detail in this chapter.

13.1 *From APIs to DSLs: Creating expressive custom code structures*

Before we dive into the discussion of DSLs, let's better understand the problem we're trying to solve. Ultimately, the goal is to achieve the best possible code readability and maintainability. To reach that goal, focusing on individual classes is not enough. Most of the code in a class interacts with other classes, so we need to look at the *interfaces* through which these interactions happen—in other words, the *APIs* of the classes.

It's important to remember that the challenge of building good APIs isn't reserved for library authors; every developer has to do it. Just as a library provides a programming interface for using it, every class in an application provides possibilities for other classes to interact with it. Ensuring those interactions are easy to understand and can be expressed clearly is essential for keeping a project maintainable.

Throughout this book, you've seen many examples of Kotlin features that allow you to build *clean APIs* for classes. What do we mean when we say an API is clean? We mean two things:

- It needs to be clear to readers what's happening in the code. This can be achieved with a good choice of names and concepts, which is important in any language.
- The code needs to include minimal ceremony and no unnecessary syntax. Achieving this is the main focus of this chapter. A clean API can even be indistinguishable from a built-in language feature.

Examples of Kotlin features that enable you to build clean APIs include extension functions, infix calls, lambda syntax shortcuts, and operator overloading. Table 13.1 shows how these features help reduce the amount of syntactic noise in the code.

Table 13.1 Kotlin support for clean syntax

Regular syntax	Clean syntax	Feature in use
`StringUtil.capitalize(s)`	`s.capitalize()`	Extension function
`1.to("one")`	`1 to "one"`	Infix call
`set.add(2)`	`set += 2`	Operator overloading
`map.get("key")`	`map["key"]`	Convention for the `get` method
`file.use({ f -> f.read() })`	`file.use { it.read() }`	Lambda outside of parentheses

`sb.append("yes")`
`sb.append("no")`
	`with (sb) {`
	`    append("yes")`
	`    append("no")`
	`}`
		Lambda with a receiver

`val m = mutableListOf<Int>()`
`m.add(1)`
`m.add(2)`
`return m.toList()`
	`return buildList {`
	`    add(1)`
	`    add(2)`
	`}`
		Builder functions with lambdas

In this chapter, we'll take a step beyond clean APIs and look at Kotlin's support for constructing DSLs. Kotlin's DSLs build on its syntax features and extend them with the ability to create *structure* out of multiple method calls. As a result, DSLs can be even more expressive and pleasant to work with than APIs constructed out of individual method calls.

Just like other features of the language, Kotlin DSLs are *fully statically typed*. This means you still get all the advantages of static typing, such as compile-time error detection and better IDE support, when you use DSL patterns for your APIs.

As a quick taste, here are a couple of examples that show what Kotlin DSLs can do. This expression goes back in time and returns the previous day (alright, it doesn't actually time travel—it just provides the previous date):

```
val yesterday = Clock.System.now() - 1.days
```

This function generates an HTML table:

```
fun createSimpleTable() = createHTML().
    table {
        tr {
            td { +"cell" }
        }
    }
```

Throughout the chapter, you'll learn how these examples are constructed. But before we begin a detailed discussion, let's look at what DSLs are.

13.1.1   Domain-specific languages

The general idea of a DSL has existed for almost as long as the idea of a programming language. We make a distinction between a *general-purpose programming language*, with a set of capabilities complete enough to solve essentially any problem that can be solved with a computer, and a *domain-specific language*, which focuses on a specific task, or *domain*, and forgoes the functionality that's irrelevant for that domain.

The most common DSLs that you're undoubtedly familiar with are SQL and regular expressions. They're great for solving the specific tasks of manipulating databases and text strings, respectively, but you can't use them to develop an entire application. (At least, we hope you don't. The idea of an entire application built in the regular-expression language makes us shudder.)

These languages can effectively accomplish their goal by reducing the set of functionality they offer. When you need to execute an SQL statement, you don't start by declaring a class or a function. Instead, the first keyword in every SQL statement indicates the type of operation you need to perform (SELECT, INSERT, …), and each type of operation has its own distinct syntax and set of keywords specific to the task at hand. With the regular-expression language, there's even less syntax: the program directly describes the text to be matched, using compact punctuation syntax to specify how the text can vary. Through such a compact syntax, a DSL can express a domain-specific operation much more concisely than an equivalent piece of code in a general-purpose language.

Another important point is that DSLs tend to be *declarative*, as opposed to general-purpose languages, which are often *imperative*. Whereas an imperative language describes the exact sequence of steps required to perform an operation, a declarative language describes the desired result and leaves the execution details to the engine that interprets it. This often makes the execution more efficient because the necessary optimizations are implemented only once in the execution engine; on the other hand, an imperative approach requires every implementation of the operation to be optimized independently. Considering SQL again, when you make a DELETE query, you don't manually iterate each entry in your table, extract the individual fields, and decide what action should be performed. Instead, you only declare the conditions that should be met for an entry in the table to be deleted: the query-execution engine then takes this information to form an optimal query, taking into account indexes, joins, and so on.

As a counterweight to all those benefits, DSLs of this type have one disadvantage: combining them with a host application in a general-purpose language can be difficult. They have their own syntax, which can't be directly embedded into programs in a different language. Therefore, to invoke a program written in a DSL, you need to either store it in a separate file or embed it in a string literal. That makes it nontrivial to validate the correct interaction of the DSL with the host language at compile time, debug the DSL program, and provide IDE code assistance when writing it. Additionally, the separate syntax requires separate learning and often makes code harder to read.

To solve that problem while preserving most of the other benefits of DSLs, Kotlin makes it possible to write *internal DSLs*. Let's see what this is about.

13.1.2 *Internal DSLs are seamlessly integrated into the rest of your program*

As opposed to *external DSLs*, which have their own independent syntax, *internal DSLs* are part of programs written in a general-purpose language, using exactly the same syntax. In effect, an internal DSL isn't a fully separate language, but rather a particular way of using the main language while retaining the key advantages of DSLs with an independent syntax.

To compare the two approaches, let's see how the same task can be accomplished with an external and an internal DSL. Imagine you have two database tables, Customer and Country, and each Customer entry has a reference to the country the customer lives in. Your task is to query the database and find the country where the majority of customers live. The external DSL you're going to use is SQL; the internal one is provided by the Exposed framework (https://github.com/JetBrains/Exposed), which is a Kotlin framework for database access. Here's how you do this with SQL:

```
SELECT Country.name, COUNT(Customer.id)
     FROM Country
INNER JOIN Customer
```

```
        ON Country.id = Customer.country_id
GROUP BY Country.name
ORDER BY COUNT(Customer.id) DESC
  LIMIT 1
```

Writing the query in SQL directly may not be convenient: you have to provide a means for interaction between your main application language—in this case, Kotlin—and the query language. Usually, the best you can do is put the SQL into a string literal and hope that your IDE will help you write and verify it.

As a comparison, here's the same query built with Kotlin and Exposed:

```
(Country innerJoin Customer)
    .slice(Country.name, Count(Customer.id))
    .selectAll()
    .groupBy(Country.name)
    .orderBy(Count(Customer.id), order = SortOrder.DESC)
    .limit(1)
```

You can see the similarity between the two versions. In fact, executing the second version generates and runs exactly the same SQL query as the one written manually. But the second version is regular Kotlin code, and `selectAll`, `groupBy`, `orderBy`, and others are regular Kotlin methods. Moreover, you don't need to spend any effort to convert data from SQL query result sets to Kotlin objects—the query-execution results are delivered directly as native Kotlin objects. Thus, we call this an *internal DSL*: the code intended to accomplish a specific task (building SQL queries) is implemented as a library in a general-purpose language (Kotlin).

13.1.3 *The structure of DSLs*

Generally, there's no well-defined boundary between a DSL and a regular API. Often, the distinction is as subjective as, "I know it's a DSL when I see it." DSLs often rely on language features that are broadly used in other contexts as well, such as infix calls and operator overloading. But one trait comes up often in DSLs and usually doesn't exist in other APIs: *structure* or *grammar*.

A typical API consists of many methods, and the client uses the offered functionality by calling the methods one by one. There's no inherent structure, like nesting or grouping, in the sequence of calls, and no context is maintained between one call and the next.

Such an API is sometimes called a *command-query API*. In contrast, the method calls in a DSL exist in a larger structure, defined by the *grammar* of the DSL. In a Kotlin DSL, structure is most commonly created through the nesting of lambdas or through chained method calls. You can clearly see this in the previous SQL example: executing a query requires a combination of method calls describing the different aspects of the required result set, and the combined query is much easier to read than a single method call taking all the arguments you're passing to the query.

This grammar is what allows us to call an internal DSL a *language*. In a natural language such as English, sentences are constructed out of words, and the rules of grammar govern how those words can be combined with one another. Similarly, in a DSL, a single operation can be composed of multiple function calls, and the type checker ensures the calls are combined in a meaningful way. In effect, the function names usually act as verbs (groupBy, orderBy), and their arguments fulfill the role of nouns (Country.name).

One benefit of the DSL structure is that it allows you to reuse the same context between multiple function calls, rather than repeat it in every call. This is illustrated by the following example, showing the Kotlin DSL used for describing dependencies in Gradle build scripts:

```
dependencies {                                    ◁—— Structure through lambda nesting
    testImplementation(kotlin("test"))
    implementation("org.jetbrains.exposed:exposed-core:0.40.1")
    implementation("org.jetbrains.exposed:exposed-dao:0.40.1")
}
```

In contrast, here's the same operation performed through a regular command-query API. Note that there's much more repetition in the code:

```
project.dependencies.add("testImplementation", kotlin("test"))
project.dependencies.add("implementation",
    "org.jetbrains.exposed:exposed-core:0.40.1")
project.dependencies.add("implementation",
    "org.jetbrains.exposed:exposed-dao:0.40.1")
```

Chained method calls are another way to create structure in DSLs, making them easier to read. For example, they're commonly used in test frameworks to split an assertion into multiple method calls. Such assertions can be much easier to work with, especially if you can apply the infix call syntax.

The following example comes from Kotest (https://github.com/kotest/kotest), a third-party test framework for Kotlin that we'll discuss in more detail in section 13.4.1:

```
str should startWith("kot")        ◁—— Structure through chained method calls
```

Note how the same example expressed through regular JUnit-style APIs is noisier and not as readable:

```
assertTrue(str.startsWith("kot"))
```

Now, let's look at an example of an internal DSL in more detail.

13.1.4 Building HTML with an internal DSL

One of the teasers at the beginning of this chapter was a DSL for building HTML pages. In this section, we'll discuss it in more detail. The API used here comes from the kotlinx.html library (you can find more information about the library, including instructions on how to add it to your own project, at https://github.com/Kotlin/ kotlinx.html). Here's a small snippet that creates a table with a single cell:

```
import kotlinx.html.stream.createHTML
import kotlinx.html.*

fun createSimpleTable() = createHTML().
    table {
        tr {
            td { +"cell" }
        }
    }
```

It's clear what HTML corresponds to the previous structure:

```
<table>
  <tr>
    <td>cell</td>
  </tr>
</table>
```

The createSimpleTable function returns a string containing this HTML fragment.

Why would you want to build this HTML with Kotlin code, rather than write it as text? First, the Kotlin version is type safe: you can use the td tag only in tr; otherwise, this code won't compile. What's more important is that it's regular code and you can use any language construct in it. That means you can generate table cells dynamically (e.g., corresponding to elements in a map) in the same place you define a table:

```
import kotlinx.html.stream.createHTML
import kotlinx.html.*

fun createAnotherTable() = createHTML().table {
    val numbers = mapOf(1 to "one", 2 to "two")
    for ((num, string) in numbers) {
        tr {
            td { +"$num" }
            td { +string }
        }
    }
}
```

The generated HTML contains the desired data:

```
<table>
  <tr>
    <td>1</td>
    <td>one</td>
  </tr>
  <tr>
    <td>2</td>
```

```
      <td>two</td>
    </tr>
</table>
```

HTML is a canonical example of a markup language, which makes it perfect for illustrating the concept, but you can use the same approach for any languages with a similar structure, such as XML. Shortly, we'll discuss how such code works in Kotlin.

Now that you know what a DSL is and why you might want to build one, let's see how Kotlin helps you do that. First, we'll take a more in-depth look at *lambdas with receivers*: the key feature that helps establish the grammar of DSLs.

13.2   *Building structured APIs: Lambdas with receivers in DSLs*

Lambdas with receivers are a powerful Kotlin feature that allows you to build APIs with a structure. As we already discussed, having structure is one of the key traits distinguishing DSLs from regular APIs. Let's examine this feature in detail and look at some DSLs that use it.

13.2.1 *Lambdas with receivers and extension function types*

You had a brief encounter with the idea of lambdas with receivers when we talked about the `buildListbuildString`, `with`, and `apply` standard library functions in chapter 5. Now, let's look at how they're implemented, using the `buildString` function as an example. This function allows you to construct a string from several pieces of content added to an intermediate `StringBuilder`.

To begin the discussion, let's define the `buildString` function so that it takes a regular lambda as an argument. You saw how to do this in chapter 10, so this should be familiar material.

Listing 13.1   Defining `buildString()` that takes a lambda as an argument

```
fun buildString(
    builderAction: (StringBuilder) -> Unit    ◁——— Declares a parameter of a function type
): String {
    val sb = StringBuilder()
    builderAction(sb)            ◁——— Passes a StringBuilder as an argument to the lambda
    return sb.toString()
}

fun main() {
    val s = buildString {
        it.append("Hello, ")     ◁——— Uses the it function to refer to the StringBuilder instance
        it.append("World!")
    }
    println(s)
    // Hello, World!
}
```

This code is easy to understand, but it looks less easy to use than we'd prefer. Note that you have to use `it` in the body of the lambda to refer to the `StringBuilder` instance (you could define your own parameter name instead of `it`, but it still has to be explicit). The main purpose of the lambda is to fill the `StringBuilder` with text, so you want to get rid of the repeated `it` prefixes and invoke the `StringBuilder` methods directly, replacing `it.append` with `append`.

To do so, you need to convert the lambda into a *lambda with a receiver*. In effect, you can give one of the parameters of the lambda the special status of a *receiver*, allowing you to refer to its members directly without any qualifier. The following listing shows how you do that.

Listing 13.2 Redefining `buildString` to take a lambda with a receiver

```
fun buildString(
    builderAction: StringBuilder.() -> Unit        ⟵  Declares a parameter of a
): String {                                             function type with a receiver
    val sb = StringBuilder()
    sb.builderAction()         ⟵  Passes a StringBuilder as
    return sb.toString()           a receiver to the lambda
}

fun main() {
    val s = buildString {
        this.append("Hello, ")   ⟵  The this keyword refers to
        append("World!")              the StringBuilder instance.

    }                            ⟵  Alternatively, you can omit the this
    println(s)                      keyword and refer to StringBuilder.
    // Hello, World!
}
```

Pay attention to the differences between listings 13.1 and 13.2. First, consider how the way you use `buildString` has improved. Now, you pass a lambda with a receiver as an argument, so you can get rid of `it` in the body of the lambda. You replace the calls to `it.append()` with `append()`. The full form of the call would be `this.append()`, but as with regular members of a class, an explicit `this` is normally only used for disambiguation.

Next, let's discuss how the declaration of the `buildString` function has changed. You use an *extension function type* instead of a regular function type to declare the parameter type. When you declare an extension function type, you effectively pull one of the function type parameters out of the parentheses and put it in front, separated from the rest of the types with a dot. In listing 13.2, you replace `(StringBuilder) -> Unit` with `StringBuilder.() -> Unit`. This special type is called the *receiver type*, and the value of that type passed to the lambda becomes the *receiver object*. Figure 13.1 shows a more complex extension function type declaration.

Why use an *extension* function type? The idea of accessing members of an external type without an explicit qualifier may remind you of extension functions, which allow you to define your own methods for classes defined elsewhere in the code. Both

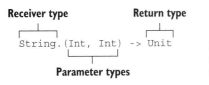

Figure 13.1   An extension function type with receiver type `String` and two parameters of type `Int`, returning `Unit`

extension functions and lambdas with receivers have a *receiver object*, which must be provided when the function is called and is available in its body. In effect, an extension function type describes a block of code that can be called as an extension function.

The way you invoke the variable also changes when you convert it from a regular function type to an extension function type. Instead of passing the object as an argument, you invoke the lambda variable as if it were an extension function. When you have a regular lambda, you pass a `StringBuilder` instance as an argument to it using the following syntax: `builderAction(sb)`. When you change it to a lambda with a receiver, the code becomes `sb.builderAction()`. To reiterate, `builderAction` here isn't a method declared on the `StringBuilder` class; it's a parameter of a function type you call using the same syntax you use to call extension functions.

Figure 13.2 shows the correspondence between an argument and a parameter of the `buildString` function. It also illustrates the receiver on which the lambda body will be called.

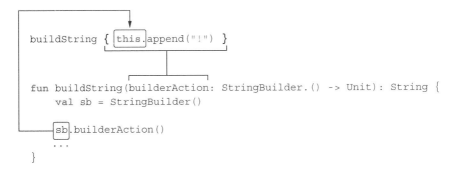

Figure 13.2   The argument of the `buildString` function (lambda with a receiver) corresponds to the parameter of the extension function type (`builderAction`). The receiver (`sb`) becomes an implicit receiver (`this`) when the lambda body is invoked.

You can also declare a variable of an extension function type, as shown in in the following listing. Once you do that, you can either invoke it as an extension function or pass it as an argument to a function that expects a lambda with a receiver.

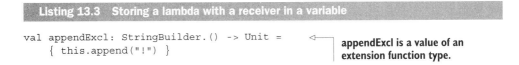

Listing 13.3   Storing a lambda with a receiver in a variable

```
val appendExcl: StringBuilder.() -> Unit =
    { this.append("!") }
```
    appendExcl is a value of an extension function type.

```
fun main() {
    val stringBuilder = StringBuilder("Hi")
    stringBuilder.appendExcl()                      You can call appendExcl
    println(stringBuilder)                          as an extension function.
    // Hi!
    println(buildString(appendExcl))                You can also pass appendExcl
    // !                                            as an argument.
}
```

Note that a lambda with a receiver looks exactly the same as a regular lambda in the source code. To see whether a lambda has a receiver, you need to look at the function to which the lambda is passed: its signature will tell you whether the lambda has a receiver (see figure 13.3) and, if it does, what its type is. For example, you can look at the declaration of `buildString` or look up its documentation in your IDE; see that it takes a lambda of type `StringBuilder.() -> Unit`; and conclude from this that in the body of the lambda, you can invoke `StringBuilder` methods without a qualifier.

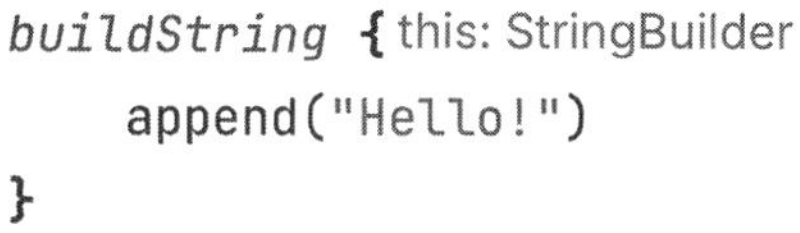

buildString { this: StringBuilder

append("Hello!")

}

Figure 13.3 Optional inlay hints in IntelliJ IDEA and Android Studio can help you visualize the receiver type of a lambda.

The implementation of `buildString` in the standard library is shorter than in listing 13.2. Instead of calling `builderAction` explicitly, it is passed as an argument to the `apply` function (which you saw in chapter 5). This allows you to collapse the function into a single line:

```
fun buildString(builderAction: StringBuilder.() -> Unit): String =
        StringBuilder().apply(builderAction).toString()
```

The `apply` function effectively takes the object on which it was called (in this case, a new `StringBuilder` instance) and uses it as an implicit receiver to call the function or lambda specified as the argument (`builderAction`, in the example). You've also seen another useful library function previously: `with`. Let's study their implementations:

```
inline fun <T> T.apply(block: T.() -> Unit): T {          Equivalent to this.block(); invokes
    block()                                                the lambda with the receiver of
    return this      ───── Returns the receiver            apply as the receiver object
}

inline fun <T, R> with(receiver: T, block: T.() -> R): R =
    receiver.block()
                          Returns the result of calling the lambda
```

Basically, all `apply` and `with` do is invoke the argument of an extension function type on the provided receiver. The `apply` function is declared as an extension to that receiver, whereas `with` takes it as a first argument. The main difference is that `apply` returns the receiver itself, but `with` returns the result of calling the lambda.

So if you don't care about the result, these functions are actually interchangeable:

```
fun main() {
    val map = mutableMapOf(1 to "one")
    map.apply { this[2] = "two"}
    with (map) { this[3] = "three" }
    println(map)
    // {1=one, 2=two, 3=three}
}
```

The `with` and `apply` functions are used frequently in Kotlin, and we hope you've already appreciated their conciseness in your own code.

We've reviewed lambdas with receivers and talked about extension function types. Now, it's time to see how these concepts are used in the DSL context.

13.2.2 *Using lambdas with receivers in HTML builders*

A Kotlin DSL for HTML is usually called an *HTML builder*, and it represents the more general concept of *type-safe builders*. Initially, the concept of builders gained popularity in the Groovy community (https://www.groovy-lang.org/dsls.html#_builders). Builders provide a way to create an object hierarchy in a declarative way, which is convenient for generating markup or describing layouts.

While it uses the same idea, Kotlin's builders are type safe, making them more robust and convenient to use. Let's look in detail at how the implementation of an HTML builder could work in Kotlin.

Listing 13.4   Producing a simple HTML table with a Kotlin HTML builder

```
fun createSimpleTable() = createHTML().
    table {
        tr {
            td { +"cell" }
        }
    }
```

To reiterate, this is just regular Kotlin code, not a special templating language; `table`, `tr`, and `td` are just functions. Each of them is a higher-order function, taking a lambda with a receiver as an argument. When you write `+"cell"`, this also simply calls a function; the HTML DSL overrides the `unaryPlus` operator you learned about in chapter 9 to add the content of the string to the surrounding `td` cell.

The remarkable thing here is that those lambdas *change the name-resolution rules—* they introduce additional functions that can be called inside their body. In the lambda passed to the `table` function, you can use the `tr` function to create the `<tr>` HTML tag. Outside of that lambda, the `tr` function would be unresolved. In the same way, the `td` function is only accessible in `tr`, and the unary plus operates on the receiver of the surrounding `td` tag (figure 13.4). Notice how the design of the API forces you to follow the grammar of the HTML language.

```
fun createSimpleTable() : String  = createHTML()
    .table { this: TABLE
        tr { this: TR
            td { this: TD
                +"cell"
            }
        }
    }
```

Figure 13.4 Optional inlay hints in IntelliJ IDEA and Android Studio help visualize the receiver types for the lambdas.

The name-resolution context in each block is defined by the receiver type of each lambda. The lambda passed to `table` has a receiver of a special type `TABLE`, which defines the `tr` method. Similarly, the `tr` function expects an extension lambda to `TR`. The following listing is a greatly simplified view of the declarations of these classes and methods.

Listing 13.5 Declaring tag classes for the HTML builder

```
open class Tag

class TABLE : Tag {
    fun tr(init: TR.() -> Unit)        ◁——  The tr function expects a lambda
}                                            with a receiver of type TR.

class TR : Tag {                       The td function expects a lambda
    fun td(init: TD.() -> Unit)        ◁——  with a receiver of type TD.
}

class TD : Tag
```

`TABLE`, `TR`, and `TD` are utility classes that shouldn't appear explicitly in the code, and that's why they're named in capital letters. They all extend the `Tag` superclass, which you will use later to add additional helpful constraints to the DSL. Each class defines methods for creating tags allowed in it: the `TABLE` class defines the `tr` method, among others, whereas the `TR` class defines the `td` method.

Note the types of the `init` parameters of the `tr` and `td` functions: they're extension function types `TR.() -> Unit` and `TD.() -> Unit`. They determine the types of receivers in the argument lambdas: `TR` and `TD`, respectively.

To make it clearer what happens here, you can rewrite listing 13.4, making all receivers explicit. As a reminder, you can access the receiver of the lambda that's the argument of the `foo` function as `this@foo`.

Listing 13.6 Making receivers of HTML builder calls explicit

```
fun createSimpleTable() = createHTML().table {
    this@table.tr {                          ◁——— this@table has type TABLE.
```

```
        this@tr.td {                    ⟵──── this@tr has type TR.
            +"cell"        ⟵─┐
        }                    └─ The implicit receiver this@td
    }                           of type TD is available here.
}
```

If you tried to use regular lambdas instead of lambdas with receivers for builders, the syntax would become as unreadable as in this example; you'd have to use the `it` reference to invoke the tag-creation methods or assign a new parameter name for every lambda. Being able to make the receiver implicit and hide the `this` reference makes the syntax of builders nice and similar to the original HTML.

Note that if one lambda with a receiver is placed in the other one, as in listing 13.6, the receiver defined in the outer lambda remains available in the nested lambda. For instance, in the lambda that's the argument of the `td` function, all three receivers (`this@table`, `this@tr`, `this@td`) are available. If you're working with deeply nested structures, this can lead to confusion because it won't be immediately obvious which receiver an expression is invoked on. For example, you could accidentally refer to the `href` property of a surrounding `a` tag from inside an `img` lambda.

Listing 13.7   Having multiple receivers in scope can lead to confusing code.

```
createHTML().body {
    a {
        img {
            href = "https://..."        ⟵──── Refers to the receiver of the a lambda
        }
    }
}
```

To avoid this, Kotlin provides the `@DslMarker` annotation, which constrains the availability of outer receivers in lambdas, as shown in the following listing. The `@DslMarker` annotation is a meta-annotation, as you have gotten to know them in chapter 12; it can be applied to an annotation class. In `kotlinx.html`, that annotation is called `HtmlTagMarker`.

Listing 13.8   Defining a marker annotation class for a DSL

```
@DslMarker
annotation class HtmlTagMarker
```

Any declaration annotated with `@HtmlTagMarker` will have additional restrictions on its implicit receivers. Specifically, you can never have two implicit receivers within the same scope if their types are marked with the same `@DslMarker` annotation. Because our tags are all subclasses of the `Tag` class, we can add the `@HtmlTagMarker` annotation there:

```
@HtmlTagMarker
open class Tag
```

Now, the receiver of the `a` lambda (`this: A`) is not available inside the `img` lambda (`this: IMG`) because both these receiver types are marked with `@HtmlTagMarker`; the same code you saw in listing 13.7 now doesn't compile. Instead, attempting to assign `href` inside the `img` block leads to the following error: `var href: String can't be called in this context by implicit receiver. Use the explicit one if necessary.`

We've explained how the syntax of HTML builders is based on the concept of lambdas with receivers. Next, let's discuss how the desired HTML is generated.

Listing 13.9 uses functions defined in the kotlinx.html library. Now, you'll implement a much simpler version of an HTML builder library, extending the declarations of the `TABLE`, `TR`, and `TD` tags and adding support for generating the resulting HTML. As the entry point for this simplified version, a top-level `table` function creates a fragment of HTML with `<table>` as a top tag.

Listing 13.9 Generating HTML to a string

```
fun createTable() =
    table {
        tr {
            td {
            }
        }
    }

fun main() {
    println(createTable())
    // <table><tr><td></td></tr></table>
}
```

The `table` function creates a new instance of the `TABLE` tag, initializes it (calls the function passed as the `init` parameter on it), and returns it:

```
fun table(init: TABLE.() -> Unit) = TABLE().apply(init)
```

In `createTable`, the lambda passed as an argument to the `table` function contains the invocation of the `tr` function. The call can be rewritten to make everything as explicit as possible: `table(init = { this.tr { … } })`. The `tr` function will be called on the created `TABLE` instance, as if you'd written `TABLE().tr { … }`.

In this toy example, `<table>` is a top-level tag, and other tags are nested into it. Each tag stores a list of references to its children. Therefore, the `tr` function should not only initialize the new instance of the `TR` tag but also add it to the list of children associated with the outer tag.

Listing 13.10 Defining a tag-builder function

```
fun tr(init: TR.() -> Unit) {
    val tr = TR()
    tr.init()
    children.add(tr)
}
```

This logic of initializing a given tag and adding it to the children of the outer tag is common for all tags, so you can extract it as a `doInit` member of the `Tag` superclass. The `doInit` function is responsible for two things: storing the reference to the child tag and calling the lambda passed as an argument. The different tags then just call it: for instance, the `tr` function creates a new instance of the `TR` class and then passes it to the `doInit` function along with the `init` lambda argument: `doInit(TR(), init)`. The following listing shows the full code used to generate the desired HTML structures.

Listing 13.11   A full implementation of a simple HTML builder

```
@DslMarker
annotation class HtmlTagMarker

@HtmlTagMarker
open class Tag(val name: String) {
    private val children = mutableListOf<Tag>()          ⟵—— Stores all nested tags

    protected fun <T : Tag> doInit(child: T, init: T.() -> Unit) {
        child.init()                    ⟵─┐
        children.add(child)      ⟵──┐   │ Initializes the child tag
    }                                     │
                                          └─ Stores a reference to the child tag
    override fun toString() =
        "<$name>${children.joinToString("")}</$name>"     ⟵─┐ Returns the resulting
}                                                            │ HTML as String

fun table(init: TABLE.() -> Unit) = TABLE().apply(init)
                                                             ┌ Creates, initializes, and
class TABLE : Tag("table") {                                 │ adds a new instance of
    fun tr(init: TR.() -> Unit) = doInit(TR(), init)   ⟵──┤ the TR tag to the
}                                                            │ children of TABLE
class TR : Tag("tr") {
    fun td(init: TD.() -> Unit) = doInit(TD(), init)   ⟵──┐ Adds a new instance
}                                                            │ of the TD tag to the
class TD : Tag("td")                                         │ children of TR

fun createTable() =
    table {
        tr {
            td {
            }
        }
    }

fun main() {
    println(createTable())
    // <table><tr><td></td></tr></table>
}
```

Every tag stores a list of nested tags and renders itself accordingly; it renders its name and all the nested tags recursively. To keep the code concise, this implementation doesn't support text inside tags or tag-specific attributes. If you are interested in the full implementation of an HTML builder for Kotlin, you can browse the source code of the aforementioned kotlinx.html library.

Because the tag-creation functions add the corresponding tag to the parent's list of children on their own, you can generate tags dynamically.

Listing 13.12   Generating tags dynamically with an HTML builder

```
fun createAnotherTable() = table {
    for (i in 1..2) {
        tr {                      ◁──┐  Each call to tr creates a
            td {                      │  new TR tag and adds it to
            }                         │  the children of TABLE.
        }
    }
}

fun main() {
    println(createAnotherTable())
    // <table><tr><td></td></tr><tr><td></td></tr></table>
}
```

By now, you have seen how lambdas with receivers are a great tool for building DSLs. Because you can change the name-resolution context in a code block, they let you create *structure* in your API, which is one of the key traits that distinguishes DSLs from flat sequences of method calls. Next, let's discuss the benefits of integrating this DSL into a statically typed programming language.

13.2.3   Kotlin builders: Enabling abstraction and reuse

When you write regular code in a program, you have many tools to avoid duplication and to make the code look nicer. Among other things, you can extract repetitive code into new functions and give them self-explanatory names. That may not be as easy or even possible with SQL or HTML. But using internal DSLs in Kotlin to accomplish the same tasks gives you a way to abstract repeated chunks of code into new functions and reuse them.

Let's consider an application responsible for generating a list of book summaries as HTML, complete with a table of contents in the beginning. Writing such HTML by hand isn't particularly difficult—a basic implementation of the application could look like the following listing.

Listing 13.13   Building a page with a table of contents

```
<body>
  <ul>
    <li><a href="#0">The Three-Body Problem</a></li>
    <li><a href="#1">The Dark Forest</a></li>
    <li><a href="#2">Death's End</a></li>
```

```
    </ul>
    <h2 id="0">The Three-Body Problem</h2>
    <p>The first book tackles...</p>
    <h2 id="1">The Dark Forest</h2>
    <p>The second book starts with...</p>
    <h2 id="2">Death's End</h2>
    <p>The third book contains...</p>
</body>
```

In Kotlin with kotlinx.html, you can use the functions ul, li, h2, p, and so on to replicate the same structure.

Listing 13.14   Building a page with a table of contents using a Kotlin HTML builder

```
fun buildBookList() = createHTML().body {
    ul {
        li { a("#1") { +"The Three-Body Problem" } }
        li { a("#2") { +"The Dark Forest" } }
        li { a("#3") { +"Death's End" } }
    }

    h2 { id = "1"; +"The Three-Body Problem" }
    p { +"The first book tackles..." }

    h2 { id = "2"; +"The Dark Forest" }
    p { +"The second book starts with..." }

    h2 { id = "3"; +"Death's End" }
    p { +"The third book contains..." }
}
```

But you can do better. Because ul, h2, and so on are regular functions, you can extract the logic responsible for building the table of contents as well as the summary into separate functions. The result may look like the following listing.

Listing 13.15   Building a page with a table of contents with helper functions

```
fun buildBookList() = createHTML().body {
    listWithToc {
        item("The Three-Body Problem", "The first book tackles...")
        item("The Dark Forest", "The second book starts with...")
        item("Death's End", "The third book contains...")
    }
}
```

Now, the unnecessary details are hidden, you don't need to manually keep track of adding items to the table of contents, and the code looks much nicer. But how can you actually implement the listWithToc and item functions?

Just like we saw in listing 13.11, we can create our own LISTWITHTOC class, which provides an entries function and keeps track of all the headline–body pairs added using the `item` function. The class is annotated with `@HtmlTagMarker` to ensure it follows the DSL scoping rules we previously discussed in section 13.2.2:

```
@HtmlTagMarker
class LISTWITHTOC {
    val entries = mutableListOf<Pair<String, String>>()
    fun item(headline: String, body: String) {
        entries += headline to body
    }
}
```

After you define the `LISTWITHTOC` class, you need to provide a way of calling it, as we've seen in listing 13.5. For simplicity, we can assume that we want to be able to add our list with table of contents directly to the `body` of our HTML. As such, we can make the `listWithToc` function an extension function of `BODY`. Its parameter `block` is the lambda in which you can specify the entries to the list. Because you want to be able to invoke the `item` function inside that lambda, you need to specify its receiver type, `LISTWITHTOC`. The `listWithToc` function creates a new instance of the `LISTWITHTOC` class, and calls the `block` lambda, which was passed as the parameter, on the instance. This executes the code specified inside the body of `block`, including all calls to `item()`, adding them to the list's `entries`. You can then use the computed `entries` list to create both the table of contents and the actual paragraphs with their respective headlines. Because your function is an extension on `BODY`, you can call the same functions as before, such as `ul`, `li`, `h2` and `p`, to append the list to the surrounding tag:

```
fun BODY.listWithToc(block: LISTWITHTOC.() -> Unit) {
    val listWithToc = LISTWITHTOC()
    listWithToc.block()
    ul {
        for ((index, entry) in listWithToc.entries.withIndex()) {
            li { a("#$index") { +entry.first } }
        }
    }
    for ((index, entry) in listWithToc.entries.withIndex()) {
        h2 { id = "$index"; +entry.first }
        p { +entry.second }
    }
}
```

> **NOTE** For simplification reasons, we've used `BODY` as the receiver type in this example. However, kotlinx.html actually also has a more generic type that could've been used instead: `HtmlBlockTag`, which represents any HTML block element. Moving from `BODY` to `HtmlBlockTag` would allow the `listWithToc` function to be invoked wherever an HTML block is expected.

This example illustrates how the means of abstraction and reuse can help improve your code and make it easier to understand. Now, let's look at one more tool that can help you support more flexible structures in your DSLs: the `invoke` convention.

13.3   *More flexible block nesting with the invoke convention*

The `invoke` convention allows you to call objects of custom types as functions. You've already seen that objects of function types can be called as functions; with the `invoke` convention, you can define your own objects that support the same syntax.

Note that this isn't a feature for everyday use because when abused, it can be used to write hard-to-understand code, such as `1()`. But it's sometimes very useful in DSLs. We'll show you why, but first, let's discuss the convention itself.

13.3.1   *The invoke convention: Objects callable as functions*

In chapter 9, we discussed in detail Kotlin's concept of *conventions*: specially named functions that aren't called through the regular method-call syntax but using different, more concise notations. As a reminder, one of the conventions we discussed was `get`, which allows you to access an object using the indexed access operator. For a variable `foo` of type `Foo`, a call to `foo[bar]` is translated into `foo.get(bar)`, provided the corresponding `get` function is defined as a member in the `Foo` class or as an extension function to `Foo`.

In effect, the `invoke` convention does the same thing, except that the brackets are replaced with parentheses. A class for which the `invoke` method with an `operator` modifier is defined can be called as a function. Here's an example of how this works.

> **Listing 13.16   Defining an `invoke` method in a class**

```
class Greeter(val greeting: String) {
    operator fun invoke(name: String) {          ◁—— Defines the invoke method on Greeter
        println("$greeting, $name!")
    }
}

fun main() {
    val bavarianGreeter = Greeter("Servus")
    bavarianGreeter("Dmitry")                    ◁—— Calls the Greeter instance as a function
    // Servus, Dmitry!
}
```

This code defines the `invoke` method in `Greeter`, which allows you to call instances of `Greeter` as if they were functions. Under the hood, the expression `bavarian-Greeter("Dmitry")` is compiled to the method call `bavarianGreeter.invoke("Dmitry")`. There's no mystery here. It works like a regular convention, providing a way to replace a verbose expression with a more concise, clearer one.

The `invoke` method isn't restricted to any specific signature. You can define it with any number of parameters as well as any return type, or you can even define multiple overloads of `invoke` with different parameter types. When you call the instance of the class as a function, you can use all of those signatures for the call.

You may actually remember seeing `invoke` earlier in the book—in chapter 10, we discussed that you can call a variable of a nullable function type as `lambda?.invoke()`, using the safe-call syntax with the `invoke` method name.

Now that you know about the `invoke` convention, it should be clear that the way you normally invoke a lambda (by putting parentheses after it, as in `lambda()`) is nothing but an application of this convention. Lambdas, unless inlined, are compiled into classes that implement the `FunctionN` interfaces (`Function1` and so on), and those interfaces define the `invoke` method with the corresponding number of parameters:

```
interface Function2<in P1, in P2, out R> {      ◁——┐  This interface denotes a function
    operator fun invoke(p1: P1, p2: P2): R          │  that takes exactly two arguments.
}
```

When you invoke a lambda as a function, the operation is translated into a call of the `invoke` method, thanks to the convention.

Let's look at a practical situation where the `invoke` convention can be used in the context of building internal DSLs with Kotlin.

13.3.2 The invoke convention in DSLs: Declaring dependencies in Gradle

Let's revisit the example of the Gradle DSL for configuring the dependencies of a module. Here's the code you saw earlier:

```
dependencies {
    testImplementation(kotlin("test"))
    implementation("org.jetbrains.exposed:exposed-core:0.40.1")
    implementation("org.jetbrains.exposed:exposed-dao:0.40.1")
}
```

You often want to be able to support both a nested block structure, as shown here, and a flat call structure in the same API. In other words, you want to allow both of the following:

```
dependencies.implementation("org.jetbrains.exposed:exposed-core:0.40.1")

dependencies {
    implementation("org.jetbrains.exposed:exposed-core:0.40.1")
}
```

With such a design, users of the DSL can use the nested block structure when there are multiple items to configure and the flat call structure to keep the code more concise when there's only one thing to configure.

The first case calls the `implementation` method on the `dependencies` variable. You can express the second notation by defining the `invoke` method on `dependencies` so that it takes a lambda as an argument. The full syntax of this call is `dependencies.invoke({…})`.

The `dependencies` object is an instance of the `DependencyHandler` class, which defines both `implementation` and `invoke` methods. The `invoke` method takes a lambda

with a receiver as an argument, and the type of the receiver of this method is again
`DependencyHandler`. What happens in the body of the lambda should already be familiar to you: you have a `DependencyHandler` as a receiver and can call methods such as
`implementation` directly on it. The following minimal example shows how that part of
`DependencyHandler` is implemented.

Listing 13.17   Using `invoke` to support flexible DSL syntax

```
class DependencyHandler {
    fun implementation(coordinate: String) {        ◁──── Defines a regular command API
        println("Added dependency on $coordinate")
    }

    operator fun invoke(
        body: DependencyHandler.() -> Unit) {   ◁──── Defines invoke to support the DSL API
        body()                        ◁─┐
    }                                    │  The this expression becomes a receiver
}                                        │  of the body function: this.body().

fun main() {
    val dependencies = DependencyHandler()
    dependencies.implementation("org.jetbrains.kotlinx
    ⇒ :kotlinx-coroutines-core:1.8.0")
    // Added dependency on org.jetbrains.kotlinx
        ⇒ :kotlinx-coroutines-core:1.8.0
    dependencies {
        implementation("org.jetbrains.kotlinx:kotlinx-datetime:0.5.0")
    }
    // Added dependency on org.jetbrains.kotlinx:kotlinx-datetime:0.5.0
}
```

When you add the first dependency, you call the `implementation` method directly. The
second call is effectively translated to the following:

```
dependencies.invoke({
    this.implementation("org.jetbrains.kotlinx:kotlinx-datetime:0.5.0")
})
```

In other words, you're invoking `dependencies` as a function and passing a lambda as an
argument. The type of the lambda's parameter is a function type with a receiver, and
the receiver type is the same `DependencyHandler` type. The `invoke` method calls the
lambda. Because it's a method of the `DependencyHandler` class, an instance of that class
is available as an implicit receiver, so you don't need to specify it explicitly when you
call `body()`.

One fairly small piece of code, the redefined `invoke` method, has significantly
increased the flexibility of the DSL API. This pattern is generic, and you can reuse it
in your own DSLs with minimal modifications.

You're now familiar with two new features of Kotlin that can help you build DSLs: lambdas with receivers and the `invoke` convention. Let's look at how previously discussed Kotlin features come into play in the DSL context.

13.4 Kotlin DSLs in practice

By now, you're familiar with all the Kotlin features used when building DSLs. Some of them, such as extensions and infix calls, should be your old friends by now. Others, such as lambdas with receivers, were first discussed in detail in this chapter. Let's put all of this knowledge to use and investigate a series of practical DSL construction examples. We'll cover fairly diverse topics: testing, rich date literals, and database queries.

13.4.1 Chaining infix calls: The should function in test frameworks

As we mentioned previously, clean syntax is one of the key traits of an internal DSL, and it can be achieved by reducing the amount of punctuation in the code. Most internal DSLs boil down to sequences of method calls, so any features that allow you to reduce syntactic noise in method calls find a lot of use there. In Kotlin, these features include the shorthand syntax for invoking lambdas, which we've discussed in detail, as well as *infix function calls*. We discussed infix calls in chapter 3. Here, we'll focus on their use in DSLs.

Let's look at an example that uses the DSL of Kotest (https://github.com/kotest/kotest), which you saw earlier in this chapter. The `testKPrefix` test will fail with an assertion if the value of the `s` variable doesn't start with `K`. Note how the code reads almost like English: "The `s` string should start with this letter."

Listing 13.18 Expressing an assertion with the Kotest DSL

```
import io.kotest.matchers.should
import io.kotest.matchers.string.startWith
import org.junit.jupiter.api.Test

class PrefixTest {
    @Test
    fun testKPrefix() {
        val s = "kotlin".uppercase()
        s should startWith("K")
    }
}
```

To accomplish this syntax in your own DSL, you would declare the `should` function with the `infix` modifier.

Listing 13.19 Implementing the should function

```
infix fun <T> T.should(matcher: Matcher<T>) = matcher.test(this)
```

The `should` function expects an instance of `Matcher`, a generic interface for performing assertions on values. `startWith` implements `Matcher` and checks whether a string starts with the given substring.

Listing 13.20   Defining a matcher for the Kotest DSL

```
interface Matcher<T> {
    fun test(value: T)
}

fun startWith(prefix: String): Matcher<String> {
    return object : Matcher<String> {
        override fun test(value: String) {
            if (!value.startsWith(prefix)) {
                throw AssertionError("$value does not start with $prefix")
            }
        }
    }
}
```

NOTE   The actual Kotest DSL defines some additional functionality in the `Matcher` interface, and extends the `test` function by returning a `MatcherResult`, used for processing matches. For brevity, we have simplified the signatures of these interfaces here. However, implementing your own `Matcher` that returns a `MatcherResult` is very similar to the code you've examined in the context of this section, and you're welcome to build your own real Kotest matcher as an exercise.

Listing 13.18 shows that applying infix calls in the DSL context is simple and can reduce the amount of noise in your code.

This was a relatively tricky example of DSL construction, but the result is so nice that it's worth figuring out how this pattern works. The combination of infix calls and `object` instances lets you construct fairly complex grammars for your DSLs and use those DSLs with a clean syntax. And of course, the DSL remains fully statically typed; an incorrect combination of functions and objects won't compile.

13.4.2 *Defining extensions on primitive types: Handling dates*

Now, let's take a look at the remaining teaser from the beginning of this chapter:

```
val now = Clock.System.now()
val yesterday = now - 1.days
val later = now + 5.hours
```

The `kotlinx.datetime` library (https://github.com/Kotlin/kotlinx-datetime) provides such a DSL for handling date and time manipulation.

The DSL itself can be described in a few lines of code. The following listing shows the relevant part of the implementation.

Listing 13.21 Defining a date manipulation DSL

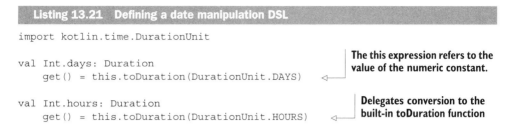

```
import kotlin.time.DurationUnit

val Int.days: Duration
    get() = this.toDuration(DurationUnit.DAYS)    ◁───

val Int.hours: Duration
    get() = this.toDuration(DurationUnit.HOURS)   ◁───
```

The this expression refers to the value of the numeric constant.

Delegates conversion to the built-in toDuration function

Here, both `days` and `hours` are extension properties on the `Int` type. Kotlin has no restrictions on the types that can be used as receivers for extension functions: you can easily define extensions on primitive types and invoke them on constants. You can, of course, use the same approach for declaring your own custom measurements. A *fortnight*, for example, refers to the period of 14 days:

```
val Int.fortnights: Duration get() =
    (this * 14).toDuration(DurationUnit.DAYS)
```

All of these extension properties return a value of type `Duration`, which is Kotlin's type for representing an amount of time between instants. Now that you have an idea of how this simple DSL works, let's move on to something more challenging: the implementation of the database query DSL.

13.4.3 Member extension functions: Internal DSL for SQL

So far, you've already seen that extension functions play a significant role in DSL design. In this section, we'll study a further trick that we've mentioned previously: declaring extension functions and extension properties in a class. Such a function or property is both a member of its containing class and an extension to some other type at the same time. We call such functions and properties *member extensions*.

Let's look at a couple of examples that use member extensions. They come from the internal DSL for SQL, the Exposed framework, mentioned earlier. Before we get to that, though, we need to discuss how Exposed allows you to define the database structure.

To work with SQL tables, the Exposed framework requires you to declare them as objects extending the `Table` class. Here's a declaration of a simple `Country` table with two columns.

Listing 13.22 Declaring a table in Exposed

```
object Country : Table() {
    val id = integer("id").autoIncrement()
    val name = varchar("name", 50)
    override val primaryKey = PrimaryKey(id)
}
```

This declaration corresponds to a table in the database. To create this table, you would connect to your database and call the `SchemaUtils.create(Country)` method within a transaction. In a project that uses an H2 in-memory database (https://h2database.com/), that would look like this:

```
fun main() {
    val db = Database.connect("jdbc:h2:mem:test", driver = "org.h2.Driver")
    transaction(db) {
        SchemaUtils.create(Country)
    }
}
```

This generates the necessary SQL statement based on the declared table structure:

```
CREATE TABLE IF NOT EXISTS Country (
    id INT AUTO_INCREMENT NOT NULL,
    name VARCHAR(50) NOT NULL,
    CONSTRAINT pk_Country PRIMARY KEY (id)
)
```

Just like with generating HTML, you can see how declarations in the original Kotlin code become parts of the generated SQL statement. If you examine the types of the properties in the Country object, you'll see that they have the Column type with the necessary type argument: id has the type Column<Int>, and name has the type Column<String>.

The Table class in the Exposed framework defines all types of columns you can declare for your table, including the ones just used:

```
class Table {
    fun integer(name: String): Column<Int>
    fun varchar(name: String, length: Int): Column<String>
    // ...
}
```

The integer and varchar methods create new columns for storing integers and strings, respectively.

Now, let's see how to specify properties for the columns. This is when member extensions come into play:

```
val id = integer("id").autoIncrement()
```

Methods like autoIncrement are used to specify the properties of each column. Each method can be called on Column and will return the instance it was called on, allowing you to chain the methods. Here are the simplified declarations of this function:

```
class Table {
    fun Column<Int>.autoIncrement(): Column<Int>    ⟵  Only integer values can
    // ...                                               be auto-incremented.
}
```

Even though autoIncrement is a *member* function of the Table class (meaning it can't be used outside the scope of this class), it's still an *extension* function of Column<Int>. This illustrates why it can make sense to declare methods as member extensions: you constrain their applicability scope. You can't specify the properties of a column outside the context of a table, since the necessary methods won't resolve.

Another great feature of extension functions that you use here is the ability to restrict the receiver type. Although any column in a table can be its primary key, only numeric columns can be auto-incremented. You can express this in the API by declaring the `autoIncrement` method as an extension on `Column<Int>`. An attempt to mark a column of a different type as auto-incremented will fail to compile.

Member extensions are still members

Member extensions have a downside as well: a lack of extensibility. They belong to the class, so you can't define new member extensions on the side.

For example, imagine that you wanted to add support for a new database to Exposed and that the database supported some new column attributes. To achieve this goal, you'd have to modify the definition of the `Table` class and add the member extension functions for new attributes there. You wouldn't be able to add the necessary declarations without touching the original class, as you can do with regular (nonmember) extensions because they wouldn't have access to the `Table` instance where they could store the definitions.

At the time of writing, the Kotlin team is designing a language feature that, among other use cases, addresses this: *context receivers*. Context receivers will allow you to specify more than one receiver type for a function. For example, the `autoIncrement` function, which needs to access a `Table` and a `Column<Int>` instance, could be declared as an extension function on `Column<Int>` with a context receiver `Table`:

```
context(Table)
fun Column<Int>.autoIncrement(): Column<Int> {
    // access properties and methods of both `Table` and `Column<Int>`
}
```

While the proposal for context receivers is still being refined, a prototype of context receivers is already available to evaluate the feature. For more information and related discussions, including instructions on how you can try out the prototype, take a look at the corresponding Kotlin Evolution and Enhancement Process (KEEP) document: http://mng.bz/67Ge.

Let's look at another member extension function that can be found in a simple `SELECT` query. Imagine you've declared two tables, `Customer` and `Country`, and each `Customer` entry stores a reference to the country the customer is from. The following code prints the names of all customers living in the USA.

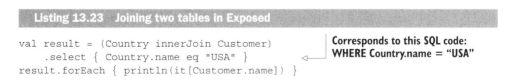

Listing 13.23 Joining two tables in Exposed

```
val result = (Country innerJoin Customer)
    .select { Country.name eq "USA" }
result.forEach { println(it[Customer.name]) }
```

Corresponds to this SQL code:
WHERE Country.name = "USA"

The `select` function can be called on `Table` or on a join of two tables. Its argument is a lambda that specifies the condition for selecting the necessary data.

Where does the `eq` method come from? We can say now that it's an infix function taking `"USA"` as an argument, and you may correctly guess that it's another member extension.

Here, you again come across an extension function on `Column` that's also a member and, thus, can be used only in the appropriate context: for instance, when specifying the condition of the `select` method. The simplified declarations of the `select` and `eq` methods are as follows:

```
fun Table.select(where: SqlExpressionBuilder.() -> Op<Boolean>) : Query

object SqlExpressionBuilder {
    infix fun<T> Column<T>.eq(t: T) : Op<Boolean>
    // ...
}
```

The `SqlExpressionBuilder` object defines many ways to express conditions: compare values, check for being not `null`, perform arithmetic operations, and so on. You'll never refer to it explicitly in the code, but you'll regularly call its methods when it's an implicit receiver. The `select` function takes a lambda with a receiver as an argument, and the `SqlExpressionBuilder` object is an implicit receiver in this lambda. That allows you to use in the body of the lambda all the possible extension functions defined in this object, such as `eq`.

You've seen two types of extensions on columns: those that should be used to declare a `Table` and those used to compare the values in a condition. Without member extensions, you'd have to declare all of these functions as extensions or members of `Column`, which would let you use them in any context. The approach with member extensions gives you a way to control that.

NOTE In chapter 9, we looked at some code that worked with Exposed while talking about using delegated properties in frameworks. Delegated properties often come up in DSLs, and the Exposed framework illustrates that well. We won't repeat the discussion of delegated properties here because we've covered them in detail. But if you're eager to create a DSL for your own needs or improve your API and make it cleaner, keep this feature in mind.

Summary

- Internal DSLs are an API design pattern you can use to build more expressive APIs with structures composed of multiple method calls.
- Lambdas with receivers employ a nesting structure to redefine how methods are resolved in the lambda body.
- The type of a parameter taking a lambda with a receiver is an extension function type, and the calling function provides a receiver instance when invoking the lambda.

- The benefit of using Kotlin internal DSLs rather than external templates or markup languages is the ability to reuse code and create abstractions.
- Defining extensions on primitive types allows you to create a readable syntax for various kinds of literals, such as durations.
- Using the `invoke` convention, you can call arbitrary objects as if they were functions.
- The kotlinx.html library provides an internal DSL for building HTML pages and can be extended to suit your applications.
- The Kotest library provides an internal DSL that supports readable assertions in unit tests.
- The Exposed library provides an internal DSL for working with databases.

Part 3

Concurrent programming with coroutines and flows

By now, you have developed a deep understanding of Kotlin as a language and its conventions. In this part of the book, you'll learn how to perform concurrent programming in Kotlin.

Concurrency is an impactful topic no matter whether you are writing server-side, mobile, or desktop applications with Kotlin. Most modern applications need to do more than one thing at once, be it serving or making network requests, keeping a responsive user interface while performing CPU-intensive tasks, or allowing users to multitask in other ways. As a Kotlin developer, you'll come across and work with concurrent code in Kotlin sooner or later, as well.

Kotlin comes with a unique and robust approach for concurrent programming based on the concept of *coroutines*, a lightweight abstraction that works on top of threads. The core primitives for concurrent programming are built right into the language, and its capabilities are extended by the kotlinx.coroutines library, which is being developed at JetBrains. Many libraries in the Kotlin ecosystem have fully embraced Kotlin's coroutines-based concurrency model and expose idiomatic and non-blocking APIs for you to use. Gaining an understanding of the concepts used by these APIs allows you to make use of these libraries to their fullest potential.

In chapter 14, you will get an overview of Kotlin's concurrency model. You will get an overview of suspending functions, coroutines, and the basic mechanics that apply when writing concurrent code with Kotlin. In chapter 15, you will explore the concept of structured concurrency, which helps you establish structure and hierarchy of your concurrent tasks and provides the facilities required for providing mechanisms for cancellation and error handling.

In chapters 16 and 17, you will learn about flows, the Kotlin way of working with multiple, sequential values over time, built on top of Kotlin coroutines, and the library of operators you can use to transform these value streams. You'll also learn about the difference between cold and hot flows, the two large categories of flows available, and get an understanding of when to use them. In chapter 18, you will dive deeper into the subject of error handling and testing your concurrent code. By the end of this part, you will have a solid understanding of concurrency-related concepts in Kotlin, and you will be able to confidently write code that uses the functionality of Kotlin coroutines.

Coroutines

This chapter covers

- The concepts of concurrency and parallelism
- Suspending functions as the basic building blocks for concurrent operations in Kotlin
- Kotlin's approach to concurrent programming with coroutines

Modern programs rarely only do one thing at a time; networked applications may need to make or serve multiple network requests but shouldn't wait for each network request to finish before starting the next one. Mobile and desktop apps may need to do anything from querying on-device databases, to using sensors, to communicating with other devices—all while redrawing their user interface 60 times per second or more.

To handle this, modern applications need to do multiple things at the same time, asynchronously. That means developers need tools to allow different operations to execute independently without blocking each other as well as coordinate and synchronize between concurrent tasks.

In this chapter, we'll take a look at Kotlin's approach to doing these kinds of asynchronous computations using coroutines. Coroutines allow you to write code that can be both concurrent and parallel.

14.1   *Concurrency vs. parallelism*

Before we dive deeper into concurrent programming with Kotlin, let's briefly define what we actually mean when we talk about concurrency—as well as its relationship to the concept of parallelism.

Concurrency is a general term used to mean that multiple tasks are being worked on simultaneously. However, it's not required for them to be physically executed at the same time—a system that intertwines execution of multiple parts of code is a concurrent system. This means that even applications running on a single CPU core can make use of concurrency: by switching back and forth between multiple concurrent tasks, even a single core can be enough to make a heavy computation while keeping the user interface responsive, as illustrated in figure 14.1.

Figure 14.1   By interleaving execution, even when running on a single core, an application can do more than one task at once. By switching back and forth between multiple tasks as required (like redrawing the user interface and performing parts of a long-running calculation), it leverages concurrency.

While concurrency is the general ability of the code to be divided into parts that could be run simultaneously, *parallelism* refers to physically executing multiple tasks simultaneously on multiple CPU cores. Parallel computations can use modern multicore hardware effectively, often making them more efficient. However, they also come with their own class of challenges—we'll discuss those briefly in section 14.7.4. Figure 14.2 shows a case of parallelism.

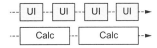

Figure 14.2   Parallelism means physically executing multiple tasks simultaneously on multiple CPU cores. In this example, long-running calculations happen in the background while the UI is being rendered.

This differentiation between the topics of concurrency and parallelism is, of course, heavily abridged—both are large fields in themselves. Books like *Grokking Concurrency* by Kirill Bobrov (2024, Manning) can provide a general overview of their topics. With Kotlin coroutines, you can do both concurrent computations and parallel computations, and you'll see both throughout this chapter.

14.2   *Concurrency the Kotlin way: Suspending functions and coroutines*

Coroutines are a powerful feature of Kotlin, providing an elegant way to write concurrent code that can run asynchronously and that is non-blocking. Compared to traditional approaches, like threads, coroutines are much more lightweight. Via *structured concurrency*, they also provide the facilities needed to manage concurrent tasks and their life cycle.

You'll start with a comparison between classic threads and Kotlin's coroutines. From there, you'll explore the basic abstraction of using coroutines in Kotlin: *suspending functions*, which allow you to write code that looks sequential without the drawbacks of blocking threads. You'll also see a comparison of coroutines to other concurrency models, like callbacks, futures, and reactive streams, highlighting the simplicity of Kotlin coroutines' abstractions.

14.3   Comparing threads and coroutines

The classic abstraction for both concurrent and parallel programming on the JVM is using *threads*, which provide you with the ability to specify blocks of code that run independently of each other and concurrently. Throughout the book, you've seen time and time again that Kotlin is 100% compatible with Java, and threads are no exception. If you want to use threads like you might in Java, you can use convenience functions from the Kotlin standard library. Specifically, you can use the `thread` function to start a new thread. In this example, you're using the function to start a new thread and display its name:

```
import kotlin.concurrent.thread

fun main() {
    println("I'm on ${Thread.currentThread().name}")
    thread {                                                ◄─────  Starts a new
        println("And I'm on ${Thread.currentThread().name}")        thread, which
    }                                                               executes the given
}                                                                   block of code

// I'm on main
// And I'm on Thread-0
```

Threads can help you make your application more responsive and help you make better use of modern systems by allowing you to distribute work across the individual cores of a multicore CPU. However, using threads in your application comes at a price. On the JVM, each thread you create typically corresponds to a thread managed by the operating system. Creating and managing such system threads can be costly, and even modern systems can only effectively manage a few thousand threads at a time. Each system thread needs to allocate a few megabytes of memory, and switching between threads is an operation executed on the level of the operating system kernel. The cost of these allocations and operations can quickly add up.

In addition, when a thread is waiting for an operation (e.g., a network request) to complete, it is also *blocked*—the thread can't do any other meaningful work while waiting for a response—it just sleeps, taking up system resources. This means you need to exercise great care when creating new threads, and you are naturally discouraged from using them in a fine-grained or short-lived manner.

Threads also just exist as standalone processes by default, which can provide a challenge when managing and orchestrating their work, especially regarding concepts like cancellation and exception handling. These constraints put a limit on the applicability of threads: you're constrained when you can create new threads (because they are expensive, and waiting for results may block them) and how you manage threads (because they have no concept of "hierarchy" by default).

Kotlin introduces an alternative abstraction to threads called *coroutines*, which represent suspendable computations. Kotlin coroutines can be used wherever you would usually use threads but provide a number of benefits:

- Coroutines are a very lightweight abstraction. You can easily run 100,000 or more coroutines on a regular laptop. Coroutines are cheap to create and manage, meaning you can use them more broadly and in a much more fine-grained manner than you would use threads, even for very short-lived tasks.
- Coroutines can suspend execution without blocking system resources and resume where they left off at a later point. This makes coroutines efficient for many asynchronous tasks like waiting for network requests or IO tasks compared to blocking threads.
- Coroutines establish structure and hierarchy of your concurrent tasks via a concept called *structured concurrency*, providing mechanisms for cancellation and error handling. When a part of a concurrent computation fails or is no longer required, structured concurrency ensures other coroutines started as children of the computation are canceled.

Under the hood, coroutines are implemented by running on one or more JVM threads (see figure 14.3; you'll learn more about this in section 14.7). This means your code written using coroutines can still make use of the parallelism the underlying threading model supplies, but you are not constrained by the limits of threads imposed by the operating system.

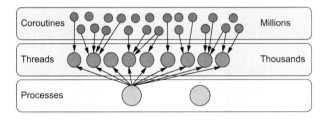

Figure 14.3   Coroutines are a lightweight abstraction on top of threads. Where a single process may have thousands of threads, you can run millions of concurrent tasks using coroutines.

Coroutines and Project Loom

Project Loom (https://wiki.openjdk.org/display/loom) is an effort to bring lightweight concurrency in the form of *virtual threads* natively to the JVM, dissolving the expensive one-to-one coupling between JVM threads and operating system threads. Since both Loom and Kotlin coroutines address similar concerns, it makes sense to take a moment to explore their relationship.

Coroutines were first introduced with Kotlin 1.1, released in 2016. Since then, they've become a mature abstraction for writing concurrent code and have been used in production applications for many years. Coroutines have been designed as a concurrent abstraction independent of the underlying execution model. In fact, their design is even decoupled from the JVM, allowing coroutines to be used when running Kotlin code on other platforms, like natively on iOS.

The primary goal of Project Loom is to enable existing, IO-heavy legacy code to be ported to virtual threads. That is where it shines the most, but it is also its core weakness. Loom was retrofitted onto the existing Java APIs for threads and IO. That means there is no language-level distinction between fast local computations and functions that might wait for information from the network for an unpredictable time (*suspending functions*, as they are called in Kotlin coroutines). This makes it harder to make sense of the code in larger codebases where local operations (like UI, caches, and state updates) are mixed with remote data access.

Java's legacy thread APIs were designed for the situation where threads are expensive and are rarely created. However, in highly concurrent code, coroutines are launched all the time. Kotlin coroutines APIs were designed from the ground up for the ergonomics of such code and are optimized for efficiency and minimal memory consumption in those situations. Kotlin coroutines are so cheap that it is often fine to create a new coroutine for a trivial operation, like incrementing a counter. Kotlin coroutines are even used to implement collection-manipulation operations on sequences with the `sequence {}` function—a feat not remotely possible at such efficiency with the Project Loom's virtual threads.

At the time of the writing, Project Loom is experimenting with retrofitting structured concurrency (a topic you will explore in depth in chapter 15) onto the legacy thread APIs it is based upon. Even though the shape of those APIs is not final, we can say that it is a far cry from the Kotlin coroutines API, in which structured concurrency takes the *central role* and underlies the core principles of the whole API design. In code that makes heavy use of concurrency, it is all too easy to make a mistake of launching a concurrent operation, forgetting to wait or cancel it, thus creating a potential resource leak. The very shape of the Kotlin coroutines API, from the ground up, is designed to ensure these mistakes are hard to make. You have to go the extra mile and write extra code to leak a coroutine. The shortest code you can write with Kotlin coroutines is always the correct one.

However, Kotlin coroutines will also be able to utilize the new functionality introduced by Loom to gain advantage of the benefits it provides—namely, integrating the code written using blocking APIs in a more efficient way. This can be achieved by providing a Loom-based virtual threads dispatcher for your coroutines. (You'll learn more about dispatchers in section 14.7.)

Learning Kotlin coroutines will teach you the useful skills of architecting your concurrent code with a clear distinction between local and remote (suspending) operations in mind and maintaining the practice of structured concurrency to avoid leaking resources. Even if, in the future, you'll be programming in an environment where these concerns are not directly or prominently exposed in the language and APIs, as in Kotlin coroutines, these are essential practices to learn for writing clean, concurrent code.

Let's explore Kotlin's model for concurrent programming from the ground up, starting with the most basic building block: suspending functions.

14.4   *Functions that can pause: Suspending functions*

One of the key properties of working with Kotlin coroutines that sets it apart from other concurrency approaches like threads, reactive streams, or callbacks, is that, in many cases, you don't need to change much about the "shape" of your code—it still looks sequential. Let's take a closer look at how *suspending functions*—functions that can pause—enable this.

14.4.1 Code written with suspending functions looks sequential

To understand how suspending functions in Kotlin work, let's take a look at a small piece of traditional application logic and see how suspending functions can improve it. In listing 14.1, you create a function called `showUserInfo` that's responsible for requesting some information from the network and displaying it to the user. The `login` and `loadUserData` functions make network requests. So far, this code doesn't use any kind of concurrency; it simply calls the functions one after the other, and then, finally, returns a value once the network request is answered.

Listing 14.1   Writing blocking code to call multiple functions

```
fun login(credentials: Credentials): UserID          Consider these
fun loadUserData(userID: UserID): UserData           functions blocking.
fun showData(data: UserData)

fun showUserInfo(credentials: Credentials) {
    val userID = login(credentials)
    val userData = loadUserData(userID)
    showData(userData)
}
```

From a computational perspective, this code doesn't actually do a lot of work. It spends the majority of its time waiting for the result of the network operation, blocking whatever thread the `showUserInfo` function is running on (see figure 14.4). As we established, blocking threads is generally not desirable because a blocked thread wastes resources: the number of system threads modern devices can handle is in the thousands. If, for example, you use this code from a networked application and block one thread per request, the blocking nature of the code can quickly turn into an upper limit to the number of requests your service can handle. If your application has a user interface, calling this function without concurrency would freeze the whole user interface until the operation completes. Such degradation in user experience and system performance clearly indicates a fault with our code.

Figure 14.4   Using blocking code means your hypothetical sample application, which spends most of its time waiting (visualized here as a square with diagonal lines) rather than working (visualized as a square with a function name), wastes computational resources.

Coroutines—more specifically, suspending functions—can help us do better. The following is the same code built as a non-blocking implementation using Kotlin coroutines. Note that the code still looks sequential; the only real difference is that the functions `login`, `loadUserData`, and `showUserInfo` have been annotated with the `suspend` modifier.

Listing 14.2 Using suspending functions to perform the same logic

```
suspend fun login(credentials: Credentials): UserID
suspend fun loadUserData(userID: UserID): UserData       Note the suspend
fun showData(data: UserData)                             modifier.

suspend fun showUserInfo(credentials: Credentials) {
    val userID = login(credentials)
    val userData = loadUserData(userID)
    showData(userData)
}
```

So what does it mean to mark a function with `suspend`? It indicates that this function may pause execution, for example, while waiting on a network response. Suspension doesn't block the underlying thread. Instead, when the execution of a function is suspended, other code can run on the same thread (see figure 14.15).

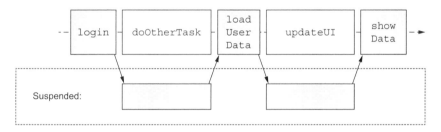

Figure 14.5 Using suspending functions means that waiting functions don't block execution. They're suspended instead and make way for any other functions that might want to run in the meantime, until they can continue executing.

Note that you didn't change the structure of your code: your code still looks and behaves sequentially, but you have gotten rid of the drawbacks of blocking code. The body of `showUserInfo` is still executed from top to bottom, statement after statement. However, while suspended, the underlying thread can proceed with other work— drawing the user interface, handling user requests, showing other data, and so on. The problems we discussed previously are no longer—calling this function from the UI thread of an application would not result in a UI freeze. While waiting for the network responses, the underlying thread is free to do other work.

Of course, this doesn't work by pure magic. It also requires the underlying libraries (i.e., the implementation of `login` and `loadUserData`) to be implemented with Kotlin coroutines in mind—and indeed, a lot of libraries in the Kotlin ecosystem expose APIs that work with coroutines. In the case of making network requests, those are libraries such as the Ktor HTTP clients, Retrofit, or OkHttp.

14.5 *Comparing coroutines to other approaches*

If you've previously used other approaches for writing concurrent code—whether in Java or a different programming language—you might be interested in seeing how they compare, and how coroutines can improve on them. Let's briefly look at three examples encompassing the most common approaches: callbacks, reactive streams (RxJava), and futures. We won't dive into their detailed design here, but you'll take a brief look at some sample implementations for the purpose of the discussion. If you haven't used these approaches before, you can, of course, skip this section.

Implementing the same logic as discussed in listing 14.1 using callbacks, you must change the signature of the `login` and `loadUserData` functions to provide a callback parameter.

Listing 14.3 Using callbacks to call multiple functions in succession

```
fun loginAsync(credentials: Credentials, callback: (UserID) -> Unit)
fun loadUserDataAsync(userID: UserID, callback: (UserData) -> Unit)
fun showData(data: UserData)

fun showUserInfo(credentials: Credentials) {
    loginAsync(credentials) { userID ->
        loadUserDataAsync(userID) { userData ->
            showData(userData)
        }
    }
}
```

Likewise, the `showUserInfo` function needs to be rewritten, using the individual callbacks. In the resulting code, you now end up with a callback inside a callback. While this may still be manageable for two function invocations, as your logic grows, you quickly find yourself in a hard-to-read mess of nested callbacks. This problem is so notorious that it has earned the moniker "callback hell."

Over time, other approaches to fighting callback hell have appeared; however, they usually still come with their own type of complexity, which you need to learn and get used to.

For example, using `CompletableFuture` avoids nesting callbacks but requires you to learn the semantics of new operators like `thenCompose` and `thenAccept`. It also requires you to change the return type of the `loginAsync` and `loadUserDataAsync` functions—their return type is now wrapped in a `CompletableFuture`.

Listing 14.4 Using futures to call multiple functions in succession

```
fun loginAsync(credentials: Credentials): CompletableFuture<UserID>
fun loadUserDataAsync(userID: UserID): CompletableFuture<UserData>
fun showData(data: UserData)

fun showUserInfo(credentials: Credentials) {
    loginAsync(credentials)
        .thenCompose { loadUserDataAsync(it) }
        .thenAccept { showData(it) }
}
```

Similarly, an implementation via *reactive streams* (e.g., using RxJava) avoids callback hell but still requires you to change the signatures of your functions—they now return `Single`-wrapped values—and to use operators like `flatMap`, `doOnSuccess`, and `subscribe`.

Listing 14.5 Using reactive streams to implement the same logic

```
fun login(credentials: Credentials): Single<UserID>
fun loadUserData(userID: UserID): Single<UserData>
fun showData(data: UserData)

fun showUserInfo(credentials: Credentials) {
    login(credentials)
        .flatMap { loadUserData(it) }
        .doOnSuccess { showData(it) }
        .subscribe()
}
```

Both approaches introduce cognitive overhead, and you need to introduce new operators to your code, both when declaring functions and when using them. Compare this to the approach using Kotlin coroutines, where you only need to mark the functions with the `suspend` modifier—the rest of your code stays the same, keeps its sequential look, and still avoids the initial drawbacks of blocking the thread. Of course, both reactive streams and futures have their use cases. As you'll see in section 14.6.3, Kotlin comes with its own flavor of futures called *deferred values*, and we'll spend all of chapter 16 and chapter 17 discussing *flows*, a reactive-stream-style abstraction available for coroutines. But as you can see, neither of these abstractions is necessary for the basic case of enabling concurrency. If you happen to have existing code written using other concurrency models, Kotlin provides extension functions that allow you to convert many of their primitives into coroutine-friendly versions.

14.5.1 Calling a suspending function

Because a suspending function can pause its execution, it can't just be called anywhere in normal code—it needs to be called in from a block of code that can also pause its execution. One such type of block would be another suspending function. This should follow your intuition: "If a function can pause its execution, then the execution of its caller may also potentially get paused." Like you've seen in listing 14.2, the suspending `showUserInfo` function can call the suspending `login` and `loadUserData` functions. Of course, it can also call regular, non-suspending functions in its body, like the `showData` function (figure 14.16).

```
suspend fun showUserInfo(credentials: Credentials) {
    val userID :UserID  = login(credentials)
    val userData :UserData  = loadUserData(userID)
    showData(userData)
}
```

Figure 14.6   IntelliJ IDEA and Android Studio highlight the invocation of functions marked with `suspend` by adding a small "suspension" gutter icon. Additionally, your IDE allows you to specify a custom color for suspending function invocations.

Trying to call a suspending function from regular, non-suspending code, will result in an error:

```
suspend fun mySuspendingFunction() {}

fun main() {
    mySuspendingFunction()
}
```

Error: Suspend function mySuspendingFunction should be called only from a coroutine or another suspend function.

So how do you actually call your first suspending function? The simplest answer is that the `main` function of your program can also be marked with the `suspend` modifier. However, when you're writing code within the context of a larger codebase or in the context of an SDK or framework like Android's, you often can't simply change the signature of your `main` function. That's why this approach is typically reserved for use in small utility programs.

A more versatile and powerful approach is using *coroutine builder* functions, which are responsible for constructing new *coroutines*. They serve as the typical entry points for calling suspending functions.

14.6   *Entering the world of coroutines: Coroutine builders*

So far, you've gotten to know suspending functions as the basic concurrency building block in Kotlin: functions that can pause execution, and that can only be called from within another suspending function or from a coroutine.

We've already discussed the intuition behind why it is okay for one suspending function to call another suspending function. Now, it's time to turn our attention to the other half of the hint given by the error message: calling a suspending function from a *coroutine*. We've used that term a few times already, but haven't really defined it up until now. Let's fix that.

A *coroutine* is an instance of a suspendable computation. You can think of it as a block of code that can be executed concurrently (or even in parallel) with other coroutines, similar to a thread. These coroutines contain the required machinery to suspend execution of the functions called in their body. To create such a coroutine, you use one of the coroutine builder functions. There are a number of functions available:

- `runBlocking` is designed for bridging the world of blocking code and suspending functions.
- `launch` is used for starting new coroutines that don't return any values.
- `async` is for computing values in an asynchronous manner.

Let's take a closer look at all of them.

> **NOTE** The coroutines-related functionality that is part of the core Kotlin compiler as well as the standard library is intentionally kept lean. Most functions discussed from this point forward aren't part of the Kotlin standard library itself but part of the first-party library kotlinx.coroutines (https://github.com/Kotlin/kotlinx.coroutines) developed by JetBrains. This allows concurrency-related functionality to evolve independently of the language release cycles. It also allows the community to provide alternative higher-level concurrency libraries that can rely on a small and stable set of core functionality. To follow along with the code in the rest of the book, make sure you specify the artifact `org.jetbrains.kotlinx:kotlinx-coroutines-core:1.7.3` or later as a dependency for your project.

14.6.1 *From regular code into the realm of coroutines: The runBlocking function*

To bridge the world of "regular" blocking code to the realm of suspending functions, you can use the `runBlocking` coroutine builder function, passing a block of code that makes up the body of the coroutine. It creates and runs a new coroutine and simply blocks the current thread until the coroutine has completed. Inside the code block passed to the function, you can make calls to suspending functions. In this example, you're using the special built-in `delay` function to suspend your coroutine for 500 milliseconds before printing the text.

Listing 14.6 Using `runBlocking` to invoke a suspending function

```
import kotlinx.coroutines.*
import kotlin.time.Duration.Companion.milliseconds

suspend fun doSomethingSlowly() {
    delay(500.milliseconds)          ◁——— Pause the function for 500 milliseconds.
    println("I'm done")
}

fun main() = runBlocking {
    doSomethingSlowly()
}
```

But wait: wasn't the whole point of using coroutines to *avoid* blocking threads? So why are we using runBlocking now? Indeed, when using runBlocking, you block *one* thread. However, within this coroutine, you're free to start any number of additional child coroutines, which won't block any further threads. Instead, they'll run concurrently, freeing up your one thread whenever suspended for other coroutines to run their code. To start such additional child coroutines, you can use the launch coroutine builder. Let's explore it in more detail and see what that looks like.

14.6.2   *Creating start-and-forget coroutines: The launch function*

The launch function is used for starting a new child coroutine. It is typically used for "start-and-forget" scenarios, where you want to run some piece of code, but aren't waiting for it to compute a return value. Let's put the previous claim about runBlocking only blocking a single thread to the test.

Because you want to get a better idea of when and where the code is running, instead of using println, let's use a simple log function that adds extra information—a timestamp as well as the thread the function is being called on:

```
private var zeroTime = System.currentTimeMillis()
fun log(message: Any?) =
    println("${System.currentTimeMillis() - zeroTime} " +
            "[${Thread.currentThread().name}] $message")
```

In this example, you use the runBlocking and launch coroutine builders to start a number of new coroutines, and use the log function to log some information about their execution:

```
fun main() = runBlocking {
    log("The first, parent, coroutine starts")
    launch {
        log("The second coroutine starts and is ready to be suspended")
        delay(100.milliseconds)
        log("The second coroutine is resumed")
    }
    launch {
        log("The third coroutine can run in the meantime")
    }
    log("The first coroutine has launched two more coroutines")
}
```

If you run this example with the -Dkotlinx.coroutines.debug JVM option (see figure 14.7) or in the Kotlin playground (where this option gets added automatically), you additionally get information about the coroutine name next to the thread name, which can be extra helpful in understanding how the coroutines works. Going forward, we'll show the output of the code snippets with this flag enabled.

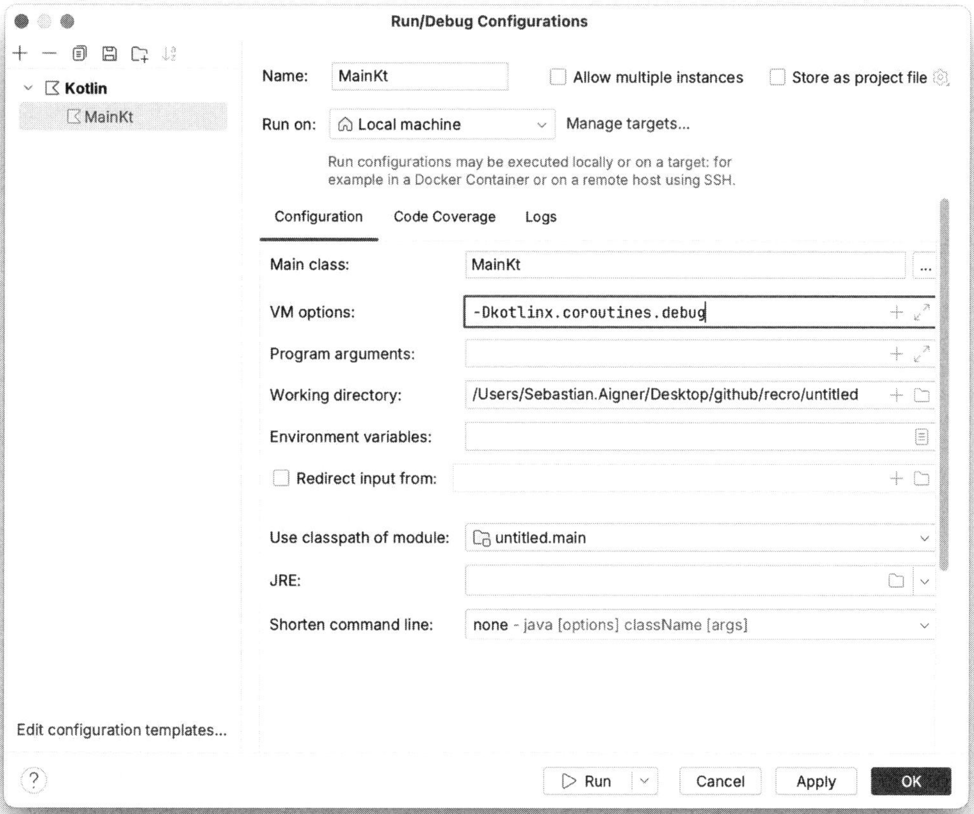

Figure 14.7   To set a JVM option from inside IntelliJ IDEA, click Run Configuration in the top-right corner and select Edit Configurations … . Then, you can add the debug option under VM Options.

Executing this code, you'll see the following output (the exact timings in the output will depend on your machine, but the line order stays the same):

```
36 [main @coroutine#1] The first, parent, coroutine starts
40 [main @coroutine#1] The first coroutine has launched two more coroutines
42 [main @coroutine#2] The second coroutine starts and is ready to be suspend
    ed
47 [main @coroutine#3] The third coroutine can run in the meantime
149 [main @coroutine#2] The second coroutine is resumed
```

In this example, all the coroutines run on one thread, called `main`. You can visualize the execution of this code as shown in figure 14.8.

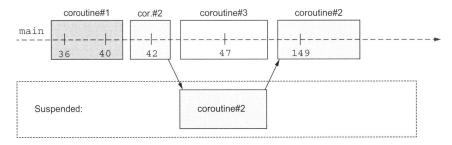

Figure 14.8 The first (parent) coroutine starts and launches two more coroutines. Coroutine 2 executes until its suspension point. It gets suspended without blocking the main thread, freeing it up for coroutine 3 to do its work, before resuming and finishing its execution.

Let's discuss the execution in detail and follow along with figure 14.8. The line represents the timeline of the main thread, and the rectangles on it are the coroutines running on this thread at a given moment in time. Below is the zone illustrating the suspended coroutines at a given moment.

Your code starts three coroutines in this example: the first (parent) coroutine started by `runBlocking` and two child coroutines started by invoking `launch` twice. When coroutine 2 calls the `delay` function, it triggers the suspension of the coroutine. This is called a *suspension point*. Coroutine 2 is now paused for the specified time and frees up the main thread for other coroutines to work on. That means coroutine 3 can begin its work. Because coroutine 3 only contains a single `log` call, it finishes quickly. After the specified 100 milliseconds, coroutine 2 resumes its work, and the execution of your whole program finishes.

Where do suspended coroutines go?

The heavy lifting for making coroutines work is done by the compiler; it generates supporting code responsible for suspending, resuming, and scheduling a coroutine. The code of suspending functions is transformed at compile time so that when a coroutine is suspended, information about its state at the time of suspension is stored in memory. Based on this information, the execution can be restored and resumed at a later point.

Thinking back to our comparison of concurrency and parallelism in section 14.1, you can probably identify this as an instance of interleaved execution without parallelism (all coroutines run on the same thread). If you do want your coroutines to run in parallel, on multiple threads, you could keep your code mostly the same, but use a multi-threaded dispatcher—something we'll discuss in section 14.7.

Using `launch`, you can start a new, basic coroutine. But, while `launch` allows you to perform concurrent computations, it doesn't easily allow you to return a value from the code inside the coroutine—the design of `launch` lends itself more toward start-and-forget tasks, which may perform some side effects (like writing to a file or a database), if you aren't interested in an actual return value. The `launch` function returns an object of type `Job`, which you can think of as a handle for the coroutine you started. You can use the `Job` object to control the execution of the coroutine—for example, by triggering cancellation (you'll learn more about coroutine cancellation in chapter 15). The case of returning a computed result is covered by another coroutine builder function, whose name and concept you might already be familiar with from other programming languages: `async`.

14.6.3   Awaitable computations: The async builder

If you are looking to perform an asynchronous computation, you can use the `async` builder function. Just like with `launch`, you give it a block of code to be executed as a coroutine. However, the return type of the `async` function is different; it returns an instance of `Deferred<T>`. The main thing you can do with a `Deferred` is await its result via the suspending `await` function.

Let's consider the following listing, which calculates two numbers asynchronously. In this listing, you simulate the calculation taking a long time by introducing a call to `delay`. You wrap the two calls to `slowlyAddNumbers` in a call to `async` before calling `await` on the deferred values returned by the `async` builder function.

Listing 14.7   Using the `async` coroutine builder to start a new coroutine

```
suspend fun slowlyAddNumbers(a: Int, b: Int): Int {
    log("Waiting a bit before calculating $a + $b")
    delay(100.milliseconds * a)
    return a + b
}


fun main() = runBlocking {
    log("Starting the async computation")
    val myFirstDeferred = async { slowlyAddNumbers(2, 2) }      Starts a new coroutine
    val mySecondDeferred = async { slowlyAddNumbers(4, 4) }     for each async call
    log("Waiting for the deferred value to be available")
    log("The first result: ${myFirstDeferred.await()}")        Waits for the results
    log("The second result: ${mySecondDeferred.await()}")      to be available
}
```

Running this code yields the following output:

```
0 [main @coroutine#1] Starting the async computation
4 [main @coroutine#1] Waiting for the deferred value to be available
8 [main @coroutine#2] Waiting a bit before calculating 2 + 2
9 [main @coroutine#3] Waiting a bit before calculating 4 + 4
213 [main @coroutine#1] The first result: 4
415 [main @coroutine#1] The second result: 8
```

Taking a look at the timestamps, you'll notice that computing the two values only took roughly 400 milliseconds in total, which is the duration of the longest computation (one takes 200 milliseconds, and the other takes 400 milliseconds). Using `async`, you start a new coroutine for each of the function calls, allowing both computations to happen concurrently (figure 14.9). Just like `launch`, invoking `async` doesn't suspend a coroutine. The root coroutine suspends when you call `await`, until a value is available.

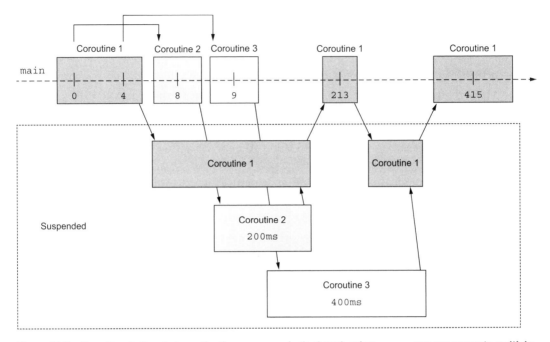

Figure 14.9   Even though the whole application runs on a single thread, using `async`, you can compute multiple values concurrently. Coroutine 1 starts two asynchronous computations and suspends until their values are available. Each new coroutine—coroutines 2 and 3—suspend internally for a bit before returning the resulting value back to coroutine 1.

You may already be familiar with the `Deferred` type under a different name, like `Future` or `Promise`. In each case, their concept is the same: a deferred object represents a value that is potentially not yet available. This value needs to be computed or retrieved. It's promised to become known sometime in the future—in other words, its computation is deferred.

Something that sets Kotlin apart from other languages is that you don't have to use `async` and `await` in basic code that calls suspending functions sequentially, as you did in listing 14.2. In Kotlin, you only use `async` when you want to concurrently execute independent tasks and wait for their results. If you don't need to start multiple tasks at once and then wait for their results, you don't have to use `async`—plain suspending function calls suffice.

NOTE You may have noticed that the `async {}` builder function and the suspending `await` functions aren't keywords in Kotlin (like `async`/`await` are in many other languages). They're simply functions provided by the `kotlinx.coroutines` library. Using your IDE's Go to Definition feature, you can even take a look at how all these functions are implemented. Suspending functions—one of the few concurrency primitives included directly in the core of the Kotlin language—proved to be such powerful low-level abstractions that functionality like `async`/`await` could just be implemented in a stand-alone library. As you'll see in chapter 16, the suspend mechanism is also versatile enough to implement a reactive-stream-style API.

Table 14.1 provides an overview of coroutine builders and their usage.

Table 14.1 Depending on your use case, you can pick one of the available coroutine builders.

Builder	Return value	Used for
`runBlocking`	Value calculated by lambda	Bridging blocking and non-blocking code
`launch`	`Job` (explored further in chapter 15)	Start-and-forget tasks (that have side effects)
`async`	`Deferred<T>`	Calculating a value asynchronously (which can be awaited)

Coroutines are an abstraction on top of threads. But which threads does our code actually run on? You already saw one special case, `runBlocking`, in which case the code is just executed on the thread calling the function. For more control over which threads to run our code on, you use *dispatchers* in Kotlin coroutines.

14.7 Deciding where your code should run: Dispatchers

The *dispatcher* for a coroutine determines what thread(s) the coroutine uses for its execution. By choosing a dispatcher, you can confine the execution of a coroutine to a specific thread or dispatch it to a thread pool, allowing you to decide whether the coroutine should run on a specific thread or number of threads. Inherently, coroutines aren't bound to any particular thread; it's okay for a coroutine to suspend its execution in one thread and resume its execution in another, as dictated by the dispatcher.

What's a thread pool?

A thread pool manages a set of threads and allows the execution of tasks (or, in our case, coroutines) on those threads. It doesn't allocate a new thread each time a new task needs to be executed, since this is an expensive operation. Instead, a thread pool keeps a number of threads allocated and distributes incoming tasks based on some internal and implementation-specific logic.

14.7.1 Choosing a dispatcher

As you'll see in section 14.8, coroutines inherit their dispatcher from their parent by default, so you don't need to explicitly specify a dispatcher for each and every coroutine. However, there are a number of dispatchers available to choose from. These help you explicitly run coroutines in their default circumstances (`Dispatchers.Default`) when working with UI frameworks (`Dispatchers.Main`) and with APIs that inherently block threads (`Dispatchers.IO`). Let's take a closer look at each of them.

A MULTITHREADED GENERAL-PURPOSE DISPATCHER: DISPATCHERS.DEFAULT

The most generic dispatcher that can be used for general-purpose operations is `Dispatchers.Default`. It's backed by a thread pool with as many threads as CPU cores are available. That means when you schedule coroutines on the default dispatcher, your coroutines get distributed to run across multiple threads, and as such, they can run in parallel on multicore machines. Unless you find yourself in a special scenario that requires confinement to a specific thread or thread pool, it's usually fine to stick with the default dispatcher when starting most of your coroutines. Remember, after all, because each coroutine simply suspends rather than blocking the thread it uses, even a single thread can handle thousands upon thousands of coroutines.

RUNNING ON THE UI THREAD: DISPATCHERS.MAIN

UI frameworks, whether you're using them on a desktop (with JavaFX, AWT, or Swing) or Android, sometimes need you to constrain the execution of certain operations to a specific thread, called the *UI thread* or *main thread*. One example of such an operation would be the redrawing of user interface elements. To safely execute these operations from a coroutine, you can use `Dispatchers.Main` when dispatching the coroutine. (Note that this doesn't mean you have to run your entire coroutine on the main dispatcher—you'll learn about a typical pattern involving `Dispatchers.Main` in section 14.7.3.)

Because there is no universal definition of what the "UI" or "Main" thread of an application is, the actual value of `Dispatchers.Main` varies, depending on what framework you are using. There are additional artifacts, such as `org.jetbrains.kotlinx:kotlinx-coroutines-swing` and `org.jetbrains.kotlinx:kotlinx-coroutines-javafx`, providing respective implementations for the main dispatcher of each framework. On Android, the `Dispatchers.Main` implementation is provided via the general `org.jetbrains.kotlinx:kotlinx-coroutines-android` artifact you use to set up coroutines on Android.

BLOCKING IO TASKS: DISPATCHERS.IO

When you're using third-party libraries, you might not always have the option to pick an API built with coroutines in mind. For those cases, when all you have is a blocking API (e.g., to interact with a database system), you might run into trouble when you call this functionality from the default dispatcher. Remember that the number of threads in the default dispatcher is equal to the number of available CPU cores. That means, if you were to invoke two thread-blocking operations on a dual-core machine, you would exhaust the default thread pool: no other coroutines would be able to run while your operations wait to complete. The IO dispatcher is designed to address exactly these scenarios. Coroutines launched in this dispatcher will execute in an automatically scaling pool of threads, which is allocated for precisely this kind of non-CPU-intensive work, where you're just waiting for a blocking API to return.

Specialty and custom dispatchers

Most application code you write with coroutines can be dispatched on one of the dispatchers you have gotten to know so far. But, of course, you might have specific requirements regarding the performance or behavior of your concurrent systems built with Kotlin coroutines. For these cases, the coroutines library provides additional functionality. For example, the `Unconfined` dispatcher allows a coroutine to run without any kind of thread confinement. If you need to specify custom constraints on parallelism for a dispatcher, you can use the `limitedParallelism` function. However, these are reserved for specialty cases. Consult the Kotlin documentation on coroutines and dispatchers (http://mng.bz/oeVZ) for more information.

Refer to table 14.2 and figure 14.10 for a comparison of the available dispatchers.

Table 14.2 Dispatchers available out of the box in Kotlin coroutines

Dispatcher	Number of threads	Used for
`Dispatchers.Default`	Number of CPU cores	General-purpose operations, CPU-bound operations
`Dispatchers.Main`	One	UI-bound logic ("UI thread"), only when in the context of a UI framework
`Dispatchers.IO`	Up to 64 threads (auto-scaling) or number of CPU cores (whichever is larger)	Offloading blocking IO tasks
`Dispatchers.Unconfined`	– ("Whatever thread")	Advanced cases where immediate scheduling is required (non-general-purpose)
`limitedParallelism(n)`	Custom (n)	Custom scenarios

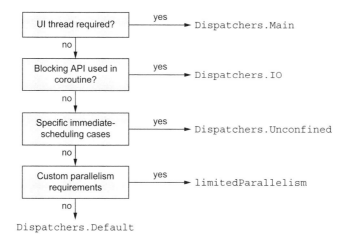

Figure 14.10 This small decision diagram helps you pick your dispatcher. Unless there is a particular reason, like working with UI threads, blocking APIs, or special cases, you can always pick `Dispatchers.Default` for your coroutines.

As you've seen, you aren't *required* to specify a dispatcher when launching a new coroutine. So the question is, where will your code be executed? The answer is, the dispatcher of the parent coroutine. We'll see how dispatchers and other elements relevant to the *context* of a coroutine are inherited in greater detail in chapter 15.

14.7.2 *Passing a dispatcher to a coroutine builder*

To make a coroutine run on a specific dispatcher, you can pass a dispatcher as an argument to the coroutine builder function. All coroutine builder functions, like `run-Blocking`, `launch`, and `async`, allow you to explicitly specify the dispatcher for their coroutine.

In this listing, you're configuring the `launch` function to start its coroutine on the default dispatcher by passing it as an argument.

> **Listing 14.8 Specifying a dispatcher as a parameter to a coroutine builder**

```
fun main() {
    runBlocking {
        log("Doing some work")
        launch(Dispatchers.Default) {          ◁─── Sets the dispatcher for the
            log("Doing some background work")        coroutine to Dispatchers.Default
        }
    }
}
```

Looking at the output of our code, you can indeed see that the first call to `log` runs on the main thread, and the second call from within the launched coroutine 2 is executed on one of the threads from the default dispatcher thread pool:

```
26 [main @coroutine#1] Doing some work
33 [DefaultDispatcher-worker-1 @coroutine#2] Doing some background work
```

Rather than switching the dispatcher for a whole coroutine, you can be more fine-grained regarding where you want specific parts of your coroutine to be executed. You do this using the function we'll look at next, `withContext`.

14.7.3 *Using withContext to switch the dispatcher within a coroutine*

Especially when working with UI frameworks, you might need to ensure your code runs on a specific underlying thread. A classic pattern when developing UI applications is to perform some long-running computation in the background and then, once the result is available, switch to the UI thread and update the user interface.

To switch dispatchers for an already existing coroutine, you can use the `with-Context` function and pass a different dispatcher (figure 14.11). In this snippet, you're launching a new coroutine that performs some background operation that might suspend. Once a result is available, you instruct the coroutine to switch to the UI thread via `Dispatchers .Main` and perform a (hypothetical) UI-specific operation:

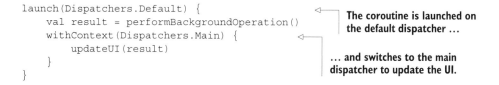

```
launch(Dispatchers.Default) {
    val result = performBackgroundOperation()
    withContext(Dispatchers.Main) {
        updateUI(result)
    }
}
```

The coroutine is launched on the default dispatcher …

… and switches to the main dispatcher to update the UI.

NOTE This example snippet uses `Dispatchers.Main`—as you've learned in section 14.7.1, which is provided by a UI framework like JavaFX, Swing, AWT, or the Android framework—so the snippet will only work in a project where one of these frameworks is configured. Switching to a different dispatcher (e.g., `withContext(Dispatchers.IO)`) works in all projects.

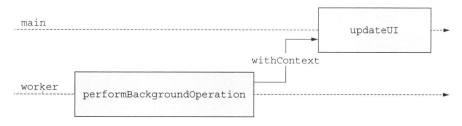

Figure 14.11 **The call to `withContext` causes the coroutine, which was originally started on the default dispatcher and running on one of its worker threads, to execute on the specified dispatcher. In this case, this is the main thread to update the UI.**

14.7.4 *Coroutines and dispatchers aren't a magical fix for thread-safety concerns*

With `Dispatchers.Default` and `Dispatchers.IO`, you've just gotten to know two built-in *multithreaded dispatchers*. A multithreaded dispatcher distributes your coroutines across more than one thread. If you've ever done multithreaded programming before, this might lead you to wonder whether you're now faced with typical thread-safety concerns. This is a good instinct to have, and it provides a wonderful basis for us to discuss the semantics of coroutines in a bit more detail.

A single coroutine is always executed sequentially—no parts of an individual coroutine run in parallel. That also means that data associated with a single coroutine doesn't run into any of the typical synchronization problems. Reading and changing data from multiple (parallel) coroutines isn't quite as easy. Let's compare two code snippets to illustrate this small but important difference. In this listing 14.9, you are launching a coroutine that increments a counter x 10,000 times.

Listing 14.9 Running a single coroutine to increment a variable

```
fun main() {
    runBlocking {
        launch(Dispatchers.Default) {
            var x = 0
            repeat(10_000) {
                x++
```

Starts a single coroutine on the multithreaded default dispatcher

```
        }
        println(x)
      }
    }
  }
}

// 10,000
```

The value of x after the coroutine has finished is exactly as expected. That's because even though the single coroutine you started runs on an arbitrary thread, its logic runs strictly sequentially. Compare this to a second code snippet in which you are launching 10,000 coroutines that increment a counter one time each.

Listing 14.10 Starting multiple coroutines to increment a variable

```
fun main() {
    runBlocking {
        var x = 0
        repeat(10_000) {                              Starts the coroutines on the
            launch(Dispatchers.Default) {    ◁──┘     multithreaded default dispatcher
                x++
            }
        }
        delay(1.seconds)
        println(x)
    }
}
// 9,916
```

In this case, the counter value is lower than expected because you have multiple coroutines modifying the same data (incrementing the counter). When some of these operations happen in parallel because you're running on a multithreaded dispatcher, some of the increment operations may overwrite each other.

Just like any other concurrent system that may manipulate data in parallel, there are a few approaches you can use to remedy this situation. As shown in the following listing, coroutines provide a `Mutex` lock, which allows you to ensure the critical section of your code will only be executed by one coroutine at a time.

Listing 14.11 Using a `Mutex` around the critical section

```
fun main() = runBlocking {
    val mutex = Mutex()
    var x = 0
    repeat(10_000) {
        launch(Dispatchers.Default) {
            mutex.withLock {
                x++
            }
        }
    }
```

```
        delay(1.seconds)
        println(x)
}
// 10000
```

You can also use atomic and thread-safe data structures made for concurrent modifications, like `AtomicInteger` or `ConcurrentHashMap`. Confining your coroutines (or, using `withContext`, their critical section) on a single-threaded dispatcher can also negate the problem but has its own performance characteristics to consider. For more details, see "Mutable Shared State and Concurrency" (http://mng.bz/ngx5) in the Kotlin coroutines documentation.

Summing this up, when you're working with coroutines, the same concurrency concerns apply as with threads: as long as data is associated with a single coroutine, your code will behave as expected out of the box. When multiple coroutines running in parallel modify the same data, you need to perform synchronization or locking, just like you would with threads.

14.8   Coroutines carry additional information in their coroutine context

In the previous sections, you've provided different dispatchers as arguments for the coroutine builder functions as well as the `withContext` function. But if you take a look at the parameter name (and type) of these functions, you'll actually notice the parameter isn't a `CoroutineDispatcher`. Really, the parameter is a `CoroutineContext`. Let's explore what that's all about.

Each coroutine carries with it additional context information in the form of a `CoroutineContext`, which you can simply think of as a set of various elements. One of those elements is, indeed, the dispatcher, deciding what thread or threads a given coroutine will run on. A `CoroutineContext` also usually contains a `Job` object associated with the coroutine responsible for its life cycle and its (potentially exceptional) cancellation. The coroutine context can also contain additional attached metadata, like a `CoroutineName` or `CoroutineExceptionHandler`.

You can inspect the current coroutine context by accessing a special property called `coroutineContext` inside any suspending function. This property isn't actually defined in Kotlin code; it's a *compiler intrinsic*, meaning its actual implementation is handled as a special case by the Kotlin compiler:

```
import kotlin.coroutines.coroutineContext

suspend fun introspect() {
    log(coroutineContext)          ◁——┐  The coroutineContext intrinsic contains
}                                      │  context information for a coroutine.

fun main() {
    runBlocking {
        introspect()
    }
```

```
}

// 25 [main @coroutine#1] [CoroutineId(1),
//     "coroutine#1":BlockingCoroutine{Active}@610694f1,
//     BlockingEventLoop@43814d18]
```

When you pass a parameter to a coroutine builder or the `withContext` function, you override this specific element in the child coroutine's context. To override multiple parameters at once, you can concatenate them using the + operator, which is overloaded for `CoroutineContext` objects. For example, you could start your `runBlocking` coroutine on the IO dispatcher and give it the name `Coolroutine`:

```
fun main() {
    runBlocking(Dispatchers.IO + CoroutineName("Coolroutine")) {
        introspect()
    }
}

// 27 [DefaultDispatcher-worker-1 @Coolroutine#1]
//    [CoroutineName(Coolroutine), CoroutineId(1),
//     "Coolroutine#1":BlockingCoroutine{Active}@d115c9f, Dispatchers.IO]
```

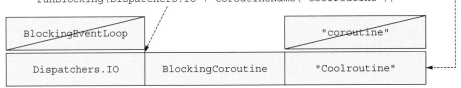

Figure 14.12   The parameters passed to `runBlocking` override the elements in the child's coroutine context: `Dispatchers.IO` replaces the special `BlockingEventLoop` dispatcher from `runBlocking`, and the name of the coroutine is set to `"Coolroutine"`.

We'll talk more about the significance of coroutine contexts in section 15.1.4. But to do so, we first need to lay the required groundwork by talking about one of the most powerful features built into Kotlin coroutines: structured concurrency, the subject of the next chapter.

Summary

- Concurrency refers to working with multiple tasks at the same time, manifesting in intertwined execution. Parallelism refers to executing physically at the same time, making use of modern multicore systems effectively.
- Coroutines are a lightweight abstraction working on top of threads for concurrent execution.

- The core concurrency primitive in Kotlin is the suspending function—a function that can pause execution. A suspending function can be called from another suspending function or from within a coroutine.
- Unlike other approaches, such as reactive streams, callbacks, and futures, suspending functions don't change the shape of your code—it still looks sequential.
- A coroutine is an instance of a suspendable computation.
- Coroutines avoid the problems caused by blocking threads, which are expensive, limited system resources.
- Coroutine builders like `runBlocking`, `launch`, and `async` allow you to create new coroutines.
- Dispatchers decide on which thread or thread pool your coroutines run.
- The different built-in dispatchers serve different purposes: `Dispatchers.Default` is a general-purpose dispatcher, `Dispatchers.Main` helps you run operations on the UI thread, and `Dispatchers.IO` is used for calling blocking IO tasks.
- Most dispatchers, like `Dispatchers.Default` and `Dispatchers.IO`, are multithreaded dispatchers, meaning you need to take extra care when multiple coroutines modify the same data in parallel.
- You can specify a dispatcher when creating a coroutine or switch between dispatchers using `withContext`.
- The coroutine context contains additional information associated with a coroutine. The dispatcher of a coroutine is part of the coroutine context.

Structured concurrency

When you use Kotlin coroutines in the context of real applications, chances are you will be managing a lot of coroutines. Major challenges when working with many concurrent operations are keeping track of the individual tasks that are running, cancelling them when they're no longer needed, and making sure that errors are handled properly.

Without keeping track of your coroutines, you run the risk of resource leaks and doing unnecessary work. Consider the following example: a user requests a network resource and immediately navigates away to a different screen. If you have no way of

418

keeping track of the (potentially dozens of) coroutines responsible for the network request and postprocessing of the information received, you have no choice but to let them run to completion—even if their result will just be discarded in the end.

Thankfully, *structured concurrency*, the ability to manage and keep track of the hierarchy of coroutines and their lifetimes within your application, is built right into the core of Kotlin coroutines. Structured concurrency works out of the box, without requiring you to manually keep track of each coroutine you start. By using structured concurrency throughout your application, there are no "rogue" coroutines to forget about or that run for longer than you plan for them to.

In this chapter, you'll take an in-depth look at Kotlin's structured concurrency mechanism and see how it enables you to confidently manage even large numbers of coroutines.

15.1 Coroutine scopes establish structure between coroutines

With structured concurrency, each coroutine belongs to a *coroutine scope*. Coroutine scopes help establish parent–child relationships between coroutines; the `launch` and `async` coroutine builder functions are actually extension functions on the `Coroutine-Scope` interface. That means that when you create a new coroutine using `launch` or `async` in the body of another coroutine builder, your new coroutine will automatically become a child of that coroutine. In this code snippet, you're starting a number of coroutines that take differing amounts of time to complete.

Listing 15.1 Starting a number of different coroutines

```
fun main() {
    runBlocking { // this: CoroutineScope        ◁─── Implicit receiver
        launch { // this: CoroutineScope    ◁─
            delay(1.seconds)                     The coroutine started by launch is a child
            launch {                             of the parent runBlocking coroutine.
                delay(250.milliseconds)
                log("Grandchild done")
            }
            log("Child 1 done!")
        }
        launch {
            delay(500.milliseconds)
            log("Child 2 done!")
        }
        log("Parent done!")
    }
}
```

When you look at the output, you'll notice that even though the body of the `runBlocking` function finishes its execution almost instantly—indicated by "Parent done!"—the program doesn't actually terminate until all child coroutines have completed:

```
29 [main @coroutine#1] Parent done!
539 [main @coroutine#3] Child 2 done!
1039 [main @coroutine#2] Child 1 done!
1293 [main @coroutine#4] Grandchild done
```

This is possible thanks to structured concurrency: there is a parent–child relationship between the coroutines (strictly speaking, the `Job` objects associated with your coroutines, as you'll see in section 15.1.4), meaning your `runBlocking` invocation knows how many of its children are still working, and continues to wait until they are all done. This hierarchy is visualized in figure 15.1. You did not have to manually keep track of the launched coroutines or their further descendants. Additionally, you did not have to manually await them—structured concurrency can keep track of that for you.

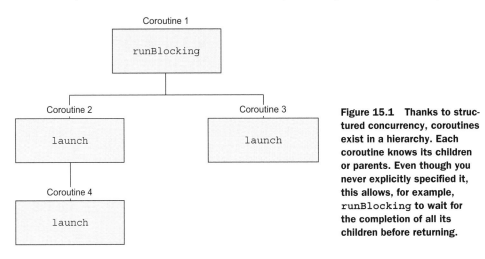

Figure 15.1 Thanks to structured concurrency, coroutines exist in a hierarchy. Each coroutine knows its children or parents. Even though you never explicitly specified it, this allows, for example, `runBlocking` to wait for the completion of all its children before returning.

As we'll explore further in section 15.2, the fact that coroutines are aware of their child coroutines and can keep track of them also enables functionality like automatically cancelling child coroutines when the parent coroutine gets cancelled. They can also help you express your desired behavior when it comes to exception handling—we will discuss this in chapter 18. (You'll learn more about how this parent–child relationship is being established on a technical level in section 15.1.4.)

15.1.1 *Creating a coroutine scope: The coroutineScope function*

As you've seen, whenever you create a new coroutine using the coroutine builders, they create their own `CoroutineScope`. But you can also group coroutines using our own coroutine scopes without having to create an entirely new coroutine. To do so, you can use the `coroutineScope` function. It's a suspending function that creates a new coroutine scope and waits for the completion of all of its child coroutines before it itself completes.

A typical use case for the `coroutineScope` function is *concurrent decomposition of work*—leveraging multiple coroutines together to perform a computation. In this example snippet, you're using it to calculate a sum of multiple concurrently generated numbers. Here, you use the fact that `coroutineScope` can return a value to return the sum of the two values from the block before logging it (visualized in figure 15.2). Because `coroutineScope` is suspending, you also mark the `computeSum` function as suspending:

```kotlin
import kotlinx.coroutines.*
import kotlin.random.Random
import kotlin.time.Duration.Companion.milliseconds

suspend fun generateValue(): Int {
    delay(500.milliseconds)
    return Random.nextInt(0, 10)
}

suspend fun computeSum() {                  ◁——— computeSum is suspending.
    log("Computing a sum...")
    val sum = coroutineScope {              ◁
        val a = async { generateValue() }        The coroutineScope function
        val b = async { generateValue() }        provides you with a scope.
        a.await() + b.await()               ◁
    }
    log("Sum is $sum")                            Before returning, coroutineScope
}                                                 waits for all child coroutines to finish.

fun main() = runBlocking {
    computeSum()
}

// 0 [main @coroutine#1] Computing a sum...
// 532 [main @coroutine#1] Sum is 10
```

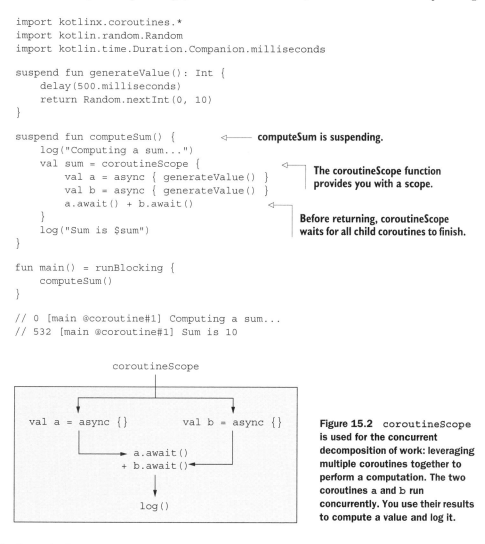

Figure 15.2 `coroutineScope` is used for the concurrent decomposition of work: leveraging multiple coroutines together to perform a computation. The two coroutines a and b run concurrently. You use their results to compute a value and log it.

15.1.2   Associating coroutine scopes with components: CoroutineScope

While the `coroutineScope` function is used for the decomposition of work, you might also find yourself wanting to build a class that defines its own kind of life cycle, managing the starting and stopping of concurrent processes and coroutines. For those scenarios, you use the `CoroutineScope` constructor function to create a new standalone coroutine scope. Unlike `coroutineScope`, this function doesn't pause execution—it simply gives you a new coroutine scope you can use to start new coroutines.

`CoroutineScope` takes one parameter: the context associated with the coroutine scope (you'll explore coroutine contexts in section 15.1.4). Here, you can, for example, specify the dispatcher used by coroutines started in this scope.

By default, invoking `CoroutineScope` with only a dispatcher creates a new `Job` automatically. However, in most practical cases, you want to instead use a `SupervisorJob` with `CoroutineScope`. A `SupervisorJob` is a special type of job that prevents uncaught exceptions from cancelling other coroutines associated with the same scope and propagating the exception further (you will explore supervisors in detail when we talk about error handling in chapter 18).

In the following listing, you create a class that can start and manage coroutines alongside its own life cycle. It takes a coroutine dispatcher as a constructor argument and uses the `CoroutineScope` function to create a new coroutine scope associated with the class. The `start` function launches a coroutine that keeps running and another coroutine that simply does a one-off task. The `stop` function cancels the scope associated with the class and, with it, the previously started coroutines (you'll explore cancellation in more detail in section 15.2).

Listing 15.2   A component with an associated coroutine scope

```
class ComponentWithScope(dispatcher: CoroutineDispatcher =
➥ Dispatchers.Default) {

    private val scope = CoroutineScope(dispatcher + SupervisorJob())

    fun start() {
        log("Starting!")
        scope.launch {
            while(true) {
                delay(500.milliseconds)
                log("Component working!")
            }
        }
        scope.launch {
            log("Doing a one-off task...")
            delay(500.milliseconds)
            log("Task done!")
        }
    }

    fun stop() {
        log("Stopping!")
        scope.cancel()
    }
}
```

You can construct a new instance of this `Component` and call `start` to have the component internally launch its coroutines. Then, you can call `stop`, which concludes the life cycle of the component:

```
fun main() {
    val c = ComponentWithScope()
    c.start()
    Thread.sleep(2000)
    c.stop()
}
// 22 [main] Starting!
// 37 [DefaultDispatcher-worker-2 @coroutine#2] Doing a one-off task...
// 544 [DefaultDispatcher-worker-1 @coroutine#2] Task done!
// 544 [DefaultDispatcher-worker-2 @coroutine#1] Component working!
// 1050 [DefaultDispatcher-worker-1 @coroutine#1] Component working!
// 1555 [DefaultDispatcher-worker-1 @coroutine#1] Component working!
// 2039 [main] Stopping!
```

Frameworks that have to manage components with life cycles often internally make use of the `CoroutineScope` function. You'll see one such example—Android's `ViewModel` class—in section 15.2.9.

> ### coroutineScope and CoroutineScope
>
> While they are named deceptively similarly, the `coroutineScope` and `CoroutineScope` functions serve different purposes:
>
> - *You use `coroutineScope` for the concurrent decomposition of work.* You launch a number of coroutines, and wait for all of them to complete, potentially computing some kind of result. Because `coroutineScope` waits for all of its children to complete, it is a suspending function.
> - *You use `CoroutineScope` to create a scope that associates coroutines with the life cycle of a class.* It creates the scope, but doesn't wait for any further operations, so it returns quickly. It returns you a reference to that coroutine scope, so you can later cancel it. (You'll explore cancellation in section 15.2.)
>
> In practice, you'll see many more uses of the suspending `coroutineScope` than the `CoroutineScope` constructor function. You typically see invocations of `coroutineScope` in the body of a suspending function, and typically see the `CoroutineScope` constructor used when storing a coroutine scope as the property of a class.

15.1.3 The danger of GlobalScope

In some samples or code snippets, you may see a special instance of coroutine scope, `GlobalScope`. As the name suggests, it's a coroutine scope that exists on the global level. Especially for newcomers to Kotlin coroutines, this might make it a tempting choice when deciding what coroutine scope to use when creating a coroutine—after all, it is available globally.

However, using `GlobalScope` comes with a number of drawbacks. Briefly summarized, using `GlobalScope` means opting out of all the benefits that structured concurrency has to offer. Coroutines launched on the global scope can't be automatically cancelled and aren't aware of any life cycle. This means it's very easy to introduce resource leaks into your application when using the global scope, or simply continue to do unnecessary work, and waste computational resources.

You can see one type of problem caused by using GlobalScope by slightly adjusting the code from listing 15.1. This code will terminate immediately, without waiting for any of the launched coroutines.

Listing 15.3   GlobalScope breaks the structured concurrency hierarchy

```
fun main() {
    runBlocking {
        GlobalScope.launch {                    ◁─── Using GlobalScope in regular
            delay(1000.milliseconds)                 application code is generally
            launch {                                 a bad idea.
                delay(250.milliseconds)
                log("Grandchild done")
            }
            log("Child 1 done!")
        }
        GlobalScope.launch {
            delay(500.milliseconds)
            log("Child 2 done!")
        }
        log("Parent done!")
    }
}

// 28 [main @coroutine#1] Parent done!
```

This code terminates immediately because using GlobalScope breaks the hierarchy typically established out of the box when using structured concurrency. Coroutines 2 through 4 have been launched in a way where the coroutine associated with runBlocking, coroutine 1, is no longer the parent (visualized in figure 15.3). Therefore, it has no children to wait for, and the program terminates prematurely.

For these reasons, GlobalScope is declared with a special annotation—@DelicateCoroutinesApi. You'll get a warning that encourages you to exercise caution: "This is a delicate API and its use requires care. Make sure you fully read and understand the documentation of the declaration that is marked as a delicate API." In general application code, cases where you should choose GlobalScope are extremely rare (one such example are top-level background processes that must stay active for the *whole* lifetime of an application). You are usually better served finding a more appropriate scope to start your coroutines: either via the coroutine builders or via the coroutineScope function.

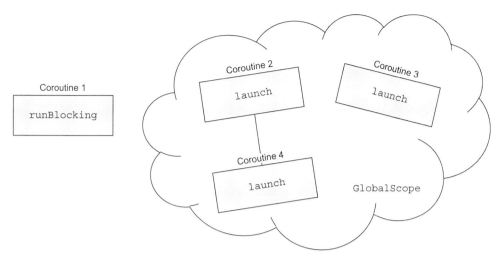

Figure 15.3   Using `GlobalScope` **breaks the hierarchy between coroutines.** `runBlocking` **is no longer a parent of the launched coroutines, meaning it has no way to automatically wait for their completion.**

15.1.4 Coroutine contexts and structured concurrency

Now that you have a high-level overview of structured concurrency, we can return to the discussion of coroutine contexts. Coroutine contexts are closely related to the concept of structured concurrency; they are inherited along the same parent–child hierarchy established between coroutines.

So what happens with the coroutine context when you start a new coroutine? First, the child coroutine inherits the parent context. Then, the new coroutine creates a new `Job` object (the same kind as you have seen in chapter 14), which is responsible for establishing the parent–child relationship—the `Job` becomes a child of the `Job` in the parent coroutine. Finally, any arguments provided for the coroutine context are applied. They may override whatever was previously inherited.

The following code snippet and figure 15.4 visualize this:

```
fun main() {
    runBlocking(Dispatchers.Default) {
        log(coroutineContext)
        launch {
            log(coroutineContext)
            launch(Dispatchers.IO + CoroutineName("mine")) {
                log(coroutineContext)
            }
        }
    }
}

// 0 [DefaultDispatcher-worker-1 @coroutine#1] [CoroutineId(1),
//     "coroutine#1":BlockingCoroutine{Active}@68308697, Dispatchers.Default]
```

```
// 1 [DefaultDispatcher-worker-2 @coroutine#2] [CoroutineId(2),
     "coroutine#2":StandaloneCoroutine{Active}@2b3ce773, Dispatchers.Default]
// 2 [DefaultDispatcher-worker-3 @mine#3] [CoroutineName(mine),
     CoroutineId(3), "mine#3":StandaloneCoroutine{Active}@7c42841a,
     Dispatchers.IO]
```

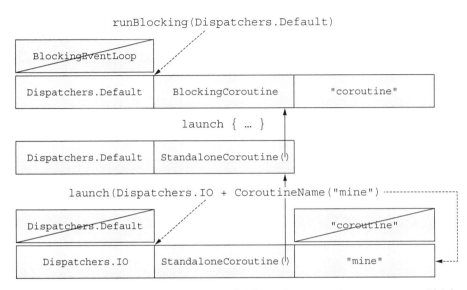

Figure 15.4 `runBlocking` **starts with a special dispatcher,** `BlockingEventLoop`, **which is overridden by the provided parameter and becomes** `Dispatchers.Default`. **It creates a** `Job` **object for the coroutine called** `BlockingCoroutine` **and initializes the coroutine name with the default value** `"coroutine"`. `launch` **inherits the default dispatcher. It creates its own** `Job` **object called** `StandaloneCoroutine` **and establishes the relationship with the parent job—the coroutine name remains unchanged. The second invocation of** `launch` **also inherits the dispatcher and creates a new child** `Job` **as well as the coroutine name. The parameters passed to** `launch` **override the dispatcher to be** `Dispatchers.IO` **and the coroutine is named** `"mine"`.

Now that you know how coroutine contexts are passed down the hierarchy of coroutines, it's easier to come up with an answer to this question: "If I `launch` a new coroutine without specifying a `Dispatcher`, which dispatcher will it run on?" The answer is *not* `Dispatchers.Default`! Rather, it is whatever the parent dispatcher was.

You can actually see the parent–child relationship between the coroutines in your code—or, more precisely, the relationships between the *jobs associated with your coroutines*. You can do so by checking the `job`, `job.parent`, and `job.children` properties on the coroutine context of each coroutine:

```
import kotlinx.coroutines.job

fun main() = runBlocking(CoroutineName("A")) {
    log("A's job: ${coroutineContext.job}")
    launch(CoroutineName("B")) {
```

```
        log("B's job: ${coroutineContext.job}")
        log("B's parent: ${coroutineContext.job.parent}")
    }
    log("A's children: ${coroutineContext.job.children.toList()}")
}


// 0 [main @A#1] A's job: "A#1":BlockingCoroutine{Active}@41
// 10 [main @A#1] A's children: ["B#2":StandaloneCoroutine{Active}@24
// 11 [main @B#2] B's job: "B#2":StandaloneCoroutine{Active}@24
// 11 [main @B#2] B's parent: "A#1":BlockingCoroutine{Completing}@41
```

Just like coroutines started with the coroutine builder functions like `launch` and `async`, the `coroutineScope` function also has its own `Job` object that participates in the parent–child hierarchy. You can convince yourself that this is indeed the case by checking its `coroutineContext.job` property:

```
fun main() = runBlocking<Unit> { // coroutine#1
    log("A's job: ${coroutineContext.job}")
    coroutineScope {
        log("B's parent: ${coroutineContext.job.parent}") // A
        log("B's job: ${coroutineContext.job}") // C
        launch { //coroutine#2
            log("C's parent: ${coroutineContext.job.parent}") // B
        }
    }
}


// 0 [main @coroutine#1] A's job: "coroutine#1":BlockingCoroutine{Active}@41
// 2 [main @coroutine#1] B's parent:
    "coroutine#1":BlockingCoroutine{Active}@41
// 2 [main @coroutine#1] B's job: "coroutine#1":ScopeCoroutine{Active}@56
// 4 [main @coroutine#2] C's parent:
    "coroutine#1":ScopeCoroutine{Completing}@56
```

This parent–child relationship established by structured concurrency also helps with *cancellation*, as you'll explore in the next section.

15.2 Cancellation

Cancellation refers to stopping the execution of your code before it has completed regularly. While cancellation may, on the surface, not seem like a particularly common occurrence, the reality is that almost all modern applications need to be able to handle the cancellation of computations if they want to be robust and efficient. There are several reasons for that.

Cancellation prevents unnecessary work. In applications with a user interface, you may start a computation or network request, and the user may simply close the window or navigate away. Without a way of cancelling the work you started, you would have to complete the computation or download the whole response over the network and then throw away the result. It can negatively impact the throughput of server-side applications, and this is especially wasteful on mobile devices, where computational resources and battery life are constrained.

Cancellation also helps avoid memory or resource leaks. Without a way to cancel work when it is no longer needed, it would be easy for rogue coroutines to hold onto resources, or keep references to data structures in memory, preventing the garbage collector from freeing up the space.

Cancellation also plays an important role when it comes to handling errors, which we'll discuss in more detail in chapter 18. In short, you often have multiple coroutines working together to compute a result—for example, you may be starting a number of asynchronous network requests, and then await all of their results. If one of the network requests fails, you might find yourself in a situation where you can't reasonably compute a result anymore—so there is no reason to wait for the completion of further (or start additional) network requests. This is a special case of avoiding unnecessary work.

Because cancellation is such a core part of building concurrent applications that behave well, Kotlin coroutines come with built-in machinery to perform as well as handle cancellations. Let's take a closer look.

15.2.1 *Triggering cancellation*

The return value of the different coroutine builders can be used as a handle for you to trigger cancellation; the `launch` coroutine builder returns a `Job`, and the `async` coroutine builder returns a `Deferred`. Both of them allow you to call `cancel` to trigger cancellation of the respective coroutine:

```
fun main() {
    runBlocking {
        val launchedJob = launch {         ⟵─── launch returns a Job ...
            log("I'm launched!")
            delay(1000.milliseconds)
            log("I'm done!")
        }
        val asyncDeferred = async {         ⟵─── ... and async returns a Deferred ...
            log("I'm async")
            delay(1000.milliseconds)
            log("I'm done!")
        }
        delay(200.milliseconds)
        launchedJob.cancel()                │ ... both of which
        asyncDeferred.cancel()              │ you can cancel.
    }
}

// 0 [main @coroutine#2] I'm launched!
// 7 [main @coroutine#3] I'm async
```

In section 15.1.4, you also learned about the fact that the coroutine context for each coroutine scope also contains a `Job`, which you can use to cancel a scope in the very same way. Despite manually triggering cancellation for a coroutine, you can also let the library automatically cancel coroutines under certain conditions.

15.2.2 *Invoking cancellation automatically after a time limit has been exceeded*

The Kotlin coroutines library also comes with some convenience functions that can help you trigger cancellation for your coroutines automatically. The `withTimeout` and `withTimeoutOrNull` functions allow you to compute a value while constraining the maximum amount of time spent for the computation.

Similar to other functions in the Kotlin standard library you have gotten to know already, the `withTimeout` function throws an exception (a `TimeoutCancellation-Exception`, to be exact) in case the timeout was exceeded. To handle the timeout, you wrap the invocation of `withTimeout` in a `try` and `catch` the thrown `TimeoutCancellation-Exception`. Analogue to this, the `withTimeoutOrNull` sibling function returns `null` when the timeout is exceeded.

> **NOTE** Don't forget to catch the `TimeoutCancellationException` thrown by `withTimeout`! As you'll see in section 15.2.4, its `CancellationException` super-type is used as a special indicator to cancel coroutines. That means that leaving the `TimeoutCancellationException` uncaught can cause the (unwanted) cancellation of the invoking coroutine (for more information, see https://github.com/Kotlin/kotlinx.coroutines/issues/1374). To avoid this dilemma altogether, use the `withTimeoutOrNull` function instead.

In the next code example, you're invoking the `calculateSomething` function, which takes about 3 seconds to complete. You invoke it first with a short timeout of 500 milliseconds, which causes the timeout to expire. The `calculateSomething` function gets cancelled, and you receive `null` as the return value. In the second invocation, you give the function enough time to complete, so you receive the actual computed value (visualized in figure 15.5):

```
import kotlinx.coroutines.*
import kotlin.time.Duration.Companion.seconds
import kotlin.time.Duration.Companion.milliseconds

suspend fun calculateSomething(): Int {
    delay(3.seconds)
    return 2 + 2
}

fun main() = runBlocking {
    val quickResult = withTimeoutOrNull(500.milliseconds) {
        calculateSomething()
    }
    println(quickResult)
    // null
    val slowResult = withTimeoutOrNull(5.seconds) {
        calculateSomething()
    }
    println(slowResult)
    // 4
}
```

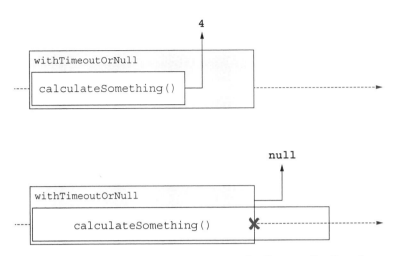

Figure 15.5 Using `withTimoutOrNull` constrains the execution time of a suspending function. When the function returns a value within the given timeout, that value is returned immediately. When the timeout expires, the function is cancelled, and `null` is returned.

15.2.3 *Cancellation cascades through all children*

When you cancel a coroutine, all of its child coroutines are also cancelled. This is a very powerful feature of structured concurrency. Because each coroutine is aware of the coroutines it started, it can always clean up after itself, without leaving any rogue coroutines running that might end up doing unnecessary work or holding extraneous data in memory for longer than required.

Even when you have many layers of indirection, like in the following listing, where you have multiple coroutines launching coroutines of themselves, triggering the cancellation of the outermost launched coroutine properly cancels even the great-grandchild coroutine.

Listing 15.4 Cancelling all child coroutines automatically

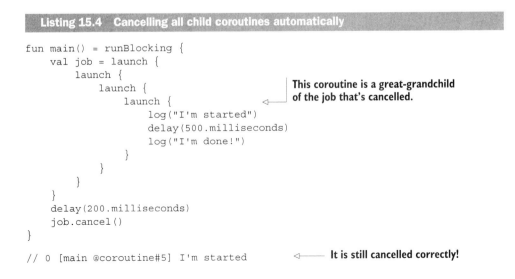

```
fun main() = runBlocking {
    val job = launch {
        launch {
            launch {
                launch {
                    log("I'm started")
                    delay(500.milliseconds)
                    log("I'm done!")
                }
            }
        }
    }
    delay(200.milliseconds)
    job.cancel()
}

// 0 [main @coroutine#5] I'm started
```

This coroutine is a great-grandchild of the job that's cancelled.

It is still cancelled correctly!

But how and where can a coroutine be cancelled?

15.2.4 *Cancelled coroutines throw CancellationExceptions in special places*

The general mechanism of cancellation works by throwing a special exception type, `CancellationException`, at special places. Those places are first and foremost suspension points.

A cancelled coroutine throws `CancellationException` at suspension points, which, as you've briefly seen in chapter 14, are places where the execution of a coroutine can pause. In general, you can assume that all suspending functions inside the coroutines library introduce such points where a `CancellationException` can be thrown. Depending on whether the scope was cancelled or not, the following code snippet would either print "A" or "ABC"—but never "AB," since there is no cancellation point between "B" and "C":

```
coroutineScope {
    log("A")
    delay(500.milliseconds)          ◁─┐ The point where the
    log("B")                             function can be cancelled.
    log("C")
}
```

Because coroutines use an exception to propagate cancellation across the hierarchy of coroutines, it's important to take care not to accidentally swallow this exception or handle it yourself. Consider the following code, which repeatedly executes some code that may throw an `UnsupportedOperationException`:

```
suspend fun doWork() {                                    The CancellationException
    delay(500.milliseconds)                               thrown here ...
    throw UnsupportedOperationException("Didn't work!")  ◁─┘
}

fun main() {
    runBlocking {
        withTimeoutOrNull(2.seconds) {
            while (true) {
                try {
                    doWork()                               ... gets swallowed,
                } catch (e: Exception) {             ◁─┐ preventing cancellation.
                    println("Oops: ${e.message}")       ┘
                }
            }
        }
    }
}

// Oops: Didn't work!
// Oops: Didn't work!
// Oops: Didn't work!
// Oops: Timed out waiting for 2000 ms
// ... (does not terminate)
```

After 2 seconds, the `withTimeoutOrNull` function requests the cancellation of its child coroutine scope. In doing so, the next invocation of `delay` throws a `Cancellation-Exception`. However, because the `catch` statement catches exceptions of all types, the code just continues looping indefinitely. You can fix this by either rethrowing the exception (`if(e is CancellationException) throw e)`) or not catching it in the first place (`catch (e: UnsupportedOperationException)`). With either of these changes, the code cancels as expected.

> **NOTE**   It's not just catching `Exception` that may cause this unwanted behavior. You need to exercise the same type of caution when working with any super-type of `CancellationException`: `IllegalStateException`, `RuntimeException`, `Exception`, and `Throwable`.

15.2.5 *Cancellation is cooperative*

All functions included with Kotlin coroutines out of the box are already cancellable. Likewise, in practice, when you are using a library that offers a suspending API, such as Ktor, you can assume that any suspending functions provided by the framework functions are internally cancellable. For your own code, however, you need to take care of making it cancellable yourself. It may be easy to assume your code is cancel-lable. But take a look at this code:

```
suspend fun doCpuHeavyWork(): Int {
    log("I'm doing work!")
    var counter = 0
    val startTime = System.currentTimeMillis()
    while (System.currentTimeMillis() < startTime + 500) {
        counter++                          ◁──────┐  Simulates some CPU-heavy
    }                                             │  computation by incrementing
    return counter                                │  a counter for 500 milliseconds
}

fun main() {
    runBlocking {
        val myJob = launch {
            repeat(5) {
                doCpuHeavyWork()
            }
        }
        delay(600.milliseconds)
        myJob.cancel()
    }
}
```

You may suspect that this code would print the "I'm doing work" text twice before get-ting cancelled. However, the actual output of this code snippet reveals that, in fact, all five iterations of `doCpuHeavyWork` complete before the program ends:

```
30 [main @coroutine#2] I'm doing work!
535 [main @coroutine#2] I'm doing work!
```

```
1036 [main @coroutine#2] I'm doing work!
1537 [main @coroutine#2] I'm doing work!
2042 [main @coroutine#2] I'm doing work!
```

Why is this? Recall that cancellation works by throwing a CancellationException at a suspension point within the function. However, despite being marked with the sus-pend modifier, the body of the doCpuHeavyWork function does not actually contain any suspension points—it performs a call to log and then performs some long-running, CPU-heavy computation (that we simulate here by continuously incrementing a counter until 500 milliseconds have elapsed).

This is why we say cancellation in Kotlin coroutines is *cooperative*; suspending func-tions need to provide the logic that makes them cancellable themselves. When your code calls other functions that are cancellable, this automatically also introduces a point where your code can be cancelled as well. For example, including a call to delay in the function body of doWork introduces a point at which your function can be cancelled:

```
suspend fun doCpuHeavyWork(): Int {
    log("I'm doing work!")
    var counter = 0
    val startTime = System.currentTimeMillis()
    while (System.currentTimeMillis() < startTime + 500) {
        counter++
        delay(100.milliseconds)        ◁───  This function call also introduces
    }                                        a point where doCpuHeavyWork
    return counter                           can be cancelled.
}
```

But, of course, you wouldn't want to delay your computation artificially only to sup-port cancellation. Instead, the Kotlin coroutines come with utility functionality that helps you make your code cancellable. Specifically, those are the ensureActive and yield functions, as well as the isActive property. Let's take a closer look at how they can be used.

15.2.6 *Checking whether a coroutine has been cancelled*

To determine whether a coroutine has been cancelled, you can just check the Boolean isActive property of a CoroutineScope. A false value indicates that the coroutine is no longer active. You can still finish your current unit of work, close any resources you may have acquired, and then return. For example, you could rewrite your loop to check whether the current coroutine scope has been cancelled:

```
val myJob = launch {
    repeat(5) {
        doCpuHeavyWork()
        if (!isActive) return@launch
    }
}
```

Rather than checking `isActive` and explicitly returning in case a `false` value is encountered, Kotlin coroutines provide another convenience function: `ensureActive`. If the coroutine is no longer active, this function throws a `CancellationException`:

```
val myJob = launch {
    repeat(5) {
        doCpuHeavyWork()
        ensureActive()
    }
}
```

15.2.7 *Letting other coroutines play: The yield function*

The coroutines library also provides another, related function, called `yield`. Besides introducing a point where your function can be cancelled, it also provides a way to let other coroutines work on a currently occupied dispatcher. To motivate this, let's take a look at this code that launches two coroutines, which each do some work:

```
import kotlinx.coroutines.*

fun doCpuHeavyWork(): Int {
    var counter = 0
    val startTime = System.currentTimeMillis()
    while (System.currentTimeMillis() < startTime + 500) {
        counter++
    }
    return counter
}

fun main() {
    runBlocking {
        launch {
            repeat(3) {
                doCpuHeavyWork()
            }
        }
        launch {
            repeat(3) {
                doCpuHeavyWork()
            }
        }
    }
}
```

If the implementation of `doCpuHeavyWork` does not have any suspension points in its implementation, you'll notice your first launched coroutine runs to completion before the second coroutine even begins to run:

```
29 [main @coroutine#2] I'm doing work!
533 [main @coroutine#2] I'm doing work!
1036 [main @coroutine#2] I'm doing work!
1537 [main @coroutine#3] I'm doing work!
2042 [main @coroutine#3] I'm doing work!
2543 [main @coroutine#3] I'm doing work!
```

Why is that? Without any suspension points in the body of your coroutine, there is never an opportunity for the underlying coroutines machinery to pause the execution of your first coroutine and start the execution of your second coroutine. Checking isActive or calling ensureActive does not change anything. These functions only check for cancellation but don't actually suspend the coroutine.

Here, the yield function helps; it's a suspending function that introduces a point in your code where a CancellationException can be thrown, and also allows the dispatcher to switch to working on a different coroutine if there is one waiting (the coroutine *yields* the dispatcher). You can rewrite the implementation of the doCpuHeavyWork function to look as follows.

Listing 15.5   Using `yield` to switch to a different coroutine

```
suspend fun doCpuHeavyWork(): Int {
    var counter = 0
    val startTime = System.currentTimeMillis()
    while (System.currentTimeMillis() < startTime + 500) {
        counter++
        yield()
    }
    return counter
}
```

With a call to yield in place, your different coroutines can now work interleaved, with coroutines 2 and 3 processing their workload alternately:

```
0 [main @coroutine#2] I'm doing work!
559 [main @coroutine#3] I'm doing work!
1062 [main @coroutine#2] I'm doing work!
1634 [main @coroutine#3] I'm doing work!
2208 [main @coroutine#2] I'm doing work!
2734 [main @coroutine#3] I'm doing work!
```

Figure 15.6 illustrates the difference between having no suspension and cancellation points, just checking isActive or ensureActive, and calling yield. Table 15.1 provides another overview of when each of the three functions is used.

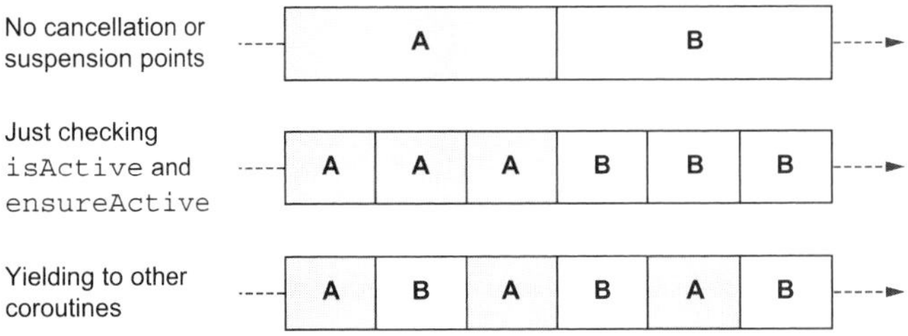

Figure 15.6   Without suspension points, multiple coroutines will always run to completion and (on a single-threaded dispatcher) without interleaving. Checking `isActive` **or calling** `ensureActive` **allows the coroutines to cancel their work prematurely at these cancellation points. Using** `yield` **to let other coroutines use the underlying thread means the coroutines can run interleaved.**

Table 15.1   Mechanisms for enabling cooperative cancellation

Function/property	Use case
`isActive`	Checks to see if cancellation was requested (to do some finishing work before stopping work)
`ensureActive`	Introduces "cancellation point"—throws `CancellationException` upon cancellation, instantly stopping work
`yield()`	Relinquishes computation resources, preventing CPU-heavy computations from exhausting the underlying thread (pool)

15.2.8   *Keep cancellation in mind when acquiring resources*

Real code often has to work with resources like database connections, IO, and more, that need to be explicitly closed after use to ensure they are properly released. Because cancellation, just like any other type of exception, can cause an early return of your code, you need to take proper care to ensure you don't accidentally keep holding on to resources after your coroutine was cancelled. In this example, you're using a `Database-Connection` object that is intended to be closed after use to "store" a string of text. However, in this snippet, you're intentionally cancelling the execution of the coroutine associated with making this request before it can close its database connection. The result is that the `close` function never gets called, and you have leaked a resource:

```
class DatabaseConnection : AutoCloseable {
    fun write(s: String) = println("writing $s!")
    override fun close() {
        println("Closing!")
    }
}

fun main() {
    runBlocking {
        val dbTask = launch {
            val db = DatabaseConnection()
            delay(500.milliseconds)
```

```
                db.write("I love coroutines!")
                db.close()
            }
        delay(200.milliseconds)
        dbTask.cancel()
    }
    println("I leaked a resource!")
}
```

You should always design your coroutines-based code to be robust in the face of cancellation. You have already seen that when cancellation happens, a CancellationException is thrown. Therefore, you can use the same mechanism you would use for regular exception handling in the context of coroutines, as well—a finally block, which is executed regardless of whether an exception was thrown or not.

Listing 15.6 Using a finally block to close resources

```
val dbTask = launch {
    val db = DatabaseConnection()
    try {
        delay(500.milliseconds)
        db.write("I love coroutines!")
    } finally {
        db.close()
    }
}
```

If the resource you are using inside your coroutine implements the AutoClosable interface, you can utilize the .use function you've gotten to know in chapter 10 as a more idiomatic shorthand for the same behavior.

Listing 15.7 Using use to automatically close resources

```
val dbTask = launch {
    DatabaseConnection().use {
        delay(500.milliseconds)
        it.write("I love coroutines!")
    }
}
```

15.2.9 Frameworks can perform cancellation for you

So far, you've manually triggered the cancellation of your coroutines, or, in the case of withTimeoutOrNull, let the coroutines library decide when to trigger cancellation. In many real-world applications, frameworks—for example, the Android platform, or the networking framework Ktor—can take care of providing coroutine scopes as well as triggering their cancellation. In those cases, your duty is to pick the right coroutine scope, and make sure that the code you write can actually be cancelled.

In the context of an Android application, the `ViewModel` class provides a `viewModel-Scope`. When the `ViewModel` is cleared—for example, when the user navigates away from the screen displaying the `ViewModel`—the `viewModelScope` is cancelled, and so are any coroutines launched in this scope:

```
class MyViewModel: ViewModel() {
    init {
        viewModelScope.launch {          ◁─┐ Launches the coroutine in
            while (true) {                   the scope of the view model
                println("Tick!")
                delay(1000.milliseconds)
            }
        }
    }
}
```

Another example is server-side applications written with Ktor. Here, each request handler has an object of type `PipelineContext` as an implicit receiver, which inherits from `CoroutineScope`. That means you can launch multiple coroutines from within the handler. This coroutine scope is cancelled when the client disconnects. If the client closes the connection to this endpoint within less than 5 seconds, the "I'm done" line will never be printed because the coroutine, which was launched in the coroutine scope of the request, will have been cancelled:

```
routing {
    get("/") { // this: PipelineContext         Launches the coroutine on the
        launch {                          ◁─┐   request-level coroutine scope
            println("I'm doing some background work!")
            delay(5000.milliseconds)
            println("I'm done")
        }
    }
}
```

This behavior prevents request-level coroutines from doing unnecessary work. When there is no client waiting for a response, there is no point in finishing all computations kicked off by the request handler. For work that should continue asynchronously regardless of whether the client is still present, you need to pick a different scope. In Ktor, the `Application` class also doubles as a coroutine scope that has the same lifetime as the Ktor application (meaning it'll be cancelled only when the application is stopped). This scope would be well suited for coroutines that should run independently of the request scope. You can access it via the `call` variable.

Listing 15.8   Starting a long-living coroutine in Ktor

```
routing {
    get("/") {
        call.application.launch {          Launches the coroutine on the
                                     ◁─┐   application-level coroutine scope
```

```
            println("I'm doing some background work!")
            delay(5000.milliseconds)
            println("I'm done")
        }
    }
}
```

Even when the client cancels the HTTP request, the launched coroutine isn't cancelled. That is because it is a child of the application coroutine scope, not the request-level coroutine scope.

By discussing coroutines, coroutine contexts, coroutine scopes, and the concept of structured concurrency, you're now equipped with the basic tools to write concurrent code with Kotlin. In the next chapter, we're going to move our attention toward flows, which help you model sequential streams of values on top of the abstractions you're now familiar with.

Summary

- Structured concurrency gives you control over the work coroutines are doing and prevents rogue coroutines from escaping cancellation.
- You can create new coroutine scopes using the suspending `coroutineScope` helper function and the `CoroutineScope` constructor function. While named similarly, they serve different purposes:
  - `coroutineScope` is designed for concurrent decomposition of work: starting a number of coroutines, waiting for them to calculate a result, and then returning that result.
  - `CoroutineScope` creates a coroutine scope used to associate coroutines with the life cycle of a class. It is typically used with a `SupervisorJob`.
- `GlobalScope` is a special coroutine scope that, while often shown in example snippets, should not be used in application code because it breaks structured concurrency.
- The coroutine context manages how individual coroutines are executed. It is inherited along the coroutines hierarchy.
- The parent–child hierarchy between coroutines and coroutine scopes is established via the associated `Job` object in the coroutine context.
- Suspension points are places where coroutines can be paused and other coroutines can begin their work.
- Cancellation is realized by throwing a `CancellationException` at suspension points.
- Cancellation exceptions should never be swallowed (caught and not processed). Instead, they should either be rethrown or not be caught in the first place.
- Cancellation is a normal occurrence, and your code should be designed to handle it.

- You can invoke cancellation yourself using functions like `cancel` or `withTimeout-OrNull`. Many existing frameworks can also cancel coroutines for you.
- Marking a function with the `suspend` modifier is not enough to support cancellation. However, Kotlin coroutines provide mechanisms that support you in building cancellable suspending functions (e.g., functions like `ensureActive` or `yield` as well as the `isActive` property).
- Frameworks use coroutine scopes to help tie your coroutines to the life cycle of the application (e.g., the time a viewmodel is shown on screen or in which a request handler is executed).

16

Flows

This chapter covers

- Working with flows as a model for sequential streams of values
- Use cases for and differences between cold flows and hot flows

In the previous chapter, you have gotten to know coroutines and suspending functions as the basic abstraction used for concurrent programming in Kotlin. In this chapter, we will change our focus to a higher-level abstraction built on top of coroutines: *flows*, which allow you to work with multiple, sequential values over time while leveraging Kotlin's concurrency machinery. In this chapter, we'll discuss the ins and outs of flows. We'll discuss the different types of flows and how to create, transform, and consume them.

16.1 Flows model sequential streams of values

As discussed in chapter 14, a suspending function can pause its execution, be it once or multiple times. However, it can only return a single value, for example, a primitive, an object, or a collection of objects. Listing 16.1 illustrates this: your suspending function `createValues` creates a list of three values. By introducing a delay of 1 second per element, you can simulate a longer-running computation. Running this code, you will notice that the function only returns once all values have been computed: after 3 seconds, you see all three values printed.

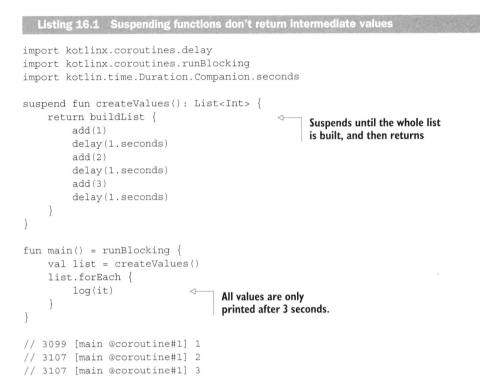

Listing 16.1 Suspending functions don't return intermediate values

```
import kotlinx.coroutines.delay
import kotlinx.coroutines.runBlocking
import kotlin.time.Duration.Companion.seconds

suspend fun createValues(): List<Int> {
    return buildList {                              Suspends until the whole list
        add(1)                                      is built, and then returns
        delay(1.seconds)
        add(2)
        delay(1.seconds)
        add(3)
        delay(1.seconds)
    }
}

fun main() = runBlocking {
    val list = createValues()
    list.forEach {
        log(it)                                     All values are only
    }                                               printed after 3 seconds.
}

// 3099 [main @coroutine#1] 1
// 3107 [main @coroutine#1] 2
// 3107 [main @coroutine#1] 3
```

However, looking at the actual implementation of the createValues function, you can see that the element 1 was actually available instantaneously. Likewise, element 2 could have already been available after 1 second, and so on. In scenarios like these, where a function computes multiple values over a stretch of time, you may want to return values asynchronously as they become available, rather than only when the function has finished executing. This is where flows come in.

In Kotlin, flows are a coroutine-based abstraction that makes it possible to work with values that appear over time. Their general design is loosely inspired by Reactive Streams, an abstraction whose implementation you may have already crossed paths with: RxJava (https://reactivex.io/) and Project Reactor (https://projectreactor.io/) are two popular implementations of Reactive Streams on the JVM.

Just like Reactive Streams, flows are a general-purpose abstraction that can be used to implement functionality like progressive loading, working with streams of events, or modeling subscription-style APIs.

16.1.1 *Flows allow you to work with elements as they are emitted*

Let's rewrite the previous createValues function from listing 16.1 to make use of flows. To do so, you use the flow builder function instead of the buildList function. To add elements to the flow, you call `emit`. After calling the function, you can use the `collect` function to iterate the elements in the flow (you will examine the `flow` builder function further in section 16.2.1 and learn about the `collect` function in detail in section 16.2.2).

Listing 16.2   Creating and collecting a flow

```
import kotlinx.coroutines.delay
import kotlinx.coroutines.runBlocking
import kotlinx.coroutines.flow.*
import kotlin.time.Duration.Companion.milliseconds

fun createValues(): Flow<Int> {
    return flow {                          Each emission is immediately
        emit(1)                     ◁──┘   passed to the collector.
        delay(1000.milliseconds)
        emit(2)
        delay(1000.milliseconds)
        emit(3)
        delay(1000.milliseconds)
    }
}

fun main() = runBlocking {
    val myFlowOfValues = createValues()        The values are printed as
    myFlowOfValues.collect { log(it) }   ◁──┘  soon as they are emitted.
}

// 29 [main @coroutine#1] 1
// 1100 [main @coroutine#1] 2
// 2156 [main @coroutine#1] 3
```

Examining the timestamps of the output, you can quickly notice that the elements from the flow are displayed as soon as they are emitted. The code does not need to wait for all values to be computed. This basic abstraction of being able to work with values as soon as they are computed, rather than having to wait until the whole batch of elements is created, is at the core of flows in Kotlin. You will explore it in detail throughout this chapter.

16.1.2 Different types of flows in Kotlin

While all flows in Kotlin expose a consistent set of APIs for working with values that appear over time, in Kotlin, you distinguish between two categories of flows: *cold* flows and *hot* flows. In brief:

- *Cold flows* represent asynchronous data streams that only start emitting items when their items are being consumed by an individual collector.
- *Hot flows*, on the other hand, produce items independently of whether the items are actually being consumed, operating in a broadcast fashion.

This description may seem a bit abstract at this point, but as you explore these two types of flows more thoroughly over the course of this chapter, their differences and similarities will become clear. We'll start with our discussion of cold flows and examine hot flows in detail in section 16.3.

16.2   Cold flows

In section 16.1.1, you've used your first cold flow to represent an asynchronous stream of numbers, which are being computed over time. Let's take a look at that code in greater detail and discuss the different aspects involved in working with cold flows: their creation, when and how they work, how flows are cancelled, and how you can use concurrency inside them.

16.2.1   Creating a cold flow with the flow builder function

Creating a new cold flow is straightforward: just like with collections, there is a builder function that allows you to create a new flow, aptly named `flow`. Inside the block of the builder function, you can call the special `emit` function, which offers a value to the collector of the flow and suspends the execution of the builder function until the value was processed by the collector—you can think of it as an asynchronous `return`. Because the signature of `flow` declares the block with the `suspend` modifier, you can also call other suspending functions from within the builder, such as `delay`.

Listing 16.3   Calling suspending functions from the `flow` builder

```kotlin
import kotlinx.coroutines.*
import kotlinx.coroutines.flow.*
import kotlin.time.Duration.Companion.milliseconds

fun main() {
    val letters = flow {
        log("Emitting A!")
        emit("A")                            ⊲——— emit offers a value to the collector of the flow.
        delay(200.milliseconds)
        log("Emitting B!")
        emit("B")
    }
}
```

It's worth noting that when you run this code, you won't actually see any output. That's because the builder function returns you an object of type `Flow<T>`, a representation of a sequential stream of values. Just like with sequences, this flow is initially inert. It's not actually executed until a *terminal operator* is invoked on the flow that kicks off the computation as defined in the builder, and any other intermediate operators that come before (you'll learn more about intermediate operators on flows in section 17.2 and take another look at terminal operators in section 17.4). This is why the flow is called *cold*: it is inert by default until it is collected.

Because invoking the `flow` builder function doesn't actually trigger any work, you can build a flow in "regular," non-suspending Kotlin code. In practice, you will often find yourself writing functions with a non-suspending signature that return multiple values over time via a cold flow. Inside the flow builder, you would then call suspending functions:

```
import kotlinx.coroutines.flow.*

fun getElementsFromNetwork(): Flow<String> {
    return flow {
        // suspending network call here
    }
}
```

Since the code inside the builder function only gets executed once it's being collected, it's also okay to define and return an infinite flow, just like with sequences, as you've seen in chapter 6. In this snippet, you're creating a `counterFlow` that emits an ever-increasing number every 200 milliseconds.

Listing 16.4   Creating an infinite flow

```
val counterFlow = flow {
    var x = 0
    while (true) {
        emit(x++)
        delay(200.milliseconds)
    }
}
```

This loop will only begin to run once the flow is actually being collected. Let's take a look at that next.

16.2.2   *Cold flows don't do any work until collected*

Calling the `collect` function on a `Flow` runs its logic, with the code responsible for collecting the flow typically referred to as the *collector*. When invoking `collect`, you can provide a lambda that gets invoked on each emission in your flow. Because collecting a flow actually executes the suspending code from inside the flow, `collect` is a suspending function; it suspends until the flow has finished. Likewise, the lambda provided to the collector may also suspend, which allows you to call out to further suspending functions. For example, the collector of a flow may write data to a database, or make HTTP requests based on the values it received from the flow.

In this snippet, you're collecting the `letters` flow. Because `collect` is a suspending function, you wrap the invocation in `runBlocking`. To illustrate that the lambda passed to `collect` is also a suspending function, you delay after collecting each element:

```
import kotlinx.coroutines.*
import kotlinx.coroutines.flow.*
import kotlin.time.Duration.Companion.milliseconds

val letters = flow {
    log("Emitting A!")
    emit("A")
```

```
        delay(200.milliseconds)
        log("Emitting B!")
        emit("B")
}

fun main() = runBlocking {
    letters.collect {
        log("Collecting $it")
        delay(500.milliseconds)
    }
}

// 27 [main @coroutine#1] Emitting A!
// 38 [main @coroutine#1] Collecting A
// 757 [main @coroutine#1] Emitting B!
// 757 [main @coroutine#1] Collecting B
```

Taking a look at the timestamps of the output, it becomes clear again that the collector is responsible for running the logic of the flow—the delay between the collection of element A and B is roughly 700 milliseconds. That is because the following sequence of events happens:

- The collector triggers the logic defined in the flow builder, causing the first emission.
- The lambda associated with the collector is invoked, logging the message and delaying for 500 milliseconds.
- Then, the flow lambda is continued, delaying for a further 200 milliseconds, before the emission (an associated collection) happens.

Figure 16.1 illustrates this, and you'll further explore this intertwined nature of execution in section 16.2.4.

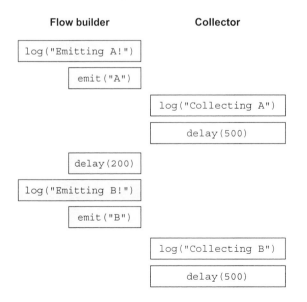

Figure 16.1   The first emission in the flow builder means the lambda associated with the collector is invoked. It logs a message and delays, before the flow builder lambda is continued. After the delay of 200 milliseconds and a log message, the control flow moves back over to the collector, collecting the second element and delaying for a final 500 milliseconds. While these operations happen intertwined, they all run on the same coroutine.

It's worth noting that just like sequences get reevaluated every time you use a terminal operator, calling `collect` on a cold flow multiple times also triggers the execution of its code multiple times. This is worth keeping in mind if your flow has side effects like making network requests—they will be executed multiple times (you'll learn about a way to avoid this behavior in section 16.3).

Listing 16.5 Collecting the same flow multiple times

```
import kotlinx.coroutines.flow.*
import kotlinx.coroutines.*
import kotlin.time.Duration.Companion.milliseconds

fun main() = runBlocking {
    letters.collect {
        log("(1) Collecting $it")
        delay(500.milliseconds)
    }
    letters.collect {
        log("(2) Collecting $it")
        delay(500.milliseconds)
    }
}

// 23 [main @coroutine#1] Emitting A!
// 33 [main @coroutine#1] (1) Collecting A
// 761 [main @coroutine#1] Emitting B!
// 762 [main @coroutine#1] (1) Collecting B
// 1335 [main @coroutine#1] Emitting A!
// 1335 [main @coroutine#1] (2) Collecting A
// 2096 [main @coroutine#1] Emitting B!
// 2096 [main @coroutine#1] (2) Collecting B
```

The `collect` function suspends until all elements of the flow have been processed. However, as you've seen in section 16.2.1, flows may potentially have infinitely many elements—meaning the `collect` function would suspend indefinitely. To stop collecting a flow before all elements have been processed, you can cancel it.

16.2.3 Cancelling the collection of a flow

You have already gotten to know mechanisms for cancelling coroutines in chapter 15. They also apply for flow collectors. By cancelling the coroutine of the collector, you stop the collection of the flow at the next cancellation point.

Listing 16.6 Cancelling the collection of a flow

```
import kotlinx.coroutines.flow.*
import kotlinx.coroutines.*
import kotlin.time.Duration.Companion.seconds

fun main() = runBlocking {
    val collector = launch {
```

```
        counterFlow.collect {
            println(it)
        }
    }
    delay(5.seconds)
    collector.cancel()
}

// 1 2 3 ... 24
```

NOTE Like other built-in suspending functions, emit acts as a cancellation and suspension point for your code.

Later on, when you take a closer look at intermediate and terminal operators, you will get to know some additional ways of cancelling the execution of flows. One such example would be the take operator, which you'll explore in chapter 17.

16.2.4 *Cold flows under the hood*

In section 16.1, you already heard that flows are an abstraction on top of the Kotlin coroutine machinery, more precisely, suspending functions. Now that you have seen the first few flows, you can take a look at how they are implemented. While knowledge of the inner workings isn't required to use flows, it can still help you build a stronger understanding of cold flows and their mechanics. Cold flows in Kotlin are a clever combination of suspending functions and lambdas with receivers, both language features you've already gotten to know over the previous chapters. The definition of cold flows as provided by coroutines is actually just a few lines long and only requires two interfaces: Flow and FlowCollector. They each define only one function: collect and emit:

```
interface Flow<out T> {
    suspend fun collect(collector: FlowCollector<T>)
}

interface FlowCollector<in T> {
    suspend fun emit(value: T)
}
```

When you define a flow using the flow builder function, the lambda you provide has the receiver type FlowCollector. This is what makes it possible to invoke the emit function from within the builder. The emit function calls the lambda passed to the collect function. In effect, you have two lambdas calling each other:

- Calling collect invokes the body of the flow builder function.
- When this code calls emit, it in turn calls the lambda passed to collect with the parameter passed to emit.
- Once the lambda expression has finished executing, the function returns back into the body of the builder function, and continues execution.

Figure 16.2 illustrates this concept for the following code snippet:

```
val letters = flow {
    delay(300.milliseconds)
    emit("A")
    delay(300.milliseconds)
    emit("B")
}

letters.collect { letter ->
    println(letter)
    delay(200.milliseconds)
}
```

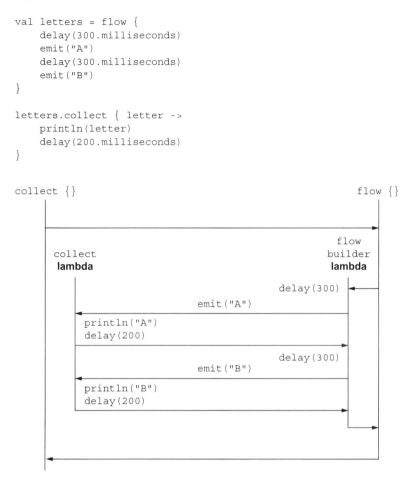

Figure 16.2 Calling `collect` invokes the lambda associated with the `flow` builder function. In this case, the lambda suspends for 300 milliseconds. The call to `emit` executes the lambda passed to `collect` and runs it to completion. Here, it executes a `print` statement and delays for 200 milliseconds. Then, the control flow returns to the lambda flow builder, which repeats this cycle for a second time, before finally returning and, thus, finishing the initial invocation of `collect`. All of these are just regular function calls; all this code is executed within a single coroutine.

As you can see, there aren't that many moving parts in a regular cold flow. Yet, they provide an extremely useful and extensible abstraction for writing code that processes streams of values while still remaining lightweight.

16.2.5 *Concurrent flows with channel flows*

The cold flows you have created so far using the `flow` builder function are all sequential. The block of code runs, just like the body of a suspending function, as a single coroutine. As such, calls to `emit` are also executed sequentially. For many cases, this basic abstraction is more than enough, but when your flow performs a number of computations that could run independently of each other, this sequential nature can prove to become a bottleneck. Consider the following listing, where you declare a flow `randomNumbers` that calculates 10 numbers using the artificially slow `getRandomNumber` function.

Listing 16.7   A regular cold flow is executed sequentially

```
import kotlinx.coroutines.flow.*
import kotlinx.coroutines.*
import kotlin.random.Random
import kotlin.time.Duration.Companion.milliseconds

suspend fun getRandomNumber(): Int {
    delay(500.milliseconds)
    return Random.nextInt()
}

val randomNumbers = flow {
    repeat(10) {
        emit(getRandomNumber())
    }
}

fun main() = runBlocking {
    randomNumbers.collect {
        log(it)
    }
}

// 583 [main @coroutine#1] 1514439879
// 1120 [main @coroutine#1] 1785211458
// 1693 [main @coroutine#1] -996479986
// ...
// 5463 [main @coroutine#1] -2047597449
```

Collecting this flow takes a little over 5 seconds because each `getRandomNumber` invocation is executed one after the other. Figure 16.3 illustrates this.

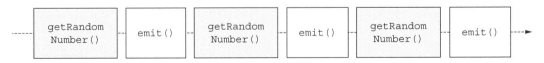

Figure 16.3   When using a regular cold flow, each random number is generated and emitted. This happens entirely sequentially.

The flow is executed sequentially, with all computations running on the same coroutine. Because the operations you perform in this code (generating numbers) are independent of each other, they seem like an ideal candidate for being performed concurrently or, if desired, in parallel. Just like with `async`, as you saw in chapter 14, this could make the execution much faster, bringing the time to compute all 10 elements down to roughly 500 milliseconds.

It might be tempting to apply what you have learned so far to introduce concurrency into your flow builder invocation by launching some background coroutines and emitting values directly from them. However, you will be greeted by an error message if you do so: "Flow invariant is violated: Emission from another coroutine is detected. FlowCollector is not thread-safe and concurrent emissions are prohibited."

```
val randomNumbers = flow {
    coroutineScope {
        repeat(10) {
            launch { emit(getRandomNumber()) }          Error: emit can't be called
        }                                                from a different coroutine.
    }
}
```

This is because the basic, cold flow abstraction only allows invocations of the `emit` function from the same coroutine. What's needed is a flow builder that allows you to build a concurrent flow that allows emissions from multiple coroutines. In Kotlin, this is called a *channel flow*, and can be constructed with the `channelFlow` builder function. A channel flow is a special type of cold flow. It doesn't provide an `emit` function for sequential emissions. Instead, multiple coroutines can use `send` to offer values. The collector of this flow still receives them in sequential fashion, and the `collect` lambda can do its work. Here, you're using a channel flow to optimize your previous implementation. Just like the `coroutineScope` function, the lambda for `channelFlow` provides a coroutine scope on which you can launch new background coroutines.

Listing 16.8 Concurrently sending elements into a channel flow

```
import kotlinx.coroutines.flow.channelFlow
import kotlinx.coroutines.launch

val randomNumbers = channelFlow {          Creates a new channel flow
    repeat(10) {
        launch {
            send(getRandomNumber())        send can be called from different coroutines.
        }
    }
}
```

Collecting this flow in the same manner as before, but now using a channel flow, you can observe that `getRandomNumber` now indeed gets executed concurrently, and the whole execution finishes in about 500 milliseconds (also illustrated in figure 16.4):

```
553 [main] -1927966915
568 [main] 222582016
...
569 [main] 1827898086
```

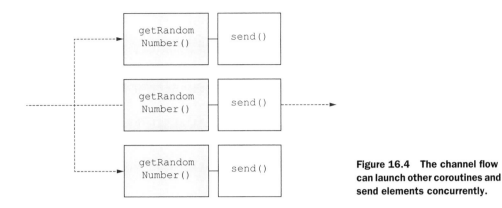

Figure 16.4 The channel flow can launch other coroutines and send elements concurrently.

With `channelFlow`, you now know of a flow builder that can be called concurrently. At this point, it might be natural to wonder if there's ever any reason to use a non-channel flow—after all, the channel flow can do everything a regular flow can, and more! So how do you decide?

Generally, regular cold flows are the easiest and most performant abstraction you can choose; while they are strictly sequential and can't launch new coroutines, they are very simple to create, their interface consists of just a single function (`emit`), and there are no additional moving parts or overhead you need to keep track of. Channel flows, on the other hand, are specifically designed for the use case of concurrent operations. They are not quite as cheap to create because they have to manage another concurrent primitive, the *channel*, under the hood. Channels are a comparatively lower-level abstraction for cross-coroutine communication. The `send` function is part of the overall more complicated interface exposed by channels.

When deciding between regular cold flows and channel flows, only pick channel flows if you need to launch new coroutines from inside your flow. Otherwise, choosing regular cold flows is the way to go.

Cold flows are a useful abstraction for working with values computed over time. Later on, in chapter 17, you'll learn about the powerful ways to apply further transformations to your flows. However, cold flows are always directly associated with their collector: each collector executes the code specified for the flow independently. In the next section, you'll learn about the second type of flow, which you can apply for broadcast-style communication of values across coroutines, as well as to manage state in a concurrent system: hot flows.

16.3 *Hot flows*

While still following the overall structure of emission and collection, hot flows have a number of properties that make them different from cold flows. Hot flows share emitted items across multiple collectors, called *subscribers*, rather than having each collector trigger the execution of the flow logic independently. This means they lend themselves for use cases where you are emitting events or state changes in your system that happen independently or aren't tied to a collector being present. This is also where they get their name from: independently of the presence of a subscriber, emissions can happen in these *hot* flows that are always active.

Kotlin coroutines come with two hot flow implementations out of the box:

- *Shared flows*, which are used for broadcasting values, and
- *State flows*, for the special case of communicating state

In practice, you'll likely use state flows more often than shared flows (and as you'll see in section 16.3.3, you can often reframe code that uses a shared flow to use a state flow instead), but it's still useful to understand how both types work. You'll first see shared flows in action and then move on to state flows.

16.3.1 Shared flows broadcast values to subscribers

Shared flows operate in a *broadcast fashion*—independently of whether a subscriber (a collector of a shared flow) is present, emissions can happen (visualized in figure 16.5). To demonstrate this broadcasting behavior, you can model a real-life broadcasting transmitter: a numbers station (see "The Spooky World of the 'Numbers Stations,'" Sorrel-Dejerine, 2014, https://www.bbc.com/news/magazine-24910397). These mysterious radio stations exist in real life and transmit encoded messages to spies around the world via open frequencies, who can listen in and try to decode these messages. (Because we don't have our spy handbook ready, though, we will have to make do with actually generating random numbers.)

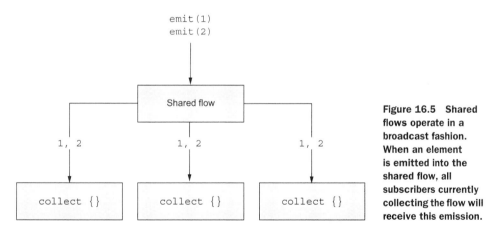

Figure 16.5 Shared flows operate in a broadcast fashion. When an element is emitted into the shared flow, all subscribers currently collecting the flow will receive this emission.

Shared flows are typically declared in a container class—in your case, the `RadioStation` class. The mutable version of the shared flow, `_messageFlow`, which can be used to `emit` values, is encapsulated as a private property of the class, while the read-only version of the flow `messageFlow`, which can be used to subscribe to the emissions, is exposed as a public property. You also define a function called `beginBroadcasting`, which launches a new coroutine on a given scope, which emits (and logs) random numbers on the message flow, as shown in the following listing

Listing 16.9   Broadcasting values using `SharedFlow`

```
import kotlinx.coroutines.*
import kotlinx.coroutines.flow.*
import kotlin.random.*
import kotlin.time.Duration.Companion.milliseconds

class RadioStation {
    private val _messageFlow = MutableSharedFlow<Int>()
    val messageFlow = _messageFlow.asSharedFlow()

    fun beginBroadcasting(scope: CoroutineScope) {
        scope.launch {
            while(true) {
                delay(500.milliseconds)
                val number = Random.nextInt(0..10)
                log("Emitting $number!")
                _messageFlow.emit(number)
            }
        }
    }
}
```

Defines a new mutable shared flow as a private property

Provides a read-only view of the shared flow

Emits a value to the mutable shared flow from a coroutine

As you can see, constructing a hot flow, like `SharedFlow`, works differently from constructing a cold flow. Rather than using a flow builder, you get a reference to a mutable version of the flow. Because emissions happen independently of whether subscribers are present, it's your responsibility to start a coroutine that performs the actual emissions. It also means that you can have more than one coroutine that emits values into a mutable shared flow without any further hassle.

Underscores when naming hot flows

You may wonder why shared flows (and state flows) follow the pattern of defining a private variable whose name begins with an underscore as well as a public variable with a name not beginning with an underscore. At the time of writing, Kotlin does not support different types for private and public variables. By defining the mutable version of the flow to be private and exposing a property that has the read-only type `Shared-Flow<T>`, you prevent exposing a mutable version of your shared flow to consumer classes, which is in the interest of encapsulation and information hiding—after all, the consumers of your class should typically only subscribe to the flow, not emit elements into it. Being able to specify a different type for a property depending on whether it is accessed from inside or outside the class is planned to be added to the language within the scope of Kotlin 2.x ("Support Having a "Public" and a "Private" Type for the Same Property," Isakova, https://youtrack.jetbrains.com/issue/KT-14663).

When you construct an instance of the `RadioStation` class and call the `beginBroadcasting` function, you will see that broadcasting begins immediately, even when no subscribers are present:

```
fun main() = runBlocking {
    RadioStation().beginBroadcasting(this)        ◁────┐ Starts the coroutine on the
}                                                       coroutine scope of runBlocking

// 575 [main @coroutine#2] Emitting 2!
// 1088 [main @coroutine#2] Emitting 10!
// 1593 [main @coroutine#2] Emitting 4!
// ...
```

Adding a subscriber works the same way as collecting a cold flow—you simply call `collect`. The lambda you provide will be executed whenever a value is emitted. However, it's important to note that subscribers only get emitted values from the beginning of their subscription. To illustrate this, you can start subscribing to the shared flow after a small delay.

Listing 16.10 Subscribing to a shared flow with a delay

```
fun main(): Unit = runBlocking {
    val radioStation = RadioStation()
    radioStation.beginBroadcasting(this)
    delay(600.milliseconds)
    radioStation.messageFlow.collect {
        log("A collecting $it!")
    }
}
```

Looking at the output, you'll notice that the first value, which was emitted after roughly 500 milliseconds, was not collected by the subscriber:

```
611 [main @coroutine#2] Emitting 8!
1129 [main @coroutine#2] Emitting 9!
1131 [main @coroutine#1] A collecting 9!
1647 [main @coroutine#2] Emitting 1!
1647 [main @coroutine#1] A collecting 1!
```

Because shared flows operate in a broadcast fashion, you can add additional subscribers that also receive emissions of the existing `messageFlow`. For example, you could add an additional subscriber on its own coroutine by adding a second call to `launch` inside the `runBlocking` block:

```
launch {
    radioStation.messageFlow.collect {
        log("B collecting $it!")
    }
}
```

It will receive the same values as all other subscribers of the same shared flow—your numbers station is *broadcasting* its values. Note that, unlike with cold flows, the collector(s) are not responsible for triggering the actual emission of elements in the flow—they are merely subscribers that will be notified when new elements are emitted.

REPLAYING VALUES FOR SUBSCRIBERS

When using a shared flow, subscribers only receive emissions that happen after they have started their subscription by calling `collect`. If you want subscribers to receive previously emitted elements, you can use the `replay` parameter when constructing the `MutableSharedFlow` to set up a cache of the latest values for new subscribers. In this example, you're setting up the message flow to replay the last five values when a new subscriber is added:

```
private val _messageFlow = MutableSharedFlow<Int>(replay = 5)
```

With this change, even when launching the collectors after a short delay of 600 milliseconds, they will still receive up to five elements that preceded their subscription. In this case, that means the subscriber will see the value emitted at 560 milliseconds, before it started its subscription:

```
560 [main @coroutine#2] Emitting 6!
635 [main @coroutine#1] A collecting 6!
1080 [main @coroutine#2] Emitting 10!
1081 [main @coroutine#1] A collecting 10!
```

This can be a convenient way to make sure subscribers always have a few of the most recent values to work with when they first subscribe.

FROM COLD FLOW TO SHARED FLOW WITH SHAREIN

Let's assume for a moment you have a function that provides a stream of values, such as temperatures that are being collected from a sensor at an interval of 500 milliseconds. This function, as provided to you, returns a cold flow.

Listing 16.11   A simple function that returns a stream of values in a given interval

```
import kotlinx.coroutines.*
import kotlinx.coroutines.flow.*
import kotlin.random.*
import kotlin.time.Duration.Companion.milliseconds

fun querySensor(): Int = Random.nextInt(-10..30)

fun getTemperatures(): Flow<Int> {
    return flow {
        while(true) {
            emit(querySensor())
            delay(500.milliseconds)
        }
    }
}
```

If you were to call `collect` on this function multiple times, for example, to output the temperature once in Celsius, once in Fahrenheit, then each collector would cause the sensor to be queried independently:

```
fun celsiusToFahrenheit(celsius: Int) =
    celsius * 9.0 / 5.0 + 32.0

fun main() {
    val temps = getTemperatures()
    runBlocking {
        launch {
            temps.collect {              ◁────┐
                log("$it Celsius")
            }                                  │  Triggers the collection
        }                                      │  of the flow twice
        launch {
            temps.collect {              ◁────┘
                log("${celsiusToFahrenheit(it)} Fahrenheit")
            }
        }
    }
}
```

Whether interacting with sensors, making network requests, or making database queries, it's often desirable to avoid interacting with external systems or performing long-running computations more than necessary. Instead, you should *share* the flow returned between two collectors—they should both receive the same elements.

You can convert a given cold flow to a hot shared flow by using the shareIn function. This conversion from cold to hot causes the code of the flow to be executed, so this function needs to run on a coroutine. For this purpose, shareIn take a scope parameter of type CoroutineScope on which that coroutine is launched.

Listing 16.12   Using `shareIn` to convert the cold flow to a hot shared flow

```
fun main() {
    val temps = getTemperatures()
    runBlocking {
        val sharedTemps = temps.shareIn(this, SharingStarted.Lazily)
        launch {
            sharedTemps.collect {
                log("$it Celsius")
            }
        }
        launch {
            sharedTemps.collect {
                log("${celsiusToFahrenheit(it)} Fahrenheit")
            }
        }
    }
}

// 45 [main @coroutine#3] -10 Celsius
// 52 [main @coroutine#4] 14.0 Fahrenheit
// 599 [main @coroutine#3] 11 Celsius
// 599 [main @coroutine#4] 51.8 Fahrenheit
```

The second parameter `started` defines when the flow should actually be started. Here, you can specify multiple different behaviors:

- `Eagerly` starts the collection of the flow immediately.
- `Lazily` starts the collection only when the first subscriber appears.
- `WhileSubscribed` starts the collection only when the first subscriber appears, and then cancels the collection of the flow when the last subscriber disappears.

It's a common pattern in Kotlin for operations that compute multiple values over time to simply be exposed as cold flows and your application code to, when needed, convert these cold flows into hot flows. Because `shareIn` participates in structured concurrency via its coroutine scope, you can be sure that when your application no longer needs the information from the shared flow, its internal logic gets cancelled when the surrounding coroutine scope gets cancelled.

16.3.2 *Keeping track of state in your system: State flow*

A special case that comes up in concurrent systems is keeping track of some value that may change over time or, put differently, the state of a value. In our previous example, this may be the values read by the temperature sensor, which represent the current temperature state in our system. Kotlin coroutines comes with a specialized abstraction to handle this case, called *state flow*. A state flow is a special version of a shared flow that makes it particularly easy to keep track of state changes of a variable over time. There are a number of topics related to state flows that are worth exploring:

- How state flows are created and exposed for subscribers
- How the value of a state flow can be updated safely, even when accessed in parallel
- The concept of *equality-based conflation*, which causes state flows to only emit when their values actually change
- How to convert cold flows into state flows

Creating a state flow works analogously to creating a shared flow: you create a `MutableStateFlow` as the private property of a class and expose a read-only `StateFlow` variant of the same variable. In this example, you're defining a view counter. Because a state flow represents a value that may change over time, but can be read at any point, you also provide an initial value as a parameter to its constructor (in this case, zero views). Instead of using `emit`, you use the `update` function to update its value.

Listing 16.13 A basic implementation of a view counter that uses a state flow

```
import kotlinx.coroutines.flow.*
import kotlinx.coroutines.*

class ViewCounter {                                          Creates a mutable state flow
    private val _counter = MutableStateFlow(0)   ◁─────      with an initial value of 0
    val counter = _counter.asStateFlow()
```

```
    fun increment() {
        _counter.update { it + 1 }
    }
}

fun main() {
    val vc = ViewCounter()
    vc.increment()
    println(vc.counter.value)
    // 1
}
```

You can access the current state represented by the mutable state flow via its `value` property; without suspending, this property allows you to safely read its value. Updating the value is done via `update`, a function that deserves a closer look.

SAFELY WRITING TO A STATE FLOW WITH THE UPDATE FUNCTION

Upon further inspection, you might notice that the `value` property is actually a read–write property; you can assign values to it as well. As such, it may be tempting to implement the `increment` function using the classic `++` operator:

```
fun increment() {
    _counter.value++
}
```

However, there is a problem with this code: these increment operations aren't *atomic*. To illustrate this problem, you can write a short code snippet that runs 10,000 coroutines that all call `increment`. By calling `runBlocking` with the default dispatcher, you make sure these are distributed over multiple threads.

Listing 16.14 Incrementing the `value` of a state flow from 10,000 coroutines

```
fun main() {
    val vc = ViewCounter()
    runBlocking(Dispatchers.Default) {
        repeat(10_000) {
            launch { vc.increment() }
        }
    }

    println(vc.counter.value)
    // 4103
}
```

As you can see, the resulting number in the counter is much lower than 10,000. This is because these coroutines are running on multiple threads. The increments are performed nonatomically, in multiple steps: read the current value, compute the new value, and then write the new value. If two threads read the current value at the same time, then one of the increment operations will effectively be dropped.

To address this, state flows provide the `update` function, which helps you make *atomic* updates to the value of a state flow. You provide a lambda expression that describes how, given a previous value, the new value should be computed (in the case of the view counter, the value should be incremented by one). If two updates to the state flow were to happen in parallel, it simply executes the update function again with a refreshed `previous` value, making sure that no operation gets lost. Rerunning the same test code from listing 16.14 with the implementation in listing 16.13 yields the correct result.

STATE FLOWS ONLY EMIT WHEN A VALUE HAS ACTUALLY CHANGED: EQUALITY-BASED CONFLATION
Just like a shared flow, you can subscribe to a state flow and its value over time by calling `collect`. In this example, you're defining a "direction selector" that exposes functions to turn a switch either to the "left" or "right" position:

```
import kotlinx.coroutines.flow.*
import kotlinx.coroutines.*

enum class Direction { LEFT, RIGHT }

class DirectionSelector {
    private val _direction = MutableStateFlow(Direction.LEFT)
    val direction = _direction.asStateFlow()

    fun turn(d: Direction) {
        _direction.update { d }
    }
}
```

You can then use this direction selector to perform a few transitions between the "left" and "right" positions. By calling `collect`, the coroutine in charge of logging these transitions will be notified whenever a new value is set:

```
fun main() = runBlocking {
    val switch = DirectionSelector()
    launch {
        switch.direction.collect {
            log("Direction now $it")
        }
    }
    delay(200.milliseconds)
    switch.turn(Direction.RIGHT)
    delay(200.milliseconds)
    switch.turn(Direction.LEFT)
    delay(200.milliseconds)
    switch.turn(Direction.LEFT)
}

// 37 [main @coroutine#2] Direction now LEFT
// 240 [main @coroutine#2] Direction now RIGHT
// 445 [main @coroutine#2] Direction now LEFT
```

When inspecting the output of this snippet, you'll notice that despite `turn` being invoked with `LEFT` as its parameter twice, one after the other, the subscriber is only invoked once. This is because state flows perform *equality-based conflation;* they only emit values to the collectors when the value has actually changed. If the previous value and the updated value are the same, no emission happens (visualized in figure 16.6). If you're observing a value twice, and at both times they have the same value, nothing has conceptually changed.

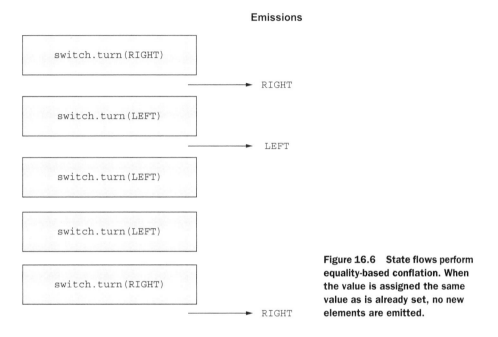

Figure 16.6   State flows perform equality-based conflation. When the value is assigned the same value as is already set, no new elements are emitted.

FROM COLD FLOW TO STATE FLOW WITH STATEIN

When working with an API that provides you with a cold flow, like you had in listing 16.11, you can use the `stateIn` function to convert a cold flow to a state flow, allowing you to always read the latest value emitted from the original flow. Just like with shared flows, adding multiple collectors or accesses to the `value` property won't execute the upstream flow.

Listing 16.15   Using `stateIn` to convert a cold flow to a hot state flow

```
import kotlinx.coroutines.flow.*
import kotlinx.coroutines.*
import kotlin.time.Duration.Companion.milliseconds

fun main() {
    val temps = getTemperatures()
    runBlocking {
        val tempState = temps.stateIn(this)
```

```
        println(tempState.value)
        delay(800.milliseconds)
        println(tempState.value)
        // 18
        // -1
    }
}
```

Unlike with shared flows in section 16.3.1, the `stateIn` function doesn't provide any starting strategies. It always starts the flow in the given coroutine scope and keeps providing its latest value to its subscribers via the `value` property until the coroutine scope is cancelled.

16.3.3   *Comparing state flows and shared flows*

You're now familiar with the two hot flows you can use out of the box with Kotlin. Both of them allow emissions to happen independently of whether subscribers are present, but their uses differ. Shared flows can broadcast events where subscribers can come and go, with subscribers only receiving emissions while they are subscribed. State flows are designed to represent any kind of state and use equality-based conflation, meaning emissions only happen when the value represented by the state flow actually changes.

In general, state flows provide a simpler API than shared flows: they only represent a single value. Shared flows may result in added complexity because it is your responsibility to make sure subscribers are present at the time they are expected to receive emissions. As such, it might be worth investing some time and trying to reframe problems you're trying to solve using shared flow, to see if you could use a state flow instead.

For example, you might find yourself designing a system where you are using a shared flow to broadcast messages to multiple subscribers. However, you'll find that an implementation like this one doesn't actually print any messages.

Listing 16.16   A broadcaster that emits all messages before the first subscriber appears

```
import kotlinx.coroutines.flow.*
import kotlinx.coroutines.*
import kotlin.time.Duration.Companion.milliseconds

class Broadcaster {
    private val _messages = MutableSharedFlow<String>()
    val messages = _messages.asSharedFlow()
    fun beginBroadcasting(scope: CoroutineScope) {
        scope.launch {
            _messages.emit("Hello!")
            _messages.emit("Hi!")
            _messages.emit("Hola!")
        }
    }
}
```

```
fun main(): Unit = runBlocking {
    val broadcaster = Broadcaster()
    broadcaster.beginBroadcasting(this)
    delay(200.milliseconds)
    broadcaster.messages.collect {
        println("Message: $it")
    }
}

// No values are collected, nothing is printed
```

Because your subscriber only appears sometime after the messages were broadcast, it won't receive any messages. Of course, you've already seen that you can fine-tune the replay cache of the shared flow. But instead, you can also reach for a simpler abstraction: the state flow. Rather than emit individual messages, a state flow would store the entire message history as a list, so that subscribers can easily access all prior messages:

Listing 16.17   Using state flow to store the entire message history

```
import kotlinx.coroutines.flow.*
import kotlinx.coroutines.*
import kotlin.time.Duration.Companion.milliseconds

class Broadcaster {
    private val _messages = MutableStateFlow<List<String>>(emptyList())
    val messages = _messages.asStateFlow()
    fun beginBroadcasting(scope: CoroutineScope) {
        scope.launch {
            _messages.update { it + "Hello!" }
            _messages.update { it + "Hi!" }
            _messages.update { it + "Hola!" }
        }
    }
}

fun main() = runBlocking {
    val broadcaster = Broadcaster()
    broadcaster.beginBroadcasting(this)
    delay(200.milliseconds)
    println(broadcaster.messages.value)
}
// [Hello!, Hi!, Hola!]
```

By reframing the problem to use state flows instead of shared flows, you can use a simpler API and allow collectors that join at a later point to see the entire history of updates.

16.3.4 *Hot, cold, shared, state: When to use which flow*

You've now taken an in-depth look at the different types of flows available in Kotlin coroutines. Table 16.1 lists the key properties of flows again, for your convenience.

Table 16.1   Hot flows and cold flows have different properties and behaviors. As such, they also serve different purposes.

Cold flow	Hot flow
Inert by default (triggered by the collector)	Active by default
Has a collector	Has multiple subscribers
Collector gets all emissions	Subscribers get emissions from the start of subscription
Potentially completes	Doesn't complete
Emissions happen from a single coroutine (unless `channelFlow` is used).	Emissions can happen from arbitrary coroutines.

As a rule of thumb, functions that provide a service (like making a network request or reading from a database) are declared using cold flows. Other classes and functions that use these flows can either collect them directly or convert them into state flows and shared flows where applicable to expose this information to other parts of the system.

Interoperability with different implementations of reactive streams

If you're working in a project that already uses a different abstraction for reactive streams, such as Project Reactor (https://projectreactor.io/), RxJava (https://reactivex .io/), or Reactive Streams (https://www.reactive-streams.org/), you can use built-in conversion functions to convert their representation into Kotlin flows and vice versa. This allows you to seamlessly integrate flows with your existing code. Refer to the documentation (https://kotlinlang.org/api/kotlinx.coroutines/) for additional information on this topic.

By themselves, both cold and hot flows already present a useful abstraction for working with values over time. However, their true power comes from *flow operators*, the subject of the next chapter, which help you manipulate flows, much in the same way you've already seen with collections and sequences.

Summary

- In Kotlin, flows are a coroutine-based abstraction that makes it possible to work with values that appear over time.
- You differentiate between two types of flows: hot flows and cold flows.
- Cold flows are inert by default and associated with a single collector. Cold flows are constructed with the `flow` builder functions. Using the `emit` functions, values can be offered asynchronously.

- Channel flows, a special type of cold flow, allow the emission of values from multiple coroutines via the `send` function.
- Hot flows are always active and are associated with multiple collectors, called subscribers. Shared flows and state flows are instances of hot flows.
- Shared flows can be used for broadcast-style communication of values across coroutines.
- Subscribers of shared flows receive emissions from the start of their subscription and those values that were replayed by the shared flow.
- State flows can be used to manage state in your concurrent system.
- State flows perform equality-based conflation, meaning they only perform emissions when their value actually changes, not when assigning the same value multiple times.
- Cold flows can be turned into hot flows via the `shareIn` and `stateIn` functions.

17

Flow operators

This chapter covers

- Operators used to transform and work with flows
- Intermediate and terminal operators
- Building custom flow operators

17.1 *Manipulating flows with flow operators*

In the previous chapter, you got to know flows as the higher-level abstraction that allows you to work with multiple, sequential values over time while leveraging Kotlin's concurrency machinery. In this chapter, we'll discuss how to manipulate and transform them. You've already seen that Kotlin provides a vast selection of operators you can use to manipulate collections (as discussed in chapters 5 and 6). Likewise, you can use operators to transform flows.

Just like with sequences, you distinguish between the *intermediate* flow operators and *terminal* flow operators analogously to our discussion in chapter 6: intermediate operators return another, modified flow, without actually running any of the code yet. Terminal operators return a result—like a collection, an individual element from the flow, a computed value, or no value at all—collecting the flow and executing the actual code (visualized in figure 17.1).

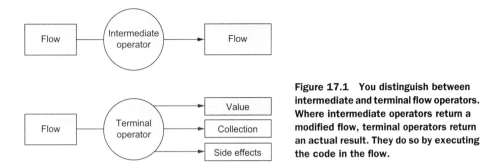

Figure 17.1 You distinguish between intermediate and terminal flow operators. Where intermediate operators return a modified flow, terminal operators return an actual result. They do so by executing the code in the flow.

17.2 Intermediate operators are applied to an upstream flow and return a downstream flow

Intermediate operators are applied to a flow and return a flow themselves. To make it easier to talk about these flows in relation to operators, the names *upstream* and *downstream* flow are commonly used; you call the flow being operated on the *upstream* flow. The flow returned by an intermediate operator is called the *downstream* flow. In turn, this downstream flow can act as the upstream flow for the next operator, and so on. Figure 17.2 illustrates this. As with sequences, calling an intermediate operator on a flow doesn't run any code: the returned flow is *cold*.

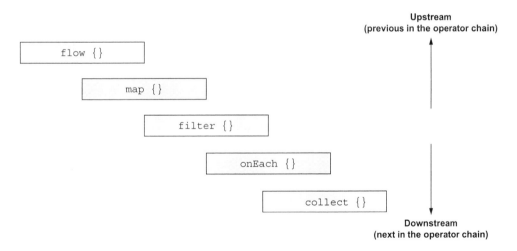

Figure 17.2 The terms *upstream* and *downstream* describe where an intermediate operator sits in the operator chain in relation to another operator. The flow that an operator is being called on is the upstream flow. The flow it returns is the downstream flow. In this example, flow is upstream of map, filter is downstream of map, onEach is upstream of collect, and so on.

> **NOTE** You may wonder what happens when you apply an intermediate operator to a hot flow. Indeed, even in this case, the behavior defined by your operator won't be executed until a terminal operator like collect is called to subscribe to the hot flow.

The great news is that you already know many intermediate operators that work with flows: a large portion of the intermediate operators from sequences are available for Kotlin flows as well, including the most popular functions, like map, `filter`, or `onEach`. They behave exactly as you would expect, just operating on the elements of a flow rather than a sequence or a collection. But there are also flow operators that provide special behavior and functionality beyond what you already know. Let's focus on them, beginning with the `transform` operator.

17.2.1 *Emitting arbitrary values for each upstream element: The transform function*

You already know you can use the map function to take an upstream flow, modify its elements, and return a new downstream flow—effectively emitting a new element to the downstream flow for each element in the upstream flow.

Listing 17.1 Mapping a flow

```
import kotlinx.coroutines.*
import kotlinx.coroutines.flow.*

fun main() {
    val names = flow {
        emit("Jo")
        emit("May")
        emit("Sue")
    }
    val uppercasedNames = names.map {
        it.uppercase()
    }
    runBlocking {
        uppercasedNames.collect { print("$it ")}
    }
    // JO MAY SUE
}
```

However, you may find yourself in a situation where you want to emit more than one element. For example, rather than just emitting an uppercase variant of each name, you may want to include an entirely lowercase variant of each name in the output stream as well. In Kotlin flows, you can do this via the `transform` function. It allows you to emit arbitrarily many elements to the downstream flow for each element in the upstream flow.

Listing 17.2 Transforming a flow

```
import kotlinx.coroutines.flow.*

fun main() {
    val names = flow {
        emit("Jo")
        emit("May")
```

```
        emit("Sue")
    }
    val upperAndLowercasedNames = names.transform {
        emit(it.uppercase())
        emit(it.lowercase())
    }
    runBlocking {
        upperAndLowercasedNames.collect { print("$it ")}
    }
    // JO jo MAY may SUE sue
}
```

In cases like these, where your initial flow simply emits a list of values that you then continue to transform via flow operators, you can also use a shorthand builder function for the flow called `flowOf`: `val names = flowOf("Jo", "May", "Sue")`.

17.2.2 The take operator family can cancel a flow

You already know functions like `takeWhile` from our discussion of sequences in chapter 6. You can use them the same way you are used to in sequences. It's worth noting that when the conditions specified by the operator are no longer valid, the upstream flow gets cancelled, meaning no further elements are emitted. For example, by calling `take(5)` in listing 17.3 on the flow returned by `getTemperatures`, as you declared it in chapter 16, the upstream flow will be cancelled after five emissions.

Listing 17.3   `take` cancels the upstream flow after collecting *n* emissions

```
    val temps = getTemperatures()
    temps
        .take(5)                  ◁─┐  Cancels the flow
        .collect {                  │  after five emissions
            log(it)
        }
}

// 37 [main @coroutine#1] 7
// 568 [main @coroutine#1] 9
// 1123 [main @coroutine#1] 2
// 1640 [main @coroutine#1] -6
// 2148 [main @coroutine#1] 7
```

Besides cancelling the coroutine scope associated with the collector, as you've seen in section 16.2.3, the `take` function is another way to cancel the collection of a flow in a controlled manner.

17.2.3 Hooking into flow phases with onStart, onEach, onCompletion, and onEmpty

To see that the flow from listing 17.3 indeed completes after collecting five elements, you can use the `onCompletion` operator, with which you can provide a lambda that gets executed after the flow either terminates regularly, is cancelled, or terminates with an exception (you'll learn how to handle exceptions in detail in chapter 18). You can modify the code from listing 17.3 to notify the user that the collection has finished either normally or with an exception. You can access the latter as a parameter for the lambda, allowing you to process it further:

```
fun main() = runBlocking {
    val temps = getTemperatures()
    temps
        .take(5)
        .onCompletion { cause ->
            if (cause != null) {
                println("An error occurred! $cause")
            } else {
                println("Completed!")
            }
        }
        .collect {
            println(it)
        }
}
```

onCompletion is part of a family of intermediate operators that allow you to perform at specific phases in the life cycle of a flow: onStart is executed when the collection of the flow begins, even before the first emission happens. onEach performs an action on each emitted element of the upstream flow, before emitting it to the downstream flow. For the special case of having a flow that terminates without ever emitting any elements, you can add the onEmpty intermediate operator to perform additional logic or some default elements.

Here, you're putting together the different operators in the process function to specify behavior for the beginning of the flow, the processing of each element, and the completion of the flow. You also specify a default case when an empty flow is processed.

Listing 17.4   Running logic in different flow phases

```
flow
    .onEmpty {
        println("Nothing - emitting default value!")
        emit(0)
    }
    .onStart {
        println("Starting!")
    }
    .onEach {
        println("On $it!")
    }
    .onCompletion {
        println("Done!")
    }
    .collect()
}
```

Calling this function with an empty and nonempty flow, respectively, you can see that the individual operators are invoked in the order of the flow life cycle:

```
fun main() {
    runBlocking {
        process(flowOf(1, 2, 3))
        // Starting!
        // On 1!
        // On 2!
        // On 3!
        // Done!
        process(flowOf())
        // Starting!
        // Nothing - emitting default value!
        // On 0!
        // Done!
    }
}
```

This is a great example to once again illustrate that these intermediate operators emit elements into their downstream flow. If you were to move the `onEmpty` operator invocation further down the call chain (e.g., right before the call to `collect`), then you would not see the `On 0!` message. That is because `onEach` would be an upstream operator in relation to `onEmpty`—it won't receive any emissions made by the downstream operator.

17.2.4 *Buffering elements for downstream operators and collectors: The buffer operator*

Real application code often does a lot of heavy lifting inside flows; when collecting the elements of a flow, or processing them with operators like `onEach`, you often find yourself calling suspending functions that take some time to complete. In this example, you simulate accessing a slow database to obtain a flow of user identifiers. Each user identifier is associated with a profile that's accessible via an even slower network resource:

```
fun getAllUserIds(): Flow<Int> {
    return flow {
        repeat(3) {
            delay(200.milliseconds) // Database latency
            log("Emitting!")
            emit(it)
        }
    }
}

suspend fun getProfileFromNetwork(id: Int): String {
    delay(2.seconds) // Network latency
    return "Profile[$id]"
}
```

Out of the box, when working with a cold flow such as the one shown previously, the producer of values suspends its work until the collector has finished processing the

previous element. You can observe this by calling the getUserIds function and calling
getProfileFromNetwork for each element:

```
fun main() {
    val ids = getAllUserIds()
    runBlocking {
        ids
            .map { getProfileFromNetwork(it) }
            .collect { log("Got $it") }
    }
}

// 310 [main @coroutine#1] Emitting!
// 2402 [main @coroutine#1] Got Profile[0]
// 2661 [main @coroutine#1] Emitting!
// 4732 [main @coroutine#1] Got Profile[1]
// 5007 [main @coroutine#1] Emitting!
// 7048 [main @coroutine#1] Got Profile[2]
```

As you can see, emissions of IDs and the request of profiles are intertwined. When an
element is emitted, the producer code doesn't continue until the downstream flow
has finished processing the element. In this implementation, that means processing
an individual element takes about 1.2 seconds. Figure 17.3 illustrates this.

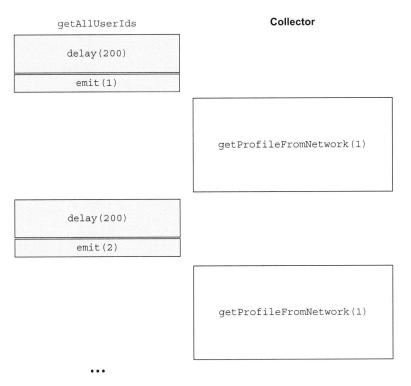

**Figure 17.3   When the flow from getAllUserIds emits an item, the producer code
doesn't continue until the downstream flow has finished processing the element.**

Even without doing more advanced optimizations, like spawning new coroutines for the processing of each element in the flow, there is another observation you can make: if the producer were to be able to produce elements without having to wait for the collector to process them, you could make the execution of your flow faster. This is exactly what the `buffer` operator allows you to do. It introduces a buffer into which elements can be emitted, even while the downstream flow is still busy processing previously emitted elements. This allows you to effectively decouple parts of your chain of operators that process a flow. By adding a buffer with a capacity of three elements, the emitter can continue to produce new user identifiers and place them in the buffer until the collector is ready to make further network requests:

```
fun main() {
    val ids = getAllUserIds()
    runBlocking {
        ids
            .buffer(3)
            .map { getProfileFromNetwork(it) }
            .collect { log("Got $it") }
    }
}

// 304 [main @coroutine#2] Emitting!
// 525 [main @coroutine#2] Emitting!
// 796 [main @coroutine#2] Emitting!
// 2373 [main @coroutine#1] Got Profile[0]
// 4388 [main @coroutine#1] Got Profile[1]
// 6461 [main @coroutine#1] Got Profile[2]
```

Comparing the execution time between the two implementations, we can see that adding the buffer reduced the execution time. That's because the flow returned by `getAllUserIds` can keep emitting items into the buffer while the collector is working. Figure 17.4 illustrates this.

Especially when the time needed to emit and process elements for your flow fluctuates, introducing buffers in your chain of operators can help you increase the throughput of your system. For example, you may be reading and processing input data of different size and complexity. The `buffer` operator is also highly customizable. In addition to the `size` parameter, it also provides an `onBufferOverflow` parameter, which allows you to specify what should happen when the capacity of the buffer is exhausted: whether the producer should suspend (`SUSPEND`), drop the oldest value in the buffer without suspending (`DROP_OLDEST`), or drop the latest value being added (`DROP_LATEST`).

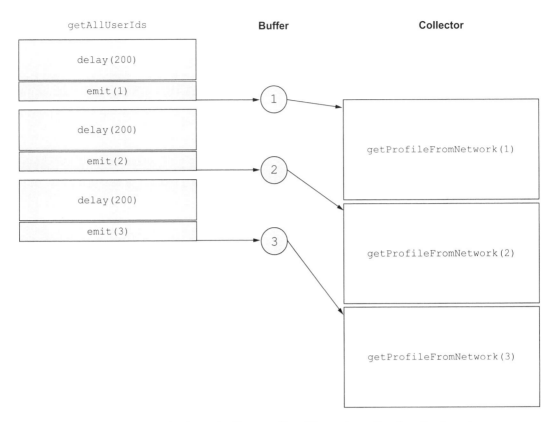

Figure 17.4   The `buffer` operator decouples the execution of the upstream flow from the downstream flow: the flow returned by `getAllUserIds` can keep emitting items into the buffer. The collector, which uses the retrieved IDs to call `getProfileFromNetwork`, can do so as elements become available, and at its own speed.

17.2.5   *Throwing away intermediate values: The conflate operator*

Another way of ensuring a producer of values can work unhindered is to simply throw away any items emitted while the collector is busy. In Kotlin flows, you can do this via the `conflate` operator. Here, you're using `conflate` together with the `getTemperatures` function from chapter 16, which reads the temperature in 500-millisecond intervals, to collect the flow every second. Looking at the output, you can see that the flow upstream of `conflate` contains all elements emitted by `getTemperatures`, while intermediate elements are discarded downstream in the collector.

Listing 17.5   Using `conflate` to ignore intermediate values

```
runBlocking {
    val temps = getTemperatures()
    temps
        .onEach {
            log("Read $it from sensor")
```

```
            }
            .conflate()
            .collect {
                log("Collected $it")
                delay(1.seconds)
            }
    }
}

// 43 [main @coroutine#2] Read 20 from sensor
// 51 [main @coroutine#1] Collected 20
// 558 [main @coroutine#2] Read -10 from sensor
// 1078 [main @coroutine#2] Read 3 from sensor
// 1294 [main @coroutine#1] Collected 3
// 1579 [main @coroutine#2] Read 13 from sensor
// 2153 [main @coroutine#2] Read 26 from sensor
// 2556 [main @coroutine#1] Collected 26
```

Similarly to `buffer`, using `conflate` decouples the execution of the upstream flow from the execution of any downstream operators. When you work with a flow whose values become "out of date" quickly, being replaced by other emitted elements, conflation can help a slow collector keep up by processing only the latest elements in the flow.

17.2.6 *Filtering out values on a timeout: The debounce operator*

In some scenarios, it might be useful to wait for a while before processing values in a flow. In this snippet, you're simulating a user typing a search query into a field by emitting an incrementally longer string whenever the user types something. Because users don't type instantaneously, but take some time to press buttons, you add calls to `delay` to simulate typing happening over time:

```
val searchQuery = flow {
    emit("K")
    delay(100.milliseconds)
    emit("Ko")
    delay(200.milliseconds)
    emit("Kotl")
    delay(500.milliseconds)
    emit("Kotlin")
}
```

Many applications aim to provide "instant search functionality," where the user can type and see results without having to press an additional Search button. If you were to collect this flow without any further processing, it would result in starting a new search request for each keystroke.

An often-used strategy is to wait for a while before actually starting the search process. While the user is still typing their query, no unnecessary search requests are made, but as soon as they stop typing for a period of time, results are displayed without any further action from the user. Using the `debounce` operator, this behavior is easy to implement in Kotlin coroutines; it only emits items into the downstream flow once a certain timeout has elapsed when the upstream hasn't emitted any items. By debouncing with a timeout of 250 milliseconds before collecting the `searchQuery` flow, only elements preceded by a pause of a quarter of a second are emitted into the downstream flow and, thus, collected:

```
fun main() = runBlocking {
    searchQuery
        .debounce(250.milliseconds)
        .collect {
            log("Searching for $it")
        }
}

// 644 [main @coroutine#1] Searching for Kotl
// 876 [main @coroutine#1] Searching for Kotlin
```

17.2.7 Switching the coroutine context on which a flow is executed: The flowOn operator

When your flow operators use blocking IO or need to work with the UI thread, the same considerations as with regular coroutines apply: the coroutine context decides where the logic of a flow is executed. By default, the collection process happens in the context in which `collect` has been invoked. But as you have seen by now, you can build quite complex data processing pipelines using flows. You may want some parts of your processing pipeline to run on a different dispatcher, or with a different coroutine context. The `flowOn` operator allows you to do exactly that—like the `withContext` function you got to know in chapter 14, it adjusts the coroutine context. Here, you're using it to switch between the dispatcher of `runBlocking`, the default dispatcher, and the IO dispatcher.

Listing 17.6   Switching dispatchers via `flowOn`

```
    runBlocking {
        flowOf(1)
            .onEach { log("A") }
            .flowOn(Dispatchers.Default)
            .onEach { log("B") }
            .flowOn(Dispatchers.IO)
            .onEach { log("C") }
            .collect()
    }
}

// 36 [DefaultDispatcher-worker-3 @coroutine#3] A
// 44 [DefaultDispatcher-worker-1 @coroutine#2] B
// 44 [main @coroutine#1] C
```

It's important to note that the `flowOn` operator only affects the dispatcher of the upstream flow—that is, the flow (and any intermediate operators) that come before the invocation of `flowOn`. The downstream flow remains untouched, which is why this operator is also referred to as being *context preserving*. Switching the dispatcher to `Dispatchers.Default` only affects `"A"`, the switch to `Dispatchers.IO` only affects `"B"`, and `"C"` is not affected by the preceding invocations of `flowOn` at all.

17.3   *Creating custom intermediate operators*

As you can tell, the Kotlin coroutines library comes with a large selection of operators that allow you to manipulate flows. But how do these operators work internally, and how can you create your own, custom intermediate operators?

Generally, an intermediate operator acts as a collector and emitter at the same time: it collects the elements from its upstream flow, performs transformations, side effects, or other custom behavior, and then emits new elements into the downstream flow. You already know all these individual pieces: collecting elements from an upstream flow is done via `collect`, and you can create a new downstream flow using the `flow` builder function. Because you only call `collect` on your upstream flow from within the `flow` builder, you ensure the operator is still cold. Only when another function calls `collect` on the flow returned by your operator will the collection of the upstream flow be triggered.

For example, you could implement an operator that computes the average of the last `n` elements in a flow of doubles. To do so, your operator would internally keep track of a list of numbers that have occurred and then emit the average of the encountered values:

```
fun Flow<Double>.averageOfLast(n: Int): Flow<Double> =
    flow {
        val numbers = mutableListOf<Double>()
        collect {
            if (numbers.size >= n) {
                numbers.removeFirst()
            }
            numbers.add(it)
            emit(numbers.average())
        }
    }
```

Just like any other intermediate operator, you could then invoke this operator on an upstream flow and collect its downstream flow:

```
fun main() = runBlocking {
    flowOf(1.0, 2.0, 30.0, 121.0)
        .averageOfLast(3)
        .collect {
            print("$it ")
        }
}
// 1.0 1.5 11.0 51.0
```

Most standard operators in the Kotlin coroutines library follow a similar pattern, although they often also contain additional code for the purposes of performance optimization, which helps multiple chained operators perform more efficiently. This is merely an implementation detail—these optimizations happen entirely under the hood, and without changing the behavior of your code.

17.4 Terminal operators execute the upstream flow and may compute a value

While intermediate operators transform a given flow into another flow, they don't actually execute any code themselves—this is triggered by the *terminal operators*. Terminal operators either compute a single value or a collection of values, or just trigger the execution of the flow, performing computations and side effects as specified. You've already seen the most common terminal operator: `collect`. It provides the useful shorthand of specifying a lambda that will be executed on each element in the flow. Now that you have seen the available intermediate operators, you can probably gather that it is equivalent to calling `onEach` before invoking `collect` without any parameters:

```
fun main() = runBlocking {
    getTemperatures()
        .onEach {
            log(it)
        }
        .collect()
}
```

Because terminal operators are responsible for executing the upstream flows, they are always suspending functions. Calling `collect` always suspends until the entire flow has been collected (or until the coroutine scope in which `collect` is called is cancelled). Other terminal operators, like `first` or `firstOrNull`, can cancel the upstream flow after receiving an element, just as you have seen with intermediate operators in section 17.2.2. For example, if you're only interested in an individual reading from your temperature sensor, you can use the `first` terminal operator or its sibling function `firstOrNull` to obtain a single value:

```
fun main() = runBlocking {
    getTemperatures()
        .first()
}
```

17.4.1 Frameworks provide custom operators

Certain frameworks in the Kotlin ecosystem also provide direct integrations with flows and expose custom operators and conversion functions. For example, the Android UI framework Jetpack Compose from Google and its sibling project Compose Multiplatform from JetBrains allow you to convert Kotlin flows into `State` objects, which are used by the machinery of the UI framework to trigger the recomposition of the user interface, redrawing elements that have changed. In this snippet, you're using the `collectAsState` function to convert a flow of integers passed as an argument to create a state object. Just like with state flows, the `State` objects from Compose expect an initial value, which you can set to `null` to indicate the absence of a value. You can then use the `temperature` variable in the Compose DSL to describe a component of a user interface. In this case, you simply put some text inside a box:

```
@Composable fun TemperatureDisplay(temps: Flow<Int>) {
    val temperature = temps.collectAsState(null)
    Box {
        temperature.value?.let {
            Text("The current temperature is $it!")
        }
    }
}
```

Flows are a powerful addition to your coroutines-based toolkit, and you've seen how they can help you write elegant code that processes values over time. In the next chapter, we will examine how errors are propagated and handled in coroutines-based applications, and we will take a closer look at how you can test your concurrent code.

Summary

- Intermediate operators are used to transform flows into other flows; they operate on an *upstream* flow and return a *downstream* flow. Intermediate operators are cold; they are not executed until a terminal operator is called.
- A large portion of the intermediate operators available for sequences are also available directly for you to use with flows. Flows also provide additional intermediate operators that allow you to perform transformations (`transform`), manage the context in which a flow is executed (`flowOn`), and run code at specific phases during the execution of a flow (`onStart`, `onCompletion`, etc.).
- Terminal operators like `collect` run the code of a flow or, in the case of hot flows, take care of subscribing to the flow.
- You can build your own operators by collecting a flow from within another flow builder, emitting transformed elements from it.
- Several external frameworks, like Jetpack Compose and Compose Multiplatform, provide direct integration with Kotlin flows.

Error handling and testing

This chapter covers

- Controlling the behavior of your code in the face of errors and exceptions
- How error handling relates to the concept of structured concurrency
- Writing code that behaves correctly when parts of your system fail
- Writing unit tests for concurrent Kotlin code
- Using the specialty test dispatcher to speed up test execution and testing fine-grained concurrency constraints
- Testing flows with the Turbine library

Over the last few chapters, you've gotten an overview of the different aspects involved when writing concurrent code with Kotlin coroutines. To ensure the robustness of your applications, there is one more aspect that needs to be covered: How does your code behave when things go wrong?

Working with concurrent applications is an inherently complex task—likely, you'll have many moving parts in your system that interact with each other. Beyond that, your application likely also interacts with other systems outside of your control. These systems may fail, or your connection to these services may be unreliable. However, even in these situations, your application should work well. One of the key aspects that enables this is proper error handling—implementing appropriate mechanisms to handle problems gracefully.

When working with Kotlin coroutines, the subject of error handling is deeply intertwined with the concept of structured concurrency, which you already explored in chapter 15. You'll spend the first half of this chapter learning more about how uncaught exceptions are handled and propagated along your hierarchy of coroutines, how errors are handled in flows, and what tools are at your disposal to control this behavior.

Another aspect of building robust software is testing. While many books could be filled with testing strategies and approaches for general-application code, you'll spend the second half of this chapter taking a closer look at how to specifically test code written using Kotlin coroutines, learning about the specialty features of running tests with virtual time, and conveniently writing tests for flows using the Turbine library. By the end of this chapter, you'll have a better understanding of how error propagation works, how you can deal with errors in flows and coroutines, and the mechanics of writing tests for your concurrent code.

18.1   Handling errors thrown inside coroutines

Just like any other Kotlin code, code written inside suspending functions or a coroutine builder might throw an exception. To handle such exceptions, it may be tempting to surround a `launch` or `async` invocation with try-catch. However, this wouldn't work. Remember that these are *coroutine builder functions*: they create new coroutines to be executed. Exceptions thrown in these new coroutines won't be caught by your `catch` block (just like, for example, exceptions thrown in a newly created thread wouldn't be caught by the code creating the thread.) So code like this, where an `UnsupportedOperationException` is thrown from within a `launch` builder, will not catch the exception:

```
import kotlinx.coroutines.*

fun main(): Unit = runBlocking {
    try {
        launch {
            throw UnsupportedOperationException("Ouch!")
        }
    } catch (u: UnsupportedOperationException) {
        println("Handled $u")                          ◁─── Not called
    }
}
// Exception in thread "main" java.lang.UnsupportedOperationException: Ouch!
//   at MyExampleKt$main$1$1.invokeSuspend(MyExample.kt:6)
//       …
```

One way to properly catch this exception is to move the try-catch block inside the block associated with `launch`. In this case, the exception doesn't cross coroutine boundaries, and you can deal with it in the same way you would if no coroutines were involved at all (see sections 18.2.3 and 18.3, later in this chapter, for a discussion on how uncaught exceptions thrown from coroutines can be handled automatically without crashing the whole application):

```
import kotlinx.coroutines.*

fun main(): Unit = runBlocking {
    launch {
        try {
            throw UnsupportedOperationException("Ouch!")
        } catch (u: UnsupportedOperationException) {
            println("Handled $u")
        }
    }
}
// Handled java.lang.UnsupportedOperationException: Ouch!
```

If a coroutine created using `async` throws an exception, calling `await` on its result rethrows this exception. That's because `await` can't return a meaningful value of the expected type and, therefore, needs to throw an exception. Listing 18.1 illustrates this. You originally expected `myDeferredInt.await()` to return an integer value, but since an exception was thrown inside the `async` coroutine computing this value, `await()` rethrows the exception. You catch it by surrounding `await()` with a try-catch block.

Listing 18.1 **An async coroutine that throws an exception**

```
import kotlinx.coroutines.*

fun main(): Unit = runBlocking {
    val myDeferredInt: Deferred<Int> = async {
        throw UnsupportedOperationException("Ouch!")
    }
    try {
        val i: Int = myDeferredInt.await()
        println(i)
    } catch (u: UnsupportedOperationException) {
        println("Handled: $u")
    }
}
```

When running this example, you can observe that the exception was caught by the try-catch surrounding `await()`. But curiously, it was also printed to the error console at the same time:

```
Handled: java.lang.UnsupportedOperationException: Ouch!
Exception in thread "main" java.lang.UnsupportedOperationException: Ouch!
    at MyExampleKt$main$1$myDeferred$1.invokeSuspend(MyExample.kt:6)
    ...
```

That's because `await` *rethrows* the exception, but you observe the original exception, as well. In this example, `async` propagates the exception to its parent coroutine, created using `runBlocking`, which prints it to the error console and crashes the program.

A child coroutine always *propagates* an uncaught exception to its parent. That means it becomes the responsibility of the parent to handle this exception. Just like in real life, the children pass their problems on to their parents if they don't know how to handle them themselves (or if it's simply more convenient to do so). In the next sections, you'll take a more detailed look at error propagation and learn about different ways the parent coroutine can handle uncaught errors from its children.

18.2   Error propagation in Kotlin coroutines

When you were first introduced to structured concurrency in chapter 15, we briefly mentioned that, besides cancellation, one of the major responsibilities of this concept is handling errors. The structured concurrency paradigm influences what happens with the parent coroutine when a child coroutine throws an uncaught exception. There are two conceptual ways for dividing work between children and, therefore, two ways of handling errors from children. They differ in whether a failure of one child should lead to failure of the parent:

- If coroutines are used for *concurrent decomposition of work*, the failure of one child means that it's no longer possible to get the final result. The parent coroutine should complete with the exception as well, and other children still working get cancelled to avoid producing results that are no longer needed. The failure of one child leads to the failure of the parent.
- The second case is when the failure of one child doesn't lead to common failure. We say that a parent is *supervising* execution of their children when the failure of one child must be handled by the parent and shouldn't lead to a whole-system crash. Typically, such supervising coroutines live at the top of the coroutine hierarchy. For example, a server process may start multiple child jobs and need to supervise their execution. Or a UI component that should stay alive even if fetching the latest data may fail. In this scenario, the failure of one child does not lead to the failure of the parent.

In Kotlin coroutines, the way how the child coroutines are handled by the parent depends on whether the parent coroutine has a regular `Job` (child failure leads to the common failure) or `SupervisorJob` (parent is supervising its children) in its coroutine context. In the next sections, you'll see this difference in detail.

18.2.1   Coroutines cancel all their children when one child fails

When examining coroutine contexts in section 14.8, you learned that under the hood, the parent–child hierarchy between coroutines is built via `Job` objects. As such, if a coroutine isn't explicitly created with `SupervisorJob` to become a supervisor, the default way an uncaught exception from one of the child coroutines is handled is to complete the parent with the exception.

A failed child coroutine propagates its failure to its parent. The parent then does the following:

- It cancels all of its other children to avoid unnecessary work.
- It completes its own execution with the same exception.
- It propagates the exception further up the hierarchy.

This process is illustrated in figure 18.1.

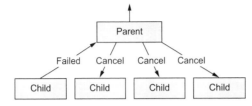

Figure 18.1   When child coroutines fail with an uncaught exception, they notify their parent. The parent, in turn, cancels all the sibling coroutines, and propagates the exception further up the coroutine hierarchy.

This behavior is different from comparable primitives in other languages (e.g., a goroutine in Go has no such behavior). Usually, this convenient cancellation of other "sibling" tasks on one task failure isn't provided out of the box and must be implemented by hand, but it is one of the big benefits of Kotlin coroutines.

This behavior is very useful for coroutines grouped under the same scope that work together to perform computations concurrently and then return a common result. When one of the coroutines within the scope fails with an uncaught exception—that is, it encounters a problem it doesn't know how to recover from by itself—the assumption is that the common result can no longer be reasonably computed. To prevent the sibling coroutines from continuing now-useless computations or holding onto resources in such a situation, they are cancelled. This avoids unnecessary work and releases their resources.

Consider listing 18.2, where you create two coroutines. The first coroutine acts as a "heartbeat" coroutine, which simply loops and prints a message on an interval. If an exception occurs, this coroutine terminates by printing the exception and rethrowing it. The second coroutine throws an exception, which is not handled, after 1 second.

Listing 18.2   Starting a heartbeat coroutine and an exception-throwing coroutine

```
import kotlinx.coroutines.*
import kotlin.time.Duration.Companion.milliseconds
import kotlin.time.Duration.Companion.seconds

fun main(): Unit = runBlocking {
    launch {
        try {
            while (true) {
                println("Heartbeat!")
                delay(500.milliseconds)
```

```
            }
        } catch (e: Exception) {
            println("Heartbeat terminated: $e")
            throw e
        }
    }
    launch {
        delay(1.seconds)
        throw UnsupportedOperationException("Ow!")
    }
}
```

As you can see in the output, the moment a sibling coroutine throws an exception, the heartbeat coroutine is also cancelled:

```
Heartbeat!
Heartbeat!
Heartbeat terminated: kotlinx.coroutines.JobCancellationException: Parent job
    is Cancelling; job=BlockingCoroutine{Cancelling}@1517365b
Exception in thread "main" java.lang.UnsupportedOperationException: Ow!
```

By default, all coroutine builders, including `runBlocking` in this example, create a regular, nonsupervisor coroutine. That's why when one coroutine terminates with an uncaught exception, the other child coroutines also get cancelled.

This behavior of error propagation affects all coroutines, not just those started with `launch`. Starting a new child coroutine with `async` exhibits the same behavior: it propagates its uncaught exception to the parent. Replacing `launch` with `async` in this example also causes the sibling coroutine to be cancelled.

18.2.2 Structured concurrency only affects exceptions thrown across coroutine boundaries

This behavior of cancelling sibling coroutines and propagating the exception up the hierarchy of coroutines only affects uncaught exceptions that cross coroutine boundaries. Because of this, the easiest approach to avoid having to deal with this behavior is to avoid throwing exceptions across these boundaries in the first place. A try-catch block confined to a single coroutine (e.g., inside the body of a suspending function) will behave exactly as you would expect. You can rewrite listing 18.2 to catch the `UnsupportedOperationException` itself.

Listing 18.3 Catching the exception inside the coroutine

```
import kotlinx.coroutines.*
import kotlin.time.Duration.Companion.milliseconds
import kotlin.time.Duration.Companion.seconds

fun main(): Unit = runBlocking {
    launch {
```

```
        try {
            while (true) {
                println("Heartbeat!")
                delay(500.milliseconds)
            }
        } catch (e: Exception) {
            println("Heartbeat terminated: $e")
            throw e
        }
    }
    launch {
        try {
            delay(1.seconds)
            throw UnsupportedOperationException("Ow!")
        } catch (u: UnsupportedOperationException) {
            println("Caught $u")
        }
    }
}
```

With this change in place, you can see that the heartbeat coroutine keeps printing its text, even after the exception was thrown:

```
Heartbeat!
Heartbeat!
Caught java.lang.UnsupportedOperationException: Ow!
Heartbeat!
Heartbeat!
...
```

> **NOTE** It's worth reminding yourself again of what you learned in section 15.2.4: be mindful of cancellation exceptions and their supertypes whenever you're catching exceptions in coroutines. Since cancellations are a natural part of the coroutine life cycle, these exceptions shouldn't be swallowed by your code. Instead, they should either not be caught in the first place, or rethrown.

The propagation of uncaught exceptions up the hierarchy of coroutines, and the cancellation of sibling coroutines that comes with it, helps enforce the paradigm of structured concurrency in your app. But, of course, a single uncaught exception shouldn't tear down your entire application. Instead, you want to be able to define boundaries for this error propagation. In Kotlin coroutines, you can do so using supervisors.

18.2.3 *Supervisors prevent parents and siblings from being cancelled*

Supervisors survive the failure of their children. Unlike scopes that use regular jobs, supervisors don't fail when some of their children report a failure (see figure 18.2). They don't cancel their other child coroutines and don't propagate the exception further up the structured concurrency hierarchy. Because of this, you'll also often find supervisors as the root coroutine, the topmost coroutine in a coroutine hierarchy.

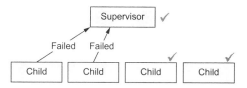

Figure 18.2 When one or more child coroutines of a supervisor fail, the sibling and parent coroutines all keep on working. The exception is no longer propagated further.

For a coroutine to act as a supervisor for its children, the job associated with it should be a `SupervisorJob` instead of a regular `Job`. It takes the same role but prevents the propagation of exceptions to parents and doesn't trigger the cancellation of other child jobs as a response. Of course, supervisors still participate in structured concurrency—they can still be cancelled and still propagate cancellation exceptions correctly.

To see the supervisor behavior for yourself, you can create a scope via the `supervisorScope` function. It's analogous to the `coroutineScope` function you explored in section 15.1.1 but has a key difference: when one of its child coroutines fails, no sibling coroutines are terminated, and the uncaught exception isn't propagated further. Instead, both the parent coroutine and the sibling coroutines keep working. So to fix listing 18.2 and keep the heartbeat coroutine running, you can wrap the invocations of `launch` in a `supervisorScope`.

Listing 18.4 Using a supervisor scope to stop the exception from propagating further

```
import kotlinx.coroutines.*
import kotlin.time.Duration.Companion.milliseconds
import kotlin.time.Duration.Companion.seconds

fun main(): Unit = runBlocking {
    supervisorScope {
        launch {
            try {
                while (true) {
                    println("Heartbeat!")
                    delay(500.milliseconds)
                }
            } catch (e: Exception) {
                println("Heartbeat terminated: $e")
                throw e
            }
        }
        launch {
            delay(1.seconds)
            throw UnsupportedOperationException("Ow!")
        }
    }
}
```

Running this code, you'll notice that the heartbeat coroutine continues working even after the exception was thrown. The supervisor has effectively prevented the child from cancelling the parent coroutine (figure 18.2 illustrates this, as well):

```
Heartbeat!
Heartbeat!
Exception in thread "main" java.lang.UnsupportedOperationException: Ow!
...
Heartbeat!
Heartbeat!
...
```

So why can you see the exception even though the application keeps running? That's because the `SupervisorJob` invokes the `CoroutineExceptionHandler` for child coroutines that were started using the `launch` builder (you'll dive deeper into this topic in sections 18.3 and 18.3.1).

Coroutine-aware frameworks often provide coroutine scopes out of the box that act as supervisors. For example Ktor's `Application` scope allows the `Application` object to be used to start coroutines that run for longer than the lifetime of an individual request handler—these coroutines can live as long as the entire Ktor application. The `Application` scope also acts as a supervisor because a single uncaught exception in a coroutine shouldn't tear down the whole application. Compare this to the `Pipeline-Context` in Ktor, which is responsible for coroutines living as long as a single request handler. Because the assumption is that multiple coroutines in the `PipelineContext` work together to compute a result (the response to the received request), a coroutine failing with an uncaught exception means no sensible result can be computed anymore—the other coroutines associated with this particular request are cancelled.

Supervisors tend to live "higher up" in the hierarchy of coroutines in your application. They're often used to associate coroutines with long-living parts of your software, such as the overall lifetime of an application or the time a window or view is visible to the user. Fine-grained functions typically don't make use of supervisors—after all, having your unnecessary work cancelled is a desirable property of error propagation in coroutines.

18.3   *CoroutineExceptionHandler: The last resort for processing exceptions*

A child coroutine propagates an uncaught exception to its parent until the exception encounters a supervisor, or until the exception reaches the top of the hierarchy—a root coroutine without a parent. At this point, the uncaught exception will go to a special handler, called the `CoroutineExceptionHandler`, which is part of the coroutine context. If no coroutine exception handler is present in the context, the uncaught exception moves to the system-wide exception handler.

> **NOTE** The system-wide exception handler is different between pure JVM projects and Android projects. In a pure JVM project, the handler simply prints the exception stack trace to the error console (as per the JVM's `UncaughtExceptionHandler`). On Android, the system-wide exception handler *crashes your app.*

You can customize the behavior of handling uncaught exceptions by providing such a `CoroutineExceptionHandler` in the coroutine context. Kotlin frameworks can provide a coroutine exception handler on their own. The server-side framework Ktor, for example, uses a `CoroutineExceptionHandler` to send a string representation of uncaught exceptions to its logging provider. Android's `ViewModel`, on the other hand, does not specify a `CoroutineExceptionHandler` in the context of the `SupervisorJob` associated with a `viewModelScope`. This means that uncaught exceptions from coroutines started using `launch` on the `viewModelScope` will result in a crash of your app (you'll learn a bit more about the details in section 18.3.1).

The definition of this handler is quite simple: it receives the coroutine context as well as the uncaught exception as parameters to a lambda. This coroutine exception handler, for example, logs the uncaught exception with a custom prefix to the console:

```
val exceptionHandler = CoroutineExceptionHandler { context, exception ->
    println("[ERROR] $exception")
}
```

`CoroutineExceptionHandler` is a `CoroutineContext` element, which can be added to the coroutine context. In this example, you create a `ComponentWithScope`, which defines a scope with a `SupervisorJob` to make it a supervisor (you've previously seen this way of creating a coroutine scope in section 15.1.2). You also specify your custom exception handler as an element of the coroutine context. To test the behavior, you start a coroutine that throws an exception.

Listing 18.5 A component with a custom coroutine exception handler

```
import kotlinx.coroutines.*
import kotlin.time.Duration.Companion.seconds

class ComponentWithScope(dispatcher: CoroutineDispatcher = Dispatchers.Defaul
    t) {
    private val exceptionHandler = CoroutineExceptionHandler { _, e ->
        println("[ERROR] ${e.message}")
    }

    private val scope = CoroutineScope(
        SupervisorJob() + dispatcher + exceptionHandler
    )

    fun action() = scope.launch {
        throw UnsupportedOperationException("Ouch!")
    }
}

fun main() = runBlocking {
    val supervisor = ComponentWithScope()
    supervisor.action()
    delay(1.seconds)
}
```

The output shows that the exception is handled by the custom exception handler:

```
[ERROR] Ouch!
```

> **NOTE** Under the hood, the direct children of the supervisor technically handle the exceptions themselves by passing them to the custom coroutine exception handler in the context, if it's available, or to the default one. For simplicity, you can think of it as the supervisor taking care of the exceptions from its children. Coroutine exception handlers are also only invoked when the topmost coroutine in the hierarchy was started using the `launch` builder—more on that in section 18.3.1.

It's worth reiterating once again that child coroutines, coroutines started on a coroutine scope or from another coroutine, delegate the handling of uncaught exceptions to their parent. This parent, in turn, delegates this handling further, all the way until the root of the hierarchy. Accordingly, there is no such thing as an "intermediate" `CoroutineExceptionHandler`; handlers installed in the contexts of coroutines that aren't root coroutines are never used.

Listing 18.6 demonstrates this. You create a root coroutine via the delicate `Global-Scope.launch` API, as discussed in section 15.1.3, and provide a custom coroutine exception handler as a part of its context. You also provide an intermediate exception handler to the `launch` coroutine. Running this code, you'll see that the only coroutine exception handler invoked is the one at the top of the hierarchy—the intermediate one doesn't get used.

Listing 18.6   Only the exception handler at the top of the coroutines hierarchy is invoked

```
import kotlinx.coroutines.*

private val topLevelHandler = CoroutineExceptionHandler { _, e ->
    println("[TOP] ${e.message}")
}

private val intermediateHandler = CoroutineExceptionHandler { _, e ->
    println("[INTERMEDIATE] ${e.message}")
}

@OptIn(DelicateCoroutinesApi::class)          ⟵── Makes the usage of a
fun main() {                                       delicate API explicit
    GlobalScope.launch(topLevelHandler) {
        launch(intermediateHandler) {
            throw UnsupportedOperationException("Ouch!")
        }
    }
    Thread.sleep(1000)
}
// [TOP] Ouch!
```

This is because the exception can still be propagated further, to the parent coroutine, as illustrated by figure 18.3.

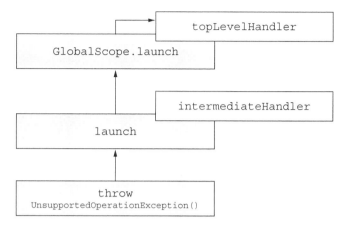

Figure 18.3 Even though the intermediate call to `launch` has a coroutine exception handler in its coroutine context, it's not a root coroutine. Therefore, the exception continues to be propagated along the hierarchy of coroutines. Only the exception handler at the root coroutine (here, `GlobalScope` `.launch`) is invoked.

18.3.1 Differences when using CoroutineExceptionHandler with launch or async

When looking at the `CoroutineExceptionHandler` (whether the default handler or a custom one), it's important to note that the exception handler only gets called when the topmost coroutine in your hierarchy was created with `launch`. Having an `async` as the topmost coroutine means the `CoroutineExceptionHandler` is not invoked.

The following two examples illustrate this. In the first one, you're starting a coroutine with `launch`, which internally starts an additional coroutine using `async`. As discussed, when the topmost coroutine under the supervisor is started using `launch`, the `CoroutineExceptionHandler` is invoked:

```
import kotlinx.coroutines.*
import kotlin.time.Duration.Companion.seconds

class ComponentWithScope(dispatcher: CoroutineDispatcher =
➥ Dispatchers.Default) {
    private val exceptionHandler = CoroutineExceptionHandler { _, e ->
        println("[ERROR] ${e.message}")
    }

    private val scope = CoroutineScope(SupervisorJob() + dispatcher +
➥ exceptionHandler)

    fun action() = scope.launch {
        async {
            throw UnsupportedOperationException("Ouch!")
        }
    }
}

fun main() = runBlocking {
    val supervisor = ComponentWithScope()
```

```
    supervisor.action()
    delay(1.seconds)
}

// [ERROR] Ouch!
```

When you alter the implementation of `action` so that the outer coroutine is started using `async`, you won't see the coroutine exception handler invoked.

Listing 18.7 An `async` coroutine that throws an exception as the direct child of a supervisor

```
import kotlinx.coroutines.*
import kotlin.time.Duration.Companion.seconds

class ComponentWithScope(dispatcher: CoroutineDispatcher =
➥ Dispatchers.Default) {
    private val exceptionHandler = CoroutineExceptionHandler { _, e ->
        println("[ERROR] ${e.message}")
    }

    private val scope = CoroutineScope(SupervisorJob() + dispatcher +
    ➥ exceptionHandler)

    fun action() = scope.async {        <-- async is now the outer coroutine.
        launch {
            throw UnsupportedOperationException("Ouch!")
        }
    }
}

fun main() = runBlocking {
    val supervisor = ComponentWithScope()
    supervisor.action()
    delay(1.seconds)
}
// No output is printed
```

The reason for this is the following: when the topmost coroutine is started using `async`, it becomes the responsibility of the consumer of the `Deferred` to handle this exception by calling `await()`—the coroutine exception handler can ignore this exception, and the calling code, which works with the `Deferred`, can wrap its `await` invocation in a try-catch block. It's important to note that this doesn't affect the *cancellation* of coroutines, though: if the `scope` in the preceding example didn't have a `SupervisorJob` installed in its context, then this uncaught exception would have still triggered the cancellation of all other coroutines that are children of `scope`.

So far, the discussion of error handling has been limited to coroutines. But what about handling errors when using flows? Let's take a closer look at this subject next.

18.4   Handling errors in flows

Just like regular Kotlin functions or suspending functions, flows can also throw exceptions, as illustrated in the following listing. When collected, this flow will emit five elements (the numbers 0 through 4) and then throw a custom exception called `UnhappyFlowException`.

Listing 18.8   A flow that throws an exception after emitting five numbers

```kotlin
import kotlinx.coroutines.*
import kotlinx.coroutines.flow.*

class UnhappyFlowException: Exception()

val exceptionalFlow = flow {
    repeat(5) { number ->
        emit(number)
    }
    throw UnhappyFlowException()
}
```

Generally, if an exception occurs during any part of a flow—while it's being created, transformed, or collected—the exception is thrown from `collect`. That means you can surround the call to `collect` with a try-catch block, which will behave as expected (of course, keeping in mind the special rules concerning `CancellationException` when doing so). This is independent of whether there are any intermediate operators applied to the flow. You can see this in the next code snippet, where you're first transforming the `exceptionalFlow` into `transformedFlow` via the `map` function. You then surround the call to `collect` with a try-catch block:

```kotlin
fun main() = runBlocking {
    val transformedFlow = exceptionalFlow.map {
        it * 2
    }
    try {
        transformedFlow.collect {
            print("$it ")
        }
    } catch (u: UnhappyFlowException) {
        println("\nHandled: $u")
    }
    // 0 2 4 6 8
    // Handled: UnhappyFlowException
}
```

As you can see by the `Handled:` prefixing the exception name, you indeed catch the exception. However, there is another way that works more conveniently, especially when you have built longer and more complex pipelines of flows: the `catch` operator.

18.4.1 *Processing upstream exceptions with the catch operator*

`catch` is an intermediate operator that can process exceptions that occur in a flow. In the lambda associated with a function, you can access the thrown exception via the parameter (which, as usual, is implicitly named `it`, by default).

Since this operator is part of the built-in set of operators, it's already aware of cancellation exceptions, meaning the block provided to `catch` won't be called in case of cancellation. Additionally, `catch` can also emit values itself, which is helpful if you want to turn exceptions into some error values that can be consumed by the downstream flow. In this example, you're catching and logging any exceptions produced by `exceptional-Flow` and emitting an error value of `-1` to the collector in these cases.

Listing 18.9 Using the `catch` operator to emit a default value in case of an exception

```
fun main() = runBlocking {
    exceptionalFlow
        .catch { cause ->
            println("\nHandled: $cause")
            emit(-1)
        }
        .collect {
            print("$it ")
        }
}
// 0 1 2 3 4
// Handled: UnhappyFlowException
// -1
```

It's important to reiterate that the `catch` operator only operates on its upstream, exclusively catching exceptions that occurred prior, in the flow-processing pipeline. You can see this in the following snippet, where the exception thrown in the `onEach` lambda, which follows after the `catch` invocation, would remain uncaught:

```
fun main() = runBlocking {
    exceptionalFlow
        .map {
            it + 1
        }
        .catch { cause ->
            println("\nHandled $cause")
        }
        .onEach {
            throw UnhappyFlowException()
        }
        .collect()
}
// Exception in thread "main" UnhappyFlowException
```

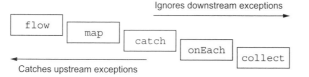

Figure 18.4 The `catch` operator only catches exceptions that occur upstream. Exceptions occurring downstream are unaffected by the `catch` operator.

NOTE To catch an exception that occurs inside the `collect` lambda, you can wrap the invocation of `collect` in a try-catch block. Alternatively, you can rewrite the logic using a chain of `onEach`, `catch`, and `collect` without a lambda. The only important detail here is that the `catch` operator is placed downstream from where the exception can be thrown (see figure 18.4). Because only upstream exceptions are handled by the `catch` operator, it's even perfectly valid to rethrow an exception from `catch` (or transform it somehow), for it to be processed by another `catch` operator further downstream.

18.4.2 Retry the collection of a flow if predicate is true: The retry operator

When you encounter an exception in the processing of a flow, rather than simply terminate with an error message, you might want to retry the operation. The built-in `retry` operator makes this quite convenient: just like `catch`, `retry` catches upstream exceptions. You can then use the associated lambda to process the exception and return a Boolean value: if the lambda returns `true`, a retry will be initiated (up to the specified maximum number of retries). During a retry, the upstream flow is collected again from the beginning, once again running all intermediate operations. You can see this in action in the following listing, which simulates an unreliable flow that tries to emit 10 elements. Each emission can fail, with a chance of 10%, so you use the `retry` operator to collect the flow again.

Listing 18.10 Retrying the collection of an unreliable flow

```
import kotlinx.coroutines.flow.*
import kotlinx.coroutines.*
import kotlin.random.Random

class CommunicationException : Exception("Communication failed!")

val unreliableFlow = flow {
    println("Starting the flow!")
    repeat(10) { number ->
        if (Random.nextDouble() < 0.1) throw CommunicationException()
        emit(number)
    }
}

fun main() = runBlocking {
    unreliableFlow
        .retry(5) { cause ->
            println("\nHandled: $cause")
```

```
        cause is CommunicationException
    }
    .collect { number ->
        print("$number ")
    }
}
```

Since this example uses some randomness, the output you see may differ, but after rerunning the snippet a few times, you may see an output that resembles the following. The output will have a number of elements being collected and then an exception being thrown, causing the operation to be retried one or two more times before all 10 elements from the flow are collected successfully:

```
Starting the flow!
0 1 2 3 4
Handled: CommunicationException: Communication failed!
Starting the flow!
0 1 2 3
Handled: CommunicationException: Communication failed!
Starting the flow!
0 1 2 3 4 5 6 7 8 9
```

It is important to note that retrying the collection runs all upstream operators as well: if any steps of the upstream flow perform side effects, you'll see them executed multiple times. In this case, you should make sure they're either *idempotent* (i.e., applying them multiple times has the same outcome as applying them only once) or that repeated execution is handled correctly otherwise.

You now have an idea of how errors are treated in code built with coroutines and flows. Next, let's move our attention to testing, another important topic when it comes to writing robust software.

18.5   *Testing coroutines and flows*

Fundamentally, writing tests for code that uses Kotlin coroutines works the same way as writing regular tests. To enter the world of coroutines from your test method, you use the special `runTest` coroutine builder.

Let's discuss first why this separate coroutine builder is needed and `runBlocking` isn't enough. The `runBlocking` builder function, which you got to know in section 14.6.1 and is used to bridge the worlds of regular Kotlin code and concurrent Kotlin code, can be used for writing tests for suspending functions and code that uses coroutines or flows. There is, however, a caveat to this approach. When using `runBlocking`, your tests run in real time—that means if your code specifies delays, these are executed in their entirety before results are calculated.

For example, you may be testing a system that aggregates sensor readings. To avoid overloading the real device, the code in the system only queries the sensor every 500 milliseconds. If you write a unit test for this part of the system using `runBlocking`, that means this test would have to wait out these delays before it can continue—even if you switched out the underlying sensor communication with a test stub! Likewise, you may develop an application that executes search requests, and before submitting each query, the system waits a few hundred milliseconds so that the user doesn't submit too many requests at once. If you were to write a unit test for this search function, each simulated request would take a few hundred milliseconds, and your tests would be slow, as a result.

As your test suite grows larger, this needlessly long execution time can rapidly compound and affect how quickly you can test your whole application—after all, the slower your tests are, the more cumbersome it becomes to run them. As a result, you'll likely run them less frequently, meaning you'll get less value out of your tests. Kotlin coroutines offers a solution for this: running your tests under *virtual time.*

18.5.1 Making tests using coroutines fast: Virtual time and the test dispatcher

Rather than executing all your tests in real time—waiting for all delays, and, as such, slowing down your tests—Kotlin coroutines allows you to fast-forward the execution of your tests by using virtual time. When using virtual time, delays are automatically fast-forwarded, eliminating the previously highlighted issues.

In the following listing, you're using `runTest` to run a test with virtual time. Despite declaring a delay of 20 seconds, this test runs practically instantaneously, in just a few milliseconds (measured here using `System.currentTimeMillis()`).

Listing 18.11 Running a test with virtual time

```
import kotlinx.coroutines.*
import kotlinx.coroutines.test.*
import kotlin.test.*
import kotlin.time.Duration.Companion.seconds

class PlaygroundTest {
    @Test
    fun testDelay() = runTest {
        val startTime = System.currentTimeMillis()
        delay(20.seconds)
        println(System.currentTimeMillis() - startTime)
    // 11
    }
}
```

`runTest` uses a special test dispatcher and scheduler to make this speedup possible. Rather than actually wait out the delays of coroutines, they are fast-forwarded.

> **NOTE** Because artificial delays are automatically fast-forwarded, `runTest` specifies a default timeout of 60 (real-time) seconds. When making proper use of the virtual time mechanism, this should be plenty. However, sometimes (e.g., when writing integration tests), you might find yourself needing more time. For those cases, you can specify a `timeout` parameter when invoking `runTest`.

Just like `runBlocking`, the dispatcher of `runTest` is single threaded. As such, any child coroutines are executed concurrently, but not in parallel to your test code by default (the exception being a child coroutine explicitly specifying a multithreaded dispatcher). Like you've seen when we explored cancellation (section 15.2.4), for other coroutines to run their code when sharing a single-threaded dispatcher, your code needs to provide suspension points, and `runTest` is no different. This is particularly important to keep in mind when writing assertions for your tests. The assertion in this test will fail because there are no suspension points in the body of `runTest`, which means there is no way for the launched coroutines to run before the assertion:

```
@Test
fun testDelay() = runTest {
    var x = 0
    launch {
        x++
    }
    launch {
        x++
    }
    assertEquals(2, x)
}
```

You should already be familiar with different ways of introducing suspension points to your code, as covered in section 14.6.2. Adding `delay(50.milliseconds)`, `yield()` or another function call that triggers suspension works to make this test pass.

Additionally, the test dispatcher comes with more fine-grained controls over the virtual time via its special `TestCoroutineScheduler`. This scheduler is part of the coroutine context (you've learned about coroutine contexts in chapter 15). Inside the block of the `runTest` builder function, you get access to a specialized scope, called `TestScope`, which exposes the `TestCoroutineScheduler` functionality for you to use (either directly via extension functions or via the `testScheduler` property). Its key functions are the following:

- `runCurrent`—To run all coroutines currently scheduled for execution
- `advanceUntilIdle`—To run all coroutines scheduled for execution at any point

To just move the virtual clock of the test dispatcher forward, you can use `delay`. Because the clock is virtual, this delay is passed instantaneously, and code that was previously scheduled for delayed execution will be executed. To get an idea of the current time the virtual dispatcher is at, you can use the `currentTime` property.

> **Listing 18.12 Forwarding the virtual clock with `delay`**

```
@OptIn(ExperimentalCoroutinesApi::class)
@Test
fun testDelay() = runTest {
    var x = 0
```

```
        launch {
            delay(500.milliseconds)
            x++
        }
        launch {
            delay(1.second)
            x++
        }
        println(currentTime) // 0

        delay(600.milliseconds)
        assertEquals(1, x)
        println(currentTime) // 600

        delay(500.milliseconds)
        assertEquals(2, x)
        println(currentTime) // 1100
}
```

When you want to run all coroutines that are currently scheduled to run, you can use the runCurrent function. If, in the process, new coroutines are scheduled for immediate execution, these are also executed directly. To run even those coroutines scheduled for delayed execution at some point in the future, you can use the advanceUntilIdle function, instead.

Listing 18.13   Running all scheduled coroutines via `advanceUntilIdle`

```
@OptIn(ExperimentalCoroutinesApi::class)
@Test
fun testDelay() = runTest {
    var x = 0
    launch {
        x++
        launch {
            x++
        }
    }
    launch {
        delay(200.milliseconds)
        x++
    }
    runCurrent()
    assertEquals(2, x)
    advanceUntilIdle()
    assertEquals(3, x)
}
```

NOTE   Other dispatchers, like `Dispatchers.Default`, don't have any knowledge about the `TestCoroutineScheduler`. As such, they're unaffected by the virtual time mechanism; a coroutine explicitly started on a nontest dispatcher will always wait out delays in full. Thus, to make your code quickly testable, it's preferable to design your code in a way that allows you to change the dispatcher (e.g., by allowing the dispatcher to be specified as a parameter). You've seen examples of this in sections 15.2.2 and 18.3, where you created components with their own life cycle that specify a `dispatcher` constructor parameter.

18.5.2 *Testing flows with Turbine*

Testing code that uses flows isn't inherently different from testing other suspending code, using `runTest`. For example, by calling `toList`, you can first collect all elements of a finite flow into a collection and then check whether all elements you expected are actually in the resulting collection.

Listing 18.14 Collecting a flow to a list

```
val myFlow = flow {
    emit(1)
    emit(2)
    emit(3)
}

@Test
fun doTest() = runTest {
    val results = myFlow.toList()
    assertEquals(3, results.size)
}
```

In projects, your flow-based code is often more complicated, may involve infinite flows, or may require you to cover more complex invariants. These cases are supported by the Turbine library, which helps write tests for flows. Turbine is a third-party library, but many Kotlin developers consider it essential for writing tests for flow-based APIs. To add the library to your project, refer to its documentation (https://github .com/cashapp/turbine). Once added, it adds a handful of new functionality and extension functions on flows that help you when writing tests.

The core of Turbine's functionality is the `test` function, which is an extension function on flows. The `test` function launches a new coroutine and internally collects the flow. In the `test` lambda, you can then use the `awaitItem`, `awaitComplete`, and `awaitError` functions together with the regular assertions of your test framework to specify and validate invariants about your flows. It also ensures all elements emitted into the flow were consumed properly by your test.

Listing 18.15 Testing a flow with Turbine

```
@Test
fun doTest() = runTest {
    val results = myFlow.test {
        assertEquals(1, awaitItem())
        assertEquals(2, awaitItem())
```

```
            assertEquals(3, awaitItem())
            awaitComplete()
        }
    }
}
```

Turbine also provides additional functionality for testing multiple flows in conjunction with each other as well as creating standalone `Turbine` objects that can be used to construct stand-ins of parts of your system for the purpose of testing. For more information on these more advanced subjects, refer to the library's documentation.

This concludes our discussion on both error handling and testing code built using Kotlin coroutines. You now have an understanding of how error propagation and handling works in Kotlin coroutines, know how to use coroutines' test functionality to make sure the tests for your code run fast, and have seen how the Turbine library makes writing tests for flows easier.

Summary

- Exceptions confined to a single coroutine can be handled the same way you would in regular, non-coroutine-based code. Extra care is required when exceptions are thrown across coroutine boundaries.
- By default, when an uncaught exception occurs in a coroutine, the parent coroutine and all sibling coroutines are cancelled. This enforces the concept of structured concurrency.
- Supervisors, used via `supervisorScope` or another coroutine scope that has a `SupervisorJob`, don't cancel their other child coroutines when one of them fails. They also don't propagate uncaught exceptions further up the hierarchy of coroutines.
- `await` rethrows the exceptions from an `async` coroutine.
- Supervisors are often used for long-running parts of applications. They often also come as built-in parts of frameworks, like Ktor's `Application`.
- An uncaught exception gets propagated until it encounters a supervisor or until the exception reaches the top of the hierarchy. At this point, the uncaught exception will move to the `CoroutineExceptionHandler`, which is part of the coroutine context. If no coroutine exception handler is present in the context, the uncaught exception makes it to the system-wide exception handler.
- The default system-wide exception handler is different for JVM and Android: on JVM, it logs the stack trace to the error console, while on Android, it crashes your application.
- The `CoroutineExceptionHandler` acts as a last resort for processing exceptions—while it can't catch exceptions, it allows you to customize the way the exceptions are logged. The `CoroutineExceptionHandler` sits in the context of your root coroutine, at the very top of your hierarchy.
- The `CoroutineExceptionHandler` only gets invoked if the topmost coroutine was started using the `launch` builder. If it was started using the `async` builder, the

handler won't be invoked; instead, it is the responsibility of the code that awaits the `Deferred` to handle the exception.

- Error handling in flows can be done by wrapping `collect` in a try-catch statement or using the dedicated `catch` operator.
- The `catch` operator only processes exceptions thrown upstream. It ignores downstream exceptions. You can even use it to rethrow exceptions for further processing downstream.
- By using `retry`, you can restart the collection of a flow from the beginning, in case of an exception, giving your code the chance to recover.
- By using virtual time via `runTest`, testing coroutines code can be accelerated. Any delays are automatically fast-forwarded.
- The `TestCoroutineScheduler`, a part of the `TestScope` exposed by `runTest`, keeps track of the current virtual time, and you can use functions like `runCurrent`, and `advanceUntilIdle` for fine-grained control over the execution of your tests.
- The test dispatcher is single-threaded, meaning you'll have to manually ensure newly started coroutines have time to run before you call your assertions.
- The Turbine library allows you to write convenient tests for code based on flows. Its core API is the `test` extension function that collects items from a flow and allows you to use functions like `awaitItem` to check the emissions of the flow under test.

appendix A
Building Kotlin projects

This appendix explains how to build Kotlin code with Gradle and Maven, the two most popular build systems used with Kotlin projects.

Building Kotlin code with Gradle

The recommended system for building Kotlin projects is Gradle. Gradle has become the de facto standard build system for Kotlin projects. It has a flexible project model and delivers great build performance, thanks to its support for incremental builds, long-lived build processes (the Gradle daemon), and other advanced techniques.

Gradle allows you to specify your build scripts in either Kotlin or Groovy. Since Gradle has chosen the Kotlin syntax as its default and recommended approach for new build script projects, we also use it in this book. As a side effect, this also means both your build configuration and your actual application are written in the same language. The easiest way to create a Gradle project with Kotlin support is via the built-in project wizard (see figure A.1) in IntelliJ IDEA, which you can find under File > New… > Project or via the New Project button on the Welcome screen.

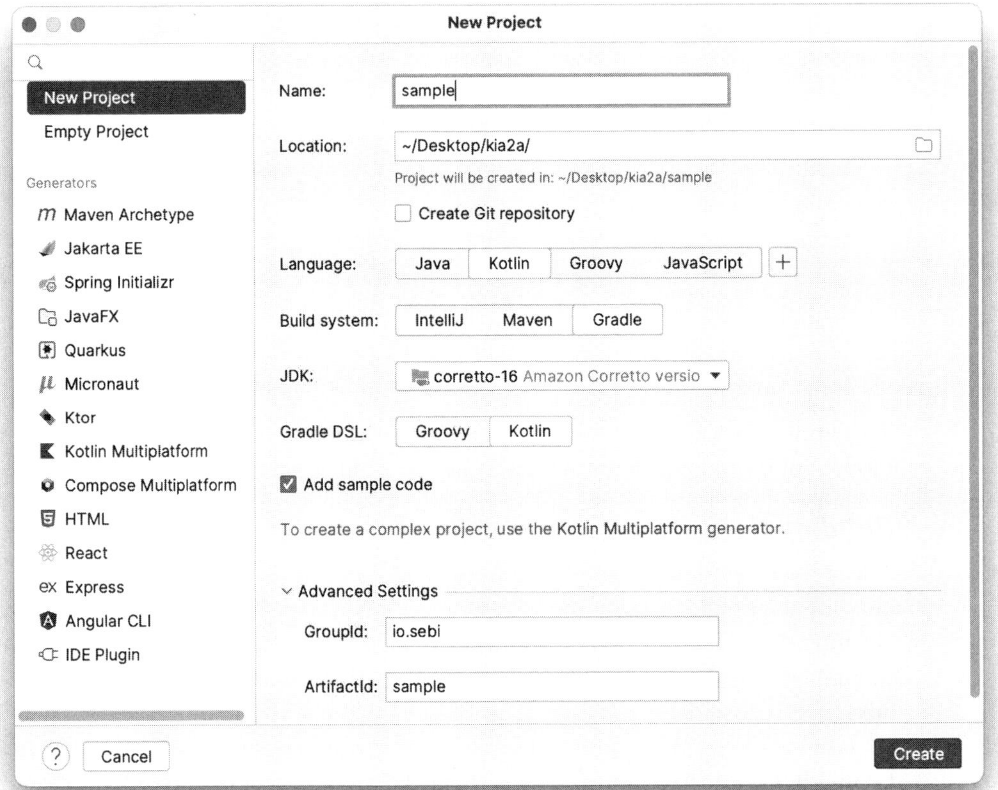

Figure A.1   The new project wizard in IntelliJ IDEA makes it easy to set up a Kotlin project.

The standard Gradle build script for building a Kotlin project looks like this:

```
plugins {
    kotlin("jvm") version "YOUR_KOTLIN_VERSION"
    application
}

group = "org.example"
version = "1.0-SNAPSHOT"

repositories {
    mavenCentral()
}

dependencies {
    testImplementation(kotlin("test"))
}

tasks.test {
```

Applies the Kotlin Gradle plug-in and specifies the Kotlin version

The Kotlin standard library is implicitly added; there is no need to specify it here.

Adds the Kotlin test library as a dependency

```
        useJUnitPlatform()
}

kotlin {
    jvmToolchain(20)
}

application {
    mainClass.set("MainKt")
}
```

By default, the script looks for Kotlin source files in the following locations: * src/main/kotlin for Kotlin production source files and src/main/java for both Kotlin and Java production source files; and * src/test/kotlin and src/test/java for the corresponding test source files. Especially when you're introducing Kotlin into an existing project, using a single source directory reduces friction when converting Java files to Kotlin.

If you're using Kotlin reflection, which you've gotten to know in chapter 12, you need to add one more dependency: the Kotlin reflection library. To do so, add the following in the `dependencies` section of your Gradle build script:

```
implementation(kotlin("reflect"))
```

If you're using Kotlin coroutines, which you spent the third part of the book exploring, you also need to add the corresponding dependency:

```
implementation("org.jetbrains.kotlinx:kotlinx-coroutines-core:1.7.3")
// if you're targeting Android, additionally add:
implementation("org.jetbrains.kotlinx:kotlinx-coroutines-android:1.7.3")
```

Please refer to the documentation (https://github.com/Kotlin/kotlinx.coroutines) to determine the latest version of the coroutines library.

Building projects that use annotation processing

Some Kotlin frameworks rely on *symbol processing* to introspect and generate code at compile time in your project. To do so, projects like `koin` (https://insert-koin.io/), `kotlin-inject` (https://github.com/evant/kotlin-inject), and Ktorfit (https://foso.github.io/Ktorfit/) use the *Kotlin Symbol Processing* (KSP) API. To add KSP support to your project, follow the installation instructions from the KSP project page (https://github.com/google/ksp).

If you are working with Java frameworks in your project that do annotation processing to generate code at compile time, you can use `kapt`, which is a Kotlin annotation processing tool that is backward compatible with Java libraries. It needs to be enabled in your build script, which you can do by adding the following line to the `plugins` block:

```
kotlin("kapt") version "YOUR_KOTLIN_VERSION"
```

If you have an existing Java project that uses annotation processing and you're introducing Kotlin to it, you need to remove the existing configuration of the apt tool. kapt handles both Java and Kotlin classes, and having two separate annotation-processing tools would be redundant. To configure dependencies required for annotation processing, use the kapt dependency configuration:

```
dependencies {
    implementation("com.google.dagger:dagger:2.46.1")
    kapt("com.google.dagger:dagger-compiler:2.46.1")
}
```

If you use annotation processors for your androidTest or test source, the respective kapt configurations are named kaptAndroidTest and kaptTest.

Building Kotlin projects with Maven

If you prefer to build your projects with Maven, Kotlin supports that as well. The easiest way to create a Kotlin Maven project is to use the org.jetbrains.kotlin :kotlin-archetype-jvm archetype. For existing Maven projects, you can add Kotlin support by choosing Tools > Kotlin > Configure Kotlin in Project in the Kotlin IntelliJ IDEA plugin.

To add Maven support to a Kotlin project manually, you need to perform the following steps:

1   Add a dependency on the Kotlin standard library (group ID org.jetbrains .kotlin, artifact ID kotlin-stdlib).
2   Add the Kotlin Maven plug-in (group ID org.jetbrains.kotlin, artifact ID kotlin-maven-plugin), and configure its execution in the compile and test-compile phases.
3   Configure source directories, if you prefer to keep your Kotlin code in a source root separate from Java source code.

For reasons of space, we're not showing full pom.xml examples here, but you can find them in the online documentation at https://kotlinlang.org/docs/maven.html.

In a mixed Java/Kotlin project, you need to configure the Kotlin plug-in so that it runs before the Java plugin. This is necessary because the Kotlin plugin can parse Java sources, whereas the Java plugin can only read .class files, so the Kotlin files need to be compiled to .class before the Java plugin runs. You can find an example showing how this can be configured at http://mng.bz/v8Op.

appendix B
Documenting Kotlin code

This appendix covers writing documentation comments for Kotlin code and generating API documentation for Kotlin modules.

Writing Kotlin documentation comments

The format used to write documentation comments for Kotlin declarations is called *KDoc*. KDoc comments begin with /** and use tags starting with @ to document specific parts of a declaration (as you might be used to from Javadoc). KDoc uses a dialect of Markdown (https://daringfireball.net/projects/markdown) as its syntax to write the comments itself. To make writing documentation comments easier, KDoc supports several additional conventions to refer to documentation elements, such as function parameters.

The following listing contains a simple example of a KDoc comment for a function.

Listing B.1 Using a KDoc comment

```
/**
 * Calculates the sum of two numbers, [a] and [b]
 */
fun sum(a: Int, b: Int) = a + b
```

To refer to declarations from a KDoc comment, you enclose their names in brackets. The example uses that syntax to refer to the parameters of the function being documented, but you can also use it to refer to other declarations. If the declaration you need to refer to is imported in the code containing the KDoc comment, you can use its name directly. Otherwise, you can use a fully qualified name. If you need to specify a custom label for a link, you use two pairs of brackets and put the label in the first pair and the declaration name in the second: [an example] [com.mycompany.SomethingTest.simple].

The following listing features a somewhat more complex example, showing the use of tags in a comment.

Listing B.2   Using tags in a comment

```
/**
 * Performs a complicated operation.
 *
 * @param remote If true, executes operation remotely      ◁
 * @return The result of executing the operation           ◁
 * @throws IOException if remote connnection fails          ◁
 */
fun somethingComplicated(remote: Boolean): ComplicatedResult { /* ... */ }
```

Documents a parameter

Documents the return value

Documents a possible exception

KDoc supports the following tags, among others:

- `@param parameterName`, `@param[parameterName]` to document a value parameter of a function or the type parameter of a generic construct.
- `@return` to document the return value of a function.
- `@constructor` to document the primary constructor of a class.
- `@receiver` to document the receiver of an extension function or property.
- `@property propertyName` to document a property of a class when declared in the primary constructor.
- `@throws ClassName`, `@exception ClassName` to document exceptions that may be thrown by a function. The value of the tag is the fully qualified name of the method to be included.
- `@see otherSymbol` to include a reference to another class or function in the "See Also" block of the documentation.
- `@author` to specify the author.
- `@since` to specify the version in which the documented element was introduced.
- `@suppress` to exclude this declaration from the generated documentation.

You can find the full list of supported tags at https://kotlinlang.org/docs/kotlin-doc.html.

From Javadoc to KDoc

Besides the difference in syntax—Markdown in KDoc and HTML in Javadoc—there are some other characteristics worth pointing out if you're used to writing Javadoc to help ease the transition.

Some Javadoc tags aren't supported in KDoc:

- `@deprecated` is replaced with the `@Deprecated` annotation.
- `@inheritdoc` isn't supported because, in Kotlin, documentation comments are always automatically inherited by overriding declarations.
- `@code`, `@literal`, and `@link` are replaced with the corresponding Markdown formatting.

Note that the documentation style preferred by the Kotlin team is to document the parameters and the return value of a function directly in the text of a documentation comment, as shown in listing B.1. Using tags, as shown in listing B.2, is recommended only when a parameter or return value has complex semantics and needs to be clearly separated from the main documentation text.

RENDERED DOCUMENTATION IN INTELLIJ IDEA AND ANDROID STUDIO Besides providing syntax highlighting and navigation for symbols in your KDoc comments, IntelliJ IDEA and Android Studio provide a *rendered view* option. You can enable it by hovering your cursor close to the line numbers next to your KDoc comment and selecting the Toggle Rendered View option. This changes the appearance of comments to a variable-width font and renders references and hyperlinks in place. This is especially handy when you're browsing sources of libraries and other read-only code, since it makes the distinction between documentation and implementation even more obvious.

```
4
5    ⌇  Toggle Rendered View  ^⌥Q
6          * Calculates the sum of two numbers, [a] and [b]
7       */
8    fun sum(a: Int, b: Int) :Int  = a + b
```

```
4
         Calculates the sum of two numbers, a and b
8    fun sum(a: Int, b: Int) :Int  = a + b
```

Generating API documentation

The documentation-generation tool for Kotlin is called Dokka (https://github.com/kotlin/dokka). Just like Kotlin, Dokka fully supports cross-language Java/Kotlin projects. It can read Javadoc comments in Java code and KDoc comments in Kotlin code and generate documentation covering the entire API of a module, regardless of the language used to write each class in it. Dokka supports multiple output formats, including plain HTML and Javadoc-style HTML (using the Java syntax for all declarations and showing how the APIs can be accessed from Java).

You can run Dokka from the command line or as part of your Gradle or Maven build script. The recommended way to run Dokka is to add its plug-in to the Gradle build script for your module. Its versioning follows the Kotlin versioning scheme. Here's the minimum required configuration of Dokka in a Gradle build script:

```
plugins {
    id("org.jetbrains.dokka") version "YOUR_KOTLIN_VERSION"
}
```

You can find information on how to generate documentation for your module in the supported formats as well as on specifying additional generation options in the Dokka documentation (https://kotlinlang.org/docs/dokka-introduction.html). The documentation also shows how Dokka can be run as a standalone tool or integrated into Maven build scripts.

appendix C
The Kotlin ecosystem

Over the years, Kotlin has cultivated a broad ecosystem of libraries, frameworks, and tools. In this appendix, we'll give you some pointers to help you explore this ecosystem. Of course, the Kotlin ecosystem continues evolving and expanding, so a book isn't the ideal medium to provide an always-up-to-date view of available libraries—online resources are better suited for this. The GitHub topic page on Kotlin (https://github.com/topics/kotlin) and community-curated lists, like "Kotlin is Awesome" (https://kotlin.link/), provide a wider overview of the Kotlin universe.

This is also a good place to remind you once more that Kotlin is fully compatible with the entire Java library ecosystem. If you can't find a Kotlin library to fit your use case, it's perfectly fine to pick a Java library. Some Java libraries even offer Kotlin-specific extensions, providing more clean and idiomatic APIs.

As a general-purpose programming language, the Kotlin ecosystem spans many topics and usage areas. The following are some of its major categories:

- Testing
- Code coverage
- Benchmarking
- Documentation
- Dependency injection
- Networked applications
- Serialization
- Database access
- Concurrent programming
- User interface development

Testing

In addition to the well-established frameworks JUnit and TestNG, which work well with Kotlin, *Kotest* (https://github.com/kotest/kotest) is a flexible test framework that supports a number of different layouts for writing tests. You already came across it during our discussion of DSLs in section 13.4.1.

The MockK library (https://github.com/mockk/mockk) provides a DSL you can use to describe simplified implementations of parts of your system for the purpose of testing—a technique referred to as *mocking*. If you're already familiar with the Mockito mocking framework, you can use Mockito-Kotlin (https://github.com/mockito/mockito-kotlin), which provides helper functions that make using the framework natural from Kotlin.

Code coverage

When you want to understand how much of the code in your code base is actually being tested, a typical approach to use is *code coverage*. Code coverage measures how many lines of code are executed when you run your automated tests, relative to the total number of lines in your program. The Kover (https://github.com/Kotlin/kotlinx-kover) library allows you to use code coverage agents like JaCoCo on your Kotlin project. It generates detailed reports that help you understand how many lines are covered by automated tests, which subsystems in your codebase could do with additional tests, and which parts already have sufficient coverage.

Benchmarking

To test the performance of your code in detail, kotlinx.benchmark (https://github.com/Kotlin/kotlinx-benchmark) provides you with a convenient way of running the same code multiple times. The library automatically accounts for factors that may skew the measurement results, such as warm-up time and possible run-time optimizations. It also provides you with detailed performance reports of your code.

Documentation

Dokka (https://github.com/Kotlin/dokka) is the de facto standard documentation engine for Kotlin projects. You have already seen it in appendix B, where we talked about documenting Kotlin code. Dokka can generate documentation for your projects, whether they are pure Kotlin, a mix of Kotlin and Java, or use Kotlin Multiplatform, and supports a variety of output formats.

Dependency injection

Dependency injection and inversion of control are two core programming patterns used in object-oriented systems. Koin (https://insert-koin.io/) and Kodein (https://github.com/kosi-libs/Kodein) are dependency injection frameworks that provide Kotlin DSLs for configuring dependencies. Dependency injection frameworks, such as Spring, Guice, and Dagger Hilt, also work well with Kotlin.

Networked applications: Servers and clients

Many modern applications need to interact with other systems via the network. *Ktor* from JetBrains (https://ktor.io/) is a modern and simple framework for creating asynchronous client and server applications. It fully embraces Kotlin's language idioms and is built entirely on coroutines as its underlying concurrency mechanism. Ktor is extensible through its plug-in system, which allows you to easily integrate it with other established libraries—for example, templating, serialization, authentication and authorization, or monitoring. Projects like Ktorfit (https://github.com/Foso/Ktorfit) extend Ktor with popular paradigms, like Retrofit-style APIs (http://square.github.io/retrofit), which are particularly popular in Android development.

The http4k toolkit (https://http4k.org/) provides functional-style abstractions for working with HTTP services, both as a server and as a client. Additionally, you can use established frameworks, like Spring, Quarkus, or Vert.x, among many others. Spring includes Kotlin support and extensions out of the box (https://spring.io/guides/tutorials/spring-boot-kotlin). Quarkus provides first-class support for using Kotlin (https://quarkus.io/guides/kotlin)—as does Vert.x (https://vertx.io/docs/vertx-core/kotlin/).

Serialization

You've seen how to build your own JSON serialization library in chapter 12, but for production applications, you will likely want to use an established and optimized library. Kotlin Serialization (https://github.com/Kotlin/kotlinx.serialization) is developed by JetBrains and provides a compiler plugin to generate high-performance serialization and deserialization code. It also supports serialization formats beyond JSON, including Protobuf, CBOR, and additional community-contributed formats. Alternatively, Moshi (https://github.com/square/moshi/) is a community-maintained library that provides parsing and encoding functionality for JSON with clean Kotlin APIs.

Database access

Several Kotlin-specific choices can help you address your database-access needs. At JetBrains, we build Exposed (https://github.com/jetbrains/Exposed), an SQL-generation framework discussed a few times throughout this book. SQLDelight (https://github.com/cashapp/sqldelight) turns the typical approach of object-relational mapping (ORM) on its head, generating typesafe Kotlin APIs from SQL queries. Additionally, you can also use traditional Java options, such as Hibernate (https://hibernate.org/) or jOOQ (https://www.jooq.org/), to address your database-access needs.

Concurrent programming

You have already seen kotlinx.coroutines (https://github.com/Kotlin/kotlinx.coroutines) as the main supporting library for concurrency in Kotlin. Additionally, a few other libraries provide convenience functionality for concurrent programming.

AtomicFU (kotlinx.atomicfu) provides atomic references and operations in Kotlin. Its API is designed as idiomatic Kotlin, and the library also works for Kotlin's non-JVM targets, where Java primitives might not be available.

kotlinx.collections.immutable (https://github.com/Kotlin/kotlinx.collections .immutable) provides *immutable persistent collections* for Kotlin—a different type of implementation for the `Collection` interface, where you can create modified copies of immutable collections without incurring the performance penalty of allocating a complete, new collection in the process. These collections are general purpose but shine especially in the context of concurrent programming.

Turbine (https://github.com/cashapp/turbine) is a testing library for flows. It provides convenience functions for testing the behavior of your flow-based APIs, automatically calling your validation code for individual or multiple flows.

User interface development

For building user interfaces, JetBrains builds Compose Multiplatform (https://jb.gg/compose), a modern, declarative UI framework based on Google's Jetpack Compose. It allows you to develop beautiful desktop applications on the JVM using a Kotlin DSL that emphasizes reusable UI components. It also allows you to build shared mobile user interfaces that work on Android, iOS, and other platforms.

index

RELATED MANNING TITLES

The Well-Grounded Java Developer, Second Edition
by Benjamin Evans, Jason Clark, and Martijn Verburg
Foreword by Heinz Kabutz

ISBN 9781617298875
704 pages, $69.99
October 2022

Get Programming with Scala
by Daniela Sfregola

ISBN 9781617295270
560 pages, $59.99
July 2021

Functional Programming in C#, Second Edition
by Enrico Buonanno

ISBN 9781617299827
448 pages, $59.99
December 2021

Modern Java in Action
by Raoul-Gabriel Urma, Mario Fusco, and Alan Mycroft

ISBN 9781617293566
592 pages, $54.99
September 2018

For ordering information go to www.manning.com